A History of
Framingham
Massachusetts

William Barry

HERITAGE BOOKS
2013

A

HISTORY

OF

FRAMINGHAM,

MASSACHUSETTS,

INCLUDING THE PLANTATION,

FROM 1640 TO THE PRESENT TIME,

WITH

AN APPENDIX,

CONTAINING A NOTICE OF SUDBURY AND ITS FIRST PROPRIETORS;

ALSO,

A REGISTER

OF THE INHABITANTS OF FRAMINGHAM BEFORE 1800, WITH GENEALOGICAL SKETCHES.

BY WILLIAM BARRY,
LATE PASTOR OF THE FIRST CHURCH IN FRAMINGHAM.

BOSTON:
JAMES MUNROE AND COMPANY.
1847.

HERITAGE BOOKS
AN IMPRINT OF HERITAGE BOOKS, INC.

Books, CDs, and more—Worldwide

For our listing of thousands of titles see our website
at
www.HeritageBooks.com

A Facsimile Reprint
Published 2013 by
HERITAGE BOOKS, INC.
Publishing Division
5810 Ruatan Street
Berwyn Heights, Md. 20740

Entered according to Act of Congress, in the year 1847,
by William Barry
in the Clerk's Office of the District Court of the District of Massachusetts

— Publisher's Notice —
In reprints such as this, it is often not possible to remove blemishes from the original. We feel the contents of this book warrant its reissue despite these blemishes and hope you will agree and read it with pleasure.

International Standard Book Numbers
Paperbound: 978-0-917890-28-4
Clothbound: 978-0-7884-6880-3

INTRODUCTION.

The following History can possess but little interest beyond the neighborhood, whose memorials it is designed to preserve. Some may even be disposed to question the propriety of dignifying with so ambitious an epithet, the simple annals of an agricultural town, or of seeking for them the distinction of a publication from the press. The public taste has, however, created a demand for such publications; and the inquisitive interest it betokens, in respect to the characters, the deeds, the personal fortunes, of the Planters of New England, is worthy of the past, and creditable to the present. Humble and unostentatious as are the annals of our New England villages, they are such only relatively, or as judged by false standards of glory and merit. The examples they display of heroic faith, of invincible courage, of generous self-sacrifice, of bold and untiring enterprise, the illustration they afford to the genius of the age, and the race that transformed the stern cliffs and gloomy forests of these Western wilds, into a cultivated and flourishing Commonwealth, the extraordinary spectacle every where presented of rising schools, amidst popular ignorance of a stern morality amidst general degeneracy, of a devout and inflexible faith amidst widespread unbelief, of a jealous and enlightened love of liberty, amidst universal despotism, all reflect honor upon the past, — are required to give completeness to New England history, and will be recalled with an ever-increasing interest, as time shall cover with the deepening mist of antiquity, the "beginnings of the Commonwealth." Well shall it be, if the record shall not gratify a vain curiosity, nor nourish a yet vainer boasting; but the rather feed a nobler emulation, a purer patriotism, a more exalted virtue, a more generous philanthrophy.

The following sketch of the settlement and the settlers of Framingham, was commenced many years since, and prosecuted during the intervals of professional labor.* The author, starting with no definite plan, found the field of research widening, and the sources of information copious and inviting, beyond his expectation. It became soon apparent that his labor would be imperfect, unless embracing much personal history, and a knowledge of the emigration of families — an investigation of almost infinite extent, and demanding much laborious and critical inquiry. Unwilling to pause in his pursuit, he proceeded to a careful examination of the records of the town and church, comparing them with such authentic papers and traditions as were preserved. His enquiries were extended to

---

* A historical sketch of Framingham was published several years previous, which was attributed to Dr. Ballard. The value of its historical facts is counter-balanced by its satire, personality, and irrelevant matter. It is a curious specimen of eccentricity.

INTRODUCTION.

the records of the neighboring towns, and to those of nearly all the towns first planted in the vicinity of Boston, to the archives of the counties and of the Commonwealth, and to the valuable historical collections in our public libraries. The result of his labors is presented in the following volume. It is unnecessary to detain the reader, by explaining or vindicating the method he has pursued, which it is hoped will sufficiently explain itself to the intelligent reader. Suffice it to say, that the author has endeavored to be accurate and perspicuous.

The materials relating to the town, derived from its records, have been digested and revised with particular care, and their deficiences have been supplied from other sources. While it would be presumptuous to claim for this work any degree of completeness, the author hopes, that whatever gratification it may impart may incite others to a continuation of the same labor, or at least, awaken a more general concern in the community, for the preservation of ancient writings and memorials, of historical interest.

It is not to be denied, that the prevailing indifference in this particular, has been of a serious nature, causing the unseasonable loss or destruction of much valuable information.*

It is highly important to enforce upon the consideration of the intelligent and public-spirited, the duty of exploring and guarding the materials both of general and of local history. Valuable books and papers should be recovered, and deposited in places of safety. Opportunities may be sought to elucidate obscurities, by consulting the recollections of the aged. Much might be done by an association of minds in our towns, whose labors could be profitably united in this department of the public good. Nor should the future, more than the past, be forgotten in a wise foresight, to provide that the public records should be in the keeping of intelligent, enlightened, and responsible hands, where their importance is understood, and their safe custody will be secured. It is a remarkable fact and deserves serious consideration, that the records of nearly all our towns for the last fifty years, are far less complete, valuable, and reliable, as sources of historical information, than for the same space at any former period. It surely ought not to be thus.

The author, in conclusion, would commend his work to the candid judgment of the reader. It was originally prepared, and has been prosecuted as a "labor of love," and under a sense of gratitude for personal favors and an ever kind and friendly regard, which has found but an inadequate expression in this work, laborious as it may have been. To the inhabitants of Framingham the work is most respectfully inscribed, with the hope and prayer, that their intelligence, liberality, and public spirit may provide the materials of a future history, of which it may not be said, that the "former days were better than these."

Framingham, September, 1847.

---

* The author can speak with the more feeling on this point, from the fact, that nearly all the papers required to illustrate the early history of the First Church, were probably in existence not many years since

HISTORY OF FRAMINGHAM.

FRAMINGHAM is situated in the S.W. part of the County of Middlesex, in the State of Massachusetts. It is bounded on the N. by Sudbury, N.E. by Wayland, S.E. by Natick and Sherburne, S. W. by Ashland, W. by Southborough and Marlborough. It lies on the late Worcester Turnpike, about midway between that town and Boston; being 21 miles distant W. from Boston, and 14 miles nearly S. from Concord. It contained in 1832 an area of 18,976 acres, of which 537 were covered with water and 324 were appropriated for roads. By the incorporation of Ashland, in 1846, a tract of about 3,000 acres was set off from Framingham to that town. The Sudbury or Concord river passes diagonally through the town, in a course from S.W. to N.E., affording good water privileges for mills and factories. With a soil of very general fertility, and occupied by a population always characterized by habits of industry, moderation and enterprise, this town has steadily advanced in general prosperity. It is now, in population, the fifth town in the County of Middlesex.

The history of the planting and settlement of Framingham goes back to an early period. Though incorporated as late as 1700, the territory had for many years previous been known as Mr. Danforth's Farms, and as early as 1670 it is found to have borne upon the County Records the name of the Framlingham Plantation. The first grant within its territory was made as early as 1640. The materials of its history, during the time referred to, are obscure and scanty. Without proprietary records, holding their estates, in many cases, by unregistered leases, living with no civil organization among themselves, scattered over an extensive tract, and obliged to seek such privileges, civil and religious, as were to be had in the nearest incorporated towns, the early settlers of the Plantation have left no record of their labors, hardships and sufferings. The most we can do, therefore, is to gather up the fragments of historical incident preserved to us, and, by the help of such imperfect lights as remain, to trace out the doings and progress of the early founders of the town.

FRAMLINGHAM PLANTATION.

For some time after the settlement of Sudbury,* there lay, to the S. of that township, a large tract of country, known only, in ancient records, as " Wilderness land." The southern boundary of that town was undoubtedly the same as now.† No settlement existed to the S. nearer than Medfield. On the W. was the newly-formed township of Marlborough, whose bounds extended S. to Sudbury river, including the present town of Southborough. The nearest settlements to the E. were in Watertown, and in the present town of Newton, then a part of Cambridge. The settlement of the Praying or Christian Indians at Natick, in 1650, led to the establishment, by the General Court, of a territorial plantation, called the Natick Plantation, which was reserved for their particular use and disposal. From the recorded survey of it, made July 29th, 1659, it appears that its westerly bounds were to " extend as far as Cochituate brook, at

---

* Sudbury was first settled in that part now called Wayland, in 1638, and received its first grant of five miles from the General Court, Sept. 4, 1639. In 1640, an additional grant was made of " a mile in length, upon the S.E. and S.W. sides " of the plantation; and subsequently, in 1649, a further grant of two miles upon its W. boundary. (Col. Rec.) Johnson describes it (Description of N. England, p. 36) as " furnish with great store of fresh marsh; but lying very low, it is much endamaged with land floods." The first minister — Rev. Edmund Brown — was ordained in Aug. 1640, and d. Jan. 22, 1677.

For further particulars respecting the first settlement of Sudbury, see the appendix.

† That this is true of that part of the boundary which now divides Framingham from Sudbury proper, appears evident from the existence there of very aged trees once marked with the initials of the name of Thomas Danforth, and long known as the T. D. trees. They were undoubtedly the original bounds of Danforth's Grants. One of these trees, a white oak of gigantic size, may be seen upon the farm of the late Mr. John Eaton.

the common passing-place or highway, that leadeth from Sudbury to John Stone's house, and from thence the bounds to be John Stone's land and Sudbury river — extending up Sudbury river four miles, to be measured by a strait line from the aforesaid common wading-place on Cochituate brook." * Within this tract, however, was land already in the occupation of English settlers, under grants from the General Court, which was excepted in the reservation to the Indians.

EARLY GRANTS.

Although the greater part of the territory of Framingham was granted to Governor Danforth, there were, in the order of time, still earlier grants.

GLOVER'S FARM. — Mrs. Elizabeth Glover, relict of the Rev. Jesse Glover, † received a grant from the General Court, of six hundred acres of land, which they ordered, October 7, 1640, to be laid out " on the E. side of Sudberry river, without the limits of the last addition, to the bounds of Sudberry, and between the said bound and the Great Pond at Cochituate br," (brook.) ‡ The particular bounds of this tract, variously called the Glover, Dunster or Pond Farm, it is difficult now to trace. That a considerable part of the grant lay within the bounds of the present territory of Framingham, is rendered probable by the following transaction. § Sept. 29, 1647, John Glover, then of Harvard College, and President Dunster, his guardian, leased for

---

* This brook is the same which runs from Cochituate or Long Pond, into Sudbury river.

† The Rev. Jesse Glover, formerly Rector of Sutton, in Surry, embarked for N. E. 1639, in the John, of London, and d. on the passage, leaving two sons — Capt. *Roger*, (in 1652, "lately slain at Edenborough,") and *John :* and three daughters — *Elizabeth*, who m. Adam Winthrop, son of the Governor; *Saara*, who m. Dean Winthrop; and *Priscilla*, who m. John Appleton, of Ipswich. Elizabeth, widow of the Rev. Jesse Glover, m. Henry Dunster, President of Harvard College.

‡ Col. Rec. 1. 289.

§ The Dunster Farm was leased for six years, to Edmund Rice, Sept. 13, 1642, for 30 bushels of corn per year the first two years; 50 bushels per year the next two years; and 100 bushels the last two years, in equal proportions of wheat, indian and rye; and, as the "Pond Farm," was conveyed, June 24, 1659, to Edmund Rice and his son Benjamin, by Joseph Hills, Edward Collins and Edmund Frost, executors of President Dunster's will. Middlesex Deeds.

ten years, to Edmund Rice, the whole farm of said J. Glover, "lying W. on said H. Dunster's land, severed by Sudbury line, and so on to Cochittuate Brooke, wherewith it is bounded southerly, as with the two Ponds." By the terms of the lease, Edmund Rice contracted to make a fence between the two farms of J. Glover and H. Dunster, easterly, "and so all the lands encompassed eyther by the foresaid brook or the Great River, westerly;" and also to keep in good repair "the fences already on the farme between the Great Pond and the River." It was further required of him to build on the premises, "during the first five or six years," a dwelling-house, "thirty foote long, ten foote high stud, one foot sill from the ground, sixteen foote wide;" with two rooms, both below or the one above the other; "All the doores well hanged, and staires, with convenient fastnings of locks or bolts, windows, glases, and well planked under foote, and boarded sufficiently to lay corne in, in the story above head." He was also to build a barn "fifty foote long, eleven feet high in the stud, one foote above ground, the sell twenty foote, if no leantes, or eighteen foote wide with leantees on the one side, and a convenient threshing-floare between the doares." The particulars of this transaction are the more worthy of notice, as connected with the first known occupation of the town by English settlers, dating, as will be seen, at a very early period. The tract above described was situated in the region, in ancient papers called COCHITUATE — the name being applied both to the great pond and to its neighboring territory.

RICE'S GRANTS. — In 1652, Edmund Rice had from the General Court a grant of 50 acres, lying a mile southerly from Cochituate Brook, or thereabouts, deeds of which tract are in the possession of his descendants in this town. In 1659, he obtained from the same source a grant of 80 acres on the "S. side of the path leading from Sudbury to Connecticot, about six miles from Sudbury." These tracts, to which large additions were afterwards made, were in that part of the town to the N.E., where the descendants of the family have continued to reside unto the present day.*

---

* Several of the sons of Edmund appear to have been proprietors, and more than one, perhaps, residents within the limits of Framingham.

STONE'S GRANTS. — May 15, 1656, " William Boman, Capt. Josiah, Roger, and James, and Keaquisan, Indians, living at Naticke," * in consideration of a valuable sum of Peage and other goods, conveyed to John Stone of Sudbury, " a parcell of broaken-up and fenced-in land, lying on the *S. side of Sudbury line*, upon the falls of Sudbury river, and bounded with ye comon land surrounding; the said land conteyning, by estimation, about 10 acres, more or less." In 1656, in answer to the petition of John Stone of Sudbury, for confirmation of the purchase of 11 acres of land bought of the Indians, the General Court " ordered that his petition be granted, as also the grant of 50 acres of land more to be added thereunto, according to his desire," &c.† In conformity to the above, Edmund Rice and Thomas Noyes laid out the above lands, May 19, 1658, " at the falls of Sudbury river." To this tract extensive additions were from time to time made by purchase, until a large part of the present territory of Saxonville and considerable tracts elsewhere, came into the possession of this family.

WAYTE'S GRANT. — In 1658, Richard Wayte of Boston, Marshal, obtained from the General Court a grant of " 300 acres of land, in the wilderness, between Chochituate and Nipnox," ‡ which was laid out as follows, viz. :

" There being a neck of land about 220 acres, more or less, and is surrounded by Sudbury river, a great pond and a small brook that runneth from said pond into the river, and from the southerly end of the said pond running to the river again, by a westerly line, according to marked trees ; and, on the westerly side of Sudbury river, to extend his bounds from the said river 20 pole in breadth, so far in length as his land lyeth against the said river. Also on the N. and N.E. of said brook and pond, he hath five patches of meadow, containing about

---

Henry, the oldest son, was the ancestor of most of the name now living here. The precise time at which he settled here it is not easy to determine. See Genealogical Register.
* Bowman's Brook, and Rogers' Field, both near Saxonville village, will be recognized as having derived their names from the above Indian proprietors and grantors. The original deed referred to, is in the possession of Mr. Abner Stone, of Framingham.

† Col. Rec. iii. 172.
‡ Nipnox is the name given to the undefined territory belonging to the Nipmuck Indians, who inhabited the interior of Mass. and lived about the ponds and streams. Their principal seats were at Oxford and on the Blackstone River. They were partly subject to the Narraganset, and partly to the Massachusetts Indians.

20 acres, more or less, being all surrounded with wilderness land; also on the N.E. side of Washakum Pond, he hath 60 acres, being bounded with said pond on the S.W. and an Indian bridge on the E., and elsewhere by marked trees — the wilderness surrounding."

The above tract, on which no settlement appears immediately to have been made, was conveyed to Thos. Danforth. The Indians quit-claimed to the latter, Oct. 1, 1684.*

RUSSELL'S GRANT. — May 6, 1659, by order of the General Court, Richard Russell,† treasurer, had laid out to him " 500 acres of land lying in the wilderness upon both sides of the path that leadeth from Sudbury towards Nipnox; and is bounded on the N.E. with Washakum pond and a swamp adjoining thereto, and on the W. by a marked tree, and the W. side of an ashen swamp, and on the S. with the upland adjoining to the southerly or S.W. point of that meadow which lieth on the westerly side of the aforesaid meadow, and on the N. extending on the N. side of the aforesaid path, and is surrounded with the wilderness." ‡ This grant also came into the possession of Gov. Danforth, to whom the Indians released all claim, Oct. 1, 1684.

CORLETT'S FARM. — The tract known by this name as late as 1750, when it was delineated on Hazzell's survey of the N. part of Framingham, was originally granted by the Court, Oct. 18, 1659, to Elijah Corlett, a schoolmaster of much celebrity at Cambridge, whose services to the infant colony are noticed in strong eulogy by the writers of his day.§

---

* From their situation, it appears probable that the elevation known as " Mount Wait," and the meadow called " Wait's meadow," may have derived their names from the first grantee of the soil.

† RICHARD RUSSELL, with his wife Maud, came from Herefordshire, England, in 1640. He resided in Charlestown, and was a Representative in 1642, and for many years after. He was chosen Speaker of the House in 1654, and in 1659 was made Assistant, which office he retained until 1669. He was also for many years Treasurer of the Colony. Hutchinson states that his son, grandson, and two of his great-grandsons were of the Council. He died May 14, 1676, aged 65. Farmer's Register. Hutchinson's Hist. Mass. Bay, I. 189.

‡ Col. Rec.

§ ELIJAH CORLETT was educated at Lincoln College, in Oxford, where he was admitted in 1626. He came to New England and settled as early as 1643, in Cambridge, where he was for more than forty years instructer of a grammar school. All accounts concur in representing him as a man of learning, piety and respectability. In N. England's first fruits he is said to have " very well approved himself

18 Oct. 1659. "In answer to the petitions of Daniel Weld and Elijah Corlett, schoolmasters, the Court, considering the usefulness of the petitioners in an employment of so common concernment for the good of the whole country, and the little encouragement that they have had from their respective towns for their service and unwearied pains in that employment, do judge meet to grant to each of them 200 acres of land, to be taken up adjoining to such lands as have been already granted and laid out by order of this Court." This farm was laid out May 22, 1661, by Mr. Thomas Noyes of Sudbury,

"A mile distant from the S.W. angle of the land formerly granted to Sudbury, also having a parcel of meadow granted to Mr. Edmund Brown, teacher to the church of Sudbury, on the S.; also being about half a mile distant northerly from the river which runneth to Sudbury, also being a mile and a quarter distant W.N. westerly, from the now dwelling house of John Stone. The said farm, for the most part bordering upon the wilderness and laying in a long square, the longest lines running W. by S. five degrees southerly," &c. *

---

for his abilities, dexterity and painfulness." Cotton Mather describes him as the "memorable old schoolmaster in Cambridge, from whose education our college and country has received so many of its worthy men, that he is himself worthy to have his name celebrated in our church history." He elsewhere commemorates him in connection with Cheever, in a familiar couplet:

"'T is CORLETT'S pains and CHEEVER'S, we must own,
That thou, New England, art not Scythia grown."

Dr. Holmes states that great effort was made for Mr Corlett's maintenance in the early settlement of Cambridge, that he was charged with the tuition of the Indian scholars intended for the college, for which service he received compensation from the Society for Propagating the Gospel among the Indians. It would seem, however, from the order of the General Court above noticed, that his labors met with a scanty reward. Poverty was the destiny of his profession in that day of small things. May we not presume that he was included among those referred to by Hutchinson, who said of Cheever, "he is not the only master who kept his lamp longer lighted than otherwise it would have been, by a supply of oil from his scholars." Corlett died, Feb. 25, 1686-7, aged 78 years, and an elegy on his death in blank verse, by N. Walter, was published. His wife's name was Barbara, and he had, besides two daughters, an only son, Ammi Ruhamah, who graduated at Harvard College in 1670, and deceased Feb. 1, 1679. This son may have been the individual referred to in the Mass. Hist. Coll. as instructer in Plymouth in 1672. Corlett was the author of a biographical notice of the Rev. Mr. Hooker, preserved in the Magnalia. Mass. Hist. Coll. 1 Ser. I. 243, vii. 22. 2 Ser. III. 173, iv. 91. Magnalia. Allen's Biog. Dict. Farmer's Register.

* Corlett, by permission of the Court, May 22, 1661, had set off to him a farm of 320 acres of land, belonging to Netus, Indian, at Nip Nap, which was described in the survey made by Edmund Rice and Thomas Noyes, as at the N. end of Nip Nap hill, being about three miles distant northerly from the Indian plantation. This farm was conveyed by him in 1685 to Ales Thomas, of Boston, widow, and Benjamin Thomson, her son. Mid. Deeds, book IX.

The above-described farm, which lay to the S. and S.W. of the present school house No. 8, was conveyed Dec. 13, 1661, by Corlett to Thomas Danforth, and by the latter reconveyed the same day to John Stone.

DANFORTH'S FARMS. — The first grants to Gov. Danforth consisted of two tracts, one Oct. 16, 1660, of 200, the other May 7, 1662, of 250 acres, "adjoining" the former, both which were included in the general survey following, which is copied from the Records of the General Court.*

"MR. DANFORTH'S FARMES LAYD OUT.

" Layd out unto Thomas Danforth, Esq., a parcel of land lying between Marlbury and Kenecticut path, and is bounded easterly by Sudbury lands, adjoining to that part of their bounds near Lannum, the land of John Stone, and a part of Natick plantation; southerly, the lands of the said Thomas Danforth and Natick lands; northerly, with the other part of Sudbury bounds towards Marlbury; and westerly, with the country lands; the said westerly line being limited by a pine tree marked with D, and standing on the N. side of that branch of Sudbury river that cometh from Marlbury,† and on the westerly side of Angellico brook; and from the said pine tree continuing a S. westerly line unto the other branch of Sudbury river that is the bounds of Natick plantation; from the said pine tree northerly, continuing unto Sudbury bounds, coming by a tree marked, in the highway that leadeth from John Stone's house to Marlbury — in which tract of land, bounded as above said, is contained 200 acres of land belonging unto John Stone, ‡ and is excepted out of that layd out unto the said Thomas Danforth; also four hundred and fifty acres of land granted by the General Court in two several grants to the said Thomas Danforth, and the remainder thereof is for the satisfaction of money disbursed by the said Thomas Danforth, for the use of the country, by the appointment of the General Court. Given under our hands the 27th of May, 1662.

" At a County Court, held at Cambridge, Oct. 7, 1662, Edmund Rice and John How, appearing in Court, acknowledged the above written to be their act according to the appointment of the General Court."

By adding to the above the Wayte Grant of 300 acres, and the Russell Grant of 500 acres, some idea can be formed of the

---

* Col. Rec IV. 413.
† Marlborough at that time included Southborough.
‡ This probably has reference to the Corlett farm, which is not excepted by name in the survey.

extent of Mr. Danforth's possessions. It will be seen that they embraced a very large part of the present territory of Framingham, between its extreme Northerly and Southerly bounds, excepting the Glover Farm and that considerable tract to the S.E. of Sudbury river, limited by Cochituate brook and Mr. Danforth's southerly bounds, which was within the bounds of the Indian plantation of Natick.*

COL. CROWNE'S GRANT. — Oct. 8, 1662. "As an acknowledgement of the great pains of Col. William Crowne in behalf of this country, when he was in England," the General Court grant-

---

* As the reader will be interested in the life and character of the individual who bore so prominent a part in the early settlement of this town, we here condense such information as we have been able to collect from various sources. Thomas Danforth was the oldest son of Nicholas Danforth of Framlingham, a town near the S.E. part of the County of Suffolk, in England. The father possessed there, according to Mather, a fine manor, and was "a gentleman of such estate and repute in the world, that it cost him a considerable sum to escape the knighthood which K. Charles I. imposed on all of so much per annum." In 1634, Thomas came to New England with his father, who settled in Cambridge, was a Representative in 1636, and died in 1638. Thomas resided in Cambridge, and in 1657 was chosen Representative to the General Court, and in 1659 became an Assistant, in which office he continued until 1679. Upon the election of Mr. Bradstreet as Governor that year, he came into the place of Deputy Governor, and held it until 1686, and three years after the revolution in 1689. In 1684 he failed of his election as Governor by 61 votes. He was Chief Justice of the Court of Oyer and Terminer held at Charlestown, and "had a chief hand under God in putting an end to the troubles under which the country groaned in 1692." In 1681 he was appointed President of the Province of Maine, where he resided for a short time. Hutchinson refers to him as having had "a great share in managing the public affairs in the most difficult times." Judge Sewall describes him as "a very good husbandman and a very good Christian and a good counsellor." An original letter from him, dated 1695, in the possession of Mr. Abner Stone of Framingham, gives a favorable impression of his wisdom, forbearance and conciliatory spirit, in the management of his private affairs. Gov. Danforth married his first wife, Mary Withington, Feb. 23, 1643-4, by whom he had 11 children, five of whom were sons; and by his second wife, Elizabeth, he had one daughter. Samuel, his eldest son, born Oct. 5, 1652, was graduated at H. C. 1671, gave early promise of distinction as a scholar, but died in London, of the small pox, Dec. 22, 1676. Gov. Danforth deceased at Cambridge, Nov. 5, 1699, aged 77, leaving several daughters. He survived all his sons. His brother, the Rev. Samuel Danforth, (H. C. 1643) was tutor at the College, and was ordained as colleague with the Rev. John Eliot, in 1650. He d. in 1674, aged 48. His brother Jonathan settled in Billerica, where he died in 1712, aged 84. He had two sisters; Anna, who m. Matthew Bridge, and was great-grandmother of the Rev. Matthew Bridge, minister of the 1st church in Framingham; and Elizabeth, who m. Andrew Belcher, and was grandmother of Gov. Belcher. (Holmes's Annals, 1699. Hutchinson's Hist. Mass. Bay, I. 189, 223. Farmer's Register. Magnalia, b. iv. p. 154.

ed him 500 acres of land, which was laid out to him, in 1663, as follows, viz.

"Laid out, &c., the 500 acres granted unto the Hon. Col. Wm. Crowne, in the year 1662, at a place near the Cold Spring, near unto the road which leadeth from Sudbury unto Connecticut, on the S. side of a branch of Sudbury river, being about nine miles from the town of Sudbury, at a place called by the Indians, Maynaguncok hill; beginning at the S. side of the said hill, and from thence a line upon a N.N.W. point 300 rods, butting on a branch of Sudbury river, and from thence a line upon a S.E. (S.S.E.) point by the river-side 360 rods, and from thence a [circular] line by the said river and by a brook 160 rods, a line from the said brook upon a W.N.W. point 240 rods, and from thence a line upon a [S.S.W. point 150 rods, and from thence a line upon a W.N.W. point 154 rods, ending where we began,] * adding four acres of meadow upon the said brook and three acres of meadow joyning to the S. line of the said farm — all which said land and meadow and butting and bounding is described by a plat under — make up the full complement of the aforesaid 500 acres. Signed by

"Thomas Noyes, Surveyor.
"App'd by Court, 25, 3, 1665."

The farm thus described, which embraced the territory of the present village of Ashland, is included in Gore's survey of Framingham, made in 1699, and referred to in the grant of this town, as defining its bounds. It was conveyed, with some improvements, July 4, 1687, to Savill Simpson of Boston, cordwainer, for £30, by Henry Crowne, Executor of Col. Crowne's Will, and the Indian title was relinquished June 20, 1693.† It was set off to Hopkinton at the incorporation of that town, Dec. 13, 1717.‡

Instead of that part of the description enclosed in brackets, the conveyance to Savill Simpson reads thus: "N.N.W. point 134 rods where the first began."

† Middlesex Deeds.

‡ Of the life and character of Col. Crowne our knowledge is imperfect. Hutchinson (Hist. I. 214) speaks of him as a "noted royalist," and as one of the "principal persons of the town," who called upon Whaley and Goffe when they visited Boston in 1660. From a letter of Charles II. to the Governor and Council of R. I. (M. H. Coll. 1 Ser. v. 224,) it appears that Col. Crowne had represented himself as having sustained severe losses by the surrender of Nova Scotia to the French, for which, through his son John, he petitioned the king to indemnify him by the grant of Mt. Hope. In the reply of the Governor and Magistrates, (p. 228,) they maintain that his losses were more imaginary than real, and that his "present demeanance was not such as should highly deserve of his majesty, being rather a burthen where he hath been than otherwise; that he hath good accommodations freely granted unto him, but very unhappy disquiets attended that Plantation during his residence there." In the same Colls. (Vl. 92) may be found a letter from Edward Randolph to Gov. Winslow, relative to his proceedings at Piscataqua. Col. Crown died at Piscataqua about the year 1687.

EAMES' GRANTS. — Thomas Eames obtained considerable grants in the S. part of the present territory of this town. At a Court held at Nonantum, Jan. 24, 1676, the Natick Indians granted him "a parcel of land now belonging to Natick, that is encompassed by the lands of Mr. Thomas Danforth, Goodman Death and John Stone." This grant, consisting of 200 acres, was confirmed to him by the General Court in 1679, and an Indian Deed of the same executed in 1695. In 1679 the inhabitants of Sherborn voted to Thomas Eames, "for building the Meeting House, to have the corner of the town where he lives." In 1677, upon his application to the General Court for relief, on the occasion of the destruction of his property by the Indians, he obtained a grant of 200 acres of land, "to be laid out in any free place not prejudicing the laying out of a plantation."

GOOKIN AND HOW'S PURCHASE. — May 19, 1682, Samuel Gookin* of Cambridge, and Samuel Howe of Sudbury, purchased of the Natick Indians 1700 acres of land, which, from subsequent conveyances appears to have extended along the road from Sudbury to Sherburne, south of Cochituate brook, including land about Indian Head and Succo pond. Confirmation of this purchase was made by the General Court Nov. 20, 1696, to the grantees and "the tertenants holding under them." †

LYNDE'S FARM. — The date and circumstances of the origin of this tract do not appear. Mention is made of it in 1689, as Lyneses' Farm. On Hazzell's survey, in 1750, it is represented in the form of an irregular triangle, the base of which extends along the S. side of the N. road to Marlborough, beginning near the present School-House No. 8, and proceeding W. as far as the old Frost place. Its S.E. line was a bound of the Corlett Farm.

---

* Samuel Gookin was a son of Daniel Gookin of Cambridge, who d. March 19, 1686-7, "a very zealous but an upright man," who was an Assistant and Major General of the Colony, but most distinguished as the associate of Eliot and the steadfast friend of the Indians. Samuel was Sheriff of the County of Middlesex. Of his brother Daniel, the first minister of Sherburne, Judge Sewall in his Diary writes, "he was a good scholar and solid divine. We were fellows together at College, and have sung many a tune in consort; hope shall sing Hallelujahs together in Heaven."

† Of this tract, in 1683, John Bent purchased 60 acres W. of Cochituate brook, and bounded on his own land; and David Stone, 200 acres; and Matthew Rice, in 1694, 300 acres, "W. side of the way from Stone's mills to John Pratt senior's land," at Indian Head. Thomas Walker, jr. and John Pratt were also early purchasers.

It contained about 200 acres, including the meadow from which the S. branch of Hop brook originates, and a ledge known at the present day as Lynde's Rocks. This tract was in Col. Buckminster's possession in 1705.

The above comprise the chief of the early grants within the territory of Framingham, occupying, as will be seen, nearly the entire domain of the town. Besides these were smaller tracts, held in general by non-residents, and in some instances grants chiefly within the limits of neighboring towns may have extended within the bounds of the plantation of Framingham.* Of these grants a considerable number were confirmed by deeds of quitclaim from the Indian proprietors of the soil, some of which are on record, and others it is presumed may yet be discovered. Nothing is more clear to an inquirer into the early history of our towns, than the manifest care of the first settlers of Massachusetts, to obtain a legal title to their lands from the native proprietors. We have somewhere met with a remark, attributed to the elder President Adams, that in all his practice at the bar, he never knew a contested title to land which was not traced back to the Indian grantors.

EARLY SETTLEMENT OF THE PLANTATION.

The precise date of the first settlement of Framingham is unknown. The first house was probably erected by Edmund Rice, soon after the year 1647, upon the farm before noticed as leased by him of John Glover, that year. An early inhabitant of the town was Elder John Stone, the oldest son of Deacon Gregory Stone of Cambridge, with whom he emigrated to this country in 1635, at the age of 16 years. While yet under age, he came to Sudbury in 1638, probably among its first settlers, where his

---

* Before 1661, Edmund Brown, minister of Sudbury, had a grant of meadow S. of the Corlett farm, and in 1678 was proprietor here of land near Doeskin or Nobscut hill. "Sherman's land" was of some extent, and lay between the house of the late Col. Trowbridge and Nobscut hill. "APPLETON'S FARM" was within the plantation of Natick, but bounded in part on Charchitawick (Cochituate) brook and pond. It was conveyed June 17, 1697, to Thomas Browne, Thomas Drury and Caleb Johnson, as joint proprietors, by John Appleton, jr. of Ipswich, whose father, John, of Ipswich, married Priscilla, daughter of the Rev. Jesse Glover. The land may therefore have been a part of the original Glover or Dunster farm. The territory of the Indian plantation of Magunkook also extended within the modern bounds of this town.

name is found in the record of the inhabitants, with the lands divided to them respectively. In what part of Sudbury he first settled is uncertain. The following extract from the Town Records may indicate the time when he left the bounds of that town, and settled within the limits of Framingham:

1645. " John Moore bought of John Stone, his dwelling house and houselot, with all other lands and meadows belonging to the said John Stone, or that shall hereafter be due unto the said John Stone by virtue of his right in the beginning of the plantation of Sudbury, also the fencings, boards, &c. about the house."

Whether he then or at a later day removed without the bounds of Sudbury, he continued to enjoy his civil rights as an inhabitant of that town, having been appointed, in 1654, to see to the fences on his side of the river, and in 1655, to the office of Town Clerk. He was also an officer of the church in that place. Deacon or (as he was often called) Elder John Stone first built at Otter Neck, near the curve of Sudbury river. His residence there is referred to in the description of the bounds of the Natick Plantation in 1659, and in Corlett's Grant, 1661. In 1665, he was freeman at Cambridge, which town he represented in the General Court, 1682 and 3. He returned thither to reside upon the paternal estate, leaving his children to cultivate the large farms he had acquired in this town. He died in Cambridge, May 5, 1683, aged 64 years.*

Henry Rice, oldest son of Deacon Edmund of Sudbury, who in 1660 was one of the first proprietors of Marlborough, before 1659 owned land in the East part of the town, and had probably settled there at that time. In 1662, John Bent was proprietor of lands now composing in part the ancient Bent farm, occupied by Mr. Gibbs. Samuel Winch was of Sudbury in 1671, and then, or soon after, was in the occupation of lands out of the South bounds of Sudbury, where he probably lived. " Winch's old house " is referred to as on the Danforth farm, in 1689. Thomas Drury, John How and others, were early settlers in that part of the town. The nearness to Sudbury doubtless led to the early settlements in that neighborhood. The inhabitants were thus enabled to ob-

---

* For further particulars see the Genealogical Register in this volume.

14   FRAMLINGHAM PLANTATION.

tain protection from danger, and to have easy access to the civil and religious privileges of an incorporated town. The individuals referred to are generally described in deeds as of Sudbury, sometimes as "out-dwellers," sometimes as "living in or near unto Sudbury."

NAME OF THE PLANTATION.

An. 1670, we find the first recorded notice upon the County Registry of Births &c., of the name of Framlingham; previously to which, and often after, this territory was described as Mr. Danforth's farm. Its name of Framlingham was derived from the birth-place of Mr. Danforth in England. The bounds of the Plantation were not distinctly defined, neither did it possess any legal organization. That the name was not restricted to the lands of Mr. Danforth, is made probable by the fact, that Thomas Eames is described as of that Plantation in 1676. Framlingham was taxed in 1674 and after. The interest which naturally attaches to the ancient name of this town, may justify a brief account of the original Framlingham in Great Britain.

Framlingham is in the hundred of Loes, County of Suffolk, in England, and lies 18 miles N.E. by N. from Ipswich, and 88 miles N.E. from London. The river Ore runs by it, and upon the W. side of the town spreads into a sort of lake. By the bounty of King Henry I., here was formerly a castle of the *Bigods*. It is described by Camden (1695) as "a very beautiful castle, fortified with a rampire, a ditch, and a wall of great thickness, with thirteen towers; within it has very convenient lodgings. From this place it was that, A.D. 1173, when the rebellious son of King Henry II. took up arms against his father, Robert, Earl of Leicester, with his stipendiaries from Flanders, harassed the country all around; and here also it was that, An. 1553, Queen Mary entered upon the government, notwithstanding the violent opposition of Dudley, Earl of Northumberland, against King Henry VIII.'s daughters." This town contains a free school, and also the chapel of Saxtead, valued in the King's books at £43 6 8, the patronage of which is in Pembroke Hall, Cambridge. The church is dedicated to St. Michael. The resident population of this parish, in 1801, was 1,854, and the amount raised by the parish rates, in 1803, was £1,129 12 0, at 5s. 4 1-2d. in the pound. Cotton Mather relates of Nicholas Danforth, (father of Thomas), that he was " of such figure and esteem in the church, that he procured that famous lecture at Framlingham, in Suffolk, where he had a fine manor, which lecture was kept by Mr. Burroughs and many other noted ministers in their turn ; to whom, and especially to Mr. Shepard, he proved a Gaius, and then especially, when the Laudian fury scorched them." Framlingham is a market town, its market being held on Saturday. The Fairs are on Whit-Monday and the 10th of October. There are two other places of the same name in England, viz. Framlingham Earl's, and Framlingham Pigot, both in the hundred of Henstead, and County of Norfolk.*

HIGHWAYS.

Of the only roads of which we first have record, one is described as the path to Quintecote, or Conecticot, which extended from Sudbury, (now Wayland), following, as nearly as we can judge, the most ancient line of travel, crossing the " fording place of Cochituate brook," passing near the house now of Mr. Uriah Rice, from thence by the route towards the railroad and Sherburne. On this line settlers gradually extended towards the S.E. and S. parts of the town, where, before 1680, we find traces of the Eameses, the Pratts, Thomas Gleason, Isaac Learned, John Death, &c.† Most of these occupied lands within the limits of the Indian plantation of Natick. Some of the number became townsmen of Sherburne, after its incorporation in 1679.

Another road, probably intersecting the former, is referred to as the " path to Nipnox," which was perhaps the line of communication between Natick and Magunkook, at the South part of the town. In 1659, is noticed the " path from Natick to John Stone's house ;" and in 1662, the " highway leading from John Stone's house to Marlbury." These probably comprise all the roads, (if such they may be termed), traversing the early Plantation.

---

* Camden's Britannia, p. 373. Carlisle's Topographical Dictionary, (1808.) Magnalia, b. iv. p. 154.

† For particulars respecting these and other early settlers, the reader is referred to the Genealogical Register.

"At a County Court holden in Charlestown, Dec. 23, 1673, John Stone sen'r of Sudbury, Serg't (John) Woods of Marlborough, and Thomas Eames of Framingham, together with John Livermore of Wattertown, (or any two of them,) were appointed and impowered to lay out an highway for the use of the country, leading from the house of the said John Livermore to a horse-bridge (then being) near the house of Daniel Stone, jun., and thence the nearest and best way to Marlborough, and thence to Quabuog," (now Brookfield.)*

The above highway was laid out, and the return made Oct. 6, 1674. It is the highway at the North part of Framingham, extending from the "New Bridge," (so called in 1750), W. towards Marlborough.† The "horse bridge" referred to, is probably explained by the following, extracted from the County Records, iii. 87:

"April 7, 1674. In answer to the petition of Samuel How, referring to some allowance to be made him, for his expenses about the bridge he had lately erected upon Sudbury river, *above the towne*, he is allowed to take toll of all travellers, for a horse and man 3d, and for a cart 6d, until there be an orderly settling of the Country highway, and some provision made for repayment to him of his disbursements."

INDIAN HISTORY OF THE PLANTATION.

As our narrative of events approaches the period of King Philip's war, it may be proper here to condense such information as we have obtained relative to the early Indian history, as connected with this township.

History and tradition alike fail of throwing much light upon the Indian tribes, who must once have inhabited this town. The spacious ponds and the river, particularly at the falls, abundantly stored with fish, undoubtedly attracted them within these borders.

---

* Co. Records.
† The identity of this road is proved by a petition, (an attested copy of which is in the author's possession), signed by fourteen persons, nearly all of Framingham, and bearing date 1722. The petition, addressed to the Court of Quarter Sessions at Cambridge, refers to the origin of the road, and represents it as "nearer and more commodious for travellers from Boston to Marlborough and the towns lying above and westward thereof, than any other road now in use, yet through neglect and disuse, unpassable." A committee was prayed for "to view the said highway and order the building of a bridge over the river there," or elsewhere, "and order the said way to be laid open and made passable for travellers." In the action of the Court upon this petition may have originated the name of the "New Bridge."

INDIAN HISTORY OF THE PLANTATION. 17

Ancient records refer to the " Indian graves " in the neighborhood of Saxonville, as well known, but the precise locality (probably upon the plain E. of school house No. 9) is now lost. The remembrance of it has passed away with the interesting and unfortunate people it commemorated.

The only information we possess, which seems to indicate their actual occupation of the territory in this neighborhood, after the settlement of the colony, is contained in a letter of John Eliot,* who, writing in 1649, says: " Some SUDBURY Indians, some of Concord Indians, some of Maestick Indians, and some of Dedham Indians, are ingenious and pray unto God, and sometimes come to the place where I teach, to hear the word." We have preserved also the religious confession of an Indian named William, of Sudbury, alias Nataous, who is probably the Netus, referred to in the note to the Corlett Grant. He is described, 1662, as living at Nipnap Hill,† three miles N. of the Indian Plantation (Natick?). Hubbard speaks of him as " very familiar with the whites." Gookin, in 1674, refers to Nattous as among " the good men and prudent " who were rulers at Natick. He is also described as a Nipmuck Captain. The Co. Records, as early as 1659,‡ notice him, by the name of Netus, as having been sued by Serg. John Parmenter, of Sudbury, for a debt. This same Netus was the leader of the Indians at the assault upon Mr. Eames' house, soon to be related.

The name of Jacob's Meadow, (E. of Indian Head), and Jacob's Further Meadow, both in this town, indicate the probable residence here of " Old Jacob," as he is named in the accounts of the praying Indians. Old Jacob (his Indian name being Aponapawquin), " was among the first that prayed to God. He had so good a memory that he could rehearse the whole catechism, both questions and answers. When he gave thanks at meat, he would sometimes only say the Lord's Prayer." Dr. Homer of Newton states that he died at the age of 90 years, recommending union to his brethren at large, and an inviolable regard to the laws of equity and to the civil authorities.§ Old Jacob will soon appear also as a participator in the " Eames' burning."

---

* M. H. Coll.
† We have been unable to identify this hill. May it not have been another name for Nobscut hill, whose position is about three miles N. from the ancient bounds of Natick.
‡ i. 157.
§ 1 M. H. Coll., ix. 198 ; v. 264.

BOMAN and ROGER have already been noticed as grantors of land near the Falls, and as commemorated in the names of Bowman's Brook and Roger's Field. Other Indian names of hills, ponds and streams, (and those in some instances corrupted), are meagre, yet pleasant memorials transmitted to us, of the aboriginal race.*

Ancient records moreover inform us, that John Awansamug, Sen., was a "chief proprietor" and "sachem" of a tract of land, extending from the S. part of Framingham into Sherburne, and beyond that town to the S. W.; and the name of "Peter Jethro's field," on an old survey, points out the local habitation, near Nobscut Hill, of an individual, whose name is somewhat notorious in the annals of King Philip's war. Capt. Tom's Hill, which lies at the E. part of the town, S. of the turnpike, upon the bounds of Natick and Framingham, probably received its name from the celebrated Wuttusacomponom, or Capt. Tom, the chief sachem of the Nipmuck Indians. Of the three last named, the following sketches may deserve a place in this History.

AWANSAMUG.—This name very often occurs in ancient deeds, and is variously written Awussomoag, Oonsumog, Wessomog, Ossamog, &c. The earliest mention made of him is in the History of Lynn,† which refers to him (if the same), as having lived at Rumney Marsh (now Chelsea), and the father of Muminquash, (James Rumney Marsh), born in 1636. He is generally known, however, as one of the "Natick Indians," in their conveyances of lands. In an account of the Praying or Christian Indians, 1659,‡ he is described as "a young man when they (the Indians) begun to pray to God. He did not at the present join with them. He would say to me, *I will first see to it, and when I understand it, I will answer you.* He did after a while enter into the civil covenant; but was not entered into church covenant before he died. He was propounded to join the church, but was delayed, he being of a quick, passionate temper." It is added, that the church would have been satisfied to receive him, had he

---

* Indian arrow-heads have been frequently found in ploughed fields in this town.
† Page 18.
‡ 1 M. H. Coll. ix. 198.

recovered from the long sickness which caused his death. Eliot elsewhere gives this Indian's confession among others.* The extent of his possessions in this region must have been considerable. Besides land in the S. part of this town, he conveyed to William Sheffield 500 acres at Chaboquassit, in Sherburne, and obtained leave of the General Court, just before his death, to sell a large tract not far from Sherburne line on the S.W., to —— Rawson. He appears to have received much kindness from Thomas Eames, of Framingham, "for sundry years until his death," of which a suitable notice is taken in an Indian conveyance to his sons. Awansamug left at his death a widow Yawataw, who signed the deed of the township of Salem in 1686, and at least two sons, Thomas and Amos; the former of whom owned a "houselot" upon the land of Thomas Eames, and was living (or a son) in Natick, June 4, 1742. Samuel Assamug, of Natick, 1682, was probably another son.†

JETHRO AND PETER JETHRO.—The early historical accounts contain notices of Old Jethro, called Tantamous, and of his son Peter Jethro, in which there is some confusion. Whether the field above named refers to one only, or both, is uncertain. Old Jethro, says Drake, lived on Nobscut Hill at the breaking out of King Philip's war in 1675. The place called "Peter Jethro's field," which was upon the present farm of Mr. Ezekiel How, is referred to in a deed dated 1693. Shattuck's History of Concord states, that Jethro was present as a witness at the purchase of Musquitaquid, or Concord, in 1635, which took place under an old tree, standing some years since near the Hotel, called Jethro's tree, and used in early times as a belfry on which the town bell was hung. This must have been the younger Jethro, as the deposition printed by Mr. Shattuck, relating to the purchase, was given in 1684, when the deponent was about 70 years old, which was eight years after the death of the older Jethro. The deposition notices that Jethro lived at Nashobah fifty years before. Gookin, writing in 1674,‡ speaks of Jethro as "a grave and pious

---

* See his letter 3 M. H. Coll.
† Mr. Willard, in his History of Lancaster, notices that "Hannah Woonsamug, an Indian woman, owned the Covenant (in that town) and was baptized Oct. 1710." Wor. Mag. II. 300.
‡ 1 M. H. Col. vii. 193.

Indian" belonging to Natick, who was sent to be a teacher at Weshakim, near Lancaster. In 1675, the older Jethro, (according to Drake), with his family of about twelve persons, then living at Nobscut Hill, were among the Indians ordered for security to Deer Island, at the breaking out of King Philip's war. Resenting the ill usage the Indians received from their conductors, he escaped in the night with his family, but was afterwards betrayed with others, by his son Peter Jethro, to the English, by whom, according to Hubbard, he was executed Sept. 26, 1676.

In 1665, "Animatohu, alias Jethro," was among the Indians who conveyed to John Haynes and others, 3200 acres of land E. of Quinsigamoge Pond. The Indian name probably belongs to the younger Jethro.

Peter Jethro, in 1683, was living with Jonathan Ting, of Dunstable; in consideration of whose kindness to him and his uncle Jeffry (called Quaquoco Noucanomon of Waymessitt), he conveyed to him a tract of land six miles square, at Machapaog, N. of Watchusett's Hill and W. of Groton, which he had previously obtained from his uncle Jeffry. In the deed Peter represents himself as without children and not likely to have any. In 1684, he was among the Indian grantors of the two-mile tract, added upon the W. line of Sudbury. Peter Jethro had derived much benefit from his intercourse with the English, and at times acted as scribe for the Indians. His treachery to his father led to the remark of Increase Mather, "that abominable Indian, Peter Jethro, betrayed his own father and other Indians of his special acquaintance unto death." A tradition exists, that since the incorporation of the town, Peter's house has been occupied by Indians, who are reputed to have been mischievous, and troublesome to their neighbors.

CAPT. TOM,— called also Old Tom, alias Wuttusacomponum, appears to have been one of the praying Indians. Among the State Files* are papers describing the character of "Tom," (perhaps the same Indian), which accuse him of lying, excessive drinking &c., and as, "in brief, a fellow very profane and of noe conscience;" and adds, that going on one occasion "to charge his gun, and wanting paper to ram in, he did teare a piece

---

* Vol. xxx, p. 57.

of the Bible," and said "he would make the word of God to flie." It is certain, however, that he was held in esteem by Gookin, who speaks of him as "the chief among these praying Indians, who also was their ruler, named Capt. Tom, &c.—a prudent, and I believe a pious man, and had given good demonstration of it many years." He again refers to him as his chief assistant at Pakachoag, being of the chief sachem's blood of the Nipmuck country, and then (1674) residing at Hassanamesit (Grafton). During Philip's war, he was pressed to join his countrymen against the English; and depositions exist among the State papers, of persons who swore to have recognized him at the attack upon Sudbury, at the Causey, "by a grumbling sign or noise" peculiar to him. On the 9th or 10th June, 1676, he was taken, with his daughter and two children, by a scout sent by Capt. Henchman, *about* 10 *miles S.E. of Marlborough*. While on trial in Boston, an urgent petition* was sent in to the Governor and Council by James Rumney Marsh and others, in behalf of 80 Indian soldiers then in the service of the English, praying for the lives of "Capt. Tom, his son Nehemiah, his wife and two children; John Uktuck, his wife and children; Maanum and her children." The lives of the women and children were spared; Capt. Tom and another were hanged the 26th (some say 22d) June; "both," says a writer, "died (as it is to be hoped) penitent, praying to God, not like the manner of the heathen." Gookin, who befriended the unhappy Christian Indians at that time of trial, after his favorable mention of Capt. Tom's prudence and piety above quoted, adds, "I had particular acquaintance with him, and cannot think otherwise concerning him in his life or at his death; though possibly in this action he was tempted beyond his strength." From the distance and position of the hill referred to as the place of Capt. Tom's capture, it is probable that "Capt. Tom's Hill" in Framingham derived from him its name.†

The success of the Apostle Eliot's labors among the natives, led to the establishment of several towns of praying Indians, of which

---

* State papers, vol. 30.

† There are traces of other Indians, bearing the name of Capt. Tom. "Thomas Ukqueakussennum, alias Captain Tom, of Waymessick," (Chelmsford), was among the grantors of the Salem township, 1686. (Hist. Salem.) In 1703, the town of Hampton was surprised by a noted warrior called Capt. Tom, a Tarratine. Drake's Book of the Indians.

the seven oldest were settled at Natick, Punkapaog (Stoughton), Hassanamesitt (Grafton), Okommakamesit (Marlborough), Wamesitt (Lowell), Nashobah (Littleton), and Magunkaquog or Magunkook, now Hopkinton.

Framingham lay midway between three of these towns, viz: Natick, Okommakamesit, and Magunkaquog. Natick — the name signifying a place of hills — was the earliest settled, and in that part now called South Natick. Gookin, in 1674, described it as containing 29 families and about 145 souls; the chief man being Waban,* about 70 years of age, and a man of great prudence and piety.†

The town of Okommakamesit, which embraced a tract of 6000 acres in Marlborough, was occupied at the same period, by about 10 families and about 50 souls. Their ruler, who deceased in 1674, was Onomog, a sachem who had been "the very soul of that place." Hutchinson gives their teacher's name as Solomon.

The town of Magunkaquog, or Magunkook, i. e. the plain of great trees, is described by Gookin ‡ as "partly in Natick, partly on land granted by the country. It lies W. southerly from Boston about 24 miles, near the midway between Natick and Hassanamesitt. The number of its inhabitants are about 11 families and about 55 souls. There are, men and women, eight members of the church at Natick and about 15 baptized persons. The quantity of land belonging to it is about 3000 acres. The Indians plant upon a great hill which is very fertile, and these people worship God and keep the Sabbath and observe civil order, as do the other towns. They have a constable and other officers. Their ruler's name is Pomhaman,§ a sober and active man and pious.

---

* Waban held a commission as justice of the peace, and is represented to have acted with great energy in the government of his people. Among other anecdotes related of him, it is said that being once inquired of, what he would do, when Indians got drunk and quarrelled, he answered: " Tie um all up, and whip um plaintiff, whip um fendant, and whip um witness." Drake.

† In 1764, only thirty-seven Indians remained in Natick; and in 1792, they were reduced to one family of five persons and two single-women. The Natick Indian town was settled in 1651; the first church was embodied, 1660. Natick was incorporated as an English district, in 1761, and as a town, 1781. 1 M. H. Coll. I. 184 note.

‡ 1 M. H. Coll. I. 188.

§ Of Pomhaman we have obtained no satisfactory information. The religious confession of Ponampam (possibly the same), is preserved to us. (3 M. H. Coll. iv. 240.) Pomham was Sachem of Showamit (where Gorton settled), and came under the government of the Mass. Colony.

Their teacher is named Job,* a person well accepted for piety and ability among them." He adds, that this town was the last setting of the old towns, and that the Indians had plenty of corn and kept some cattle, horses and swine, for which the place was well accommodated. The "great hill" referred to, which is now called Maguneo Hill, and on which ancient apple trees were standing a few years since, lies to the S.W. of the village of Ashland, at a short distance from the Railroad. The precise bounds of the Indian territory are not known; but from the extent of the grant, they undoubtedly continued within the ancient territory of Framingham, as the farm of Savil Simpson began at the foot of the hill. It is probable that a part, at least, of the Magunkook tract was granted by the General Court to Sherburne, and was included in the "4000 acres adjoining unto Magunkoog Indian Hill," which they gave to the Natick Indians in exchange for land to the E. of Sherburne which they received from the latter, in 1679.† The burial place of the Magunkook Indians is still identified, as the spot on which stands the brick school-house, near the house of Mr. Samuel Valentine. Skeletons have been disinterred, within a few years, near the highway.

Some interest attaches to this Indian community, not only from their proximity to this town, but from the part they took in the destruction of Thomas Eames' house in Framingham, the only event of Philip's war particularly connected with the town, which will soon be related. The Indians of Magunkook, with those of the other praying towns, were brought under serious suspicion at the opening of the war. The greater part of the Christian Indians were disarmed, and sent to Deer Island, where, according to Gookin, they suffered extreme hardships. The inhabitants of Magunkook were among those who most readily yielded to the enticements of Philip, so that after the war their plantation was broken up.‡

Hutchinson i. 119. Sav. Wint. ii. pp. 120, 155. Israel Pumhamun was one of the Natick Indians who conveyed land to John Coller, Aug. 24, 1699.

* Job, whose Indian name was Kattewanit, was at Hassanamesit at the beginning of Philip's war. He was friendly to the English, and rendered them much service as a spy.

Among the Indians of Magunkook before the war, were William Wanuckhow or Jackstraw, his sons Joseph and Apumatquin or John, Joshua Assatt, John Dublet, son-in-law of Jacob, the latter afterwards of Natick.

† See State files.

‡ Before the war, the whole number of praying Indians in all the

The formidable combination under King Philip, spread consternation through the colonies of Plymouth and Massachusetts, and threatened a general ruin of the whites. The designs of that crafty chieftain had been suspected as early as 1671, which led to the dangerous expedient of a general disarming of the Indians. The first act in the tragic war which followed, was the attack upon the people of Swanzey, June 24, 1675. Others succeeded in various places, until the memorable Narraganset fight, on the 19th Dec. 1675, upon the issue of which, Philip retired into the western parts of Massachusetts.

A few weeks after that event, occurred the incident we are now to relate.* Thomas Eames, who a few years before had leased the "Pelham Farm," at Sudbury, settled, near 1670, within the bounds of the Plantation of Framingham. He built his house on the southern slope of Mount Wayte, between the Sudbury river and Farm pond, at a distance of about seven miles S.W. from the ancient town of Sudbury, and about three miles E. from the Indian town of Magunkook. A partial depression of the surface, with the surrounding apple trees, still indicate the spot, which is upon the farm of Mr. Harrison Eames. His family consisted, at the time now referred to, of a wife and nine children.† On the 1st of February, (some accounts say the 2d,) 1675-6, during the absence of the father, who had gone to Boston to obtain a supply of ammunition, a party of about 12 Indians, headed by Netus, approached the house, one of them remaining in the corn-fields at a distance, probably as a watch. Tradition states that two of the children were surprised at the well, and seized; and that the mother, who had resolved never to be taken alive, made a brave resistance, and being employed at

---

towns was estimated to be between eleven and twelve hundred. After its close, scarce half that number could be found. Gookin says, that "through God's favor, some of them were preserved alive, and are reconciled again to the English, and now live among the rest of the Christian Indians."

* Besides the well-known authorities for the particulars of this event, the author has discovered the original minutes of the magistrate, (Thomas Danforth), who examined the actors in the affair; and also a petition and deed, to which the sons of Mr. Eames were parties, detailing some of the circumstances.

† Six of the children were by his second wife, then living. Their names were Thomas, Samuel, Margaret, Nathaniel, Sarah, and Lydia; the oldest about twelve, the youngest about three years of age. One only of his sons is known to have been married at this time, who probably lived at Watertown. See Watertown Records.

the time in making soap, poured upon the assailants the boiling fluid. The Indians soon succeeded in firing the house, and either killed or took captive the entire family; at the same time destroying the barn, with the cattle and stores.

Of the exact numbers killed and taken captive, the accounts are contradictory and irreconcilable.* The nearest estimate we can form is, that of the ten members of the family, the wife and three or four of the children were killed, and the rest carried into captivity. Hubbard notices, that the wife of Eames' son died the following day, having, as another account says, been previously tomahawked and scalped. Of this statement we have found no confirmation. Tradition informs us that the captives were first taken in the direction of Lancaster, and that one of the sons was present at the attack upon the garrison of Sudbury, the following April.† It was probably the same son, who, in the spring following his capture, succeeded in making his escape. Having been early instructed, in such an event, to go in the di-

---

* Drake quotes two authorities, one of which gives seven as killed, and two children taken; the other, "they killed seven people in a barbarous manner, and carried some away captive." Drake himself says, without giving his authority, " in all, seven persons were killed or fell into the hands" of the Indians. According to Hubbard, (p. 84) Mr. Eames' "wife was killed and his children carried captive," and he adds, that "the next day his son's wife died." The Indian deed to the sons of Eames says, they "killed his wife and three children, and captivated five more, whereof only three returned, who are now dwelling on the said (Eames') lands." The sons in their own petition to the Gen. Court, represent, that "they slew his wife and five children, and four only of those whom they took into captivity returned." The facts known are as follows: Eames, in his inventory detailing his losses, states his family to have consisted of "a wife and nine children." As his oldest son, John, was probably living at Watertown, it is to be presumed that he was not included in the family. His wife having had children by her first husband, it is probable that some of them lived with her. There is no reason for supposing, that any of the family escaped death or captivity. The whole number, then, killed and taken captive, was probably ten. Of this number three only of the children can be accounted for, viz. Samuel, Margaret and Nathaniel, all of whom returned, and were subsequently married. According to the confession of the Indians, there were two daughters among the captives. It is certain therefore that as many as four captives were carried away. As it is probable, moreover, that not all the captives ultimately returned, the best conjecture we can form is, that four or five, including the wife, were killed, and the rest taken captive, of whom three returned. As the sons of Eames who returned were quite young at the time of their captivity, and as there is reason to believe, that the captives were separated soon after the catastrophe occurred, the discrepancy in the different statements in which they were parties, is less surprising.

† He is said to have reported, that the Indians suffered severely by the fire from the garrison, and that an aged squaw lost six sons, all of whom were brave and distinguished warriors.

rection of the rising sun, after a bold and perilous journey of some 30 miles in the wilderness, he reached in safety an English settlement; an act of singular courage in a boy of eleven or twelve years.*

We learn from the confession of the Indian actors in this domestic tragedy, that near the month of June following the event, the two daughters of Mr. Eames were "at a great hill about midway between Watchusett and Penecooke, in good health, and not in a starving plight;" that Mattahump † had one of the daughters, and Pumapen the other. They were supposed, in August, to be in the neighborhood of Fort Aurania, (Albany). Respecting the subsequent fate of the captives, we know little more than that two sons and one daughter were happily restored to their desolated home and friends. Tradition throws an air of romance upon the fortunes of Margaret, the daughter. The colonial government having despatched some agents to obtain the release of captives detained in Canada, one of their company was in his own turn captivated by the attractions of the daughter of Mr. Eames, whose release he had obtained, and whom he soon after made his wife. The Cambridge Records are authority for the fact, that Joseph Adams married Margaret Eames, in 1688.‡

---

* "The next day, (i. e. March 12, another account says May), a youth of about eleven years of age made his escape from the Indians, who was taken prisoner when his father's house was burnt and his mother murthered, on the first of February last; and though the boy knew not a step of the way to any English town, and was in continual danger of the skulking Indians in the woods, and far from the English, yet God directed him aright and brought him to the sight of *plantane*, (the herb which the Indians call English-foot, because it grows only amongst us and is not found in the Indian plantations), whereupon he concluded he was not far from some English town, and accordingly following of the plantane, he arrived safely among us." (Drake's old Indian Chronicle, p. 122). From the age above given, it is probable that the name of the boy was Samuel Eames.

† Mattahump was probably the Mautamp, Sachem of Quabaog, who, in 1665, witnessed the sale of Brookfield, and was hanged with others, Sept. 26, 1676. Hubbard, pp. 35, 75.

‡ It is quite probable that one or more of the children remained in Canada; a not uncommon event, and in some cases the result of preference on the part of the captives, who became so accustomed to their change of life, as to lose all attachment to their English society and friends. Hutchinson states in his history (ii. 140), that the captives who have been carried to Canada, have often received very kind usage from the French inhabitants. A tradition exists, that a sister of Capt. Isaac Clark of Framingham, who with her mother (then of Maine), had been taken by the Indians to Canada, was there sold to the French; among whom she lived so contented and happy, that when money was sent for her redemption, she refused to leave; sending word that the money was not sufficient to supply her table.

The following inventory exhibits the particulars of the loss sustained by Mr. Eames.

"An inventory of the loss of Thomas Eames, when his house was fired by Indians at Framingham near unto Sudbury, in the County of Middlesex, the first of February, 1675-6.
Imprimis — A wife and nine children.

Item — A house 34 feet long, double floores, and garret, and cellar, and a barn 52 foot long, leantir'd one side and two ends,	£100.00 00
It. 4 oxen,	024.00 00
It. 7 cows, fair with calf,	028.00 00
It. 2 yearlings,	003.00 00
It. 1 bull,	002.00 00
It. 2 heifers, fair with calf,	006.00 00
It. 1 heifer,	002.00 00
It. 8 sheep, fair with lamb,	003.12 00
It. 30 loads of hay in yᵉ barn at 8s. per load,	012.00 00
It. 10 bush. wheate, at 6s. p. bush.	003.00 00
It. 40 bush. rye, at 4s. 8d. p. bush.	008.00 00
It. 210 bush. of indian, at 3s. p. bush.	031.00 00
It. Hemp and flax, in yᵉ barne,	001.00 00
It. Fire arms, with other arms and ammunition,	006.00 00
It. Butter 20s., cheese 40s., 2 barrels and a half of Pork, and 4 flitches of bacon 10 lb.	013.00 00
It. Carpenter's and joyner's tooles,	005.00 00
It. 2 great spinning wheeles and 2 small wheeles, 4s., 4 for cards,	001.00 00
It. 6 beds, 3 of them feather beds, and 3 flock, 6 Ruggs, 12 blankets,	005.00 00
It. 1 chest of lynen with yᵉ sheets and shifts,	010.00 00
It. A livery cupboard with what was in it,	002.00 00
It. My wife's lynen and wearing apparel, and children's cloathing, and my own cloathing, with clothing that was my former wife's,	025.00 00
It. Pewter, brasse, and Iron ware,	014.00 00
It. Churns and other dairy vessells, with other wooden lumber,	005.00 00
Total,	330.12 00

The actors in the affair we have related, did not long escape the hands of justice. Netus, the leader of the party, was killed March 27th, at Marlborough, by a party of English under the command of Lt. Jacobs, and his wife was sold. Annecoeken, another, was dead before the close of summer. Aug. 11th, a warrant was issued by Thomas Danforth, Magistrate, for the ar-rest of "Joshua Assatt, John Dublet, son-in-law to Jacob, William Jackstraw and two of his sons, the name of the one Joseph, also Jackstraw's wife, all of them late of Moguncog Indians."* Three of them, viz. William Wanuckhow, alias Jackstraw, and his two sons, Joseph and John, were taken and examined by Mr. Danforth the 14th of the same month, before whom they made confession of the act, assigning as its cause, "their missing of corn, which they expected to have found at Mogoncocke." They also accused two others, Joshua Assatt, then absent in the English service at Marlborough, under Capt. Hunting, and Awassaquah, who was sick "at the Ponds." † The three were committed to prison, and Joseph was indicted, with probably the others, who

---

* The constable was also ordered to warn Peter Ephraim's wife to appear before the magistrate. Peter lived at Brush hill, on Natick lands exchanged with Sherburne in 1679, not far distant from Framingham, where he had broken up land. He was a Nipmuck Indian, whose religious confession is given by Eliot. He rendered valuable services to the English in Philip's war, and as commander of a company of friendly Indians, accompanied the English to Rehoboth. Ancient accounts state that while the English became discouraged, "Ephraim continued and captived forty-two, besides killing eight." He was of Natick, in 1695. His wife's name was Wuttawtinnusk. Peter's hill, a part of Natick, probably derived its name from him.

† We subjoin a copy of the original minutes of this examination, which are on file in the handwriting of Mr. Danforth, in the archives of the State. Vol. xxx. p. 211. The names in *Italics* undoubtedly indicate the individuals accused:

"Camb. 14, 6, 76.
"*Netus* — dead and his wife sold.
"*Annecoeken* — dead.
"*Aponapawquin* als. Jacob.
"*Acompanatt* als. James Philip.
"*Pakananunquis* — Joshua Assatt, with C(apt.) Hunting.
"*Apumatquin* als. John.
"*William*.
"*Joseph*.
"*Pumapene* of Quabaug, and his sonne, abt. 40 years old.

"*Awassaquah* — at (the) ponds, sick.
—[?]—of Nashaway (absent).
ye wife of Aquetokush, and is sold already.
"Joseph Indian, son of William of Mogoncocke, being examined, do say and confess, that himself with those others named by the Marshal, were the persons that destroyed Thomas Eames' family, in the beginning of February last; that the same was occasioned by their missing of corn which they expected to have found at Mogoncocke, and by that means were provoked to come and do the spoil, killing of some and carrying captive the rest, and burning house, barn and cattle; and do confess that he himself carried away on his back one of Eames' sons. Also he saith that about 2 mo. since, he enquired concerning Goodman Eames' two daughters, and understood they were at a great hill about middleway between Watchuset and Penecooke, and were in good health and not in a starving plight.
"Apumatquin, alias John, being examined, do confess the same thing as above; to be the truth; only he saith he knows nothing how it is with Goodman Eames' daughters at present, not having heard lately any thing concerning them.
"Wm. Jackstraw being examined, do confess the same thing as above; owns that his sons Joseph and John above examined, were present at the desolation of Gn. Eames' family, and

were tried September 18th. How many of their accomplices, if any, were afterwards brought to justice, does not appear. Gookin states that "three were executed about Thos. Eames his burning." The execution took place the 21st of September. "Two of the murderers," according to the petition of the Eames' sons, " Old Jacob, a chief man sometime at Natick, and Joshua Assunt, returned and were pardoned, and lived at Natick many years after." The close of this war of so disastrous issues to the Indians, undoubtedly dictated a course of forbearance and clemency to the accused; since justice had already been satisfied by the blood of three of their accomplices.

For the severe loss sustained in this affair, computed, as we have seen, at £330, (a large sum for those days), Thomas Eames received a small indemnity. The General Court granted him, "various considerations thereunto moving," 200 acres of land. He also sued the Indians at law, and obtained from them a tract of 300 acres. But no recompense in land or treasure could restore to him his desolated home. He survived the calamity a few years, and died about a week before the 4th anniversary of the event, Jan. 25, 1680, aged about 62.*

The return of peace, after the destructive hostilities of this Indian war, was soon followed by the arrival of new settlers in this territory, particularly towards the S. part. In 1674 the inhabitants of Bogestow, now Sherburne, receiving from the Court a grant of six miles square, and becoming soon organized as a civil

---

that himself was one of the company, but kept at a distance, a little off in the corn fields.

"Isaac Beech being present at this examination do say, that Joseph above-named, confessed the same thing to him and John Prentice.

"For encouragement to Joseph, who was first examined, to tell the truth, (they at first denying all), I told him I would speak to the Governor to spare his life, in case he would tell me plainly how all the said matter was acted.

"Taken the day and year above-said, before   THO. DANFORTH.

"Jno. Speene, Interpreter.

"Confessions were owned by the prisoners at the bar 18. 7. '76.
    "E. R. S."

"Wm. Jackstraw saith, that Mattahump hath one of Gn. Eames' daughters, and Pumapen (the other), and they were alive at planting time; and he thinks they may be yet (towards Fort) Auranea (Albany), but (uncertain where.)

* On the State Files (xxx. p. 122) is a paper (without date, probably about 1680), recounting the abusive treatment received by Mary Parkes of Sherburne (æ. 39), from an Indian who encountered her returning from a visit to "Corporal Rice's." The particulars are not worthy of notice. She reached her home in safety, after a severe fright.

community, several of the inhabitants of this Plantation were admitted there as townsmen.* Most of these were received conformably to an act of the General Court in 1679, requiring that "all other farmes that are nighest Sherborn meeting house, shall likewise be in the bounds of Sherborn, and do duty and receive priviledge therein;" to which the following proviso was annexed: "*Provided always, that the tract of waste lands scituate and lying indifferently accomodable for Sudbury and Marlborough as well as Sherborn, and are now belonging to Thomas Danforth, Esq. Deputy Governor, be excepted.*" † This action by the Court possesses some interest, as the origin of the "difficulties with Sherburne," which caused no small contention, after the incorporation of Framingham as a township. The arrangement was doubtless made in aid of that young township, which, according to an early Rate, contained only 16 taxable polls.‡

1680. The largest body of the settlers of this territory being at this period in the neighborhood of Sudbury bounds, some interest is connected with the following extract from the Records of that town, illustrating the care of the early planters in the instruction and moral training of the rising commonwealth. The statement was prepared in conformity to an act of the General Court, requiring returns to be made relative to the support of the ministry, the maintenance of schools, and the general order of families, in respect to habits of regular industry and good morals. Early in the year, the selectmen had reported their "having gone over the houses throughout the town, from house to house, and inspected and made enquiry;" and "do find that all children and young persons are in a forward and growing way as to reading

---

* The records of Sherburne bear the names of the following who were admitted as inhabitants :— Thomas Eames, Jan. 4, 1674-5 ; John Death, Jan. 1677-8 ; Thomas Gleason, July 8 1678 ; Tho. Pratt, Sen., Zacry Padelford, John Eames, Isaac Learned and Tho. Pratt, Jr., April, 1679. Thomas Eames was early one of the Selectmen, and was on the committee for building the meeting house, and received a grant "for building" the same. John Eames was Selectman in 1682. The Rev. Daniel Gookin, (H. C. 1669 and Librarian of the college), son of Major Gookin of Cambridge, was settled in Sherburne as the first minister, in 1681, with a salary of £40, and d. Jan. 8, 1717-8, æ. 67.

† State Files — Towns.

‡ By virtue of the act referred to, Sherburne claimed, in 1701, a tract of land, within the limits of this town, included between the W. bounds of Washakum and Farm (or Great) Ponds, the Indian bridge or Beaver Dam, and Sudbury river, including Larned's and Gleason Pond, and the land to the N. of them.

and catechising, and as to work and employment, they find them generally diligent and in a hopeful thriving way in all respects."*

The account after some details, adds, " that though there be no stated school, the inhabitants being scattered, they have two school dames each side of the river that teacheth small children to spell and read, which is so managed by their parents and goodmen at home, — after such sort, as that the Selectmen returned from all parts a comfortable and good account of all these matters, and render them *growing in several families beyond expectation, hardly reprovable anywhere, encouraging in most places and in others very commendable, so as that the end is accomplisht hitherto ;* and for teaching to write and cypher, there is Mr. Tho. Walker, and two or three others about town that do teach ; and the selectmen having also been made acquainted that ye Court expects their inspection, touching persons who live from under family government or after a dissolute and disorderly manner, to ye dishonor of God and corrupting of youth ; the selectmen, after personal enquiry into all families and quarters, in and about this town, do return this answer, *that they find none such amongst them.*"

Who can estimate, how far we are indebted to the noble spirit speaking in these tones of homeliness and simplicity, for the intelligence, the enterprise, the moral and religious spirit which have since characterized this Commonwealth!

New roads, soon after this period, were probably opened in the Plantation, as appears from the following extract from the County Records.†

" Oct. 7, 1684, Lt. Edward West, Obadiah Morse, Thomas Read, Jonathan Whitney, Jon. Fay, and John Collar, are appointed a committee to lay out highways leading from Sudbury, Sherborn, Marlborough and Framingham, and the Falls upon Charles River, so as may be most convenient for the accommodation of travellers from Town to Town, both for man and beast."

As no return is found upon the Record, what particular action was had by the commission does not appear. The same Records inform us, that Dec. 16 of the same year, John Eames recovered of the town of Sherborn £5 in country pay, for killing 10 wolves.

1691. A great flood is noticed as having occurred in this region on the 1st of March of this year, and the " greatest flood

---

* The number of rateable males in Sudbury at this time was 62 ; the number of families " in and about the town," 59 ; and the pay of the minister £80, a quarter part in money.
† iv. 131.

by several feet perpendicular, that ever was remembered by English or Indians then surviving." *

1692. This year is memorable, as the date of the outbreak of the celebrated Witchcraft delusion; in the course of which, the lives of many innocent persons were sacrificed to a "blind zeal and superstitious credulity." It is so far connected with our present history, as having caused the emigration, soon after, to this Plantation, from Salem village, now Danvers, of the families of Clayes and Nurse, who, with their descendants, still remaining in the town, have been useful and respected members of the community. They settled about a mile W. from the centre of the Plantation, and the neighborhood has since been known by the name of SALEM END.

The melancholy delusion referred to, commenced in Essex County — the chief seat of its violence — Feb. 1691-2, in the family of Mr. Parris, a minister of Salem Village, and soon spread into other parts of the Colony. It was communicated to this country from England, where several years before had been published Glanvil's Witch Stories, and the trials of the Suffolk Witches, books which circulated in New England, and with the added authority of so great a man as Sir Matthew Hale, who countenanced the superstition, made a deep impression upon the minds of the grave people who dwelt amidst the gloom of the wilderness, and were harassed by continual privation and danger. Among the numerous families who suffered from this infatuation, were the two above named. March 1, 1692, Rebecca, wife of Francis Nurse, and Sarah, wife of Peter Clayes, of Salem Village, were committed with others to the prison in Boston, on the charge of witchcraft. The fate of the former was singularly unhappy. At her trial the jury could not agree in a verdict, and on the second return to the Court had not found her guilty. Persisting, however, in her refusal to answer certain questions, about an expression she had used, her silence was made constructive proof of guilt, and she was accordingly condemned to death. She was excommunicated July 3, from the old church of Salem, and on the 19th of the same month was hung. Many testimonials were given of her good character and domestic worth, without effect. The 31st of

---

* I M. H. Coll. x.

the following month, the wife of Mr. Clayes was removed to the Ipswich prison; but the fury of the delusion abating, she escaped with her life, having, as tradition says, been conveyed by night to Framingham. Mary Easty, a sister of Rebecca Nurse, (as was Sarah Clayes), also Abigail Williams, probably the sister or niece of Mr. Clayes, appear to have been implicated, in the course of events. It is painful to reflect, that this delusion was encouraged by men of high distinction in the Colony, both in the church and state. One of them (Judge Sewall) afterwards bewailed his participation in it, and asked "pardon of God and man."

The gradual increase of settlers at Lanham and the E. part of Framingham, on the borders of Sudbury, some of whom probably attended public worship in that town, without bearing their due portion of town charges, led the selectmen of that place, in 1691, to apply to the General Court for relief. The following order was accordingly passed.

"At an adjournment of the Gen. Court of their Maj. Colony of the Mass. Bay, in Boston, March 8, 1691-2:

"In answer to the petition of the selectmen of Sudbury, ordered: that the outdwellers adjoining unto the said Town, comprehended within the line beginning at Matth. Rice's, from thence to Cornet Wm. Brown's, Corporal Henry Rice's, Thomas Drury's, Tho. Walker, Jun., John How, and Samuel Winch's (not belonging to any other towne), be annexed unto the Town of Sudbury, and continue to bear their part of all duties, and partake of all priviledges there, as formerly, until further order."

In pursuance of this order, which applied (except perhaps in the case of the first two), to inhabitants of the present town of Framingham, we soon find traces of town action within the borders of this town.

"In 1693, Daniel Stone and John Adams, were chosen fence viewers from Lanham, Daniel Stone's Mill to Sherborn bounds.

"Jan. 10, 1693-4. Voted and agreed &c., that Daniel Stone, Jr., Nath. Stone, Samuel Winch, John Adams, Corporal Bent, David Stone, Mr. Henry Rice, David Rice, Thomas Drury, Thom. Walker, John How, shall be rated to the highway according to former custom and usage; and shall work out their rates about the making and maintaining of the bridge and Casway, at Dan. Stone's river, and at Cochecheuat brook the bridge and casway there, in good repair, &c.

"Also voted and agreed, &c., That Corporal Samuel How, Mr. Thomas Read, (John) How, John Gibbs, Math. Gibbs, Edmond Bowker, Tho. Read, Jun., Tho. Frost, Benj. Wight, John Sheers, shall be rated to the highway rate as formerly, and shall work out their rates at Lanham bridge and Casway, &c."

In Feb. 1693-4, among the schoolmistresses appointed by the selectmen " for the younger sort of children," (Samuel Wright having been appointed to teach and instruct children and youth to read and write and cast accompts), we find " at the S. end of the town, the wife of our brother Daniel Stone, and at Lanham, the wife of brother Reade, Sen." and the selectmen " entreat the persons above named to accept thereof."

The neighborhood above referred to, contiguous to the present bounds of Wayland, was known soon after this period as the " Sudbury Farms." The success of Sudbury in sharing the dispersed inhabitants of this unappropriated region, inspired hopes in another quarter.

Feb. 3, 1695. At a town meeting in Sherburne, relative to an enlargement of their town bounds, by the addition of " land joining to the farm of Henry Rice, to make one township," embracing such " farmers as are willing to join our township," it was proposed " to run a straight line from the S. corner of Henry Rice's to the cartway, crossing Cochituate brook, near where Course brook meets with Cochituate brook." The projected union, however, met with no successful issue.

The time had arrived when the Incorporation of the Plantation began to be seriously meditated. Its territory was becoming settled in all directions. It contained a population estimated at near 200 souls. Great inconvenience was experienced from the want of schools, and the remoteness of public worship. The community possessed among their number men of enterprise and energy. An individual had become a proprietor of lands in the Plantation, who was destined to act an important part in the future establishment and administration of the town. As early as 1693, Joseph Buckminster, of Muddy River, now Brookline, then about 27 years of age, a man who to a considerable estate, united great resolution and ardor of character, was in possession, jointly with Joseph White, of a tract of land, the commencement of the large interest he afterwards acquired. Accordingly, in 1696, a petition was formally preferred to the General Court, praying that the inhabitants might be incorporated as a township. This first movement was for the time lost; the petition having been laid over to the session of the following year.

The winter of 1696 – 7 was remarkable for an extreme severity, extending from the middle of November to the middle of March. The Records of Sudbury notice it as "the terriblest winter for continuance of frost and snow, and extremity of cold, that ever was remembered." Much sickness and mortality arose from the prevalence of coughs and colds. Other contemporaneous accounts state, that at Boston, sleighs and loaded sleds passed on the ice from Boston as far as Nantasket. What added to the sufferings of the colonists, was the great scarcity of food, grain never having been higher.

Before proceeding to give, in orderly detail, the proceedings which issued in the establishment here of a township, it may be proper to notice a transaction of some importance, viz. the transfer of Mr. Danforth's control of the chief of his large estate in the Plantation to Joseph Buckminster, which involves various particulars of interest, as connected with subsequent events. Mr. Danforth had disposed of his lands to the tenants who had settled upon them, by lease, for a long term of years.* He now conveys almost the entire estate, in like manner, to Mr. Buckminster. The original instrument bears date March 25, 1699, and is on record among the Middlesex Deeds. After the usual introduction, we extract the following : —

"That whereas the said Thomas Danforth hath a tract or parcell of land, and a part of those lands commonly called Framingham, lying &c., in the wilderness, and is bounded by Sudbury on the northerly side thereof, by Marlborough on the westerly side, and the easterly side is bounded partly by land now occupied by Simon Mellins, John Collar Sen. and the Whitneys', and southerly, by Sherborn line : also, within said tract or parcell of land, is contained sundry parcells of land and meadows, that are appropriated to sundry other persons and not to the said T. D. : also within said tract of land is comprehended one neck of land, bounded by Sudbury river, southerly, S. westerly, and S. easterly, and a small branch of said river northerly, running towards Marlborough line, and said line is the westerly bounds thereof, which said neck of land, (excepting only 600 part thereof to be laid out in — distinct

---

* The rents were paid for many years; until, by some means unexplained, the tenants were able to resist the demand. Tradition states that the legal evidences had been surreptitiously destroyed. The late Mr. Ebenezer Eaton is said to have been the last agent for collecting rents.

places and no more), the said T. D. reserveth to lye in common, for the accommodation of those that do or shall occupy other, the said lands of the said T. D., as for the tennants and farmers of him, the said Joseph Buckminster, in manner as he, the said T. D., shall hereafter appoint and order, reserving also to Simon Mellins and John Collar, and the farms by them occupied, all the meadows lying upon Sudbury river, as far downward as the aforesaid branch of the said river, and so much of the upland as shall be set out to them for the accommodating the fencing of said meadows, and to the other farmers of the said lands of the said T. D. conveniency for passage of their cattle to the said neck of land, and an highway of 20 pole wide or more, in manner and place as shall be requisite and meet, as said T. D. shall appoint — also 600 acres of land to be laid out in one entire place, and to bound southerly upon the path leading from Dea. Stone's to Marlborough; also for the accommodation of the meeting house and settlement of the minister, said T. D. reserveth 140 acres, and is laid out in two or more places, as they, the above named T. D. and J. B., have ordered and appointed — all the remainder of the said tract of land to him the said T. D. appertaining," &c.

Without specifying the bounds, he proceeds to lease the same to the said Joseph Buckminster, for the term of 999 years, at a rent of £22 per annum, current money; and in default of money, in good merchantable corn, (not exceeding one-sixth part Indian corn or oats), butter, and well fatted beef or pork, (boars and bulls excepted), at the current money price.

The reader will recognize in the reservations above noticed, the origin of the Common lands, and of the grant for the support of public worship; which last we shall have occasion to refer to, in connection with the building of the second meeting house.

On the 5th of November succeeding the above act, Gov. Danforth departed this life, aged 77, after a long course of active service to the colony, leaving honorable proof of his liberality to the Plantation, whose establishment he had so long superintended.*

The proceedings which ultimately resulted in the incorporation

---

* In his will, bearing date Sept. 1, 1699, he gave to the College "three tenements on lease to Benj. Whitny, John Whitny and Isaac Bowen, situated at Framingham." He left also to his executors 600 acres at Framingham, on Doeskin hill, and 160 acres at the same place, "that John Green should have had." To Thos. Foxcroft, he gave one quarter of "Buckminster's lease," half of the same having been previously conveyed to his dr., Wid. Mary Phipps. The tract of 160 acres referred to, was the so called "HALF MILE SQUARE," which soon came into the possession of George Walkup, by whom one half was conveyed to Jonas Eaton, in 1708. A part of the tract is now owned by Deacon Jona. Greenwood, and a large part by the heirs of the late Mr. John Eaton.

of this town, appear to have been protracted, and attended with inconvenient embarrassment and delays. The petition which was referred to the session of 1697, met with no success that year. On a renewal of the petition the following year, the Court appointed a committee to meet in the Plantation and give hearing to all persons concerned; upon whose return, a resolve, after due deliberation, was passed by the House in favor of the incorporation of the place, but was non-concurred in by the Council. At the summer session petitions were renewed, praying the concurrence of the Council. But the relations of many of the inhabitants to Sudbury and Sherborn, threw embarrassment upon the action of the Court, and caused further postponement. A remonstrance (without date) was sent in by the Rev. Daniel Gookin of Sherborn, setting forth the grounds of opposition to the measure, and an additional remonstrance from inhabitants of that town.* The occupants of the so called "Sudbury Farms," † also threw in a petition adverse to their separation from Sudbury, on the ground of their peaceable connection with that town, where they had been at much charge for the building of a meeting house, and the maintenance of the ministry; though their opposition was subsequently withdrawn, and they were probably included among those who prayed to be annexed to the town, after its incorporation had been effected.

---

* The following is an abstract of Mr. Gookin's remonstrance:
I. The small number of families in Sherborn, not exceeding "3 score and four."
II. That the proposed seceders "have had the privilege of taking up lands in such parts of the town which they themselves have acknowledged to belong to Sherborn."
III. That to accommodate them "the meeting house was, to the great disadvantage and dissatisfaction of the first planters, placed at least a mile and an half nearer to those inhabitants that are now laboring to get away from us."
IV. That should these be suffered to go, "there will forthwith be some other families of this town will attempt the same thing, and so in a short time Sherborn will be reduced (as it were) to a mere nullity."
The petition of the inhabitants of Sherborn adds, that the land to be taken from that town, had been received in exchange for lands on the S.W. part of their town, now belonging to the Indians, and that so serious a loss would "disenable" them for the settling of new inhabitants. They urge moreover, that these inhabitants (proposing to be annexed to Framingham), have already taken up in Sherborn "in way of dividend near 500 acres of land;" and that if they be taken, it will disenable them to make good their engagement, for the maintenance of their reverend minister.

† The following farmers united in this petition, viz: John Bent, Daniel Stone, Matthew Rice, John Loker, Nathaniel Stone, John Adams, Elnathan Alling (Allen), Caleb Johnson, Samuel Allen, Isaac Rice, Matthew Stone.

In prosecution of their design, the inhabitants of the Plantation, in 1698 or 9, had built a meeting house for the accommodation of the town. The particulars of this event are not given, and are probably lost to us irrecoverably. All that is known is, that it was erected within what is now the old burying ground, its first minister, at his decease, having been buried (according to an undoubted tradition) beneath where the pulpit stood. The building was not immediately finished. In conformity too to an order of the General Court, in Oct. 1699, a survey of the proposed township was completed by Jno. Gore, surveyor, which has fortunately been preserved.

This survey, (the oldest we possess of the Plantation), bearing the date above named, is on a scale of 200 rods to the inch. It generally presents nearly the modern bounds of the town; excepting that it includes the farm of Mr. Savil Simpson, (now in Ashland), and contemplated the annexation of a tract of Natick land, west of Cochituate Pond, which would have made the west margin of the pond, in its whole extent, the E. bound of the town. This tract, however, (consisting of over 1200 acres), was included in dotted lines, and was not granted by the Court. The survey also embraced, as did afterwards the township, two irregular pieces of land, since known as FIDDLE NECK and THE LEG. The former, which derived its name from its figure, was a neck or goar of land, beginning near Bigelow's paper mill, where it was about 200 rods wide, and extending west a distance of near two and a half miles, the lines terminating at the westerly extremity in a point. It bordered during its whole extent upon the river, which formed its south bound, and the Boston and Worcester rail road track runs through it longitudinally. This tract was subsequently set off to Southborough. The LEG was a tract about 280 rods long and 150 rods wide, in the form of an oblong square, extending from the N. bound of Framingham at the extreme west, north into Marlborough, and was set off to the last named town in 1789.

The above named survey possesses some interest, in indicating the then settled parts of the Plantation, which included 33 houses N.W. of the river, and 31 S.E., making an aggregate of 64 houses. It also designates the location of the meeting house then built. On the S. bounds, as represented, considerable changes were subsequently made at the incorporation of Hopkinton and

Holliston. The original survey is to be found among the State files, and appears to have been referred to in the orders of the General Court establishing the township.*

As an off-set to the objections raised by Sherborn, to the incorporation of Framingham, the following paper was presented to the General Court; which, as it contains details of interest, and illustrates the character and motives of the actors at that period, we give in *extenso*.

" To his Excellency, Richard, Earl of Bellemont, Capt. General and Governor in Chief of his Maj. Province of the Mass. Bay in N. England, &c., and the Honored Court now assembled in Boston.

" We underwritten, do humbly petition, that agreeable to our former petition to the Honored Court, (relating to a township), we may now be heard in a few things.

" 1. Inasmuch as our former petition hath been so far considered by the Honored Court, as that the lower house have seen good to grant it, and your Honours have seen good to order us to procure a draft of the place we petition for, drawn by a sworn Surveyor, we have faithfully obeyed your orders herein.

" 2. In which Plot we have not knowingly taken in the lines or bounds of any town, only according to our petition that if the Indians were permitted to make sale of any of their lands, that then we might have the refusal of those scrips of land that interfere upon us; agreeable hereunto, we have run the line across some small bitts of Indian land, which otherwise would have made the line very crooked, which is now strait, which thing is plainly specified in the Plot, and the surveyor can inform your Honours therein; and if so be that any town shall charge us with running in upon their lines or bounds, we humbly desire that your Honours would cause them to produce the plot of their township, which will plainly evidence the contrary.

" 3. Inasmuch as that for a long time we have lain under a heavy burden, as to our attendance on the Publick Worship of God, so that for the most part our going to meeting to other places on the Sabbath, is our hardest day's work in the week; and by reason of these difficulties that attend us therein, we are forced to leave many at home, especially our children, where to our grief, the Sabbath is too much profaned; and being desirous to sanctify the Sabbath as to the duty of rest required, as far as we can with conveniency; these motives moving us, we have unanimously built a Meeting House, and have a minister

---

* In addition to the above, we possess a careful survey of the N. part of the town, taken in 1750 by R. Hazzell, Esq., extending W. from the " New Bridge " on Sudbury river to the house of the late Col. Trowbridge, and from the Sudbury line S. nearly two miles at its largest width. In 1832, an excellent plan of the town was prepared on surveys by Col. Jonas Clayes and Warren Nixon, Esq., which was printed, and is now in general use.

among us, and we now humbly petition to your Honours, to countenance our present proceedings.

"We contain in the plot we have taken above 350 souls, whereof not above a quarter part, can constantly attend the worship of God in other places, by reason of the length and badness of the ways; and we could have taken others in our plot that are out of the bounds of any town, but we would not deprive others of that privilege we petition for. Those families specified in the plot, are not in the bounds of any town; and are, some four, some five, some six, some seven miles from any other meeting; and very few of them above two miles distant from the meeting house, which we have built among ourselves.

"4. And whereas some do say, Sherborn town cannot raise their minister's salary without some of these families, which lie next to Sherborne town; we desire to inform your Honours that they never raised their minister's salary by reason of us, and none of them can say but that they are abundantly more able now without us, than they were at first with us; and now their meeting house is built, and their minister settled among them, and they contain more than three score families.

"5. And whereas some of Sherborne do say, that their meeting house was placed to accommodate some of these families, we desire to inform the Honored Court, that Sherborne meeting house is placed considerably nigher to the other side of their town bounds opposite from us, than to that side next to us: and it stands as nigh as can be thought in the center of those families which are in Sherborne town, without respecting us who are out of their town. We had no hand in settling of their town, and do humbly petition that we may not be so burthened to gratify their wills, when we are able to subsist by ourselves. We desire to inform the Honored Court, that we never had any voice in petitioning for Sherborne township; and to demonstrate further that Sherborne meeting house was not moved a mile and a half to accommodate any of us, as they say, their Pastor's house was erected and his lot laid out, before their meeting house was erected, and their Pastor goes now half a mile to meeting towards the other side of the town, opposite from us; and if their meeting house had been a mile and a half further, he must have gone two miles, which is irrational to conclude, that he should go so far to meeting.

"6. When Sherborne was granted to be a township, the Honored Court obliged them to settle 20 new families among them; and we fear that the Honored Court takes us for some of those families. It was for their sakes, if any, that their minister is settled as he is, and their meeting house placed as it is.

"7. And as for what privilege we have received from Sherborne, we have paid at an excessive rate for it: seven years after the settlement of the town, we could have bought as much of the same land for half the money that we gave for the settlement of their town and their meeting house, and Pastor's house: and as for what lands we have in Sherborne, we are contented that they should do duties in Sherborne.

"8. We petition neither for silver nor gold, nor any such worldly interest; but that we may have the worship of God upheld among us and our children; for this, we humbly repair to his Right Hon. Lordship and most Excellent Governor, under the shadow of whose wings we rejoice that we may rest for patronage and protection, and all of the Honored Court, now sitting, the Fathers of our Land; to whom we humbly petition to consider and do, for the enlargement of the Kingdom of our Lord and Saviour Jesus Christ, for the good of our souls, and the souls of our children, that they may not be like the heathen; and be pleased to grant us to be either a town or Congregation.

" Finally, if any of Sherborne or any other town, shall pretend any thing to the Honored Court, which may lead to the hindrance of a grant of our petition, (by reason of those many false informations that have been carried into your Honored Court to deceive), we humbly petition that we may have admittance to speak for ourselves.

" JOSEPH BUCKMASTER,
" PETER CLOICE,
" JOHN EAMS,
" JOHN HOW,
" ISAAC LEARNED,
" THOMAS DRURY,
" In behalf, and by the consent of the rest."

The above petition was probably presented the following year, and on the 5th of June, 1700, a hearing was granted to the inhabitants of Framingham, notice having been served upon Sherborne. The following act of the Court soon followed:

" At a Great and General Court or Assembly, for his Majesty's Prov. of the Mass. Bay in N. England, begun and held at Boston, upon Wednesday, the 29th of May, 1700,* in the 12th year of his Majesty's Reign, being convened by his Majesty's writts :

" Upon a full hearing of the matters in difference between the town of Sherborne and the inhabitants of the Plantation of Framingham, containing all that tract of land formerly granted to Tho. Danforth, Esq., next adjoyning to Sherborne upon the north and northerly :

" Ordered, That the said plantation called Framingham be from henceforth a township, retaining the name of Framingham, and have and enjoy all priviledges of a town according to law, saving unto Sherborne all their rights of land granted by the General Court to the first inhabitants, and those since purchased by exchange with the Indians of Natick, or otherwise, and all the farms lying within the said township, according to former grants of the General Court.

" ISAAC ADDINGTON, Secretary."

July 4, 1700. A petition was sent to the General Court, signed by Thomas Drury, David Rice, Thomas Walker, John Prat and John How, in behalf of the rest (several others of Fa mes

---

*This date is in Old Style, and, conformably to the present style, would fall on the 10th of June.

adjacent to Sudbury), praying to be annexed to Framingham, assigning that "the said town of Sudbury have for above a year denied your Petitioners the liberty of voting and other town privileges, utterly disclaiming them as not belonging to the said town, though your Petitioners have contributed to the building the Meeting-house and maintenance of the minister, and have paid several town rates and done many town duties." Whereupon, on the following day (July 5) it was "ordered, that the Petitioners and other the farmes lying betwixt the Northerly end of Cochitawick Pond and the line of Framingham, be laid and annexed to the town of Framingham; and enjoy all immunities and privileges with other the inhabitants in said town, and that they and their estates be liable to bear a proportion of charge in the said town."

July 11, 1700. The "petition of Joseph Buckmaster and John Towne, in behalf of the inhabitants of Framingham," was presented to the Court, asking whether the purchased as well as granted lands of Thomas Danforth, were not meant and comprehended in the order establishing the Township. The General Court accordingly passed the following, viz:

"RESOLVED, That all the lands belonging to Tho. Danforth, Esq., as well by purchase as Court grant, at the time of settling the town of Sherborne, in May, 1679, and excepted in the Court's confirmation of the township of Sherborne, be and belong unto Framingham; and that the inhabitants of the said town do convene and assemble at their meeting house, on the first Tuesday in August next, and then and there make choice of Selectmen and other town officers, to serve until March next, at which time the law appoints the choice of town officers."

It may be proper to add in this place, that the following year, June 5, 1701, the Selectmen of Framingham having asked to have the line run between Sudbury and Framingham, the General Court

"ORDERED, That the line between Sudbury and the farmes annexed to Framingham, as set forth in the Platt, exhibited under the hand of John Gore, bearing date, March 8, 1700-1, be and continue the boundary line between the said farmes and Sudbury forever, viz: from the northerly end of Cochittwat pond to the bent of the river by Daniel Stone's, and so as the line goes to Framingham and Sudbury line."

By the above proceedings the long deferred hopes of the Plantation were at length consummated; though questions of boundary were yet to be adjusted—the indefiniteness of the terms of the town grant, leaving unsettled the conflicting claims of the new town and Sherborne.

THE TOWN OF FRAMINGHAM.

FROM ITS INCORPORATION IN 1700.

GENERAL MISCELLANY CONNECTED WITH THE CIVIL HISTORY OF THE TOWN.

1700, AUGUST 5. The first Town Meeting was held, at which the following officers were chosen: Joseph Buckminster, David Rice, Thomas Drury, Jeremiah Picke, Peter Clayse, Sen., John Towne and Daniel Ston, SELECTMEN; Thomas Drury, TOWN CLERK; Simon Millen and Thomas Frost, CONSTABLES; John How and Benjamin Bridges, ASSESSORS; Thomas Walker, TOWN TREASURER; Abial Lamb, Sen., COMMISSIONER; John Prat, John Haven, Peter Clayse, Jr. and Samuel Winch, SURVEYORS OF HIGHWAYS.*

---

* The following year were chosen also four Tythingmen, four Fence Viewers, four Swine Drivers and one Grand Juryman. Other officers were subsequently added, as Clerk of the Market, Deer Rieves, (beginning about 1739 and ending about 1795), Sealer of Leather, Surveyor of Hemp and Flax, &c. In 1740 was chosen a weigher of bread, and in 1764 a Surveyor of Wheat and Flour. The Selectmen were chosen " to order the providentials of the town." Two constables were at first chosen for the E. and W. sides of the river. To this office was committed the collection of rates, which was attended with vexatious delays, sometimes to the serious injury of the incumbent, whose property might be distrained in the event of delinquency in his collections. In 1740, the penalty for refusing the office was £5, and was sometimes paid. In 1703, oaths were administered indiscriminately to all town officers, from the Selectman to the Hog Constable. Town meetings were generally warned by posting notifications; on extraordinary occasions, by notice " from house to house." They were commonly held in the meeting house; on one occasion, July 23, 1729, the inhabitants adjourned to the " house of Mr. Moquet," a noted publican. The town were in early times convened to give

1700, Aug. 21. Voted in Town Meeting, that Mr. Joseph Buckminster, Isaac Larned and John Heaven should be the men to go and discourse with a lawyer about our aggrieved neighbours.*

Sept. 16, 1702. Manual labor was valued (in a rate) at 2s. per day, and oxen work at 18d. per day, and a breaking-up plow at 18d. per day.

Oct. 28, 1703. A rate being made in part payable in "corn at market price," corn was reckoned at 2s. per bushel, and rye at 3s.

April 5, 1704. John Eames, Sen. brought a woolf's head to

in their "invoice," and the Selectmen generally acted as Assessors, one of their number performing the service.

It may be worthy of note to add, that on the Sudbury Records, the "Selectmen" were first so called an. 1650; previously to that time, the designation used was, "to dispose of town affairs." They were in some towns called "Overseers" at a later date. On the same Records, the title of "Town Clerk" first appears about 1661; that officer having been before chosen without title, "to attend and write town orders, to make town rates, &c." The deputy to the General Court was first called "Representative," on the Framingham Records, an. 1703.

* This vote had relation to difficulties with Sherborne, originating in the order of the General Court, an. 1679, annexing certain farms contiguous to the bounds of Sherborne, to that town. In conformity with that order, seven families within the present limits of Framingham, became incorporated with that town. Whether this arrangement was intended to be permanent or otherwise, the bounds of Sherborne appear not to have been defined; and as new settlers came upon the lands of the individuals annexed, and formed no connexion with Sherburne, the territorial rights of the latter became involved and uncertain. At the incorporation of Framingham, 17 families living on what was termed "Sherborne Row," some holding leases from Mr. Danforth, were embraced in the "disputed territory." As the rights of Sherborne were reserved in the grant of this township, the question of jurisdiction naturally arose. The nonpayment of rates to Sherborne, led to civil actions, in which this town were disposed to aid their "wronged neighbors." In 1701, Mr. Stephen Francis of Medford, Mr. Josiah Converse of Woburn, and Lt. John Ware of Wrentham, were appointed by the Court to go upon the place and settle the line. Their action was satisfactory to Framingham, but failed of a peaceful adjustment of the matter in dispute. The question remained open from year to year, causing much confusion and uneasiness, until the winter of 1708-9; when the affair was amicably adjusted by the annexation of the 17 families to Framingham, and a grant to Sherborne of 4,000 acres of land W. of Mendon, as an equivalent for their loss.

"June 16, 1709. It appearing by the return of the Representatives of Sherborne and Framingham, and the votes of the said towns, that the late orders of the General Assembly for their settlement are agreeable to them: Ordered, therefore, that the line between the towns be forthwith run; and that the 17 families late in controversy be included within Framingham line, and be accounted part of that town for ever; and that Sherborne have the 4,000 acres confirmed to them, upon their offering the platt, as is directed by the former order of this Court." Col. Rec.

Thomas Drury, a Selectman, and John Prat, Constable, to be dealt with as the law directs.

May 14, 1716. Voted that Caleb Bridges should have 1s. for mending the stocks, and Lt. Drury 1s. for a plank to do the same.

Dec. 2, 1717. Voted that Ensign Benjamin Bridges be joined with the Selectmen or some one of them to undertake in the matter of defence of our town respecting Margarite Sergeant, alias Margarite Allin, whom the town of Weston are endeavoring to impose upon our town of Framingham.*

Oct. 3, 1721. At a meeting of the inhabitants "to choose suitable persons to receive out of the Province Treasury the town's quota of bills" of credit, voted that the town will take the sum of money allotted to them by the General Court for the use of the town.

Voted that Col. Buckminster, Lieut. Isaac Clark and Lieut. Drury be the men to receive this money for the town out of the Treasury.

Oct. 10th. Ens. John Death, Nath'l Eamms, Thomas Pratt, Thomas Gleason and Isaac Gleason, entered their dissent against the town's receiving the said bills.†

Feb. 9, 1730–1. A formulary of a petition relating to Cam-

---

* This case involved the two towns in a long and expensive litigation. The result appears to have been favorable to Framingham. "Feb. 16, 1718-9; The Selectmen do agree, that John Gleason or Thomas Drury shall go to the clerk of the Superior Court for an execution, whereby Margratt Allen, commonly called Pegge, may be removed from the town of Framingham to the town of Weston, where she properly belongs." The laws regulating habitancy at this period caused much inconvenience in towns, to the poor and the stranger within their gates. Instances often occur on the Records of this town, as of others, wherein individuals and families were in due form "warned out of town," and some of forcible removal, lest they should become a public charge.

† The following Nov., the town voted to let out the bills upon good personal security, not under six per cent., and in sums not exceeding £10, nor less than £5. July 16, 1728, Edward Goddard, Thos. Stone and Peter Clayes were chosen Trustees, to receive and let out the town's share of a further emission by the General Court of £60,000. The amount of the first mentioned emission was £50,000. By reason of the war expenses of the colony, and the depreciation of former bills of credit, money had become scarce. A controversy arose between the friends of a public and private bank, which resulted in favor of the former. The bills were to be loaned at 5 per cent. to the towns, and 1-5 part of the principal was to be paid annually. The evils of an irredeemable paper currency followed to such a degree, that an act of Parliament was passed for restraining the colonies in this particular. Hutch. II. 208; Holmes' Annals, sub an. 1748.

bridge great bridge over Charles river, was read to the town in the meeting, and voted in the affirmative, as being the town's mind that it would be of public benefit that the said bridge be cashiered.

Aug. 9, 1733. At a town meeting in part "to consider the petition for a new county now lodged in the General Court, the town of Framingham being one of the towns named therein, to join with several other towns of Suffolk and Middlesex in said new county," the town "voted not to join with the petitioners, but four persons appearing in the affirmative."

Nov. 26, 1739. Voted that Mr. Henry Emmes and Capt. Thomas Buckminster be a committee to take care for the preservation of the deer.

1740. About this time the Selectmen sent in a remonstrance against a petition before the General Court, from certain inhabitants of Framingham, "together with divers others belonging to Marlborough, Sudbury and Stow," praying to be made a township, with a tract four miles square.*

Jan. 8, 1741-2. The inhabitants of Framingham obtained a grant of a tract of land "of the contents of six miles square, lying N. of the Indian Town, so called, on Housatonic river, or as near there as the land will allow."†

---

* State Files.

† Various ineffectual attempts had been previously made by the inhabitants in their corporate capacity, to obtain grants of land from the General Court. They were probably induced to take this step, by the fact, that their township had been granted to an individual, and not, as in other towns, to the company of settlers. The earliest movement was made Feb. 26, 1701-2, soon after the town's incorporation, to obtain permission for the purchase of about 1000 acres W. of Cochituate pond, from the Natick Indians; some of the meadows therein having been "let out to sundry of our inhabitants (by the Indians of Natick), about 25 years." (State Files.) The House granted the prayer, but it was negatived by the Council. A similar petition was presented June, 1713. The Court ordered that Capt. Daniel Fisher, Capt. Joseph Morse and Mr. Thomas Sawin, be a committee to go upon the place &c. and report. The petitioners failed in their prayer. June 24, 1714, Framingham "petitioned for a tract bounded by Marlborough, Sutton, Mendon and Framingham;" and a com. was ordered upon the same, but without success. (Col. Rec. ix. 405.) At the same time Col. Joseph Buckminster obtained from the Court confirmation of "300 acres of land," "lying between the towns of Framingham and Mendon, upon a grant made to Mr. Thomas Mayhew, an. 1643, and purchased by the petitioner" from his heirs. Nov. 21, 1715, Maj. J. Buckminster secured a grant of 2,000 acres, which he offered to the town, in case the grant could be obtained for them; in which event he would "move his grant to another place." The land probably lay "adjoining to Meganka." It does not

The resolve granting a township called New Framingham, described above, was passed Jan. 8, 1741–2, as follows : *

"Jan. 8, 1741. On the petition of the inhabitants of the town of Framingham, read and ordered, that the petition be received, and the prayer therof granted; and that the petitioners be allowed and impowered, by a Surveyor and Chainmen on oath, to survey and lay out a township of the contents of six miles square, adjoining on the N., on the Indian town, so called, lying on Housetonnock river, or as near that place as the land will allow, not interfering on any former grants ; and that they return a plat thereof to this Court within 12 months for confirmation ; and for the more effectual bringing forward the settlement of the said new town, ORDERED, that there be 79 equal shares, the home lotts to be laid out in a suitable and defensible manner, one of said shares to be for the first settled minister, and one for the school ; that there be 60 families settled on 60 of the other shares or house lotts, in three years from the confirmation of the plan ; who shall each have an house built thereon of 18 feet square, at the least, and seven feet stud, and six acres of land, part thereof ploughed or brought to English grass, and fenced, and build and finish a convenient meeting house for the publick worship of God, and settle a learned orthodox minister ; that said 60 settlers give bond to the Treasurer of this Province, in the sum of £25, for complying with the terms of the grant. And if any of said settlers fail of performing the conditions of settlement aforesaid, then his or their right, share or interest in said town to revert to and be at the disposition of the Province ; and the Province Treasurer shall immediately sue out their bonds.

"Nov. 19, 1742, a plan was reported and accepted, and the lands were confirmed to Caleb Bridges and others."†

appear that their petition prevailed. Aug. 15, 1721, the town's Representative was instructed to present a petition, " when he sees fit," for a grant of country land for the town. The town desired a grant within the limits of Hopkinton. The trustees of the Hopkins fund having secured that tract, a committee was appointed to solicit the influence of the trustees in favor of a grant for the town elsewhere. Nov. 18, 1729, the town renewed their petition, and a tract was surveyed the following year, the location not indicated. These successive applications resulted in no advantage to the inhabitants at large.

* See Col. Rec. sub an.

† The names of all the grantees of this tract do not appear. Hezekiah Rice owned lots Nos. 11 and 12. Matthias Bent sold his share to John Nurse, in 1743. Peter Gallop was a proprietor, as were also James Boutwell, Samuel Jackson, and Caleb Bridges. John Butler was " one of the ten, who, by vote of the Society, were admitted with them, a proprietor or grantee &c." At a meeting of the proprietors, Oct. 19, 1742, it was voted to call the town Richfield, until the legislature should give it a name. It was afterwards called New Framingham ; and later, by its present name of Lanesborough. The settlement was commenced about 1754 or 1755 by Capt. Sam'l Martin, a Mr. Brewer, and Mr. Steales, who were driven away by a party of Indians, in the second French war. Capt. Martin was the only one who returned. Among the earliest settlers after those above named, were Nathl. Williams, Samuel Tyrrell ; John, Ephraim, Elijah and Miles Powell,

1743. A bounty was and had been previously paid for taking birds and squirrels.*

April 18, 1749. A notification, signed by Joseph Richardson, appeared in the Boston Gazette, addressed to all who "usually met at the house of Mr. Francis Moquet, in Framingham, on the affair of a petition on the Canada Expedition in the year 1690," warning them of a further meeting, at Sudbury, in June.†

Sept. 23, 1754. After a large debate by the town on that part of an Excise Bill which relates to the private consumption of wines and spirits distilled, a full vote passed that they apprehend it to be reasonable and for the interest of the Province, that the charges of the government should be defrayed in part by an excise on wine and spirits distilled; and that this excise ought to be so extended as that all persons (save those who are exempted in said bill), should be obliged to pay excise for the wine and distilled spirits which they consume.

May 23, 1757. Voted that a number of the inhabitants be

(brothers); Lt. Andrew Squier, Jas. Loomis and Ambrose Hall; these settled as early as 1759. William Bradley, James Goodrich, Thaddeus Curtis, Ebenezer Squier, Benjamin and Joseph Farnum, came in soon after. The only name indicating a possible origin from Framingham, is Brewer. Some of the names suggest a conjectural origin from Marlborough or Sudbury. The greater part of the settlers were from Connecticut. The town was incorporated June 20, 1765, and then included a large part of the present town of Cheshire. In March 1764, a church consisting of eight members was organized, over which was ordained, Ap. 17, 1764, the Rev. Daniel Collins, Yale Coll. 1760, who continued his ministry until his death. He d. Aug. 26, 1822, in the 84th year of his age. Besides the Congregational church, there is now a Baptist, and an Episcopal church. The last is at present the largest. It is well endowed with a fund of about $6000, a Glebe and a Parsonage house. The Rev. Samuel B. Shaw, B. Un. 1819, has been Rector of this church near 16 years. To his friendly attentions the author is indebted for much of the information here given. The town of Lanesborough possesses valuable resources in its beds of iron ore and extensive quarries of excellent marble. Its population in 1840, was 1,090.

* The policy of sanctioning by public rewards, the destruction of these animals, was very early introduced into our towns, and has been continued until quite recently. In March 1798, the bounty for killing crows in April, May, or June, was 25 cts. for old and 12 1-2 cts. for young crows. In April it was reduced to three cents on crows, and a half cent on redwing black birds. The year following, the town voted "that each man kill his own black birds, and pay himself." In 1804, one cent each was paid for chirping squirrels, and the bounty on crows was continued for several years subsequent.

† The meeting above referred to, was probably held for the recovery of an indemnity for services rendered in that expedition. It may be worthy of notice, to add, that about the year 1752, several of the inhabitants of Framingham were among the proprietors of land in Kennebec No. 4. Whether the land was acquired by grant or by purchase, does not appear.

taken from the N. Constable's ward and added to the S.W. Constable's ward, viz: Timothy Stearns, Thomas Temple's old place, Widow Willson, Upham's place, Mr. Brown, John Permenter, Amos Permenter and his sons, John Darling, Amos Darling, Barret and Robinson.

May 23, 1757. Voted that the Widow Gleason's effects that she left when she died, be divided among those neighbours that have been kind to her, in contributing for her support.

1760. Voted that Capt. Isaac Clark shall not be rated this year.

Dec. 29, 1760. Capt. Josiah Stone gave Maj. John Farrar, Town Treasurer, a note of hand of £6.4s., on demand, for the town's use; and also Mr. Benoni Pratt a note for £1.18.7, for said town's use.

March 6, 1769. Voted that the Town Clerk, for the future, shall enter in the town book all the persons that shall come to dwell in this town; viz., their names, last place of settlement, or, if not known, the last place of abode, and the time when they came into town.

1771. The vote was tried whether the town did approve of the practice of shooting fowls, and it passed in the negative.

1772. Voted that Jesse Eames, Collector, be hereby directed not to distrain those persons that occupy College land, for their Province tax raised on those lands, till further orders from the town.

June 22, 1778. Committees of the towns of Framingham and Westborough met, "to complete an amicable settlement of the lines" between said towns.

1794. The price of wood for the minister was estimated at 9s. per cord.

1796. A town law was passed, "forbidding cattle to go at large from April 1 to Nov. 15; the owner to forfeit for each day's offence, 25 cents per head."

1799. A dog tax was imposed, but was afterwards refunded.

Nov. 7, 1814. Voted that the laws made for the due observation of the Lord's day, be carried into effect.

1825. The Selectmen were authorized, at discretion, to place durable bounds on the lines between Framingham and the adjoining towns.

1830. The town granted $75 " to pay for a survey of the town, and procuring a map of the same."

The town chose a committee " to secure a location of the Insane Hospital here," and authorized them to offer $500 for a site.

1831. The town granted $25 for ringing one of the church bells at 12 M. and 9 P.M.

The town voted upon a proposed amendment of the constitution relating to the commencement of the political year—yeas 10, nays 33.

1833. Voted to build a town hall. The committee appointed to report upon the subject, proposed the erection of a house 40 feet by 68, with a colonnade at the E. and W. ends, at an estimated cost of $4,200.

1834. Voted, that in the opinion of the inhabitants of the town, the public convenience does not require that any license be given for the sale of ardent spirits.

BRIDGES.

May 22, 1701. Voted, that the inhabitants will make a foot bridge upon the E. side of the river, from the great bridge that leads out to the meeting house, as far as is convenient and needful to be made.

May 12, 1712. Voted, that there be a cart bridge over Sudbury river, where the way is laid out from Simon Mellen's unto our public meeting house, near the now dwelling house of Ebenezer Singletary.

May 18, 1713. Voted, that there be a foot bridge built from the cart bridge already built over Sudbury river, by our public meeting house, over the intervale or lowland unto the upland.

March 17, 1718. Voted a grant to John How, for answering the town's presentment for our great bridge, by the meeting house.

1723. Voted, that the old bridge by Mr. Simpson's be repaired.

1729. A bridge was built between Hopkinton and Framingham.

Dec. 24, 1735. The small bridges and causeways on the W. side of the land of John Drury, were laid out as a part of the public highway; the sluice next to said Drury's dwelling house to be kept open and in good repair by him.

May 21, 1739. Ezekiel Rice received a grant of £3.2.6, for timber for the great bridge.

March 1, 1741–2. Granted £40 old tenor, to build a bridge where the old bridge is, near where the old meeting house stood.

March 7, 1742–3. Put to vote, whether the town will grant money to build the bridge called Coller's Bridge, and the bridge called Singletary's Bridge, both anew; and it passed in the negative.

Oct. 12, 1747. Voted to repair the causeway belonging to the bridge by Dea. Daniel Stone's, and that said causeway be 15 feet wide; also voted, that the causeway on the N. side of said bridge be raised level with the top of said bridge, as it now stands.

March, 1794. Voted to have a row of posts erected from the bridge the upper side of the causeway, to Mr. Eli Bullard's bark house; and a foot bridge made convenient to pass with a hand pole.

TOWN HIGHWAYS LAID OUT.

April, 1701. From the meeting house as the road goes by Mr. John Swift's; and so on the S. side of John Town's door by his house; and so over the new bridge over Stony brook; and so over the plain to the corner of Benj. Nurse's land; thence over a little spruce swamp, S. side of it, to Peter Cloyce, Sen.; and so up to John Nurse's, &c.; and the highway runs from James Travis' to Caleb Bridge's door; and so to the common.

Jan. 1702–3. Beginning at the house of John Whitney, and following the occupied way to N.W. corner of John Haven's field, S. of his house; thence N. as the way is to stones W. of Simon Melin's house; thence N. to the river, S. of John Town's house, and to the way laid from the house of Peter Cloyce, Sen.

1706. About this time, Joseph Buckminster was allowed to make and maintain a highway from his house to the meeting house; and in consideration thereof, to be exempt from labor on the highways elsewhere, seven years.

March 15, 1706. Beginning by the bridge by John Town's,

running W. below the hill, to Elnathan Palmer's house on the S. side of the river; there over the river to Philip Pratt's land; thence between the lands of Philip Pratt and Simon Mellen, to a highway formerly laid out; said way to be two rods wide.

March 8, 1707 – 8. Return of a highway, from the meeting house bridge to the highway from Sudbury to Sherborn, to run straight from the bridge to a hollow, commonly gone up and down in by the people when it is miry and dirty, riding the way usually occupied over the Thorngutter; so N. side of the little Cranberry place and over the Thorngutter, to Pratt's plain; thence on the edge of the plain by Sucker (Succo) pond, and close to the corner of John Pratt's field, to the way leading from Sudbury to Sherborn.

April, 1708. On petition of Geo. Walkup and Jonas Eaton, laid out a way through the land of John Winch; 2d, through land of John and Joseph Gibbs; 3d, through land of Samuel Winch, as the way now is; 4th, through land of Nathl. Stone; 5th, through lands of Jeremiah Pike, Sen., to run by the line of Abraham Belknap's land, till it meets the way from J. Pike's house to the meeting house.

March 14, 1708 – 9. A highway returned, beginning at land of John How, so running through land of Thomas Walker, and after passing the fences, to be two rods wide down the brook; one part of said way to be laid upon the lands of Dea. David Rice, and the other part on lands of John Bent; and to run over the foot bridge now standing, and so through land of Thomas and Caleb Drury, to the land of Caleb Johnson, Sen.

April 11, 1709. Return of highway from Benjamin Ball's to the common, — from said Ball's house across the plain, by the W. end of James Cloyce's field; so over the plain to a brook; and over the brook between lands of John Provender, Sen. and Philip Pratt, till it comes to Nathaniel Pratt's; and so through his land and John Provender's, till it comes to the common.

July 15, 1709. Return of highway, from Mr. Simptson's farm, into the highway that leads to our meeting house, — beginning at the river, at the S. corner of the land bought by said Simptson of Capt. Joseph Buckminster; so E. into a way formerly occupied; so near the river, till it comes to the upper end of James

Coller's meadow; there to cross the river, and run, as the way lies, to the highway from the Havens to our meeting house.

Jan. 10, 1709-10. Return of a way for Amos Waite to meeting — beginning at a path N. of said Waite's house, running W. side of a hill unto Samuel How's land; and from thence a strait line W. side of said How's land, to a heap of stones near the old road from Samuel How to Marlborough.

Return of highway from John Sheres to the meeting house, — beginning at said Sheres' land; thence to land of Jonathan Lamb and Joseph Wetherbee, as the way now is, and between their lands, and so as the path now is to Ab. Belknap's and Jeremiah Pike's land; and between their lands to Jeremiah Pike's shop; and so as the way now is, to the way from Samuel Winch's to the meeting house.

March 6, 1709-10. John Jaques doth give unto the Sherborn Row an highway through his land; — beginning at the most northerly corner of Zech. Padelford's field; thence to S. corner of Isaac Lerned's meadow; so to continue on the E. side of his land next the meadow, until it comes to the Stone's dam; and so on to the highway from Pratt's plain to the bridge, near the meeting house.

May 27, 1713. Return of highways, for the accommodation of the 17 families taken off from Sherborn and others, for their convenience to go to meeting, mill and market. — Beginning at a walnut tree, on the way leading from the Mellens' to the S. side of the great meadow; so by the way as now is, and marked trees, to Richard Haven's house; thence as the way is, to land of John Adams; so N.W. of marked trees, to run as the old way did lie, unto Daniel Stone's mill, — the way to be two rods except where obstructed; — also a way to turn off the bridge by John Adams' house, and to run as it now is to the way that comes from the Rice's end; — also a highway turning out of the highway by John Gleason's house, and to run down by his barn, till it comes to a white oak, standing on the S. side of a slew.

April 23, 1719. Return of a highway, from Samuel Lamb's land to John Singleterry's ditch, said ditch being the N.E. bounds of said way, till it comes to Jonathan Rugg's land; then through his land, as the way now is, to a marked tree; then between the land of said Rugg and the land of Jonathan Bruer, as far as their lands join; then N. of said Bruer's land to his N.E. corner; then to an oak on a ledge of rocks, S. side of the road; thence to a stake and stones by the side of Caleb Bridge's fence.

Feb. 26, 1721–2. Return of highway, beginning at a highway from Samuel Lamb's to the meeting house; thence S. on the E. side of Eben. Harrington's line, to a marked tree, the bound between said Harrington's and John Drury's land; thence to land now or formerly of Ens. Rice, now in possession of his son, Abraham Rice; thence by marked trees, to the common or unimproved lands S. of said Rice's land.

1722. Messrs. Samuel and Nathaniel Eames having made proposals relating to Beaver Dam bridge, — Voted, that a town highway shall lie and be, as now occupied, to Beaver Dam bridge, and so through to Sherborn line; and that the bridge be continued where it now is.

Nov. 4, 1723. A town road laid out to Lt. How's, — beginning at the road from Lamb's to the meeting house, which road lieth W. side of a marked oak, standing by said road near the turn of Mr. Swift's fence, which is E. from Ball's bridge, so called; which road is laid two rods wide, till it comes into the road from our meeting house to Marlborough, which road runs upon Benjamin Ball's land.

1724. Return of highway, from the country road leading from Sudbury to Marlborough, to a highway from John Shears to the meeting house, laid out as follows, viz. — between lands of Thomson Woods and John Parmenter, to lands wholly of said Parmenter; then successively through the latter, Col. Buckminster's land, Thompson Wood's, Robert Jenneson's, Nath. Wilson's, Jona. Jackson's, Stearns', and Joshua Eaton's land, where it meets the other town way abovesaid.

Feb. 4. 1724–5. Return of highway on both sides of Beaver Dam, viz. — beginning at a tree, marked with the letter W, upon the Sherborn line, E. of said tree; then to a heap of stones, the bounds of Oliver Death; thence making a bow into Corporal Eames' land; thence (still bowing), to a stake at the foot of the bridge; thence a straight line to another W tree near Beaver Dam bridge, which is the tree where Sherborn men began to lay out the way more than 20 years ago, (as Ens. Death informed us); thence two rods E.; thence by various marked trees to a black oak marked W, by a town highway formerly laid out.

April 26, 1731. Laid out a highway from Mr. James Cloyes' house to Southborough line, as far as the lane now goes; thence by marked trees to John Nurse's land; and so N. of his orchyard to the N. side of his N.W. corner; thence as the road now is, to Southborough line.

Nov. 27, 1732. A highway return, beginning at Mr. John Pierce's house; so running E. over Cochitawic brook, as the road now is, to the N.W. corner of Mr. Steven Jennings' cornfield; so over the same to a tree, the bound between Mr. Tho. Kendal and said Jennings; so E. on said K.'s land between said K. and said Jennings, till it comes to Jennings' E. corner mark; thence to the road from Rice's end to Sherborn line. Also, a highway from the house of Mr. Eben. Stone, N.E., as the way is used, to the land of Mr. Tho. Kendall; so through said K.'s land to Steven Jennings' corner mark, — said mark standing on the Indian Graves (so called); thence to Sudbury line as the way is now used.

March 18, 1733-4. A highway from Jona. Jackson, through Timo. Stearns' land, to Mr. Joseph Maynard's (as it is now occupied), was accepted by the town.

1735. Return of highway, beginning at Southborough highway, near the house of Daniel Mixer; so down, as the way is, to Ichabod Hemenway, Jun's. house; thence S. side of Jona. Morse's house, to a small pine N. side of the old path in the low land, about 30 rods from said Morse's; thence to Col. Buckminster's dam; and thence, as the way is used, over the other dam; thence to the corner of the fence between Edward Wright and Serg. Treadway; thence S. to an oak in said Wright's field; thence to the line between Col. Buckminster and said Wright; thence, as the line runs, to the path from the said Wright's to the meeting house; thence, as the way is, to the road from Mr. Tredway's to the meeting house.

Feb. 2, 1735-6. Return of a highway from Benj. Ball's corner, over the land of Jona. Maynard, to an oak near the brook; thence near the N.W. corner of Benj. Tredway's barn; so over said T.'s land, to a pine on the N. part of the hill; thence over Col. Buckminster's land, to near the crotch of Mr. Tredway's land; and so on the line between Mr. T. and William Pike, to the meeting house land.

7 March, 1736 – 7. The highway from the old meeting house place to William Pike's, is discontinued, so far as it goes over Col. Buckminster's and Mr. Treadway's land; and laid out from the house of Francis Moquet, by the end of Bear Hill, to the meeting house.

March 24, 1737. Return of alteration of the highway from the old meeting house to Rice's end, near to Sucker (Succo) pond; — the alteration to begin at the corner of Ezekiel Rice's fence near Sucker brook, and the way to run over said brook, to a stake and stones on the brow of the hill; thence E., by marked trees, to the way formerly laid out.

July 15, 1737. Return of a highway from Southborough to Sudbury; viz. — beginning at Southborough line, on land of Mr. Isaac Gleason; through his land as the way is, said G.'s fence to be the S. bound; thence through Mr. Eben. Frizzell's land as the way is, said F.'s fence to be the S. bound; thence through Mr. Timo. Stearns' land, as the way is, to the way from Lt. Willson's to the meeting house, — said Stearns' N. fence to be the S. bound; — thence in said way to the foot of the hill near the N.W. corner of Lt. Winchester's fence; thence through said W.'s land, as the way is, to Capt. Clark's N. corner; thence between lands of Capt. Clark and the widow Frost, to the N. side of Jona. Clarke's frame; thence to the crotch of the paths leading, one to Stone's mills, the other to the new bridge; thence along Stone's path, near the corner of Ebenezer Pike's new broke up land; thence N. over to said new bridge path; thence as the way is, to said new bridge.

Nov. 14, 1737. Return of highway, viz. — from near Amos Gates' house, through his land to Isaac Clark's gate; through said Clark's land, as the path is now trod, to land of Cornet Matthias Clark; thence to the road from Marlborough to Stone's mills.

Dec. 26. 1737. Return of a way from Singletary's bridge, through Jona. Maynard's land to the bridge near Benj. Tredway's, — beginning at said Maynard's fence, at the E. end of said bridge, by marked trees to the Salem end road.

May 12, 1738. Return of a way from the house of Matthias Bent, to the road about 20 rods E. of Dea. Adams' house, — beginning at said Bent's house, running by marked trees along by the S. side of Dea. Adams' orchard; and so to the old road leading from Mr. Thomas Stone's to Mr. Moquet's.

Return of a road, beginning at Jonathan Rugg's N.W. corner; thence N.W., by marks, to a stake and stones on Southborough line.

Alteration of the road from Rev. Mr. Swift's new house, to the old meeting house bridge.

March 5, 1743 – 4. The town accepted the following way; — beginning at Singletary's bridge; thence, as the way is, to near Mr. Richard Mellen's; thence W. side of a stone wall, into the way leading by Daniel Mellen's barn; thence, as the way is, by Joseph Haven's to the road leading from Coller's bridge; thence by W. end of Elkanah Haven's house; thence, as the way is, to Mr. Nathan Haven's stone wall; thence by said wall, into the road formerly laid out by said Nathan Haven.

March 5, 1743 – 4. Accepted an alteration of the road by Mr. John Parmenter's house to the country road, — by various marks, over the brook below the saw mill; thence to the country road, within Eben. Hager's land.

May 8, 1744. Alteration of a highway, — turning out of the old road at the corner of Mr. Jona. Morse's fence, S. of his barn; thence N.E. into the old road; thence, as the old road is now trodden, to the Colonel's dams.

Alteration of a highway, — turning out of the old road, near the lane coming from Lt. Rice's door; running a little W. of the old road; coming into it again on a hill near Mr. Moquet's fence.

March 3, 1745 – 6. Record of a highway, — beginning at the end of the lane from Jona. Morse, to the highway from Ball's bridge to the meeting house; E. from Mr. Benj. Ball's fence, — said fence to be the W. bounds of said road; — thence, as now used, to James Clayes' house; and also from the house of Mr. Caleb Bridges, till it comes into the aforesaid highway to the meeting house.

Oct. 12, 1747. Alteration of the road by the Rev. Mr. Bridges' house.

March 7, 1747-8. Alteration of a road (probably at the N.W. corner of the town) — beginning near the road now occupied, by the land of John Bullen; thence E. by marks, by the path coming from William Upham's, into the road formerly laid out.

March 4, 1750-1. Return of highway from Sudbury line, near Jona. Robinson's, to the great road in Sudbury, by the house of David How, innholder, of Sudbury; — beginning two rods N. of Robinson's N.E. corner on Sudbury line; and thence S., bounding E. on Sudbury line, to the great road by David How's.

March 1, 1756. The town accepted a private way from Nathan Haven's house to Holliston line; — also an alteration of a private way, from the great road coming from Hopkinton to Benj. Barnard's, to William Ballard's.

Nov. 22, 1756. Accepted a highway laid out, — beginning at the river between Hopkinton and Framingham; thence on Elisha Bemis' land, by marks, to Theo. Peirce's land; thence by marks to Southborough line.

March 6, 1758. Return of a highway from Sudbury line by Cornet Eaton's to the meeting house, — beginning at Sudbury line, to said Eaton's tan house; thence S.E. to his gate; thence, as the road is, through Geo. Walkup's land, to Tho. Winch's lane; thence, as said lane goes, to the place where old Mr. Streeter's house formerly stood; thence S.W.; thence by marks to the W. fence of the lane leading over the bridge over Hop brook; thence, as now trod, to the meeting house.

Road laid out, — beginning at Stone's mills; running E. to Hezekiah Stone's fence; thence N. towards Sudbury, as the way is, having lands of Hez. and Micah Stone for the E. bounds, till it comes to Moses Stone's land; thence to Silvanus Hemenway's land; thence to Sudbury line, as the way is now trod, to Landham.

March 5, 1759. Highway through George Walkup's and G. Walkup, Jun's. land, discontinued as an open highway; but reserved as a bridle way.

March 1, 1762. Voted, to accept as a town way, the road from Capt. John Butler's corner at the foot of the Rice's hill, to the road leading from Daniel Adams' to Stone's mills. Also, an alteration of the way, turning out of the country road, a little W.

TOWN HIGHWAYS.

of Tho. Kendall's barn, and running to Stephen Jennings his house.

March 2, 1763. Return of a townway, — beginning at the end of the road bounded W. on land of Eben. Singletary's original lot, — said road extending S., to the land of Simon Pratt and James Glover.

Return of highway, — beginning at Jona. Hemenway's house; thence W. by Ralph Hemenway's house, over a bridge and causeway, to the country road, a little to the E. of Mr. Eben. Boutwell's house.

Alteration of a town way leading from Jona. Barret's to the highway, toward the great road in Sudbury, a little above David How's field.

March 9, 1767. Return of a town way, — beginning at a large rock at the end of a stone wall on Marlborough road, now in possession of Joshua Fairbank; thence S. on Micah Gibbs' land, and widow Fairbank's, to Mr. Brinley's land; thence on said Gibbs' land, wild land of Mr. Brinley and Mr. John Mixer, to land now improved by Jos. Nichols and John Eames; thence to the country road leading by said Nichols.

Return of a town way, from the corner of Cornet Abr. Rice's stone wall, by William Merret's, Daniel and Cornelius Claflen's.

1771. Alteration of a town way near Mr. John Fisk's.

1772. Alteration of the road by Wm. Merrit's.

1774. Return of a highway, laid out from the end of the road from Cornet Abr. Rice's, to Timothy Pike's; and thence W. to the lot No. —, in the river range: thence by marks to Geo. Stimpson's land; thence meeting a road laid out by Hopkinton.

1779. The town accepted the exchange of a way laid out through lands of David Rice, 2d.

1781. Accepted a town way, — beginning by the road W. of Simon Pratt's house; thence S. to an oak N. of Daniel Tombs' house; thence to the corner of lot No. 14, river range; thence to the head of the lane near Capt. Ballard's house.

1795. A road was laid out from Capt. John Jones' mill to Mr. Nathan Dadman's, and to the town road N. of said Dadman's house.

April, 1797. Accepted an exchange of the above road.

1799. Accepted an alteration of the road near Lt. Cornelius Claflin.

Table of Annual Grants for Highways and Bridges.

1701 - - £ 20	1748 - -	£ 400, old tenor.
1723 - - - 30	1759 - - -	150
1736 - - - 100	1771 - - -	250
1737 - - - 200	1789 - - -	100
1741 - - - 250	1798 - -	$ 800 *

POUNDS.

March 2, 1702. Voted, that there shall be a pound set up upon the W. side of the river, by the bridge.

Oct. 28, 1703. Voted, that there shall be a pound set up upon the land of John Town, joining to Mr. Swift's land, by the road.

April 10, 1719. Voted, that the town's pound be removed and set up upon Col. Buckminster's land, adjoining or near to Benj. Tredway's land, by a certain pond hole.

June 15, 1719. The above location having been found inconvenient, ordered that the pound be set between the two highways, one leading from the plain, the other from Singleterry's bridge to the meeting house, so as to join Mr. Swift's land; and to be set up near the top of the hill.

May 8, 1733. Mr. Maynard made offer of land for a town pound, by the oak tree upon the hill near his dwelling; which was accepted by the town.

1741. Granted £ 7.11 to Henry Eames for building the pound in said town.

1755. A grant was voted to Lt. Hezekiah Rice for building a pound.

1781. Voted to build a new pound and set it where the old one stood.

---

* The annual appropriations since 1798, have been generally $800, to the present time. The only years before 1835, when they exceeded that sum, were in 1818 and 1819—having been, the former year $1200, and the latter $1000. The roads in this town are kept in good repair at so moderate a charge. The allowance to such as worked out their highway tax, was in 1737, 5s. per diem for a man, and the same for a cart and four oxen, or two oxen and a horse. In 1754, the allowance was 4d. per hour.

FISHERIES.

The river and ponds in Framingham have, from the earliest times, afforded an abundant supply of fish, until the obstructions of the former, by dams, impeded the communication with the sea. In 1743, Josiah Drury and David Gregory were appointed by the town to take care of the fish.

March 1, 1762. " Voted, that Messrs. James Clayes, Isaac Fisk and Joshua Harrington be a committee to view the Stones' mill dams in said town, and consider of the necessity and conveniency of opening a passage way through said dams, to let the fish called alewives pass up into the pond called Farm pond, to cast their spawn." The subject was dismissed the May following.

March 7, 1763. Pursuant to an act, &c. to prevent the destruction of the fish called alewives, and other fish, " Mr. Wm. Brown and Mr. Bezaleel Rice were chosen to see that the passage ways mentioned in said act (within our bounds) are open, &c.; and also to appoint the proper place or places for the taking such fish with scoop nets or otherwise, and to limit the particular times and days for the taking the same." Committees were in like manner chosen in succeeding years.

March 8, 1792. An act was passed by the General Court, " to enable the town of Framingham to regulate and order the taking of shad and alewives within the limits of said town;" and a farther act was passed June 15, 1821, regulating the pond fishery.

April 2, 1792. The town voted that the fish called alewives and shad, be taken only one day in the week, that to be on Tuesday; and to be taken only at one place, and that to be within 15 rods of Dea. Wm. Brown's fulling-mill dam.

Voted, to choose a committee to let out the catching the alewives to the highest bidder; whoever purchases the privilege is to sell them for no more than 4d per score.*

---

* The proceeds of the fisheries were given for some years to the singers, and hence were called the " singers' fish privilege." The only fish now taken in the town are pond fish, which are found in considerable abundance, though the regulations established by law are but little regarded. The fine fishing afforded by the ponds, formerly attracted numerous visiters from Boston. Trout, which were once abundant in the small streams, have nearly disappeared.

CIVIL HISTORY.

POPULATION.

Years.	Houses.	Families.	Males under 16.	Females under 16.	Males over 16.	Females over 16.	Polls rateable.	Polls r. and non r.	Free White Females.	Colored.	Total.
1696											near 200
1699	64										over 350
1708		75(?)									
1710							111				
ab't 1760	198						301	331			
1763–5	205	234	325	302	306	347					1,280
1776											whites,1,574
1777					384						
1778						337					
1781		•						370			
1784								389			
1791	221	292	350		394				828	26	1,598
1810			354	354	437	517				13	1,670
1820*			445	404	510	661				17	2,037
1830										15	2,313
1840										7	3,030
1845											about 4,000

VALUATION ABOUT 1760.†

301 polls rateable,   ⎫
30 " non-rateable, ⎬ 331 polls.
                      ⎭

198 dwelling houses,	at 60s. each,	-	£594.
28 work houses,	at 25s. "	- -	35.
8 mills, -	at 80s. "	-	32.
1 iron work, - -	at 60s. "	- -	3.
7 servants for life,	at 40s. "	-	14.
£60.13 0 Trading stock, at 6 per cent.		- -	3.12.09
£936.17 4 money at interest at 6 per cent.,		-	56.04.02¾
162 horses, -	- at 4s. 9d.	- -	38.09.06
265 oxen, - -	at 4s.	- -	53.00.00
724 cows, -	- at 3s.	- -	108.12.00
886 sheep &c., -	at 3d.	- -	11.01.06
35 swine, -	- at 12d.	- -	1.15.00
1,023½ cow pastures,	at 10s.	- -	511.15.00
20,665 bushels grain,	at 8d.	- -	688.16.08
1,716 barrels of cider,	at 2s.	- -	171.12.00
447½ tons of English hay,	at 12s.	- -	268.10.00
1,021¼ tons of meadow hay, at	6s.	- -	306.09.00
			£2897.17.07¾

* In 1820, 308 were engaged in agriculture, 22 in commerce, and 140 in manufactures. In 1840, 715 were engaged in agriculture, 463 in manufactures, 3 in navigation, 15 in the learned professions and engineering; 16 were revolutionary pensioners, 6 insane and idiotic. Official Returns.

† This valuation, it will be understood, is a reduced one.

COLORED INHABITANTS.

We possess a few data relating to this class of the inhabitants of the town, who, during the first century succeeding its incorporation, until the adoption of the Constitution, were generally held as slaves. Slavery, however, in New England, existed in its most mitigated form, and to a very limited extent. In 1708, the number of slaves was computed at 400 in Boston, and 150 in the rest of the State. In 1754 and 5, a census of negro slaves gave the entire number in the State at 2,717; none, however, were reported from Framingham. Yet before 1743, five slaves, (three males and two females), were owned by the Rev. Mr. Swift; and there is reason to believe that there were then others in various families of the town. In the valuation of 1760, (several of Mr. Swift's slaves having left the town), the number of "servants for life" reported, was seven. In 1764-5, the number of "negroes" in Framingham is given at 25, the entire colored population of the State being 5,312. The number of persons of color in this town has gradually diminished. The census of 1840, returns but seven.*

---

* The names of Mr. Swift's slaves, disposed of in his will dated Sep. 1743, were a negro man Francis, a legacy to his son, the Rev. John Swift of Acton; Guy, a negro man, to his son-in-law, the Rev. Philips Payson of Walpole; Nero, to his son-in-law Eben'r Robie. He also left two women, Dido and Esther, for the service of his wife until her decease; after which, they were to be the property of his daughter Martha, the wife of Maj. John Farrar.

NERO, (his entire name being Nero Benson), had married Dido (Dingo) in 1721, and served as trumpeter in Capt. Isaac Clark's troop in 1725. His religious scruples appear to have been respected by his master, the Hopkinton church record informing us, that Sep. 20, 1737, "Nero, servant to Rev. Mr. Swift, applied for admission to the church." This occurred at a period of much contention in the church of Framingham, which will be explained in that branch of our history. Tradition preserves a favorable account of Nero's character. He had several children. A son William was owned at one time by Joseph Collens, of Southborough. Esther, above named, was probably daughter of Nero and afterwards lived in a Haven family. His descendants are yet living in this town. Of other individuals of this class, we are induced to give the following memoranda.

Jane, colored servant to Col Buckminster, was bap. in 1722. Primus, servant to Aaron Pike, was bap. in 1744. Mereah, servant to the widow Frost, in 1746; Jenny, servant to Lt. Winch, and Vilet, servant to Jonathan Rugg, in 1746; Flora, servant to Dea. Balch, in 1747, and named in his will 1755; Flora, Brill and Titus, servants to Mrs. Winchester, in 1748; Hannover, servant to Nat. Belknap, in 1755; Phebe, servant to Simon Edgel, in 1767. In 1716, John Stone held as a slave, Jone, wife of John Jackson, of N. London, Conn., who commenced a process to recover her freedom. Oct 9, 1733, Thomas Frost

64   CIVIL HISTORY.

CASUALTIES AND REMARKABLE EVENTS.

1717. About this time, a Gleason house was destroyed by fire, near the site of Mr. Charles Clark's present house.

1717. The great snow of this season is referred to in a Journal kept by the Rev. Mr. Swift, as follows, viz.: "Feb. 24. We had no meeting by reason of a very deep snow, that fell on the

bought of Jona. Smith of Sud., for £60 current money, a negro man named Gloster, æ. about 30 years. Dill, a negro woman in the service of Dea. Daniel Stone, died Dec. 13, 1767. Plato Lambert, probably a negro, born in 1737, was taken when an infant, by Mrs. Martha Nichols of Framingham.

KATA HUNKER, as he is commonly called, was probably the same person rated as Cato Hart in 1786. He was slave to Joseph Haven, Esq., and was born in his house (now occupied by Mr. Francis Cooledge). A grandson by the name of Primus, was lately an inmate of the Poor House.

BRIN, (otherwise called Blaney Grushy), is said to have been a slave of Col. Micah Stone. He was at the battle of Bunker Hill, and served on other occasions during the war. He died Feb. 1820.

PETER SALEM — alias Salem Middlesex — was originally the slave of Capt. Jeremiah Belknap, and was sold by him to Maj. Lawson Buckminster. He married in 1783, Katy Benson, a granddaughter of Nero, and lived for a time, where is now a cellar hole on the farm of the late Mr. Richard Fiske, near the pond. He served in the war of the Revolution as waiter to Col. Thomas Nixon, of Framingham; and at the opening of the war was present at the battle of Bunker Hill. Emory Washburn Esq., in his interesting Hist. of Leicester (Worc. Magazine II, 113), says of him — "There was residing here, till within a few years, a black man, who, we have good reason to believe, was the one who shot Maj. Pitcairn, whose death forms so affecting an incident in that bloody affray. History relates that he was shot by a negro; and from the story of the one we allude to and many corroborating circumstances, we are led to conclude that he was the person who did the deed. The person to whom we refer was named Peter Salem. * * * * * * * Maj. Pitcairn was shot as he was mounting the redoubt, and fell into the arms of his son. His loss was a severe one to the British, and added not a little to their regret at the events of that day." Peter died in Fram., Aug. 16, 1816.

But the most noted individual of the class under consideration, was PRINCE, sometimes called Prince Young, but whose name is recorded as Prince Yongey, and Prince Jonar, by which last name he is noticed in the Town Rec. in 1767. He was brought from Africa when a young man of about 25 years, having been a person of consideration in his native land, from whence, probably, he derived his name. He was first owned by Col. Joseph Buckminster, and afterwards by his son, the late Dea. Thomas. He married, (by name Prince Yongey) in 1737, Nanny Peterattucks, of Framingham, (the name indicating Indian extraction) by whom he had several children, among them a son, who died young, and a daughter Phebe, who never married. Prince was a faithful servant, and by his general honesty, temperance and prudence, so gained the confidence of his first master, Col. Buckminster, that for about a quarter of a century, he was left with the management of a large farm, during his master's absence at the General Court. He occupied a cabin near the Turnpike, and cultivated, for his own use, a piece of meadow, which has since been known as Prince's meadow.

REMARKABLE EVENTS.

Thursday before, and a great storm on that Sabbath." Contemporary accounts represent the depth of the snow, as about six feet. "March 10. The Lord's supper adjourned till the next Sabbath, by reason of the restraint of the season by deep snow."* The annual Town meeting, which was to have been held March 4, " provided the town can come roundly together, and are not hindered by reason of the extremity of the season," was not held until the 18th of the same month.

1719, April 12. " A contribution recommended for Mr. John Dunton, who had been burnt out a little before."†

1720, Feb. 21. Under this date, Mr. Swift notices a great deluge, (Diluvium magnum), but with no particulars.

1724, Oct. 18th. " Contribution for David Prat, my neighbour, who was burnt out, £24.14.6."‡

1727, Oct. 29. Mr. Swift enters the following notice of the great earthquake. " Nocte subsequente fuit terræ motus valde terribilis, circiter horas 10m. and 11m."

1736. " Voted that 30s. be paid or abated to Moses Haven, late constable, in consideration that the like sum is said to have been burnt of the town's money, *when his house was burnt.*"§

1736, Aug. A very fatal disease prevailed in this and neighbouring towns, of which many died.

1747, April 29th. " The wife of Mr. David Harrington of Framingham, returning from market at Boston, while crossing a river in that town, fell from her horse and was drowned."

1749, Oct. The house of Robert Sever was destroyed by fire.||

He chose the spot as resembling the soil of his native country. During the latter part of his life he was offered his freedom, which he had the sagacity to decline; pithily saying, "massa eat the meat; he now pick the bone." Prince shunned the society of persons of his own color, and though accustomed to appear in public armed with a tomahawk, was a great favorite with the young, whom, under all provocations, he was never known but in one instance to strike. He had been sufficiently instructed to read, and possessed the religious turn characteristic of the African race. In his last sickness, he remarked with much simplicity, that he was "not afraid to be dead, but to die." He passed an extreme old age in the family of Dea. Thos. Buckminster, and died Dec. 21, 1797, at the age of 99 years and some months. Numerous anecdotes are yet related, illustrating the simplicity, intelligence, and humor of "Old Prince."

* Swift.
† Swift.   ‡ Swift.
§ Town Rec.
|| Mr. Sever, after this event, peti-

1754. The first four months of this year are made memorable by the occurrence of a fatal distemper, known as the "great sickness."*

1755, Nov. 18. A terrible earthquake took place "a little after four o'clock, in a serene and pleasant night, and continued near four and a half minutes; the shock was the most violent ever known in the country."† Tradition has preserved among us the memory of this event, and the consternation it produced. Its effects were less destructive here than in some other towns. ‡

1756–7. A Journal kept by Mr. Henry Eames of this town, represents the total depth of snow, fallen this winter, at nearly six feet.§

1766. About this time, the house of Deac. Daniel Stone was destroyed by fire.

1769. A school house was consumed by fire, in the N. part of the town.

---

tioned the Court to grant him indemnity for the loss of several bills (Old Tenor), burnt by the destruction of his house while he and his wife were absent, which "consumed all the little substance he had in this world." He added that he and two sons were at the taking of Louisburg, "and one of them is there still." The Court ordered him to be paid £3.15. State Files.

* The mortality was greatest in Holliston, where 53 deaths occurred — according to a petition in the State Files, "one eighth part of the entire population, some families having been quite broken up." The number of deaths in Sherburne was between 20 and 30. Of the precise number of deaths in this town, we have no authentic return; not more than seven being recorded on the town books. The Goddard family appear to have been the chief sufferers. The Rev. David Goddard, (minister of Leicester), deceased here Jan. 19th; his mother, Feb. 4; and his father, the Hon. Edward Goddard, Feb. 9th. Others of the family were sick, but recovered. Mr. Joshua Hemenway was also a victim to the malady. The reader will find a particular account of the symptoms, &c. of this distemper, in the Rev. Mr. Fitch's Century Sermon, delivered at Holliston Dec. 4, 1826, and printed.

† Holmes' Annals.

‡ Vide the Rev. John Mellen's sermon describing its effects at Stirling.

§ "Dec. 17, 1756, snow 15 inches deep.

"Snow 20th day, 15 inches more.

"Snow 23d day, 7 or 8 inches more.

"Cold rain 26th day; 27th, warm three days, then some rain.

"Jan. 3, 1757, cold N.W. snow, about two or three inches.

"Jan. 9, about noon very hot fog, then rain.

"17th, very cold N.W. wind.

"22d, rain and thaw very fast.

"24th and 25th, snow to the value of 10 inches; the night after, eight inches more.

"30th and 31st, thawed away the most of the snow that came last; the whole depth above 4 ft. and 4 inches.

"Feb. 2, snow and hail seven inches deep.

"5th, snow 7 inches deep more.

"6th, rain most of the day.

"7th, snow three inches deep.

"10th, S. wind and rain, till the snow wasted the most of it."

1777, June 3. Mr. Abraham Rice and Mr. John Clayes, were killed by lightning, during a very short thunder squall.*

1785, April 12. The Hon. Josiah Stone, aged 60 years, was suddenly killed by falling from the carriage of his mill. He had been long held in honorable esteem by his townsmen, and had filled many offices in the civil and military service of the Commonwealth.

1786, Nov. 5. Jesse Eaton died suddenly in the meeting house, while in the act of singing.

1787, Aug. 15. About 3 o'clock, P. M., a hurricane passed through the N. part of the town, doing considerable damage.†

---

* The following particulars were taken by the author from Mr. Josiah Clayes, now living, who was son of one of the victims, and a spectator of the scene. Mr. Laban Wheaton was at the time preaching in the first Parish, and had employed Mr. John Clayes, (who lived in a house a few rods E. of the one now occupied by his son Josiah), to try a horse he had proposed to buy. On the day above mentioned, a little after noon, the neighbors assembled at Mr. Clayes' house to see the animal, viz. Peter Parker, Abraham Rice, Simon Pratt and his son Ephraim. Old Mr. Parker had rode away upon the horse at some distance, when a cloud began to rise in the N.W. On Mr. Parker's return, the company, who during his absence had retired to the house, went out to see him ride, at which time a few drops of rain were falling. As Mr. Parker rode up, Mr. John Clayes stepped out of the gate, leaving the others leaning against the fence within; and as he took the horse by the reins, the lightning struck every individual of the company to the ground. Mr. Rice and Mr. Clayes, with the horse, were instantly killed. Mr. Parker lay as if dead, but gradually recovered his consciousness, though a long time elapsed before he was fully restored to his usual health. The boy recovered quickly. Mr. Pratt suffered much, and for a long time after the event. Josiah Clayes, then a boy, went for Dr. Stone, who was absent at Natick; but before his return, Mr. Fiske, a neighbor, had procured Dr. Hemenway, who gave what relief he could to the sufferers. The horse was struck in the head, and the lightning descended each side of the neck and both fore legs to the shoes, singeing the hair in its course. Mr. Clayes was struck in the head, and the fluid passed along the neck — leaving a blister in the breast — down both legs, which showed traces of its course, but left his shoes uninjured. Having hold of the horse's bridle, the animal fell upon him. All were singed in body and dress, having on, at the time, woollen clothes. The boy was a little distant from the company. The shower was very brief, and Mr. Clayes thinks there was but a single clap of thunder. This event excited great interest at the time, and a long elegy was written by Miss Lydia Learned, (who to the gift of teaching added a devotion to the poetic Muse), and was afterwards printed. The reader will probably be satisfied with the following stanzas, which were inscribed upon the grave-stone of the victims of the disaster.

" My trembling heart with grief o'erflows,
While I record the death of those
Who died by Thunder sent from Heaven,
In 17 hundred seventy seven.

Let's all prepare for Judgment Day,
As we may be called out of Time,
And in a sudden, awful way,
Whilst in our youth and in our prime."

† It came, as nearly as we can learn, from the direction of Marlborough. It demolished the barn and ten feet of the house of the late Mr. Phinehas Gibbs; overturned a dwelling house occupied by a Shattuck

The same year a school house was destroyed by fire, in the E. part of the town.

1793. The small pox made its appearance in the town.*

1797. The house of Mr. William Ballard, at the S.W. part of the town, was destroyed by fire.

1800. We give below a schedule of the disasters by fire in Framingham, as far as known to the author, since the commencement of the present century.†

---

family, leaving the lower floor; two children, lying upon a bed asleep, were found uninjured. A Mrs. Saunders, living with the Shattucks, was carried by the violence of the wind to a considerable distance, and was seriously injured. Mrs. Shattuck was blown about ten rods. A feather bed was found three miles distant from the house, and in it were recovered thirty dollars in specie, which had previously been placed there for safe-keeping. The hurricane made an even path, several rods in width, through the woods—passed in the direction of the Nixons and Edmunds from the Frost house, where it seemed to ascend into the atmosphere, and soon afterwards re-appeared at Weston, where further damage was experienced.

* A few years earlier the disease probably existed here; as in February, 1777, a proposition was made to build a small pox hospital, but was negatived by the town; and instances of death from the disease occurred at a period still prior. In September, 1792, according to the Records, "it having been proposed by the physicians of the town, to receive permission to *inoculate with the small pox,*" the town voted "not to have the small pox in town, by inoculation, nor any other way, if it can be prevented." May, 1793: "voted, that the Selectmen be a committee to prosecute any person that shall spread the small pox, by inoculation, or any other way." At the same time, the town granted £30 to assist the sick, and appointed a committee of distribution. A hospital was provided at the house of Mr. George Pratt. The disease was introduced into the town by one David Butler, who came to Framingham from Peterboro', and falling sick with the disease, his nurses, to the number of seventeen, took the infection, and five persons besides Butler, died. Aug. 12, 1793, Peter Clayes was paid by the town for supplies furnished to the hospital. In 1810, the town chose Dr. J. B. Kittredge, Dr. Timo. Merriam, and Maj. Benjamin Wheeler, a committee to devise a system for inoculating with the kine pock.

† 1822, Nov. 24. Capt. Higgins' house; same year, Mr. Gilman's house.

1826, April. The barn of Mr. Levi Eaton.

1828, Dec. The woollen factory at Saxonville.

1831. In the Spring, the shop of Mr. Dexter Hemenway.

1834. In the Summer, the cotton factory at the E. part of the town.

1835-6. In the Winter, the house of Mr. Edward How, a mile E. from the village.

1837. The bake-house of Mr. Child, near S. house, No. 8.

1839. Mr. Edmund Capen's barn; supposed to have been an incendiary act.

1841, Oct. The poor house was destroyed, one of the inmates having clandestinely placed a lighted lamp in a closet, from which the house took fire.

1842, March. The paper mill of Calvin Shepard, Jr. Esq.

1843. In the autumn, the saw-mill belonging to William Buckminster, Esq.; also, Mr. Gill's house, in the S. district, No. 8.

1844—Summer. The barn of Maj. Benj. Wheeler; the same year, a shingle-mill, belonging to Wm. Buckminster, Esq.

1846, March. A shop belonging to Col. Timothy Eames.

PROVISION FOR THE POOR.

For many years after the incorporation of the town, no stated provision for the poor was required, individual instances of suffering being met as the exigency arose. The first certain instance of public relief, occurs upon the Record Feb. 1, 1736, when " an order was directed to Mr. Micah Stone by the Selectmen, desiring him to pay into the hands of Mr. Ralph Hemenway, the sum of £5, (out of the money paid by fines of persons chosen to serve as Constables in March last), to be improved and bestowed by said Hemenway, at his best discretion, for the relief of Stephen Streater's family ; and one other order to said Mr. Stone, to pay out of the same fines, 18s. to Edward Goddard, for three pair of Indentures, for binding out three poor children."

May 21, 1739. " Granted to John Nurse, the sum of £4, for boarding John Provender."

Nov. 26, 1739. An article was, for the first time, placed in the town warrant, " to see if the town will grant a suitable sum for the support of the poor." The article was debated and not voted upon, when the meeting was dissolved.

1741. The town first chose overseers of the poor. The persons elected were Amos Gates, John Bent and William Ballard.

May 16, 1743. " Voted, that at every Publick Thanksgiving, and also every publick fast, there be a contribution for the support of the poor in said town."

About the year 1747, one or two individuals only received public support, who were boarded in various places.

Aug. 29, 1754. Upon an article in the warrant, " to see what method the town will take relating to Moquet, who is now at the Rev. Mr. Gardner's of Stow, and claims the assistance of the town : Voted, that the overseers be directed for the future to make provision for him in a decent manner."

Feb. 14, 1757. It having been proposed to make provision for a French family, then in town, and also to provide a work house,

---

In 1816, an unsuccessful movement was made in town meeting to obtain a fire engine. In 1818, individuals having offered to purchase one for the use of the town, seventy dollars were granted by the latter for an engine house. In 1847, the Legislature passed an act establishing a Fire Department in this town. There are now three engines.

the town voted the 7th of March, prox., " that the overseers of the poor, shall (if they can) provide a house and land, by hiring the same for the French family, in said town, for the year ensuing, that they may provide subsistence for themselves. Voted, that Mr. William Brown take care of the poor in said town that shall be put into the work house, that they may be kept at work, and subsisted with such things as are necessary and convenient for their support."*

May 21, 1764. Voted, that Mr. Ralph Hemenway, Capt. Josiah Stone, and Mr. John Haven, be a committee to provide the town with a work house, and take care of the poor, and commit them to said house, &c.

Sept. 1, 1766. Voted to build a work house, 32 feet long and 16 feet wide, and seven and a half feet stud between joints. Voted, that there shall be a cellar under one of the rooms as big as said room, the walls of said house to be enclosed with white pine boards, and sealed with the like boards: also voted that said work house be built on said town's land, called the meeting house land, in the most convenient place, as the committee shall think proper.

Voted, that Lt. Sam. Gleason, Capt. Jona. Brewer and Capt. Josiah Stone, be a committee to build the work house, and that £50 be granted for this object.

1767. The town of Reading recovered £60 of Framingham, for the support of paupers.

1768. Chose nine overseers.†

1771. Joseph Buckminster, Esq., gave a deed of gift of a half acre of land, adjoining to the meeting house lot, to accommodate the work house and school house; for which the town unanimously voted him their thanks.

---

* Tradition informs us that the house once occupied by Mr. Swift, was obtained in conformity with the above vote. An aged lady, who has lately entered upon her 97th year, remembers distinctly the French family referred to, with their wooden shoes and striped silk cloaks!

† June 4, of this year, the Overseers made a Report, which was accepted by the town, embodying their regulations, specifying the hours of labor, the employment of the paupers, (chiefly the picking of oakum), the misdemeanors which were to be made punishable " by stripes on the naked back not exceeding ten stripes, by setting on the stocks or otherwise," at the discretion of the Overseers. Begging from house to house was forbidden under like penalties; and half of the proceeds of each pauper's labor was to be disposed of, at the discretion of the Overseers, for their greater advantage.

1774. A motion being made "to discontinue the annual contributions for the poor, since they are so very little of late," the same was negatived.

1800, April. The town voted to sell the work house to the highest bidder.

Oct. 13, 1813. Col. Micah Stone, by his will, made the town residuary legatee of his estate, providing that "the annual interest be applied (under the directions of the selectmen for the time being), for the support of his children, grand children, and great grand children, (if any of them should stand in need of support); otherwise, it may be applied to the support of the poor of said town; but no part of the Principal is ever to be expended." The amount accruing from this legacy was about $10,000.

In 1827, the town appointed a committee to purchase a Poor farm. In 1832, a new committee was chosen for the same object, the expense of the farm to be paid out of the Stone fund. The farm of Mrs. Solomon Fay was accordingly purchased, at a cost of $3,500. Additional charges were incurred — for enlarging and repairing the house, &c., $711.51 — live stock, $355 — farming tools, $206.22 — household furniture, $191.44. Total, $4,964.17.*

The number of persons supported by this town, varies with different years, but has rarely exceeded 16, composed chiefly of the aged, infirm, or idiotic. Considering that the population of the town now exceeds 4000, this fact presents in a favorable view the general thrift and prosperity of the community. The appropriations for the support of the poor, at different periods, are, viz: —

1755. - - - - £20	1810. - - - - $1100
1764. - - - - 50	1812. - - - - 800
1789. - - - - 150	1816. - - - - 1000
1797. - - - - $304	1823. - - - - 600
1800. - - - - 500	1827. - - - - 400
1802. - - - - 600	1828. - - - - 300
1805. - - - - . 500	1830. - - - - 100
1806. - - - - 700	

The average annual appropriation, from 1800 to 1834, was near $633.

---

* This house was consumed by fire Oct. 1841, and a much larger and more commodious one occupies its place. It is the practice of the town to hire a family to take charge of the farm and poor house, with its inmates.

EMIGRATIONS.

The spirit of change and adventure, so characteristic of New England, has left marked traces in the history of Framingham; which, from an early period, has sent forth numerous colonies, to people the wild lands of this and other States.

The first emigration of note from this town occurred about the year 1713, when a considerable number of families became grantees of the town of Oxford, and were prominent in the establishment of that flourishing town.*

At the incorporation of Hopkinton, (Dec. 13, 1717), and of Holliston, (1724), many families removed into those places. In the former town the Mellens and Havens were conspicuous.

At, or soon after, the incorporation of Rutland, (1722), several of the inhabitants of Framingham are found to have resided there, and the names of some are conspicuous in the early records of the town.† Shrewsbury (incorporated 1727) received from

---

* The township of Oxford, (whose Indian name was Manchage), with an area of eight miles square, "in the Nipmug country," was originally granted, in 1692, to Joseph Dudley, William Stoughton, and others. They soon after brought over thirty families of French Protestants, and set apart 12,000 acres in that place, for their use. The French settlers built for their protection, on a hill southeast of the present village of Oxford, a fort, whose ruins, with the vines planted by these fugitives from persecution, yet remain, interesting memorials of their short sojourn in the place. The massacre of one of their families by the Indians, and the hardships and perils of that wild region, induced them soon to forsake their lands; and the entire township, (with a single reservation to Gabriel Bernon), was conveyed, in 1713, to thirty-eight individuals, among whom, eleven at least were inhabitants of Framingham, viz: John, Ephraim, and Israel Town; Daniel Eliott, and his sons, Daniel and Ebenezer; Isaac and Ebenezer Larned; Thomas Leason, (Gleason), Benj. Nealand, and Abial Lamb. In addition to these, we find the names of Samuel Barton, Hezekiah Stone, and probably others, who then, or soon after, became inhabitants of the place. At the first meeting for the formation of the church, three of the four persons present, viz: Lt. John Town, Abial Lamb and Saml. Barton, were from Framingham; the first-named was chosen Deacon. The covenant of the church was adopted from that of the first church in this town, and at the ordination of their first minister, Mr. John Campbell, March 1, 1720-1, Dea. Haven and Ens. Benj. Bridges appeared as delegates from Framingham, and Mr. Swift gave the fellowship of the churches. Mr. Swift appears, from his journal, to have preached at Oxford, May 10, 1719; on which occasion he baptized eight persons, viz: Elijah and Francis Town, Abigail Learned, Mercy Gleason, Prudence and Lidia Eliot, Hephzibah Shumway, and Sarah Hunkins.

† Rutland was granted, twelve miles square, and the Indian Deed, chiefly to the heirs of Maj. Simon Willard, is dated 1686. The names of William Brintnal, David Bent and

the Goddards, Drurys, and other families, contributions to its settlement. The records of Templeton, in 1735, present among the first proprietors of the township, the names of John and Henry Eames, John Provender and Isaac Learned; and others soon followed from the families of Lamb, Shattuck, &c. Nichewaug, (now Petersham), contained, in 1750, a number of settlers from Framingham, as did, a little later, Poquaig, (Athol), in which last place the Havens, Goddards and Drurys were represented by men of influence and respectability. At a later period, the towns of Westmoreland, Marlborough, and Fitzwilliam, in New Hampshire, received (particularly the last named town) a considerable number of families from this place; and soon after the close of the war of the Revolution, several removed to Whitestown,* in the vicinity of Utica, New York.

We have referred to a few only of the places, more or less distant, in which this town may lay claim to its dispersed sons and daughters. The passion for emigrating to the far West has never prevailed here to any extent. With the towns contiguous to this, there has been a continual interchange of families. The unceasing tide of emigration has borne away, in many cases, entire families, whose names, once numerous and respected, have now become extinct. Of the 59 different family names found here in 1710, but 22 are known to be represented, by lineal descendants of the same name, at this time.†

Joseph Stevens, several of the Stones, and others, were among the early settlers of the place from this town. Wm. Brintnal preached there as a candidate. Joseph Stevens became a deacon of the church, and held many civil offices. His family suffered severely in the Indian wars. John Stone, Esq. died in that place Oct. 11, 1776, æ. 73. The Rev. Jos. Buckminster, a native of Framingham, was settled over the church of that place, Sept. 15, 1742, where he continued "an able, faithful and worthy minister," until Nov. 3, 1792, when he deceased. The Rev. Joseph Willard, (before of Sunderland), the first minister, was killed before his ordination, by the Indians, after a resolute defence, in which, like the Rev. John Whiting, slain at Lancaster in 1697, he bore not the sword in vain, having killed one and wounded another. See an account of the massacre at Rutland, Boston Gazette, Aug. 19, 1723.

* We recall as many as eight individuals, viz: Robert Eames, Nathaniel Hemenway, Joseph and Uriah Jennings, Luther Clayes, Richard Sanger, Joseph and Needham Maynard, who emigrated to that place. The Hon. Needham Maynard became distinguished, and held a seat upon the Judicial Bench. He died at the advanced age of eighty-nine, a few years since.

† The reader who may desire additional information respecting the emigrations from this town, may obtain some materials in the Genealogical Register, at the close of the volume.

EDUCATION.

Schools. — Some delay appears to have been experienced in the establishment of schools after the town's incorporation, (probably arising in part from the scattered state of the inhabitants), which rendered the town liable to the penalty imposed by law for such neglect.*

1704–5, March 5. Voted, that Lt. Jos. Buckminster should have 5s. for going down to answer the town's presentment.

1706, Sept. 3. Voted, that Dea. Josh. Hemenway be our schoolmaster for the year ensuing; and that Benj. Bridges and Peter Cloyse, Jun. should agree with him, what he shall have for his pains.

1708, April 5. Voted, that Jona. Rice shall have 6s. for answering the town's presentment.

1710, April 3. Voted, that Dea. Josh. Hemenway shall be schoolmaster, &c. henceforward; and when he has a mind to lay it down, he will give the town timely notice to provide another.

1712–3, March 2. Lt. Tho. Drury and Ebenezer Harrington were chosen schoolmasters, to instruct the youth of Framingham in writing; and the selectmen are appointed to settle school-dames in each quarter of said town.

1713, Oct. 7. £10 were granted to Dea. J. Hemenway as schoolmaster for four months, beginning Nov. 13.

1714, Dec. 8. Voted, that the school be kept the present winter season in five places, viz. one mo. at the house of John Gleason; one mo. at the house of Tho. Pratt; one mo. at the house of Sam. Winch; one mo. at the house of Cornet Sam. How; and one mo. at the house of Benj. Bridges.†

1716, March 5. Voted, to build a school house 20 or 30 poll. from the W. end of the meeting house, where the land may be convenient.

---

* In 1701, the penalty upon towns for neglecting to provide grammar schools, was £20. It was required that the school-master should be approved by the ministers of the town, and the ministers of the two next adjacent towns, or any two of them, by certificates under their hands.

† The following year, the places selected were "Benj. Bridges, Joseph Haven's, Thos. Drury, Saml. Winch, and Isaac Heath's, three weeks at each place; nine weeks south side of the river, and eight weeks on the north side."

1716, Aug. 10. Voted, to build a school house, 22 feet long, 16 broad, and six feet between the joints. Voted, to raise £16 for this object. £1.10 was afterwards added.

1716, Dec. 17. Voted to have a moving school in the four quarters of the town. Mr. Goddard consented to teach four weeks in each place, for £15; and all taught at his house to pay 6d. per head, per week.*

1717-8, Feb. 10. A committee having reported their inability, after "the utmost diligence," to obtain a schoolmaster, and the town having been again presented, another committee was appointed, 5 Aug. to obtain one, " and that forthwith;" also voted, that the gentlemen of the committee first go to Capt. Edward Goddard and see upon what terms he will serve the town; and if he will serve the town as cheap, or something cheaper, than another, then the committee are to make a full bargain with him for a year.

1724, July 21. Voted, that the committee to engage a teacher first treat with a scholar of the College; and that they be desired to treat with Sir Stone, and acquaint him that the town is desirous to enjoy him as their schoolmaster. The same year, granted £6.2s. for repairing the school house.

1745. The town appointed a committee to consider what might be proper for the town to do relating to building school houses in said town.

1748-9, March 6. Voted, that the town will this year have a grammar school kept, the winter half year, in the centre of the town; and raise an equal sum, to be laid out for the benefit of schooling in the outskirts of said town.

Aug. 22, 1749. Voted, to accept the following report:

" That the centre of the town be allowed to be at the publick meeting house; that the bounds of the centre school be as followeth, viz.: from the centre to Messrs. Moses Learned, Joseph Bixby, Nathaniel Pratt, John Drury, John Clayes, Ichabod Hemenway, John Bruce, Amos Gates, Josiah Warren, Jona. Clark, Tho. Winch, Jun., the two Boutwells, John Jones, Thomas Coller, Dea. Adams, Lieut. Rice, Francis Moquet, and Joseph Hemenway's; that the outskirts, not included in the forementioned circumference, be divided into eight schools, as follows, viz.: from David Sanger's to Ebenezer Marshall,

---

* The places selected were " Edward Goddard's, (formerly Samuel Barton, Senior's), Eben. Winchester's, John Eames, Jr's., and John Stone's."

be allowed to be two schools, to be divided between Nathaniel Emmes and Micah Haven's; and Salem side (so called) outskirts be one school; that all the outskirts N. from Stoney Brook, as far as Samuel Fairbank's, be one school; that Col. Brinley's Farm Road, by Joseph Berry's to Sudbury line, be the E. bounds of the next school; and all the outskirts from Jona. Edmunds, to Nathaniel Sever's, and Moses Cutting's, be another school; and all the outskirts from Sam. Stratton's to the bridge over the river by Dan. Stone's, be another school; and from Dan. Gregory's to Sam. Stone's, thence to David Emmes', be the W. bounds of the last school in the outskirts. Furthermore, we report, as our opinion, that there be a convenient school house built at the publick meeting house, and also, that the school begin there the first of Oct., and end at the last of March yearly."

Aug. 22, 1749. Voted, that Messrs. Henry Eames, Joseph Stone and John Parker be a committee to build a school house at the meeting house, as soon as may be.

1750, May 14. Upon an article to see if the town will choose a meet person, in each district of the outskirts, to draw their respective parts of money, Tho. Temple, Noah Eaton, Daniel Stone and Bezaleel Rice were chosen for that service.*

1750, Oct. 22. A committee reported in favor of constructing 4 school houses in the outskirts, viz. one at or near Capt. Goddard's N. draw bars, on the path leading to Hemenway's bridge; the 2d W. from the house of Ens. Richard Haven's, (on the road), N. between Benj. Haven's and Eben. Marshall's lands; the 3d on the road between Mr. Tho. Stone's and Mr. Daniel Gregorie's, on the S. side of the little brook crossing said road; the 4th between Capt. Clark's and Mr. Jona. Edmonds, in or near the road between said houses.

Granted £ 80, lawful money, to build four school houses, each 20 by 14 feet.

1750. The town was presented for not having a grammar school.

1755, May 26. Voted, that the women's schools be kept in the summer season, to the amount of half the money granted; the other half to be expended for a moveable grammar school.

1756. Voted, that the schooldames' board be paid in the same

---

* This vote appears to indicate the origin, in this town, of the District or Prudential Committee.

manner as the schoolmasters' are paid, viz. that each person that has boarded them bring in their accompt for allowance.*

1761. £ 10 were granted to repair the school houses.

1765, June 3. Voted, that there be two masters employed six mos. in the winter half year.

1768, May 16. The town voted to have one grammar school, the year, at a charge of £ 50; and that each squadron keep a woman's school 16 weeks in the year; having liberty to employ men, instead of women, to keep the schools, as the major part of each squadron can agree. The sum of £ 25 was voted for the support of the women's schools.

1769. A school house having been destroyed by fire, in the N. part of the town, voted to rebuild near Jona. Edmunds' house, 21 by 16 feet; also voted to rebuild at Salem End, 16 feet square.

1774, March 31. The following report upon the school divisions, was accepted:

" 1. That it is necessary to the convenience of the N. part of the town, that there be a school house near Mr. Silas Winch's, and to move the house by Capt. Gibbs here. 2d. A house built between Mr. Childs' and the crotch of the road, near Mr. Trowbridge's. 3d. To accommodate the W. part of the town, to erect a house between Dr. Hemenway's and Mr. Charles Dehouties' (Dougherty's). 4th. To convene Salem end with the common, to move the house by Mr. Benj. Mixer's, and set it between Mr. John Parker's and Mr. John Clayes'. 5th. To accommodate the S. part of the town, to move the house near Mr. Jesse Haven's, up to the road near Mr. Adams'. 6th. To erect an house on the N. side of the way leading from Mr. Sam. How's to the widow Larnard's, near the corner."

1774. Voted, that there be two women's schools kept in each ward, in the summer season.

1774. Voted, that there be four mos. grammar school, and six mos. with two writing schoolmasters, kept in the winter or dead season of the year.†

---

* Two shillings per week was allowed for the board of women, and four shillings per week for men. In 1763, the board of the female teachers was increased to two shillings eight pence. At this time, the women's schools, in some districts, had been divided. In 1794, Lt. John Jones taught the Centre school eight weeks, at 60s. per month, and boarded himself at 6s. per week.

† In 1792, the town voted to build a school-house in the east part of the town, and to place the south school-house at the west corner of Capt. Ezra Haven's land. The year following, it was voted, to build that year a brick house in the centre, and one

In 1795, the No. of School wards in the town was nine, containing the aggregate No. of 618 scholars.* In 1798, the whole No. of scholars was 659, (probably including, in both cases, all between 4 and 18 years of age).

1798. The town first chose a committee to inspect the public schools. The following year, the school money was divided among the several districts, according to their number of polls respectively. In 1808, was adopted the rule of division, which, with occasional modifications, has been continued to the present time. Of the $700 dollars appropriated for schools, $175 were divided equally among the nine districts, and the residue, according to the polls from 4 to 18 years of age. A few years previously, (May 5, 1800), a committee of nine persons was appointed to prepare articles for the government of the schools; and several useful regulations were reported the following month, and adopted. In 1833, by a vote of the town, it was ordered, that the superintending committee should receive pay for their services.

The public schools of Framingham have, for many years, received the benefit of a judicious and watchful oversight; and the general intelligence and enterprise which have long marked the community, bear witness to their healthful and vigorous condition. A wise and liberal spirit, it is hoped, will never be wanting to perceive and to appropriate such improvements as the experience and investigations of wise and good men are yet destined to bring to light.

---

at Salem end. In 1798, $120 were granted to the north district, provided the district will build a good brick school-house, and supply what it may cost more. In 1804, $150 were granted to build a school-house in the north-west ward. In 1811, $600 for a house in the E. district. In 1812, $400 for a house in the south-east district. The year following, $500 for a house in the W. district, twenty-six by twenty-eight feet. In 1814, $550 for a house in the S. district. In 1816, $600 for a house in the centre; and the E. district, was divided. In 1817, $525 for a house at Salem end. In 1818, $470 for a house in the south-west district. In 1822, district No. 10 was formed, and $525 granted for a house. Since that period, three new districts have been established, and a large proportion of the houses have been rebuilt, in a greatly improved style, both as regards convenience and health; wood being preferred to brick, after a due trial of both materials.

* The S. ward contained eighty-two scholars; the south-west, sixty-one; west, fifty-one; south-east, fifty-two; new ward, forty-five; north-west, eighty-four; centre, ninety-seven; north, 53; east, ninety-three.

EDUCATION.

The following is an imperfect list, derived chiefly from the Records of the town, of the individuals employed, for one or more years, as schoolmasters in Framingham, during the 18th century:

1706.	Joshua Hemenway.		1757.	Dr. —— Sparhawk.
1713.	Thomas Drury.		1759.	John Haven, H. U. 1757.
1713.	Ebenezer Harrington.		1769 ?	James Parker.
1715.	Edward Goddard.		1774.	Dr. Samuel Cooley.
1715.	Abraham Cozzens.		1776.	Joseph Nichols.
1720.	Robert Pepper.		1780 ?	John Jones.
1725.	James Stone,	H. U. 1724.	1780.	—— Man.
1726-7.	J. Bridgham,	H. U. 1726.	1789.	Daniel Stone, Jr.
1730.	P. Hemenway,	H. U. 1730.	"	J. Maynard, H. Coll. 1775.
1732.	S. Kendall,	H. U. 1731.	"	John Trowbridge.
1733.	J. Swift, Jr.,	H. U. 1733.	1790.	Samuel Bullard.
1736.	Josh. Eaton,	H. U. 1735.	1791.	Micah Stone.
1739.	Ch. Gleason,	H. U. 1738.	"	Hiram Walker.
1740.	J. Buckminster,	H. U. 1739	1794.	John Gleason.
1752.	—— Webb.		1798.	Eli Bullard, Y. C. 1787.*

The following table exhibits the annual town grants for schools, at different periods.

1713.	- -	£10	1760.	- - £40	1825.	- -	$1100
1714.	- -	25	1765.	- - 65	1834.	- -	1300
1716.	- -	15	1768.	- - 75	1835.	- -	1500
1720.	- -	30	1793.	- - 80	1837.	- -	1800
1736.	- -	45	1799.	- - $500 †	1840.	- -	2000
1741.	- -	70	1801.	- - 600	1842.	- -	2200
1746.	- -	140	1805.	- - 700	1844.	- -	2500
1756.	- -	30	1814.	- - 900			

FRAMINGHAM ACADEMY.

This Institution, which, for more than half a century, has maintained a flourishing existence, contributing largely to the intelligence and prosperity of the town, deserves a respectful notice in a History of Framingham.

It had its origin in 1792; early in which year, the " proprie-

---

* In addition to the above, tradition affords the names of Jonas Clark, David Sanger, George and Ephraim Stimson, and Isaac Clark, the last in 1793, Elisha Frost, 1794.

† In addition to the above, from the year 1798 to 1824, the town annually granted the interest on $1,000 in aid of the Academy, which sum ought properly to be considered a part of its annual grant for schools.

tors of the brick school house " organized a society, whose object was defined, " to disseminate piety, virtue and useful knowledge ; " the number of its members was limited to 25.* The character of the enterprise is indicated by the following regulations in their first by-laws, providing that " no person shall be admitted as preceptor in the school, unless he has received a collegiate education, and been endowed with a degree of Bachelor of Arts in some University ; " and that every branch of useful science may be taught, " a primary regard being had to the initiation of youth into the principles of piety and virtue."

The proprietors proceeded, at once, to the construction of a brick school house, with two stories, which was completed at a charge of £176.9.6.; and the school was opened Nov. 27, 1792, under the instruction of Mr. James Hawley, afterwards Tutor at Harvard College. The school continued in a prosperous state ; and received in 1798, a grant of the interest on $1000 from the town, which was annually granted until 1824.† March 1, 1799, the General Court granted the petitioners therefor, an act of Incorporation, as the Framingham Academy, providing for a body of Trustees, in number, not to exceed nine, nor to be less than seven. The liberality of the legislature provided, in addition, " a grant of a tract equal to the half of a township, six miles square, of any of the unappropriated lands within either of the Counties of Lincoln, Hancock, or Washington, excepting the lands on the Penobscot river." This tract was sold in 1803, to Messrs. Jonathan Maynard and Samuel Weed, and the proceeds constituted a fund, the interest of which was applied in aid of the Institution.

The Academy, for a long series of years, has been conducted by a succession of educated teachers, with variable but general success, attracting many pupils from distant places, and maintaining

---

* The names of the first proprietors were, David Kellogg, Jona. Hale, David Brewer, Simon Edgell, Elijah Stone, Peter Clayes, Ezra Haven, Joseph Bennet, Matthias Bent, Jr., John Trowbridge, Jr., Samuel Frost, Jr., Jona. Rugg, John Fisk, Ebenezer Eaton, Thomas Buckminster, Jona. Maynard, Elisha Frost, Barzillai Banister, Lawson Buckminster, and Lawson Nurse. Sam. Ballard and Andrew Brown were afterwards admitted.

† The terms of the grant were :— " Granted $1,000 to support the Academy school, or the interest of the same to be paid annually, provided it will exempt them from keeping a grammar school, and the Legislature will make a grant of half a township at the eastward." In 1824, the illegality of the grant caused it to be withdrawn, but " no censure was cast on the trustees or preceptor."

a respectable rank among the kindred seminaries, which have since been so largely multiplied in the Commonwealth. With competent instructers, it has prepared many young men for our Colleges. In 1826, John Trowbridge, Esq. devised, by will, a legacy of $500 to the Trustees, the interest of which has been since applied, agreeably to the provisions of the donor, in aid of young men of this town preparing for College. In 1838, at the decease of Mr. Micah Stone, a gentleman whose high character for probity and enterprise, won the confidence and esteem, as his various acts of liberality, entitle his name to the enduring gratitude of this community, a legacy of $3,000 was received by the Trustees. The interest of this sum was to be applied to the reduction of the charge of tuition, to pupils belonging to the town, with the proviso, that it should not be reduced to a less charge than three dollars per quarter. The year preceding, (1837), the Trustees, at a cost of about $3,000, replaced the old school house by a new and more commodious structure of stone. The various benefits derived to the inhabitants of the town, from a seminary so early founded, and by its liberal provisions rendered accessible to all who have desired its privileges, are beyond computation. Without courting an ephemeral popularity, it has pursued its steady course of beneficence for more than half a century, numbering among its alumni, names which have repaid its cherishing care by lives of honorable distinction, and adding largely to the general intelligence and cultivation of this community.

The names of the Trustees, from the incorporation of the Academy to the present time, we present below: the first column of years indicating the date of their accession, and the second (as far as known) of their retirement or decease, respectively.

Hon. Artemas Ward, Jr.,	1799 to 1825
Rev. David Kellogg, D.D.,	1799 to 1825
Rev. Josiah Bridge,	1799 to 1802
Rev. Jacob Bigelow,	1799 to 1803
Hon. Jona. Maynard,	1799 to 1803
Peter Clayes, Esq.,	1799 to 1804
Maj. Jona. Hale,	1799 to 1802
Col. David Brewer,	1799 to 1822
Capt. Samuel Frost,	1799 to 1810
Rev. Samuel Kendall, D.D.,	1802 to unk.
Eli Bullard, Esq.,	1802 to unk.

CIVIL HISTORY.

Rev. Asa Packard,	1803 to 1820
Dr. Tapley Wythe,	1803 to 1812
Col. John Trowbridge,	1804 to 1824
Jeremy Stimpson, Esq.,	1810 to 1820
Maj. Benjamin Wheeler,	1813
Rev. Ralph Sanger,	1814
Rev. Joseph Field, D.D.,	1820 to 1824
Hon. Josiah Adams,	1820
Hon. Rufus Hosmer,	1821 to 1825
Rev. Rufus Hurlburt,	1822 to 1832
Rufus Brewer, Esq.,	1824 to 1844
Rev. John B. Wight,	1824 to 1837
Isaac Fisk, Esq.,	1825 to 1830
Col. Moses Edgell,	1825
Hon. Abner Wheeler,	1828 to 1843
Rev. Artemas B. Muzzey,	1830 to 1833
Rev. Charles Train,	1832
Rev. George Chapman,	1833 to 1834
Rev. William Barry,	1836
Rev. David Brigham,	1837 to 1839
Hon. Samuel Greele,	1844
Dr. Simon Whitney,	1845
Rev. Increase N. Tarbox,	1847

The successive Treasurers of the Board, have been — Peter Clayes, Esq., Col. John Trowbridge, Rufus Brewer, Esq., and Col. Moses Edgell.

The following presents a list, nearly complete, of those employed as Preceptors of the Academy, since its institution:

1792.	James Hawley, a graduate of		H. C., 1792
1793.	John Park,	"	D. C., 1791
1795.	Eli Bullard,	"	Y. C., 1787
1798.	Joseph Emerson,	"	H. C., 1798
1800.	Samuel Weed,	"	H. C., 1800
1806.	B. H. Tower,	"	H. C., 1806
1806.	William T. Torrey,	"	H. C., 1806
1807.	John Brewer,	"	H. C., 1804
1808.	Charles Train,	"	H. C., 1805
1810.	John Cotton,	"	H. C., 1808
1811.	George Morey,	"	H. C., 1811
1813.	Mason Fisher,	"	H. C., 1813
1814.	Aaron Prescott,	"	H. C., 1814
1815.	George Otis,	"	H. C., 1815
1816.	Augustus Whiting,	"	H. C., 1816
1818.	George R. Noyes,	"	H. C., 1818

FRAMINGHAM ACADEMY. 83

1819.	Walter R. Johnson, a graduate of		-	-	H. C.,	1819
1820.	Enos Stewart,	"	-	-	H. C.,	1820
1821.	John M. Cheney,	"	-	-	H. C.,	1821
	George Folsom,	"	-	-	H. C.,	1822
	Alfred W. Pike,	"	-	-	D. C.,	1815
	Omen S. Keith,	"	-	-	H. C.,	1826
	David W. Fisk,	"	-	-	B. U.,	1825
	Duncan Bradford,	"	-	-	H. C.,	1824
	Barzillai Frost,	"	-	-	H. C.,	1830
	Jacob Caldwell,	"	-	-	H. C.,	1828
	Rufus King,	"	-	-	H. C.,	1838
	Charles W. Goodnow,	"	-	-	A. C.,	1838
	Marshall Conant, A. M.,		-	-	-	
	Thomas Russell,	"	-	-	H. C.,	1845
	John A. Hastings,	"	-	-	H. C.,	1846

We subjoin, in a note, some memoranda extracted from the Records of the Trustees, which may be worthy of preservation.*

---

* The assessments upon the original proprietors, (at three several times), amounted to over $20 for each proprietor. July, 1794, £3.7.11, were received from the sale of tickets for the exhibition.

Dec. 29, 1794, voted that balls shall not be held in the school-house, during the existence of the constitution this day adopted.

May 23, 1795. Chose a committee to let the Hall to the Free-masons for one year.

Oct. 5, 1795. The thanks of the trustees were voted to Joseph Park, for the donation of a pair of globes.

1796. The charge of tuition was 1s. per week.

Jan. 1798. A committee was chosen to petition for an act of incorporation.

Dec. 3, 1798. Voted, that the singers have the use of the hall, gratis, for six weeks.

1804. Voted to employ a Preceptress, to teach immediately after the Summer vacation, with a grant not exceeding $100; the tuition to be twelve and a half cents per week.

1808. A vote of thanks to Jona. Maynard for twenty ornamental trees.

1810. An amount subscribed for a bell was put at interest, until able to purchase.

1811, May 8. Notice was given that the Rev. Saml. Kendall, D.D. would deliver an address to the students, at 2 o'clock, P. M.

1822. Voted to build a house for the Preceptor. [This refers to the so-called boarding-house adjoining the Academy, which was built at a charge of about $3,500.]

1824. A committee was appointed to purchase a bell; authority was also given to build a cupola for the same.

1837. Abner Wheeler, Josiah Adams, and Moses Edgell, Esqs., were appointed the Building Committee, to superintend the construction of the new school-house.

In 1794, the amount accruing from the charges of tuition, probably for the year, was £100.18.6. In 1810, the emoluments of the Instructer were about $500 per annum. Of late years, with variations, they have averaged near $700 annually. No means exist of determining the aggregate number of pupils who have enjoyed the benefits of this seminary. For many years past, the average number of scholars has been about fifty; some terms exceeding eighty, and others falling as low as forty. Several hundred dollars have been expended, within a few years, for the purchase of apparatus.

CIVIL HISTORY.

GRADUATES.

The following individuals, natives of Framingham, or residents in the town during their Collegiate course, have graduated at the various Colleges.*

Phinehas Hemenway,	H. Coll.	1730
David Goddard,	"	1731
Elias Haven,	"	1733
John Swift,	"	1733
Nathan Haven,	"	1737
Joseph Buckminster,	"	1739
Amariah Frost,	"	1740
John Mellen,	"	1741
John Wilson,	"	1741
Ebenezer Winchester,	"	1744
Samuel Haven,	"	1749
Jason Haven,	"	1754
Moses Hemenway,	"	1755
John Haven,	"	1757
Eliab Stone,	"	1758
Moses Adams,	"	1771
John Reed,	Y. Coll.	1772
Solomon Reed,	"	1775
Samuel Reed,	"	1777
Jonathan Maynard,	H. Coll.	1775
Moses Haven,	"	1782
Timothy Reed,	D. "	1782
Jacob Haven,	H. "	1785
Joseph Bixby,	"	1791
Daniel Stone,	"	1791
John B. Fisk,	D. "	1798
William Ballard,	H. "	1799
Moses Madison Fisk,	D. "	1802
John Brewer,	H. "	1804
Jones Buckminster,	"	1804
William Haven,	B. "	1809
John L. Parkhurst,	"	1812
Dana Cloyes,	Mid. "	1815
Joseph Bennet,	H. "	1818
Jeremy Parkhurst,	Y. "	1819
Edward Frost,	H. "	1822
Increase Sumner Wheeler,	"	1826
John T. Kittredge,	A. "	1828

* In the table, H. stands for Harvard (College); B. for Brown; Y. for Yale; D. for Dartmouth; A. for Amherst; Mid. for Middleboro'; W. for Williams'.

GRADUATES. 85

Joshua Trowbridge Eaton,	Y. Coll.	1830
Peter Parker,	" "	1831
Abner B. Wheeler,	H. "	1831
Arthur Savage Train,	B. "	1833
William Jones Buckminster,	H. "	1835
Edward Stone,	B. "	1835
Edward Brewer,	H. "	1836
Oliver J. Fisk,	B. "	1837
Charles R. Train,	" "	1837
Charles P. Johnson,	A. "	1839
James W. Brown,	W. "	1840
Benjamin A. Edwards,	B. "	1841
Robert Gordon,	H. "	1843
Rufus Franklin Brewer,	" "	1845
Cornaris Esty,	Y. "	1845

PROFESSIONAL MEN.

PHYSICIANS. — The earliest regular Physician known in this town, was Dr. Bezaleel Rice, who probably practiced from about 1720, and remained in practice here until 1740, if not later.*

A Dr. Nichols is noticed upon the Records, about 1740.

Dr. John Mellen was in practice here, and employed by the town, in 1748; but nothing more is known of him.

Dr. Ebenezer Hemenway, who lived on the Southborough road, was for many years in practice, commencing in 1750, and continuing as late as 1777.

Jeremiah Pike, noted as a bone-setter, was here in 1750; he removed (probably to Rutland) about 1780.

Dr. Richard Perkins, H. C., 1748, a native of Bridgewater, and brother to the wife of the Rev. Mr. Bridge, was in town in 1758; he remained but a short time.

Dr. Elijah Stone, who possessed a large share of the practice of the town, began probably about 1766, and deceased in 1804, aged 68.

Dr. John B. Kittredge came to Framingham about 1791, and has remained since in the practice of his profession, in this and

---

* John Page was in this town an. 1712, and soon after removed to Sutton, where he deceased about 1731, and was entitled " Physician." A Dr. Wilson practiced here about 80 years since, and was probably Dr. John Wilson, of Hopkinton, or Sherburne. Dr. Robie, of Sudbury, and Dr. Sparhawk, of Natick, also extended their practice within the limits of Framingham.

the neighboring towns, possessing an estimation and confidence, strengthened by a successful professional career of more than half a century.

Dr. Timothy Merriam, a native of Concord, Mass., began practice here, near the same time as the preceding, and deceased Sept. 17, 1835, aged 76.

Dr. Simon Whitney, H. C., 1818, established himself in the town about 1822, and has remained to this day, in extensive and successful practice.

LAWYERS.

For many years after the settlement of the town, no regular representative of the legal profession existed within its borders. The common exigencies of the community, in the preparation of wills, conveyances, &c., were sufficiently provided for by the clergymen and justices of the town.*

The first professional lawyer established here was Eli Bullard, Esq., a graduate at Yale College, who became an inhabitant of Framingham about the year 1791, and deceased in 1824. Josiah Adams, Esq., who studied law with Tho. Heald, Esq. of Concord, was admitted to the bar in June, 1807, and continues to this day in professional practice. William Buckminster, Lawson Kingsbury, Omen S. Keith,† and Charles R. Train, Esquires, have respectively occupied offices in this town; the last named gentleman only, remaining in regular practice.

INDIAN, FRENCH, AND REVOLUTIONARY WARS.

But little information is preserved to us, illustrating the dangers, the defences, and the military movements of this town, dur-

---

* Mr. Swift's handwriting is generally found in ancient wills. Edward Goddard, Joshua Hemenway, Tho. Drury, and the two Col. Buckminsters, were all serviceable to the town as conveyancers. Mr. Bridge also contributed his aid, as similar occasions arose.

† Mr. Keith read law with the Hon. R. Hosmer, of Stow, and J. Adams, Esq., of Framingham; became, in 1833, an associate in practice of the latter, and remained in town but a few years, when he transferred his office to Boston. He died at Brooklyn, N. Y., March, 1847; and his remains were interred at Cambridge. He was greatly esteemed for his liberality of mind, his warm affections, and unbending integrity.

ing the troubles with the Indians, which at various times occurred after its incorporation. A tradition exists, that a fort was constructed by the first Col. Buckminster. If this account is to be relied upon, it was erected probably in the neighborhood of his own farm, which was subsequently the Brinley farm. Of its locality and history, nothing is known. From the same source we derive the information, that there were garrisoned houses in various parts of the town.* These are probably referred to in the following vote of the town.

April 3, 1710. "Voted £10 to raise a stock of ammunition, to be kept in the four several places in the town."

March 24, 1711-2. Voted to procure an addition to our stock of ammunition: — to John Town, £1; to Jonathan Rice, £7.10sh.; and for the town stock, £4.†

A company of troopers, commanded by Capt. Isaac Clark, was early established in Framingham; about 30 of whom were inhabitants of the town. This company was in service about three weeks in the year 1725. A few years earlier, in 1722, we find the muster-roll of a company under the command of Col. Buckminster, who served from August to November of that year, and also the roll of the so called "Rutland Scout," commanded by Serg. Thomas Buckminster, who served from July 25 to August 26th.‡

This period must have been one of general alarm in all our towns. Tradition faintly shadows the scene, in its relations of

---

* Aged persons state that there was a garrison at Mr. Charles Clark's, near the school house No. 2; one also at Salem end. There were probably still others.

† March 8, 1715-6. The powder and shot of the town stock were weighed by the selectmen. The weight of the barrel, bag and powder was 120 lbs. The weight of the bullets, flints, and bags to put them in, 150 lbs. June 15, 1719, Capt. Drury and Ens. Bridges were appointed to take charge of the town's ammunition, and have it brought and secured in the vault, over the body of seats, in the meeting house; and Edward Goddard to procure a lock for the vault. May 28, 1733, voted that Messrs. Tho. Stone and Tho. Winch be desired to view the town stock of powder and ammunition, to see whether the same be duly preserved, and whether it needs to be changed. Feb. 28, 1788, the town stock consisted of nine fire-arms, 150 wt. powder, 381 wt. balls, 275 flints.

In 1800, the town accepted the report of a committee, recommending that the ammunition be kept in the meeting house. In 1805, a committee was chosen to build a Magazine. As the practice of warming churches is of recent date, their security in former times, as places of deposite, will be understood.

‡ The names of the men who served in these companies, as also of others who served during the French and Revolutionary wars, will be found in the Appendix.

individual exposure in the field, and of midnight assaults upon the ill-protected garrisons, where affrighted neighborhoods sought a precarious shelter. Our town records fail of handing down any distinct memorials of the sufferings and perils of the early settlers in this township. The relations of the aged, though involved sometimes in uncertainty, must therefore possess a high degree of interest, in the absence of documentary information.*

---

* Of the general insecurity of the period to which we refer above, the accounts handed down by the aged, leave no doubt. Men were obliged to take with them their arms into the field, and neighbors united in labor, for greater security. Women could safely go into the barn-yards at milking, only with the presence of their husbands. An aged woman of this town heard, from her grandmother, an account of this practice; the latter adding, that her husband's presence was, after all, of no great service; for instead of watching for Indians, he would throw himself upon his back, and sing loud enough to be heard through the neighborhood.

An aged inhabitant of this town relates an instance of narrow escape from death, on a like occasion, which occurred to his grandmother. Having gone alone to the yard to milk, about two hours before sunset, she carefully looked around to see if there were Indians in the neighborhood. Supposing herself secure, she proceeded to her work, and while in the act of milking, an Indian, (who, as was their custom, had disguised himself with brakes, and crawled along upon his belly), suddenly struck her in the back with a knife. She instantly sprung, and by the effort twitched the knife from the Indian's grasp; and before he could rise, had advanced so far, that she succeeded in reaching the house, with the knife in her back. An alarm was immediately given, by three successive discharges of a musket, which soon brought a reinforcement from the neighborhood of what is now called the Silk Farm, where was a garrison well provided with powerful dogs and arms. On pursuing, however, they found no traces of the Indian. The woman survived her injury.

From the same source, we learn that there was a garrison-house about midway between the houses of the late Col. Brewer and the late Mr. Peter Parker, on the N. side of the road; the cellar hole having been filled by Mr. John Parker, now living. The garrison house was enclosed by long close-set pickets, with a gate on wooden hinges. On a dark night, when the families were all within the garrison, two men having been stationed in the watch-box at the gable end, the dogs, (of which the largest, most savage, and quick-scented, were selected), began to show signs of uneasiness. The garrison was aroused, and guns were fired in the direction of the gate. The alarm soon ceased; and the following morning, blood was discovered near the gate, and tracked across the swale of land in the direction of the Badger house, where it disappeared.

As an illustration of the stealthiness with which an Indian could approach his victim, we have heard related the following. An Indian, in time of peace, was boasting to one of our settlers, that he could touch him while at work in the field, without his knowledge. The latter promised him a sum of money upon his doing it. A few days only elapsed, and the man was startled at his work by finding himself suddenly seized by the heel; and, on turning, he met the face of the Indian, demanding his reward.

Mr. Uriah Rice, now in his 90th year, distinctly remembers to have seen Indians, rapidly crossing a meadow, where he had wandered while a boy. He also relates, that Capt. John Butler, of this town, had, during the French war, made himself obnoxious to the Indians, three of

FRENCH WAR.

Of the extent to which this town participated in the French war, we are able to afford but little information beyond the muster-rolls to be found in the Appendix to this history. John Nixon, who afterwards distinguished himself in the service of the Revolution, his brother Thomas, and Josiah Stone, held the post of Captain in the expedition to Crown Point, in 1755. Several subordinate officers and privates, from Framingham, were also engaged on the same occasion. Colonel Buckminster was at this period in commission, and his name appears in the supply of reinforcements for the army. Several individuals lost their lives in the service of their country, during this war, whose names, as far as known, will afterwards appear.

WAR OF THE REVOLUTION.

The inhabitants of this town early espoused and vigorously maintained, the common cause of the country, in the trying events which preceded and accompanied the war of the Revolution.

The passage of the stamp act led to the following instructions to Joseph Buckminster, Esq., representative for the town in the General Court.

Oct. 21, 1765. We instruct you to promote and readily join in, such dutiful remonstrances and humble petitions to the King and Parliament, as have a direct tendency to obtain a repeal of the Stamp Act.

We further instruct you, that you do not give your assent to any Act of Assembly, that shall imply the willingness of your constituents, to submit to any taxes that are imposed, in any other way, than by the Great and General Court of this Province, according to the institution of this Government.

We further add, that you take care that money raised in this Time of Distress and Trouble, may not be used to any other purpose, than

---

whom came into the town, inquiring for him, with the purpose of revenging some former injury. Information was given to Capt. Butler, which enabled him to secure his safety.

But few Indians have been known residents within the town, since its incorporation. For some years, during the last century, a family are said to have lived at the ledge of rocks, lately quarried by Col. Jonas Clayes. A natural recess, formed by overhanging rocks, was their dwelling place. Individuals have been sometimes employed in the service of families.

what is intended by the Act for supplying the Treasury ; and as to other Affairs that shall come under consideration, we submit to your wisdom and prudence.

Sept. 26, 1768. Mr. Thomas Temple was chosen to join the committee, in convention with others, at Fanueil Hall, in Boston, to consult upon such measures as may be for the safety of the Province.

March 1, 1773. A committee, consisting of Dea. Wm. Brown, Maj. John Farrar, Jos. Buckminster, Esq., Dr. Eben. Hemenway, Joseph Nichols, Josiah Stone, and Mr. Eben. Marshall, was appointed, to take into consideration a letter from the Boston committee; who, on the 15th of the same month, presented their report, (which was unanimously accepted), asserting the privileges of the Colonies, and concluding in the following language :

"From all which it appears our absolute duty to defend by every constitutional measure, our dear privileges purchased with so much blood and treasure. Let us prudently endeavour to preserve our character as freemen and not lose that of good and loyal subjects. Let us jointly labour after (and Heaven grant we may obtain) that magnanimity of soul, by which we may be enabled to resist injuries, and let the world know, that we are not governed by feud and faction."

Jan. 25, 1774. The town resolved, "That we ourselves, or any for or under us, will not buy any teas subject to a duty, nor knowingly trade with any merchant or country trader, that deals in that detestable commodity. And since such means and methods are used to destroy our privileges, which were purchased by the dearest blood of our ancestors, those that stand foremost in a proper defence of our privileges, shall have our greatest regard ; and if any shall be so regardless of our political preservation, and that of posterity, as to endeavor to counteract our determination, we will treat them in the manner their conduct deserves."

May 18, 1774. The town chose a committee of correspondence ; viz. Joseph Haven, Esq., Josiah Stone, Dea. Wm. Brown, Mr. Eben. Marshall, Lt. David Haven, Jos. Buckminster, Esq., and Maj. John Farrar.

June 27. The town met on notice, "the fullest and most general ever known in this town on any civil occasion; when the meeting was opened by solemn prayer for divine direction, and after reading some letters and other papers, the committee of correspondence presented the following covenant, and the same was read distinctly several times, and considered, and very largely debated several hours; after which the question was put, whether the town do accept the said covenant as it now stands; and it passed in the affirmative, almost unanimously." *

Sept. 9. Capt. Josiah Stone, Joseph Haven, Esq., and Dea. Wm. Brown, were chosen delegates to the Provincial Congress, to assemble at Concord in October. Voted, that the selectmen be directed to procure and purchase, at the town's expense, five barrels of powder, and 4 or 5 cwt. of bullets or lead.

Sept. 30. The town voted to instruct their representative, Capt. Josiah Stone, "to adhere firmly to the charter of the Province, and not consent to any act that can possibly be construed into an acknowledgement of the validity of the act of the British Parliament, for altering the government of the Massachusetts Bay; more especially to acknowledge the Hon. Board of Counsellors, elected last May, by the General Court, as the only rightful and constitutional Council of the Province."

The town at the same time ordered the purchase of 20 fire arms and field pieces; on the 3d Oct. the organization of two militia companies, besides the troop; and a resolve was passed the 8th Nov., "that all public monies, belonging to the Province, shall be paid to the Receiver General appointed by the Congress."

Jan. 2, 1775. Voted that a contribution be made to the town of Boston under their present distress. Capt. Josiah Stone, and Dea. Wm. Brown were chosen delegates to the Congress, and a company of minute men was ordered to be formed, according to the advice of the Provincial Congress.

1775. Raised a Province tax of £100.

May 6, 1776. The first call of a town meeting "in the name of the Government and People of the Massachusetts Bay." †

July 1, 1776. Granted £7 per man, for all that will voluntarily enlist themselves into the continental service.

---

* It is to be regretted that this paper was not placed upon record.

† It is worthy of remark, that this was the sole change caused by the revolution, in the municipal organization and management of our towns, the meetings having been summoned as above, instead of " in his Majesty's name," as was before the practice. Similar revolutions in other countries, have introduced radical alterations in the civil and social institutions of the community. The American revolution introduced no extensive organic change; the elements of the newly constituted government having existed previously.

July 8, 1776. Voted, that Lt. Wm. Maynard be employed to purchase 10 good fire arms, and Mr. John Pratt to purchase 20 blankets.

A company marched with Capt. Edgell to Ticonderoga.

March, 1777. Chose a committee to engage men for the service, on any terms. A bounty was granted of £ 30 to every soldier who enlisted for 3 years, (and in Sept. £ 40 for the same service).

The treasurer was authorized to hire the sum of £ 1000.

June 23, 1777. Voted, that Maj. John Trowbridge inspect any that shall be thought inimical to the U. S. of America.

March, 1778. A committee was appointed to provide clothing for the soldiers in the Continental Army from this town.

May, 1778. A requisition was made upon the town for 10 men, — 8 to fortify North River.

June 5, 1778. The town voted upon the proposed Constitution or form of government. Yeas 5. Nays 77.

June 18, 1779. A requisition was received for 9 men to complete the town's quota. (The families of those in service were at this period supplied by a committee of the town).

June 18, 1779. The town secured the services of 6 Frenchmen as substitutes.

Aug. 9, 1779. Capt. Benj. Edwards and Josiah Stone, Esq., were chosen delegates to the convention at Cambridge.

Aug. 9, 1779. Voted, to approve the resolve of the convention at Concord, to regulate prices, &c., and that a committee of 10 men be chosen to state the prices of labour, country produce, manufactures, inn holders, &c.

Mr. Dan. Sanger and Capt. Simon Edgel were chosen delegates to the convention at Concord, in Oct.

June 5, 1780. The town acted on the Bill of Rights. Accepted the 1st and 2d Articles by a vote of 107 to 8; the 3d Article by 113 to 18. The others were also accepted, till the Article on Representation, which was thought unequal, and as to qualifications for voters, exceptionable. Voted, to choose a committee to prepare an amendment.

Dec. 27, 1780. Granted £ 35.000 to purchase the beef now called for.

The town being called upon to raise 20 men, for 3 years or during the war, granted £ 50.000 to hire them.

Nov. 12, 1781. The town agreed with Capt. Jona. Maynard, to supply him with $150 for each man, and $100 in one year and $50 to be paid in two years; and he engages to procure the men for that money. (The town had been fined for not furnishing its quota.)

We have preferred not to interrupt the order of the preceding extracts from the Town Records, to notice the particular events of the war in which the citizens of this town participated. In reference to these, it may be remarked, that when the tidings of the advance of the British on Concord, reached this town, the inhabitants hastened at once to the scene of action.* On this occasion, Cols. John and Thomas Nixon had the command of the First Regiment of Massachusetts Militia, and acquitted themselves with much honor.

The part taken by the citizens of Framingham in the battle of Bunker Hill, was highly creditable to their bravery and patriotism. Among the officers present, or in command, were the two Col. Nixons, Col. William Buckminster, and Col. Jona. Brewer; and the late Hon. Needham Maynard acted as aid to General Warren; all of whom were natives of this town, and nearly all received wounds in the bloody contest.† Col. Nixon was stationed

---

* Mr. Ezekiel How informed the author that he and his neighbor Benj. Berry, ran on foot the entire distance to Concord, (near 12 miles), in two hours. The first object that struck him, on his arrival, was a British regular weltering in blood. It being his first experience of the horrors of war, he was so shocked that he almost fainted. "But," he added, "they pushed me along, and a few hours afterward, I could see men dying around me with as much indifference as if they were sheep." Noah Eaton, 2d, and his brother Jonas, were at Lexington. The former, having discharged his piece, retired behind a knoll to reload, where he suddenly encountered a British regular, with a loaded gun. Noah presented his empty musket, threatening to kill the soldier; when the latter surrendered, returned with his captor to Framingham, and lived in his service. Daniel Hemenway, it is said, was the only man wounded from this town on that occasion.

† Col. Buckminster received a ball through his shoulder, and Colonel Brewer was wounded through the lower part of his arm. Col. John Nixon was severely wounded, and was afterwards commissioned, on account of his bravery and experience in the French war, as a Brigadier General. Lt. Jona. Maynard was in the engagement; and his brother William, an officer, received a bullet in his hip, which he bore with him to his grave. John Maynard, acting ensign, brother of Needham, was discovered by the latter, wounded and unable to walk, who happily succeeded in carrying him safely to Cambridge. The Hon. Needham Maynard, to whom we are indebted for many particulars of this battle, was present at the last celebration of that event in 1843; about which time, he gave a minute account of the incidents of the battle, in the presence of several intelligent persons. His narrative may be found printed in the Boston Semi-Weekly Advertiser, Ju-

on the Mystic side. Col. Brewer's regiment, numbering about 150 men, was in the open field during the greater part of the engagement.

In the subsequent engagements of the war, this town was duly represented; and not a few of its citizens lost their lives in their country's service. The Records of the town enumerate various instances in which the militia were called out, and in which their services were generously remunerated.* The extent of the charges and sacrifices, at this eventful period, borne by this town, in common with others in the Commonwealth, must be left to conjecture. The distress which pervaded the country, impoverished by harassing and expensive campaigns, and the interruption of regular industry, burthened with debts, and oppressed by a depreciated and almost worthless currency, was a severer trial of the patriotism and virtue of the people, than the threats of despotic power, or the dangers of the battle field.†

SHAY'S REBELLION.

Upon the occurrence of this outbreak against the civil authority, the three companies of the town met, Jan. 15, 1787, to enlist

---

ly 4, 1846. We have already spoken of the exploit of Peter Salem, who is believed to have killed Maj. Pitcairn in this battle.

* 1. The men who went to Cambridge, to man the lines, Jan. 29, 1776.
2. The men who went with Capts. Broad and Trowbridge, 3 mos. to the Jersies, Nov. 30, 1776.
3. The men who went with Col. Stone and Capt. Gleason to Providence, from May to July, 1777.
4. The men who went to guard the stores at Sherburne, 1777.
5. The men who went with Capt. Winch, to Ticonderoga, and the taking of Burgoyne, Aug., 1777, 4 mos.
6. The men who went with Lt. Drury, on the secret expedition to R. I., Oct., 1777.
7. The men who went with Lt. Claflin, to Cambridge and elsewhere, to guard the public stores.
8. Those who went with Lt. John Eames, 2d, 3 mos., from 1 Jan. 1778, to R. I.

9. Those who went to Cambridge, with Capt. Holmes, to guard the Convention prisoners, Apr., 1778.
10. Those that went with Capt. Edgell to R. I., June, 1778, 6 mos.
11. Those that went to Cambridge, July, 1778, 5 1-2 mos., to guard the prisoners.
12. Those that went with Maj. Trowbridge, to R. I., when the gallant attack was made on the enemy, and safe retreat, 6 weeks, Aug., 1778.
13. Those that went with Sargt. Abel Stone, to Providence, Oct., 1778, 3 mos. in service.

To all the above, the town voted bounties, "double 9 times their nominal sum."

† The extent of the depreciation of the currency, in 1790, is indicated in the following extract from the Journal of Dea. Tho. Buckminster: "Dec. 3. Sold 2710 old continental dollars, to Mr. Jonathan Wheeler, Jr., of Grafton, for 2s. 9d. per hundred. Total, £3.14.4."

men for 30 days. Volunteers in sufficient force tendered their services, who rendezvoused at Weston on the 20th, and after more than a month's service, reached home, on their return, the 27th of the following month. This force was composed chiefly of young men, the older remaining behind, ready for service if called for. A body of the latter is said to have proceeded as far as Worcester; but finding that the rebellion had been effectively subdued, soon returned.

ECCLESIASTICAL HISTORY OF FRAMINGHAM.

MEETING HOUSES.

The first meeting house, as we have already noticed, was built before the incorporation of the township, in 1698 or 9; but of its size, construction or cost, no particulars remain to us. It probably was finished but in part, as appears from the following:

March 31, 1700–1. Voted, to gather £10 of money, by way of rate, for the finishing of the meeting house; and that Peter Cloyes, Sen., John Death, Sen., and Jeremiah Pike, Sen., be a committee to employ a carpenter, and lay out this money for the best advantage.*

Sept. 8, 1700–1. Voted, That Mr. Jos. Buckminster should have liberty to set a pew, upon which side of the great doors he pleased, in the meeting house; also voted, that there should be a table made and set in the meeting house, before the Deacon's seats.

Jan. 13, 1701–2. Chose to seat the meeting house, Jeremiah Pike, Sen., John Death, Sen., John Haven, John Town, Sam.

---

* Oct. 3, 1705, an additional rate of £10 was granted, "for the better finishing of the House; and a still further grant of £15, Apr. 5, 1708, "towards the finishing of our meeting house, and the payment of sundry debts."

Winch, Peter Cloyes, Sen., Tho. Walker, Josh. Hemenway, and John How.

Voted, to leave to the Committee's discretion, to seat by age or by rate.

Voted, to set up (for) Mr. Swift a pew.

Voted, that there shall be a pew made for those men's wives that sit at the table, at the N. corner of the meeting house.*

March 6, 1709-10. Voted, that there shall be a decent body of seats set upon the meeting house, with a hanging table before the Deacon's seats.

Jan. 8, 1710-11. The Selectmen made arrangements with Tho. Gleason, to repair damage done by the wind to the roof of the meeting house. Expense £2.0.7.

March 24, 1711-2. Voted, that the Selectmen, &c., procure from the Executors of Mr. Danforth's will, a title to the lands on which our publique meeting house standeth, as it is referred (to) in Mr. Buckminster's lease.

March 23, 1714. Voted, that Mr. Edward Goddard, Jona. Rice, and Tho. Drury, be a committee to see if those persons that have pews, will give liberty to have them removed, that so we may have a decent body of seats set up in the body of the meeting house; and to see about the confirmation of the land, given

---

* The distribution of the members of the congregation, at this period, was a measure demanding great prudence and discretion. The action of the committee was over-ruled in the case of particular individuals, who were allowed, by special favor, to build pews, or hold a particular seat. Jno. Jaquish, 1702, was permitted to build a pew behind the men's seats, on condition of taking care of the meeting house for 7 years. Jeremiah Pike had the same privilege, "provided he cuts a door to come into it, through the end of the meeting house, and takes in two families more with him." In 1705, difficulties arose about the seating new comers. March 24, 1711-2, the town chose Thomas Pratt, Sen., Peter Cloyes, Simon Mellen, John Gleason, Phil. Pratt, Jerem. Pike, and Sam. Stone, "to regulate those disorders, in our publique meeting house, which shall be laid before them." Also "declared by the sign manual of the Inhabitants of Framingham, that the cutting off of seats, or any seat, in the meeting house, and, also, the *cutting of Holes through the walls of the aforesaid meeting house, either for doors or windows,* or on what pretence soever, without license for the same, obtained of the town; and also the Building or enlarging of Pews in the said meeting house, without the said Town's License, first for the same obtained, are disorders to be regulated by the aforesaid committee." The committee were also empowered, on inspecting the house, "to take away all Pews or enlargements, for which there appears no Grant upon record; and also to repair all breaches on the walls of the meeting house, without the town's license, either cut or broken."

by the Hon. Mr. Danforth, for the use of the town, for setting of a meeting house, and for a burial place, and training place.
April 6, 1715. Voted, that the meeting house be enlarged 10 feet in breadth, on the back side; and that the back part of the house be removed. Granted for the same £70.* Voted, that Tho. Drury, Sen., Jona. Rice, Benj. Bridges, John Whetney, and Edward Goddard, be a committee to agree with Mr. John How for the above repairs, accordingly.†
July 19, 1715. Maj. Jos. Buckminster, John Stone, Jona. Rice, Jos. Pratt, Moses Haven, Jeams Clayce, Dan. Mexer, John Gleason, Jerem. Pike, were chosen the committee to seat the meeting house.

Voted, that their rule for seating be, according to every man's rate or proportion in the £70 granted for the repairing of the meeting house.‡

---

* Thomas Stone entered his dissent to paying any part of the £70. Mr. How demanded £85 when the work was completed, and in 1720, sued the town for the recovery of his full claim.

† The agreement with Mr. How is recorded as follows: "to remove the back part of the meeting house, with the pulpit and the posts on each side of the pulpit, ten foot backward; thereby making the house square; to place and put on a roof of the same form and workmanship as the Marlboro' meeting house, &c.; to inclose the sides and ends of the ten foot breadth, with good boards and clapboards, the old stuff to be improved as far as it will go; to make and place a good floor, a table and body of seats below, &c. as in Sudbury meeting house; to make galleries and gallery stairs, floors and seats, as the town or their committee shall appoint; to make and place a good floor of joists, for the vault overhead; and to line the same with a good floor of planed boards under the joists; to whitewash the same; to lathe, plaster, and whitewash the walls; to provide glass to the value of 40 sh., in addition to what glass there already is, &c; and to make windows, frames and casements for the same; to provide at his own cost all timber, boards, shingles, nails, &c," — the whole to be done "in every respect, strong, substantial, and workmanlike." Aug. 9, 1715, the town "voted to have three doors to the meeting house, one at each end, and the great doors in the foreside, and the rest of the doors to be clapboarded up; that so the house may be kept secure." Pews were allowed to be built by individuals; the required dimensions, in general, being six feet by four and a half or five.

‡ The committee were directed "to have respect but to one single poll in every man's rate, and that rate and age be the two things observed only; and, as for the dignity of the seats, the table and the fore seats are accounted to be the two highest; the front gallery is accounted, in dignity, equal to the second and third seats in the body of the meeting house; and the side gallery is accounted equal to the fourth and fifth seats in the body of the meeting house." Sept. 27th, the town approved "the committee's work" in the seating; and as complaints had been made, voted "that the deacons, viz. Dea. Rice and Dea. Hemenway, are desired to take special notice of all disorderly persons on the Lord's day, that do not keep to their own seats appointed for them, but keep others out of their seats, whereby the Sabbath is profaned;

SECOND MEETING HOUSE.

Feb. 3, 1724–5. At a meeting called "to determine upon a place where, and the time when, to erect a new meeting house," the meeting was divided upon a motion to remove the place to the centre ; "and there appeared a great majority who were for continuing the place." "The question being put whether the town desires to begin to build, the Summer now advancing, and to proceed therein, so as to complete it in about three or four years, or sooner; it passed in the affirmative by a great majority ;" twenty-five persons, chiefly from the N. and N.W. parts of the town, entered their dissent against both votes.*

April 19, 1725. "Col. Buckminster and others, proposed to have the exact centre of the town found, and to have the meeting house placed in the nearest convenient place thereto : " on which, the vote being taken, it was declared in the negative. A proposal was then made by Col. Buckminster, "to set the meeting house on the most accommodable place on the E. side of the great hill, which lies W. of the meeting house, &c. ; and that himself would procure conveniency of land for a house and ways thereto, on his land lying near the place ; " and the vote thereon was in the negative.

Voted, that £100 be granted for and toward the building of a new meeting house. (Nov. 29th, the sum of £100 was added). Chose Caleb Johnson, James Clayes, and John Gleason, to agree with a workman, not being an inhabitant of the town, to build a house, in length 60 feet, and in breadth 50 feet, the height to be suitable to the length and breadth, and for one tier of galleries.†

---

and that they admonish for their misbehavior in that respect." The house was newly seated in 1722.

It may not be improper to observe here, that during the period of the Indian troubles, (as tradition informs us), it was customary to keep a sentry upon Bear hill, during the hours of public worship, to give alarm upon the approach of Indians.

* Their names were Jos. and Tho. Buckminster, Abr. Belknap, Sen., Eben. Winchester, Ralph Hemenway, Edw. and James Wilson, Sam. Frost, Tompson Woods, Eben. and Sam. Frissel, Amos and John Parmenter, Jonas Eaton, Uriah and Matthias Clark, Tho. and Daniel Winch, Moses and Jerem. Pike, John Trowbridge, Jona. Jackson, Amos Wait, Timo. Stearns, Isaac How.

† Nov. 29, 1725, the committee, (others having been added), viz : John Whitney, Samuel How, Peter Clayes, John Gleason, James Clayes, Ichabod Hemenway, and Thomas Stone, agreed with Eph. Bigelow, of Holliston, to construct the frame of a house, 60 feet long, 50 feet broad, and 23 feet between the joints, the com-

SECOND MEETING HOUSE.

To give, in detail, the proceedings of the town, in relation to a controversy which was protracted during a period of more than eight years, would occupy a larger space than our limits permit. We shall accordingly condense in a note, the most important particulars.*

mittee to provide the timber; the contractor to receive £120 bills of credit. (The original is among the papers in the County Clerk's office, Boston).
* May 17, 1725. The town having adjourned to view the place, voted to have the house at the spot indicated by Col. Buckminster, if the N. inhabitants will peaceably fall in; otherwise near the old house. No result following this vote, Col. Buckminster, (probably claiming by his lease, or otherwise, the meeting house land), commenced a cellar, and drew timber upon the same; and the town, Nov. 29, voted to warn him by a committee, to fill the cellar, and remove the timber; and also authorized the use of the pine trees, upon the same land, for the meeting house. Apr. 4, 1726, a vote was passed, to place the house on the S. side of the road from the meeting house to Bear Hill, "near opposite to a place called the square." Col. Buckminster declared "that the land was his, and his resolution to obstruct the setting of a meeting house there." May 16, 1726, the last named place being thought by some "too flat and moist, and also so near the hill, that the shade of the trees would darken it, and another place being proposed and viewed by the town, it was voted that the house be erected there; and that a committee defend the town's title to the land." May 30th, Col. Buckminster proposed to place the house on the E. side of the river, near to Joseph Stone's. The N. inhabitants voted in the affirmative, but the majority in the negative; and the town voted that the house be placed round the present meeting house, and to annul all former votes, and to supply new timber, in the room of that carried away by Col. Buckminster, unless returned at or before the 21st June. July 4th, the town adjourned to view another place; voted to place the house at the W. end, as near the old house as may be.

July 25, Thomas Stone, Joseph Haven, and John Jones, of Hopkinton, were appointed a committee to sue those who had trespassed on the meeting house timber, cutting, carrying it off, and mutilating it. Dec. 12, proposals of agreement were presented to the town, as follows, viz:— "to have the town exactly measured, and the true centre determined, by a skilful surveyor and chainmen, upon oath; and that a line be drawn from said centre to the meeting house, and the new meeting house be set up exactly half way between," as near as the land shall permit, &c. This agreement being satisfactory, Jan. 25, 1726-7, Col. Wm. Dudley was made choice of for surveyor, and Mr. James Brewer and Deacon Fisk, of Sudbury, and Lieut. Samuel Brigham and Ensign Zorobabel Ager, of Marlborough, for chainmen. A proposal, in March, to suspend the survey, was dismissed.— Meanwhile, a petition had been sent from the N. inhabitants, to the General Court, Aug. 26, 1726, praying for a committee to view and report; otherwise, to be set off as a separate precinct; which was answered by a committee of the town: and Dec. 6, 1726, the articles of agreement were confirmed by the Court.

May 26, 1727, the Selectmen publicly notified the town, to give information of any engaged "in putting fire to, and cutting" the meeting house timber. Oct. 13, the Selectmen petitioned the General Court, complaining of "divers unwarrantable actions and proceedings of Jos. Buckminster, Esq., and others, referring to the placing of a meeting house, &c.;" and especially of a warrant given out by Francis Bowman, Esq., for the call of a town meeting clandestinely obtained, which, at their prayer, the Court "superseded." Nov. 17, the town

March 25, 1734. After debate, the meeting was adjourned for three quarters of an hour, to view several places in nomination to build a new meeting house on. After the people returned, the town voted, "to erect and build a new meeting house at an oak tree, marked, standing on Mr. Wm. Pike's land, at the N. end of Bare Hill. Mr. Pike declared in town meeting, that the town should have two acres of land there for £6 money. The town granted £400 for the object; £200 to be paid in Dec. next, and the other £200 to be paid in April next after.

voted to proceed no further, "under their present difficult circumstances;" and granted £4 to repair windows, or set up fallen seats. Eight successive votes were passed by the town, between Sept. 1728 and March 1734, refusing to repair the old house. May 19, 1729, Matth. Gibbs was appointed "to do what is needful to secure the galleries of the meeting house, by raising them, and fastening the pillars." June 18, 1730, Col. Joseph Buckminster was forbidden, by the Selectmen, to dispose of the timber prepared for the new meeting house. June 29th, "Wm. Ballord, Deacon Joshua Hemenway, Peter Clayes, John Whitney, Elkanah Haven, and Thomas Mellen, were chosen to enquire as to the ground of complaint against the town, by Col. Buckminster, for claiming a right to the land, whereon the timber for a meeting house was laid."

Dec. 1, 1730, Col. Buckminster made a proposal to the town, to make good all the timber for the meeting house he has made use of, either in his barn frame, or any other way to his private use. The proposal was accepted; after which it was moved to *divide the town* by the Constable Wards; which was negatived. Jan. 1, 1730-1, a "Petition of Moses Haven, and a great number of the inhabitants of Framingham, living on the E. and S. sides of the river," was presented to the General Court, praying a division of the town. (Court files). Feb. 19, Samuel How and others petitioned the Court to divide the town into two precincts, by a line running S.E. and N.W.; and according to Col. Dudley's platt, to cross the centre of said town. The House passed an order of notice; but the Council non-concurred. (State files). The town refused, Feb. 5, to decide upon a proposal to divide, by an E. and W. centre line. On the 1st of the same month, the town voted not to build at the half-way centre. March 15, the town chose Col. Buckminster, Lt. John Gleason, and Tho. Stone, to prefer a petition to the General Court, to send a committee, to hear all parties, and set out a particular spot for their meeting house. April 19, the town voted, 54 to 15, to build at the place called the square. June 29, voted, 58 to 41, not to build "at Capt. Ward's centre;" also voted, 62 to 45, not to build at the "middle centre." Voted, 55 to 34, not to choose a committee of another town, to stake out a spot. Also voted, 45 to 12, not to ask for a commissioner from the General Court. Dec. 6, the town again voted, 56 to 46, to build on Tredway's land, (near Bear Hill); but refused, Dec, 27, to choose a committee to agree with a workman. After other ineffectual attempts, the question was put, June 27, 1732, whether the town would build on the land of Mr. Wm. Pike, N. side of the road from Bare Hill to his house; and it was negatived. May, 1733, Richard Haven was appointed to secure the galleries from hazard. Jan. 21, 1733-4, Ensign Micah Stone and Edw. Goddard, were chosen to answer the town's presentment respecting the meeting house.

We have now approached the happy end of this prolonged controversy, which appears to have terminated in a disposition to unanimity, as relieving to the reader, as it must have proved to the parties concerned.

May 20. Col. Buckminster, Ens. Pike, and Mr. Caleb Bridges were chosen to agree with a workman, agreeably to the town's instructions, — which were, to build a house, 55 feet long, and 30 feet between the joints, and 40 feet wide, or 42 feet, if the committee shall see cause.

Nov. 11. Voted, to assess £14 to pay Mr. Wm. Pike for four acres of land, on which to place the meeting house.

May 19, 1735. Lt. Sam. Moore, Henry Eamms, Amos Gates, Ens. Jos. Stone, Michal Pike, Capt. Buckminster, and Uriah Drury, were chosen a committee, " to provide for the raising of the meeting house." *

July 21, 1735. Voted £150 towards the charge of finishing the meeting house.

Oct. 1, 1735. Voted to give the old meeting house frame to Mr. Swift.†

March 8, 1736. William Ballord, Rich. Haven, Henry Eames, John White, and Joshua Hemenway, were appointed to proportion the pews, and to find who the highest payers are; and report to the town.‡

March 10, 1737-8. Ens. Pike, Messrs. Benj. Treadway, Abr. Rice, Wm. Ballord, and William Pike, were appointed to seat the meeting house. §

---

* The directions by the town were " to procure one bbl. rum, three bbls. cider, six bbls. beer, with suitable provision of meat, bread, &c. for such, and only such, as labor in raising the meeting house; that the said provisions be dressed at a private house or houses, and that the same, (together with the drink), be so brought to the frame; and if a sufficiency of victual be brought in by particular persons, then that the town in general be not charged for the same; if otherwise, then the committee to procure and pay for the same. July 7, the town granted to this committee £68.19; to the committee for their service, 10s. each; and £2.05 more were expended by the committee."

† Persons had volunteered to take down the old house "on Tuesday, the 12th Aug."; and the materials were to be sold, as far as not available in the new house.

‡ May 17, the town appointed the

ministerial pew as the first on the left hand of the pulpit; and reserved a pew for the town's use, in the N. E. corner. They also designated the particular pews to be occupied by individuals, respectively; " the several persons to enjoy their pews, provided they build the same, and finish the meeting house as high as the lower range of girts, within the space of six months; the backside of the pews to be cilled, by being double-boarded up to the lower part of the windows; and then up to the girts, to be boarded, lathed and plastered, and white washed; and at all times, keep the glass against the pews in good repair; and in case of neglect, to forfeit their pews to the town." Nov. 15, liberty was granted to such as desire it, " to make windows to their pews," under the inspection of the building committee; they, (the owners of pews), to provide glass.

§ The town directed the seating

May 21, 1739. Granted £ 50 for the better finishing of the meeting house.

The same year, several persons were fined £ 5 for cutting the posts of the meeting house, for the convenience of their pews; and £ 20 penalty was ordered, for the like offence in future.

1771. Voted, that the meeting house be new shingled on the back side, and new clapboarded all round, with new doors and sash glass; also that the outside be well painted. Granted £ 80 for the same.*

THIRD MEETING HOUSE.

May 6, 1805. Voted, that the town will build a meeting house at some future day. Voted, that Lt. Abner Wheeler, Lt. John Eames, Messrs. John Park, James Wilson, Josiah Clayes, and James Morse, Lt. Joshua Trowbridge, Capt. Sam. Frost, and Capt. Josiah Stone, be a committee to locate the ground where the said house shall be erected.

Voted, that Eli Bullard, Esq., Col. David Brewer, and Lt. Abner Wheeler, be a committee to consider when the house shall be built, its size, and the manner of erecting it, whether by individuals or the town; to obtain plans, and receive proposals. The above committees reported in May. The first proposed to build near the gun house, on the town's land. The town adjourned to view the spot, and accepted the recommendation.

The other committee reported, that the house should be 76 by 68 feet, with a tower at one end and a porch at the other; and that it should be built by the town, in 1807. The whole expense was estimated at $ 13.000, and they proposed to raise the sum of

according to each one's proportion of all the taxes assessed for the meeting house; that to those arriving at sixty years of age, should be added 4d. per year to each one's rates; and that the seats be dignified as in the old meeting house, till they come to the fifth seat below; and the rest to fall in successively. May 22, 1738, voted that Mr. Thos. Mellen and Mr. Benj. Nurse be seated in the deacons' seats; Mr. James Clayes, in the second seat in the body of seats; and Mr. Tho. Eames in the fore seat in the side gallery. May 20, 1754, and March 1, 1762, committees were appointed to new seat the house, upon similar rules as before. Dec. 18, 1788, the assessors were chosen to seat the meeting house anew. After this period, all notice of this ancient practice ceases.

*The second meeting house was three stories high, with double galleries; and was placed a few rods to the S. (a little E.), of the third meeting house, just replaced by a new one, on the same site.

$2000. The report was accepted, excepting the part relating to the size and form.

May, 1806. The town directed, that the dimensions of the building should be 65 feet square; and voted to have a tower only, (and not a porch).

Nov. 18. A committee was appointed to estimate the difference of cost between brick and wood; and upon their report, the town voted to build of wood.

May 6, 1805. Col. David Brewer, Lt. Abner Wheeler, and Eli Bullard, Esq., were chosen agents of the town, with full powers to carry their votes into effect.

March 2, 1807. The town reconsidered their vote as to the location, and voted to purchase a certain tract of land of Messrs. Martin and Nathan Stone, and also of Capt. Simon Edgel, and to set said new meeting house thereon; and chose a committee to procure deeds of the same.

May 4, 1807. Voted, that the selectmen dispose of the privilege of selling liquors on the common during the time of raising the new meeting house.

May 26, 1807. Began to raise the meeting house. 1 June, finished raising it.*

1807. The town authorized a committee to purchase of Capt. Edgell sufficient land for stable ground, and to mark out a plan.

In 1810 the following correspondence, (on record), accompanied an act of liberality which deserves honorable notice, and commends the piety and public spirit of the generous donor.

FRAMINGHAM, MAY 7, 1810.

To the Inhabitants of the Town of Framingham, assembled in Town Meeting :—

GENTLEMEN :—Having arrived at an advanced period of life, and being sensible that I must soon be numbered with the dead, I often think of the place in which my existence was begun, and which has been my home, through infancy, manhood and age. In reviewing the

---

* The Meeting House was dedicated Feb. 24, 1808; on which occasion a discourse was preached by the Pastor, the Rev. David Kellogg, from Haggai ii. 7. "And I will shake all nations, and the desire of all nations shall come; and I will fill this house with glory, saith the Lord of Hosts." The Discourse was appropriate to the occasion, and contained several forcible passages. The pews, which had been appraised at $12,300, (the aggregate expense of the house, including the bell, having been $12,913 01), were sold at auction, Jan. 11, 1808, by John Fiske, for $14,884. The contractors for building the house were David Brooks of Prince-

progress of my past years, a thousand incidents unite to endear to my heart the spot of my nativity, and the Town of Framingham ; and while I express my affection for my fellow townsmen, I recollect with the deepest gratitude, the bounties of an all-kind God, who, by giving me something more than a competency, has put it in my power to prove the sincerity of my professions, by a small donation. Among the numerous blessings of life, I have ever considered as one of the greatest, that the preaching of the Gospel, and the public worship of our Maker, have been continued among us, with regularity and order. To encourage the continuance of this laudable practice, and to add dignity and solemnity thereto, it was my intention to have furnished the Meeting House, which has lately been erected, with a public Bell ; and although I have delayed to execute the intention, until a Bell has been otherwise procured, yet I am still desirous it should be considered a present from me. For which purpose, I request you to accept the sum of four hundred and thirty-seven dollars, and sixty-four cents, which I have deposited in your Treasury, being the original cost of the bell.

Permit me, Gentlemen, to express my earnest wishes for the peace and prosperity of my native Town, and to add my most ardent hope, that the weekly knell which shall call us to devotion, may have a happy agency, in preparing us for a joyful meeting in the eternal world.

Micah Stone.

Which being read, voted, unanimously, that the Inhabitants of Framingham highly value, and sincerely reciprocate, the friendly and affectionate sentiments expressed in the letter of Micah Stone, Esq., this day received, and request him to accept their thanks for his generous donation ; and while they lament the probability, that the life and usefulness of their much respected and beloved fellow townsman, will soon be at an end, they have the satisfaction to believe, as they most ardently hope, that the evening of his days will be unclouded, and afford him a joyful prospect of a brighter day, in the eternal world : and they cannot but anticipate with pleasure, that the weekly knell which shall call them to devotion, will also remind them of the virtues and example of a departed friend.

And in order to manifest their gratitude for the generosity, and their respect for the character, of Colonel Stone, the Selectmen are directed to cause the bell to be rung on his birth day, during his life, and to be tolled, for a suitable time, at his death ; and the Town Clerk is also directed to file and record his letter, and to furnish him with an attested copy of this vote.

The third meeting house was built in a style of elegance for its day, and for many years was the place of assemblage for almost

---

ton, and Mr. Warren of Charlestown. May 23, 1808, the Town voted to build a Town House out of the old Meeting House, the expense not to exceed $500. In 1820 was passed a vote to paint the Meeting House ; and an unsuccessful attempt was made to procure stoves for the same. In 1823, the sum of $150 was granted to procure stoves for the Meeting House, and also a stove for the Town House.

the entire community, who worshipped together within its walls. Notwithstanding its great dimensions, it was frequently crowded, and many recall with pleasure, mingled with regret, the recollections of that golden age, when through this ample town there was but one fold and one shepherd. The unavoidable revolutions of opinion have since multiplied the churches of this, as of other towns; a result not to be deplored, so long as a generous toleration and Christian charity shall allay all party jealousy, and the only rivalry or contention shall be for noble and worthy ends.*

MINISTERS OF FRAMINGHAM.

The precise date of the first preaching in this town is unknown. The earliest notice on the Records, is given the 21st of Aug. 1700; when it was voted by the town, that if Mr. John Swift, of Milton, continues to live with us, to be a settled minister among us, that then he shall have, for his own proper use, 100 acres of land, and 10 acres of meadow.†

May 13, 1701. Chose Peter Cloyes, Sen., Benj. Bridges, John How, John Haven, John Town, and Sam. Winch, to go to three ordained ministers for their opinion, whether Mr. John Swift be a person well qualified for the work of the ministry, according as the law directs.‡

---

* The house above referred to, was taken down in August, 1846; and a new and more elegant one in the Gothic style, is now being erected upon its site. The building Committee are Messrs. Josiah Stedman, Moses Edgell, William H. Knight, Rufus Brewer, Simon Whitney, Increase S. Wheeler, and George Phipps.

† The town also voted, to give Mr. Swift £60 in money, yearly, and find him in his wood; to fence in 20 acres, and break up 10 acres of land, and also to give £100 towards the building of a house, one-fifth of the same in money. They also voted to raise the salary, by a rate; "and it shall be paid by contribution, every man to paper his money; and that which is not papered, to be accounted as strangers' money." David Rice and John How were appointed to receive the contribution money, and pay it to Mr. Swift every week, and keep an account of every man's money.

Mr. Swift appears to have received just before this period, an invitation from Marlborough. "July 12, (1700), voted, unanimously, by church and town, to invite Mr. Swift to help with our present pastor, (Rev. Wm. Brinsmead), if God shall raise him up." Marlb. Rec.

‡ The committee applied to Rev. James Sherman, of Sudbury, Rev. Grindal Rawson, of Mendon, and Rev. William Brattle, of Cambridge, who gave a full testimonial of Mr. Swift's qualifications, which is placed upon record. Mr. Swift appears to have continued his labors from Aug., 1700, to the time of his ordination.

May 22. Legally voted, to give a call to Mr. John Swift, of Milton, to abide and settle with us as our legal minister. Chose Abiall Lamb, Dav. Rice, Benj. Bridges, John Haven, John Town, Peter Cloyes, Sen., Sam. Winch, and Tho. Drury, to give the call.

The only account existing of the ordination of Mr. Swift, and the institution of the church, is contained in the following memorandum, by Mr. Bridge, in the Records of the Church; viz: —

FRAMINGHAM, OCT. 8, 1801.

Then a church was embodied in this place, consisting of 18 members, over which the Rev. Mr. John Swift was ordained, (the same day), a Pastor. The names of those who (laid the) foundation of said church, were these, viz:—Henry Rice, Dn. David Rice, Dn. Joshua Hemmingway, Thomas Drury, Thomas Walker, John How, Simon Mellen, Peter Cloice, Benj. Bridges, Caleb Bridges, Thomas Mellen, Benj. Nurse, Sam'l Winch, Thomas Frost, John Haven, Isaac Bowen, Stephen Jennings, Nath. Haven.

The Covenant of said church was as follows:

We do, under a soul-humbling and abasing sense of our utter unworthiness of so great and high a privilege, as God is graciously putting into our hands, accept of God, the Father, Son, and Holy Spirit, for our God, in covenant with us; and do give up ourselves and our seed, according to the terms of the everlasting covenant, to be his, under most sacred and inviolable bonds; promising, by the help of his grace and strength, (without which we can do nothing), that we will walk together in a church state, as becomes saints, according to the rules of his holy word; submitting ourselves and seed unto the government of the Lord Jesus Christ, as King of his church; (afterwards it was added), *and to the watch and discipline of this church* — managing ourselves towards God and man, all in civil and sacred authority, as those ought, who are under the teachings of God's Holy Word and Spirit; alike declaring it to be our resolution, that we will, in all things, wherein we may fall short of duty, wait upon God, for pardoning mercy and grace, in and through our dear Lord and Saviour Jesus Christ. To whom be glory forever. Amen.

To persons, upon their admission into the church, it was said:— And we, the church of Christ in this place, do promise to carry it towards you, as a church of Christ ought, to its particular members, according to the rule of God's Holy Word. This we also promise, in and through our dear Lord Jesus Christ. To whom be glory forever.*

---

* Mr. Bridge adds: "The above written was copied from a paper drawn by the Rev. Mr. Swift sometime before his death. Attest, Mat. Bridge. And it appears that for above forty years, the Rev. Mr. Swift disciplined his church consistent with the above mentioned covenant, as became a Wise, Faithful, Religious and Prudent Pastor, and Departed this Life, (much lamented), April y_e 24, 1745."

The above Covenant has been preserved in substance in the 1st church

May 18, 1702. The town quit-claimed to Mr. Swift the tract of land in his possession.*

The Records of the Church during the ministry of Mr. Swift being lost, the remaining sources of information illustrating its history, are scanty. A private journal, in the form of a Sabbath Diary, kept by Mr. Swift, and extending from Dec. 30, 1716, to July 14, 1728, is preserved to us; in which allusions are made to passing events, and which supplies, to some extent, the lost records, (if such have existed).†

The only event of particular interest recorded in this volume, was connected with one of the Deacons of the church; about which, in 1719, the " advice of the Elders at Boston," was received and complied with; though not to the peaceable adjustment of the difficulty. Feb. 12, 1722, a council convened at Framingham, whose result was read the following Sabbath. The 18th of Aug. following, full satisfaction was given by Deacon Hemenway, the individual referred to, and the peace of the church was restored.

About the year 1726, appeared the first known indications of a contentious spirit in the church, which was destined to disturb its harmony through a course of years; and which resulted, at length, in a temporary division of the parish. The origin of the unhappy breach is clearly traced to an individual of conspicuous zeal, formerly of the old church in Boston, (Capt. Edward Goddard), who entertained high notions of the importance and authority of the office of Ruling Elder, in which he found little sympathy from the pastor of this church. Having succeeded in attaching a number of adherents to his particular views, (in 1732

---

to the present time. It was adopted by the churches of Hopkinton, Oxford, Acton, and perhaps others; in the Records of some of which, it is found recorded in the hand writing of Mr. Swift. No doctrinal confession appears upon the Records of this church, during the entire period of its existence.

* The above is described as beginning at the W. end of the Bridge over Sudbury River; thence to the N. end of Duck Pond at the E. end of Mr. S.'s house; thence N.W. to John Town's land; thence S. to Sudbury River; thence E. and N.E. to the afore said Bridge. Also a piece of meadow on the N. side of the (then) Meeting House. Also a piece of do. N. of Bare Hill. Sept. 16, 1702, a Rate of £10 was ordered " for breaking up our Rev. Pastor's land." Oct. 3, 1705, the Town voted £20 to cross-plow the same, and break up, the next June, as much as will make 15 acres, and cross-plow it in *the fall of the leaf* next after."

† The Journal alluded to, contains the entries of baptisms, admissions to the church, &c., during the period named, and is of much value even in its incidental notices.

about 16 persons), he with others sought admission into the church of Hopkinton.* Mr. Swift asked advice of the Boston Association, the nature of which, (if given), is unknown. The withdrawal of a considerable number of the members of his church, under such circumstances, must have contributed, in its results to the peace of the town and the church in succeeding years, in hastening the declining health of Mr. Swift, already worn by domestic affliction.

June 29, 1741. The town dismissed the matter in the warrant, relative to the settlement of another minister, while Mr. Swift is living.

March 7, 1742–3. Voted by the town, that there be a monthly lecture set up, according to Mr. Swift's writing, sent into the town meeting.

Aug. 13, 1743. At a meeting, "to see if the town will come into some method to provide help for Mr. Swift, he being unable to preach," Deac. Adams and Mr. Caleb Bridges were chosen to wait on the Rev. Mr. Swift, to advise with him; and Deac. Adams and Deac. Pike to supply the pulpit for the present.

March 5, 1743–4. Voted, to proceed to proper methods in order to settle a minister with the Rev. Mr. Swift at this time; and Ens. Stone, Deac. Balch, and Mr. Joseph Haven, were chosen, " to provide suitable gentlemen to supply the pulpit in order for settlement."

Feb. 6, 1744–5. At a meeting " to see if the town would concur with the church's vote in choosing Mr. John Newman to be their minister, it passed in the Negative."

April 24, 1745. The Rev. Mr. Swift departed this life.

The Rev. John Swift was born in Milton, March 14, 1678–9, and was son of Thomas and Elizabeth Swift. He was grandson of

---

* From the Ch. Rec. of Hopkinton, it appears that Edw. Goddard, Tho. Mellen, Benj. Whitney, Simon Mellen, Richard Haven, and Simon Goddard were received from Framingham, Jan. 10, 1732-3. Others applied afterwards, which led to the convention of a council in that town, in 1735, upon the result of which, Dea. Josh. Hemenway, Wm. Ballord, Elk. and Moses Haven, Moses Haven, Jr., and Joshua Hemenway, Jr., were received Sept. 19, 1735. May 26, 1737, Susannah Goddard, Esther and Abigail Mellen, Susannah Drury, Abigail Hemenway, aad Susannah Goddard, Jr., were, in like manner, received from this church. Sept. 20th, Nero, Mr. Swift's servant, also applied for admission.

The action of the church at Hopkinton, in receiving the members of Framingham, appears to have produced great disaffection and division for several years, in that church. Vide the Hop. Ch. Rec.

Thomas Swift, who came over with the first settlers in Dorchester in 1630; and when the greater part of them removed to Connecticut, in 1635, he remained behind. Mr. John Swift was educated at Harvard College, where he graduated in 1697, and was ordained at Framingham, Oct. 8, 1701. He soon after was married to Sarah, daughter of Timothy and Sarah Tileston, of Dorchester; by whom he had six children. His only son, John, a graduate of Harvard College, was ordained over the church at Acton. His ministry in this town, as far as is known to us, was conducted with faithfulness and prudence; and not a notice occurs, in all the transactions of the town and church, in any degree qualifying the respect and estimation in which he was held. He was, on many occasions, called to act in council with other ministers,* where his judgment and discretion were highly approved. The advice of his church, in some instances, was sought from abroad; and he frequently preached at fasts, instituted on particular occasions, in other churches. He notices his preaching the Thursday lecture, in the place of Mr. Checkly, April 20, 1727; and on the 31 May, 1732, he preached the annual election sermon, which was printed. Of his ability as a preacher, we have no means of judging. His printed sermons are marked with a pure and classical taste. He was free from all affectation of style as well as extravagance of zeal, or rashness of opinion. The subjects of his ordinary pulpit discourse, (as one may infer from his own Diary), were often suggested by passing events. Some of these discourses bear marks of extemporaneous composition. Thus he notes on one occasion, his preaching from the words, "The voice of the Lord is upon the waters; the God of glory thundereth;" adding, "it being a day of thunder." On another, "Behold! this day I am going the way of all the earth;" with an allusion to a neighbor, who was then dying. A day of extreme severity suggested the text, "Who can stand before his cold;" and a few weeks later, doubtless while the snow drifted through the crevices of the ancient and dilapidated meeting

---

* Nineteen instances are noticed in his journal, in the space of about eight years. Besides Councils of Ordination, he attended a Council at Woodstock 1719, at Worcester and Westboro' 1720, at Watertown and Norton in 1722, at Sandwich and Yarmouth in May, at Leicester in June, and again at Sandwich in July 1728. The advice of his church was sought from Gloucester, March 19, 1723.

house, the motto of his sermon was, a " covert from the storm." The halt of a detachment of soldiers in the village, proceeding to the eastward, induced him to discourse from the words, " a devout soldier." And again, " it being a very rainy day," with rare felicity, he adopted for his text the appropriate verse, " For the earth which drinketh in the rain that cometh oft upon it, and bringeth forth herbs meet for them by whom it is dressed, receiveth blessing from God; but that which beareth thorns and briars is rejected, whose end is to be burned."

During the contentions, which must have been sorely harassing to the church and himself, in the latter part of his ministry, he (if we may judge from a letter to the Rev. Dr. Colman, of Boston, in our possession, and his own memoranda), bore himself with singular candor, calmness, and discretion. It was a time marked by not a little pretension in individuals ambitious of notoriety, and arrogating superior light and grace. The following extract from a funeral discourse on the excellent Mr. Breck of Marlboro', in 1731, will exhibit his style as a writer, and the light in which he regarded his own profession.

"You have lost a learned Teacher or Instructer. It hath been observed that religion and learning revived in the world together; that the light that Erasmus brought into the schools, helped Luther's labors in the church. 'T is the sophistry of the Devil to decry humane learning in the ministry. There is a generation who call themselves the children of light; who cry down a learned ministry as needless; and pretend that their own knowledge of the word of God, (such as it is), like Jacob's vision, is by the Lord brought to their hands. But you find that when Christ sent forth his apostles, rather than they should want learning, he miraculously gave them the gift of Tongues, and doubtless all the humane learning therewith that they needed. Moses was skilled in all the learning of the Egyptians. St. Paul was brought up at the feet of Gamaliel, and was able out of Aratus, Anacreon, Menander, and Epimenides, to confute the Heathen Poets. Heaven gave to this, his servant that you have lost, such powers, on which he made such improvements in learning, as that he was a grace to that Academy where he had his education."

Mr. Swift was a member of the ministerial association of this vicinity, (afterwards called the Marlborough Association), whose first meeting for organization was held at his house, June 5, 1725.*

---

* This association was formed " with (the) design and aim herein to advance the interest of Christ, the service of their respective charges,

Numerous attestations exist to the estimation in which he was held by his professional brethren, which led to the remark by the late Rev. Dr. Harris, to the writer of this sketch, that he was " a wise counsellor and a good man, of a well cultivated mind, and held in great esteem in the churches." He appears to have experienced severe domestic affliction; his wife having, for several years, been subject to mental alienation; at which period, he received substantial evidence of the sympathy and consideration of his people.* During the last four years of his life, the failure of his health disabled him, a large part of the time, from professional service; and after a protracted illness, he expired the 24th April, 1745; having ministered to this people for the space of near 45 years, and in the 44th year from his ordination. As a mark of respect for his long and faithful services, the town voted, Sept. 2, 1746, a grant of " £125, old tenor, to defray the funeral charges of their late Reverend Pastor, and to purchase a decent Tomb-stone."† An appropriate monument was accordingly erected, and the inscription, in Latin, upon the following page, was placed upon the slab.

---

and their own mutual edification in their great work." They agreed to meet four times in a year, choose a moderator and clerk from time to time, &c. The articles were then signed by
John Swift, Pastor in Framingham.
Robert Breck, " Marlborough.
John Prentice, " Lancaster.
Israel Loring, " W. Sudbury.
Job Cushing, " Shrewsbury.
John Gardner, "* Stow.
Eben'r Parkman, " Westborough.

In process of time, the association became so numerous, and the members at so great a distance, that it spontaneously divided, Aug. 10, 1762. See 1 M. Hist. Coll. x. 89.

* The sickness of Mr. Swift's family obliged him to erect a building for a study, remote from his house, which was built near the present house of Col. Hastings. It was the building occupied by the French family, before spoken of; and was subsequently removed near the bridge, and was occupied by Mr. Gregory as a store. March 12, 1712-3, the town voted to add £10 to his salary, " his family being visited by sickness." Mr. Swift's salary, during the principal part of his ministry, was £70. Various grants were made to him, by reason of the depreciation of the currency; and in one instance " in consideration of provisions being dear." Historical truth obliges us to add, that in 1733, such was the amount of his arrearages, (arising probably from the great number of seceding members), that the case was carried to the Court of Sessions.

† It is to be regretted, that for some years, this monument has been in a dilapidated state, by reason of which the slab has been broken, and mutilated. The thoughtful liberality of an individual has partially restored the structure, which, it is hoped, may yet be preserved, with a due respect for the honored dead.

Hic Jacet,
Qui obiit, A. D. 1745, Aprilis 24to,
Ætatisque anno 67mo,
Vir ille Reverendus D. JOHANNES SWIFT,
Dotibus et nativis et acquisitis ornatus;
Docendi Artifex, Exemplar vivendi,
Felix, dum vixit,
Mores exhibens secundum Divinas Regulas
Episcopo necessarios;
Commiscens Prudentiam Serpentis, Columbæque
Innocentiam;
Commercium cum eo habentibus
In vita percharus,
Atque gratam sui, etsi mœstam, Memoriam
Post mortem, Iis relinquens:
Qui per varios casus, variaque Rerum Discrimina
atque usque ad mortem,
Raram discretionem, Modestiam, Patientiam,
Voluntatique Supremi Numinis, Submissionem
Spectandam prœbens:
Jam tandem in Domino requievit,
Adoptionem,
Scilicet, Corporis obruti Redemptionem,
Expectabundus.

In the Boston Evening Post of May 13th, 1745, we find the following notice of his death:

Framingham, May 8. On the 24th of the last month, died here, after a long and tedious indisposition, the Rev. Mr. John Swift, the first Pastor of the church in this place, in the 67th year of his age, and the 45th of his ministry. As he was a gentleman of considerable natural powers, so he acquired a considerable degree of human knowledge and useful learning. He particularly excelled in Rhetoric and Oratory, and as a critic in the Greek language. His piety was sincere and eminent. His preaching was sound and evangelical. As a Pastor, he was diligent, faithful and prudent; and in his conversation, he was sober, grave, and profitable, yet affable, courteous, and pleasant. He was a lover of hospitality; and kept his heart and his house open to all good people. When he received injuries at any time, he bore them with singular discretion and meekness; and the various trials and sorrows with which he was exercised, especially in the latter part of his life, gave occasion for showing forth his wisdom, humility, patience and resignation to the divine will. He was had in high esteem by the Association to which he belonged, and respected by all who had any acquaintance with his real character and merits.

Two discourses by Mr. Swift were printed, and are preserved in the library of the Mass. Historical Society.

I. A funeral discourse, delivered at Marlborough, on occasion of the death of the Reverend and learned Mr. Robert Breck, late Pastor of the church there; who died Jan. 6, 1730–31, in the 49th year of his age. By John Swift, A. M., Pastor of the church in Framingham. Boston, N. E.: Printed by J. Kneeland and T. Green, 1731.

II. A sermon preached at Boston, before the Great and General Assembly of the Prov. of the Mass. Bay, in N. E., May 31, 1732; being the Anniversary for the election of his Majesty's Council for the Province, by John Swift, M. A., and Pastor of the church in Framingham. Printed at Boston, in N. E., by B. Green, 1732.

After the decease of Mr. Swift, a call was given to Mr. William Vinal, by the church; in which the town voted to concur, June 25, 1745; but the following day, they voted, " that they will not make any grant for the settlement, or the salary of the said Mr. Vinal;" and the 15th July following, the selectmen were appointed to inform Mr. Vinal of the votes passed at their last meeting.

THE SETTLEMENT OF REV. MATTHEW BRIDGE.

Dec. 2, 1745. The town voted to " concur with the church, in their choice of Mr. Matthew Bridge to be their minister;" at the same time voting to grant, as his yearly salary, £260, old tenor bills of public credit, or that which shall be equivalent, to the acceptance of Mr. Bridge; also, a settlement of £600, old tenor.*

Jan. 20, 1745–6. The town voted that Wednesday, come four weeks, be the day appointed for the ordination; and that provision be made at the house of Mr. Jos. Stone, for the ministers, messengers, &c.†

The ordination of Mr. Bridge took place on the 19th Feb. 1745–6; the council having been invited to assemble at 12

---

* Mr. Bridge's salary was, in general, £80 lawful money. In 1748, £140, old tenor, was granted to him, in addition to his salary, " in consideration of the great rise in the necessaries of life."

† Messrs. Amos Gates, Hezekiah Rice, Henry Emms, Eben. Winchester, Abraham Rice, Francis Moquet, and Stephen Jennings, were chosen by the town, to provide for the ordination; Messrs. Caleb Bridges, Jr., and John Jones, Jr., to " strengthen the meeting house;" and Messrs. Ezek. Rice, James Clayes, Jr., Gideon Bridges, John Bent, Jr., Phinehas Rice and Timo. Stearns, " to take care of the meeting upon the ordination day." March 3, the sum of £109.8.2 was granted to pay the charges of the ordination.

o'clock, on the day preceding.* At a meeting of the church on the 18th, Col. Buckminster, Ens. Stone, Deacons Adams and Pike, and Mr. Bridges, were chosen "to be the mouth of the church to the Council." The day following, at an adjournment of the church, (the Rev. Oliver Peabody presiding), Mr. Bridge was formally voted and admitted a member of the church in Framingham. The only questions submitted to Mr. Bridge, which appear on record, regarded : 1. His intention to conduct himself according to "the congregational principles of church discipline and the platform of the same, and the general practice of these churches;" 2nd. His willingness, "in any matter of importance, to take the vote (of the church) by uplifted hands;" both of which having been answered in the affirmative, the church, by a "great majority," expressed their satisfaction.

The proceedings of the council not being placed on Record, the particular action of that body is unknown. From papers, probably authentic, we learn, that the elements of dissatisfaction, before noticed, far from being allayed, had spread more widely, and assumed an attitude of open opposition. The dissensions experienced here, were shared with other parts of New England; and the preaching of Mr. Whitefield in the town, the preceding summer, served doubtless to fan the flame of division.†

The following Declaration was prepared, and submitted to the Council, for the ordination of Mr. Bridge.‡

To the Rev. and Hon. Elders, and Messengers of the churches, chosen by the church of Framingham, to assist in the ordination of the Rev. Mr. Bridge :

Whereas we, the subscribers, inhabitants of said Town, and some of us members in full communion with said church, having dili-

---

* The ministers, (with their churches), invited, were Rev. Messrs. Hancock, of Lexington, Appleton, of Cambridge, Loring, of Sudbury, Peabody, of Natick, Williams, of Weston, Cook, of Sudbury, Turell, of Medford, Porter, of Sherburne, Stone, of Southborough, Williams, of Waltham, Barrett, of Hopkinton, and Swift, of Acton. It was proposed to the church, to invite Messrs. Sewall and Prince; but the vote was passed in the negative.

† From a religious diary kept by Mr. Ebenezer Goddard, of Framingham, we extract the following : "July ye 5, 1745, that dear servant of God, Mr. Whitefield, preached at Framingham." It is said that he preached in a barn.

‡ The above is taken from a printed vindication, which, from the initials, (E. G.), appended to it, we may presume to have proceeded from the hands of Capt. Edward Goddard. The part in italics is so printed in the original.

gently observed the scope and tenor of Mr. Bridge's preaching, while under Tryal, do hereby declare our great dissatisfaction therewith; for that many such doctrines, as we esteem to be of the greatest importance, are wholly omitted, or, at best, slightly touched on, in his sermon — particularly *the doctrine of Original Sin ; the imputation of it ; the total loss of the Image of God in the fall of Adam ; the wrath and curse of God consequent thereon ; the Freeness and Sovreignty of Divine Grace, in electing some to everlasting Life, and the provision made in the way of the New Covenant, for their Salvation by Jesus Christ ; the Nature and Necessity of Regeneration, and an Almighty Power of the Spirit of God, for the production of the New Creature, and renewing the Image of God upon the Soul in Sanctification ; the nature of that Faith whereby the Souls of Believers are united to Christ ; the Doctrines which relate to the Person, Natures and offices of Christ ; the way of a Sinner's Justification, by the Imputation of the Righteousness of Christ ; as also, those discriminating Doctrines, which shew the difference between that Faith, that Repentance, and that Obedience, which is merely legal, superficial and servile, and that which is evangelical.* And though we neither did nor could reasonably expect, that all these Doctrines could be distinctly insisted on, opened and applied in a short space of Time, yet it is to us inconceivable, how any one who approves of, and has a relish for, such doctrines, could, in his preaching so many sermons, (as Mr. Bridge did before his choice), keep such Doctrines under concealment, so as not (at least) to say enough upon them, to distinguish his Doctrines from such schemes of Doctrine, as are calculated to explode or enervate all the soul-humbling and Christ-exalting doctrines of the Gospel.

On this account we desire that this venerable Council will consider us, as wholly dissenting in the settlement and ordination of Mr. Bridge, and countenance us in our just plea of Liberty, to hear and judge for ourselves, and to try the Doctrines we hear, by the Holy Scriptures, the only Standard of Truth, and Rule of Faith and Practice; and to provide and attend a publick ministry, which may be agreeable to our Understanding of those Sacred Oracles, especially, since it is no new or strange Doctrine which we desire to adhere to, but the pure Doctrines of the Gospel, as we find them avowed in the Assembly's Catechism and the Confession of Faith, owned and consented to by the Elders and Messengers of the Churches, met at Boston, anno. 1680. And for the Settlement of such a Ministry, we have determined to use all proper Endeavors, and desire your Prayers for success therein. And subscribe, Your brethren and humble servants,

Jonathan Hemenway, Simon Mellen Jr., Dan. Haven, John Hill, Rich. Mellen, James Haven, Isaac Fisk, Daniel Mellen, Elkanah Haven, Ebenezer Goddard, Eben. Singletary, Richard Haven, John Hemenway, Joseph Nichols, Nathan Haven, John Haven, Eb. Hemenway, Jr., Tho. Temple, Micah Haven, Joshua Hemenway, James Cook, Benj. Haven, Joshua Hemenway, Jr., John Bruce, Richard Haven, Dan. Stone, Benj. Whitney, James Mellen, Edward Goddard, Benj. Whitney, John Bruce, Moses Haven, Jr., William Ballord.

Framingham, Feb. 1745.

"The ordination of Mr. Bridge being accomplished,* the dissenting party applied for, and obtained advice of, a council of churches, pursuant to which, a number of them were embodied into a church." This event took place probably between the months of April and November of the same year; † after which, the new church invited Mr. Solomon Reed to become their pastor, who was instituted in his office in the month of January, 1746 – 7, by an ordaining council, regularly convened. Probably soon after the organization of the church, a meeting house was built on the Southborough road, near the house of Mr. Joseph Morse. The Records of this church are lost; and from the long interval which has elapsed since its discontinuance, there are none living who possess any personal knowledge of its history. From the Records of the town, it appears that repeated applications were made by the supporters of Mr. Reed, to be discharged from all taxes for the maintenance of the first church; and upon the refusal of the town to grant their prayer, unavailing petitions for relief were presented to the General Court.‡

---

* Mr. Bridge's notice of the event states that he was ordained "upon the old Foundation."

† As early as April 2, Nathan, James and John Haven, Dan. Brewer, and Eb. Singleterry, desired a dismission to form a second church, which the church refused. May 2, their request was repeated (in which they were joined by Joseph Haven and James Cook), but unanimously refused. Nov. 17, Eliz. and Abigail Mellens, Lydia, Silence, Mehitable, Sarah, Mehitable, Lydia and Mehitable Haven, Mary Munsell and Hannah Mayhew, applied for a recommendation to the second church; and a Committee was appointed to take advice upon the subject. Mr. Bridge notes, that before the Committee was able to report, the party were embodied. The following April, "eighteen sisters," of the first church, applied for dismission and recommendation to the second church, which is the last similar application noticed.

‡ March 2, 1746-7. The Town rejected the petition of Edward Goddard Esq., to be released from all assessments for Mr. Bridge's Settlement and salary. March 20, a Committee was chosen to make answer to the complainants' prayer for relief, to the General Court. March 6, 1748-9, it was proposed to the Town, either to release the petitioners from assessments for Mr. Bridge's support, or that the town collectively maintain both ministers. "After a large debate," the proposition was negatived. Nov. 27, 1749, Edward Goddard and forty-two others renewed their prayer for a discharge from the Parish Rates, or a reference to arbitrators; both of which proposals were rejected. March 5, 1749-50, the same prayer was submitted, with a proposition to submit the matter in dispute to a council of Ministers. The Town persisted in their refusal to accommodation. September 6, of the same year, the Town "refused" to make a grant of money to Mr. Caleb Bridges Jun., in consideration of his extraordinary trouble in collecting his rates the year past. In 1752, Edward Goddard, Ralph Hemenway, Thomas Temple, Eben. Goddard, and William Brown, commissioners for the second church in Framingham, petitioned the General Court for relief, "not being able, by po-

By the decease, in 1754, of Mr. Goddard, whose name and influence seem to have been predominant in all the movements of the new church, the society sustained a severe loss, which probably hastened, if it did not cause, its early extinction. The precise time of its dissolution is unknown. The dismissal of Mr. Reed probably occurred towards the latter part of the year 1756;* but no general movement was made towards a reconciliation with the first church, until a few years later.

The Rev. Solomon Reed, minister of the second church, was born in the town of Abington, about the year 1718, and was educated at Harvard College, where he graduated in 1739. He was ordained over the second church in Framingham, in Jan. 1746-7, and was probably soon after married to Abigail Houghton, of Connecticut, by whom he had five children during his residence in this place, one of whom was the late Rev. John Reed, D.D. pastor in Bridgewater, and a Representative in the Congress of the United States.† He remained in the ministry in this town, until the year 1756; after which, he was installed in the North Parish of Middleborough, called the Titicut Parish, (composed partly of inhabitants of Middleborough and partly of inhabitants of Bridgewater), where he remained until he died, about the year 1785. He appears to have been held in much consideration by his people in this place, among whom he was settled, (in the words of Mr. Goddard), to "the great satisfaction of the society." ‡ A descendant § writes, that "he was esteemed an able, pure, zealous, devout preacher of the Orthodox order, was highly

---

sition, to have a separate precinct," and representing themselves as not making up one fifth of the inhabitants of the Town. (Court Files). The Court gave them no relief.

* A church meeting was held Nov. 4, 1756, to consider the petition of Mr. Moses Haven, "to return to his duty and privileges with the Church." "Voted, every man as one, that since Mr. M. H. had no other objection against returning, but his relations to the Society, termed Mr. Reed's Church, which relation he was apprehensive would soon be dissolved, therefore it was prudence for him to wait, till he were satisfied how that affair would turn."

† For particulars relating to the family of the Rev. Solomon Reed, reference may be had to the Genealogical sketches at the close of this volume.

‡ In the printed paper before referred to, Mr. Goddard says, "I am persuaded that there are a number of upright Nathaniels in that Society, (the second), who meet with such precious cordials under Mr. Reed's ministry, as they would not exchange for all the Riches, Honors, and Pleasures of this world.

§ The Hon. John Reed, Lt. Governor of this Commonwealth, to whose obliging attention we are indebted for some of the above particulars.

respected and esteemed by his society, and lived a quiet and peaceable life. He instructed and prepared in his family, as the custom then was, a considerable number of young men for college." *

After the retirement of Mr. Reed from his ministry in the second church, no definite overtures towards a restoration of peace and harmony appear, until June 4, 1759.† At this time the first church, " having some months past come to a resolution that such as had lately been of Mr. Reed's party, and were now desirous to return, and profess to do so, in full charity, should be heartily welcome, but finding that motion insufficient with respect to a number," voted to send them a letter, inviting them to join in a mutual council, which was sent by the hands of Dea. Pike and Mr. Moses Haven. A reply was received, proposing a mutual conference, which was held July 10 ; when it was " unanimously agreed to by both parties, that a council be called, and that each society or church be allowed to bring every thing into the council, (when convened), that the council will receive." ‡

Sept. 18. The council convened, of whose action and decision it is recorded, that " the council went into a full hearing of the reasons or objections that the said church and society had to offer, against submitting to Mr. Bridge as their minister, and unanimously came to a result, in which their objections are judged insufficient. They are advised and urged to return to their union with the said church, and the said church are advised to receive them." §

---

* From all accounts it seems probable that Mr. Reed, in his early manhood, engaged warmly in the new movement, which at that period agitated the New England churches, and whose adherents were denominated *New-Lights*. An anecdote of him in this connection is still preserved among the aged. Being interrogated by some members of the first church as to his religious sentiments, one of the company categorically demanded if he was a " New-Light ?" Mr. Reed promptly answered, " No — I am not a New Light; I am an old light *new snuffed;* " a witticism, which bears comparison with the well known saying of Dr. Byles, that he had heard much said of New *Lights;* he would like to hear more of New *Livers*.

† In March, of the same year, the town " negatived the request of Tho. Temple, Eben. Goddard, and others, to draw out of the town treasury," their assessment for the support of the ministry, " for the encouragement of the second church."

‡ The ministers, (with their churches), agreed upon to constitute the council, were the Rev. Messrs. Pemberton, of Boston, Dunbar, of Stoughton, Stone, of Southborough, Wells, of Attleborough, Hutchinson, of Grafton, Eliot, of Boston, and Wigglesworth, of Ipswich. The Record states, that all the votes, at the above meeting, " were passed with an entire and sweet unanimity."

§ The proceedings consequent upon this decision are not noticed. It

July 11, 1754. "A vote was passed by the church, desiring seven brethren, viz. John Clayes, Benj. Pepper, John Farrar, Bezaleel and David Rice, Sam. Dedman, and Dan. Adams, together with Mr. Eben. Marshall, to take immediate care to qualify them to set the Psalm in publick; and as soon as they are properly qualified, to lead the assembly in that part of Divine Worship." *

March 7, 1757. "Voted, (by the town), that if the tythingmen see any of the youths in said town disorderly in the public worship, and they will not forbear by being once stamped at by any of the tythingmen, in such case said tythingmen are desired to call them by name."

Sept. 2, A.D. 1775, departed this life, in the 55th year of his age, and 30th of his ministry, the Rev. Matthew Bridge, Pastor of the Church of Christ in Framingham.†

The Rev. Matthew Bridge was born in Lexington, July 18, 1721, and was the son of Matthew and Abigail Bridge, of that town. He descended from John Bridge, who settled early in Cambridge, and from his son Matthew, who married Anna Danforth, sister of Lt. Gov. Danforth, the original grantee of the territory of Framingham. Mr. Bridge was educated at Harvard College, where he graduated in 1741. He was at one time en-

---

is understood that some were re-instated in the church. The others probably united in the formation, soon after, of a Baptist Society, of which some account will be given in this volume. A Mss., probably written by Mr. Eben. Goddard, has fallen into the writer's hands, commenting upon the decision of the council, in 1759; from which it appears that the grievances of the complainants were, 1, their dissatisfaction with Mr. Bridge's sermons; 2d, Mr. Bridge's having received members from the 2d church, not in full standing; 3d, the continued opposition (of Mr. B.'s church) to the revivals in the land; the 4th appears to have had relation to the alleged injustice they had suffered, in being obliged to pay taxes for the support of the 1st church and its minister. Another charge, (the nature of which is unknown), was understood by the council to have been withdrawn.

* An aged lady has informed the writer that Mr. Bridge was a good singer, and frequently met with his people to instruct them, there being no other singing master. She adds, that he was at first opposed in an attempt to introduce a new hymn book, but succeeded, by a gratuitous distribution among certain persons, in encouraging its use. The introduction of stringed instruments was a severe shock to the piety of some, one of whom, on a certain occasion, when a violin was disabled, exulted that "the Lord's fiddle was broken." When Billings's music was introduced, and the tune of "David the King" was sung, an aged man cried out, "hold, hold," and seizing his hat, left the church. Watts' Psalms and Hymns were introduced, by a vote of the church, Nov. 22, 1792.

† Church Records.

gaged as a teacher in Worcester. He was ordained minister of the First Parish in Framingham, Feb. 19, 1745 – 6, and married, soon after, Anne, daughter of the Rev. Daniel Perkins, of Bridgewater,* by whom he had seven children, three of whom were sons. His ministry in this town, though disturbed at its commencement by serious dissensions, embarrassing to a young man, was marked by uniform firmness, and a spirit of conciliation, which ultimately reinstated, in a good measure, the peace and harmony of the church. Though not distinguished as a preacher, he is uniformly represented as a man of benevolent feelings and attractive manners; and by a faithful service of his people, he secured a general and lasting attachment. At the breaking out of the war of the Revolution, Mr. Bridge, in common with other clergymen, volunteered his services as chaplain to the American army, which was then stationed at Cambridge. While in the discharge of this duty, he was seized with an epidemic disease, which prevailed in the camp; to which he fell a sacrifice a week or two after his return home, on the day above named.†

The only Sermon published by Mr. Bridge, was a Discourse delivered at the Ordination of Mr. Eliab Stone, over the Second Church in Reading, May 20, 1761; and printed by Thomas and John Fleet, Boston, 1761.‡

Oct. 18, 1779. A committee was chosen by the town to build

---

* Mr. Perkins's second wife was Madam Hancock, the mother of Gov. John Hancock.

† We have been favored with a memorandum of an interview with the late Mr. Ebenezer Eaton, in 1832, who "described Mr. Bridge's personal appearance as dignified and imposing. He was more than six feet high; his hair very black, which he wore in curls over the cape of his coat; his eyes black, his figure erect and 'boney,' resembling that of General Washington, by whose side he had seen him stand, when the army was stationed at Cambridge. Mr. Eaton stated that he was much beloved by his people, and esteemed by those of other towns. He was extremely benevolent in his feelings. "He was good himself, and wished to make every body else so." Mr. Bridge's widow was remarried, after his decease, to the Rev. Timothy Harrington, of Lancaster, April 11, 1780, whom she survived. She deceased at Framingham, May 12, 1805., æ. about 81 years. The Boston Gazette, of Sept. 11, 1775, contains a notice of Mr. Bridge's decease, confirming the general impression of the amiableness of his character, and the affectionate esteem in which he was held by his people.

‡ The only manuscript writing of Mr. Bridge, in preservation, is a "Diary," kept in his early years. A granddaughter, in placing it in the author's hand, remarked, "that it gives a specimen of the extreme simplicity of his early life and manners." We may add, that it affords full evidence of his early habits of piety, and of an inquisitive interest in theological reading.

a monument over the grave of the Rev. Mr. Bridge. Probably by reason of the Revolutionary distresses, this purpose was postponed; and though again brought before the town in 1801, it has remained to this day unexecuted.

SETTLEMENT OF THE REV. DAVID KELLOGG.

After the decease of Mr. Bridge, a committee was chosen by the town, Oct. 9, 1775, to unite with a similar committee of the church, to supply the pulpit. For more than three years the pulpit was variously supplied.* The distracting events of the Revolution undoubtedly contributed to delay the re-establishment of the ministry. April 5, 1778, Mr. David Kellogg preached, probably for the first time.† Dec. 7th, by a vote of 123 to 14, (the vote of the church was 48 to 7), he received an invitation from the town to become their minister, to which, April 25, 1779, he gave a negative answer. Negotiations were, however, continued, the supply of the pulpit remaining in his hands, until July 3, 1780,

---

* March 4, 1776. The committee were directed to employ Mr. (Laban) Wheaton, 1 mo.; and after that, Mr. (Moses) Adams, 1 mo. June 3d, it was voted to engage Mr. Bigelow six weeks. Mr. Wheaton, who greatly interested the people, obtained, Feb. 18th, 1777, a vote of the town, concurrent with that of the church, inviting him to become their minister, and offering him £200 settlement and £100 salary. Mr. Wheaton declined the invitation, and preached a farewell sermon to the people, July 13, 1777. Mr. Wheaton afterwards entered upon the profession of the law, in which he became successful, and was advanced to important public offices. It may be interesting to add, that a few years since, when over 80 years of age, he visited the Rev. Dr. Kellogg; on which occasion he recounted, with much gratification, the reminiscences of his early labors in the town, and expressed a regret that he should have relinquished the profession; adding, that all the success and honors of public life appeared to him, in review, poor, in comparison with the useful and unpretending labors of the Christian Ministry. His name was long cherished with respect in the town. Aug. 10, 1777, Mr. (probably Solomon) Reed preached, and for numerous succeeding Sabbaths. January 4, 1778, Mr. (Ezra) Ripley preached, and supplied nine Sabbaths. July 12, Mr Willard, of Mendon, preached. In Sept. Mr. Eliot preached, and at other times subsequently. In Sept. and Oct., Mr. Guild and Mr. Gannet supplied for one or more Sabbaths, "the contract for each day, the price of eight bushels of Indian corn at market." Nov. 18, 1778, was observed as a day of fasting and prayer, by a vote of the church, preparatory to their choice of a minister. Feb. 18, 1777, the town voted that all male persons, upwards of 21 years of age, be voters in the choice of a minister.

† The texts on which he preached, are preserved. They were, Isaiah, xlv. 22 — Rev. iii. 20. Dec. 6, 1779, the town voted to give Mr. Kellogg $4 per day for preaching, "to be as good as money was five years ago."

when proposals were voted by the town, to the satisfaction of Mr. Kellogg, upon which he consented to become their minister.*

The ordination of Mr. Kellogg took place on Wednesday, Jan. 10, 1781; † previously to which, he was, by letter from the church in Dresden, admitted a member of the church in Framingham. To the church he gave a satisfactory announcement of his intention, "to conform to the same mode of discipline" practiced by his predecessor, and "to the Cambridge Platform, (eldership excluded), agreeably to the custom of these New England churches."

Nov. 22, 1792, the church voted, at the request of the pastor, "that the Scriptures should be read in publick on the Sabbath, and a Bible procured for that purpose." In March following, the town granted $8 for the purchase of a Bible.

1803. The town voted $60 to support a singing school. ‡

The ministry of Mr. Kellogg affords no incidents of general interest, demanding notice in these sketches. He continued in

---

* The town voted a settlement of £346.13.4, to be paid in Indian corn, at 2s. 8d. per bushel, and rye, at 3s. 4d.; or money to purchase the same. They also voted to give him £100 as his yearly salary, to be paid in Indian corn, at 3s. per bushel, and Rye, at 4s. In case of disability, by infirmity or age, to supply the pulpit, he was to receive but half his salary. July 10, voted to give Mr. K. annually 20 cords of wood, upon the same rule as the salary. The salary of Mr. K. greatly varied. In 1801, it was $500. In 1803 and 1821, $450. For several years, $666.67. Once, (in 1817), it was $750, with the addition, in every case, of $50 or $60 per annum, for wood. The average salary, including wood, from 1800 to 1825, was about $628. Taking the original settlement into consideration, his average emoluments may be estimated at more than $700 per annum.

† The churches invited were those of the Rev. Messrs. Stone, of Southborough, Harrington, of Lancaster, Prentice, of Holliston, Badger of Natick, Buckminster, of Rutland, Bridge of East Sudbury, Brown, of Sherburne, Fitch, of Holliston, and Biglow, of Sudbury. The "day was rainy," and Messrs. Buckminster, Stone, Bridge, Fitch and Biglow, were the only clergymen present, the first named being moderator of the council. The discourse was preached by Mr. Bridge, from 2 Cor. v. 20. "Now then we are ambassadors for Christ, &c." It is noticed that Mr. Parsons deceased before the ordination. The church voted to "make no extraordinary provision for a promiscuous multitude, as has been customary on such occasions; thinking the practice repugnant to the rules of the Gospel, and tends to such vain sporting, as is utterly inconsistent with the solemnities of the day."

‡ The singing schools were generally kept at the hall of the Academy. The same hall was also used, during the intermission of public worship, as a place of retirement and refreshment, for such as did not return to their homes. Apartments in private houses were in some cases hired, for the same object, by select companies, where a comfortable fire was provided, in cold weather. "Noon houses," as they were termed, were quite indispensable, before modern invention had discovered the important art of warming churches.

the discharge of his ministry in this populous town until the year 1825, at which time, by reason of " the infirmities, the usual attendants of old age," he requested the church to settle a colleague to assist him in his labors. Nov. 14, the same year, the town voted, to " concur with the church in procuring assistance for the Rev. Dr. Kellogg, in his ministerial labors;" and chose Josiah Adams, Abner Wheeler, and Dea. Luther Haven, a committee " to supply the desk the ensuing winter, should he be unable to supply himself."

April 3, 1826. Luther Belknap and others addressed a petition to Abraham Harrington, Esq., of Hopkinton, praying for the organization of the First Parish, according to law. A warrant was accordingly issued for a meeting, to be held April 24; at which the parish was duly organized. From that period ceased all connection between the parish and the civil authority of the town.

The connection of Dr. Kellogg with the First Parish continued for the space of almost fifty years; and was terminated, by his retirement, about September, 1830.

The Rev. DAVID KELLOGG was born in Amherst, Mass., in the year 1755 ; and was son of Daniel Kellogg, born in Old Hadley, who married Esther, only daughter of Ephraim Smith, of South Hadley. His grandfather was Nathaniel Kellogg, an extensive land proprietor and surveyor in Old Hadley. He early commenced his studies preparatory for college, which he pursued, principally under the tuition of the Rev. David Parsons, first minister in Amherst. He received his first degree at Dartmouth College, 1775; immediately after which, he engaged in the study of divinity, under the direction of his venerated pastor. After completing his preparatory studies in theology, he preached at Concord and at Framingham. His labors in this town, (where he perhaps succeeded the Rev. Ezra Ripley, afterwards of Concord),* commenced April 5, 1778, and were continued, to the satisfaction of the town, until Dec. 7, when he received a nearly unanimous

---

* Tradition reports, that the contrast in appearance and manners, between the two candidates, caused them to be variously regarded, by the aged and the young. The bearing of Mr. Ripley, while young, was grave almost to austerity ; while that of Mr. Kellogg was easy, affable and free. The measured and stately step of the former, in ascending the pulpit stairs, was thought more evangelical than the quick and graceful gait of the latter.

invitation from the church and parish to become their pastor. To this invitation a negative answer was returned the succeeding April. The troubles and distresses of the war interposed unavoidable hinderances to the immediate re-establishment of the ministry, under circumstances mutually satisfactory to the candidate and the town. Mr. Kellogg continued, however, to supply the pulpit until July 3, 1780, when the invitation was repeated; and the proposals of the town proving satisfactory, his ordination took place Jan. 10, 1781.

The ministry of Mr. Kellogg was peaceful and harmonious. Possessed of respectable talents, united with a character marked by energy, decision, and self-reliance, his manners ripening into mingled dignity and ease, his voice full and commanding, he maintained, through the remarkable vicissitudes of opinion and sentiment which agitated the period of his ministry, — extending through half a century, — a character of unquestioned sincerity, consistency, and uprightness, which commanded respect and confidence. As a preacher, his manner was energetic, his style and diction correct, somewhat formal, yet forcible. He inclined, in discussion, to be logical and argumentative, and courted not the flow and embellishment of a more popular oratory. His devotional services were particularly felicitous and impressive. In his theological opinions, he could not, with strictness, be appropriated by any religious party, although, towards the close of his life, he expressed his sympathy and preference for the society of those who adhered to the Calvinistic system. As a Congregationalist of the old school, he was settled in the Christian ministry; and to the principles, usages, and habits of thought of the times contemporaneous with his settlement, he adhered to the last. To the writer of this sketch, he once freely expressed his disapprobation of the innovations which had crept into the Congregational polity, and avowed his fixed predilection for the ancient order of the New England churches. In the admission of members to the church, without the form of public investigation into the religious experience and belief of the candidate, and in the rejection of all formularies of opinion, as conditions of Christian fellowship, he continued, to the close of his ministry, a faithful adherent to the deliberate and confirmed convictions of his early years. Though many may regard with surprise and regret, that he shared so little in the stirring changes of opinion, the strife of controversy, or the novelties of speculation, which have distinguished the last thirty years, it is to be remembered, that he was already an old man, of matured habits, constitutionally moderate, a lover of peace, and of a will not easily swayed by the changing breezes of popular opinion. On the whole, it may be said of him, that he was a true, upright, and wise man, a worthy representative of genuine Congregationalism, in the palmy days of its union and strength. As a proof of the estimation in which he was generally held, he received from the college at which he was educated, the honorary degree of Doctor of Divinity.

After a protracted ministry of almost half a century, Dr. Kellogg voluntarily retired from his pastoral office, about the month of September, 1830; after which, he continued for many years to reside upon his estate, in the enjoyment of a vigorous and "green old age." Many will recall with pleasure, his venerable form, slightly bowed, his tall and robust figure, his fresh yet placid countenance, his dignified and courteous manners, as he moved among us, almost sole survivor of the generation who had welcomed him to the sacred office, as their Christian pastor and guide. Within a year before his decease, occurred an incident expressive of the honorable estimation in which he was held by the inhabitants of the town. May, 1843, members of all the religious societies united in a tea-party, at the town hall, at which he was invited to meet them. His appearance was greeted with a warm welcome; and he improved the occasion to enforce sentiments of mutual toleration and Christian harmony, worthy of durable remembrance.

Dr. Kellogg was seized, but a few days before his death, with the illness which terminated his earthly stay.* He passed away gradually, and with little suffering; and on the 13th of August, 1843, slept with his fathers, at the advanced age of 87 years. The funeral service was performed in the first church, where he

---

* It is worthy of notice, as illustrating the vigor of his constitution, that on Wednesday, he was able to walk to the house of the author of this history, to sit for his portrait. The following day he was too ill to walk. On Friday and Saturday, he was able to sit to the artist for a few minutes at his own house, and on Sunday he deceased.

had so long ministered to his people, and in which the inhabitants generally united in demonstrations of respect for his memory.*

The only publications by Dr. Kellogg, are as follows, viz: —

1. The Nature, Obligation and Importance of Christian Compassion; illustrated by a Sermon preached before the Middlesex Lodge, &c., in Framingham, June 24, 1796. Boston: Printed by Tho. Fleet, Jun., Cornhill. 1796.

2. An Address on Presenting the Right Hand of Fellowship, at the Ordination of Rev. Mr. Dickinson, of Holliston.

The successors in the pastoral office, of the Rev. Dr. Kellogg; are as follows, viz: — Rev. Artemas B. Muzzey, (Harvard College, 1824), ordained June 10, 1830, retired May 18, 1833. Rev. George Chapman, (Harvard College, 1828), ordained Nov. 6, 1833, deceased June 2, 1834. † Rev. William Barry, (Brown University, 1822), installed Dec. 16, 1835, retired Dec. 16, 1845. Rev. John N. Bellows, ordained April 15, 1846.

Deacons of the First Church.

Chosen.		Chosen.	
Oct. 1701.	David Rice.	June, 1763.	Daniel Stone.
" "	Joshua Hemingway.	April, 1771.	William Brown.
Mar. 1717.	Moses Haven.	April, 1782.	Gideon Haven.
June, 1726.	John Adams.	April, 1794.	Tho. Buckminster.
	Peter Balch.	" "	Matthias Bent, Jr.
	Moses Learned.	April, 1817.	Luther Haven.
Aug. 1751.	Jonathan Morse.		John Temple.

---

* The funeral sermon was delivered by the Rev. David Brigham, Pastor of the Hollis Evangelical church, in which Dr. Kellogg, with his family, worshipped. The other services were performed by Mr. Barry of the first church, and the Rev. Mr. Haven, Sen. of Hopkinton. Dr. Kellogg preached but once in the first church after his retirement. It took place about the year 1838.

† Mr. Chapman's ministry was very brief. Few have entered the sacred office under circumstances more encouraging and auspicious. His early death disappointed the sanguine hopes of an extensive circle of friends, to whom he was ardently attached, as well as the just expectations of his people, who fully appreciated his intelligence, sincerity, and devotion. He died of a pulmonary disease, having administered the communion, for the last time, Jan. 5· 1834.

BAPTISMS, ETC., IN THE FIRST CHURCH.

Of the ministry of the Rev. Mr. Swift, our recorded information is confined to the interval between Jan. 1716–7, and July 1728.

	Males.	Fem.	Total.
During this period, there were baptized,	198	182	380
During Mr. Bridge's ministry, from 1746 to 1775,	440	413	853
During the interval from 1775 to 1781,	52	68	120
During Mr. Kellogg's ministry, from 1781 to 1829,	366	442	808
	1056	1105	2161

Admitted Members of the Church.

During Mr. Swift's ministry, from Jan. 1717 to July 1728,	34	82	116
During Mr. Swift's ministry, (for the same period), by letter,	8	5	13
During Mr. Bridge's ministry, from 1746 to 1775,	81	102	183
During the Interval, from 1775 to 1781,	11	14	25
During Dr. Kellogg's ministry, from 1781 to 1829,	69	175	244
During Mr. Kellogg's ministry, (for the same period), by letter,	12	34	46
	215	412	627*

---

* No regular record of marriages appears on the church books, until the commencement of Dr. Kellogg's ministry. The difficulty of determining with precision the number of cases of adult baptism, has led to the omission of any estimate of the same. As the period of eleven and one half years in Mr. Swift's ministry, of which we possess Records, occurred about midway between his ordination and decease, an approximate estimate of the whole number of baptisms performed by him may be arrived at, which would amount to about 1454; of which, (supposing the same proportion in the sexes), 757 would be males, and 697 females. The aggregate number of baptisms therefore, (including adults), from 1701 to 1829,

THE BAPTIST CHURCH IN FRAMINGHAM.

The first recorded notice of the origin of this Society, is contained in the town Records, March 7, 1763; when an article was presented in the Town Warrant, "to see if the town will abate the ministerial rates to a number of persons of this town, who pretend (profess) to be of the persuasion of the Anabaptists, and have sent in their names to the selectmen." The following year, March 12, the town voted, " that the minister's rate, for 1763, of Jos. Byxbe, James, Elkanah, Elkanah, Jr., Squier, James, Jr., and Isaac Haven, James Mellen, Simon Pratt, Eben. Singletary, and Eben. Bullard, be abated."*

The above society, which probably originated from the dissolution of the second Congregational church, continued for many years under the care of various ministers of the Baptist persuasion, of whom the chief was Edward Clark, who preached in this town for the space of about 10 years.†

Jan. 30, 1811. The Rev. Charles Train, a graduate of H. College in 1805, was ordained Pastor of this church, and June may be estimated at 3235; of which 1615 are males and 1620 females. During the ministry of Dr. Kellogg, but two adults were baptized between 1781 and 1815. Between 1815 and 1829, the number was 27.

* Similar votes were afterwards recorded in 1772 and 1776. In 1783, a committee was chosen to prevent a law-suit for recovery by the Dissenters of their ministerial tax, and an agreement was made, based on their paying half their tax.

† From the best information we possess, it is probable that Mr. JOSEPH BYXBE was the first preacher. His successors were NATHANIEL GREEN, who lived and died at Leicester, where he was the founder of a Baptist Church ; SIMEON SNOW, who lived at Upton, preached in Framingham and Weston, two or three years; afterwards became a Congregational minister at Thomaston Me., where he died at an advanced age ; NOAH ALDEN, of Bellingham, who baptized here in 1773, and preached occasionally; —— LAMPSON, of whose ministry we have no particulars ; ELISHA RICH, (a gunsmith by trade), who resided here for a time, preached afterwards at Chelmsford, and subsequently moved to the West; and EDWARD CLARK, who came to Framingham about 1780, and remained until 1790, when he removed to Medfield. After the lapse of several years, he returned to Framingham, and died on a visit at Mansfield, about 1810 ; his remains were brought to this town for interment.

The Society obtained the meeting house built by Mr. Reed's church, which had been used as a granary, and removed it to what is now called the Silk Farm, from whence it was subsequently moved further S. The present Railroad track crosses its site. The society previously worshipped in what was then called the Dean (now Park) house ; of which two large chambers were united to form a spacious hall. The attendance between 70 and 80 years since, averaged about 50 persons, from this and neighboring towns. The Society was destined to a successful enlargement, under the ministry of others at a later period.

22, 1812, the society obtained an Act of Incorporation by the name of the First Baptist Society. Under the judicious and earnest care of their new Pastor, the society increased in numbers. A new impulse was given to its prosperity, at a later period, by the erection of a new meeting house, near the centre of the town. It was dedicated, with appropriate services, Jan. 1, 1827. Mr. Train's ministry terminated Sept. 1839; since which period, he has remained in the town, enjoying the esteem and consideration due to a long course of useful service to the public, and a respectful sympathy in his protracted bodily sufferings.*

Mr. Train was succeeded by the Rev. Enoch Hutchinson, installed Aug. 21, 1840, retired Jan. 8, 1841; the Rev. James Johnston, who commenced (without installation) June 27, 1841, retired Sept. 1, 1845; the Rev. Jonathan Aldrich, (B. Un. 1826), who commenced (without installation) Sept. 27, 1846.

THE METHODIST CHURCH.

The Methodist Episcopal Church in Framingham was instituted in 1788, by the labors of the Rev. John Hill, from Virginia; at

---

* Mr. Train first preached to this church, Dec., 1807, at which time the society had become almost extinct. About twenty families professed the sentiments of the Baptist denomination, and five persons only had been baptized. At the ordination of Mr. Train, the Rev. James Reed, of Attleborough, prayed; the sermon was preached by the Rev. Joseph Grafton, of Newton; the charge was given by the Rev. William Collier, of Charlestown, and the Right Hand of Fellowship, by the Rev. William Gammell, of Medfield; the concluding prayer was made by the Rev. Aaron Leland, of Vt. Of the ordaining council, every member has deceased. In 1811, this society took the name of the Baptist Church of Weston and Framingham; Mr. Train officiating at both places, alternately, until the connection was dissolved, Nov. 1826; at which time the church in Framingham consisted of 100 members. Between Sept. 1815 and Sept. 1816, 53 persons were baptized by Mr. Train, and the religious interest extended into the first parish. Mr. Train's salary was at first about $200 per year; from 1823, it was $300; and so continued until 1829, when it was raised to $400; and four years after, to $500. Until the year 1822, he received pupils into his family, some of whom were prepared by him for college. Mr. Train rendered very valuable service to the town, as a Superintendent of the public schools, for more than thirty years. In March, 1833, he met with a fall, by which his life was endangered, and from the effects of which he has since experienced severe bodily suffering. Nov., 1843, the inhabitants of the town united in a social assembly, at the Town Hall, as a testimony of their respect and affectionate regard for the late pastor of the First Baptist Church. Mr. Train had previously received decisive marks of the confidence of this community, in his election, for several consecutive years, as a Representative or Senator in the General Court.

which time, it consisted of seven members.* They first assembled for religious worship in a private house, belonging to Mr. Benjamin Stone, in the N. part of the town; his widow survives, and occupies the same house. For several years, this society was visited by various preachers, among whom were Jesse Lee, Bishop Asbury, Ezekiel Cooper, George Pickering, and other "pioneers of Methodism in New England." Without a regular ministry, they maintained, with few interruptions, their weekly meetings, until 1822; when an interesting revival increased their number to thirty. At this period, the church was incorporated with the Needham circuit, and became one of the places of regular appointment for preaching. In 1833, the society commenced the erection of a house of worship, near the house of Mr. Benj. Stone, which was finished in Sept. 1834. The dedicatory sermon was preached by the Rev. Abel Stevens, of Boston, then only 19 years of age.† The society was legally organized the same year. In 1844, for the better accommodation of the inhabitants at Saxonville, the house was removed to a central part of the village, and an addition was made to its dimensions. A neat and convenient parsonage has since been built, which is in the occupation of their present Pastor.

The preachers who have successively ministered to this society, since the erection of their house of worship, are as follows, viz.: C. Vergin, Peter Sabin, N. B. Spaulding, Paul Townsend, Tho. Tucker, L. P. Frost, Geo. Pickering, Willard Smith, N. S. Spaulding, and Chester Field, the present Pastor.‡

THE SAXONVILLE RELIGIOUS SOCIETY was incorporated, Feb. 23, 1827; and their meeting house, constructed on an elevated site, and within a beautiful grove, was dedicated Sept., 1827. A church was organized, May 26, 1833. The successive Pastors of this society, are as follows, viz.: Rev. Corbin Kidder, (Amherst

---

* They were, Isaac Stone, Benjamin Stone, and Jonathan Hill, with their wives, and Matthew Stone.

† An incident connected with the age of the preacher, is remembered with much interest. The Rev. Dr. Kellogg was present at the service. When, at its close, the youthful speaker descended from the pulpit, the venerable patriarch rose from his seat at the altar, and laying his hand upon the young man's head, said, with much feeling and impressiveness, " Let no man despise thy youth!"

‡ To the attentions of Mr. Field, the reader is indebted for the particulars of the above sketch.

College, 1828), ordained, July 30, 1834, retired, Oct. 25, 1837; Rev. Isaac Hosford (D. Coll. 1826), ordained Feb. 14, 1838, retired, March 10, 1847; Rev. B. G. Northrop, ordained, March 10, 1847.

A society of UNIVERSALISTS was formed Nov. 1829, and erected a place of worship, which was dedicated with appropriate services, Sept. 1832. This society have employed ministers without the forms of regular settlement. The names of those whose term of service has extended to the period of one year or more, are as follows, viz.: Rev. Thomas J. Greenwood, who preached eight years; Rev. Isaac Brown, one year; Rev. Joseph O. Skinner, four years; Rev. Horace P. Stevens, two years; and the Rev. David J. Mandell, the present minister, one year.

The "HOLLIS EVANGELICAL SOCIETY" was formed Jan. 20, 1830, and their place of worship was dedicated, Sept. 15th, of the same year. The Pastors of this society, in the order of succession, are, the Rev. George Trask, (Bowd. College), ordained, Sept. 15, 1830, retired April 6, 1836; the Rev. David Brigham, (Union College), installed, Dec. 29, 1836, retired, May 9, 1844; the Rev. Increase N. Tarbox, (Y. College. 1839), ordained, Nov. 20, 1844.

A CATHOLIC Church has been erected in the vicinity of the Carpet Factory, at Saxonville, and was opened for public worship, Sept. 14, 1845.

BURYING GROUNDS, MORTALITY, ETC.

The old burying ground, which surrounded the first meeting house, has been in use since the incorporation of the town. Grave stones (in some instances of a rude character, the names graven probably by the hands of surviving realatives), were very early placed, and are interesting memorials of the ancient Fathers of the town.* A new burying ground, for the use of the inhabitants

---

* March 22, 1708-9. Samuel Barton was appointed grave Digger, with authority to receive 3s. a grave for grown persons. In 1741, three grave

of the S. part of the town, was set apart by the town, about the year 1827. A movement has been recently made towards the establishment of a Rural Cemetery, which, it is hoped, will be successfully accomplished.

HEALTH AND LONGEVITY.

But few towns have been more remarkable for the general health of their inhabitants, and the absence of prevalent and fatal epidemics, than this. At no period in its history, has the mortality been particularly alarming; and deaths among the young, are comparatively rare.* The simple habits of an agricultural population, united with the general purity of the atmosphere, have undoubtedly contributed to prolong life beyond its ordinary duration, to an extent perhaps uncommon.

---

diggers were chosen by the town, and five to make coffins. In May 1735, the Pastor and Deacons were desired to move the congregation to contribute for a burying cloth. May 17, 1762, the thanks of the town were voted to Capt. John Butler, for his present of a burying cloth. March 3, 1794, a committee was chosen " to purchase a burying cloth, and also a convenient carriage to carry a corpse." May, 1799, the town granted $20 to build a house to deposit the carriage in. In 1803, a committee was chosen " to provide a decent hearse." In 1805, " voted to have the burying ground fenced with a good four-foot wall, and to have two gates on the road." Granted $300. (The expense of a hearse-house was probably included in the grant). The same year, a question of title to the burying ground land arising, between the town and Dea. Tho. Buckminster, the same was settled by a quit-claim deed from the latter, of about five acres 20 rods of land, including the graves, and a note of $50 from him; the town giving, in return, a quitclaim of the remainder of the land in dispute. 1809, authority was given to individuals, to build tombs. 1811, posts were ordered for the burying ground. 1813, Jona. Maynard was authorized " to take the grass from the burying ground for five years, on condition that he erect the fallen grave stones, clear out all cobble stones, mow all bushes, keep the wall and gates in good repair, for the same term, and suffer no cattle to depasture thereon, said Maynard to pay $5, being the sum for which the privilege was sold at auction, in town meeting." In 1827, voted to provide a hearse and burying cloth for the South burying ground. The condition of the centre burying ground, though doubtless intended to be carefully provided for by the town, is far from what it ought to be. The neglect of the more ancient monuments, is particularly to be regretted, and is unworthy the respect due to the dead; most of all, to the founders of the town.

* The author seriously regrets to have mislaid papers, from which an exhibit could be prepared, of the actual mortality of the town, during the last 20 years. It may be worthy of remark, that of the whole number of deaths which occurred under his personal cognizance, within the space of ten years, viz: 73, 16 were of children in very early infancy; 8, from 1 to 10 years of age; 2, from 10 to 20; 7, from 20 to 30; 4, from 30 to 40; 6 from 40 to 50; 3, from 50 to 60; 4, from 60 to 70; 12, from 70 to 80; 8, from 80 to 90, and 3, over 90.

TABLE OF LONGEVITY.

The following comprise the names, as far as known, of persons who have deceased in this town, at the age of 85 years, or upwards. The figures at the right denote the years, and when known, the additional months, if any.*

Names.	Date of death.	Age.
Mrs. Margery Darling,	June 9, 1819,	85
Miss Lois Wright,	1813,	85
John Stone, Esq.,	Aug. 1, 1827,	85
Thomas Pratt,	Feb. 6, 1741,	85
William Ballord,	Oct. 8, 1777,	85,6
John Kendall,	Nov. 16, 1840,	85,6
Isaac Fisk,	Dec. 22, 1799,	85,8
Nathaniel Kendall,	Aug. 21, 1844,	85,10
Capt. Daniel Stone,	April 3, 1813,	ab. 86
Widow Mary Bennet,	April 9, 1838,	86
Mrs. Ruth Rice,	May, 1822,	86
Miss Abigail Pratt,	Jan. 18, 1837,	86,9
Dea. Matthias Bent,	1799,	87
Widow Hannah Eaton,	March 8, 1795,	87
Job Darling,	March 26, 1814,	87
Capt. Simon Edgell,	Oct. 3, 1820,	87
Rev. David Kellogg, D. D.,	Aug. 13, 1843,	87
Mrs. Catharine Hill,	1846,	87
Mrs. Lucy Rider,	March, 1807,	87,6
Jonathan Edmunds,	Jan. 8, 1816,	87,8
Mrs. Sarah Clark,	May 17, 1761,	88
Mrs. Zebiah Fisk,	Jan. 25, 1837,	88
Mrs. Ruth Haven,	Sept. 21, 1814,	88
Mrs. Deborah Hemenway,	July 7, 1846,	88
Mrs. Mary Littlefield,	1838,	88
Mrs. Sarah Pike,	Jan. 28, 1823,	88
John Bent,	Sept. 16, 1818,	88,4
Timothy Stearns, (unm.)	Jan. 3, 1820,	88,4
John Eames,	March 13, 1832,	88,5
Mrs. Bathsheba Hemenway,	July 19, 1828,	88,10
Mrs. Beulah Patterson,	May, 1829,	88,10
Phinehas Gibbs,	1846,	89
Mrs. Elizabeth Stone,	July 24, 1830,	89
Mrs. Mary Trowbridge,	1844,	ab. 89
Mrs. Abigail Bent,	Nov. 1814,	89,9
Maj. Lawson Buckminster,	Feb. 26, 1832,	89,10

---

* The author has also memoranda, containing the names of 4 who died at the age of 80; 8 aged 81; 8, aged 82; 7, aged 83; and 6 aged 84. Of the total number of these (33), 25 are males. Of the above list of 68 persons æ. above 85 years, 30 are males, and 38 females. Of the 36 under 90, 17 are males; of the 32 over 90, 13 are males. Six of the above were unmarried — 1 male and 5 females. Colored persons, 1.

Mrs. Mary Hunt,	Jan, 1843,	90
Miss Elizabeth How,	about 1813,	90
Miss Sarah Stone,	Nov. 24. 1829,	90
Silas Winch,	Sept. 19, 1834,	90,2
Amos Parmenter,	Feb. 26, 1785,	90,11
Mrs. Auna Manson,	June, 1843,	91
Mrs. Mehetabel Edgell,	Feb. 5, 1835,	91,4
Mrs. Elizabeth Winch,	April, 1833,	91,6
Ebenezer Hemenway,	Dec. 11, 1831,	91,7
Ezekiel How,	March 26, 1847,	91,10
Ebenezer Eaton,	Aug. 23, 1842,	92
Mrs. Lydia Gallot,	Nov. 1821,	92
Widow Mary Morse,	Dec. 7, 1842,	ab. 92
Mrs. Mary Buckminster,	Sept. 17, 1842,	92,3
Henry Rice,	Feb. 10, 1710–11,	ab. 93
Mrs. Olive Eaton,	Sept. 20, 1842,	93
Mrs. Hannah Haven,	Jan. 8, 1842,	94
Widow Patience Rice,	Jan. 2, 1796,	94
Mrs. Anne Stone,	May 20, 1819,	94,1
Joshua Parmenter,	Oct. 19, 1822,	94,7
Mrs. Hannah Kendall,	1822,	95
Widow Mary Rice,	Dec. 16, 1785,	95
Mrs. Mary Shattuck,	June 14, 1822,	95
Miss Sarah Stearns,	Feb. 8, 1825,	95,2
William Walkup,	May 1836,	95,8
Dea. Gideon Haven,	Dec. 1829,	95,9
Dea. Jonathan Morse,	March 5, 1801,	96
Mrs. Susanna Morse,*	Feb. 1, 1847,	96
Abraham Pike,	Jan. 1810,	97,11
Widow Sarah Walkup,	1792,	98
Prince Yongey, (colored),	Dec. 21, 1797,	99,4
Capt. Isaac Clark,	May 26, 1768,	102

TOPOGRAPHY OF FRAMINGHAM.

THE territory of Framingham embraces several localities referred to in its Records. "STONE'S END," is the name formerly given to the present village of Saxonville, whose soil was, to a considerable extent, in the possession of the Stone family.

---

* The longevity of this lady, (who deceased while this work was in preparation for the press), with that of her ancestors, is particularly remarkable. Her grand-father was born in 1665, who had a brother, her great uncle, born in 1641; i.e., three generations of the family cover the term of 206 years.

"Rice's end," refers to that part of the town, which is in the neighborhood of the house of Mr. Uriah Rice. "Salem end," has already been noticed, as situated about one mile west from the centre. "Guinea end," was the ancient name of the tract of land at the S. part of the town, near the Railroad station. It derived its name from the neighboring meadows, called the "Guinea meadows."*

THE COMMON.

The history of the Common lands in Framingham is lost, with the Records of the proprietors; of which only mutilated fragments remain.† By a reference to Mr. Danforth's lease to Col. Buckminster, on a former page, the reader will discover in what terms the original reservation of the common lands was made. Intimations are given in Dr. Ballard's sketch of Framingham, (p. 27), that owing to the fertility of the tract reserved, it was "by mutual consent of the proprietor and town exchanged, for a differently situated tract." The Records of the proprietors, (to which Dr. Ballard may have had access, though he does not refer to them), might throw light upon this transaction, of which no notice is to be found on the Records of the town.‡ The tract designated in later years as the Common, lies in the S.W. part of the town; a considerable part of which has been recently set off to the town of Ashland. The organization of the proprietors was dissolved about the year 1785; when the last of the lands, (about 40 acres), were sold, near Wild Cat Hill, to Mr. John Parker. The proceeds of this sale were suitably appropriated to the purchase of a public library.

---

* This name is said to have originated from the circumstance, that the meadows were first purchased for a guinea. Besides the localities above named, were "Pike Row," a name given from the Pike family, who lived on the road running E. from the house of L. Belknap, Esq.; and "Sherburn Row," the range of houses connected with Sherburn, before the incorporation of this town.

† The loss of these Records is seriously to be regretted; and affords proof of the extreme hazard of leaving records of historical and public interest, in private and irresponsible hands.

‡ The fragments of the Proprietors' Records preserved, demonstrate, that two of the bounds of the common lands, were the Southborough line and Sudbury river.

TOPOGRAPHY OF FRAMINGHAM.

THE CENTRE COMMON.

This tract, which, since its enclosure, and the improvements made upon it, has been rendered an attractive ornament to the village, was originally known, (from its resemblance, in shape, to a flat iron), as *the heater*. The first improvements on Record took place in 1785; when a committee was chosen " to set the bounds of the corner of the meeting house land, proper to be subdued;" and the town voted, that " Lawson Buckminster may subdue and improve the same three years, if he will lay it down even and smooth." In 1796, a committee was chosen to effect an exchange of land with Deac. Tho. Buckminster, " in order to straighten the line across the Common, and make it more convenient." May 6, 1800, the town passed a vote, prohibiting all persons tying horses to the trees upon the common field, around the public meeting house, or in any way damaging said trees, under the penalty of one dollar. Aug. 9, 1808, Capt. Richard Fisk, Eli Bullard, and Abner Wheeler, were chosen to dispose of as many of the trees now standing on the public Common, as they may think proper; and also the manure where the old meeting house stood; and expend the proceeds, in setting out ornamental trees, in such places, as said Committee may think proper. In May, 1809, a committee reported, that the whole sum expended for levelling the Common around the meeting house, was $232.61, which sum the town allowed. In 1810, it was voted, that the meeting house agents superintend the setting out of trees around the new meeting house; said trees, so set out, to stand during the town's pleasure. Nov. 2, 1818, Josiah Adams, Solomon Fay, and Rufus Brewer, were chosen to purchase a piece of land adjoining the meeting house Common; and the sum of $50 was granted to level said land; liberty was at the same time granted to set out trees, to ornament the Common, without expense to the town. In 1819, a committee was appointed to take legal measures for laying out roads, on the E. and W. sides of the Common, and for discontinuing all other roads already laid out across said Common. In 1819, the committee for levelling the Common, were authorised to draw $75 from the town Treasury. In 1820, John Ballard, 2d, was agreed with to subdue bushes on the E. side of the

Common. April 4, 1825, the town authorized the selectmen " to appoint a committee to get the Common fenced." Since the last named date, a private subscription, amounting to near $700, has been raised in the town, for the farther improvement of the Common, and of the entire village in the centre, by planting additional ornamental trees. The judicious liberality, which for so many years has been directed to beautify the town, has not been disappointed, and is destined to meet new returns, as time shall perfect the original design. Few of our inland villages are more attractive to the eye of the stranger.*

THE BRINLEY FARM.

The traditionary interest connected with this locality, justifies a brief notice of it in these sketches of the town's history. The tract so called, was the same originally settled and occupied by the first Colonel Buckminster.† It was by him, and his sons Joseph and Thomas, conveyed to Francis Brinley, Esq., of Roxbury, Feb. 1, 1742, for the sum of £8,600 in bills of public credit. It contained about 860 acres, of which it was estimated that 400 acres were improved. The general bounds of the tract, whose configuration was too irregular to be now described in detail, were, on the N., the lands of Eben. Winchester and John Trowbridge; E., the highway from J. Trowbridge's house to the meeting house; S., the lands of John Hemenway, Jona. Morse, Col. Buckminster, and Edward Wright; W., the lands of Tim. Stearns, Moses Pike, Wm. Dunn, Jos. Angier, and John Bruce. The tract contained a mill privilege, W. of N. from Col. Buckminster's house, not many rods distant.

Oct. 20, 1746, the town granted " £23.3.4, old tenor, to

---

* It would be impossible to afford an adequate idea of the labor required for the improvements above referred to, by reason of the great inequalities of the surface to be overcome. The public spirit in which the inhabitants of the town generally co-operated in the enterprise, forbids particular notice of individual zeal and liberality.

† Col. B. (according to a survey of the above tract, made by John Jones, Surveyor, of Hopkinton, Jan. 26, 1741-2), lived near, or upon, the spot now occupied by Mr. Vose, who conducts the " Wheeler farm; " and his son, (then Capt. Buckminster), lived about 250 rods E. of S. from his father's house, probably at or near Dea. Belknap's.

make up the deficiency of Col. Brinley's rate, for the settlement and ordination of our Rev. Pastor."

The history of the occupation of this tract is too imperfectly preserved, to allow exactness of dates in all cases. By whom it was cultivated the first 18 years, after Mr. Brinley's purchase, does not appear. Col. Brinley became surety for Geo. Cradock, to Sir Peter Warren, Admiral of the British Navy, to whom he mortgaged the farm, and possession was afterwards obtained under the mortgage.* Mr. Nathaniel Brinley, son of Francis, hired the farm for several years of Oliver De Lancey, attorney of the proprietor, at a rent of £30 sterling per annum. Mr. N. Brinley first occupied the premises about the year 1760; and employed, it is said, some 15 or 20 negroes in its cultivation. Daniel Shays, who gave a name to the rebellion of 1786, at one time worked in Mr. Brinley's employ.† At the commencement of the revolution, Mr. Brinley, whose political principles ranked him with the tories, left the town; and an unsuccessful attempt was made in town meeting to confiscate the estate, of which we extract the following from the Record:

March 4, 1776. "To see if the town will, in answer to a petition from several of the inhabitants, take any order concerning the farm lately occupied by Nathl. Brinley, or the utensils thereto belonging; and act thereon as the town shall judge proper."

In Nov. 1778, it was again proposed " to give such direction to the selectmen, respecting the farm in this town, belonging to the heirs of Sir Peter Warren, as the town shall judge proper." But no action upon the same is recorded. At this period, the farm was exposed to serious depredation and waste by unscrupulous trespassers, who entered upon the land and removed its timber. In ——, Edward Brinley, Esq., of Weston, brother of Nathaniel, leased and took possession of the farm. After occupying it one year, John Eames, John Taylor and others, claimed to have purchased the estate, and to hold a bond for a deed of the same; upon which Mr. Brinley removed, and Eames and others took possession. In 1785, Levi Thayer, of Milford, Mass., alleged his

---

* Sir Peter Warren married Susanna, sister of Oliver De Lancey, of New York, who acted as attorney to the widow of Sir Peter, in the recovery of the estate.
† Worcester Magazine.

purchase of the same tract, for £4,500 sterling, by a deed claimed to have been executed in London by Oliver De Lancey, and placed on record; the genuineness of which was disputed by the relatives of the supposed grantor. He, however, entered upon the possession of the estate. Mr. E. Brinley, Jan. 21, 1793, obtained a power of attorney from John Watts, in behalf of the proprietors, with full powers to superintend the farm, and bring all trespassers to justice; and a civil process was commenced against Thayer, then in the occupation of it.* By the decease of the original proprietors, the right of property in the farm had now fallen to the Earl of Abington, Viscount Gage, and Lord Southampton, heirs of Sir Peter Warren.† In 1795, Col. McGregor and John Rogers, Esq., purchased for £400, one third of the farm from the attorney of Lords Gage and Abington; and by their agent at London, the remaining third. In 1802, William Maxwell, of New York, a merchant, purchased of the widow of John Rogers, and of the Trustees of Col. McGregor, their rights in the estate, and the same year disposed of the same to the Hon. John Lowell.‡

The proprietors of this farm holding under Mr. Lowell, have enjoyed peaceable possession of a tract, so long disputed among contending claimants. A considerable part was purchased by Maj. Benjamin Wheeler, from whom it has derived the name of

---

* Various portions of the farm had, from time to time, been conveyed and reconveyed; and about the date last referred to, "one part was occupied and claimed by Jos. Roberts, and another by one Bannister." Mr. Brinley wrote, in 1795, "that a Mr. John Gardner has been here twice, from N. York state, in order to sell the farm at auction, under Levi Thayer's title. The people of Framingham wish to purchase, as he will sell on very low terms." He also writes, "I have combated a great deal of ill-treatment, to prevent the entire destruction of the estate." Mr. Brinley had endeavored to purchase the estate from the English heirs, for which he offered £1200. But the negotiation met with no success. He appears to have taken a laudable part in the preservation of the property, which, at this period, he described, perhaps with some exaggeration, as "without a rod of fence, and the buildings good for nothing." Forty acres of the land had, some years before, been sold for taxes.

† Lord Abington married a daughter, the two others, grand-daughters, of Sir P. Warren. John Watts and Peter Kemble, of N. York, were attornies for Lord Gage.

‡ In a memorandum in our possession, it is stated that Mr. Lowell gave $2000 for the rights purchased of McGregor, and £900 for a quit-claim from the heirs in England. Some apology is, perhaps, needed, for the particularity of the above notice of these various transactions. We have inserted it as matter of history, and to clear up the obscurity in which the title to this estate was long involved.

the "Wheeler Farm," which has undergone valuable improvements, under the liberal and judicious management of himself and his son, Mr. I. S. Wheeler, the present possessor of the farm. The mill privilege on this farm long since fell into disuse.*

The township of Framingham possesses in general a fine soil, well furnished with water, and capable of easy cultivation; it also contains numerous meadows, from which abundant materials have been derived for the improvement of the uplands.† The town is well wooded, affording excellent timber of hard wood; though the forests have of late years sensibly diminished.‡ Great attention has been devoted to orcharding, in which the inhabitants have manifested much liberality and foresight. The finest varieties of the apple, pear, peach, plum, &c., have been introduced, and are under successful cultivation; and nurseries have been attempted by various individuals. The fruit production of the town, must in a few years be a large source of emolument to the community. A marked and intelligent spirit of improvement has of late been exhibited, among the agricultural population of the town.§

The surface of the town is generally level, or rising by easy swells. Its mineral productions demand no particular notice. Good granite is found in considerable quantities, of which some is hammered for mill stones and house building.‖ Indications of the

---

* About 1806, Luther Belknap, Esq, bought 112 acres of Mr. Lowell. Jona. Maynard was also a purchaser in 1803.

† Since the valuable properties of peat muck have become known, the farms in this town have been greatly improved. Of the practicability of reclaiming swamp land, a striking example was furnished, near the centre of the village, about 20 years since, by Maj. Benj. Wheeler. A stranger would, with difficulty, believe that the beautiful and fertile meadow to the west of the centre common, was once covered with water and brush, and altogether valueless.

‡ Good wood now sells at about $5 the cord in this town. It is to be feared, that in not a few instances, a permanent loss is likely to accrue to the town, by clearing lands far more valuable for timber, than for cultivation or pasturage. It may be here observed, that there are several white oak trees of remarkable size in this town; two, near the house late of Dea. Matthias Bent, one of which is supposed to be more than 200 years old. The "T. D." tree, on the farm of Mr. John Eaton, is of such gigantic size, that seven persons are said to have found a shelter in the hollow of it, during a shower of rain. Mr. Eaton cut off a large part of the top, a few years since, as it shaded his mowing.

§ Meetings for the advancement of agricultural science have, of late years, been held, with a good degree of regularity, in the town; and a newspaper, entitled the Massachusetts Ploughman, has been conducted by William Buckminster, Esq., and published at Boston and Framingham. By its extensive circulation, it has contributed largely to diffuse valuable information.

‖ A tradition exists, that the Indians of Maguncook came to Wild Cat

presence of lime stone have been discovered in the N. part of the town. Large bowlders are to be seen widely spread upon the tract, E. of Nobscot Hill, indications of early Geological changes in that region.*

HILLS.

NOBSCOT, OR DOESKIN HILL, lies upon the N. bounds of Framingham, and has a conspicuous elevation, which renders it visible at a great distance.†

GIBBS' MOUNTAIN, lies near the N.W. corner of the town, N.W. from the house of the late Mr. Micah Gibbs.

WILD CAT HILL, late in the S.W. part of the town, at the "Common," is now included in Ashland.

BALLARD'S HILL, late in the S. part of the town, W. from the house of J. Ballard, Esq., is now chiefly in Ashland.

MERRIAM'S HILL, lies N. of Ballard's Hill.

MOUNT WAIT, is the name given to a beautiful conical hill, S. of Sudbury river, and about one mile S. from the centre village.

BEAR, OR BARE HILL, is an elevation contiguous to the centre village, on the S.

INDIAN HEAD HILL, lies S. of the late Dea. Bent's.

CAPT. TOM'S HILL, is on the bounds of Framingham and Natick, and lies E., a little S. from the house of the widow Eaton.

LT. GLEASON'S HILL, is on the S.E. corner of the town, near the Railroad.

WALNUT HILL, probably near Ezekiel How's.

RIVERS AND STREAMS.

1. CONCORD, or SUDBURY RIVER. — This river is found on Wood's map of New England, in 1635, by the Indian name of

---

Hill, in the neighborhood of which they professed to have found lead. We give the tradition as it has been repeated to us.

* A rocking bowlder, in the W. part of Framingham, is referred to in Hitchcock's Geol. of Mass., p. 376, and Silliman's Journal, VII.

† In ancient deeds and surveys the name of Doeskin is sometimes given to Nobscot Hill The late Mr. John Eaton informed the author, that the hill N. of his old house had been called Doeskin Hill.

Musquitaquid. It is first formed by the confluence of two streams originating in Westborough, one a little S. of Wessonville, the other N. of Fay's mountain; after their junction it unites with Whitehall brook, whose source is Whitehall pond, in the S.W. part of Hopkinton. These two streams unite about 100 rods N. of the N.W. line of Hopkinton, and form what was formerly called the Hopkinton river. The river then follows a nearly Easterly course about four miles, to a point near Bigelow's paper mills, where it receives from the S. as a tributary, the Indian brook. About a mile farther E., it receives from the S. the Cold Spring brook, near Shepard's paper mill. Its course here turns northerly into Framingham, about one and a half miles, where it receives the waters of Stoney brook, coming from the N.W., from Southborough. From this point it is called Sudbury river, and flows about three miles, in a course nearly N.E., to the village of Saxonville, where the Cochituate brook discharges the water of Cochituate or Long Pond. The river then turns northerly, entering Sudbury, and is finally lost, after receiving various tributaries, at its confluence with the Merrimack at Lowell. This stream is generally sluggish, and from the vegetable substances it receives in its passage through extensive meadows, its water bears a dark color. There are now but two mill sites in this town on the Concord river; Brown's mills, and the mills at Saxonville.

STONEY BROOK rises in the N. W. corner of Southborough, flows in an irregular course S.E., receiving the waters of Angle brook, which rises in the S. part of Marlborough, and flows S.E., uniting with Stoney brook W. of Framingham bounds. It enters Framingham about 100 rods N. of the turnpike, flows S.E. to its junction with Hopkinton river, about one fourth of a mile S.E. from Mr. Bullard's machine shop; which derives from Stoney brook a water privilege of some value.

COCHITUATE BROOK, (sometimes written Wachetuwot and Cochitawick), rises at a point on the W. side of Cochituate Pond, in Framingham, and running about one third of a mile to the S.W., receives the waters of Course brook; it then flows in a course generally to the N.W., furnishes a supply of water to the large carpet Factory of Mr. W. H. Knight, and soon after discharges into the Sudbury river, near Saxonville.

HOP BROOK, rises in the N. part of the town, and flows E. and northerly, crossing the bounds of Sudbury and Framingham, E. of the old house of Mr. John Eaton.

BEAVER DAM BROOK, once called Steep Brook, is formed of the S. and E. outlets of Washakum Pond, and flows in a direction N. of E., S. of Mr. Sylvanus Phipps' house, into Sherburne.

BAITING BROOK, is the name anciently given to the brook which crosses the road near Mr. Amasa Kendall's house, and empties into Sudbury river.

ANGELLICO BROOK, is referred to as the W. bound of Mr. Danforth's farm.*

CHERRY MEADOW BROOK, is described as on the Corlet farm, and a bound of land sold to Samuel Winch, Sen.

INDIAN BROOK, is referred to as near Cochituate brook on the E.

BIRCH MEADOW BROOK, referred to in ancient deeds.

SQUARE MEADOW BROOK, now called Dadmun's Brook, flows into the Sudbury river, near the house of W. Dadmun.

DUNSDELL BROOK,† crosses the road near the house late of E. Jones, now occupied by Mr. Hudson, and flows into Sudbury river.

BOARDMAN'S BROOK flows from the N. into Sudbury river, at Saxonville, above the falls.

STRAWBERRY CORNER BROOK, is referred to, 1710, in the will of Henry Rice of this town.

COURSE BROOK, rises near the Worcester Turnpike, on the east border of the town, and flows in a nearly N. Easterly course, into Cochituate broook.

The "GREAT DRAIN,"—a brook so called at Rice's end.

MEADOWS, SWAMPS, ETC.

GUINEA MEADOWS, in the S.E. part of the town, extending about two miles from S.W. to N.E.‡

POD MEADOW, at the N.E. corner of the town, about 12 acres in extent, owned by Mr. Luther Stone.

---

* Could this have been the modern Angle Brook?

† The origin of this name is unknown. In Sudbury, 1697, Mary Bacon conveyed to Josiah Haynes, a farm S.W. of the great river, at a place commonly called "Dunsdale." A William *Densdell* lived, probably at Chelmsford, about 1674. Mid. Deeds, V. 115.

‡ Mr. Abel Eames was informed by his grand-father, that this meadow was once accidentally set on fire, and burned to a superficial extent of two miles, doing serious damage to the soil.

INDIAN HEAD MEADOW, E. of Indian head hill.

JACOBS' MEADOW, owned by John Bent, 1717. It is perhaps the same called also "Indian Jacob's Meadow."

FLAGG MEADOW, owned by Tho. Read, Sen., 1693, in the N. part of the town.

BEAVER HOLE MEADOW, owned by Caleb Johnson 1716, in the E. part of the town.

COLLER'S MEADOW, beyond Mrs. Dadmun's house.

BENJAMIN'S MEADOW, at Rice's end.

WAIT MEADOW, S. of the river, near the site of the first meeting house.

RATTLE SNAKE MEADOW, "between Sudbury and Framingham;" sold by M. and J. Gibbs to Nath. Stone, 1697.

JACOBS' FURTHER MEADOW, in the S.E. part of the town.

WILD CAT MEADOWS, near Mr. Eben. Clafflin's house.

DUNSDELL MEADOW, on Dunsdell brook.

BIRCH MEADOW.

JACKETT MEADOW, on the lower part of Baiting Brook. The last three owned, 1696, by Daniel Stone.

ASHEN SWAMP, near Washakum Pond.

WOLF SWAMP, on the Corlett Farm, near the present Frost house.

DEER SWAMP, between Mr. Bennett's and the Bent farm.

ROE SWAMP, between Mr. Charles Fiske's and the old Walker place.

PRATT'S PLAIN, about one mile E. from the centre village.

WILLOW PLAIN, about 40 rods N. of Mr. Curtis Childs' house.

BRIDGE FIELD, now occupied by the carpet factory.

ROGERS FIELD, an extensive tract W. of the falls.

LAKES AND PONDS.

COCHITUATE LAKE, or LONG POND, situated on the N.E. bounds of Framingham, lies in Framingham, Natick, and Wayland. In ancient deeds and surveys, it bears, in general, the name of Cochituate, sometimes of Cochichawick, and in a few instances of Wachituate; which last is given to it on Gore's Survey of "the farmes and quantity of a parcel of land, commonly called Framingham," executed in Oct. 1699. Its extent, in a right line from N. to S., is about three and a half miles; but following its irregular windings, its length is considerably greater. Its breadth, at the widest part, exceeds half a mile. Its circumference, at the water's edge, when at its medium height, measures 10 miles and 23 feet.

This lake presents the appearance of two bodies of water, united by a narrow strait, over which passes the railroad from Saxonville. Of the two divisions, the northerly part is the longer; which is itself divided into two ponds, communicating by a passage less narrow than the former, which is crossed by the new road from Framingham to Newton. Both these straits were ancient " crossings " or " fording places." Over the first and the narrowest, a road was anciently constructed of loose stones, traces of which are still discoverable beneath the surface, at a depth of about three feet. The greatest depth of water in the lake, at its highest flood, is about 69 feet, which is in its southerly section; the greatest depth in the middle section, is 61 feet; and in the northerly section, 48 feet. The area of the entire lake at low water, when the surface is even with the flume at the outlet, has been ascertained, by recent surveys, to be 489 acres; when raised 17 inches above the flume, 504 acres; when three feet above, 559 acres; when six and a half feet above, 659 acres; and when eight feet above, 684 acres. In the southerly section is a small island, called Gipsy Island.

"Cochituate Pond" possesses a degree of historical interest, the contiguous territory having been a place of resort to the aboriginal race, numerous traces of whose ancient habitancy in the neighborhood, are frequently to be discovered, and more particularly about the southerly " crossing." The fishery of this lake must have been to them important and valuable. Since modern enterprise has obstructed the channel of communication with the sea, its primitive consequence has ceased.

The celebrated Dunster Farm, the property of Pres. Dunster,* lay contiguous to the northerly bounds of the lake. The first christian habitation in its immediate vicinity, was probably erected, a few years later, by Edmund Rice. Settlements soon ex-

---

* The Dunster Farm, as conveyed in 1659, began where the " two ponds come nearest together,' (i.e., Dudley and Cochituate Ponds); and extended to the fording place of Cochituate Pond.

tended along the Cochituate brook, by which the waters of the pond are discharged into Sudbury river. This entire region, sometimes denominated COCHITUATE, is full of historical interest, as the locality in this township where the footsteps of civilization are first traced.

The waters of Cochituate Pond appear to have been unappropriated to mechanical uses, until near the war of the Revolution; when a fulling mill was erected towards its outlet. After the termination of the war, a grist mill was put in operation by Deacon Wm. Brown, nearer the pond. Within a few years, the enterprise of an individual, (Mr. William H. Knight,) who in 1830 obtained possession of the water privilege of the pond, greatly enlarged its resources, and rendered it an important tributary to the industry and prosperity of the town. In 1834, the attention of the public was directed to this pond, as a desirable and abundant source for the supply of fresh water to the metropolis. The rival claims of other proposed sources, delayed the issue, until June 25, 1846; when the water privilege and the extensive manufacturing establishment connected with Cochituate pond, both in the possession of Mr. Knight, were purchased by the city of Boston, upon terms liberal and mutually satisfactory to the parties. A plan for the construction of an aqueduct, at an estimated cost of $1,681,599, (exclusive of the city reservoir and distribution), was soon adopted; and the ground was first broken, with public ceremonies, Aug. 20, 1846.*

That a negotiation of such importance, as touching the industrial prosperity of the town, should pass without misgivings or opposition from its inhabitants, could hardly be expected. Independently of all calculations of interest or apprehensions of pecuniary loss, there is involved somewhat of natural regret in beholding the water courses which have irrigated their ancient fields, dried up, and an important source of municipal prosperity, alienated to other uses.

But humanity and patriotism alike forbid such reflections, in view of the grandeur and immensity of the benefit this enterprise is destined to accomplish; and that not for a limited period, but

---

* The Board of Water Commissioners, intrusted with the execution of this project, consists of Nathan Hale, James F. Baldwin, and Thomas B. Curtis, Esqs.

through the succession of uncounted generations. If to give a cup of cold water to the parched lips of a single sufferer, was accounted meritorious and honorable, how immeasurably greater the privilege and satisfaction of supplying one of the most important elements of health, and aids to purity and virtue, to the crowded and swelling population of a great city.

FARM POND, (sometimes called in ancient surveys, Great Pond), probably derived its name from the "Danforth Farm." It lies a little E. of S. from the village, and its northerly point is about 100 rods S. of Sudbury river, with which it communicates by a small stream, once a passage for shad and alewives into the pond. This pond extends about one mile in length, the Boston and Worcester railroad passing near its southerly margin. At its widest part its breadth is near half a mile. It contains an area of 193 acres. This pond is beautifully situated, and is often resorted to by fishing parties.*

WASHAKUM POND, (now abbreviated to Shakum Pond), is thus named in ancient conveyances. It lies about 170 rods from the S. point of Farm Pond, is of irregular shape, and contains an area of 89 1-2 acres. Its waters are discharged by Beaver Dam Brook, flowing easterly into Sherburne.†

LEARNED'S POND lies to the E. of Farm Pond, and derived its name from Isaac Learned, who early settled near it. It is in a sequestered spot, and has no known communication with other bodies of water. It covers 36 acres.

GLEASON'S POND, (anciently called Bigelow's Pond and Little Pond), lies a few rods to the E. of Learned's Pond, and covers about 13 acres.

SUCCO POND, (generally called Sucker Pond), lies near the junction of the Worcester Turnpike and the old road to Boston, about one mile from the centre village. It covers three and a half acres, and communicates with a still smaller pond of one and a half acres, to the N. of it.

---

* There exists a tradition, that a trunk of money was for some time supposed to have been deposited in Farm Pond; which at times was seen to approach the surface, but disappeared at the advance of any one.

† There is a pond in Sterling of the same name, "Washacum." "Wech-ecum signifies sea, or the largest collection of water; and Washacum is probably a modification of that word. W, with an aspirate, is sometimes placed in the Indian dialects, to signify great, or large in the superlative degree." Worc.,Mag., I. 383, note.

MILLS AND FACTORIES IN FRAMINGHAM.

MILLS.

The first mill in this town was built by Elder John Stone, near the Falls. The precise date of its establishment is unknown. It was perhaps in existence in 1659; but first receives a distinct notice, 1672. It continued in the possession of his descendants, until the establishment of factories near the Falls.

Savill Simpson constructed a mill on the Hopkinton River, where is now the Ashland Factory, soon after the year 1707.

John How " set up about 4 or 5 years before, a certain water mill on his own land in Framingham, very convenient to the towns of Framingham and Sherborn, it standing on the river between the two towns; which has been of great service to a great number of said towns, there being no other grist mill within six miles of (it) but Mr. Simson's."*

Col. Buckminster early put up a mill upon the stream, near his house, on what was afterwards the Brinley farm; it stood there in 1741.

A small grist mill was built upon the brook, near the present poor house; but was long since discontinued.

A grist mill S. of the house of Mr. Aaron Bullard, was disused many years ago.†

A grist and saw mill was built on the site of Shepherd's paper mill, before the establishment of the latter.‡

A trip hammer establishment, owned by Mr. Ebenezer Marshall, existed near the above, before 1760; where were manufactured scythes, hoes, axes, mill cranks, &c. A saw and grist mill now occupy the site.§

Deacon Wm. Brown built a grist mill on Cochituate brook, near the house of his grandson, Col. J. Brown.‖

---

* How's petition, 1716. State Files.
† In 1760, there were eight mills and one iron work in Framingham.
‡ This mill was owned about 40 years by Isaac Dench.
§ The sawmill was built by Richard Sears, about 1816. Mr. Sears sold to Calvin Bigelow, who built a grist mill. The property has since belonged successively to Messrs. Jas. Whitmore, Wm. Greenwood, and N. S. Cutler.
‖ Tradition gives the date of its origin near the termination of the

Maj. Lawson Buckminster built a saw mill N. of his house, which is now in the possession of his son, Wm. Buckminster, Esq.

The grist and saw mill near the house of Deac. Bent, on Sudbury River, was built about the year 1824, by Lawson Buckminster, Jr., and Joseph Brown. The privilege is now owned by the N. E. Worsted Co. of Saxonville.

Mr. George Bullard's machine shop, on Stoney Brook, was built about 1830.

FACTORIES.

The Framingham Manufacturing Company was incorporated, Feb. 6, 1813, with a capital limited to $80,000;* and built a mill on the site of Deac. Brown's mill, which was destroyed by fire. Feb. 4, 1824, was incorporated the Saxon Factory Co., for the manufacture of wool, with a capital of $300,000. This Company constructed mills at the Falls of Sudbury River.†
June 11, 1829, was incorporated the Saxon Cotton and Woollen Factory; the proprietors named in the act being Jos. Head, Henry Gardner, Edward Miller, Henry H. Jones, and others.

Feb. 16, 1832, the name of this Co. was changed to that of the " Saxon Factory."

In 1837, the N. E. Worsted Co. purchased of the Saxon Co. their property, and removed hither from Lowell their worsted machinery.

In 1845, this Company possessed three mills, with 16 sets of machinery, consuming annually 2,000,000 lbs. of wool. They

---

Revolutionary War. A fulling mill was built, probably before, on Cochituate brook, N.W. from Col. Brown's house. Maj. Andrew Brown, son of Dea. Wm., conducted it. (He also built fulling stocks in the grist mill). The fulling mill was succeeded by a small factory for spinning cotton, built by Luther Rice; and a partner conducted it. The building came into the possession of Col. J. Brown, by whom it was sold to Mr. W. H. Knight, who there commenced his establishment, (afterwards removed), for the manufacture of carpets. Col.

Micah Stone also owned a fulling mill, near the falls.

* Among the proprietors were Calvin Sanger and others, of Sherburne; Benj. Wheeler and Luther Belknap, of Framingham.

† Mr. Washburn states in his History of Leicester, (Worc. Mag.), that the " Leicester Manufacturing Company," incorporated in 1823, "afterwards united and was incorporated with the Saxon Factory in Framingham, under the style of the Saxon and Leicester Factories."

manufactured annually 113,000 yards of flannel and bockings, valued at $56,500; 90,000 lbs. of woollen yarn, not made into cloth, valued at $27,000; 40,000 pairs of blankets, valued at $120,000; 350,000 lbs. of worsted yarn, not made into cloth, valued at $175,000; and 2,300 pieces of worsted bunting, valued at $14,950. The capital employed by the company amounted to $400,000; and the number of operatives, 227 males, and 190 females.

CARPET FACTORY.—The establishment for the manufacture of carpets was commenced in 1830, by Mr. William H. Knight, who purchased of Col. J. Brown the site of the old fulling-mill, on Cochituate brook. Dec. 30, 1839, Mr. Knight purchased the "bridge lot," and the following year constructed a new dam about 80 rods below, upon the same stream, and removed thither his factory, to which, with outbuildings, large additions were subsequently made. He also purchased, July 1844, the privilege formerly connected with Deacon Brown's mill which, for many years had belonged to Mr. Isaac McLellan, of Boston; where he also constructed a factory for the spinning of woollen yarn. The remarkable success of Mr. Knight's enterprise and liberality was soon manifested in the rapid growth of the neighborhood; converting a quiet and rural region, into an active and flourishing village. In 1845, Mr. Knight was in possession of 3 mills, consuming annually 465,000 lbs. of wool, and manufacturing 199,037 yards of carpeting, valued at $149,530. The number of operatives in his employ, was 191 males, and 41 females; total, 231. In 1847, the manufacture had increased to 1500 yards per diem.*

The two establishments above referred to, with their appendages, constitute the village of Saxonville; whose rapid growth, and prosperity, for the space of ten years past, on both sides of the river, afford favorable evidence of the ability and enterprise which have conducted this branch of our industry. A spacious hall has recently been erected in this village, at the

---

* Since writing the above, the greater p^rt of the valuable establishment of Mr Knight, which, with the water privilege of Long Pond, had been previously sold to the city of Boston, has been destroyed by fire. The casualty occurred March 20, 1847, at 4 1-2 o'clock, A. M. The value of the buildings destroyed, is estimated at $40,000; and of the stock, $22,000.

charge of the town, where literary and scientific lectures are well attended. The character of this place for morality and social order, compares favorably with that of similar establishments in the Commonwealth. Its location is commanding, and affords many beautiful views, when observed from various directions. There are three churches in this village, a Congregational, a Methodist, and a Catholic ; and ample accommodation is provided for the instruction of the young in schools. A branch rail-road, connecting with the B. and W. Rail-road, at Natick, opened in 1846, affords easy communication with Boston.

MANUFACTURE OF STRAW BONNETS.

This branch of industry, which has afforded a profitable employment to a large number of the inhabitants of this town, was commenced by Mrs. Uriah Rice, and individuals of the family of Eames, about 45 years since.* Maj. Benj. Wheeler engaged in it in 1807, as did also Capt. John J. Clark and others. Major Wheeler traded at the South, and the annual amount of his business in this article, in some years, exceeded $30,000. The aggregate product of this manufacture, in the town, reached $50,000. In 1845, the number of straw bonnets manufactured here was 31,000, valued at $20,100. The value of braid manufactured, was $450. Fifty females were employed in the manufacture.†

MISCELLANEOUS STATISTICS FOR 1845.

1 Axe Manufactory; articles manufactured, 1000; value, $700; hands employed, 1.

1 Cutlery; value of manufactures, $200; capital, $200; hands, 1.

---

* This article of manufacture had been previously introduced, about 1800, in other neighboring towns. Capt. Adams, of Franklin, and Mr. Hall, of Wrentham, conducted the business to a considerable extent. Braid early brought 3 and 3 1-2 cents per yard.

† This information, with other, relating to the industry of the town, is obtained from returns to the Secretary of the Commonwealth. The number of persons employed in the Bonnet manufacture, is probably exclusive of those who only braid the straw. A new establishment for the prosecution of this business, has been recently commenced by Messrs. Richardson and Manson, which gives promise of a revival of its former prosperity.

INDUSTRY OF FRAMINGHAM.

2 Paper Manufactories; stock used, 225 tons; paper manufactured, 360,000 lbs; value $52,500; capital employed, $45,000; hands, 33.

2 Establishments for repair of Watches, &c.; income, $450; capital, $200; hands, 2.

2 Manufactories of Saddlery, &c.; value of manufactures, $1,200; capital, $300; hands, 4.

1 Hat Manufactory; hats made, 1200; value, $2,500; capital, $700; hands, 4.

3 Manufactories of Chaises, Wagons, &c.; value of manufactures, $3,300; capital, $1,500; hands, 6.

3 Cabinet Manufactories; value of manufactures, $1,200; capital, $800; hands, 3.

1 Tin Ware Manufactory; value of manufactures, $4000; capital, $500; hands, 4.

2 Grist Mills; income, $1730; 3 Saw Mills; income, $1,250; capital, in both, $7,500.

1 Tannery; hides tanned, 350; value of leather, $736; capital, $1,000; hands, 1.

Boots manufactured; 35,000 pairs; Shoes, 44,000; value of both, $49,450; hands, males, 60; females, 25.

Value of building stone prepared, $500; hands, 2.

Value of lumber prepared, $950; hands, 1.

Fire Wood prepared, 2,020 cords; value, $7,070; hands, 5.

Sperm oil used in manufactories, 6,744 gallons; value, $6,100; whale oil, 1,936 galls.; value, $900; lard oil, 31,140 gallons; value, $21,700; anthracite coal consumed in the same, 1000 tons; value, $6,500.

1 Bakery; value of bread baked, $8,000; capital, $600; hands, 4.

3 Millinery establishments; value of millinery manufactured, $2,000; hands, females, 10.

1 Bookbindery; income, $2,500; hands, males, 3; females, 2.

Caps manufactured, 500; value, $500; hands, females, 2.

6 Wheelwright establishments; value of manufactures, $3,000; hands, 6.

The same year there were in town 13 sheep, value, $50; wool, 52 lbs., value, $20; horses, 317, value, $17,203; neat cattle, 1,383, value, $27,700; swine, 450, value, $3,200; Indian corn produced, 15,448 bushels, value, $11,586; wheat, 25 bushels, value, $25; rye, 1,241 bush., value, $993; barley, 408 bush., value, $306; oats, 3,710 bush., value, $2,741; potatoes, 34,584 bush., value, $8,646; other esculent vegetables, 968 bush., and 15 tons, value, $502; hay, 3,212 tons, value, $40,378; fruit raised, 22,381 bush., value, $5,013; butter made, 66,690 lbs., value, $11,337; cheese, 2,950 lbs., value, $177; value of milk sold, $1,090.

MEMORANDA.

The Framingham Bank was incorporated March 25, 1833; the persons named in the act of incorporation, were Micah Stone, Dexter and Sullivan Fay, Elijah Perry, Rufus Brewer, &c. The names of the successive Presidents of this Bank, are, Josiah Adams, Micah Stone, and Oliver Dean. Rufus Brewer, Esq., has held the office of Cashier, during the whole period.

The Boston and Worcester Rail-road Corporation received its charter, Jan. 23, 1831. The opening in 1835, of this road, which passes through the south part of Framingham, essentially affected the travel in Framingham centre, and particularly on the Boston and Worcester Turnpike, (inc. June 10, 1808), where about seventeen stages had previously passed daily. The value of the turnpike was so seriously impaired, that the road was relinquished about four years since.

1795. The "Middlesex Lodge" of Free Masons was instituted in this town; and has continued its meetings, without interruption, until the present time. Its semi-centennial anniversary was observed, with suitable ceremonies.

VALUATION OF FRAMINGHAM, AT SUCCESSIVE PERIODS.

1800, - - - $168.940	1830, - - $ 802.040
1810, - - - 268.260	1840, - - - 1.380.360
1820, - - - 327.900	1847, - - 1.755.010

APPENDIX.

SETTLEMENT OF SUDBURY.*

THE following is the order of the General Court, establishing the township of Sudbury, September 4, 1639.

"The order of the Court upon the petition of the Inhabitants of Sudbury is, that Peter Noyes, Bryan Pendleton, J. Parm(enter), Edmond B(rown), Walter Hayne, George Moning and Edmond Rise, have commission to lay out lands to the present Inhabitants, according to their estates and persons; and that Capt. Jeanison, Mr. Mayhewe, Mr. Flint, Mr. Samu. Sheopard and John Bridge, or any three of them, shall in convenient time repaire to the said towne, and set out such lands and accommodations, both for houselots and otherwise, both for Mr. Pelham and Mr. Walgrave, as they shall think suitable to their estates, to be reserved for them, if they shall come to inhabit there in convenient time, as the court shall think."

Conformably to the above, the first division of lands was made (without date), in 1639; the second division, April 20, 1640; the third division, Nov. 18, 1640. The following are the names, (arranged alphabetically), of those who shared in the lands divided; the numbers indicating the several divisions.

Wyddow Baffumthwyte 1, 3.
Robert Beast, 1, 2, 3.
Andrew Belcher, 1, 2, 3.
John Bent, 1, 2.
John Blandford, 1, 2, 3.
Mr. Edmund Browne, 1, 2, 3.

Thomas Browne, 1, 2, 3.
William Browne, 1, 2, 3.
Thomas (?) Buckmaster, 1, 2.
Thomas Cakbrad, 3.
Henry Curties, 1, 2, 3.
Robert Darvell, 1, 2, 3.

---

* Sudbury, in England, on the rivar Stour, is in the hundred of Babergh, and Co. of Suffolk. It has three parishes, containing 3,283 souls; possesses a city organization, and has sent two members to Parliament. There was here, in 970, an ancient religious order. The church, in 1374, was purchased by Simon de Sudbury, then Bishop of London, and his brother John, by whose efforts it was made collegiate. Here was also a Priory of Benedictine Monks, a Hospital, and a house of Black Friars. Sudbury is said to have been one of the first seats of the Flemings, brought over by Edward III., to teach the English the art of manufacturing their own wool. Sudbury, i.e., the "Southern burough," received its name from its position towards Norwich, i.e., the Northern village. It is populous, and thrives by the cloth trade. Camden, Carlisle, Tamer, and Morse.

PROPRIETORS OF SUDBURY.

John Freeman, 1, 2, 3.
Edmond Goodenow, 1, 2, 3.
John Goodenough, 1, 2, 3.
Thomas Goodnow, 1, 2, 3.
Hugh Griffyn, 1, 2, 3.
John Hayme, 1, 2, 3.
Thomas Hayme, 1, 2.
Walter Hayme, 1, 2, 3.
John How, 1, 2, 3.
Robert Hunt, 1, 2.
Wyddow Hunt, 3.
Theo. Islyn, 1, 2, 3.
Solomon Johnson, 1, 2, 3.
William Kerly, 3.
John Knight, 1, 3.
Henry Loker, 1, 2, 3.
John Loker, 1, 3.
John Maynard, 1, 3.
George Munnings, 1, 2, 3.
Richard Newton, 1, 2, 3.
Mr. Peter Noyse, 1, 2, 3.
Thomas Noyse, 1, 2, 3.
William Parker, 1, 2.
John Parmenter, Sen. 1, 2, 3,
John Parmenter, Jun. 1, 2, 3.
Mr. William Pellam,* 1, 2, 3.
Bryan Pendleton, 1, 2, 3.
Henry Prentise, 2, 3.
John Reddicke, 1, 2, 3.
Edmund Ryce, 1, 2, 3.
Henry Rice, 1, 3.
Wyddow Ryte, 1, 2, 3.
John Stone, 1, 2, 3.
Joseph Taynter, 1, 3.
Nathaniell Treadaway, 1, 2, 3.
William Ward, 1, 2, 3.
John Waterman, 3.
Anthony White, 1, 2, 3.
Richard Whyte, 1, 2.
Thomas Whyte, 1, 2, 3.
Goodman Witherill, 1, 2.
John Woods, 1, 2, 3.

The following received grants, or owned lands, in Sudbury, at the dates annexed to their respective names.

Thomas Axdell, about 1642.
Ambrose Beers, about 1642.
Thomas Bisbige, 1645.
Antient Cakbread, 1640.
Wid. Sarah Cakbrad, 1645.
Robert Davis, 1642.

---

* Besides the above, the proprietors made grants, in 1644, to Herbert Pelham; although it does not appear that he became an inhabitant. He owned, for many years, "the Island," so-called, which from him derived the name of "Pelham's Island." It contained, in 1725, 387 ac., 68 per.; and was sold by Edward, Edward, Jr., and Tho. Pelham, all of Newport, R. I., Nov. 4, 1711, to Isaac Hunt and Samuel Stone, Jr.; who, the same month, sold a part to Jonathan Fiske and George Reed. Herbert Pelham, Esq., was one of the council of Mass., in Eng., 1629, and put £100 into the common stock of the colony; was of Cambridge, N. E., 1638, and "Townsman" there, 1645, and also Assistant of the Col.; Commissioner of the united Colonies, 1646. In 1650 he had returned to England; and his residence is afterwards referred to as in "Ferrers, in Bewer's hamlet, county of Essex." He was buried at Bury St. Mary, county of Suffolk, in Eng., July 1, 1673. By his will, dated Jan. 1, 1672, he gave to his son, EDWARD, (of Newport, R. I., w. Freelove), his lands in Sudbury. He also left children, WALDEGRAVE, (the eldest), who was buried in England, Nov, 12, 1699, leaving a son, Herbert, and a daughter, Jemima Hunt; HENRY; PENELOPE, wife of Josiah Winslow, Esq. and mother of Isaac, and Elizabeth (Burton). Herbert Pelham was an early proprietor at Watertown, and an original patentee of Conn. He married a daughter of Mr. Waldegrave.

Capt. William Pelham was Selectman in Sudbury, 1645 and 6; his house lot was at the N.E. end of the town; he also commanded "the band of Sudbury." Johnson, (p. 193), speaks of him as then in England. Camb. and Sud. Rec.; Private Papers; Hutch. i. 144, note, (who supposes Herbert of the same family with the Duke of Newcastle); Sav. Wint. i. 8, note 1, ii. 19; Mid. Deeds, 1693. Mr. Savage supposes Herbert to have been brother to Gov. Winthrop.

APPENDIX.

Hugh Drury.
Robert Fourdum, 1642.
Sergeant John Grout, 1640.
Thomas King, 1643.

John Rutter, 1642,
Robert Slate, 1641.
John Toll, about 1640.

"The names of those tok the (oath of fidelity) July 9, 1645."

Thomas Axdell.	Edward Iron.	Thomas Noyes.
Andrew Belcher.	Solomon Johnson, Jun.	William Kerley, Sen.
Robert Bent.	Thomas Kings.	Thomas Plimton.
Henry Curties.	John Lokar.	Henry Rice.
John Hayme.	John Moores, Sen.	John Rutter.
Josiah Hayme.	Richard Newton.	Phillemon Whale.
William How.		

"They that tooke the oath of fidelity since." *

Richard Barnet.†	Henry Kerley.	Richard Sanger.
John Bent, Jun.	William Kerley, Jun.	John Smith.
Peter Bent.	Peter Kinge.	Richard Smith.
Robert Best.	John Maynard, Jun.	John Ward.
John Goodenow, Jun.	John Moores, Jun.	Obediah Warde.
John Groute.	Peter Noyes, Jun.	Richard Ward.
John Johnson.	James Pendleton,	Thomas White, Jun.
Solomon Johnson, Sen.	Edward Rice.	John Woodward.

NAMES OF MEN FROM FRAMINGHAM, WHO HAVE SERVED AT VARIOUS TIMES IN THE WARS.

In the expedition to Port Royal, Sept. 16, 1710, Joseph Buckminster was captain of grenadiers, in Sir Charles Hobby's regiment; and sailed in the brigantine Henrietta. The following persons, in the same expedition, were probably of Framingham. David Rice, d. Ap. 20, 1711; Jonathan Provender; Benjamin Provender, d. Jan. 21, 1711; Joseph Adams.

On the Muster Roll of Sergt. Thomas Buckminster's "Rutland Scout," who served from July 25, to Aug. 26, 1722, (in all 21 men), are the names of the commander, David Pratt, Philip Pratt and Thompson Wood, of Framingham. The regiment from which they were detached, was commanded by Col. Jos. Buckminster.

On the Muster Roll of the men posted under the care of Col. Buckminster, from Aug. to Nov. 1722, (in all 25), are the names of Gid-

---

* On a mutilated page are the following imperfect christian names, the sirnames having been torn from the book, viz: John, Edw, Jame, Willi, Danie, Thom, Math, Samu, Robert, Jonathan, Robert.   † Or, Barnes.

SOLDIERS FROM FRAMINGHAM.

eon Bridges, Hachaliah Bridges, Jeremiah Belknap, Oliver Keyes, Simon Goddard, and Benoni Hemingway, of Framingham, all of whom were in service from eight to fifteen weeks.

The Muster Roll of the company of troopers under the command of Capt. Isaac Clark, from Aug. 21, to Sept. 18, 1725, is as follows, viz:—

Isaac Clark, Capt., Framingham. Eben. Leland, Corp., Sherburne.
Jonathan Lamb, Lieut., " Jonas Eaton, " Fram.
Joseph Weare, Cornet, Sherburne. Eleasar Rider, " Sherburne.
Nath. Eammes, Corp., Fram.

SENTINELS.

James Clayes, Framingham. Samuel Walker, Framingham.
John Bent, " Thomas Stone, "
Joseph Haven, " John Stacy, "
Josiah Rice, " Jonathan Nutting, "
Daniel Pratt, " Oliver Death, "
Matthias Clark, " Samuel Williams, Sherb.
Thomas Winch, " Joseph Lealand, "
Jacob Pepper, " Asa Morse, "
Abraham Rice, " Edward Larnard, "
Ezekiel Rice, " Isaac Lealand, "
Robert Sever, " George Fairbank, "
Samuel Frissel, " Joseph Morse, "
Phinehas Rice, " Jonathan Fairbank, "
Moses Haven, " David Morse, "
Uriah Drury, " Jonathan Dewing, "
Joseph Brintnal, " Samuel Stone, Clerk, Fram.
Bezaleel Rice, " Tho's. Bellows, Marlb., trumpeter.
George Walkup, " Nero Benson, Fram., "
Isaac Stanhope, Sud.

SOLDIERS IN THE FRENCH WAR, ETC.

1740. Jona. Jackson, of Fram., æ 22, husbandman, was drafted for the W. India service.

1745. At the taking of Louisburg, Robert Sever and two sons, of Fram., were in the service.

1747. On Capt. Brown's muster-roll, on the alarm from Sept. 23, to 27th, are the names of the following, from Framingham:

Thos. Winch, Lieut. Jona. Maynard, Sentinel.
Daniel Gregory, Corp. Isaac Read, "
Daniel Stone, Clerk. Micah Gibbs, "
Jona. Belcher, Trumpeter. Joseph Brintnal, "
Nath'l. Seaver, " Elias Whitney, "
Thos. Winch, Sentinel. Benj. Eaton, "
Samuel Winch, " Wm. Brown, "
Phineas Winch, " Daniel Stone, "

158   APPENDIX.

John Bruce,   Sentinel.   Matth. Gibbs,   Sentinel.
John Hemenway,   "   John Gould,   "
Sam'l. Frost,   "   ,

   In the Co. of Capt. Jona. Harris, despatched upon the expedition to
Crown Pt., and in service from Mar. 27, to Sept. 8, 1755, are the following from Framingham :

John Nixon, Capt., 16 w. 5 d.   Eben'r. Boutwell, Corp., 30 w. 1 d.
Jona. Gibbs, Lieut, 38 w.   John Mathis, Priv., 30 w.
Amos Gates, Sarg't., 27 w. 4 d.   Geo. Walkup, Drum Major.

   Sept. 20, 1755. On the roll of Capt. Josiah Stone's Co., in Col.
Josiah Brown's regiment, going to Crown Point, are the following,
mostly from this town:

Capt. Josiah Stone.   John Nichols.
Lt. Benj. Fasale.   Richard Rice.
Ens. John Stone.   Peter Jenison.
                                   Nathan Winch, Jr.
         PRIVATES.   John Jenison.
Elisha Kendall.   Ephraim Shaddock.
David Haven.   Nath'l Muzzey.
Daniel Whitney.   Isaac Gibbs, Jr.
Eben'r. Haven.   Daniel Rice.
David Clark.   Joseph Stone.
Samuel Morse.   Phinehas Graves.
Benajah Morse.   James Stuart.

   To the above, we add the names of others from this place, who, according to tradition or written record, are believed to have served in
the same war.

Jonathan Robinson.   Benjamin Berry.
Ebenezer Cutting, (died 1762).   Ens. Thomas Nixon, 1756.
Jonathan Gibbs, 1761.   Capt. John Nixon,   "
Daniel Haven,   ⎱ in Canada,   Joseph Dunn,   1759.
Ebenezer Haven, ⎰ 1759.   William Dunn,   "
Thomas Stone, (died).   Capt. Jona. Rice,   "
David Sanger, (d. 1755).   Joshua Eaton.
Peter Rice, 1755.   Jonas Darling.
Robert Eames.   Phinehas Rice.
Jonathan Brewer, (an officer).   John Stone, (prob. d. 1755).*

   * Among the State Files, from   ment, to reinforce the army destined
which we have derived much of our   to Crown Point." We were unable
information, is a return Sept. 17, to detect any names of persons from
1757, by Col. Buckminster, "of vol- this town.
unteers and imprest men in his regi-

REVOLUTIONARY SOLDIERS.

The names of those, natives or citizens of the town, who served as officers or privates during the War of the Revolution, in the continental service or the militia.

FIELD OFFICERS.

Gen. John Nixon.
Col. Thomas Nixon.
Col. Micah Stone.

Col. Jonathan Brewer.
Col. William Buckminster.
Maj. John Trowbridge.

CAPTAINS.

Capt. Joseph Winch.
" Jonathan Maynard.
" Samuel Frost.
" Peter Clayes,
" Elijah Clayes.

Capt. John Gleason.
" Simon Edgell.
" Thomas Drury.
" Micajah Gleason.

LIEUTENANTS AND SUBALTERNS.

—— Claflin.
—— Drury.
John Eames.
Joseph Mixer.
William Maynard.
John Maynard.
Thomas Nixon, Jr.
Charles Dougherty.

Micah Dougherty.
John Trowbridge.
Luther Trowbridge.
Samuel Fairbanks.
Lawson Buckminster.
Needham Maynard.
James Marshall.

NON-COMMISSIONED OFFICERS AND PRIVATES.

William Arnold.
Abijah Abbot.
Phinehas Butler, (pensioner).
Joseph Belcher.
Ezra Belcher.
Jacob Belcher, (pen).
Abel Benson, trumpeter.
David Brewer, (pen).
Joseph Bennet, (pen).
Lawson Buckminster, (pen).
Rev. Matt. Bridge, (chaplain, d).
Phinehas Bemis.
David Cutting, (d).
Benjamin Clark, (wounded).
John Claflin.
Daniel Claflin.
Joel Coolidge, (pen).
Cornelius Claflin.
Nathan Dadmun.
Jonathan Dadmun.

Daniel Dadmun.
David Drury.
James Dalrymple, (pen).
Samuel Eames, (d).
Noah Eaton.
Eben. Eaton, (pen).
Luther Eaton, (pen).
Jonas Eaton.
Brigham Eaton.
Jotham Eames.
Noah Eager.
Zaccheus Fairbanks.
Corman Fairbanks. (d.)
Joshua Fairbanks.
Allan Flagg,
David Fisk, (pen.)
Moses Fisk, (pen.)
Elisha Frost.
Francis Gallot, (d.)
John Gallot, (d.)

APPENDIX.

Charles Gates, (d.)
George Gates.
Edmund T. Gates.
Henry Gates, (wd.)
Amos Gates.
Abel Greenwood.
Jona. Gleason.
Blayney Grusha.
William Hemenway.
Isaac Hemenway, (prob. d.)
Jona. Hemenway, (pen.)
Samuel Hemenway.
Thaddeus Hemenway.
Daniel Hemenway.
Ebenezer Hemenway.
Parley How.
Joseph How.
Isaac How, (pen.)
Simon How.
Ezekiel How, (pen.)
Jona. Hill.
Aaron Hill, (pen.)
Benj. Holden, Jr.
John Holbrook, (d.)
Cato Hart.
David Haven, (d. '77.)
Grant Haven.
Nathan Knowlton, (pen.)
Simon Learned.
Moses Learned, (d. '80.)
John Lamb, (pen.)
John Lennard.
Nathan Mixer, (d. Bennnington).
Timothy Merriam, (pen.)
Gilbert Marshall.
Fred. Manson, (pen.)
Josiah Nurse, (d. '77.)
Asa Nurse.
Thos. Nixon, Jr., (pen.)
Jos. Nixon.
Eph. Newton.
Solo. Newton, (d.)
James Newton.
Eben. Newton, (pen.)
Alpheus Nichols, (pen.)
Isaiah Nurse.
Lawson Nurse.
Jos. Nichols.
Jos. Nichols, 2d.
Samuel Ordway.
Moses Pike, (d.)
Timo. Pike.
John Pike, (d.)
Nath. Pratt, (pen.)
Eph. Pratt.
John Pratt.
John Park.
Aaron Parkhurst.
Nath'l Polly.
Benj. Parker.
Ezekiel Rice.
Hezekiah Rice.
Jonathan Rice, (prob. d.)
Peter Rice, (d.)
Phinehas Rice, (pen.)
Uriah Rice, (pen.)
Daniel Rice.
David Rice, Jr.
Bezaleel Rice.
John Rice, (d.)
Gideon Rider.
Jos. Richards.
Peter Salem.
John Stacy.
John Stone.
Samuel Stone.
Winsor Stone.
Jos. Tombs, (pen.)
Josiah Temple, (wd.)
Azariah Walker.
Azariah Walker, Jr.
Barechias Waite.
Josiah Waite, (d.)
Eph. Whitney, (d. '75.)
Jona. Whitney, (d.)
Silas Winch, (pen.)

SOLDIERS FROM FRAMINGHAM.

Framingham, Feb. 13, 1775.
A Return of Capt. Nixon's Company of Minute Men.

Thomas Nixon, Captain.
Micah Gleason, 1st Lieut.
Jno. Eames, 2d Lieut.
Samuel Gleason, Ensign.
Ebenezer Hemenway, Clerk.

NON-COMMISSIONED OFFICERS AND MUSICIANS.

Serg., Jno. Gleason.	Corporal, Alpheus Nichols.
" Shubel Seaver.	" Gideon Rider.
" Jona. Hill.	" Asa Nurse.
" Thos. Buckminster.	" Eben. Winch.
Fifer, Thos. Nixon, Jr.	Isaac Hemenway, drummer.

PRIVATES.

Jona. Adams.	Moses Eames.	Needham Maynard.
Badger Brown.	Nath'l. Eames.	Jos. Nichols, 3d.
Jno. Bent.	Jno. Farrar.	Fortunatus Nichols.
Ezra Belcher.	Josh. Farrar.	Jno. Nurse.
Daniel Bridge.	Moses Fisk.	David Rice, Jr.
Joseph Belcher	William Farrar.	Josh. Sever.
Andrew Brown.	Jacob Fairbanks.	Sam. Stone, Jr.
Jos. Brown.	Jona. Hemenway.	Josh. Tower.
Peter Clayes.	Jno. Hemenway.	Jona. Temple.
Abel Childs.	Nathan Hemenway.	Josiah Wait.
Charles Dougherty.	Parley Howe.	David Waight.
Micah Dougherty.	Francis Howe.	Azariah Walker.
Elisha Drury.	Joseph Howe, Jr.	Jos. Winch.
Aaron Eames.	Simon Howe.	Barechias Waight.
Ebenezer Eames.	Sam. Jones.	

Captain, 1; Lieut., 1; Ensigns, 2; Clerk, 1; Sergeants, 4; Corporals, 4; Drummer and Fifer, 2; Privates, 45. Total, officers included, 60.

APPENDIX.

Each man's proportion to a tax of £10, to procure a stock of ammunition, June 27, 1710.

[N. B. — The reader will observe a line separating the names into two nearly equal divisions. It was probably intended to distinguish those who lived N. from those who lived S. of the river.]

Name	sh.	d	Name	sh.	d.
John Bent,	03	02	Samuel Barton,	01	11
David Stone,	02	02	Benj. Ball,	01	03
Jonathan Rice,	05	03	Benj. Nurs,	02	11
Dea. David Rice,	02	08	Benj. Bridges,	02	10
Thomas Drury,	03	06	Jeames Travis,	01	02
Thomas Walker,	02	06	Eben. Herenton,	00	10
Caleb Drury,	02	00	Peter Clayes,	02	04
Thomas Stone,	00	10	Jeames Clayes,	02	02
John How,	02	10	John Nurs,	01	04
Samuel Stone,	01	04	Jona. Provender,	00	09
John Pratt,	02	04	Caleb Bridges,	01	09
Joseph Pratt,	02	03	Daniel Eleatt,	01	07
David Pratt,	02	03	Daniel Eleatt, Jr.	00	11
Jonathan Pratt,	01	04	Jonathan Rugg,	01	07
Jabesh Pratt,	00	09	John Singletary,	01	00
Thomas Pratt,	02	01	Samuel Lamb,	01	03
Daniell Pratt,	00	09	Jonathan Cutler,	00	09
John Gleason,	02	05	John Death, Jr.	00	03
Thomas Gleason,	01	07	Eben. Pratt,	00	03
Isaac Gleason,	01	07	Isaac Lerned, Sen.	03	02
Zacariah Paddellford,	01	04	John Adams,	01	11
John Eames,	03	01	Nathan Haven,	00	09
John Eames, Jr.	00	11			
John Death,	03	03	Capt. Joseph Buckminster,	04	04
Samuel Eames,	02	01	Dea. Daniel Stone,	02	02
Nath. Eames,	03	02	Nath. Stone,	04	06
Nath. Haven,	02	05	John Stone,	02	06
John Whettny,	02	02	Joseph Gibbs,	03	00
Moses Haven,	04	08	Thomas Frost,	02	00
John Haven,	01	08	Samuel Frost,	01	03
Elknah Haven,	01	08	Isaac Clerk,	03	02
Jeames Coller,	01	11	John Gibbs,	01	02
Mr. Sevell Simptson,	03	07	Samuel Gibbs,	00	00
Thomas Mellen,	03	03	Joseph Sever,	01	09
Simon Mellen,	03	09	Isaac Heath,	01	02
John Jaquish,	01	00	Jones Eatten,	01	05
Philip Pratt,	01	03	Jorg Wolkup,	02	07
John Provender,	01	00	Joseph Wetherbe,	02	04
Samuel Holland,	01	00	Jonathan Lamb,	01	08

ASHLAND. 163

	sh.	d.		sh.	d.
John Shers,	01	11	Isrell Town,	00	10
Tompson Wood,	01	02	Ephrim Town,	00	09
Benj. Neland,	01	02	John Brus,	01	04
Abiall Lamb,	02	02	Eccobod Hemenway	01	09
Samuel Frisell,	01	00	Amos Waite,	01	01
Jos. Parker,	00	10	Daniel Mexter,	02	01
John Wood,	01	03	Benj. Willerd,	01	03
Samuel Winch,	02	03	Benj. Provender,	00	09
David Winch,	00	09	Philip Gleason,	00	09
Micell Pike,	01	03	Caleb Jonson,	00	10
Jerem. Pike,	02	00	Nath. Willson,	01	08
William Pike,	01	02	Nath. Willson, Jr.	00	09
Jeames Pike,	01	03	Thomas Frostt, Jr,	01	03
John Jones,	00	09	Dea. Josh. Hemenway,	02	00
Abr. Bellknop,	01	11	Samuel How,	02	00
Edward Wright,	01	02	Matthew Gibbs,	01	03
John Town,	03	00	John Frostt,	00	09

THE TOWN OF ASHLAND.

Ashland was incorporated March 16, 1846; having been previously known as Unionville, the name being applied to a neighborhood embracing parts of Hopkinton, Holliston, and Framingham.

The first town meeting was held March 30, 1846, when the following persons were elected to public office in the town, viz: —

Daniel Eames, *Moderator.*

Calvin Shepard, Jr.
Josiah Burnham,
Dexter Rockwood, } *Selectmen.*
Andrew Allard,
Albert Ellis,

William F. Ellis,
Daniel Eames, } *Assessors.*
Simeon N. Cutler,

Benjamin Homer, *Town Treas'r.*

A Post Office was established in the village, in January, 1835; Matthew Metcalf, Esq. receiving the first appointment as Post Master.

The first preaching in the village dates from April, 1834, when the Rev. James McIntire commenced his labors A church, consisting of 21 members, was gathered Jan. 21, 1835, and the society was organized in due form of law, Feb. 17th. The meeting house was dedicated Jan. 21, 1836, on which day Mr. McIntire received ordination as pastor. Mr. McIntire retired Sept. 11, 1838, and was succeeded by the Rev. Joseph Haven, ordained Nov. 6, 1839, who retired Dec. 16, 1846. The Rev. Charles L. Mills was ordained Feb. 11, 1847.

EXPLANATION.

In the following Register will be found the names, as far as known, of all the individuals and families who were inhabitants of Framingham before the year 1800. In many of the sketches are introduced branches from other towns, which, for the sake of distinction, are printed in smaller type.

The paragraphs under each family name, are regularly numbered for convenient reference. When a number in small type is placed *before* a name, as, "¹ George," it is to indicate, that he is the first son, or a descendant from the first son, of the progenitor in the sketch. When a number, in the same type, is placed *after* a name, as, " George ¹²," it is to indicate the No. of the paragraph where his family is introduced. When at the beginning of a paragraph, a number, enclosed in parentheses, follows the name, as, " James s. of John (4)," the number in parentheses refers back to the paragraph, (No. four), where the father's family is given. Where several generations are included in the same paragraph, they will be easily distinguished by the various kinds of type in which the names are printed.

The practice of numbering the children in a family, is, for convenience, preserved in some instances, where the particular order of birth is unknown.

ABBREVIATIONS.

adm. administered.
b. born.
bap. baptized.
ch. church.
chil. children.
cov. covenanted.
d. died.
dr. daughter.
dism. dismissed.
Fram. Framingham.
f. father.

Holl. Holliston.
Hop. Hopkinton.
m. married.
Marlb. Marlborough.
Nat. Natick.
prob. probably.
prop proprietor.
pub. published.
rem. removed.
Roxb. Roxbury.
s. son.

Sal. Salem.
Sherb. Sherburne.
Southb. Southborough.
Sud. Sudbury.
T. Rec. Town Records.
unm. unmarried.
w. wife.
Wat. Watertown.
Westb. Westborough.
wid. widow.
Worc. Worcester.

GENEALOGICAL REGISTER.

ABBE, AARON and w. Anna. Their s. JOHN, was b. Sep. 1, 1781.

    AARON, of Hop. had *James*, b. 1765; *Tamezin*, '67; *William*, bap. '68; *Joshua*, '69; *Sarah*, '71; *Jerusha*, '73; *Joseph*, '77. Mrs. Anna of Hop. m. David Mading of H. Ap. 5, '87.

    2. SAMUEL, rated in F. about 1783. [Sam. Albee of Hop., m. Hannah Rider, 1748.]

    JOHN, of Hop. had *John*; *Mary*, bap. 1761, m. Josiah Bent; *Joseph*, bap. '65; *Amos B.*, bap. '69. BENJAMIN, (and w. Hannah), of Medfield, 1653. SAMUEL, and w. Mary, of Salem vill. 1683. OBADIAH, m. at Malden, Elizabeth Wilkinson, 1701. OBADIAH and w. Jane, of Holl., 1734.

ABBOT, GEORGE, was a Town officer in Fram., 1731.

    2. SAMUEL, (s. of Sam. Jr. and w. Abigail of Sud., and g. son of Sam. and w. Joyce, of Sud.), m. Martha Jennings; covenanted in Fram. 1774; and had BETSEY, bap. May 15, 1774; POLLY, bap. Aug. 15, '74, and d. young; JOSIAH, b. Sep. 26, 1775. m. Ruth Estabrook of Holden; PATTY, bap. June 14, '78, d. young. SALLY, m. Amariah Forrester; NABBY, bap. June, '83, m. Thomas Hastings, Ap. 3, 1803. Sam., the father, d. of small pox, in Sherb., 1791. His wid. m. Noah Eaton, and d. Nov. 1834.

    3. ABNER (b. Aug 25, 1770, s. of Ephraim and Sarah, of Sud., g. son of Samuel Jr. and Abigail of Sud.), and w. Phebe, lived in Fram. 1 year, about 1792; had 1 dr. here, and removed to Westb.

    1696, JOHN ABBUTT of Andover, bought of Benj. Chamberlain of Sud., and by w. Jemima, had in Sud. *Jemima*, 1699; *John*, 1701, prob. of Stow, 1722; *Mary*, '04; *Sarah*, '07; *Hannah*, '10.

    SAMUEL, m. Joyce Rice, both of Sud., 1705; and had *Joyce*, 1706; *Martha*, '12; *Samuel*, '14; *Samuel*, '16, m. Abigail Mirick, 1737, and had John, 1738; Ephraim, '40, m. Sarah Curtis, '69; Jason, '42; Sarah, '45, m. Lemuel Veasey, '71; Samuel; Rebecca, '49; Abigail, '51; Abraham, '54; Abijah, 56, m. Rachel Jennings.

ADAMS, JOHN,* of Sud. m. Hannah Bent, and lived near the carpet factory, in Fram. He had, JOHN, b. Mar. 12, 1684; DANIEL, 1685; HANNAH, 1688.

WILLIAM, of Sud. and w. Elizabeth, had JAMES, b. Mar. 31, 1674; JOHN, Mar. 8, '76; RICHARD, Aug. 22, '78.

RICHARD, of Sud. (wounded in the Narraganset fight), and w. Rebeckah, had RICHARD, Ap. 11, 1680; REBECKAH, '82; SARAH, '83; JOHN, Oct. 26, '86.

Note. — SAMUEL, was rated in Fram. about 1705.

2. JOHN, of Fram., s. of John (1), m. Elizabeth Goddard, of Roxbury, June 27, 1706. J. (and w.) adm. to the ch. 1722; Deacon, 1726. His chil. were, 1. SARAH, b. June 27, 1707, m. Daniel Greenwood of Newton, May 6, '28; 2. ELIZABETH, b. Mar. 23, '08-9, m. Jonas Stone of Rutland, Nov. 5, '31; 3. HANNAH, b. July 30, '12, m. Daniel Mellen, Feb. 3, '35-6; 4. DEBORAH, b. July 27, '14, m. Robert Eames, July 16, '40; 5. ZERVIAH, b. Mar. 17, '16-7, m. Samuel Brown of Sud, May 19, '42; 6. MARY, b. Mar. 5, '18-9, m. Joseph Hemenway, July 4, '43; 7. JOHN, b. Feb. 14, '20-1; 8. JOSEPH,³ and 9. DANIEL,⁴ twins, b. Aug. 12, '23. Deac. Adams lived on the farm now of Mr. Josiah Abbot.

3. JOSEPH, s. of John (2), m. Prudence Pratt, and lived near Mr. Seth Herring's. His chil. were, 1. JOHN, b. Oct. 26, 1744, m. Lydia Jennings, with w. cov. July '65, and lived in N. Salem, m. there a second w. and d. there; 2. KATY, bap. Ap. 13, '46, m. Moses Drury, lived in Fitzwilliam; 3. MOLLY, bap. Jan. 17, '48, m. 1st, Josiah Wait, 2d, — Morse, d. in Dublin, N. H.; 4. JOSEPH, bap. July 9, '49, d. of small pox, unm.; 5. TIMOTHY, bap. Mar. 3, '51, m. in Dublin; 6. PRUDENCE, bap. Nov. 12, '52, m. Gershom Twitchell, Dublin; 7. SARAH, bap. May 26, '54, m. — Harris; 8. DEBORAH, m. John Hemenway, May 2, '76; 9. HANNAH, m. Moses Perry, of Hop., d. in E. Boylston; 10. ABIGAIL, m. Abner Morse, d. in Dublin; 11. ELIZABETH, d. in Dublin; 12. JONATHAN, m. Hannah Parkhurst, Feb. 25, '79; 13. ELISHA, had 2 wives, lived in Me. Joseph, the father, moved to Dublin, N. H., about 1776; where he m. Esther Grout, and had 2 chil., ESTHER, and —.

4. DANIEL, s. of John (2), m. Elizabeth Balch, Sep. 22,

---

* JOHN, of Sud., may have sprung from the Wat. family, who were numerous, and extended probably into Waltham and Lexington. John and Daniel Adams were among the early proprietors of Templeton, in 1735.

1748 ; and with w. was adm. to the ch. Mar., '49. Their chil. were, 1. ELIZABETH, b. Ap. 29, '50, d. May 16 ; 2. MARY, b. June 20, '51, d. July 8 ; 3. PETER, b. Sep. 20, '52 ; 4. DANIEL, b. Feb. 11, '55 ; 5. LUTHER, b. June 5, '57 ; 6. NATHAN, b. Ap. 17, '60 ; 7. ELIZABETH, b. May 26, '63. Daniel and w. were recommended to the ch. in Rutland, Jan. 1765.

5. MOSES, (s. of Moses and Deborah, of Sherb., now Holl., and g. son of Moses and Lydia, of Sherb., and g.g. grand son of Henry and Elizabeth, of Medfield), b. Feb. 27, 1721, m. Lois Haven, Nov. 1744 ; moved from Holl. into Fram., and lived in the house afterwards of John Fisk, Esq. Their s. MOSES, was b. Oct. 4, 1749. Moses the father d. July 23, 1756, æ. 35. His wid. moved to Hop,, and d. there the same year, æ. 32.

6. MOSES, s. of Moses (5), a grad. of H. C., 1771, m. Abigail, dr. of Hon. Josiah Stone, and was received from the ch. in Camb., and with w. cov. June 13, '73. Their chil. b. in Fram., were, 1. LOIS, b. Sep. 7, '73, m. John Park, M. D. ; 2. ANNE, b. Jan. 18, '76, m. Rev. Nicholas B. Whitney, of Hingham. The f. was ord. minister of Acton, June 25, '77 ; where he had, 3. MOSES, b. Nov. 28, '77, (H. C. 1797), m. Mary L. Tuttle, of Littleton ; 4. NABBY, b. Jan. '80, m. Luke Bixby ; 5. JOSIAH, b. Nov. 3, '81, (H. C. 1801), studied law with Tho. Heald, Esq., and was adm. to the bar, June 1807, m. Jane Park, of Windham, N. H., and settled as a lawyer in Fram. He has been a member of the Executive Council, and chairman of the Hon. Board of Co. Commissioners ; 6. JOSEPH, b. Sep. 25, '83, (H. C. 1803), lawyer at W. Camb., m. Almira Fiske, d. June 10, 1814 ; 7. CLARISSA, b. July 13, '85, m. Caleb Hersey, of Hingham. The Rev. Moses d. Oct. 13, 1819, æ. ab. 70 ; his w. d. Dec. 7, 1812, æ 63.

7. BULKLEY, (s. of John), came to Fram. fr. Lincoln, and m. Persis Stone, Feb. 1785.

The Adams family have been numerous in Medfield, Sherb., and Holl. BENJAMIN, and w. Persis, were of Marlb., 1732.

AIERS, NATHANIEL, was taxed in Fram., ab. 1705.

ALEXANDER, BATHSHEBAH, m. Nathan Kazer, both of Fram., July, 1778.

Families of this name occur on the Marlb. Rec., as early as 1749.

ALLEN, OBADIAH and w. cov. in Fram., Sep. 16, 1722.

OBADIAH, (prob. their s.), was bap. Aug. 4, 1723. JAMES, was rated in Fram., 1758.

Obad. was g. g. son of WALTER, of Charlestown, who d. ab. 1681. JOHN, s. of Walter, was of Sud., 1681. JOSEPH, s. of Walter, m. Ann Brazier, 1667, and had in Wat., *Abigail*, b. 1668; *Rebeckah,* '70; *Hannah*, '74; *Joseph*, '77. DANIEL, s. of Walter, d. in Sud., ab. 1706. His chil. were, *Samuel*, w. Abigail; *Thomas*, b. 1670; *Ebenezer*, b. 1674; *Elizabeth*, m. Jos. Fletcher; *Mary*; *Abigail*, m. Moses Palmer, of Stonington; *Lydia*; *Elnathan*, who m. Mercy Rice, and had Obadiah, in Wat. b. Jan. 19, 1694–5; and in Sud., Ann, b. 1702; Israel, '05; Mary, '08; Mary, '11; Thankful, '13. Sud. Rec. bear the names of many descendants from Walter.

ALLERD, ISAAC, was in Fram. before 1750. He built the Tho. Stone house, wh. he sold to Tho. Coller. He rem. to Southb. His chil. were, 1. ISAAC; 2. ELIZABETH, m. Jos. Comings of Southb., Sep. 11, '53; 3. LOIS.

2. ISAAC, s. of Isaac, (1), m. Lois Pike, Mar. 17, 1752, cov. Sep. 9, '53. Their chil. were, 1. ANDREW, b. May 6, '53; 2. ISAAC, (one of whose sons became a physician).

3. ANDREW, s. of Isaac, Jr., (2), m. Zerviah Haven, 1774; and had, 1. ISAAC, b. Sep. 26, '75; 2. ANDREW, b. Feb. 23, '78. The f. moved to Holden, and d. in the Rev. War. His wid., Zerviah, returned to Fram., and m. Joseph Frail, of Hop., Nov. 25, 1784.

Roxbury Rec.; Goodwife Allard, a French-woman, d. Aug. 11, 1717.

ALMY, ABIGAIL, (b. in Hop.), m. Daniel Knowlton, both of Fram., Feb. 17, 1743.

AMES, NATHAN, s. of Nathan and Mary, b. in Fram, Jan. 13, 1745.

AMSDEN, SILAS, d. in Fram., Feb. 4, 1797.

ANGIER, JOSEPH, the first of the name in Fram., was, perhaps, the Joseph, of Medford, 1684. He was in Dorchester, in 1694; where, by his w. Elizabeth, he had, 1. ELIZABETH, b. Dec. 8, 1694; 2. MARGARET, Mar. 21, '97; 3. JOSEPH^2, June 20, 1702; 4. BENJAMIN^3, June 22, '04; 5. MARY, b. in Fram., Aug. 31, 1709. Jos. the f. settled on "Work Hill," back of Mr. Charles Capen's house. He was, for several years, afflicted with a cancerous complaint, which caused his death. He d. Nov. 30, 1718. His wid. Eliz. d. Jan. 24, 1732.

2. JOSEPH, s. of Jos., (1), m. Elizabeth Bruce, Dec. 16, 1719, and had, 1. JOSEPH, b. May 13, 1721, m. wid. (Judith) Salter, June 16, 1743, and d. Jan. 24, '47; the wid. Judith m.

Andrew Morse, June 26, '55; 2. JOHN⁴, b. Oct. 1, '23; 3. ELIZABETH, b. Feb. 8, 1727–8, d. Feb. 8, '30; 4. ELIZABETH, b. Oct. 20, '30, m. Sam. Stanhope, of Sud., Nov. 6, '55; 5. MARGARET, b. June 25, '33, m. Daniel Hemenway; 6. SAMUEL⁵, b. Mar. 6, 1735; 7. LYDIA, b. May 18, '39, m. Solo. Ward, and lived in Southb.

3. BENJAMIN, s. of Joseph, (1), m. Sarah —, and had, 1. SARAH, b. Sep. 25, 1729; 2. MARY, b. Oct. 24, '31, m. Stephen Harris, of F., May 27, '52; 3. BENJAMIN, b. at Marlb., 1735; 4. SILAS⁶, b. at Marlb., 1737; 5. TIMOTHY, b. in Fram., Feb. 28, '40, m. Mercy Haven, in Hop., '66; 6. JOHN⁷, bap. June 29, '46; 7. SARAH, b. July 24, '47.

4. JOHN, s. of Joseph, (2), m. Bethiah Liscom, in Southb., Feb, 22, 1752. His child. were, 1. CHARLES, b. Sep. 20, 1752, m. Elizabeth Newton, and 2, — Nixon; 2. ANN, b. Aug. 1, '54, m. — Hudson, of Westb., and d. Sep. 18, '85; 3. MOLLY, b. Ap. 10, '56, d. unm. Oct., '79. [These 3 were b. in Fram.; the following in Southb.] 4. LYDIA, b. Jan. 27, '58, m. Deac. — Bragg, of Shrewsbury; 5. JOSEPH, b. June 17, '60, d. '60; 6. JOHN, M. D., b. July 4, 1761, m. ——, practiced in N. H. and Natick, Mass., and d. in Fram., Jan. 1843; 7. ELIZABETH, b. Aug. 12, '63, d. Jan., '69; 8. MITTY, b. Aug. 11, '65, m. — Horn, of Southb., and d. 1843; 9. HANNAH, b. Aug. 18, '67, m. William Taylor; 10. CALVIN, b. Oct. 15, '69, m. Anne Parker; 11. ELIZABETH, b. Ap. 19, '72, m. Zedekiah Haven; 12. LUTHER, b. Aug. 21, '75, m. 1, Anna Mixer, 2d, wid. — Richardson. John, the f., m. a 2 w. Wid. — Hastings, of Stow, and d. Aug. 3, 1793. Bethiah, w. of John, d. Dec. 7, 1779.

5. SAMUEL, s. of Joseph, (2), m. Tabitha Newton, of Southb., and lived on the family estate in F. His chil. were, 1. LEVINAH, b. Sep. 3, 1765, d. Jan. 26, '67; 2. PERSIS, b. Dec. 18, '66, m. Cyrus Woolson, June, '84; 3. JOSEPH⁸, b. June 21, '69. Mr. Samuel d. in Fram., Ap. 21, 1793.

6. SILAS, s. of Benjamin, (3), by w. Elizabeth, had, 1. BENJAMIN, b. May 27, 1762; 2. SYBBIL, b. May 15, '64; 3. SILAS, b. Ap. 19, '66; 4. BETTY, bap. Oct. 1, '69; 5. JOEL, bap. Nov. 4, '70.

7. JOHN, of Fram., (prob. s. of Benj. 3), m. Mary —, and had, 1. MARY, b. July 15, 1766; 2. JOHN, b. Jan. 10, '69.

8. JOSEPH, s. of Samuel, (5), m. Fanny Moore, Sep., 1791; and had 1. ANNA, b. Dec. 5, '91, d. æ. ab. 22; 2. JOSEPH, b. Feb. 25, '94, m. Ruth Bailey. Joseph, the f., d. —; his wid. m. Ephraim Hager, of Fram.

NOTE. After much research by the author, the origin of the first Joseph, of Fram., remains obscure. Edmund, of Camb., had no son Joseph. He (E.) had a br. " Bazall, of Dedham." The chil. named in the settlement of Edmund's estate, 1704, are, SAMUEL, (b. Mar. 17, 1654), minister at Rehoboth and Wat.; RUTH, m. Sam. Cheever; ELIZABETH, m. Jona. Pierpont; MARY, m. John March, 1700; SARAH, m. Rev. Christopher Tappan. Edmund's w. Ruth, who d. 1656, was daughter " of that famous light, Dr. Ames." URIAN, s. of Rev. Samuel, was of Sudbury —.

ARNOLD, WILLIAM, b. in Dedham, came when young to Fram., and m. Mary Morse. Their child. were, 1. JOHN, b. Mar. 24, 1773, d. Oct. 30, '76; 2. NATHAN, b. June 7, '74, d. Nov. 1, '76, (both d. of dysentery, and were buried in 1 coffin); 3. WILLIAM, b. Mar. 12, '76, d. Nov. 1; 4. WILLIAM, b. Oct. 13, '77, killed by an explosion at Ft. Indep., June 28, 1803; 5. NATHAN, b. Jan. 9, '80, lives unm. at Cherryfield, Me.; 6. JOHN, b. July 21, '81, m. Cath. Spink; 7. LEONARD, b. Feb. 4, '83, m. Eliz. Chandler, lives in Fram.; 8. THOMAS, b. Aug. 2, '85, m. Sarah Frost, lives in F.; 9. POLLY, b. July 22, '89, d. Jan. 16, '09; 10. RELIEF, b. Oct. 3, '91, m. Henry Richardson, Esq., lives in F. Wm. the f. d. 1813, æ. 70. Mary, his w. d. 1836, æ. 83.

ARTHUR, JOHN, and w. Abigail had a dr. ABIGAIL, b. May 8, 1722, who m. James Holden, Aug. 25, 1748. Abigail, w. of John, d. May 13, 1722.

PRISCILLA m. in Marlb. Samuel Grant, 1752.

BACON, JOHN, was bap. in Fram., Oct. 19, 1721.

2. JOHN, m. in Natick, Abigail Sawin, 1744; and had 1. JOHN, b. Sep. 18, 1745; 2. ABIGAIL, b. Nov. 5, '47; 3. TIMOTHY, b. Mar. 29, '51; 4. MOSES, bap. in Fram., Oct. 28, '53; 5. DAVID and 6. JONATHAN, bap. in F. Aug. 22, '56; 7. MARY, bap. in F. Aug. 5. '59. These names are all entered on Nat. Rec.

3. WILLIAM, of Nat., s. of Wm. of Dover, m. Keziah, dr. of Abel Perry, and had 1. Keziah, b. Sep. 1780, m. Francis Bacon; 2. ELIZABETH, b. Mar. 7, 1782, m. in Fram. Joseph Buckminster, Ap. 18, '99. Keziah, wid. of William, m. Capt. Thos. Buckminster, of Fram., Feb. 1794.

The Bacons have been numerous in Nat. Henry was there in 1744; Stephen, in '43; Henry, in '47; Jerem., in '54. They prob. descended from the Bacons of Wat. and Camb.

BADGER, JOHN, (who prob. lived in the bounds of Nat.) m. Prudence (How?) and with w. cov'd in Fram. Ap. 27, 1759; their chil. bap. in Fram. were, 1. JOHN, bap. Jan. 1, 1764, m. Mary Haynes, ; 2. HEPHZIBAH, Nov. 18, '64, d. unm. in Nat.; 3. PRUDENCE, May 17, '67, m. in Fram. Daniel Trowbridge, June '85; 4. EUNICE and 5. MOLLY, Dec. 5, '73. MOLLY m. —— Wadkins of Hop.

BADLAM, EZRA, was in Fram. 1764.

BAILEY, PRISCILLA, m. Jonathan Underwood, both of Fram., Jan. 22, 1740.

2. JOSEPH, (s. of Daniel and w. Rebeckah, bap. at Hop. 1760), m. in Nat., Mary Kendall, 1788, lived in Dublin, N. H. and Nat., and moved into Fram. ab. 1798. Jos. d. 1817, æ 57.

NOTE. — Richard and w. Grace of Sud. 1756.

BAKER, NATHAN and w. Mary, cov'd in Fram. Ap. 3, 1774. MARTYN, s. of do., bap. Ap. 24, '74.

BALCH, PETER, m. in Medford, Elizabeth Dwight, 1725, was in Fram. ab. 1740, and lived on the farm now of Adam Hemenway, Esq. He was Selectman (1744), and Dea. of the church, and held in much esteem. His chil. were 1. TIMOTHY, d. Feb. 7, 1741 ; 2. SARAH, m. John Pike of Fram. ; 3. ELIZABETH, m. Daniel Adams, of Fram., Sep. 22, 1748. Deac. Peter owned land in Sturbridge, and d. in F. Dec. 27, '55, (Rec. ; 56, g. stone), æ. 70. He left a negro servant Flora.

NOTE. — The origin of Dea. Balch we have failed of discovering, unless he was a descendant of John of Beverly, memb. of Salem ch. 1626, who came from Bridgewater, Somertsh., Eng. Dea. Benj. of Beverly, who m. Sarah Newmarch, 1675, had a son Peter.

BALL, BENJAMIN, came to Fram. and settled near Salem end; m. Mary Brewer, Mar. 29, 1704. His chil. b. in Fram. were, 1. BENJAMIN, b. Dec. 17, 1704 ; 2. JOHN, b. July 16, 1706, m. Margaret Hemenway, 1734, and had in Hop. *Lydia,* bap. 1737 ; *John,* '39 ; *Benj.*; '44 ; *Abraham,* '47 ; *Benjamin,* '49 ; *Abigail,* '54 ; 3. ABRAHAM, b. Dec. 29, 1707, m. Martha Bridges, of Fram., Jan. 13, '32, and had in Holl. *Lois,* b. 1732 ; *Sarah,* and *Mary,* twins, b. 34 ; *Martha,* '37 ; *Bathshebah,* '40 ; 4. JACOB[4], b. May 28, 1712 ; 5. THOMAS[2], b. Aug. 16, 1714 ; 6. MARY, b. Feb. 11, 1716-7, m. William Wright of Fram. Jan. 22, '37-8 ; 7. ABIGAIL, b. Feb. 16, 1719-20, m. Simon Mellen Jun. of Fram. Ap. 27, '42 ; 8. DANIEL[3], b. Dec. 29, 1722.

2. THOMAS, s. of Benj. (1), m. Hannah Wright of Fram. Feb. 17, 1739-40, and had HANNAH, b. Mar. 19, '40.
3. DANIEL, s. of Benj. (1), m. Patience Gleason of F., Aug. 25, 1748, cov'd July 23, '49, and had, DANIEL, b. Ap. 9, '49; ABIGAIL, b. Mar. 4, '50.
4. JACOB, s. of Benj. (1), m. in Sud., Deborah Belknap of F., Jan. 9, 1749; Deb. the w. adm. to the ch. of F. Ap. '53. Their chil. in F. were SHADRACH, b. Feb. 4, 1749; SAM., May 8, '52.

NOTE. — JOSEPH, of Southb. m. Bathshebah Bellows, May 6, 1731, and had *Betty*, '32; *Joseph*, '34; *Lydia*, '36; *Lucy*, '38; *Prudence*, '39. ISAAC, of Holl. m. Rachel How, of Marlb. 1738. MARGARET, of Hop. (prob. wid. or dr. of John,) m. Tho. Shaddock, 1757. ELIZABETH, of Fram. m. Ephraim Goodnow, of Sud., Feb. 1764. Wid. Sybil Ball's, (prob. from Southb.) real estate tax was abated for 1761-2. (Fram. Rec.) The family of Ball were numerous in Concord and Watertown. John, of Concord, came from Wiltshire, England, and was made free 1650, d. Nov. 1, 1655. Farmer.

BALLARD, or BALLORD. The Ballards of Fram. prob. sprung from WILLIAM,* who (then æ. 32) came over in the James, 1634, with Elizabeth, æ. 26; HESTER, æ. 2; Jo. (JOHN) æ. 1. Mr. Lewis states that William was a farmer, and lived on the Boston road, W. of Saugus river, was admitted freeman, 1638, (May 2), and in the same year was a member of the Quarterly Court at Salem. He adds, that his chil. were John, Nathaniel, and Elizabeth.† Before Mar. 1, 1641, William of Lynn, had deceased, making a nuncupative will, by which he gave half of his estate to his w. and half to his chil. (the names of neither being given). Suff. Prob. B. 1.‡

2. JOHN, s. of William, had at Lynn, 1. SARAH, b. 1669; 2. REBECCA,

---

*Farmer supposes William of Lynn to have removed to Andover. A William took the freeman's oath, May 18, 1631, three years before W. of Lynn came over. William, Sen. of Andover, d. 1689, his inventory, (£206.18.6,) dated Oct. 23; and his est. was settled Sept. 28, 1691. He left a w. Grace; his sons were *Joseph, William* and *John*; the other *heirs* in the settlement were Samuel and Joseph Buterfield, John Spalden, and Abigail Ballard.

† Hist. of Lynn, p. 25. Mr. Lewis supposes Elizabeth to have married George Abbot. We find the marriage, in Andover, of Elizabeth with Geo. Abbot, 1689. On the Charlestown Records, " Elizabeth of Lynn," m. Allen Bread, 1684. Both dates are late for a dr. of William, Sen.

‡ An inventory of William, "formerly of Linn, decd." is recorded at Ipswich, dated Oct. 1, 1695, John,

s. of deceased, being admr. In 1697, John, s. of Wm., divided with his br. Nathaniel, his father's est., and in 1721 gave a deed of certain lands to his own s. John. On the birth registries, both at Salem and Lynn, the earliest entries of Ballards are, of the chil. of Nathaniel, beginning in 1666; of William, in 1668; of John, in 1669. The William was perhaps another son of William, Sen., of Lynn. It is hardly probable that he removed to Andover, as there are entries there of chil. of William, in 1655. The will of a William, of Charlestown, is dated July 5, 1679; he left, prob., no male issue; but names his dr. Elizabeth Collier, of Woodbridge, N. J., and her sister, Mary Hodley, late Farrington.

Tradition assigns Wales as the origin of the Ballards. This family name is numerous at Worcester, in England.

b. 1671; 3. JANE, b. 1674; 4. JOHN, Shipwright and Deacon, at Lynn, his will dated Jan. 21, 1765; f. by w. Sarah, of *John; William*, (who d. at Lynn, ab. 1794, f. of John, b 1751, m. Mary Newhall, and d. in Boston, 1824, and Sarah, m. —— Bancroft, and 2d, John Stocker); *Sarah*, b. 1704, m. —— Duglass; *Rebecca*, m. Thomas Berry, of Boston; *Ebenezer*, b. 1716, (f. of Mary, Ebenezer, and John); *Martha*, m. John Work; *Jane*. m. Dea. John Lewis; and *Mary*, m. Eph. Rhodes; 5. PRISCILLA, b. 1680; 6 WILLIAM, b. and d. 1683; 7. DOROTHY, b. 1684. [Sal. Rec. John m. Susanna Story, 1681]

3. NATHANIEL of Lynn, s. of William, had by w. Rebeckah, 1. MARY, b. 1666, m. Dea. Moses Haven, of Fram.; 2. NATHANIEL, b. '70, d. '72; 3 SUSANNA, b. '73; 4. ELIZABETH, b. '75, prob. unm. 1722; 5. HESTER, b. '77; 6. SARAH, b. '81; 7. ABIGAIL, b. '83; 8. JEMIMA,(Sal. Rec. '83); 9. WILLIAM[4], b. Ap. 23, '86; 10. NATHANIEL, b. —, d. 1733. Nathaniel the f. d. at Lynn, Jan. 12, 1721–2; his w. Rebeckah d. May 16, 1724. (Sal. & Lynn R.)

4. WILLIAM, s. of Nath'l (3), had at Lynn by his first w., 1. WILLIAM[5]; 2. SAMUEL[6]; he then m. 2d Deborah Ivory, Oct. 17, 1721 (Lynn Rec.) and was adm'd to the ch. in Fram. Mar. 17, 1728, where he had 3. MARY, b. July 27, 1722, m. Richard Seaver of Roxb. Nov. 13, '45; 4. NATHANIEL, b. July 17, '23, lived S. from David Fiske's, and d. in F. ab. Aug. 1767, when his wid. Abigail administered on his est.; 5. EBENEZER, b. Aug. 30, '24, prob. d. young; 6. STEPHEN, b. Mar. 4, '25–6, m. Margaret Atwood of Holl. Feb. 7, '49; 7. JOHN[9], b. Aug. 26, '27; 8. ESTHER, b. Jan. 17, '29–30; 9. TIMOTHY, and 10. ZACHEUS[11], twins, b. Mar. 21, '30–1; 11. SILVANUS[10], b. Feb. 10, '32–3; 12. JOSEPH, m. Betsey Valentine of Hop., and lived at Sugar Creek, Penn. William the f. lived on the place now of Mr. Joseph Ballard, was Selectman 1728, and 1736, and d. Oct. 8. 1771, in his 86th year.

5. WILLIAM, Jun., s. of Wm. (4), m. Hannah Peirce, Aug. 25, 1741, and had, 1. BEULAH, m. Samuel Ballard; 2. ANNE, m. Ephraim Pratt, and lived in F. and N. Y.; 3. ESTHER, m. Jona. Flagg, Jun. and d. in Fram., 1844; 4. Ebenezer, d. unm. in Fram.; 5 SARAH, m. —— Chandler, Esq., in Oxford, and lived in Woodstock, Con. Wm. the f. was a miller; his house was destroyed by fire 1797; he d. Dec. 1802, at an advanced age.

6. SAMUEL, s. of Wm., (4), m. —— Pickering, and had, in Boston, 1. WILLIAM, b. June 13, 1741; 2. SAMUEL[7]; 3. EBENEZER, d. unm. in Brookfield; 4. —— m. Col. —— Pope, of N. Bedford. Samuel, the f. d. in Boston, ab. 1793.

7. SAMUEL, s. of Sam. (6), m. Beulah Ballard, and had in Boston, 1. ELIZABETH, m. Matthew Stone, of Fram.; 2. SUSAN, m. John Dinsdale, and 2d —— Gurney; 3 .SARAH, m. Benj.

Fletcher, of Chelmsford ; 4. NANCY, d. unm. in Hop. Sam. the
f. m. 2d, Rebecca Minzy, and had, 5. ABIGAIL, m. —— Philips,
of Medway ; 6. REBECCA, m. — Jones, of Randolph ; and in Fram.
7. HARRIET ; 8. MARY, d. unm. in F., ab. 1832 ; 9. CHARLOTTE,
d. unm. in F. ; 10. WILLIAM, d. in F. æ. ab. 9. Samuel the f.
moved to Fram. after 1790, where he d. 1803 ; when his family
removed to Dorchester.

8. WILLIAM, s. of Sam. (6), m. first, Sarah Sears, and
had 1. BETSEY, d. 1785 æ. ab. 18; 2. SARAH, d. young;
3. SARAH, d. young; 4. WILLIAM, d. young; 5. a dr. d.
young. The m. d. 1773, æ. ab. 30, and Wm. m. 2d, Anne
Marshall, and had, 6. WILLIAM, b. July 6, 1776, H. Coll. 1799, a
Physician, m. Eliza Moores, and d. in F. 1827, the author of
a historical sketch of the town ; 7. MEHETABEL, b. Aug. 26. 1777,
m. Benj. K. Hager, Oct. 6 '96, lives in Baltimore ; 8. EBENEZER
MARSHALL, b. Nov. 1779, m. Sukey Fisk, Ap. 16, 1804, and d. in
F. Jan. 1823 ; 9. SAMUEL, b. Aug. 27, 1781, m. Abi Wright, 2d,
wid. Lucy How, 3d, wid. Nancy Ash ; 10, JOHN, b. Feb. 1783, m.
Elizabeth Jones, and 2d, Abigail Torrey ; 11. JOSEPH, b. Mar. 1784,
m. Hannah Fisk ; Justice of the Peace, lives at Brighton ; 12.
SALLY SEARS, bap. Dec. 1787, m. John H. Jones of Hop. ; 13.
MARY COTTON, bap. May, 1789, m. Nath'l Munroe ; 14. ELIZA,
m. Samuel Curtis of Boston. William the f. d. June 13, 1818,
æ. 77 ; Anne his w. d. Mar. 29, 1807, æ. 58.

9. JOHN, s. of William (4), m. Hephzibah Hemenway of F.
May 27, 1752 ; and had in Fram. 1. ——, d. '53 ; 2. JOSHUA, b.
Ap. 14, '54, m. in Athol, Anne Raymond, June 15, '75 ; 3.
JOHN, bap. Nov. 20, '57 ; (the foll. on Athol Rec.), 4. JOHN, b.
Oct. 13, '59, d. at Fort George, '76 ; 5. MOLLY, b. Ap. 19, '62,
m. —— Gregory, Esq. John the f. was Deacon of the ch. at
Athol. His w. Hephzibah d. at A. June 3, 1811, æ. 83.

10. SILVANUS, s. of William (3), m. Judith Boyden, in F.
May 7, 1755. He lived in the Cooledge house. His chil. were
1. TIMOTHY, b. Mar. 31, 1756, m. Keziah Bullard, Dec. 30, '78 ;
Keziah m. 2d. —— Legg, of Upton ; 2. SILVANUS, b. Aug. 10,
'58 ; 3. MARY, b. Aug. 31, '61 ; 4. JUDITH, b. May 20, '63 ; 5.
BENJAMIN, b. Ap. 29, '65 ; 6. REBECKAH, bap. Oct. 4, '72, m.
Ezekiel Kendall. Silvanus the f. d. in Fram.

11. ZACCHEUS s. of William (4), m. Elizabeth Cloyes, and

lived near Shepard's Paper Mill. His chil. were 1. ELIZABETH G. b. May 20, 1759; 2. WILLIAM, b. Oct. 26, '61, m. —— Haven, and d. in F. 1791, f. of William, Nancy, &c; 3. SARAH, b. Jan. 5, '64; 4. MARY, b. Aug. 8, '65; 5. MEHETABEL, b. May 31, '67; 6. MARTHA, b. Ap. 16, '69; all in Fram. The foll. in Oxford; 7. LYDIA, 1774; 8. ALICE, '79. Zaccheus d. prob. in Fram.
12. ANNE, was b. in Fram. Oct. 30, 1779. EBENEZER, was a hatter in Fram. 1764.

BANCROFT, NATHANIEL and w. Mehetabel, of F., had NATHANIEL, b. Oct. 15, 1748.

BANISTER, Maj. BARZILLAI, s. of Joseph and Mary of Brookfield, b. Feb. 4, 1750, m. Deborah Cushman, from Conn.; and had in Goshen, Mass., 1. IRENE; 2. DOLLY; 3. twins, d. young; 5. TRYPHENA, m. in Fram. Amos Parmenter, Ap. 8, 1798; 6. SOPHIA; 7. DEBORAH; 8. ABIGAIL; 9. LUCY. Deborah w. of Barz. d. in F. Aug. '97. B. m. in Fram. a 2d w. Nancy Fairbanks, Ap. 23, '98. Maj. B. came to Fram. ab. 1792; lived on the farm of Mr. Aaron Bullard, and afterwards kept a store.

2. JOSEPH, s. of Nathan of Boylston, and neph. of Maj. B. (1), m. Elizabeth, dr. of Dr. Elijah Stone, of Fram., left F. with Zedekiah Sanger for the Mohawk, Jan. 13, '94. His wid. and a dr. EVELINE returned to F. after Jo.'s death, and her dr. Eveline d. in F. Aug. 11, 1830, æ. 29. Elizabeth, w. of Joseph, d. in F. Feb. 3, 1833, æ 67.

Note.—CHRISTOPHER, of Marlb., 1657, d. ab. 1679. He m. Jane Goodnow, dr. of Thos., and had *Mary*, b. 1672; *Joseph*, '75; *Thomas*, '77. Lt. JOHN, who m. Ruth Eager, 1695, d. July 19, 1730, æ. 59. Lt. John had *John*, b. 1696, d. 1779; *Ruth*, b. '99; *Mary*, 1700; Ruth, '02; *Jane*, '05; *Huldah*, '07; *Martha*, '10; *Sarah*, '13.

BARNARD, BENJAMIN, of Fram., conveyed land to Abraham Nurse, 1768. SARAH of Fram. m. Joshua Gardner, of Sherb., Mar. 16, 1746.

Note.—Benjamin was prob. s. of Benj. and Sarah, of Wat., b. 1694, and in 1705 had for guardian, his uncle, Paul Wentworth, of Rowley. He m. (then of Hop.) in Wat., 1726, Mary Wellington. Mary was adm. to Hop. Ch., and dr. *Sarah* bap. 1728. ROBERT, (and w. Reb.), of Marlb., 1724, m. 2d w. Elizabeth Bayley, '29. BENJAMIN and w. Lucy, of Marlb, 1738. JAMES, of Sud., divided the Bruswicke, or Horsecraft farm, with f. in-law, Sam. Jenison, of Wat., 1699. JOHN, of Wat., d. 1646.

BARRET, JONATHAN and w. Mehetabel, of Fram., had 1. BENJAMIN, b. Oct. 25., 1726; 2. NATHAN, b. June 18, '31,

d. May 20, '57; 3. SARAH, b. Nov. 6, '33, d. Nov. 2, 1815, unm; 4. JOSEPH, and 5. AMOS, b. Sep. 10, '36; 6. JAMES, b. Jan. 14, '38–9; 7. prob. ABIGAIL, m. Moses Hayden of Sud. Ap. 1. '63. Jona. the f. lived beyond Mr. Eph. Hager's.

2. JOSEPH, s. of Jona. (1), cov'd and was bap. in F. Jan. 7, 1759, and his dr. HANNAH was bap. Ap. 21, '59. JOSEPH and w. Abigail of Sud. (prob. the same), had NATHAN, b. 1759; JOSEPH, b. '61. Joseph the f. was in the Rev. service, 1777, then prob. of Fram.

3. HEPHZIBAH (prob. dr. of Tho. and Eliz. of Marlb., b. 1708), m. in F. Eleazer How, Jan. 26, '31–32.

Note.—The origin of Jonathan is unknown, unless he was the Jona. s. of Jona. and Abigail, of Reading, b. 1705. James, of Malden, (s. of James, the f. æ. 36, 1653). had *John*, 1675; and *Jonathan*, b. '78. A James was of Sud., 1683. JOHN, prob. s. of Humphrey, of Concord, m. Mary Pond, in Sud., Sep. 1656, and d. in Marlb., July, 1711, leaving a s. *John*, who m. Deborah How, 1688. THOMAS and w. Lydia, from Camb., were in Marlb., 1670. JAMES and w. Tabitha, of Sherb., had a dr. *Sarah*, 1736. Rev. SAMUEL, of Hop., d. 1772, æ. 72. GEORGE and w. Mary, were of Hop., and had *Maning*, 1731; *George*, '33; *James*, '35; *Thornton*, bap. '40.

BARTON, SAMUEL, of Fram. and w. Hannah, had 1. SAMUEL, b. Oct. 8, 1691, m. Elizabeth Bellows of Marlb., May 23, 1715; 2. MERCY, b. May 22, '94, m. —— Town; 3. JOSHUA, b. Dec. 24, '97; 4. ELISHA, b. Ap. 22, 1701; 5. CALEB, b. Feb. 9, '04–5, m. 1st, Mary ——, who d. '47, m. 2d, Susanna March, '48, (Oxf. Rec.), and had *Abraham*, '50, and *Jacob*, '52; 6. JEDIDIAH, b. Sep. 18, '07, m. Lydia ——, and f. at Oxf. of *Abraham*, b. '32; *Isaac*, '40; 7. MEHETABEL, b. Aug. 22, '10, m. Sam. Dunkin, and d. in Worc. '42, æ. 32; 8. EDMUND, b. Aug. 5, '14. Samuel, the f. lived beyond Mr. Wm. Temple's, was dism. to the ch. in Oxford, Jan. 15, '21. His will was proved, Sep. 23, '32.

Note. MATTHEW and w. Sarah, of Salem, had *Matthew*, 1682. JAMES, of Boston, ropemaker, 1690. JAMES, prob. of Newton, 1697. TIMOTHY, of Southb., m. Hepsibah Stow, Oct., 1753.

BATT. A family of this name is reputed to have lived, anciently, where is a cellar hole, N. side of the Southb. road, E. of Mr. Dan. Hemenway's.

Note.—WILLIAM, of Sud., who m. Mehetable Warren, Wat., 1735, had dr. *Beulah*, b. 1739. SARAH, of Southb., m. John Pannel, 1737. JOHN m. Mary Farwell, at Chelmsford, 1665.

BEARD, JAMES, cov. in Fram., Sep. 30, 1722. MARY, bap. Sep. 20, 1724.

BEHONY, PETER, w. and children " warned out of Fram." 1732; living in Fram. 1747.

BELCHER, ANDREW, of Sud., m. Elizabeth Danforth, dr. of Nicholas, Oct. 1, 1639, and had, in Sud., 1. ELIZABETH, b. Aug. 27, 1640; 2. JEMIMA, b. April 5, '42; 3. MARTHA, born July 26, '44. In 1645, And. the f. sold his house, land, and rights, in Sud., to John Goodnow, and had at Camb., 4. ANNA, b. ——; 5. ANDREW, b. Jan. 1, '47. 2. 1673, Tho. Danforth conveyed " to his loving kinsman," ANDREW, Jr., (s. of preceding), 150 ac. of land, (in Fram.), bounded S. by John Stone, N. by the path to Marlb., (the most S'ly path), E. and W. by land of Thos. Danforth. According to Farmer, Andrew, Jr., was father of Gov. Jonathan Belcher. In 1682, Andrew of Camb. was entitled mariner.*

3. JONATHAN,† m. Hannah Seaver, was of F., tailor, 1732; and had 1. JONATHAN; 2. DANIEL, b. June 14, 1736 (Sud. Rec.); 3. HANNAH, b. Mar. 10, '43, d. young; 4. ANDREW, b. June 16, '48, d. young; 5. JOSEPH, bap. July, '55; 6. EZRA, m. Susanna Dadmun, Mar. 18, '94, and d. 1826, æ. 75; 7 SHUBAEL, d. young. Jona. the f. lived in Fram., on the N. path to Marlb.; his descendants live on the S. He d. 1787, æ. over 80. Hannah his w. d. 1796, æ. 84.

4. JONATHAN, s. of Jona. (3), m. Sarah Hartshorn, of Walpole. His chil. were 1. JACOB; 2. JOHN; 3. MOLLY; 4. HANNAH, m. Ephraim Pratt, June, 1788. Jona. the f. m. a 2d wife, and moved to E. Hartford.

5. DANIEL, s. of Jona. (3), m. Hannah Winch, and had 1. DANIEL; 2. JASON, m. Anne Winch, Nov. 9, 1800; 3. BETSEY, d. young. Daniel the f. d. Nov., 1787; and his wid. m. Benj. Dudley.

6. JOSEPH, s. of Jona. (3), m. Hannah Kendall, May, 1782. Their chil. were 1. MARY, b. Feb. 6, '83, m. Stephen Lord, Vt.; 2. MARTHA, b. Dec. 26, '86; 3. JOSEPH, b. June 21, '88, d. 1828; 4. HANNAH, b. Mar. 28, '91; 5. THOMAS, b. Sep. 3, '93, d. 1821; 6. CURTIS, b. June 1, '96, d. 1814; 7. ELIZABETH, b. Ap. 11, 1800. Joseph the f. d. 1833, æ. 78. His wid. was living 1845.

7. JACOB, s. of Jona. Jun. (4), m. Anne Rice, Mar., 1782. Their chil. were 1. REBECKAH; 2. JOHN, d. unm. in Brighton,

---

* JONATHAN of Boston, and w. Mary, had *Andrew*, b. Nov. 7. 1706; *Sarah*, April 22, '08; *William*, April 12, '12; *Thomas*, May 14, '13.

† March 12, 1721-2, guardianship was ordered of the chil. of RICHARD, of Charlestown, deceased, whose wid. Ruth, m. — Harris; viz. of JONATHAN, æ. 15; JOSEPH, æ. 13; MARY, æ. 9; RUTH, æ. 5; DANIEL, æ. 3; RICHARD, oldest son, had administration. (Mid. Prob.)

1838, æ. 54; 3. SARAH; 4. WILLIAM, d. unm. 1824, æ. 31. Anne the m. d. 1838, æ. 78.

8. JOHN, s. of Jona. Jun. (4), m. Hannah Williams, (Rec.; the family give her name Sarah), June, 1787. Their children were BENJAMIN; JONATHAN; JOHN; CHARLES; NANCY, m. Rufus Walkup; SARAH; ALMIRA.

BELKNAP. Of the original representatives of this family, ABRAHAM was of Lynn, 1637, d. in Salem, 1643, (Farmer), f. of ABRAHAM and JEREMIAH (Lewis). JOSEPH was of Salem, 1644. (S. Rec.) 2. SAMUEL and w. Sarah, had at Salem, 1. MARY, b. 1658; 2. ABRAHAM, b. June 4, '60; 3. SAMUEL, b. May 1, '62; and at Haverhill, 4. JOSEPH, b. March 25, '72, d. '72; 5. PATIENCE, b. Sep. 17, '75. Sarah, w. of Samuel, d. at Hav., April 18, '89.

3. ABRAHAM, s. of Samuel (2), m. at Hav. Elizabeth Ayer, 1691. Their children recorded at Hav. were, 1. MARY, b. Oct. 21, '91, m. Benj. Nurse, of Fram., (2d w.), June, 1737; 2. HANNAH, b. Jan. 13, '94-5; at Reading, 3. SAMUEL, b. Nov. 19, '93, d. Jan. 30, '94-5; 4. ABRAHAM, b. July 28, '95; at Fram., 5. SAMUEL, b. June 19, '97, d. June 2, 1716; 6. ELIZABETH, b. Jan. 21, 1700-1, m. Robert Campbell; 7. JEREMIAH, b. June 8, 1704; 8. NATHANIEL, b. Sep. 22, '06; 9. JEDIDIAH, b. Nov. 4, '09; 10. THANKFUL, b. Aug. 15, '14, m. William Rogers; 11. EXPERIENCE, b. and d. June 7, '17. Abr. the f. lived where is a cellar hole, on the farm of Luther B. Esq. He d. ab. 1728; and in his will gave £10 for the poor of the town. His w. Elizabeth d. ab. 1730.

4. ABRAHAM, Jun., s. of Ab. (3), a tailor, m. Abigail Bigelow, Mar. 8, 1727. Their chil. were, 1. SAMUEL, b. Mar. 17, '28; 2. ABIGAIL,* b. Sep. 25, '29. Abraham (probably the same) m. Mary Brown, Feb. 26, 1740-1, and had by her, CHARLES, b. Feb. 26, '41-2; MARY, bap. May 6, 1751; ISAAC, bap. Ap. 29, '53. Ab. the f. of Natick, d. ab. 1754. (Mid. Prob.)

5. JEDIDIAH, s. of Ab. (3), m. Deborah Streeter, by whom he had 1. DEBORAH, b. July 31, 1732, m. Jacob Ball Jan. 9, '49; 2. EBENEZER, m. Silence Winch; 3. MARY, b. Jan. 16, '34, m. Richard Tozer, of Southb., Feb. 14, '53; 4. HEZEKIAH, m. in Worc., and d. Wethersfield, Vt.; 5. JEDIDIAH, b. Aug. 29, '37, d. unm.; 6. ELIZABETH, b. Feb. 8, '39, m. Benj. Allen, Holden; 7. STEPHEN, bap. Oct. 4, '47, m. Ruth Eaton, lived at Roxb. a tailor, lame, and with w. returned to Fram., ab. '1786; 8. Jo-

seph, bap. May 21, '50, m. Olive Glazier, d. Wethersfield, Vt. Jedidiah the f. was lame, as were some of his posterity.

6. NATHANIEL, s. of Abr. (3), m. Sarah ——, and had 1. ESTHER, b. Aug 23, 1734, d. June 8, '41 ; 2. BENJAMIN, b. Mar. 27, '38, d. June 1, '41 ; 3. ABRAHAM ; 4. NATHANIEL, b. May 20, '40, d. May 20, '41 ; 5. DAVID, b. May 13, '42 ; 6. SARAH, b. Jan. 28, '43, m. —— Brigham, Wcstb. ; 7. ESTHER, b. Aug. 10, '46 ; 8. NATHANIEL, b. Sept. 22, '48, lived in Dublin ; 9. HANNAH, b. Dec. 17, '50, m. David Chambers '81, lived at Bolton ; 10. MITTY, b. June 16, '57. Nathaniel the f. had dec. before '62, His wid. m. again and more than once.

7. JEREMIAH, s. of Abr. (3), m. Mary Pratt, Aug. 10, '32, who d. —, and he m. Hannah, wid. of Rich. Rice, Nov. 30, '38, by whom he had, 1. JEREMIAH, b. Sept. 19, '39 ; 2. MARTHA, b. June 23, '45, d. young ; 3. ELIAS, b. Apr. 26, '49, d. young. Capt. Jeremiah was Selectman 3 years, and d. Dec. 7, '74. Hannah, his w. d. Sept. 21, '74, æ. 60 y. 2 m. 23 ds.

8. JEREMIAH, Jun., s. of Jere. (7), m. Hephzibah Stone, and had, 1. MARY, b. Oct. 9, 1761, m. John Jones, d. '98 ; 2. MARTHA, b. Aug. 2, '63, m. Jotham Haven, d. May 5, 1838 ; 3. JESSE, b. June 6, '65 ; 4. HEPHZIBAH, b. Jan. 24, '67, m. Jos. How of Sud., d. Oct. 1842 ; 5. LUTHER, b. May 7, '69, m. 1. Susannah Gates, Dec. '93, who d. July 27, '97 ; m. 2. Zibah Brown, of Sud., Mar. '99. (Luther, Esq. has been 22 years a Selectman, 17 y. T. Clerk, 4 y. a Representative, and held a Justice's commission) ; 6. DANIEL, b. Feb. 9, '71, m. Mary Parker, of Carlisle ; 7. ENOCH, b. July 7, '73, m. Ruth Luke, Oct. 29, '97 ; 8. RUTHY, (and a twin who d. young), b. Feb. 12, '79, m. Sam. Case ; 9. SALLY, b. Oct. 15, '81, m. Nath. Prentiss, of Holl. Apr. 12, 1801. Capt. Jerem. lived on the place now of his s. Luther, Esq., was a Selectman 2 years, d. May 26, '16, æ. 76. His wid. d. Sept. 24, '20, æ. 79.

9. ABRAHAM, s. of Nathaniel (6), m. Ursula Messenger, of Wrenth., by whom he had, 1. ANNE, b. Aug. 22, 1764, m. Jona. Rice, Apr. '82 ; 2. LEVINAH, b. Sept. 2, '67, d. unm. ; 3. NELLY, bap. Oct. 15, '70, m. Abel Rice ; 4. JOSHUA, b. Aug. 27, '75, d. unm. ; 5. ELISHA, b. Sept. 1, '81, m. Miliscent Frost, Dec. 16, 1804. Mr. Abraham d. June 12, 1805, æ. 67. Ursula, his wid. d. ab. 1807, æ. 72.

10. JESSE, s. of Jere. (8), m. Sybil Sawtel, July, 1788, and had, 1. JESSE, b. Dec. 19, '88; 2. JOSEPH, b. May 30, '90; 3. PERSIS STONE, b. Jan. 25, '92; 4. FRANCIS, bap. May, '95; 5. HARRY, bap. Jan, '97. Jesse, the f. d. May 31, 1834.

Note.—JEREMIAH m. Martha Rug, 1727. (Lanc. Rec.) JOHN m. Ruth Farr, 1736. (Southb. Rec.)

BELLOWS, THOMAS, of Marlb. m. Martha Maveric of Fram., May 29, 1716; cov. in F. Sept. 15, '17; had in Marlb. 1. ELIAS, b. May 12,'17, bap. in Fram. Sept. 5; 2. MARGARET, b. Oct. 16, '18, bap. in F. April, '19, and prob. d. in Fram. 1788; 3. ESTHER, b. Jan. 25, '20–1, bap. in Fram. April, '21; 4. LYDIA, b. Southb. April 30, '22; 5. ZERUIAH, b. Marlb. Jan. 15, '22–3, bap. in Fram. July, '24; 7. MARTHA, b. Marlb. Dec. 26, '24; 8. KEZIAH, b. Hop. March 15, '27, m. in Fram. Moses Parker, April 3, '47; 9. THOMAS, b. Southb. Feb. 28, '31–2; 10. ABIGAIL, b. do. March 6, '34; 11. MAVERIC, b. Hop. '35; 12. JAMES, b. do. '36.

Note.—JOHN, sen., of Marlb., (Farmer says from Concord), m. Mary Woods, and had *Isaac*, 1663, d. ab. 1746; *John*, '66; *Thomas*, '68; *Eliezur*, '71; *Daniel*, '73; *Nathaniel*, '76. (at Concord); and *Samuel*, who d. 1680. John, sen., d. 1683. His s. Eliezur was f. by w. Esther, of *Thomas*, b. Sept. 30, 1693. The posterity of John have been numerous in Marlb. and Southb.

BEMIS, ELISHA, m. Anna Newton, of Southb., had 1. ELIJAH, b. June 25, 1778, m. Sally Woolson, Oct. 9, 1805; 2. JOSEPH. E. the f. d. in Southb., 1817, æ. 64.

2. JOSIAH, br. of Elisha (1), m. in Fram. Patty Matthews, April, 1791.

3. SALLY, of Fram. m. Richard Haven, of Lancaster, Nov. 25, 1792.

Note.—PHINEHAS was drafted in Fram., 1778. He was prob. the Phin. of Southb., who by w. Lydia, had *Lydia*, b. Mar. 18, '72. JOSEPH and w. Sarah, were of Wat., 1647. Samuel and w. Sarah, of Sud., 1717.

BENNET, JOSEPH, came from Concord to Fram., m. Mary Swift, and had 1. JOSEPH, b. Jan. 12, 1775, d. April 25, '98; 2. POLLY, b. Feb. 19, '78, m. Abner Wheeler, Dec. 23, '98, d. April 12, 1836; 3. ELAPHAL, b. Nov. 20, '79, m. Perkins Boynton, Nov. 1802; 4. BETSEY, b. Jan. 26, '82; 5. SALLY, b. Aug. 9, '83, m. Isaac Warren; 6. REBECKAH, b. Dec. 25, '85, m. Benj. Wheeler; 7. NATHANIEL SWIFT, b. Jan. 11, '88, m. Hannah B. Wheeler; 8. LUCY, b. Dec. 31, '89, d. unm. Sept. 17,

1835; 9. EBENEZER, bap. Oct. '91, d. '92, of convulsions, caused by a hen flying against a window; 10. PAMELA, b. April 5, '93, m. John Ballard, 2d, of Fram., and now of Athens, O.; 11. JOSEPH, b. May 13, '98, (H. C. 1818), m. Mary Lamson, Pastor at Woburn. Joseph, the f. was sutler in the continental army. He d. Feb. 12, 1816, æ. 64; his wid. Mary, d. Ap. 9, '38, æ. 86.

Note.—JOSIAH and w. Phebe, of Sudb., had *Hannah*, b. 1733; *Keziah*, '35.

BENSON, NERO, (servant of Mr. Swift), m. Dido Dingo, May 26, 1731, and had 1. WILLIAM, b. 1732; 2. ESTHER; and perhaps others. Nero was trumpeter in Capt. Clark's company, 1726, and a legacy to Ebenezer Robie, 1743.

2. WILLIAM, s. of Nero (1), m. Sarah Perry of Sud. (a white woman), by whom he had 1. KATY, b. April 8, 1763, m. Salem Middlesex, alias Peter Salem, Sept. '83; 2. ABEL, b. 1766, m. Rhoda Jahah, dr. of Cæsar J. of Nat., Sept. '84, and d. a revolutionary pensioner, 1846; 3. POLLY, b. '73, m. —— Jonas, in Boston; 4. SALLY, b. '82, d. æ. 18; 5. WILLIAM, d. young. William was at one time owned by Joseph Collins, of Southb. (Fram. Rec). He d. 1790, æ. 62.

BENT, JOHN* came from Penton, Eng., 1638; rec'd. a division of

---

* The mother of John was Agnes. She had a dr. Agnes, who m. 1st, — Barnes, by whom she had *Richard*, and *Elizabeth*, who probably m. Tho. Plimton. After the death of her 1st husband, Agnes, Jr. m. in Eng., Thomas Blanchard. In 1639, (her son John having embarked "within less than a year" previously), Agnes the mother, then aged and infirm, her dr. Agnes and husband, and infant child, with her two children by her former husband, embarked in the "Jonathan," for N. Eng. Agnes the mother, who, before the emigration of her son, lived with him at Penton, had been placed probably at Andover; from whence she "came up to London in a wagon, with the carriers, and was with Tho. Blanchard's family about a month, in London, and there was a gathering among the Christians at (Rugla?) to help them over." Fifteen days out, Agnes, the daughter, died, making a nuncupative will, (afterwards allowed), and "a gathering was made in the ship to help put her child to nurse." But the child d. "shortly after in the ship." Near the Bank of Newfoundland, Agnes, the mother, "fell sick," and continued so. "About the time the ship came to anchor in Boston harbour," she died, and her son-in-law "procured to carry her to shore, to be buried." Thomas Blanchard was of Braintree, 1646, and of "Mystic side, Charlestown," 1651. Elizabeth Plimton was, in 1652, wife of John Rutter, (J. R. then æ. 37). Richard Barnes had, in 1649, for guardian, John Grout. Richard, Sen. d. at Marlb. Jan. 22, 1707-8, having by w. Deborah (Dix), *Deborah, Sarah*, b. 1669, *Edward, Richard*, b. '73, and *Abigail*, b. '83, m. Peter Bent. The above information was derived in part from the files of the Mid. Co. Court, where an action was had by Richard Barnes against his father-in-law, to recover a legacy from his mother. The same files contain a receipt, dated April 12, 1639, for £50, the amount of 9 full and 2 half passages, at £5 each, for passage of Peter Noyes and family; viz. Mr.

182 BENT.

meadow in Sud., 1639, and was selectman, and on the com. to assign timber, 1641. He was one of Maj. Simon Willard's troopers, at Dedham, Nov. 11, 1654, and a Prop. of Marlb., 1656. By his w. Martha, he had 1. PETER, who lived, 1659, at Lanham, m. Elizabeth ——, and had Peter, b. Oct. 15, 1653; Elizabeth, b. '58; Patience; Agnes, b. 61, m. Solo. Johnson, '84; Martha; John, b. '63; Hopestill, b. '72, m. Eliz. Brown, 1701; and Zaccheus, d. '90. (Peter and w. Eliz., of Camb., had John, b. 1676); Peter, the f. of Marlb., d. prob. in Eng., about 1678; 2. JOHN, b. 1635; 3. JOSEPH, b. May 16, 1641, m. Elizabeth ——, and had Elizabeth, b. 1673; and Joseph, '75. The f. was accidentally killed by a pistol shot from Peter, 1675. (Mid. Co. Rec.); 4. AGNES, m. Edward Rice; 5. MARTHA, m. Samuel Howe, 1663, and d. 1680. John, the f. d. in Sud. Sep. 27, 1672. His wid. Martha, d. May 15, 1679.

2. JOHN, Jr., s. of John (1), m. 1st, Hannah Stone, July 1, 1658, and had, 1. HANNAH, b. May, 6, 1661, m. John Adams; 2. JOHN³, b. Nov. 29, '89; 3. DAVID⁴. John the f. m. a 2d w., Martha, dr. of Matth. Rice. He was one of the earliest settlers in Fram.; bought, in 1662, of Henry Rice, land W. side of Cochit. Brook, and in 1683, of Gookin and How, 60 ac. near his own land, all in Fram. He prob. lived where is now a cellar hole, S.E. of Mr. Gibbs' house. John the f. was buried in Fram., Sep. 15, 1717, æ 82.

3. JOHN, s. of John, Jr. (2), m. Hannah Rice, Nov. 15, 1711. His chil. were, 1. MATTHIAS⁸, b. July 2, 1712; 2. HANNAH, b. July 10, '14, m. 1st, Richard Rice, 1734, 2d, Jerem. Belknap, '38; 3. MARTHA, b. Mar. 7, 1719-0, m. Sam. Brewer, Mar. 10, '40, lived at Paxton; 4. JOHN⁶, b. May 4, '30. John the f.'s will was dated 1754. He d. in Fram.

4. DAVID, s. of John, Jun. (2), m. Mary Drury, Jan, 1, 1712-3; and had, 1. JOHN⁵, b. Oct. 22, '13; 2. DAVID, b. Mar. 22, '16-7, d. Aug. 17, '26; 3. MARY, b. Aug. 5, '18, m. David Goodnow, of Sud., '41; 4. LYDIA, b. Ap. 6, '21, m. William Beal, of Natick, '39; 5. SARAH, b. Jan. 12, '26-7, m. Bezaleel Rice, Mar. 13, '51; 6. DAVID, (posthumous), b. Mar. 30, '30, m. 1st, Lucy Moore, '51, 2d, Martha Browning, and had chil. in Rutland, where he d. Feb. 15, '98, æ 67. David the f. lived on the now Gibbs farm, and d. Feb. 15, 1729-0.

Noyes, John Waterman, Nicholas, Dorothy and Abigail Noyes, William Stret, Peter Noyes, Anis Bent, Eliz. Plimton, Rich'd Barnes, Agnes Blanchard. The following persons came in the same ship, (the Jonathan), their age estimated in 1652: Thomas Gould, æ. 45; Sam. Hide, æ. 42; Frances, w. of Goodman Cooke, of Charlestown, æ. 44; Mark Hums, of Boston, æ. 33; Anthony Somerby, of Newbury, and Nicholas Noyes, also of Newbury, 1653. Peter Noyes appears to have lived in the neighborhood of John Bent, in England.

5. JOHN, s. of David (4), m. Elizabeth Reed, of Sud., 1737, and rem. his father's house to where Mr. Gibbs lives. His chil. were, 1. SAMUEL, b. Feb. 23, 1737-8, d. May 29, '42; 2. BETTY, b. Nov. 3, '41, d. June 20, '42; 3. BETTY, b. May 1, '43; 4. LUCY, b. Jan. 26, '45; 5. SAMUEL, b. July 19, '49. John the f. d. ab. 1750. (Prob. Rec.). His wid. Betty, adm. to the ch. May, '51, m. Joshua Harrington, Oct. 3, '51.

6. JOHN, s. of John (3), m. Molly Stacy, Oct. 23, 1751; and with w. adm. to the ch., June 6, '52. Their chil. were, 1. LYDIA, bap. Mar. 2, 1746; 2. JOHN[10], b. July 16, '52; 3. JOSIAH, and 4. MARY, twins, b. Oct. 29, '55; Josiah m. Mary Abbe, of Hop. and had chil. in Petersham; Mary m. John Trowbridge, Ap. 23, '76; 5. MARTHA, b. Ap. 14, '58. John the f. was buried, Sep. 16, 1818.

7. ELIJAH, s. of Hopestill of Sud., and g. son of Peter, and g. g. son of John, (1), m. Susannah —. His chil. were, ELIJAH, b. in Fram., Oct. 7, '39; and in Sud., DORCAS, '42; SILAS, '44, lived in Rutland; SUSANNA, '48; JOEL, '50; STEPHEN, '52; RUFUS, '55; ABIGAIL, '57; NATHAN, '60.

8. MATTHIAS, s. of John, (3), m. Abigail Stone, Feb. 26, 1746, and had, 1. ANNE, b. Oct. 14, '47, m. John Eames; 2. MATTHIAS[9], b. Sept. 15, '52. Matthias the f., who was Selectman 13 years, d. 1799; and his wid., Abigail, d. Nov., 1814, æ. 90; "neither for 50 years required the attendance of a physician."

9. MATTHIAS, s. of Matthias, (8), m. Mrs. Mary Coolidge, dr. of Nath. Bridge, of Waltham; and had, 1. POLLY, bap. Aug. 1781, d. young; 2. NABBY, b. Sep. 10, '82, d. Sep. 28, 1841, author of "The Happy Merchant," and other Tales, pub. by the Mass. S.S. Union; 3. NANCY, b. July 8, '84; 4. MARTIN, bap. Oct. '86; 5. MATTHIAS, bap. Aug. '88. Mrs. Mary the m. d. Dec. 26, '90, æ 35. The f. m. 2d, Isabella Babcock, Jan. 21, '96, by whom he had several chil. Matthias was Deac. of the ch., and d. Feb. 4, 1826, æ 73. Mrs. Isabella d. Jan. 3, 1817, æ 51.

10. JOHN, Jr., s. of John, (6), m. Sarah Stone, (g.g. dr. of Rev. Mr. Swift), and had, 1. PATTY, b. July 31, 1782, m. Isaac Dench; 2. SALLY, b. Mar. 10, '84, m. John Hemenway; 3. JOHN, b. Ap. 27, '87, entered the U. S. service, d. unm. The wid. Sarah d. Sep. 1843, æ 83.

11. THOMAS, s. of Thomas, of Sud., g. son of Hopestill, who was g. son of John, (1), b. July 4, 1738, m. Submit Parker, and was adm. from Sud. ch., June 19, 1768. His chil. b. in Fram. were, 1. ALVAN, b. June 3, '69, m. Olive Rice ; 2. POLLY, b. Ap. 5, '71 ; 3. BETSEY, bap. July 18, '79. Tho. the f. lived on the Coolidge farm.

Note.—Wid. LUCY was adm. to the ch. in F. July, 1782. Lucy, relict of Peter, (prob. s. of Hopestill, Jr., of Sud., and b. 1741), d. in F., Jan. 27, 1783, æ. 40. HOPESTILL, of Sud., s. of Peter, and g. s. of John, (1), was f. of *Peter*, b. 1703, m. Mary Parris, '27 ; *Thomas*, b. '06, m. Mary Stone, '33 ; *Hopestill*, b. '08, m. Beulah Rice, '33 ; *Elijah*, b. '13 (7) ; and *Micah*, b. '16, m. Grace Rice, '37 ; all of whom had chil. in Sud. PETER, of Marlb., m. Abig. Barnes, 1705, and d. Mar., 1717, f. of *Peter, John*, and *Jabez*. JOHN, EBENEZER, JOSEPH, and RACHEL, were of Milton, from 1721 to '37.

BERRY, JOSEPH, m. Thankful Shears, Jan. 27, 1719–0 ; and had, 1. ALICE, bap. June 18, '21 ; 2. ABIJAH, bap. July 14, '23, prob. d. young ; 3. SHEARS, b. Dec. 25, '25, m. Esther Woodward, '50, lived in Oakham ; 4. THOMAS, b. Mar. 16, '26–7. The f. m. 2d, Hephzibah Benjamin, and had, 5. BENJAMIN, b. Ap. 14, '33 ; 6. THANKFUL, b. Oct. 14, '35, m. (Gen.) John Nixon, Feb. 7, '54 ; 7. MARY, b. May 29, '37, m. Amos Parmenter ; 8. ABIJAH, b. Dec 5, '38, d. unm., Marlb., ab. 1810 ; 9. LYDIA, b. Ap. 5, '39, m. Joel Newton, Southb., '62. Jos. the f. owned the farm now of Ezek. Howe, and sold to the f. of Mr. Howe. The wid. Hephzibah's bond of Adm'n. on her husb. is dated Nov. 7, '57.

2. BENJAMIN, s. of Jos. (1), m. Anna Knight, Sud., Feb. 1, 1760; and had in Sud., REBECKAH, b. May 11, '61, m. Abel Parmenter, d. 1835 ; and ANNA, b. Ap. 3, '72, living unm., (1842), in Sud. Benj. the f. lived some time in Fram., near Mr. Ezek. Howe, with whom he went to the Concord Fight. He lost an arm in the Rev. Service, and d. in Oakham, Mar. 1800. His wid. d. 1817, æ 75.

Note.—ANNA, m. in Southb., Thos. Wetherbee, 1757. In Stow, JOHN and w. Thankful, had *John*, 1720 ; ALLES, '21 ; ABIGAIL, '23. THOMAS was of Sud., 1707.

BIGELOW, JOHN, the original N.E. ancestor, whose name is variously written Bigullah, Biggullough, Bigalow, and Bigelow, and later Biglo, and Biglow, took the oath of fidelity at Wat., where he lived in 1636, and m. Mary Warren, Oct. 30, 1642. His chil. were 1. JOHN, b. Oct. 27, '43, housewright, prob. went to Conn. ; 2. JONATHAN, b. Dec. 11, '46, who, by w. Elizabeth, had *Jonathan*, b. 1680, m. Elizabeth Bemis, 1702, lived in Weston, and had Jonathan, b. 1707, lived in Westminster, m. Mary Snow, of Lanc., 1730, and Mindwell Coolidge, of Wat., '34 ; 3. DANIEL ;

4. MARY, b. Mar. 14, '48–9, m. Michael Flagg, '73; 5. SAMUEL, b. Oct. 28, '53; 6. JOSHUA, b. Nov. 5, '55; 7. JAMES, m. Eliz. Childs, 1693, who d. '07, and 2d Hannah, or Joanna Erixson, 1708, and had *Patience*, b. 1696, m. Sam. Wood; *Abraham*, '99; J.'s est. set. 1731, (of Weston); 8. ELIZABETH, b. June 18, '57, m. (John) Sternes; 9. SARY, b. Sept. 29, '59, m. Isaac Larned, July 23, '79; 10. MARTHA, b. Ap. 1, '62, m. (John) Woods; 11. ABIGAIL. b. Feb. 4, '63–4, m. Benj. Harrington, '84; 12. HANNAH, b. and d. '65; 13. a s., b. and d. '67. John, the f. m. 2d Sarah Bemis, Oct. 2, 1694, and d. July 14, 1703, æ. 86. He bought, 1649, of Jos. Knight, an estate adjoining his own. His will was proved July 28, 1703. Inventory, £627 12s. John had a grant at Wat., he to do smith work there.*

2. SAMUEL, s. of John, (1) m. Mary Flagg, of Wat., 1673; had in Wat., 1. JOHN, b. May 9, '75, m. Jerusha Garfield, '96, was taken captive by Ind. at Lanc., and carried to Canada, 1705. J. lived in Marlb., and had *Jerusha*, b. '97; *Thankful*, b. '99, m. John How, '24; *Joseph*, b. 1703, m. Martha Brigham, '25, lived in Boylston; *John*, b. 1704, lived in Holden; *Comfort*, b. '07, m. Jos. Brigham, '28; *Freedom*, '10, m. John Bowker; *Anna*, b. '12; *Gershom*, b. 14, (had in Marlb., Timotheus and Ivory, by w. Mary); *Jotham*, b. '17, went to Guilford; *Benjamin*, b. '20, m. Levinah Thomas, '44, lived in Hartford; *Sarah*. b. '24, m. John Langdon, '45; 2. MARY, b. 1677, m. David Bruce, of Marlb, '99; 3. SAMUEL, b. 1679, m. Ruth War ren, 1705, and had in Marlb., *Mary*, '05; *Samuel*, '07, (f. of Silas, H. C. '65, ord. at Paxton, '67); *Cornelius*, b. '10, m. Mary ——, d. Brookfield; *Jedidiah*, b. '14, m. Thamezin Hemenway, Fram., '37, lived in Grafton; *Ruth*, b. and d. '16; the m. d. Ap. 1716, and Sam. m. 2d Mary Gleason, of Sud., 1716, and had *Jason*, '18, m. Abig. Will or Witt, '48, d. Brookfield; *Ruth*, b. '19; *Amariah*, b. 22, m. Lydia Brigham, '47, lived in Boylston; *Martha*, b. '24. Sam., the f.'s est. sett. 1734; 4. SARAH, b. 1679, m. Josiah How, of Marlb.; 5. THOMAS, b. Oct. 24, 1683, m. Mary Livermore, '05, and had in Marlb., *Thomas*, '06, m. Elizabeth, (and had in Marlb., Thos. and other chil.); *Mary*, '07, m. —— Goddard; *Grace*, '09, m. Jos. Hager; *Uriah*, '11, (killed accidentally when young); *Abraham*, '13, lived in Weston, (m. 1. Abigail Bullard, 2. Anna Fiske, and was twelve years a member of the Gen. Court); *Isaac*, '15, d. '36; *Jacob*, '17, (m. Susannah Mead, Dec. 14, '38, and had in Walth., Mary, '39; Jacob, Feb. 19, '42–3. (g. stone says Mar. 2, '43), H. C. '66, ord. at Sud. Nov. 11, '72, d. Sept. 12, 1816, and m. Elizabeth d. Dec. 13, 1816, æ. 71; Susannah, '44; Thomas '51; Samuel, '54; Abijah, '56; Sarah, '58); *Sarah*, m. Elisha Livermore, 1744; *Josiah*, b. 1730, m. Mary Harrington, 1749; Lt. Thos., the f. d. in Waltham, Oct. 6, 1756, æ. 73; his will was proved Nov. 15; Mary, his w. d. there 1753, æ. 70; 6. MARCY, b. Ap. 4, 1686, m. Thos. Garfield; 7. ABIGAIL, b. 1687; 8. ISAAC, b. Mar. 1691, (an Isaac m. Mary Bond, 1709); I. prob. lived in Colchester, Conn.; 8. DELIVERANCE, b. 1695, m John Sternes. SAMUEL, the f. d. ab. 1733, æ. 80; his w. Mary d. 1720. (In his will he speaks of sons-in-law, Thomas Read, and Daniel Warren).

3. JOSHUA, s. of John (1), m. Elizabeth Flagg, Oct. 20, 1676, and had in Wat., 1. JOSHUA, b. Nov. 25, 77, m. Hannah Fisk, 1701, lived at Weston, and had *Johsua*, b. Feb., '01–2, (who lived in Worc.,† and was f. of William, b. 1727, m. Marg. Gates, '53, lived in Athol; Thaddeus, of Worc.; Asa, of Brookfield; Esther; Anna; and Hannah, b. 48); *Hannah*, b. 1704; *Nathan*-

---

* The family name has by some been derived from Bedloe. The trisyllabic orthography on our earliest records seems to present an objection to this conjecture.

† The house of Mr. Joshua, of Worc., was destroyed by fire near Jan. 30, 1750, and a dr. æ. 16, and a son, æ. 18, were burned to death.

iel, b. 1706; *Lydia*, b. '09, m. Isaac Parkhurst, '33; *Elizabeth*, b. '11; *Mary ; Abigail ;* and *John*, b. '14, moved to Westford. Joshua, the f. d. ab. 1728. Inventory, £1012 ; his wife Hannah administered May 20 ; 2. BENJAMIN, b. Jan 20, 1683-4; wounded in the public service, before 1708, (Col. Rec.), and killed by a fall from a horse, ab. 1709; 3. ELIZABETH, b. Aug. 3, 1687, m. —— Harrington ; 4. DAVID, b. Ap. 30, 1694, d. in Spain ; 5. JOSEPH, (or Josiah), b. Dec. 29, '95; 6. DANIEL, who moved to Boggachoag, (now Ward), in Worc., m. Elizabeth Whitney, and had in Worc., *Daniel*, b. Jan. 4, 1729, m. 1. Mary Bond, '51, (f. of Hon. Daniel, (of Petersham), Mary, Hannah, Elijah, Sophia, and Augustus ; the 2 last by a 2d w., wid. Mary Ballard) ; *David*, b. Sept. 19. '30, m Sarah Eaton, '52, and Debo. Hayward, '64; *Elijah,* b Mar. 2, '37, scalded æ. 3 ; Col. *Timothy*, b. Aug. 2, '39, m. Anna Andrews, (dr. of Samuel and w. Anna, a Rankin of Scotland,) and was f. of Nancy ; Hon Timothy, of Groton, H. C., '86 ; Andrew ; Rufus ; Lucy ; and Clarissa ; *Silence*, b Jan. 29, '42, m. Jona. Gleason, of Worc. ; and *Nathaniel*, d. æ. 2. Daniel, the f. went in the expedition to Canada, 1711 ; 7. EBENEZER, b. Sep. 4, 1698, of Worc., 1722, and by w. Hannah, f. of *Josiah*, b. 1722 ; and *Hannah*, b. '24 ; Eben., the f. a carpenter, d. in Cuba ; 8. GERSHOM, b. 1701, m. Rachel —, (who d. at Ward, 1800, æ. 103), and lived in Sutton ; 9. ELIEZER, b. 1705, m. Mary Fisk, '24, and was f. of *Benjamin*, (of Portsmouth) ; *Elisha*, bap. July '28, m. Sarah Goodridge, '57 ; *Mary*, b. '30; *Joshua*, '33, (moved to Genessee); *Jabez*, b. '36 ; *Ann*, '40 ; *Esther*, '44. Eliezer the f. d. in Westminster; (whither he removed, June 9, 1742, with his aged father), Feb. 24, '62, æ. 56. (His. West.) Joshua the f. was wounded in King Philip's war, and rec'd. a grant of land. He d. in Westminster, Feb. 21, 1745, æ. 90. His w. Elizabeth d. in Wat., 1729.*

4. DANIEL, s. of John, (1), settled in Fram., near the E. margin of the small pond by Mr. Charles Clark's.† He m. Abial, d. of Tho. Pratt, Sen., by whom he had, 1. ABIGAIL, b. Oct. 28, 1689, m. Abraham Belknap, Mar. 8, 1727 ; 2. DANIEL, b. Nov. 24, '91 ; 3. ABIAL, b. Jan. 20, '93, m. Jona. Stone, Oct. 11, '16 ; 4. SUSANNA, b. Mar. 4, '95-6, m. Stephen Jennings, June 9, '15 ; 5. EPHRAIM, b. May 12, '98, m. Lydia Johnson, '29, and had in Holl., *Joseph*, b. 1730, m. Lydia Brown, '56 ; *Abiel*, '32 ; *Lydia*, '37 ; *Deborah*, '42 ; *Asaph*, '46 ; Eph. the f. d. Oct. 18, '56 ; his wid. d. Feb. 5, '70, æ 60 ; (E. framed the 2d meeting house in Fram.) ; 6. LYDIA, b. Jan. 2, '02, m. Martin Pratt, Sep. '31. The wid. Abial had adm'n. on the est. of Daniel, the f., 1715.

5. DANIEL, s. of Daniel, (4), m. Rebeckah Eames, June 27, 1723, and cov. Mar. '26. Their chil. were, 1. REBECKAH, bap. May 15, '26, d. July 3, '29 ; 2. DANIEL, bap. Oct. 29, '27, d.

---

* Family tradition adds to the names of Joshua's children, Jonathan, Jabez, (a merchant in Bristol, Eng.), and John, who lived in Colchester.

† The road ran between his house and the pond.

Mar. 30, '30; 3. JOSEPH, b. Oct. 28, '29, d. May 18, '30; 4. DANIEL, b. July 16, '32; 5. REBECKAH, b. May 10, and d. July 26, '34; 6. ANN, d. June 29, '38. Reb. the m. d. July 7, '38, and Dan. the f. m. 2d, Prudence Stone, July 17, '46. The inventory of Daniel the f.'s est., was presented, 1752.

6. DANIEL, s. of Daniel, (5), m. Martha Pratt, Mar. 20, 1754, and had, 1. AMOS, b. Sep. 15, '55, m. Anne Brown, lived in N. H.; 2. DANIEL, b. June 14, '58; 3. REBECKAH, b. Oct. 14, '60, unm.; 4. MITTY, b. Dec. 6, '62; 5. MARTHA, b. Aug. 27, '65; 6. THOMAS, b. Ap. 28, '68; 7. ANNA, b. June 26, '71. Daniel the f. lived near Mr. Charles Clark's, survived his w., and d. ab. 1793.

7. DANIEL, s. of Daniel (6), m. Elizabeth Gallot, Mar. 1783; and had, 1. MOLLY, bap. May, '84; 2. JOSEPH, bap. Oct. '86; 3. FRANCIS, bap. Dec. '88; 4. PETER, bap. Apr. '91; 5. BETSEY, bap. Nov. '94. Daniel the f. moved into N. H., ab. 1800.

8. ASAPH, s. of Ephraim, g. son of Daniel (4), m. Martha Gleason; and had 1. DEBORAH, b. Feb. 4, 1778, m. Seth Herring; 2. POLLY, b. June 8, '81; 3. SALLY, b. '86, m. Simon Baker, d. ab. 1813. Lt. Asaph the f. d. 1823. Martha his w. d. 1830. Lt. A. lived on the place now of Mr. S. Herring.

9. NATHANIEL, b. 1706, s. of Joshua [and w. Hannah], and g. son of Joshua, (3), m. Hannah Robinson, in Newton, Nov. 22, 1733; and had in Weston 1. HANNAH, b. 1734; 2. ELIZABETH, b. '36; 3. LOIS, b. '41, d. young; 4. LOIS, b. '46, m. in Fram., Levi Metcalf, and d. in Fram. 1832, æ. 86; 5. NATHANIEL, bap. 1750. Nath. the f. moved with his family to Fram., was Tything-man here, 1767, and adm. to the ch., by letter from Weston, Sep. 10, '69. He lived near Mr. Abner Haven's; m. 2d. Mary, wid. of Nath. Stacy, and d. in F.

10. NATHANIEL, s. of Nath. (9), m. Susannah Jennings; and had 1. ANNE, m. John Rice, Leom.; 2. HANNAH, m. Eph. Colburn, lived in N. Y.; 3. LYDIA, m. —— Tucker, of Shrewsb.; 4. NATHAN, d. unm. in Whitestown, N. Y.; Susannah the m. d. Feb. 23, 1773; and Nath. m. 2d. Anne Rider, Oct. '82, and had 5. JOHN, m. Betsey Follansbee, Leom.; 6. ISAAC, m. Nancy Josselyn, and 2d., Mrs. —— Champney, of N. Ipsw.; 7, DAVID, m. Candace Hale, Leom. and lives in Fram.; 8, NATHANIEL, m. Cath. Tyler, Leom.; 9. PERKINS, m. Relief Patrick, of Jeffry,

N. H.; 10 DEXTER, m. Lydia Brigham, of Marlb., lives in Fram.;
11. SUSANNAH, m. 1st. —— Baker, 2d. —— Keyes; 12. JOSI-
AH, m. Exion Patterson, of Harvard; all b. in Fram., except Josiah, who was b. in Leominster, whither the f. moved, and d. æ.
82; his w. Anne d. Dec., 1845, æ. 87.

11. JOSEPH, and w. cov. in Fram., May 27, 1759; and
s. JOSEPH was bap. Feb. 10, '60. [He was prob. the Joseph
who m. Sarah Hebins (or Stebins) of Leicester, 1756. Jos., of
Fram. had a br. John Stebins, 1759. (Mss. papers.) Joseph,
bap. 1760, may have been the Jos. (and w. Ruth) who had in
Fram. *Ruth*, b. 1799.]

12. DANIEL, m. Hannah Bixby, both of Fram., Mar. 20, 1754.

BISCOM, WILLIAM, was in Fram. before 1744; perhaps
the same as Briscoe; which see.

BIXBY, JOSEPH, and w. were adm. to Hop. Ch. 1728; and their chil.
JOSEPH, LYDIA, and ABNER, were bap. THOMAS, of Hop., had s. ISAAC,
bap. 1741.

2. JOSEPH, of Hop., m. Mehetabel Rugg of Fram., Mar. 30,
1732; and had in Hop. 1. JOSEPH, b. 1735; 2. HANNAH, b. '37;
3. LYDIA, b. '40, d. in Fram., Mar. 9, 1765; 4. JONATHAN, b.
'42; 5. BETTY, b. '44; 6. NATHAN, b. '46; and in Fram., 7.
JOHN, b. Oct. 8, 1750. Note—MEHETABEL, who m. in Fram.
James Haven, Nov. 16, 1752, is said to have been the eldest dr.
of Joseph and Mehetabel.

3. ABNER, m. Thamezin Nurse, 1734; and had in Hop., 1.
ELIZABETH, bap. 1737; 2. ABNER, bap. '42; 3. MARY, b. '48;
4. JOSEPH, b. '51; and in Fram., 5. BETHIAH, b. Sep. 20, '62.
Abner the f. and w. were recommended from Fram. to the ch. in
Partridgefield, Dec. 26, '73.

4. JOSEPH, Jun., s. of Jos. (2), m. Sally Haven; and had
in Fram. 1. SALLY, b. Feb. 14, 1767, m. Wm. Clark, of Norfolk, Va., June 10, '92; 2. JOSEPH, bap, Nov. 27, 68, H. C. '91,
d. unm.; 3. JOSIAH, bap. July 29, '70, unm.; 4. PATTY, b. Aug.
18, '72, m. Joseph W. Page, of Boston, Feb. 16, 1800; 5. HIT-
TY, b. Ap. 25, '75, m. Daniel Stone, M.D., of Sharon., Nov. 30,
1802; 6. LUKE, b. Oct. 25, '77, m. Abigail Adams, of Acton, a
merch. in Boston; 7. NANCY, b. July 22, '80, d. unm. Joseph
the f. d. in Fram., and was buried Apr. 20, 1786. His wid. d. in
Sharon.

5. NATHAN, s. of Joseph (2), m. Martha Twichell, of Sherb., Oct. 3, 1771; and had in Fram. JULIA, b. July 8, 1772.

SARAH, of Hop., m. William Richards, Feb., 1757. Mrs. SALLY, of Hop., m. Wm. Wesson, Feb. 9, '89. NATHANIEL and w. Mary, had chil. in Oxford, from 1763. SAMUEL, d. in Sutton, ab. 1743. (Worc. Prob.) JOSEPH Bigsbe was of Ipswich, 1659, and DANIEL, of Andover, 1675. JOSEPH, of Boxford, m. Sarah Gold, 1682, and d. ab. 1704, having had *Sarah, Joseph, Jonathan, George, Daniel, Benjamin, Marcy,* and *Abigail.*

BLACK, —— and w. appear upon the T. Rec. 1722. He was probably Hugh Black, who, in 1730, occupied a farm in Fram. near Hop.

BLAIR, SAMUEL, and w. Mary. Samuel was buried in Fram., Aug. 23, 1724; and a posthumous ch. SAMUEL, b. Nov. 20, 1724. (T. Rec.)

2. WILLIAM; letters of guardianship were granted in Worc. Co., 1733, for ROBERT, æ. ab. 11; SAMUEL, æ. ab. 8, (bap. in Fram. Nov. 1, 1724); and John, æ. ab. 13, chil. of William, late of Fram. (Worc. Prob.) [William Blair owned a lot at Rutland, 1720.]

3. ROBERT; lett. of g. ship granted in Worc. Co., 1734, for JOHN, æ. ab. 14, s. of Robert, late of Fram. [Robert, of Sud. had *Elizabeth* and *Mary*, b. (or bap.), April, 1724.]

4. JAMES, in 1730, occupied land (prob in Fram.), near Hop. [James, of N. Braintree, d. ab. 1756, leaving w. Mary, and chil. *Mary, Sarah, Rebeckah, John, Edward,* and *Ann* (Shaw).]

MATTHEW, of Hop., m. Mary Hambleton, 1727, and had *Elizabeth*, bap. '28; *Matthew*, '32. 1754, MATTHEW, of Blanford, m. Jane Alexander.

BLANCHARD, JOSEPH, m. Nancy Wait, Oct. 1789.

BLODGET, ABIGAIL, adm. to the ch. Feb. 1, 1746, and m. Samuel Gates, Ap. 11, 1751.

BOUTWELL, EBENEZER, and sister Abigail, cov. Feb. 19, 1721. ABIGAIL, bap. Aug. 12, '22.

2. EBENEZER, and w. Thankful, had 1. PHEBE, b. June 9, d. 20th. 1733; 2. EBENEZER, b. Sep. 10, 1735. Eb. the f. lived E. from No. 8 School House. He was b. in Reading, Oct. 23, 1700, and s. of James and Abigail of R.

3. JAMES, had in Sud, by. w. Judith, 1. JAMES, b. Ap. 9, 1726; 2. WILLIAM, b. May 4, '28; 3. JUDITH, b. July 27, '30; 4. CATHARINE, b. Oct. 7, '32; 5. KENDALL, b. Ap. 1, '37; 6. SARAH, b. Jan. 12, '35; 7. TIMOTHY, b. Jan. 1, 39-40. James the f. lived

in Fram., near EBENEZER (2), and owned a right in the township of New Framingham. He d. in Leominster. His will and inventory (£375) in Worc. prob., 1752.

4. EBENEZER, Jun., s. of Eben. (2), and w. Ann cov. Ap. 1759, and had, 1. JAMES, b. Feb. 11, 1759; 2. JESSE, bap. July, '66; 3. JOSIAH, bap. July 31, '68; 4. THANKFUL. bap. July 15, '70; 5. ANNA, bap. Oct. 9, '74; 6. MOLLY, bap. July 6, '77; 7. ENOCH, bap. June 14,'78. EBEN. and w. recom'd by the ch. July, 1782.

5. JAMES, s. of James (3), m. Rachel Walkup, Mar. 9, 1744, and lived in Fram. The wid. Rachel d. ab. Feb. 1789. [REBECCA, dr. of James, bap. in Fram. June 27, 1773.]

Note.—JAMES, b. in Reading, 1699, was s. of James and w. Eliz., and g. son of James, who m. Rebeckah Kendall, 1665.

BOWEN, ISAAC, (b. in Roxbury Ap. 20, 1676, s. of Henry, who m. Elizabeth Johnson, 1658), came to Fram. about 1698, and leased land from Mr. Danforth in the S. part of the town. He remained in town about 4 years, and sold to Moses Haven, of Lynn, Nov. 18, 1702. He had in Fram. by w. Hannah, HENRY b. June 30, 1700, and on returning to Roxb., had MARY, 1704; ISAAC, '07; SARAH, '09, d. '16; JOSIAH, '11; PENUEL, '15; SARAH, '17. Hannah, w. of Isaac, d. Jan. 22, '17-8.

BOYDEN, JOSEPH, was rated about 1757. JUDITH, m. Sylvanus Ballard, May 7, 1755. Joseph lived at Guinea end.

BRADISH, JOSEPH, on Sud. Rec. 1662, was in Fram. 1672. His chil. by w. Mary, were, 1. MARY, b. Ap. 10, 1665; 2. SARAH, b. May 6, '67; 3. HANNAH, b. Jan. 14, '69, m. Joseph Stanhope, '85; JOSEPH, b. Nov. 28, '72.

Note.—Jos. was s. of Robert, who was of Camb., 1635, and had by w. Mary, (who d. Sep., 1638), Joseph, b. 1638; and by w. Vashti, Samuel, b. 1639, d. '42; James; John; Hannah, m. Ezekiel Morrell; and Mary, m. (Matthew?) Gibbs. Robert, the f. d. ab. 1659. JAMES, m. in Marlb., Damaris Rice, 1708, and was f. of Hepsebah, b. 1709; Sarah, '11; Robert, '12; Mary, '15; James, '17. JOHN was of Hardwick, 1747. ROBERT and JONAS m. in Athol, ab. 1754.

BRECK, or BRICK, DANIEL, m. Patty Learned, both of Sherb., Aug. 29, 1790; and had in Fram., PATTY, b. Ap. 15, '94; and ELIJAH, b. Feb. 2, '96. Daniel d. in Sherb. 1838, æ. 80. Patty d. 1843, æ 81.

Note.—JONAS and w. Mary, had chil. in Sherb., from 1735. THOMAS and w. Mary, were of Medfield, 1663. Rev. Robert, bap. Dec. 10, 1682,

H. C., 1700, s. of John, of Dorch., ord. at Marlb., Oct. 25, '04, d. at M., Jan. 6, 1731, æ. 49.

BREWER,* JOHN, of Sud., m. Elizabeth, dr. of Henry Rice ; and had 1. JOHN, b. 1669, m. Hannah Jones, of Wat., July, 5 '93 ; 2. ELIZABETH, b. May 21, '71; 3. HANNAH ; 4. JAMES, b. Sep. 10, '75, (Deacon at Sud. m. Elizabeth Grout, 1703, 2d Abigail Smith, '19, 3d. Wid. Johanna Singleterry, of Fram., June 22, '31, f. of *James*, who m. Mary Smith, 1731; Dea. J. d. Nov. 18, '64); 5. SARAH, b. Jan. 14, '78, m. in Fram., Caleb Bridges, Nov. 26, 1700 ; 6. MARY, b. 1680, m. in Fram., Benjamin Ball, Mar. 29, 1704; 7. ABIGAIL, b. Ap. 5, '82, m. David Parmenter, 1713; 8. MARTHA, b. Mar. 5, '85; 9. JONATHAN, b. June 21, '89. John, the f. d. Jan. 1, 1690–1. His widow's est. (£292.8s) was settled Mar. 12, 1693–4.

Note.—John, above, was prob. s. of John and w. Anne, of Camb., who had 1 *John*, b. 10 Sep., (or April), 1642 ; 2. *Hannah*, Jan. 18, 1664–5, who m. in Sud. Daniel Goble, Feb. 25, 1664.

2. JONATHAN, s. of John (1), lived in Fram., on the place now of Edw. Goodnow ; and with w. Arabella cov. Ap. 17, 1717. Their chil. were 1. SAMUEL, b. Nov. 4, 1716 ; 2. ABNER, b. July 10, '18, an eccentric man, d. unm. ; 3. PETER, b. Ap. 17, '20 ; 4. ELIZABETH, b. June 2, '22, m. David Pratt, Jun., May 20, '45 ; 5. ABIGAIL, bap. Mar. 29, '24, m. Edmund Town, of Hoosack Fort, Jan. 16, '55 ; 6. JONATHAN, b. Feb. 3, '25–6 ; 7. MOSES, b. Mar. 26, '28, m. Elizabeth Davis, Dec. 4, '51, and had in Sud. *Jonathan,* 1752 ; *Elisha,* '54 ; *Moses,* '57 ; *Elizabeth,* '61 ; 8. DAVID, b. Dec. 24, '31, f. of Col. David, of Fram. b. ab. 1751 ; 9. MARTHA, b. June 16, '34 ; 10. ELIAB, b. May 14, '37. Jona. the f. d. in Fram.

3. SAMUEL, s. of Jona. (2), m. Martha Bent, Mar. 10, 1740 ; and had in Fram., 1. JASON, b. Sep. 24, '41 ; 2. MARTHA, b. Aug. 9, '43 ; and in Rutland, 3. LUCY, '45 ; 4. NATHAN, '47 ; 5. JOHN, '49 ; 6. ABIGAIL, '52 ; 7. SAMUEL, '58 ; 8. ELIZABETH, '60.

4. JONATHAN, s. of Jona, (2), m. Frances Buckminster; and had in Fram. SUSANNAH, b. Aug. 4, 1764 ; and FRANCIS, b. May 26, '66. Col. Jonathan lived also in Wat. and Boston, was in command of a reg't. at Bunker Hill, and was buried Jan. 9, 1784.

5. PETER, s. of Jona. (2), m. Abigail (prob. a mistake for Elizabeth) Pratt, Dec. 22, 1748 ; and had a dr. SARAH, bap. in Fram., Dec. 28, 1760. His child. b. in Southb. were 1. PETER, b. May 1. 1750, unm. ; 2. JOEL, b. JULY 24, '52, m. Lavoisie and Polly Newton ; 3. ELIZABETH, b. Sep. '24, '54, d. unm. ; 4. LUCIA, b. Apr. 27, '57, m. Jos. Tuttle ; 5. SARAH, b. Dec. 18, '60, m.

---

* The name is frequently recorded, BRUER.

Reuben Newton; 6. JASON, b. Jan. 13, '64, m. Anne Morse, f. of *Charlotte*, who m. in Fram. Jesse Davis, Dec. 23, 1804; and also of *Elizabeth*, who m. John Lloyd, of Milton, in Fram. Aug. 9, 1805. Elizabeth w. of Peter d. 1794, æ. 71.

6. DAVID, s. of David, g. son of Jona. (2), m. Comfort Wheeler, and had in F. 1. JOHN, b. Apr. 10, 1781, H. C. 1804, a physician, lives unm. in Phila.; 2. NABBY, bap. Nov. 2, '82, m. Simon Cutler; 3. CYRUS, b. Mar. 10, '83, d. unm. July 27, 1822; 4. DARIUS, b. Aug. 31, '85, m. Harriet Buckminster; 5. RUFUS, b. Jan. 24, '88, m. Mary Nurse, Deputy Sheriff, Cashier of Fram. Bank, and Justice of the Peace; 6. BETSEY, b. Ap. 3, '90, m. Otis Fairbanks, and d. Aug. 15, 1824; 7. DAVID, b. Ap. 8, '92, m. Olive Nurse; 8. DEXTER, bap. Ap., '95, m. Jane ——, and 2d. Mary Ann Cloyes; 9. HENRY, bap. June, '98, m. Susannah Nurse. Col. David lived at Salem End, greatly esteemed by his fellow townsmen; was Selectman 7 years, and d. in Fram. Dec. 17, 1834, æ. 83. His w. Comfort d., Mar. 9, 1833, æ. 76.

7. DANIEL, was rated in Fram. ab. 1742, and member of the ch. 1746. [He was perhaps the Daniel of Hop., who had chil. *James*, bap. in Hop. 1740; and *Mary*, bap. '44].

JOHN, s. of John (1), had by w. Mary, in Sud. and Wat., *Josiah*; *Daniel*, b. Aug. 4, 1704; and *William*, b. '07. Lt. John, the f. d. 1709, and his wid. Mary had admin. In Sud., HANNAH m. Henry Loker, 1647; and MARY m. Jona. Willard, Jan. 8, 1691. In Hop., JOHN and w. Hannah, had *David*, b. 1732; *Sarah*, '34; *Isaac*, '36; *Joseph*, '39.

BRIDGE, MATTHEW, b. at Lexington, July 18, 1721, H. C., 1741, ord. at Fram. Feb. 19, 1745-6, m. 1747, Anne, (b. 1724) dr. of Rev. Daniel Perkins, of W. Bridgewater, who m. Anna Foster, Nov. 6, 1721. Their chil. were 1. MATTHEW, b. Aug. 16, 1748, d. young; 2. ANN, b. Sep. 11, '49, d. young; 3. DANIEL, b. July 19, '51, adm. to ch. Nov. 15, '72, settled in Canada, and d. Feb. 27, 1828, father of the wife of George Brown, late minister of the U. S. at the Sandwich Islands; 4. SARAH, b. Jan. 9, '53, m. Rev. David Kellogg, May 27, '81, and d. Feb. 14, 1826, æ. 73; 5. ELEANOR, b. Oct. 10, '54, m. Capt. Samuel Ingersol, of Salem, May 31, '81, and d. Nov. 10, 1819; 6. RICHARD PERKINS, bap. Nov. 6, '56, m. Mary, dr. of Rev. Timothy Harrington, of Lancaster, settled as a Physician in Petersham, and d. Aug. 22, 1797, æ. 40. His wid. m. Dr. Fisher, of Beverly; 7. MARY, bap. Sep. 7, 1760, d. Feb. 21, 1842.

The Rev. MATTHEW d. in Fram. Sep. 2, 1775, æ. 54. His wid. m. Rev. Timo. Harrington, of Lancaster, and d. in Fram. May 12, 1805.

Note.—Rev. Matthew descended from JOHN, of Camb., 1632, who came to N. E. a widower, with two sons, MATTHEW; and THOMAS, who died before 1665, f. by w. Dorcas, of *Dorcas*, b. Feb. 16, 1648-9. † John was deacon at Camb., and selectman many years; he was also a commissioner to lay out Sudbury lands, in 1639. He sold, in 1649, land at Rocky Meadow, Cambridge. He m. a 2d w. Elizabeth Saunders, of Billerica, and his will was proved Oct. 3. 1665; (Inventory, £372. 3s. 6d.) MATTHEW, s. of. Deac. John, m. Anna, dr. of Nicholas Danforth, and had 1. JOHN, b. June 15, 1645; 2. MARTHA, b. Jan. 19, '48-9, d. 1649; 3. MATTHEW,* b. May 5, '50, d. May 29, 1738, f. by w. Abigail, (who d. Dec. 14, 1722, æ. 55), of *Mary*, b. 1688; *Anna*, 1691; *Matthew*, Mar. 1, '93-4, m. Abigail Bowman, Mar. 24, 1719, and d. at Waltham, Mar. 25, 1761, (f. of Rev. Matthew, b. July 18, 1721; Anna, b. 1723; Nathaniel, 1725, m. Mary Coolidge, and lived in Waltham; and Sarah, b. 1728); *Abigail*, b. 1696; *Joseph*, b. 1698; *John*, b. 1700, (f. by w. Anna, of Anna, b. 1730; Mary, '33; Sarah, '35; John, '37; Josiah, '39, H. C., 1758, ord. at E. Sud., Nov. 4, 1761, and d. June 20, 1801; and Ebenezer, '42); *Elizabeth*, b. 1703; *Samuel*, b. 1705, m. Martha Bowman, '38; *Martha*, b. 1707; 4. SAMUEL, b. Feb. 24, (or 17), 1652-3; 5. THOMAS, b. June 1, 1656; 6. ANNA, and 7. ELIZABETH, both bap. Aug. 17, 1659. Matthew, the f. d. Ap. 28, 1700; his w. Anna d. Dec. 2, 1704.

BRIDGES, BENJAMIN, prob. s. of Edmond and Sarah, and b. at Topsfield, Jan. 2, 1664-5, settled near Salem end, in Fram., before its incorporation; and by w. Elizabeth had, 1. DELIVERANCE, b. Sep. 10, 1690, m. James Wilson, Jan. 21, 1719-0; 2. ELIZABETH, b. July 28, '92, m. Isaac Whitney, Sep. 27, 1722; 3. JUDITH, b. Sep. 10, '94; 4. SARAH, b. Mar. 25, 1702, m. Moses Haven, Ap. 14, '20; 5. GIDEON, b. Aug. 21, '04-5, m. Mary Wilson, May 23, '23, and f. of *Anne*, b. in Fram., April 28, '25; 6. MEHETABEL, b. Oct. 17, '06, m. Daniel Hovey, of Oxford, Nov. 24, '26; 7. MIRIAM, b. Sep. 19, '11. Capt Benj. was 9 years a Selectman, and d. Aug. 28, (T. Rec.) 1725, æ. 61.

2. CALEB, prob. s. of Edmond and Sarah, and b. at Salem, June 3, 1677, m. in Fram., Sarah Brewer, Nov. 26, 1700; by whom he had 1. BATHSHEBAH, b. Jan. 19, 1702-3, d. Nov. 1, '39; 2. HACHALIAH, b. May 30, '05, m. Sarah Rug, 1728, (and f., in Southb., of *James*, b. '29, m. Mary Brown, '51; *Jonathan*, b. '30, d. '36; *Nathan*, b. '33, m. 1. Sarah Parker, '55, 2. Tamar

---

* An ancient Bible, with a date of 1610 written on the title page, and bearing also the autograph of Matthew Bridge, 1710, is in the possession of Miss Bent, of Framingham. Sternhold and Hopkins' Psalms are bound with it.

† Dorcas m. D. Champney, Camb.

Hutson, '57 ; *Sarah*, b. '35, m. John Chamberlain, '53 ; *Hachaliah*, b. '37, m. Betsey Pond, and lived in Holl. ; and *Benjamin*, b. '39, lived in Holl. H. the f. d. Sep. 27, '39, and his est. was settled 1751. His wid. m. James Work) ; 3. CALEB, b. Aug. 24, 1708 ; 4. MARTHA, b. Mar. 28, '10, m. Abraham Ball, of Holl., Jan 13, '32 ; 5. BETHIAH, b. Feb. 14, '12–3, m. Benjamin Nurse, Nov. 22, '49 ; 6. BENJAMIN, b. Sep. 19, '14, d. Oct. 6, '39 ; 7. SARAH, b. Aug. 26, '16, d. Nov. 18, '39; 8. and 9. DAVID, and JONATHAN, twins, b. Mar. 19, 1719–0 — David m. Keziah Drury, Ap. 25, 1750, Jona. d. Ap. 4, 1720. Caleb the f. was a mason and lived near Salem end.

3. CALEB, s. of Caleb (2), m. Elizabeth Stanhope, Sep. 23, 1731, and had in Hop. 1. ELIZABETH, b, July 13, '32; 2. ISAAC, b. Ap. 15, '34 ; 3. EDMON, b. July 10, '36 ; 4. CALEB, b. Jan. 22, '38. C. and w. were dismissed to the ch. in Fram. 1743, and had in Fram., 5. and 6. GIDEON, and ANNA, twins, b. Sep. 18, '44.

4. GIDEON, m. Isabel Nichols, and had in Fram., BENJAMIN, b. Dec. 14, 1762 ; MARY, b. 20 Oct. '64.

Note.—Edmond, æ. 23, came over in the James, 1634. EDMUND was of Lynn, 1637, and d. 1686. (Farmer). Edmond, of Topsfield, m. Sarah Towne, 165(9), and had at Topsfield, *Edmond*, b. Oct. 4, 1660 ; *Benjamin*, b. Jan. 2, '64–5 ; *Mary*, April 14, '67 ; and at Salem, *Hannah*, 1669 ; *Caleb*, June 3, 1677. Elizabeth, w. of E., of Ips. d. Dec., 1664. Edmond m. in Ipswich, Mary Littlehale, Ap. 6, 1665. The will of Edmund, sen., blacksmith, of Ipswich, who d. Jan. 13; '84, was proved Mar. 31, 1685 ; in it he names his w. Mary, and his chil. *John, Josiah, Faith* Black, *Bethiah*, and *Mary*. The Inventory of an Edmond, sen., (prob. of Salem), was presented Nov. 28, 1682, by Francis Nurse, and John How. (Essex Prob.)

BRIGGS, SUSANNA, b. in Fram. May 23, 1740.

BRINLEY, FRANCIS, Esq., of Roxbury, bought, Feb. 1, 1742, the so called Brinley Farm.

2. NATHANIEL, s. of Francis, occupied ab. 1760, the above named farm, and continued on it until the commencement of the Revolution, when he left the Town.

3. EDWARD, Esq. of Weston, s. of Francis, occupied the same farm one year, ab. 1778.

4. BETHIAH, m. Aaron Pike, both of Fram., Feb. 1794.

BRINTNAL (or Brinmall), THOMAS, of Boston, had by w. Esther, 1. SAMUEL, b. Dec. 2, 1665; 2. THOMAS, b. Nov. 1, 1669; 3. NATHANIEL, b. 1671; 4. JOHN, b. Mar. 3, 1672, d. in Boston, 1731, f. of *John*, who m. Deborah, dr. of Wm. Mellins, ab. 1712; 5. JOSEPH, b. Mar. 3, 1673; 6. MEHETABEL. b. 1685. Thomas, f. or son, was a prop. of Rutland, 1686.

2. THOMAS, s. of Thomas, (1), m. Hannah, dr. of Maj. Simon Willard, May 23, 1693, and had THOMAS; WILLIAM; (the following on Sud. Rec.); PARNAL, b. Sep. 27, 1696; PAUL, b. Mar. 20, 1701, m. Mary Rice, '24, and had chil. in Sud.; NATHANIEL, b. 1703, d. 1728; JERUSHA, b. Oct. 15, '04; DOROTHY, b. Dec. 21, '06, m. Eph. Morse, '36; SUSANNA, b. Ap., 170(7). Thos., the f. d. in Sud., Aug. 2, 1733.

Note.—PHINEHAS, m. Sybilla Rice, 1716, and had chil. in Sud.

3. JOSEPH, was in Framingham 1717; and was perhaps the Jos. who d. in Sud. June 28, 1731, æ. 40.

4. WILLIAM, s. of Thomas, (2), Y. C. 1721, m. Zerviah Buckminster of Fram., Dec. 19, 1729, and had in Sud., BUCKMINSTER, b. Sep. 29, '30; ANNA, b. Jan. 12, '32-3, d. in Rutland, Aug. 10, '36; and in Rutland, DORITHY, b. July 13, '36; and in Fram., CALEB, b. Nov. 4, '38; WILLIAM. b. Aug. 12, '40, d. June 22, '41. Mr. William the f. preached as a cand. at Rutland, 1721; taught school in Sud. 4 years, first in 1722, and in Rutland 1735. He was ordered, Aug. 1725, to the command of some troops to protect the inhabitants of Rut. (State Files.)

5. Mrs. SUBMIT, of Fram., m. Mr. Richard Taylor of Sud., July 23, 1741.

BRISCO, WILLIAM, m. Dinah Cutting in Fram., Oct. 22, 1740.

BRITTAN, SAMUEL, prob. in Fram. 1737, (T. Rec.)

BROWN, THOMAS, owned land near Saxonville, 1697. MARTHA, m. Philip Gleason, May 6, 1714. Wid. —— Brown adm. to the ch. Oct. 10, 1725. MARY m. in Fram. Abraham Belknap, Feb. 26, 1740-1. MARY m. in Fram. James Bridges of Southb. Ap. 24, 1751. JAMES m. in Fram. Rebecca Eaton, Oct. 18, 1733, (and had in Sud. *Thomas*, b. Mar. 26, '36). ZERUIAH, w. of Samuel, recommended to the ch. in Sud. Aug. 4, '54. SUSANNAH m. John Nurse, Nov. 8, 1781. ANNE, m. Amos Bigelow, Feb. 1784. MARTHA m. Daniel Cutting of N. Marlb. Nov. 1796. NATHANIEL, of Fram. m. Elenor Hayden of Sud. Dec. 29, 1761 and had chil. in Sud. LUCINDA m. Josiah Gegger of Nat. Nov. 14, 1804. POLLY, dr. of Ruhama, bap. Aug. 1787.

2. THOMAS, and w. Mehetabel adm. to the ch. July 7, 1765; had in Fram., JOHN, b. Aug. 14, 1765, and RHODA, b. June

4, '72. Thomas lived near Mr. Adam Hemenway's, and removed from Town. [Thomas Jun. was on a highway rate, 1775.]

3. AARON, m. Martha Walker, of Fram. and had ENOCH, bap. Aug. 8, 1769, d. young; MARTHA, bap. Aug. 19, '70, m. Jesse Winch; POLLY, m. Eben. Whitney, of Nat.; NANCY, m. Josiah Child. of Nat.; REBECCA, bap. Oct. 1, '78, m. Sam. Haynes; NABBY, bap. Oct., '85.

Aaron the f. who was br. of Nathaniel above, d. of the small pox in the house now of George Pratt.

Note. — It is probable that some of the above descended from Deac. WILLIAM, an early prop. of Sud., who m. Mary Bisby (or Bisbidge), Nov. 15, 1641, and was f. of 1. MARY, b. May 18, 1643, m. Benj. Rice, ab. '62; 2. Maj. THOMAS, b. May 22, '44, (or 5). m. Patience Foster, 1667, who d. Aug., 1706, æ. 52. and Mrs. Mary Phipps. of Camb.; Maj. T. d. in Sud., May 7, 1709, and his remains were laid in the Chapel Bur. Ground, Boston. He gave, in his will, rights "in the parishes of Hedcom and Tenterden, Co. of Kent, in Eng.;" 3. Cornet WILLIAM, m. Margaret Stone, 1676, d. 1705, and his est. was settled, 1707; 4. HOPESTILL, Esq., b. July 8, 1656, m. Abigail Haynes, '85. lived near Nobscot, and d. 1729; 5. EDMUND, b. Nov. 27, '53, m. Elizabeth ——, and was shopkeeper in Boston, 1694; 6. ELIZABETH, b. July 23, 1659. JABEZ was of Sud., 1667. RICHARD, (w. Mary), 1663. The Rev. EDMUND, of Sud., (who m. Anne, wid. of John Loveren, of Wat.). d. June 22, 1678. THOMAS, was of Sud., 1637.

4. WILLIAM, came from Lexington to Fram., and built the mill called by his name, near the house of his g. son, Col. Brown. He was a Selectman 3 years, Deacon of the ch., and took an active part in the proceedings of the Town, at the period of the Revolution. His chil. were 1. BETTY, b. Dec. 11, 1747, m. Samuel Gleason, lived in Barnet; 2. ROGER, b. Sep. 12, '49, m. Mary Hartwell, of Lincoln, was f. of Col. James Brown, of Fram. and d. in Concord; 3. KEZIAH, b. July 5, '51, m. Alex. Parkman; 4. WILLIAM, b. Mar. 22, '53; 5. (Maj.) ANDREW, b. Jan. 26, '55, d. unm., Dec. 28, 1803; 6. JOHN, bap. Aug. 5, '59, d. young; 7. RUHAMAH, bap. Aug. 5, '59, d. young; 8. FREDERICK FERDINAND, bap. Nov. 8, '61,; 9. JOHN, bap. Sep. 11, '63, m. Martha Rice; 10. EBENEZER, bap. Mar. 29, '67; 11. POLLY, bap. Aug. 6, '69, m. Samuel Parris, of Wayland; 12. (Col.) JOSEPH, m. Deborah Sanger, lived in Petersham, and d. Sep. 3, 1814, æ. 56; and his w. d. Oct. 15, 1832, æ. 70. Deacon William d. in Fram. Dec. 13, 1793, æ. 70. His wid. was bur. Feb. 1810.

5. EBENEZER, s. of William, (4), m. Keziah Nixon, and had

in Fram., 1. RUHAMAH, bap. Ap. 1789, m. Luther French; 2. POLLY, bap. Ap. '91, m. Rev. —— Colburn, late of Wells, Me.; 3. JOSEPH, m. Sally Wood, of Medway; 4. NANCY, bap: July '95, m. Sam. Dudley; 5. WILLIAM, bap. May, '97, m. in Mexico; 6. EBENEZER, bap. June, '99, went to sea; 7. ANDREW, m. in Canada; and 8. BENJAMIN, m. Wid. Lucy Ann Leland. Eb. the f. d. on his way to Canada with his family.
  6. FREDERICK F., s. of Wm. (4), m. Ruth Eames, July, 1786; and had in Fram. BETSEY, and KEZIAH, bap. May 1789, and in Petersham, RUHAMAH; JOSEPH, and others. The f. is now (1847), living in Pet.

Note.—Deac. William, was s. of Deac. Joseph, who m. in Wat., Ruhamah Wellington, 1699, and had in Wat., *Ruhamah*, b. 1701; *Daniel*, '03; *John*, '06; *Joseph*, '08, (Deac. in Holl., f. of Joseph, who m. Lydia Twichell, 1756); *Josiah*, (who lived in Sterling); and in Lexington, *Benjamin*, b. June 30, 1720, (m. Sarah Reed, Dec. 23, '42, Deac. in Lex., and d. 1801); and *William*, Deac. in Fram. Deac Jos., the f. d. in Lex., Jan. 11, 1764, æ. 85. JOHN, (and w. Hester), had in Marlb., *John*, b. 1664; *Hester*, b. and d. '67; *Thomas*, b. '71. The f. sold to Tho's Rice, 1678, moved to Wat., and d. 1696, leaving *John*, *Thomas*, *Daniel*, and *Joseph*; and 4 drs., who m. John Justin, John Adams, Thomas Darby, and John Hartshorn. JOHN, of Wat., says Farmer, had a s. John, b. 1636; a John (w. Dority), d. in Wat., 1636, æ. 36. WILLIAM, of Sherb., by w. Rebecca, had *William*, 1698, and *John*, '99. JAMES, of Marlb., m. Mary Claise, Dec. 7, 1727.

BRUCE, ROGER, had by w. Elizabeth, in Marlb., 1. SAMUEL, b. Mar. 24, 1691, m. Elizabeth —, and f. of *Joseph*, b. 1726, in Marlb. and *Samuel*, b. 1729, and *Roger*, '34, both in Southb. (the f. prob. moved to Bolton); 2. ABIJAH, b. Nov. 27, 1693, m. Mary Woods, 1719; and in Fram. 3. ELISHA, b. Sep. 14, '95, m. Silence ——, and f. of *Jotham*, b. in Worc. 1720, and lived in Southb.; and *Elisha*, b. in Southb. '31; 4. REBECKAH, b. Feb. 22, 1698; 5. SARAH, b. Mar. 2, 1700; and in Marlb. 6. DANIEL, b. Feb. 22, 1701, m. Bathshebah Bowker, '32, and had in Marlb. *Abraham*, *Benjamin*, *John*, *Daniel* and others; 7. THOMAS, b. Jan. 5, 1704, m. Sarah ——, and d. at Bolton, 1743, æ. 39; 8. HANNAH, b. Feb. 18, 1706; 9. DELIVERANCE, b. Sep. 9, '09; 10. DAVID, b. June 9, 1711, had 2 wives and many chil. in Southb., among them *David*; *Phineas*; *Josiah*; *Moses*. Roger the f. d. in Southb. Sep. 16, 1733. His will was proved, Feb. 6, '34.

JOHN, by w. Elizabeth, had in Fram., 1. ELIZABETH, b. Nov. 8, 1695, m. Joseph Angier, Dec. 16, 1719; 2. BENJAMIN, b. Ap.

1, '98 ; 3. MARGARET, b. July 16,1700 ; 4. LYDIA, b. Oct. 13, '02 ; 5. MARY, b. Ap. 12, '06 ; 6. MARTHA, b. June 23, '08 ; 7. JOHN, b. Mar. 7, 1710–1 ; 8. JOHN, b. May 12, '14. 9. JONATHAN, d. Ap. 18, '15. Elizabeth w. of John, Sen. d. (prob. 1739) æ. 65.

3. JOHN, Jun., s. of John (2), m. in Marlb. Mary Potter, Jan. 11, 1733–4 ; and had in Fram., 1. KEZIAH, b. Oct. 12, 1734 ; 2. EPHRAIM, b. Ap. 29, 1736 ; 3. SARAH, b. Feb. 26, 1737–8, m. in Hop. Joseph Chaddock, '56 ; 4. CHARLES, b. Oct. 13, '39 ; 5. EPHRAIM, b. Jan. 13, '42 ; 6. MOLLY, b. Aug. 7, '44 ; 7. JOHN, b. Nov. 30, '45 ; 8. LYDIA, b. Nov. 30, '48 ; 9. LUCY, b. June 6, '50 ; 10. CHARLES, b. July 15, '53. John the f. was recommended to the ch. in Brookfield, 1770.

4. BENJAMIN, s. of John (2), m. Abigail Morse of Sherb., Dec. 16, 1719 ; and had in Fram. 1. LOIS, b. Oct. 16, 1719 ; 2. EUNICE, b. Jan. 27, 1723–4. [JONATHAN, bap. May 15, 1726, was perhaps s. of Benj.]

5. ELISHA, and w. Mary had in Fram., EUNICE, b. June 15, 1763. [ELIJAH, s. of Elijah was bap. June 30, 1765.]

6. EPHRAIM, s. of John. Jun. (3), and w. Elizabeth had in Fram., 1. NATHAN, b. Oct. 6, 1764 ; 2. OLIVE, b. Jan. 12, 1766.

7. DAVID, Jun., s. of David, g. son of Roger (1), had in Southb. SAMUEL, 1765 ; TIMOTHY, '68 ; and ABIGAIL, bap. in Fram. Sep. 13, 1771.

8. JOTHAM, (s. of Elisha, g. son of Roger (1),) w. Miriam, and chil. PERSIS, STEPHEN, JOTHAM, and MARY, with Jotham's mother, a widow, came from Hop. to Fram. 1774. *Note*—Jotham m. in Southb. Miriam Newton, 1742, and had in South., *Hezekiah*, 1742 ; *Hephsebah*, '45 ; *Persis* '47 ; *Jesse*, '50 ; *Reuben*, '52.

9. ELISHA, of Fram., m. Esther Breck in Southb. 1762 ; and had in Southb., HEZEKIAH, ELISHA, and others.

Note. — DAVID, of Marlb., m. Mary Bigelow, of Wat., Feb. 2, 1699–0, and had *David*, 1700, who m. Mary Brigham, 1727 The f. d. 1701. Dr. Stearns notes that JOHN and w. Elizabeth, in Sud , had *Hannah*, b. 1672 ; *Mary*, '80 ; *Eunice*, '84 ; *Martha*, '85. JOHN and w. Mary, of Sud., had chil. from 1753 to 1766. WILLIAM and w. Abigail, had in Marlb., *Nathaniel, John*, and others, from 1747 to 1761.

BRYANT, SAMUEL, and w. Lydia cov'd Ap. 12, 1752. THOMAS, their s. was bap. Apr. 1752.

Note.—Samuel was prob. s. of Thomas, of Sud., (from Reading), who m. Abigail Frink, and had *Abigail, Thomas, Sarah, Susannah,* and *Samuel,* b. Nov. 1, 1729. (Dr. Stearns' mss.) THOMAS, and his br. ABRAHAM, at Sud., were sons of Thomas and Mary, of Reading.

BUCK, ISAAC, was rated in Fram. ab. 1754. EBENEZER was in Fram. 1764. RUTH, was in Fram. 1763. JOSEPH, of Fram, m. in Hop. Hephsebah Bruce, 1768. Joseph lived near Eben. Claflin's. An aged man of this name is said to have d. in Fram., on the morning of the dark day.

BUCKMINSTER, or BUCKMASTER*. THOMAS BUCKMASTER, the progenitor of this family, came, according to tradition, from Wales, and is named in the Col. Records, Ap. 30, 1640, when he received a grant amounting to £10, from the General Court.† He was made free, May 6, 1646. He lived at Muddy River, (now Brookline), where he d. Sept 20, (Bos. Rec. say 28), 1656. His will, dated Sep. 2, '56, is recorded in Suff. Prob. His wid. Johanna, m. Edward Garfield, of Wat., Sept. 1, 1661; and admin. on her est. was had, 1676. E. Garfield's will was proved, 1672. The children of Thomas were 1. LAWRENCE, made his will, Nov. 27, 1645, then "going to England," and d. prob. unm., during his absence; his will was proved July 4, 1646. (Suff. Prob.) 2. ZECHARIAH; [Z. and w. Hannah had *Zechariah*, b. Nov. 28, 1658. (Bos. Rec.) Zechariah m. Sarah Webb., 7, 1, 1654-5. Zech. was among the early settlers of Sherb., in 167-, and was there 1692. (Mid. Co. Rec.) Sarah, wid. of Zech., d. at Roxb., June 27, 1704]; 3. ELIZABETH, m. Thomas Spowell, and had a dr. *Mary ;* two chil. are referred to in her f.'s will; 4 MARY, m. (Henry?) Stevens, and two chil. are referred to in her f.'s will; 5. DORCAS, m. Clement Corbil, or Corben, Mar. 7, 1654-5; 6. THOMAS, m. Mary, who had adm. on Thomas, carpenter, Feb. 1, 1659. T. had a dr. Mary, in 1646, (Lawrence's will); 7. SARAH, m. John Lawrence, Sep. 30, 1657; 8. JOSEPH ; 9. JABESH.‡ In his will, Thomas refers to Joseph and Jabesh, as his youngest sons. Vide State files — Estates I. 171; also, the bond of Joseph to his mother, June 25, 1663; same year, deed to Joseph from his mother Joanna Garfield. (Suff. Deeds.)

Note.—HANNAH, dr. of —— Buckmaster, bap. at Roxb., 1646. MARIE, m. in Charlestown, Jos. Widney, 1664. LYDIA m. in Roxb., John Clarke, 1680. MARY m. in Camb., Benjamin Dana, May 24, 1688. ABIGAIL m. in Andover, John Gutterson, (s. of William, and b. 1661), Jan. 14, 1689; MARY, cov. at Roxb., 1684. SUSANNA m. Daniel Loring, of Boston, (his 2d w.), 1717.

---

* Buckmaster is the name given upon the Records to all of the first and second generations. In a deed to Joseph, son of Thomas, the original ancestor, dated July 23, 1660, (Suff. Deeds), the name of Buckminster first appears, and is given to Joseph as grantee in the deed. The bounds of the land conveyed, are described as "on a lot late of Tho. Buckmaster dec'd, father to the aforesaid Jos. Buckmaster, party to these presents." (we think the former is most probable; the name is evidently altered from Thomas), received a part in the division of meadows in Sud., prob. ab. 1639. "BUCKMASTER'S houselot" is referred to, 1643, as near John Freeman's house. The individual does not appear to have resided long in Sudbury.

† Thomas or James Buckmaster,

‡ Farmer gives the name of John, as perhaps a son of Thomas. We have found no verification of this conjecture. There is a John Buckman on the Boston Rec.

2. JOSEPH, s. of Thomas, (1), m. Elizabeth, (b. Jan. 31, 1647-8,) dr. of Hugh Clarke. E. cov. at Roxb., 1666. Their children were 1. JOSEPH, b. July 31, 1666; 2. ELIZABETH, (posthumous), bap. in Roxb., 10, 11, 1668. Joseph, the f. d. in 1668. (Suff. Prob.) Elizabeth, the m. was buried in Fram.

3. JOSEPH, s. of Jos. (2.), was adm. to the Roxb. ch., 1684, m. Martha Sharp, dr. of John Sharp, of Muddy River, May 12, 1686. His chil. were 1. ELIZABETH, m. in Fram. John Wood, Mar. 3, 1704-5; 2. MARTHA, m. Ebenezer Winchester, Feb. 13, 1717-8, and 2d. Rev. James Bridgham, of Brimfield, Nov. 1, 1739; 3. JOSEPH, b. 1697; 4. THOMAS; 5. JOANNA, m. 1. John Eames, 2. John Butler, Mar. 19, 1740; 6. SARAH, m. Dr. Bezaleel Rice, June 23, 1720; 7. SYBILLA, m. John White, Jan. 24, 1728; 8. Zerviah, b. in Fram., July 26, 1710, m. William Brintnal, Dec. 19, 1729.

Col. Joseph the f., was a prop. of lands in Fram., 1693. The precise date of the removal of his family to the Town, is unknown. In deeds, dated 1702, he conveys as of Muddy River. He was adm. to the ch. by letter, Jan. 5, 1718. He was Selectman, 1700 and for 17 years in all; was Representative 12 years, and in the commission of the Peace many years. His estate in the town was large, his title to which involved him in protracted lawsuits which continued after his decease. He held several military commissions, commanded a Co. of Grenadiers, in Sir Charles Hobby's regiment, in the expedition to Port Royal, and subsequently had the command of a regiment of the Colonial militia. Tradition describes him as a man, tall and athletic, of great physical power, and of a resolute spirit. After participating largely in the events connected with the early history of the town, he d. Ap. 5, 1747, æ. 81 years. The remains of his mother and 2 wives were buried in the same grave. He m. 2d. Martha Dall, of Boston, Feb. 7, 1716, who d. Feb. 1724-5. He left a "negro woman, Nanny," valued in his Inventory at £80. For numerous conveyances to and from Col. Joseph, of land in and near Boston, see Suff. and Mid. Deeds.

4. JOSEPH, Jun. s. of Jos. (3.), m. Sarah Lawson, of Hop., June 18, 1719; by whom he had 1. JOSEPH, b. Mar. 1, 1719-0, H. C. 1739; ord. in Rutland, Sep. 15, 1742; m. in Weston, Mrs. Lucy Williams, June 30, 1743, and d. Nov. 3, 1792, æ. 72, f. of *Joseph*, b. Sep. 5, 1744, d. May 23, 1745; *Sarah*, b.

June 15, '47; *Lucinda*, b. Sep. 28, '49; *Joseph*, b. Oct. 3, '51, Y. Coll. 1770 and D. D., ord. at Portsmouth, N. H.; *Solomon*, b. Feb. 19, '54, m. Betty Davis, and 2 Hannah Rice, and moved to N. H., near Keene; *Hannah*, b. Ap. 13, '56; *Elizabeth*, b. Ap. 4, '58; *Wm. Stoddard*, b. June 6, d. Oct. 5, '61; *Isabell*, b. Oct. 25, '64; * 2. MARTHA, b. Aug. 20, 1726, m. Obadiah Curtis, of Boston, Dec. 28, '51; 3. ANNE, b. Dec. 3, 1728, m. Rev. Abraham Williams, of Sandwich, Sep. 11, '51; 4. SARAH, b. Ap. 26, 1733, d. Mar. 9, '41-2; 5. WILLIAM, b. Dec. 15, 1736, m. —— Barnes, rem'd. to Barre, 1757, com'd. the Co. of Minute men of B., and was dangerously wounded at Bunker Hill. Col. William d. June 22, 1786. [See a Biographical sketch of him, Worc. Mag. I. 79]; 6. FRANCES, b. Nov. 23, 1738, m. Col. Jona. Brewer; 7. LAWSON, b. Ap. 8, 1742. Sarah, the m. d. Sep. 11, 1747. Her husb. m. Wid. Hannah Kiggell, and had, 8. THOMAS, b. Aug. 18, 1751. Col. Joseph, Jun., who, (after passing through the subordinate ranks), rec'd his commission of Col. about 1738-9, was conspicuous in the transactions of the town; was for 28 years a Selectman; 32 years Town Clerk; Representative 19 (perhaps 28) years. He lived at first on the Brinley Farm, and later, near the burying ground; and d., after a long life of public service and personal worth, May 15, 1780, æ. 83. His w. Hannah d. Oct. 25, 1776.

5. THOMAS, s. of Jos. (3), m. in Medfield, Mrs. Sarah Baxter, Mar. 1, 1721-2, and had 1. WILLIAM, b. Jan. 23, 1722-3; 2. THOMAS, b. Feb. 25, '23-4, d. Sep. 30, '36; 3. ELIZABETH, b. Oct. 30, '26, d. young; 4. MARY, b. Nov. 5, '28; 5. ELIZABETH, b. Sep. 12, '30; 6. FRANCES, b. July 12, '32, d. Sep. 25, '36; 7. SAMUEL, b. July 3, '34; 8. THOMAS, b. Jan. 26, '36, d. Ap. 18, '37; 9. SARAH, b. Oct. 24, '39, d. Feb. 6, '41; 10. SUSANNAH, b. May 11, '41. Thomas the f. moved to Brookfield.

---

* The Rev. Joseph, of Rutland, is spoken of by Whitney, (Hist. of Worc. Co.), as "the able, faithful and worthy minister of R." Eliot (Biog. Dic.) calls him a "Sublapsanan Calvinist," and adds, that he engaged in controversy, and published several writings, among them Dissertations upon Gospel Salvation. His wife is said to have been dr. of Rev. William Williams, s. of Rev. William Williams, of Hatfield. Her mother was dr. of Rev. Dr. Stoddard, of Northampton. The Rev. Jos. Buckminster, D.D., of Portsmouth, N.H., (father of the Rev. Joseph Stevens Buckminster, of Boston), was son of the Rev. Joseph, of Rutland. For a notice of Dr. B. of Portsmouth, see Alden's Coll. Alden mistakes the number of generations between Dr. B. and the progenitor of the family.

6. LAWSON, s. of Jos. (4), m. Mary, dr. of John Jones, of Hop., May 4, 1769, and had 1. SARAH, bap. July 1, 1770, m. Daniel Stone, Jr., July, 1788, and d. Ap. 19, 1845, æ. 75, (see obituary Ch'n Register) ; 2. BETTY, b. Aug. 25, 1772, d. July 4, '93 ; 3, JOHN, b. May 6, '74, d. in Hop. unm., Mar. 14, '98 ; 4. RUTH, b. Sep. 17, '76, m. Eli Bullard, Esq., May, '94 ; 5. LAW-SON, b. May 16, '79, m. Nancy Howe, d. Ap. 5, 1835 ; 6. NANCY, b. Aug. 26, '81, m. Daniel Bell, U. S. Army, July 17, 1801, and d. at Darien, Geo., July 10, 1811 ; 7. WILLIAM, b. Jan. 22, '84, a lawyer in Fram., m. Sarah Larrabee. S., the w. d. July 24, 1842, æ. 54 ; 8. JONES, b. Dec. 5, '85, d. in Tenn., Ap. 3, 1806 ; 9. MARY J., b. Jan. 19, '88, d. Nov. 9, 1805 ; 10. CAROLINE, b. Mar. 27, '90, m. Capt. John J. Clark ; 11. FANNY, b. Mar. 29, '92, m. George Morey, Esq. ; 12. HARRIET, b. Oct. 7, '93, m. Darius Brewer, lives in Dorchester ; 13. ELIZABETH, b. Oct. 8, '96, m. Levi Eaton.

Maj. Lawson, the f., served in the Rev. War, and was a Lt. under Capt. Winch, at White Plains. He was 24 years Town Clerk ; 1 year T. Treasurer ; and 5 years a Selectman ; and for many years kept a public house. He d. at the venerable age of ab. 90, Feb. 26, 1832. His w. Mary d. Sep. 17, 1842, æ. 92 y. and 3 mos. (For obituary notice of Mrs. Mary, see Ch'n Register.)

7. THOMAS, s. of Jos. (4), m. Hannah Rice, and had 1. JOHN K., b. Oct. 2, d. Nov. 6, 1773 ; 2. JOSEPH, b. Oct. 6, '74, m. Betsey Bacon, Ap. 18, '99 ; 3. HANNAH, b. Sep. 9, '76, m. Dan. Gregory, Oct. 3, '95 ; 4. THOMAS, b. Aug. 21, '79, m. Mary Patterson, and d. Mar. 7, 1817 ; 5. ANNA, b. June 3, '82, d. Sep. 30, '84 ; 6. PAMELA, b. Feb 23, '84, d. Jan. 2, 1801 ; 7. DAVID, b. Mar. 2, '86, m. Ellen Means or Meads, 2d Dorcas Scammond, lives in Saco ; 8. PATTY, b. Jan. 6, '88, m. Abijah Stone, of Westborough ; 9. ANNA, b. July 4, '90, m. Charles Fiske ; 10. SUSAN, b. May 10, '92, m. Dr. John Cotton, of Plym. late of Marietta, O. Mrs. Hannah the m. d. July 1, 1793, æ, 42. Capt. Thomas m. 2d Kezia Bacon, Feb. 4, '94, and had by her 11. DEXTER, b. Nov. 14, '94, d. Dec. 21, '99 ; 12. DEXTER, b. Mar. 13, 1800, d. unm. July 31, '35 ; 13. MARY, b. June 9, '96, lives unm. in Nat. Thomas the f. was Deac. of the 1st ch. ; 9 years a Selectman ; and 4 years T. Treasurer ; and for many years kept

a public house near the centre of the town.* He d. July 7, 1826, æ. ab. 75. His wid. Keziah d. Feb. 1833.

Note.— MARY m. Tilly Rice, 1748, in ——. EDWARD, of Dedham, 1786, was a volunteer to suppress Shay's rebellion.

BULL, JACOB, was rated in Fram. ab. 1755.

BULLARD, SETH, (b. at Holl., Feb. 17, 1709, s. of Benj. and w. Tabitha, and br. of Jona. of Barre and Benj. of Holl.) m. Sarah Twitchell, and had in Holl., 1. EBENEZER, b. 1737 ; 2. SARAH, m. Solo. Walker ; 3. MARY, b. 1746, m. Sam. Claflin ; 4. COMFORT, b. 1751, prob. d. young. Sarah the m. d. '51, and her husb. m. 2d Lydia Haven, and moved to Fram. ab. 1761, and was chosen Warden, 1768. He lived first on Rich. Fiske's farm, and 2d on the farm of Geo. Bullard, where he d. 1775, and his wid. left town.

2. EBENEZER, s. of Seth (1), m. Betsey Haven, and had in Holl. 1. BETSEY, b. Ap. 9, 1759, m. Moses Fiske, of Fram.; and in Fram. 2. LYDIA, m. Ezekiel Rice ; 3. SALLY, m. John Parkhurst ; 4. POLLY, b. in Athol, m. —— Porter ; 5. DANIEL, b. in Templeton, m. Wid. —— Nutt; 6. EBENEZER, b. in Petersham, d. æ. 9 ; 7. SETH, b. in Athol, m. —— Newton, of Southb. Ebenezer the f. occupied the Geo. Bullard farm, where he d., 1792. His wid. left town, and d. 1811.

3. ELI, (s. of Henry, of Medway), Y. C. 1787, m. in Fram. Ruth Buckminster, May, 1794; and was f. of 1. CHARLES, b. July 4, 1796, d. at sea ; 2. NANCY, b. Dec. 20, '99, m. Otis Fairbanks ; 3. EDWARD ; 4. MARIA. Eli, Esq., practised as a lawyer in Fram., was Preceptor of the Academy, and Town Clerk 8 years. He d. 1824, æ. 65.

4. AARON, (b. June 7, 1770, s. of Samuel, Esq., of Holl. by his w. Lydia Partridge), m. Jerusha Littlefield, came to Fram. Ap. 8, 1793, and settled on the Maynard Farm, before occupied by Maj. Banister. He was f. of 1. DANA, b. Jan. 4, 1796, m. 1st, Elizabeth Goodnow, 2d, Mary Ann Tarlton ; 2. GEORGE, b.

---

* Feb. 22, 1775, Capt. Brown and Ens. D'Bernicoe, were ordered by Gen. Gage, to sketch the roads, passes, &c. between Boston and Worcester. They went disguised like countrymen; and in their journal note their stay twice at Mr. Buckminster's, in Framingham, who kept a public house. They relate that during the stay on their return, a military company exercised near the house ; after which, one of the commanders made a very eloquent speech, recommending patience, coolness and bravery. M. H. Coll. 2d Ser. IV. 209, 211.

July 30, '98, m. Mary Bullard, of Wayland; 3. CYRUS, b. Ap. 22, 1801, m. Lucy Goodnow; 4. LYDIA P., b. Dec. 4, 1803, m. Hollis Clayes; 5. EMELINE, b. Nov. 4, 1811, m. H. W. Coolidge. A. the f. d. in Fram., May, 1846.

Note.— The Bullards have been numerous in Dedham, Medfield, Sherb., Holl., &c. The Sherb. families appear to have descended partly from the Dedham, and partly from the Wat. Bullards. Benj. was of Wat., 1644. Benj. of Boggestow, in 1673, conveyed land in Wat., near Fresh Pond, to Justinian Holden. He was f. by w. Martha, of *Samuel*, who m. in Sherb., Deborah Atherton, June, 1691, and d. Dec. 11, 1727. Aaron descended from Benj. and w. Eliz., of Medfield and Sherb., through Isaac, (d. 1742), Samuel, (d. 1793), and Samuel, Jr., (d. 1815).*

BULLEN, SAMUEL, and w. Prudence, had in Fram., JOHN, b. Nov. 17, 1728; SAMUEL, b. Feb. 26, '30–1. S. the f. lived in the N. part of F., and sold to John Trowbridge. (Court R.)

2. JOHN, by w. Elizabeth, had in Fram., LOIS, b. Ap. 15, 1747; SAMUEL, b. Mar. 23, '49; JEDUTHAN, b. Jan. 21, '51; ASHBELL, b. Feb. 18, '53. July 13, 1755, " Elizabeth (the m.) had a letter by the hand of her father Adams, to the ch. in Wrentham, where she went to reside." (Ch. Rec.). E. was a wid. 1759.

Note.— The Bullens of this and neighboring towns, prob. sprung from SAMUEL and w. Mary, of Dedham and Medfield, who had *Mary*, b. 1642; *Samuel*, '44; *Elizabeth*, '46; *Joseph*, '51; *Ephraim*, '53; *Melatiah*, '55; *Elisha*, '56; *Eleazer*, '62, d. do; *Bethiah*, '64; and *John*, who m. Judith Fisher, and was f. of Samuel, b. 1702. Ephraim and Elisha had child. in Sherb., the 1st (Eph. whose est. was settled Sep. 13, 1697), f. by w. Grace, of Ephraim, John, and Mary, who m. John Sherman; the 2d, f. of Elisha, Sam., and Jonathan.

BURNHAM, JOB, from Hop. ab. 1769, m. Tabitha Newton, dr. of Wm., and had 1. SALLY, b. in Hop., Aug. 28, 1769, m. John Gallot, Ap., '94; 2. JOHN, (b. in Fram. as were all succeeding), d. young; 3. SUSANNAH, m. Abr. Loker, of Nat.; 4. DANIEL, m. Patty Dadmun; 5. MOSES, m. Lois Gleason, and Hannah Young. The f. then m. 2d. Nabby Merrit, and had 6. NABBY, d. young; 7. NATHANIEL, b. 1781, d. unm., æ 28; 8. MARY, d. æ ab. 19; 9. NICHOLS, d. æ 16. Job, the f. lived on a pasture, near S. House No. 4.; removed to Littleton, where he d. Mar. 1, 1803, æ ab. 64. His wid. Nabby d. May, 1817.

---

* William d. at Charlestown, his will, (proved March 17, 1686–7), dated July 5, 1679, he being then about 85 years of age. His w. was Mary; he had sons *Isaac*, (f. of William), *Nathaniel*, and a dr. *Elizabeth*.

Note.— Job was s of Josiah and w. Anne, of Hop., who had *Job*, b. at Chebacco, 1738; *Ruth*, d. unm. æ. 74; *Lydia*, m. Timo. Johnson; *Hannah*, m. John Muzzey, of Dublin; *Joshua*, m. Anne Osburn, and lived for a time in Fram.; and *Josiah*, m. Patty Bullard, of Holl. JEREMIAH, of Hop., was dismissed to Ipswich ch., 1754.

BUTLER, JOHN, proposed to cov. in the Fram. Ch. Jan. 29, 1723-4, and had by w. Elizabeth, 1. ELIZABETH, bap. in Hop., 1727; 2. JOHN, b. Mar. 28, '29, (Hop. Rec.); 3. PHINEHAS, b. June 3, '32, m. Bathsheba Graves, Ap. 27, '65, was an invalid pensioner, and d. in Fram. Jan. 16, 1806, æ. 73 1-2 years; 4. JOSEPH, b. Aug. 15, '34; 5. WILLIAM, b. Ap. 18, '38; 6. JOHN WOOD, b. Ap. 27, '40. Elizabeth the m. d. Ap. 27, 1740, and her husb. m. 2d Wid. Joanna Eames, dr. of Col. Buckminster, Sen., Mar. 19, 1740-1. Lt. John the f., a shoemaker, lived near Phinehas Rice's. His will, written Mar. 1744, (he being then bound for Cape Breton), was proved Ap. 20, 1747.

2. JOHN, Jun., s. of John (1), m. Hannah Drury, and had, MERCY, b. Jan. 6, 1763, d. July 30, '64. Capt. John built where Micajah Rice lives. He was in the Wars, and is said to have excited the enmity of the Indians, who once came to Fram. in quest of him; but he received notice of their design and secured himself. He is said to have had a s. WILLIAM, who was perhaps the W., of Cavendish, Vt., who m. in Fram., Catharine Dadmun, Feb. 25, 1797. Capt. John d. Mar. 20, 1795.

JOSEPH, s. of John (1), m. Sarah ——, and had in Nat. 1. JOSEPH, b. Aug. 28, 1757; and in Fram. 2. SARAH, b. Jan. 27, '59; 3. JOHN, b. Feb. 19, '61; 4. MARY, b. Feb. 3, '63; 5. BELA LINCOLN, b. Nov. 22, '64. Jos. the f. kept tavern in Fram., and also for a time in Concord. He lived where the f. of Mr. Joel Rice lived.

Note.— JOSEPH and w. Sarah, of Medfield, had *Joseph*, born 1665. THOMAS was of Hop., 1745, and d. 1766. JEREMIAH, his s., m. in Holl., Martha Morse, 1755, and had *Aaron*; *Joel*, bap. 1764; and prob. others. ELIZABETH m. in Southb., Reuben Comings, 1757. PETER and w. Sarah, of Marlb., had *John*, 1732, and others.

CAMBRIDGE, TOBY, m. Rose Mingo, Jan. 4, 1738-9.

CAMPBELL, DANIEL, b. in Glasgow, Scotland, Oct. 17, 1760, came to America, 1776; and was of Worcester, when he m. BEULAH How, of Fram., Sep. 22, 1780. His chil. b. in Fram. were 1. JAMES, b. Jan. 15, 1781, m. Fanny Babcock, of Milton; 2. JANE, b. Nov. 22, '83, d. Feb. '84; 3. FANNY, b. Jan. 22,

'85, m. Jerem. Sprague of Hingham, and 2d, Israel Gilman, of Sandwich, N. H. ; 4. EUNICE, b. June 2, '87, m. Wm. Durand of Boston, and d. ab. 1836 ; 5. WALTER, b. Feb. 24, '90, unm. ; 6. BEULAH, b. May 1, '92, m. Boylston Fulham, of Fitchburg, lives in Boston; 7. BETSEY, b. Jan. 15, '95, m. Levi Lord, of Boston, d. ab. 1819; 8. and 9. twins, b. Aug. 17, '97, viz: DANIEL, d. unm. æ. 24, and NANCY, m. Levi Lord, (his 2d w.), lives in Orange ; 10. JOHN, b. Oct. 15, '99, d. unm. Beulah the m. d. ab. 1823. Daniel the f. d. Dec. 20, 1838.

CARLILE, MARY, m. Samuel Walker, Jun., Sep. 28, 1738.

Note.—BARTHOLOMEW, and w. Hannah, of Sud., had *James*, 1686; *Hannah*, '87.

CARTER. " A child of Mr. Carter bap. Sep. 16, 1764." (Ch. Rec.)

Note.— In Sud., THOMAS m. Elizabeth White, 1682. JONATHAN and w. Susanna, 1741. JAMES and w. Priscilla, 1754.

CHAMPNEY, JONATHAN, in Fram. 1764. [Jonathan and w. Damaris, of Southb. had *William*, 1767 ; *Betty ; Benjamin ; Samuel ; Nathan* ; and others.]

2. NOAH, lived near the Trowbridge farm, and d. there. He had by w. Mary, ABNER, b. Jan. 14, 1770; WILLIAM, b. Mar. 29, '73 ; MILLY ; and ELLEN.

Note.—NOAH and w. Martha, of Camb., had *John*, 1727; and *Noah*, 1732. RICHARD and w. Jane, of Camb., 1635.

CHANDLER, THOMAS ; his son REUBEN bap. June, 1786.

CHENEY, JOHN ; his w. Elizabeth d. June 13, 1730. JOHN of F. m. Mary, dr. of Noah and Mary Clap, of Sud., Dec. 25, 1730. JESSE, s. of John, bap. Oct. 20, 1754.

JOHN and w. Mary, of Sud. had *Elias*, b. 1734. JOHN and w. Keziah, had Hester, 1748. JOHN and w. Hannah, had *Jesse*, b. 1754 ; *Abigail ;* and *Elias*. JOHN and w. Elizabeth, of Newton, had chil. from 1706 to '27 ; J. and E. in Weston, 1726 to '29. Cheneys lived in Medfield, 1663.

CHILD, JOSIAH, m. Experience Reed of Sud., Oct. 10, 1753 ; and had in Fram., 1. SARAH, b. Sep. 4, 1755, m. Phinehas Bemis of Southb.; 2. ABEL, b. Nov. 9, '57, m. Hannah Eaton, f. of *Asahel ; David ; Winsor ; Phebe ; Anne ; Noah ; Martha ; Nathan ; Mary ; Curtis*, and *Abel ;* 3. JOSIAH, b. Aug. 23, 1761, bap. June 10, '70, m. Nancy Brown, Mar. 31, '96, lives in Nat.; 4. DANIEL, b. Ap. 20, '64, d. May 25, '67 ; 5. ELIZABETH, b. Ap. 30, '66, m. Amos Johnson, of South. Aug. '86 ; 6. DANIEL, bap. July 26, '72, m. Abigail Haven, of Marlb. June 16, '96, drowned ab. 1824; 7. LYDIA, bap. Oct. '75, drowned in a well. Josiah and w. adm. from ch. in Rutland, May 23, 1779.

<small>Josiah had a brother Abiathar. JOHN, in 1755, was paid in Fram., for mending the meeting house glass. Deac. EPHRAIM, of Wat., d. 1663. This family is numerous on the Wat. and Newton Records.</small>

CHRISTY, JOHN, and w. in Fram. before 1722. HESTER, bap. May 1, 1720.

CHURCHILL, MERCY, in Fram. about 1770; built near Buckminster's saw mill, and d. in Fram. Nov. 2, 1818.

CLAFLIN, DANIEL, m. in Fram., Rachel Pratt, and had in Hop. DANIEL, bap. 1727, m. Mercy Wethe, in Holl. 1750; Mercy, w. of Daniel, d. in Fram. Aug. 3, 1798; 2. TIMOTHY, bap. 1729, m. Mary Gould, in Sutton, '51; 3. RACHEL, b. 1731; 4. CORNELIUS, b. Mar. 13, '33-4. Rachel the m. d. 1736. Daniel the f. d. in Fram., old and decrepid, ab. 1775.

<small>DANIEL, of Hop., m. Susanna Carril, 1736, and had *Hepsibah*, '37; Sarah w. of Daniel, d. 1743. In Hop., ROBERT m. Elizabeth Jeffers, Oct., 1734; CALEB m. Mary Tilton, 1735; EBENEZER m. Hannah Smith, 1739; CORNELIUS m. Elizabeth Carril, 1738; all of whom had chil. in Hop. SARAH, m. in Fram., David Pratt, Mar. 10, 1723-4.</small>

2. CORNELIUS, s. of Dan. (1), m. in Hop. Deb. How, 1753; and had in F., 1. JOHN, b. Ap. 8, '54; 2. INCREASE, bap. May 7, '58, m. Sarah, dr. of Geo. Stimson, Ap. 1782, removed to N. Y.; 3. ABIGAIL, bap. Nov. 2, '60, m. Eph. Newton, Mar. 1784, moved to Delhi, N. Y.; 4. HANNAH, b. Nov. 7, '62, d. unm. 1839; 5. WILLIAM, b. Nov. 16, '65, m. Sally Dougherty, Oct. 6, '94, and f. of *Patty; Betsey; Nancy; William*, and *Milton*. Wm. the f. d. in Fram.; 6. ASA, bap. Ap. 16, '69, m. Jenny Dougherty, Ap. '93, and f. of *Micah; Alvin; Abijah; Ebenezer; David*, and *Olivia*. Asa the f. d. in. Fram. Jan. 1817; his w. d. 1829; 7. SARAH, m. Benjamin Morse, Nov. 1792, and d. in Fram.; 8. ELIZABETH, b. Ap. 11, '75, m. Nath'l Pike, of Hop. Cornelius the f. d. Aug. 1, 1818, æ. 84. Deborah his w. d. 1821.

3. JOHN, s. of Cornelius (2), m. Henrietta Stimson, of Fram.; and had in F. 1. AARON, b. Aug. 25, 1778; 2. BETSEY, b. Mar. 2, '81; 3. HENRIETTA, b. Ap. 23, '83; 4. JOHN, b. Oct. 9, '85. John the f. moved to N. Y. state, ab. 1790.*

<small>* Antipas and w. Sarah, of Lexington, (at one time prob. of Sud.), had *Sarah*, 1706; *Robert*, '08; *Noah*, '10; *Nehemiah*, '13. Robert Mackloff-</small>

CLAP, EDWARD, rated in Fram. ab. 1720. This family was numerous in Sud., and connected with the Claps of Dorchester.
CLARK, or CLARKE, ISAAC, m. Sarah Stow, of Marlb. and had, 1. MARTHA, b. ab. 1694, m. Maj. Joseph Willard, of Grafton, July 5, 1715–16, and d. at G. 1794, æ. 100; 2. SARAH, b. Aug. 5, 1701, m. Thomas Drury, Jun., June 10, 1719; 3. MARY, b. Dec. 31, 1705, m. William Coy; 4. MATTHIAS, m. Lydia Eaton, Oct. 17, 1729; [Cornet Matthias was in Fram. 1738. He d. in Leicester]; 5. JONATHAN, b. July 9, 1706, d. May 2, 1709; 6. ISAAC, b. Mar. 25, 1709; 7. JONATHAN, b. 1712; 8. REBECKAH, b. Sep. 30, 1716, m. Lt. Samuel Stone, June 14, 1737. Capt. Isaac the f. bo't, 1705, of Col. Buckminster, 90 ac. of Lynde's land. He commanded a Co. of Troopers in Fram., and d. May 26, 1768, at the extreme age of 102. Sarah his w. d. May 17, 1761, æ. 88. "He lived 70 years with the wife of his youth. His offspring that descended from him was 251." (G. Stone.)*

len, of Wenham, had *Daniel*, b. Jan. 25, 1674, and several daughters. Tradition in the Claflin family gives their name as originally McLaughlin. Hopkinton was settled by many Scotch emigrants. Were the Claflins among them? The Claflins of Fram. have generally lived near the common.

* ISAAC was son of Thaddeus, "a man of standing and enterprise," who came from Ireland, lived at "Clarke's Point," Portland, was one of the commandants there, and m. Elizabeth, 2d dr. of Michael Mitton, (whose w. was Elizabeth, only dr. of George Cleeves), about 1662; and his eldest dr., Elizabeth, m. Capt. Edward Tyng, (whose daughter Elizabeth m. a brother of Dr. Franklin), and another daughter m. a Harvey, and was a wid. in Boston, 1719. Lt. Thaddeus was killed by the Indians at Munjoy's Hill, 1690, and his wid. d. in Boston, 1736, æ. 92. (Maine Hist. Coll. I 203, 208, and 214). Mrs. Beulah Patterson, b. 1740, g. dr. of Capt. Isaac, of Fram., stated before her death, (thus writes Rev. Joseph Allen, of Northb.), that Isaac came from Falmouth, and that his mother and his sister Rebeckah were taken by the Indians and carried captive to Canada, where the mother died. Rebeckah was sold to the French Canadians, among whom she lived so contented, that when money was sent for her ransom, she refused to leave; sending word that "the money sent was not sufficient to supply her table for a single day." Tradition relates, that Capt. Isaac learned the carpenter's trade at Marlborough, and settled at Fram., in the wilderness, æ. 25, near or at Mr. Joel Tayntor's. When Gen. Amherst halted with his army at Marlb., on his march to Canada, 1759, (he encamped near the pond, and had his quarters at the tavern), he invited Capt. Clark, then much advanced in years, to breakfast with him. The latter rode to Marlb. on horseback, and his vigor and vivacity so delighted his host, that he was invited to accompany the General in a review of his troops. While riding his young horse, the General said, "Capt. Clark, you have a fine horse there; if you will sell him, I will give you his full value." The old man answered, "No! General. He was born on my farm; I raised him for my own use, and now I mean to wear him out." Capt. Clark re-

2. ISAAC, s. of Isaac (1), m. Mary Stone, Ap. 21, 1740; and had BEULAH, b. July 23, 1740, m. David Patterson.

3. JONATHAN, s. of Isaac (1), m. Anne Wilson, May 2, 1745; and had 1. JONAS, b. 1745; 2. BENJAMIN, d. unm. in Fram. ab. 1815; 3. PHINEHAS, d. unm. at sea; 4. WILLIAM, m. Hannah Moulton, of Wayland, and d. 1821; 5. ANNE, m. and lived in Boston and Maine. Jona. the f. lived at the N. part of Fram. and d. ab. 1789. Anne his w. d. 1797, æ. 81.

4. JONAS, s. of Jona. (3), m. Mary How, and with w. adm. to ch. Oct. 6, '65. Their chil. were 1. MOLLY, b. Aug. 8, '64, m. Abr. Eager, of Marlb. Dec. '85; 2. ELEANOR, b. Ap. 24, '66, m. Seth Grout of Wethersfield, Vt.; 3. ISAAC, b. Nov. 20, '67, m. Wid. Tabitha Winch, and d. in Fram. 1846; 4. ANNA, b. Oct. 20, '69, d. young; 5. JONAS, b. May 1, '71; 6. BETTY, b. July 28, '72, m. Jona. Holden, of Winsor, Vt.; 7. ANNA, b. Oct. 20, '74, m. Samuel Lovejoy of Winsor, Vt.; 8. PATTY, b. May 15, '74, m. Dumarel Grout, of Wethersfield, Vt.; 9. SALLY, b. Sep. 20, '76, m. Elijah Pike, of Hop., after of Petersham; 10. PHINEHAS, b. July 10, '78, m. Sally Margate, of Weston, now in Penn.; 11. ABRAHAM, b. Mar. 26, '80, m. Lydia Clark; 12. MOSES, b. Oct. 14, '81, unm.; 13. HITTY, b. Jan. 7, '85, d. May 15, 1805. Jonas the f. kept school, was a ready penman, and d. Dec. 1819, æ. 74. His w. Mary d. 1811, æ. 66.

5. URIAH, d. in Fram. Feb. 24, 1725. His est. was administered by his only son, PEASE, the wid. refusing; Benjamin, of Wat. a surety. [Uriah, of Wat. m. Mary Pees, of Camb. 1701.]

6. PEASE, s. of Uriah (5), had in Fram., URIAH, b. Oct. 29, 1728. Pease's est. was administered, Jan. 1728.

7. WILLIAM, s. of Isaac Jun., of Hop., m. Sally Bixby, and had in Fram., LUKE BIXBY, b. Feb. 21, 1793. William, the f. d. at the South.

---

tained his vigor to a remarkable degree, and on his centennial birth-day, rode on horseback to and from Col. Trowbridge's. He was a man of temperate habits and correct morals. He was several times chosen messenger of the church. His conjugal connection was protracted far beyond the common bounds, and has, (to our knowledge), been exceeded in duration but in one instance in this town. Mary, w. of Wm. Hunt, Esq. d. in F., Jan. 1843, æ. 90, having lived with the husband of her youth 71 y. 8 m. The late Mr Jona. Patterson, of Northborough, g. g. son of Capt. Clark, had in his possession, a year or two since, an ancient silver headed cane, marked with " Jonathan Clark, 1697."

8. EDWARD, from R. Island, was minister of the Bap. Ch. in Fram. near 20 years. He m. Elizabeth Luke, and had SALLY, b. May 16, 1782, d. Dec. 22, 1784; and ALMA, m. Artemas Parker.

9. CALEB, taxed in Fram. 1734; he was prob. the Caleb, of Sud. who had CALEB, b. 1742, BENJAMIN, SETH, CALVIN, JONAS, and others.

HUGH and w. Elizabeth, had at Wat., JOHN, b. Oct. 13, 1641; URIAH, b. June 5, '44; ELIZABETH, b. Jan 31, '47-8, m. Col. Joseph Buckminster. In 1681, Hugh and w. Elizabeth, of Roxbury, conveyed to s. John, of Muddy River, 67 acres in New Cambridge, (Newton).

JOHN, of Newton, m. Elizabeth Norman, 1684, and his will was proved Mar. 25, 1695. Inventory £660. His chil. were, 1. JOHN, m. Ann Peirce, of Dorchester, 1697, and f. of *Mary*, b. 1698; *John*, b. Sep. 22, 1700; *Thomas*, b. 1704, m. Mary Bowen, 1728, and d. at Hop., June 30, 1775, f. of Peter, b. 1729; Jonas, 1730, H. C., 1752, ord. at Lexington; Thomas; Penuel, &c.; *Isaac*, b. 1707, m. Experience Wilson, and lived in Hop., f. of John, Abigail, Isaac, Samuel, of Hubbardston, Stephen, and a dr.; and by 2d w., of Lemuel, William, and Avis; *Atherton*, b. 1711, m. Patience ——, and lived at Hop., f. of Atherton, Peter, Penuel, &c.; 2. WILLIAM, b. June 20, 1686, d. 1737, f. at Newton, by w. Hannah, of *Caleb, William Sarah*, and *Joanna*; 3. ANN, b. 1688; 4. MARTHA, b. 1690; 5. ESTHER, b. 1692; 6 HANNAH, b. 1693; 7. MOSES, b 1695. JOHN and w. Susanna were of Sud. 1742, and had *Peter, John, Jonathan, Luther*, &c. ARTHUR, of Sherb. 1719, was from Lincoln.

CLEMENSE, MARY, bap. Nov. 23, 1747. "Oct. 14, 1764, were bap. JOHN, JOSEPH and BENJAMIN, chil. of Mary Clemense, now w. of —— Green, of Upton, by profession, Anabaptist." Ch. Rec. 1771, John Clemens, æ. ab. 80, came from Upton to Fram. (T. Rec).

CLEVERLAND, ENOCH, in Fram. 1716, (T. Rec).

CLOYES. This name is variously written Clayes, Cloyse, Cloise, and Cloice, now Clayes and Cloyes.

1. JOHN CLOISE* was, by profession, a mariner, and settled first at Watertown. Oct. 31, 1639, he is referred to in the Col. Records, in connection with his servant, Peter Tylle, whom he was "to teach his trade of a seaman, by himself or others." His house at Wat. was "burned down," ab. 1656, when he, (then of Charlestown), with w. Jane, sold his land, &c, at Wat., to Samuel Stratten. He received a part in the division of wood at Charlestown, Mar. 1, 1658; and July 25, 1660, conveyed land in Charlestown to Giles Fifield. The same year, at Falmouth, Me., he signed a petition to the General Court., and in 1670, was living on the W.

---

* See a petition of Alexander Gordon, dated 1653. (Mid. Co. Files). A. G. came over with Mr Cloise, in the ——, Mr. John Allen, master; was imprisoned with others at Tuttellfield, whence they were redeemed by monies paid by Mr. Dan. Stone, of Camb. Oct. 15, 1652, Alex Gorthing, (prob. the same), Scotchman, "lately being arrived in New England, was apprenticed to Goodman Stratton, of Wat., in presence of John Cloyse," &c. (Mid. Deeds).

side of Presumpscot River. He is supposed to have been killed by the Indians, in 1676. He is said (His. of Portland) to have had two wives, Abigail and Juliann, the latter being, in 1667, 47 years of age His chil. b in Wat., were 1 JOHN, b. Aug. 26, 1638; 2. PETER, b. May 27, 1639; 3 NATHANIEL, b. May 6, 1642, m Sarah (Mills?), and w. Sarah, was received to Charlestown church, Jan. 8, 1698. He also had, 4. ABIGAIL, m. Jenkins Williams; 5 SARAH m. Peter Housing; 6. THOMAS m. Susannah. dr. of George Lewis, and had *Mary*, b July 6, 1677 ; *Thomas*, who d. in Boston, before 1735, without issue; *George*, who m Lydia Deall, 1717, and lived in Salem, 1735; and *Hannah*. Thomas, the f. was killed by the Indians, May, 1690; the inventory of Thomas, " late of Casco Bay," is dated Dec. 2, 1700; * 7. MARTHA, b. at Charlestown, Oct. 13, 1659.

2. PETER, s. of John (1), lived at Wells, Me., and afterwards, in 1692, at Salem. He removed about the time of the Witchcraft delusion to Fram., settled at Salem End, where he d. July 18, 1708. From his will, dated three days before his death, it appears that his chil. were 1. MARY, (then a wid.), who m. Joseph Trumbull, and lived in Fram.; 2. HANNAH, m. Daniel Elliot, (lived in Fram. and Oxford) ; 3. HEPHZIBAH, m. Ebenezer Harrington, of Wat., Feb. 3, 1707–8 ; 4, ——, who prob. m. —— Waters or Wallers; 4. ALICE, m. —— Bridges ; 5. JAMES ; 6. PETER. Peter Sen. had 3 wives, viz: HANNAH, (m. of Mary) ; SARAH, (m. of Hepzibah and Alice). His 3d w. was Susanna Beers, of Wat., whom he m. Jan. 2, 1704. (Susa. was prob. dr. of Robert Harrington of Wat.) Peter Sen. was T. Treasurer 1701, Moderator of several Town Meetings, and Selectman, 3 years.

3. PETER, s. of Peter (2), m. at Salem, Mary Preston, Dec. 13, 1693, and had in Fram. 1. ELIZABETH, b. Sep. 22, 1694; 2. MARY, b. Nov. 15, '96, m. in Marlb., James Brown, Dec. 7, '27; 3. MARTHA, May 12, '99 ; 4. ABIGAIL, b. Mar. 31, 1701 ; 5. EXPERIENCE, b. Nov. 19, '02, m. John Parker, and d. Feb. 23, 1783 ; 6. SUSANNAH, b. Dec. 13, '04, m. Simon Goddard, Nov. 2, '27 ; 7. REBECKAH, b. Dec. 6, '06 ; 8. PETER, b. June 21, '13, d. Ap. 17, 1736 ; 9. JOSIAH, b. Aug. 27, '15. Peter the f. was Selectman 9 years, and none of his descendants, (except through his daughters), are living in Fram.

---

* The Hist. of Portland states, that Thomas was at Saco, 1671, and in 1674 lived at Falmouth, between Round Marsh and Capisic ; that two of the sons of John, sen., viz.: John and Nathaniel, moved to Wells, and m. sisters, drs. of Thomas Mills. Peter, s. of John, was living at Wells, before John and Nathaniel moved there. Julian, w. of John, had a dr. Sarah Spurwell. We may add here, that the Charlestown Rec. contain the marriage, in 1664, of John with Mary Long. Also, the birth, July 1, 1657, of Mary, dr. of John and w. Sarah. Farmer notes Nathan, of Mass., admitted freeman, 1660.

4. JAMES, s. of Peter (2), m. Mary ——, who was adm. to the ch. 1727, and had in Fram., 1. ESTHER, b. Ap. 27, 1702, m. Daniel How, of Shrewsbury, 1725; 2. KEZIAH, b. Dec. 8, '05, m. Wm. Goddard, of Shrews., Jan. 26, 1726-7; 3. JOHN, b. Sep. 25, '07; 4. JAMES, b. June 10, '10; 5. MARY, b. Oct. 1, '12, m. Deac. Jona. Morse, May 16, '34; 6. HANNAH, b. Ap. 4, '17, m. Josiah Wilson, of Hop. Ap. 22, '35.

5. JOHN, s. of James (4), m. Elizabeth Morse, Dec. 10, 1730; and had 1. MARY, b. Nov. 3, 1731, m. Rev. Amariah Frost; 2. RUTH, b. Feb. 19, '33, prob. d. young; 3. JOHN, b. Mar. 22, '35-6. John m. 2d Zerviah Town, Nov. 22, 1748, and had 4. ELIZABETH, bap. Feb. 8, '49-0, m. —— Ballard, lived in Penn. Zerviah, w. of John, d. 1766. John the f. d. ab. 1790.

6. JAMES, Jun., s. of James (4), m. Lydia Eames, July 24, 1735; and had 1. PETER, b. Oct. 30, 1736, d. young. Lydia the m. d. Nov. 8, '36; and James the f. m. Abigail Gleason, May 28, 1740; and had 2. JOSIAH, b. Sep. 30, '41; 3. JAMES, b. Feb. 13, '42-3; 4. ELIJAH, b. Sep. 5, '44; 5. LYDIA, b. Aug. 7, '46, m. Simon Tozer; 6. ABIGAIL, b. Aug. 7, '52, m. John Mayhew, and d. in Fram. 1825; 7. PETER, b. Mar. 28, '54. James the f. was Selectman 5 years, and d. Jan. 1798; his w. Abigail d. Ap. 1798.

7. JOHN, Jun., s. of John (5), m. Desire Perry, of Sherb. Mar. 25, 1762; and had 1. DESIRE, b. Ap. 13, '63, m. Sam. Haven, d. in N. Y.; 2. JOSIAH, b. Feb. 4, '65, m. Eunice Luke, who d. June 22, 1836, æ. 64, and 2d Eunice Dadmun; 3. LUTHER, b. Jan. 23, '67, m. Sally Temple, of Marlb. 1795, lives in Utica, N. Y.; 4. DANIEL, b. Ap. 20, '70, m. —— Lee, in Utica; 5. POLLY, b. Ap. 25, '73, m. Rob. Eames, of Whitestown, N. Y., Jan. 24, '93; 6. RUTH, b. Aug. 5, '77, m. Wm. Gleason. John the f. was killed by lightning, June 3, 1777, æ. 41. His wid. Desire m. Daniel Hemenway, and d. 1809.

8. JAMES, s. of James (6), m. Mehetabel Gates, (b. in Spencer), and had, 1. RUTH, b. Dec. 24, 1767, and m. Uriah Jennings, of Whitestown, N. Y., Dec. '90; 2. MEHETABEL, b. Ap. 24, d. May 27, '70; 3. a stillborn child, Sep. 18, '71; 4. JAMES, b. July 31, '73, d. Sep. 18, '77; 4. EZRA, and 5. MICAJAH, twins, b. Dec. 23, '76 — E. m. Lydia Hill, and d. at Buffalo, 1840; M. m. Dorothy Morse, Jan. 26, 1800, lives in Eaton, N. Y.; 6.

James, b. July 30, '81 ; 7. Elijah, b. Dec. 15, '83, m. Aseneth Morse, lives in F. ; 8. Jonas, b. Ap. 14, '88, m. Susannah Morse, lives in F. James the f. was Selectman 4 years, lived on the farm late of his s. Elijah, and d. Dec. 9, 1809. Mehet. his w. d. Nov. 2, 1822, æ. 76 1-2 years.

9. ELIJAH, s. of James (6), m. Abigail Pepper ; and had in Fram. 1. Sarah, b. Jan. 8, 1763, m. Fortunatus Nichols, Sep. '83 ; 2. Elijah, b. Dec. 23, '64, m. Levinah Hemenway, Mar. '90, and d. May 22, 1815 ; 3. Benjamin, b. Mar. 20, '67, m. —— Larrabee, had 10 sons and d. in Charlestown No. 4 ; 4. Abigail, b. Aug. 29, '69, prob. d. young ; and in Fitzwilliam, 5. Joseph, b. Sep. 20, '71, m. —— How and d. in Shrewsb. ; 6. Nathan, b. Oct. 17, '73, followed the seas ; 7. Betsey, b. Nov. 15, '75, went to Dudley with her m. and m. a Phipps. Capt. Elijah the f. d. at White Plains, in the Rev. War. His wid. Abigail m. Maj. Nath. Healey, of Dudley.

10. PETER, s. of James (6), m. Polly Nixon, Jan. 1785, and had, 1. Polly, b. July 22, 1785, m. —— Harris of Bridgeport, Vermont ; 2. Sophia, b. Sep. 25, 1786, d. unm. 1804 ; 3. Nancy, b. June 5, '88, d. young ; 4. Amy, b. Mar. 23, '90, m. —— Hemenway, and d. young ; 5. Dana, bap. Oct. '92, M. Coll., Vt., a minister at Plainfield ; 6. Francis, bap. June '94, m. —— Crowfoot, of Vt. ; 7. George, bap. July '96, m. in Shelburne, Vt, ; 8. Sukey, bap. Nov. '98, d. 1802. Capt. Peter was a Selectman 6 years, and a Trustee of the Academy. He moved to Bridgeport, Vt., in the Spring of 1803, and d. there.

COGGIN, MARY, m. William Ward, of Worcester, Feb. 20, 1732-3. [John, and Josiah were of Sud., ab. 1733.]

COLE, JOHN, was bap. in Fram. Mar. 10, 1723. Jonathan, bap. May 2, 1725. Samuel of Fram. m. Sarah Boutel of Reading, in Wob., 1728.

2. ONESIMUS, m. Jemima Leland, both of Sherb., Oct. 16, 1771 ; and had (prob. in Sherb.) Thaddeus ; Samuel ; John ; Joseph ; Sally ; Polly ; Rhoda ; Jemima ; and ——. Jemima the m. d. Oct. 2, 1792, æ. 40. Her husb. m. 2. Betsey Wheeler, of Concord, Nov. 7, 1793 ; and had in Fram. Calvin ; Eliza, d. young ; Abigail ; Sukey ; Francis ; and Rebeckah. O. the f. lived near Mr. Charles Clark's and elsewhere, and d. Oct. 8, 1814, æ. 63. His wid. Betsey m. ——Hill.

COLLER, or COLLAR, JOHN early took the oath of fidelity, at Wat. John and w. Hannah, of Camb., had JOHN, b. Mar 6, 1661, and THOMAS, b. Dec. 14, '63. (Camb. Records). John, sen., owned land in Fram. and Sud., 1693. He bought of Benj. and Ebenezer Rice, Apr. 4, 1691, S. of Sud. bounds. [MARY m. in Marlb, Samuel Holland, Jan. 9, 1695-6. HANNAH, m. in Wat., James Cutting, 1679. NATHANIEL, of Sud., m. Mary Barret, Oct. 10, 1693, and was of Chelmsford, 1698; Nath., of Stow, d. at Annapolis Royal, 1711, (prob. without chil.) JANE m. in Boston, Tho. Walker, 1706. RICHARD commanded a brigantine from Boston, 1715.]

2. JOHN, s. of John, (1). d. in Nat., and his will was proved Oct., 1718. He had a w. Elizabeth, and chil. 1. THOMAS; 2. JOHN, m. Sarah Morse, of Needham, Jan. 13, 1720; 3. PHINEHAS, m. Hannah Daniels, of Sherb., Jan. 1, 1730, and had *Elizabeth*, 1731; 4. URIAH; 5. JOSEPH; 6. HEZEKIAH, b. ab. 1714, m. in Sud., Elizabeth Rice, March 1, 1743, and had *Lydia*, b. May 13, '44, m. Samuel Dunn, and d. young; 7. SUSANNA; 8. PRISCILLA, m. Peter Gallop, of Fram., Jan. 10, 1733-4; 9. SYBILLA, m. in Newton, Joseph Bartlett, Feb. 11, 1730-1. In 1705, the Nat. Indians petitioned the Court for liberty to sell to John, Jr., carpenter, 200 acres of land, for building their meeting house.

3. THOMAS, s. of John (2), m. 1. Alice Alden of Needham, Ap. 9, 1719, and 2. Elizabeth Dunton of Sud., Jan. 19, '20-1, and had ALICE, b. in Nat. Mar. 26, 1729, m. Tho's Stone of F., and d. 1782. Tho. the f. was in Fram. 1749 and deer-rieve 1757. He built the old Thomas Stone house, occupied after by his s. in law. He d. 1770; his w. d. 1780.

4. JAMES, by w. Elizabeth, had in Fram. 1. JAMES, b. Jan. 20, 1695-6; 2. JOSEPH, b. Dec. 16, 1702, m. Mercy Travise in Hop., 1729, and f. of *Joseph*, bap. 1729; *Daniel*, b. Sep. 7, '32, and rated in Fram. ab. 1757. JAMES the f. had also JONAS, b. 1713, d. 1795 at Oxford; and ELIZABETH, who m. Daniel Tombs, 1739. J. the f. m. 2d Hannah Twitchell, 1746, and d. in Oxford, 1749. (Worc. prob.)*

5. JAMES, Jun., s. of James (4), was adm. to Fram. ch. Feb. 16, 1718; and had in F., 1. JONATHAN, b. May 8, 1718; 2. DAVID, bap. Sep. 10, 21; 3. SARAH, bap. in Hop. '24. J. was dism. to Hop. ch., Nov. 19, '27.

Note. — Mrs. Mercy Collar, m. in Fram., Christopher Nixon, Aug. 16, 1748. HANNAH m. James Beale, in Weston, Sep. 5, 1718. MARY, of Needham, m. Nath. Dewing, of Weston, 1763. OLIVER was an early prop. at Oxford. Coller's Meadow is early named in Fram. Records, as in the S. W. part of Fram. Collars lived near Mr. Charles Clark's.

COLLINS, JOSEPH, and EBENEZER, rated in Fram. about 1768. This name is found on the Southb. Rec.

COOK, EDMUND, a field driver in Fram., 1705.

---

* In 1755, James Coller, æ. 55, deposed (Clerk's Off. C. C. P. Boston) that he had lived six months at Arousick Island, near the mouth of the Kennebeck, and 33 years at Richmond fort.

2. JAMES, m. Lydia Fisk in Newton, Nov. 24, 1737 ; and had in Fram., 1. JONATHAN, b. Dec. 3, '38 ; 2. LYDIA, b. Jan. 22, '39-0 ; 3. STEPHEN, b. June 24, '41 ; 4. ENOCH, Jan. 4, '44 ; 5. ZEBEDIAH FISK, Feb. 26, '46 ; and at Newton, 6. ELIZABETH, b. July 8, '48.

Note. — Stephen and w. Rebeckah, of Newton, had *James*, b. Jan. 23, 1688-9 ; *Samuel*; and *Peter*. ANDREW was of Sud., 1702 ; THOMAS, of Hop. 1726.

COOLIDGE, OBADIAH, and family are noticed in the T. Rec. as in Fram. 1729.

2. JOEL, s. of John and w. Elizabeth, of Sherb., came to Fram. 1788, and bought of wid. Sarah Bixby. He m. Martha Ware, of Sherb., and had in S. 1. CHARLES, b. '82, d. unm., 1803, in S. C. ; 2. MEHETABEL, b. Mar. 24, '84, m. Silvanus Phipps ; 3. SOPHIA, b. '87, m. Dr. Daniel Stone, of Sharon, and d. 1820 ; 4. PATTY, b. July 23, 1789, m. Josiah Fisk ; 5. SALLY, b. Mar. 27, '92, m. David Haven ; 6. FRANCIS, b. May 3, '97, m. Mahala Stone, of Dublin ; 7. HENRY WARE, b. May 3, '97, m. Emily Bullard, and d. Oct. 16, 1841 ; 8. JOSEPH B., b. Dec. 21, '99, lives in Boston. Joel the f. was Selectman 1708, and d. Oct. 5, 1841, æ. 82. Martha his w. d. Sep. 23, 1825, æ. 69.

COY, or MACOY, WILLIAM, m. Mary Clark, of Fram., and had, 1. WILLIAM, bap. Sep. 5, 1725 ; 2. MARY, bap. July 24, '26. Wm. and w. cov'd Sep. 5, 1725, and was in Fram. 1730.

2. NATHANIEL, m. Sarah Eames, of Fram., Feb. 4, 1725-6 ; and had 1. SARAH, b. Aug. 27, 1726, m. John Mistrick, Aug. 12, '47 ; 2. ABIGAIL, b. July 12, d. 14th, 1728. Sarah w. of Nath. d. July 23, 1728, æ. 27.

ARCHEBALD and w. Margaret, of Newton, (m. 1692), had *Hannah*, 1693 ; *William*, '95 ; *John*, '98 ; *Nathaniel*, '01 ; *Abigail*, '04 ; *Edward*, '06 ; *Elizabeth*, '12, d. '16 ; *Nehemiah*, '14 ; *Mary*, '20. Daniel Macoy, tailor, was of Camb., 1678, and of Cambridge village, 1679. John Coye killed at Brookfield, 1675.

CRAIGIE, JOHN, rated in Fram. 1784.

CROSBY, MARY, adm. to the ch. July 7, 1754. [JOSEPH m. Hannah Maynard, in Marlb., 1714, and d. in Worc. 1744.]

CRUMMIEL, JACOB, and w. Nanny had in Fram., 1. ELIZABETH, b. Feb. 25, 1770 ; 2. JACOB, b. Ap. 22, '73. Jacob the f. was taxed ab. 1790.*

---

* It is said that an old lady by the name of Franklin was of his family, and that he represented himself as having been saved at the earthquake of Lisbon.

CUSANS, COZENS or CUZZENS, ABRAHAM, taught school in Fram. 1715. Martha was bap. July 13, 1718. Martha dism. to the ch. in Sherb. Ap. 23, 1723.

Abraham bought in Sherb., 1684, on Chestnut and Dopping Brooks, m. in Wob. Mary Eames, '84, and had in Sherb., *Abraham*, '85, m. Abigail Wilkinson, of Charlestown, 1709; *Isaac*, '88, f. by w. Martha, of Martha, 1717; Joseph, and others, and d. 1754, in Holl.; *Jacob*, and *Joseph*, '92; and *Mary*, or *Mercy*, '95. The descendants have lived near the S. bounds of Fram. Isaac was of Boston, 1656.

CUTLER, JONATHAN, rated in Fram. 1710, m. Abigail Gale, Jan. 10, 1716-7, and w. adm. to ch. June 15, 1718. Their chil. were 1. Jonathan, b. Mar. 26, 1719; 2. David, b. Oct. 7, '21. The wid. Abigail had admin. on Jonathan's est., 1722.

Thomas and w. Tabitha, of Sud., 1707. Jonathan, who d. in Holl., 1762, æ. '52, (his w. Abigail). was from Medfield. Jonathan, of Marlb., m. Deliverance Hartshorne, 1764. Jonathan and w. Abigail, of Weston, 1724. Jonathan, of Killingsle, m. in Wat.. Abigail Bigelow, 1710. Nathan, s. of Nathan, bap. in Fram., Oct. 2, 1774.

CUTTING, HEZEKIAH, was Highway Surveyor in Fram. 1727. Keziah, was bap. Sep. 26, 1725. Lydia bap. Dec. 10, '27.

Hezekiah and w. Mary, of Sud. had *William*, b. 1713, d. 1716; *Mary*, b. 1717, m. Jonas Richardson, '37. Hezekiah, (b. 1688), and Thomas, (b. 1685), both of Sud. were sons of James, of Wat. who m. Hannah Coller, 1679. Dinah, of Fram. (prob. b. in Sud. June 21, 1718,) dr. of Thomas and w. (Mary Nobles), m. Wm. Briscoe, Oct. 1740.

2. MOSES, m. in Wat. Mercy Stratten, 1736, and lived in F. on the farm now of Sam'l Cutting. His chil. were, 1. Moses, d. young; 2. Daniel, bap. May, 1749; 3. Eben. d. in the French war; 4. Moses, m. Mary Whitcomb, '70, and d. in Troy, N. H. ab. 1841; 5. David, was burnt to death during the Rev. war, in a barn, where he lay with a broken leg; 6. Samuel; 7. Joseph, bap. Feb. 3, 1754, m. Anna Ball, 1795, and d. in N. Marlb.; 8. Lucy, bap. June 12, '57, m. Silas Cutting, and lately lived in Worc. Moses the f. d. ab. 1786. Moses was b. in Wat. Feb. 14, 1712, s. of Jonathan, (who m. Sarah Flagg, 1710), and g. son of James who m. Hannah Coller, 1679.

3. DANIEL, s. of Moses (2), m. Submit Ball, 1771, moved to N. Marlb., and had eight chil., of whom was Daniel, b. Mar. 2, 1782, m. Mary Rugg, Oct. 21, 1806, and lives in Fram.

Daniel the f. m. 2d wid. Martha Brown, came to Fram. 1796, and lived beyond Mr. E. Hager's. He brought three chil. viz: LEVI; AZUBAH, b. 1788, lives in N. Haven; and SUBMIT, b. 1792, m. John Wheeler, lived at Rutland and Hardwick. Daniel the f. d. in Fram., 1812, æ. 63.

1. SAMUEL, s. of Moses (2), m. Anne Winch, and had, 1. ELIZABETH, m. Aaron Stone, of E. Sud. Sep. 10, 1795, and d. ab. 1804; 2. NELLY, m. Luther Stone, of Wendell, Feb. 21, 1803; 3. SALLY, m. Aaron Stone; 4. NANCY, m. Abel Dearth; 5. SUSAN, m. Joseph Potter; 6. EBENEZER, d. young; 7. HANNAH, d. young; 8. SAMUEL, m. Eliza Brackett. Sam. the f. d. 1832, æ. 82; w. Anne d. 1837, æ. 77.

RICHARD, of Wat., d. Mar. 21, 1696, "an aged man," leaving *Zechariah; James; Susanna;* and *Lydia,* b. Sept. 1, 1666. JOHN, of Wat. m. Susanna Harrington, 1671, and d. 1689, f. of *Susanna, Mary, Elizabeth, John, Robert,* b. 1683, m. Abigail Sawin, 1715, (f. at Sud., of Robert, Sarah, Samuel, Isaac, Jerusha, and Silence).

DADMUN, SAMUEL, m. Martha Jennings in Fram., May, 27, 1714. [1718, Martha and her chil. are referred to on the Town Rec. A dr. of Samuel m. —— Wadsworth.]

2. SAMUEL, prob. s. of Sam. (1), m. Lois Pratt of Fram., and had 1. NATHAN, b. Mar. 7, 1742, d. young; 2. DANIEL, b. Mar. 27, '44; 3. NATHAN, b. June 16, '47; 4. TIMOTHY, bap. Mar. 28, '50; 5. MARTHA, bap. Mar. 25, '52, d. unm. July 26, 1833; 6. ELIJAH, bap. Oct. 19, '55; 7. SAMUEL, first lived in Princeton, m. Dorcas Stone, of Fram., Oct. 1787, and d. in Templeton, 1821, æ. 61; 8. JONATHAN; 9. LOIS, bap. May 20, '64, m. Isaac How, June, 1785, lived in F.; 10. SUSANNAH, bap. Feb. 5, '69, m. Ezra Belcher, Mar. 18, '94, lives in Fram. Samuel the f. lived near Stone's Mills, and d. 1794. Lois his w. d. 1808.

3. NATHAN, s. of Samuel (2), m. Hannah Sanger; and had 1. JOSEPH, b. May 14, 1774; 2. JEDUTHAN, b. Dec. 23, '75, m. Lois Jones Dec. 18, 1800; 3. ELEANOR, b. Mar. 18, 1777, m. Elias Grout; 4. SARAH, b. Jan. 10, '79, m. Eli Eames of Holl., lived in Vt. or N. H.; 5. HANNAH, b. Jan. 11, '81, m. Wm. Clark, of Hop., Jan. 11, 1801; 6. BATHSHEBAH, b. Dec. 26, '82, m. Jacob Prescott, (lives in Vt.); 7. NATHAN, bap. Sep. '88, m. Burrowdale Jackson; 8. MARY, bap. Sep. '88, m. John Clark, and d. 1843. [The births above are as given on the

T. Rec.) Nathan the f. d. 1827; w. Hannah d. Nov. 19, 1821, æ. 75.

4. DANIEL, s. of Samuel (2), m. Martha Hyde of Newton; and had, 1. PRUDENCE, b. Dec. 10, 1775, m. Luther Knowlton, Dec. 28, 1800, and d. Oct. 1843; 2. EUNICE, b. Ap. 23, '77, m. Josiah Clayes; 3. ASENETH, b. June 28, '78; 4. MARTHA, b. Oct. 11, '79, m. Dan. Burnham, of Littleton, Nov. 20, 1804; 5. JOHN, b. Feb. 17, '81, m. Betsey Mellen, d. in Fram. Sep. 1833. Daniel the f. lived at Salem end, and d. in Fram. June 2, 1791, æ. 47. His wid. Martha d. Ap. 25, 1828, æ. 83.

5. ELIJAH, s. of Samuel (2), m. Bathshebah Parmenter, in Sud., Feb. 28, 1781; and had in Fram., 1. BETSEY, b. Mar. 15, '84; 2. LUCINDA, b. Mar. 22, '86; 3. CYNTHIA, m. Abijah Hemenway. The f. moved to Marlb., and had DANIEL; MARTIN; ELIJAH; and EUNICE.

6. TIMOTHY, s. of Samuel (2), m. Sybilla Winch, lived near Saxonville, and had, 1. JOEL, d. young; 2. KATY, bap. July, 1781, m. William Butler, of Cavendish, Vt., Feb. 25, '97; 3. POLLY, bap. July, '81, m. William Dadmun, Mar. 5, 1800; 4. NANCY, bap. June, '82, m. Wm. Swan, of Dorchester. Timo. and w. adm. to ch., July, 1781. T. the f. d. in Fram., Feb., 1832, æ. ab. 82.

7. JONATHAN, s. of Samuel (2), m. Eunice Dunn, Ap., 1781, and had WILLIAM, who m. Polly Dadmun, and d. in Fram., 1834. Jona. the f. lived near the Belchers, and d. in F.

8. JOSEPH, s. of Nathan (3), m. 1st, Betsey Pike, and had WILLARD; BETSEY; LOAMMI; JOSEPH; and MARY. He m. 2d, Milly Pike, moved to Littleton, ab. 1800, and back to Fram., ab. 1842. He had in all 16 chil., 3 of them sons.

Note. — The Dadmuns are said to be of Scotch extraction.

DALRYMPLE, (commonly called Darumple), JAMES, had 1. ANNE, bap. June, 1798, d. unm.; 2. WILLIAM, d. in Canada, ab. 1814, æ. 25. James lived at Salem end, and moved to Marlb.

[James is said to have been s. of James, a Scotchman, who was taken prisoner from the Americans in the Revolutionary War, asked permission to step aside, and succeeded in escaping, although many guns were discharged at him. James m. in Sud., Azubah Parmenter, Dec. 7, 1780. ASENETH, of Fram., m. Sam. Clark, of Hop., Nov. 25, 1806. ROBERT m. in Newton, Sarah Fuller, 1768.]

DANIELS, ISRAEL, and w. Anna. A. adm. from the ch. in

Medway, Aug., 1799. DAVID, s. of Israel, bap. Oct. '99. Anna the w. d. Mar. 3, 1800, æ 33. Israel 'm. Levinah Daniels, Mar. 19, 1801.

Note.— JOSEPH was in Medfield, 1660.

DARLING, JOHN, and w. Abigail, lived in the N. part of the town; and had, 1. ABIGAIL, b. June 2, 1736; 2. JOHN, Mar. 24, '37–8; 3. AMASA, Mar. 13, '43; 4. TIMOTHY, Aug. 12, '47. Abigail the w. adm. to the ch., Feb. 5, 1748. [SARAH, of Fram., m. Isaac Wheeler, of Holden, Aug. 18, 1752. JOHN, s. of Samuel, bap. June 18, 1758. THOMAS, rated in Fram., ab. 1738.]

2. AMOS, m. Hepsebah Bruce, in Southb., May 9, 1745, and, with w. cov. in Fram., Nov. 17, '48; and had in F., 1. JOSEPH, b. Oct. 29, 1746; 2. ELIZABETH, b. Mar. 2, '48, m. Eleazer Rice, of Marlb., 1772; 3. JONAS, b. June 4, '53, m. Molly Knights, of Marlb., had 8 chil. in Marlb., and d. in Sterling; 4. LUCY, b. Aug. 13, '55, m. Daniel Rice, of Marlb.; 5. AMOS, b. June 16, '57, m. Laovisie Hager, of Marlb.; 6. HEPHZIBAH, b. Dec. 8, '59, m. Levi Wilkins, of Marlb., d. 1840; 7. LYDIA, b. July 10, '62, d. unm., '89; 8. DANIEL, b. July 24, '65, m. Rebeckah Arnold, of Marlb., and 2d, Charlotte Hunting, lived in Marlb., and d. in Fram., 1844. Amos and w. recom'd to the ch. in Marlb., Aug., 1788, about which time his farm was set off to Marlb. [JACOB, s. of Amos, was bap. in F., Nov. 27, 1748.]

3. TIMOTHY, s. of John (1), and w., ——, had, 1. TIMOTHY, bap. Oct. 28, 1770; 2. NABBY, bap. Nov. 25, 1770.

4. JOSEPH, s. of Amos (2), m. Eunice Flagg, in Marlb., 1773; and had, 1. MOLLY, b. May 8, 1774. The f. m. 2d, Sarah Houghton, and had, 2. JOHN, b. Ap. 1, 1781. Jos. lived in Fram. with Amos his f., and moved to Brattleboro', ab. 1781.

5. MARGERY, wid. of Joseph, d. in Fram., June 9, 1819, æ 85. JOB d. in F., Mar. 26, 1814, æ 87.

[The tradition of the family relates, that Amos came from Danvers, and that his g. grand father came from England, when there were fourteen houses in Salem. THOMAS, (only s. of John, who d. 1713), and w. Joana, were of Salem, 1690. DANIEL (w. Lydia) d. in Mendon, ab. 1746, f. of Daniel, Samuel, Peter, William, and 4 drs. TIMOTHY was of Lunenburg, 1753. BENJAMIN, of Wrentham, (who had brs. John and Elias), d. before the Rev'n., an aged man, and was f. of Rev. David, of Surrey, N. H., who d. 1836, æ. 81. Judge Joshua, of Heneka, N. H., was prob. a relative of this last.]

DAVIS, ELIZABETH, m. Moses Brewer, Dec. 4, 1751.
AMOS, m. Dorothy Rice, July 28, 1799.

ROBERT, of Sud., d. 1655, and had drs. *Sarah*, and *Rebeckah*, a brother John, and a sister Margaret Burnet; his widow was named Bridget. RANDALL, (and w. Susa.), of Sud., had *William* and *Amos*, 1746; *Richard*, and *William*. JOHN and w. Rebeckah, were of Marlb., 1758.

DEAN, JOSEPH, lived at the S. part of Fram. in 1753. 2. JONAS, (who lived near the Poor House), and w. Rebeckah, had JOHN, b. Oct. 22, 1788.

DANIEL was of Sud., ab. 1663. JOSEPH and w. Rebeckah, of Sud., had *Mary*, 1696, *Pelatiah*, *Daniel*, and *Sarah*; and were of Wat., about 1705.

DEARBORNE, the w. of Deac. (Simeon) Dearborne was recom. to the Ch. in Wakefield, between 1784 and 1787.

DEATH, JOHN, in Sud. 1672, bought of Benj. Rice, 1673, 40 acres on Connecticut old road, near Beaver Dam, by Jacob's further meadow and a little pond. J. was received to Sherb. Jan. 1, 1677–8, and was rated in Fram. 1710, and on Town Committees in Fram. 1700, and after. His chil., by w. Mary, are 1. JOHN, b. in Topsfield, Jan. 2, 1676; 2. HEPHZEBAH, b. June 5, 1680, (Sud. Rec.), m. David How, Dec. 25, 1700; and on Sherb. Rec., 3. LYDIA, b. Mar. 26, '82, m. in Wat., Jona. Lamb of Fram. 1708; 4. SAMUEL, b. Sep. 12, '84; 5. RUTH, b. July 20, '88, m. in Wat. Samuel How, Nov. 23, 1715. [MARY, m. Samuel Eames of Fram. Jan. 6, 1689–0.]

2. JOHN, Jun., s. of John (1), was rated at Fram. 1710. He m. Elizabeth Barber, Jan. 17, 1698-9; and had 1. JOHN, b. and d. 1710. His w. d. May 28, 1710, and he m. 2d Waitstill —, and had in Sherb. 2. HENRY, b. 1714, m. Rachel Leland, and f. of *Benoni; Henry; Elizabeth; John; Rachel;* and *Mary;* 3. MARY, b. 1716, m. Daniel Leland, '37; 3. RUTH, b. 1721, m. John Wesson of Fram., '40; 4. ABIGAIL, b. 1723, m. Wm. Greenwood, '45; 5. JOHN, b. 1726; 6. WAITSTILL, b. 1729, m. Caleb Greenwood, '49; 7. HEPSEBAH, b. '31, m. Moses Adams, '51; John Esq. m. Mrs. Martha Perry, Nov. 22, 1750, and d. in Sherb. Dec. 14, 1754, æ. 77. (G. Stone).

3. OLIVER, prob. s. of John (1), m. Martha Fairbanke, Ap. 17, 1697, and had, 1. OLIVER, b. Mar. 26, 1698 (Sh. Rec.); and on Fram. Rec., 2. CALEB, b. Jan. 7, 1699-0, d. Mar. 14, 1711; 3. JOHN, b. May 30, '02, m. Hannah Morse, 1729, and f. of *Jotham*, b. 1730, who lived in Holl., Athol, &c.; *John*, of Hop. and Tem-

pleton, m. Jerusha Cody, 1753; and *Martha;* 4. MARTHA, b. Ap., 1704. Oliver the f. d. in Fram. Mar. 3, 1704-5; his wid. Martha m. Eben. Leland, Jun., of Sherb., 1708.
4. OLIVER, Jun., s. of Oliver (3), with his w. Abigail, cov. 1726. Their s. CALEB, b. Sep. 10, 1726.
5. CALEB, s. of Oliver (4), had by w. Abigail, 1. OLIVER, b. Jan. 27, 1754, d. unm.; 2. PARLEY, b. Sep. 16, '55; 3. ABIGAIL, b. Mar. 22, '57, m. Obadiah Morse of Sherb.; 4. EBENEZER MESSENGER, b. Dec. 2, '62, d. unm.; 5. CALEB, b. May 6, '67. Caleb and w. recom. to Ch. in Sherb., Oct. 2, 1771.

ELIZABETH, of Sherb., m. James Perry, of Holl., 1728. This family have, in later years, written their name DEARTH. The family in Fram., lived in the S. part of the town.

DENCH, EUNICE, (dr. of Roger), m. William Maynard, Mar. 12, 1797. LAWSON, (s. of Roger), left Fram. ab. 1798, and m. in Boston, Mary Stoddard.

Capt. ROGER, of Boston, mariner, m. Anne Lawson, g. dr. of Savil Simpson, and was f. in Hop., of GILBERT, b. 1742, (who m. Anne Gibbs, 1761, and was f. of *Gilbert, Isaac, John, &c.*); and ROGER, who by w. Eunice, had *Lawson, Roger, John, &c.* The wid. Dench was buried in Fram., Oct. 26, 1825.

DEPISTA, KATA, dr. of Charles, bap. May 10, 1772.

DEUIN or DEVIN, BEULAH, adm. to the Ch. May 22, 1748.

DILL, a "negro woman," servant to Deac. Daniel Stone, d. Dec. 13, 1767, æ. 26.

DINGO, DIDO, (servant to Mr. Swift), m. Nero Benson, May 26, 1721.

DIX, —— lived where is now the Fram. Hotel, ab. 1780.

DODGE, MARGERY, w. of Jabez, d. Sep. 13, 1755, æ. 60. (G. Stone in Fram.) [Jabez was of Hop. 1737.]

DOLBIER, BENJAMIN, came from Weston to Fram., 1769. (T. Rec.) [Benjamin and w. Hepsebah, of Newton, had *Timothy,* 1762; and *Benjamin,* '64.]

DONACHY, WILLIAM, cov. and was bap. Mar. 13, 1720. JEAN, bap. Mar. 26, 1721; MARY, bap. Aug. 4, 1723.

DOUGHERTY, or DORITHA, CHARLES, m. Hannah Hemenway; w. Hannah cov. and bap. Nov. 10, 1765. Charles and w. Hannah adm. by letter from Brookfield Ch., Sep. 8, 1771. Their chil. were 1. WILLIAM, m. in Fram., Betsey Walkup, Jan. 1788; 2. SAMUEL, bap. Oct. 8, 1769, d. Jan. '71; 3. KATE, b. Dec. 23,

'71; 4. HANNAH, b. Feb. 27, '73; 5. CHARLES LEE, b. Sep. 15, '76; 6. LUCY, b. Feb. 11, '78; 7. REBECKAH, b. Feb. 6, '80. Charles the f. moved from town, ab. 1785.

2. MICAH, cousin to Charles (1), m. Betty Pratt, and had, 1. PATTY, b. Dec. 26, 1771, d. May 22, '89; 2. JANE, b. Nov. 9, '73, m. Asa Claflin Ap. '93, and d. 1833; 3. SALLY, b. Oct. 9, '75, m. Wm. Claflin, Oct. 16, '94; 4. REBECKAH, b. Jan. 30, '78, d. May 21; 5. WALTER, b. Feb. 19, '80, d. at Savannah; 6. BETSEY, b. July 19, '81, m. Silas Pratt; 7. DAVID, b. Aug. 28, '83, d. unm.; 8. DANIEL, b. Jan. 11, '86, d. young. Lt. Micah the f. d. Jan. 27, 1788. " Widow Dougherty buried Nov. 5, 1825." [The Doughertys originated in Ireland.]

DRURY, HUGH, had a grant of land in Sud., 1640 or '41; 1642, occupied house and land mortgaged for debt by Wm. Swifte, of Sandwich; 1646, sold to Edward Rice his house and houselot. He was f. by w. Lydia, of 1. JOHN, b. in Sud., May 2. 1646, m. Mary ——, was a carpenter in Boston, and d. ab. 1678, f. of *Thomas* and *John*; 2. THOMAS.[2] Hugh, a carpenter, d. in Boston, 1689; and his w. Lydia, d. 1675, æ. 47, (both interred in the Chapel Burial Ground). Hugh names in his will, proved July 30, 1689, his brothers Henry, Joseph, and Edward Rice. Hugh m. in Boston, Mary Fletcher, 1676. (Suff. Deeds).

2. THOMAS, s. of Hugh (1), m. Rachel, dr. of Henry Rice, Dec. 15, 1687. His chil. were 1. CALEB,[3] b. Oct. 5, 1688; 2. THOMAS,[10] b. Aug. 29, '90; 3. JOHN[11]; 4. MARY, m. David Bent, of Fram., Jan. 1, 1712–3; 5. RACHEL, m. George Fairbank, Dec. 1718; 6. LYDIA; 7. ELIZABETH, b. June 22, 1701, m. (Isaac ?) Morse; 8. MICAH,[12] b. May 2, 1704; 9. URIAH,[14] b. Jan. 17, 1706–7.

Tho. Esq., settled in the E. part of Fram., and was distinguished in town affairs. He was the first Deputy to the Gen. Court, 1701; T. Clerk, 11 years; Selectman, 13 years. In his will, proved Nov. 11, 1723, he names his cousin, Mary Ball.

3. CALEB, s. of Thomas (2), m. Elizabeth Eames, Oct. 10, 1706; and had 1. JOSIAH,[4] b. Sep. 17, 1707; 2. DANIEL, b. Ap. 25, '09, m. Sarah Flag of Sud., July 14, '29, and was in Shrewsbury, 1739; 3. JOHN, b. June 18, '11, m. Anne Gleason Nov 22, '33, and had in Nat. *Elizabeth*, 1748; 4. CALEB,[8] b. May 22, '13; 5. ASENETH, b. Jan. 9, '14; 6. SEUILL (or Seville), b. Jan. 11, '14–5, d. June 2; 7. ZEDEKIAH, b. Ap. 30, '16; 8. EBENEZER, b. Oct. 5, '18; 9. JOSEPH, b. Dec. 19, '20, m. Lydia Willard of Sherb., 1744, and had in Sud. *Zeruiah, Ephraim, Joseph;* and

in Nat. *Elizabeth*, and *Peter.;* 10. ELIZABETH, b. July 30, 1721, m. Tho. Winch, Dec. 20, '43. Caleb the f. d., ab. 1733. (Mid. Prob.)

4. JOSIAH, s. of Caleb, (3), m. Hannah Barron of Sherb., Oct. 9, 1733; and had 1. SARAH, b. Dec. 8, 1734, m. Richard Rice, Jan. 16, 1755, and d. in Me.; 2. ELIJAH, b. Nov. 30, '37; 3. JOSIAH, b. June 29, '40; 4. MOSES,[5] b. Aug. 4, '42; 5. HANNAH, b. May 27, '44, m. 1. Micajah Gleason, 2d, Gen. John Nixon, and d. 1828; 6. NATHAN,[6] b. Sep. 27, '46; 7. ASA, b. June 29, '48, m. Dolly Gleason, and had in Nat. *Elijah*, 1769; *Sally*, '78; and *Keziah*, '83, m. in Fram. Wm. Perry of Nat., Dec. 31, 1801. Capt. Asa d. June 26, 1816; 8. ELISHA,[7] b. Ap. 21, '49, d. young; 9. ELISHA, b. Aug. 5, '53. Josiah the f. was killed by an ox team, in Wayland.

5. MOSES, s. of Josiah (4), had by w. Cata, 1. SARAH, bap. Mar. 18, 1764; 2. KATY, bap. Jan. 1, '64; 3. JOSIAH, bap. July 13, '66. Moses the f. moved to Fitzwilliam.

6. NATHAN, s. of Josiah (4), m. in Sud. Abigail Rice, May 6, 1773, and had 1. NABBY, bap. May 22, 1774, m. Rev. Mr. Robinson, of Westboro'; 2. HANNAH, bap. July 14, '76, m. Moses Gleason; 3. NANCY, b. Feb. 21, '79, d. Aug. 19. Capt. Nathan d. Ap. 1, 1782, æ. 35. Abigail, his w. d. Aug. 22, 1779, æ. 26.

7. ELISHA, s. of Josiah (4), m. Salome Rice in Sud., Mar. 26, 1778; and had ELISHA, d. June 7, 1781, æ. 7 mos. E. the f. d. Feb. 22, 1782, æ. 29. His wid. Salome m. John Baker, of Westboro', Feb., 1786.

8. CALEB, s. of Caleb (3), m. Mehetabel Maynard, May 27, 1735, and had 1. CALEB,[9] b. Sep. 16, '35; 2. MEHETABEL, b. July 26, '37, d. young; 3. JONATHAN, b. May 28, '39, d. young; 4. ELIZABETH, b. Aug. 5, '41; 5. WILLIAM, b. July 4, '43; 6. JONATHAN, b. Mar. 23, '44–5; 7. ZECHARIAH, b. July 23, '48; 8. MEHETABEL, Oct. 15, '50, her mind was long disordered; 9. ABEL, b. May 29, '52, d. Feb. 22, '69; 10. NEEDHAM, b. June 15, '54, d. Jan. 17, '55; 11. NEEDHAM, b. Feb 15, '56; 12. SYBILLA, b. Jan. 21, '58, d. Nov. 22, '59; 13. ELIJAH, b. Dec. 22, '59. Mr. Caleb lived on the place now of Mr. Joseph Brown, and d. Nov. 5, 1760.

9. CALEB, s. of Caleb (8), m. Zerviah Rice; and had 1.

CALEB, b. 1775, d. unm; 2. JOHN, d. unm. in Nat.; 3. ABEL, moved to N. Salem, and m. in Fram., Nabby Broad of Nat., Dec. 1, 1803; 4. DAVID, and 5. JONATHAN, twins, d. unm; 6. ANNE, m. Josiah Rutter, June 29, 1806, and 2d, Deac. Luther Haven, and d. 1843. Caleb the f. d. ab. 1805; his w. d. a few years before.

10. THOMAS, Jun., s. of Tho. (2), m. Sarah Clark, June 10, 1719; and had THOMAS, b. Jan. 12, 1720–1.

11. JOHN, s. of Tho. (2), m. Susannah Goddard, May 21, 1719; and had 1. MARY b. Mar. 21, '19–0, m. Nath'l Sanderson, Oct. 4, '39, d. in Petersham; 2. SUSANNAH, b. Feb. 2, '21–2; 3. KEZIAH, b. Feb. 1, '23–4, m. David Bridges, Ap. 25, '50; 4. JOHN, b. Mar. 27, '26, d. June 9, 1742; 5. WILLIAM, b. June 4, '28, lived in Philipston; 6. THOMAS, b. June 15, '30, lived in Phil.; 7. EBENEZER, b. Oct. 14, '32, lived in Spencer; 8. GRACE, b. Ap. 13, '34, d. Nov. 30, '40; 9. LYDIA, b. Nov. 12, '36; 10. EXPERIENCE, b. May 7, '38; 11. EDWARD, b. Aug. 22, '39, d. young; 12. JOHN, b. July 15, '42, m. at Athol, Lydia Smith, July 3, '65, and f. of *Joel; David; John*, &c.; 13. GRACE, b. Feb. 8, '43; 14. RACHEL, b. Feb. 13, '44; 15. EDWARD, b. June 8, '48, m. Experience Goodale, of Charlton, and f. of *Jonathan*, and others, and d. at Athol, Aug. 1786. John the f. lived in the W. part of Fram. His Inventory (£1250), is dated Ap. 25, 1754; his wid. Sus. adm. His wid. m. Joseph Haven, Dec. 5, 1760.

12. MICAH, s. of Tho. (2), m. Abigail Eames, Sep. 10, 1724; and had 1. MARY, b. June 1, 172(9), m. John Crooks of Hop. Nov. 7, '51; 2. ELIZABETH, b. Oct. 21, '31; 3. MICAH, b. Oct. 13, '33, d. young; 4. DAVID, b. Feb. 17, '35; 5. HANNAH, b. June 27, '39, m. Capt. John Butler; 6. RICHARD, b. May 31, '41; 7. MICAH,[13] b. June 13, '43; 8. HENRY, b. Sep. 12, '45; 9. ROBERT, b. Aug. 26, '49. Micah, Sen. d. in Fram.

13. MICAH, Jun., s. of Micah (12), m. Lucy Howe; and had 1. MOLLY, b. Oct. 3, 1772, m. 1st, Abijah Parmenter, July, 1790, 2d, Eleazer Smith, of Walpole, Machinist; 2. DAVID, lived in Vt.; 3. LUCY, m. Wm. Stickney, of Boston. Micah the f. was eccentric, dressed like a hermit, and d. in Fram.

14. URIAH, s. of Tho. (2), m. Martha Eames, Dec. 1, 1726; and had 1. MARTHA, b. Oct. 1, 1727; 2. RACHEL, b. Feb.

7, '28-9, m. Jos. Jennings, Jan. 23, '52; 3. SYBILLA, b. June 21, '31, d. unm.; 4. URIAH, b. Mar. 16, '32-3, d. young; 5. THOMAS,[15] b. Mar. 9, '34-5; 6. SAMUEL, b. Dec. 4, '36, d. young; 7. LYDIA, b. Dec. 7, '40, d. young; 8. URIAH, b. Ap. 12, '43; 9. LYDIA, b. Oct. 5, '45; 10. SAMUEL, b. Mar. 23, '47-8, prob. d. young. Uriah the f. was a Selectman 2 years, and d. ab. 1754. (Mid. Prob.).

15. THOMAS, s. of Uriah (14), m. Martha Eames of Holl., Aug. 13, 1753; and had 1. SYBILLA, b. Oct. 28, 1753, d. unm. ab. 1805; 2. URIAH, b. Feb. 4, '55, d. Feb. 16; 3. THOMAS, b. Mar. 25, '56, m. Grace Rice, Dec. 21, '80, 2d, Lois Wood, of Newton, Sep. 15, 1794, and moved to W. part of Mass., ab. 1808; 4. SAMUEL, b. Oct. 18, '58, pub. in Nat. to Betsey Dun, 1789; 5. DAVID, b. Oct. 20, '60, m. Lydia Dudley, (f. of *Mary*, who m. Jonas Dean of Walth., Feb. 5, 1808), and d. in Nat. ab. 1812; 6. ISAAC, bap. Nov. 14, '62, d. young; 7. MARTHA, bap. Jan. 20, '65, m. Calvin Eames, lived in Canada; 8. POLLY, bap. Dec. '67, m. Luther Eaton, Dec. '89, and d. 1796; 9. NELLY, bap. Jan. 14, '70, m. Luther Eaton; 10. LUCIA, bap. Feb. '72, d. young; 11. LUCY, bap. Mar. 14, '73; 12. ISAAC, bap. Aug. 4, '76, m. in Boston, and d. ab. 1824. Capt. Thomas the f. lived near Deac. Luther Haven, and d. Ap. 19, 1790.

16. SARAH, bap. Feb. 9, 1724. ABIGAIL, bap. Jan. 29, 1727. THO'S bap. Mar. 26, '27. ELIZABETH, m. Tho. Winch, Dec. 20, 1743. ELIZABETH, m. Tho. Winch, July 17, 1754. LYDIA, m. Peter Sleeman of Charlton, Jan. 16 (or Feb.), 1758. SUSANNAH, m. John Haven, Mar. 27, 1746.

ELIJAH m. Dolly Perry, in Nat., 1792. JOHN m. in South., wid. Thankful Horne, July, 1767, and f. of *Winsor.* JOHN, m. in Southb., Abigail Rolf, 1771.

DUDLEY, PETER, m. in Southb., Experience Newton, Dec. 12, 1754, and had in Fram. 1. MARY, b. Oct. 14, 1755, m. Beriah Pratt; 2. PETER, b. Oct. 14, '58, m. in Hop., lived in N. Y.; 3. LEVINAH, b. Dec. 7, '60, m. Thaddeus Hemenway, Jan. '82, lived in N. Y.; 4. EXPERIENCE, b. Feb. 15, '64, d. unm. in N. Y.; 5. NATHAN, b. May 5, '66, m. Mercy Sheffield, Mar. 30, '86, lived in N. Y.; 6. ABRAHAM, b. Oct. 14, '68, m. in N. Y.; 7. SARAH, b. Dec. 29, '72; 8. CHARLES, b. Sep. 1, '75; 9. ANNE, b. Sep. 12, '77. Peter the f. lived near Luther Newton's, and moved to N. Y. ab. 1790.

2. JOHN, (s. of Benj. of E. Sud.) m. Zerviah Rice, May 3, 1792; and had 1. JOHN, bap. Nov. '93 ; 2. HANNAH, and 3. MARY, twins, bap. Feb. '95 ; 4. CALEB ; 5. NATHAN. John moved to Petersham.

3. BENJAMIN, by w. Sybil, had SILVA, b. Feb. 13, 1795; PHEBE, b. Feb. 9, '97. Sybil the w. d. in Sud. Sept. 17, 1824, æ. 50 ; and his 2d w. Anna, d. Jan. 2, 1838, æ. 57.

1718, Isaac Rice of Sud., by will, gave half of a farm at Indian Head, in F. to Benj. Dudley, whom he had brought up. JOSEPH, and w. Mary, were of Sud., 1757 ; WILLIAM and w. Judith, 1763 ; and EBENEZER, and w. Grace, 1758 ; all had chil. PETER, of Hartford, m. in Marlb.. Abigail Gleason, 1741. In Fram., BENJAMIN m. wid. Hannah Belcher. Mrs. Dudley d. Sept. 28, 1820.

DUNKEN, or Dunkin, JOHN, had by w. Sarah, ABIGAIL, b. Dec. 3. 1718 ; REBECKAH, b. Ap. 3, d. July 3, '21.

Note. — JOHN, (w. Sarah), of Worc., d. ab. 1740, leaving *Simeon, John, Samuel, Daniel,* and s. in-law, James Haws. Also, at Worc., JOHN, Jr., and w. Sarah, 1728. DANIEL was there, 1740, and moved to Petersham. SAMUEL, was of Roxb., 1674.

DUNN, WILLIAM, " a member of the Ch. of Scotland," had, in 1766, communed with the Fram. Ch. about 30 years, (Ch. Rec.), and had ANN, bap. Ap. 26, 1747 ; ELIZABETH, bap. June 10, 1750. [WILLIAM, of Fram., m. in Sud. Eunice Goodnow, May 4, 1758].

2. JOHN, of Fram. m. Grace Kelley, in Hop., June, 1751, and had in Fram. 1. SARAH, b. Mar. 14, '52, m. Ithamar Rice of Sud.; 2. JOHN, b. Aug. 25, '53, d. unm.; 3. EDWARD, b. June 2, '56 ; 4. MARY, bap. May 18, '60, m. Daniel Jones, May '86 ; 5. LETICE, bap. May 18, '60 ; 6. EUNICE, m. Jona. Dadmun, Ap. '81 ; 7. WILLIAM, m. Mitty Hemenway, June '88 ; 8. CATHARINE, m. Eben. Wiley, of Sunderland ; 9. JOSEPH, m. in Chester, N. York.

Note. — The Dunns lived near Cochituate Pond.

DUNTON. "A contribution was recommended (Ap. 12, 1719), for Mr. John D. who had been burnt out a little before." (Swift's Journal).

Note. — JOHN of Sud., m. Sarah Beal, 1722, and had *Timothy*, 1715; *Samuel,* '19; *Anna,* '21. THOMAS and w. Sarah, of Sud., 1722, had *Elizabeth, Elijah,* and *John.* A Thomas d. at Western, 1758. (Worc. Prob.) JOHN, a wheelwright, moved, ab. 1714, from Reading to Sud., where he d. ab. 1720, leaving a w. Ruth, and chil. *John, Thomas, Ruth, Elizabeth, Mary, Sarah,* and *Hephzibah.* SAMUEL was of Reading, 1655.

DURSTON, ABIGAIL, cov. and was bap. Oct. 8, 1727.
DYER, NATHANIEL, rated in Fram. ab. 1755.
EAGER, ABRAHAM, m. Polly Clark, Sep. 1785.

ABRAHAM, (w. Lydia), ZECHARIAH, (w. Elizabeth), ZERUBBABEL, (m. Hannah Kerly, 1697), had chil. in Marlb., from ab. 1693. WILLIAM and w. Ruth, of Camb., had *Zerubbabel*, 1672, and others.

EAMES, THOMAS, and w. Margaret, had at Dedham, 1. JOHN, b. May 16, and d. Sep. 17, 1641 ; 2. JOHN², b. Oct. 6, '42 ; 3. MARY, b. May 24, '45. Thomas the f. m. 2d at Camb. Mary, wid. of Jona.Padelford (see Padelford), ab. 1662, and had 4. THOMAS, bap. at Camb. July 12, '63 ; at Sud., 5. SAMUEL¹⁴, b. Jan. 15, '64–5 ; 6. MARGARET, b. July 8, '66, m. Joseph Adams, '88 ; 7. NATHANIEL¹⁹, b. Dec. 30, '68 ; and at Fram., 8. SARAH, b. Oct. 3, '70 ; 9. LYDIA, b. June 29, '72.

Thomas was surety for Robert Eames at Mid. Co. Court, 1651, and gave a deposition, Oct. 5, 1652, then æ. 34 or thereabouts, and of Medford. In 1668, he had leased "Mr. Pelham's farm," in Sud.* About 1670, he settled in Fram. on the S. declivity of Mt. Wait ; was received as an Inhab. of Sherb. Jan. 4, '74–5, and early chosen a Selectman ; was on the Com. for building the Meeting House, and received a grant for building the same. His house in Fram. was burnt by the Indians, Feb. 1, 1676–7, and his wife killed with some of his chil., and others taken captive. (See a former part of this volume). Thomas the f. d. Jan. 25, 1680, æ. ab. 62 years. Administration on his estate was granted to John, his oldest son, 1680. (Suff. Prob.)

Note. — MARGERY was adm. to Charlestown church, 1635. ROBERT, was of Ch'n, 1651. ROBERT, of Woburn, (his wid. Elizabeth m. Capt. Wm. Bond, of Wat.), had *Samuel* ; *John*, d. 1654 ; *Elizabeth*, b. 1659, prob. m. John Eames, May, 82 ; *Mary*, b. 1661, m. Abr. Cozzens, '84 ; *Samuel ; John*, 1653, and others. ROBERT, and w. Rebeckah, of Andover, had *Hannah*, 1661 ; *Daniel, John, Dorothy, Jacob* and *Joseph*. ROBERT, d. at Dracut, ab. 1671, and in his will refers to his cousin Richard, s. of sister Dorothy Newman, "dwelling at Fannam, (Farnham?), in Surrey, in Rattlesham." HENRY, (w. Elizabeth), messenger to the General Court, had in Boston, *William*, 1674, (prob. of Long Island) ; *John, Mary, Benjamin, Henry*, and *Samuel*. MARK and w. Elizabeth, had in Charlestown, s. *John*, 1650. JOHN was of Groton, 1716—the family numerous, and believed to have gone from Andover. GERSHOM, of Marlb., (w. Hannah), had *Hannah*, 1671, who d. 1721. G. the f. d. at Wat., Nov. 25, 1676. ROBERT, (prob.

---

* "Ordered that Tho. Eames, during his lease upon Mr. Pelham's farm, shall pay to the minister fore pound (per) anam, and 20sh. to every £20 rate, &c." (Sud. T. Rec.) In 1667, he leased of the town a piece of meadow near Doeskin Hill, for a peck of wheat.

from Malden), was of Marlb., 1744. ROBERT, (prob. his son), d. at Marlb., Feb., 1821, æ. 84. ANTHONY was of Hingham, 1637. (Sav. Wiut., II. 221 et seq.) DAVID and w. Mehetabel, of Dedham, had chil. from 1691. JETHRO, of Lancaster, 1718. BENJAMIN, of Wat., m. Mehetabel Cheney, 1725, and was of Hop., 1725. ELIZABETH, of Wat., m. Thomas Blaynford, Dec. 18, 1673.

2. [1]JOHN, s. of Thomas (1), had by w. Mary, 1. MARGARET, b. and d. in Wat. 1676 ; 2. ANNA, m. —— Flagg; and on Sherb. Rec., 3. MARTHA, b. Feb. 28, '78, m. —— Smith. Mary the m. d. Ap. 3, '81, and John the f. m. 2d Elizabeth Eames, May '82, and had, 4. PRISCILLA, b. Feb. 2, '82-3 ; 5. ELIZABETH, b. Ap. 11, '85, m. Caleb Drury, Oct. 10, 1706 ; 6. JOHN[3], b. Jan. 10, '87 ; 7. THOMAS[6], b. July 22, '94 ; 8. MARY, b. Jan. 4, '97, m. John Pike, Sep. 8, '26 ; 9. HENRY[8], b. Ap. 28, '98 ; 10. ABIGAIL, b. Mar. 9, 1705, m. Micah Drury, Sep. 10, 1724. John the f. settled in the S. part of Fram. Plantation, was received as Inhabitant of Sherb., Ap. 1679, Selectman of Sherb. 1682, and of Fram. 1701. His will bears date May 18, 1727. He d. Dec. 14, 1733. Elizabeth his w. d. June 26, 1727. Mr. Swift notes her death as "my landlady Eames."

3. [1]JOHN, s. of John (2), m. Joanna Buckminster, June 23, 1712, and had in Fram. 1. ELIZABETH, b. Nov. 15, 1713 ; 2. ROBERT,[4] b. July 15, 1714 ; 3. JOHN, bap. Aug. 10, 1718 ; and in Hop. 4. JOANNA, b. June 26, '20, m. Ephraim Stone, July 24, '45 ; 5. THOMAS, b. Oct. 3, '22 ; 6. WILLIAM, b. Aug. 31, '24 ; 7. AARON, b. July 27, '26, m. Ann ——, and had in Rut'd, *Robert*, b. 1749, of Sud. 1773 ; *Aaron*, b. '51, (m. Kezia Goodnow of Sud. and f. of Asahel, Betsey, who m. John Bellows, Esq., of Boston, and Aaron) ; *Thomas*, '53 ; and in Sud. *Charles, Calvin, Mary, Luther, Silas, Joanna, Benjamin*, and *Ann ;* 8. BENJAMIN, b. July 9, '33 ; 9. ABIGAIL, b. Nov. 15, '36 ; 10. PRISCILLA, b. and d. May 17, '38. John the f. d. —. His wid. Joanna, m. John Butler, Mar. 19, 1740.

4. [1]ROBERT, s. of John (3), m. Deborah Adams, July 16, 1740, and had 1. JOHN,[5] b. Dec. 15, 1742 ; 2. MOLLY, b. Nov. 7, '44, d. Aug. 17, '47 ; 3. ROBERT, b. Mar. 30, and d. Aug. 27, '47. Rob. the f. d. Aug. 18, 1747, and his wid. Deb. m. Dr. Ebenezer Hemenway, Nov. 29, 1750.

5. [1]JOHN, s. of Robert (4), m. Ruth Stone, lived on the Southb. road, and had 1. MOLLY, b. June 8, 1763, m. Uriah Rice, June, '84 ; 2. RUTH, b. Mar. 18, '65, m. Ezra Rice, July, '90, and

d. Nov. 1832; 3. ROBERT, b. July 24, '67, m. Polly Cloyes, June 24, '93, moved to Whitestown, N. Y.; 4. HULDAH, b. Feb. 17, d. Mar. 11, '69; 5. JOHN, b. May 28, '70, m. Sally Sanger, d. in N. Hartford, 1823; 6. HEZEKIAH, b. July 8, '74, d. Aug. 2, '75; 7. ANNA, b. Mar. 26, '76, m. Nathan Manson, d. Ap. 10, 1806; 8. DEBORAH, b. Feb. 10, '78, m. Nath. Whitney, of Sherb., d. in N. Y., 1841; 9. HEZEKIAH, and 10. ASA, (twins), bap. May 27, '80 — H. m. Percy Butler, d. in N. Y; A. m. —— Butler, d. do; 11. NATHANIEL G., b. Ap. 9, '82, d. unm. in Batavia, N. Y.; 12. MATTHEW B., b. Dec. 6, '85, d. in Paris, N. Y., Aug. 10, 1816; 13. SALLY, b. Sep. 9, '87, m. —— Smith of N. Hartford. John the f. was Selectman 10 years, and d. Ap. 18, 1806, æ. 63. His w. Ruth d. May, 1809.

6. [1]THOMAS, s. of John (2), m. Abigail Leonard, and had THOMAS[7], b. May 20, 1729. T. the f. was deaf and dumb; lived first, near Daniel Sanger's, and afterwards in a house built for him near Aaron Pratt's, by the Town, a Mr. Peck of Boston, giving him the use of land for the purpose.

7. [1]THOMAS, Jun., s. of Tho. (6), m. Rachel Graves, Sep. 21, 1748, and had 1. THOMAS, b. Dec. 28, 1748; 2. REBECKAH, b. Oct. 23, '50; 3. ANN, bap. Dec. 31, '52; 4. ELIJAH, bap. May 11, '55; 5. RACHEL, bap. Ap. 2, '58; 6. JERUSHA, bap. Aug. 22, '62. Tho. the f. lived by Aaron Pratt's, (a cellar hole remains), and moved from town, ab. 1765.

8. [1]HENRY, s. of John (2), m. Ruth Newton, of Marlb., Nov. 7, 1722, and had 1. PHINEHAS, b. Sep. 2, 1723, m. Abigail Blanden, of Newton, Feb. 20, '52, and d. Mar. 6, '52; 2. MARY, b. Mar. 15, '24–5, m. Micah Haven, Jan. 16, '43–4, and 2d Jerem. Pike; 3. HENRY,[9] b. Ap. 30, '26; 4. RUTH, b. Ap. 30, '27, m. Jona. Rice, Oct. 29, '46; 5. GERSHOM, b. Feb. 16, '28–9, d. unm. Feb. 16, '52; 6. HANNAH, b. Ap. 8, '31, m. —— Morse; 7. TIMOTHY[13], b. Nov. 23, '32; 8. BETTY, b. Dec. 10, '34, m. Benajah Morse, '58; 9. LYDIA, b. Mar. 20, '36–7, m. Jacob Pratt and d. æ. 96; 10. JESSE[11], b. July 14, '39; 11. JOHN[12], b. Oct. 30, '43. Capt. Henry, the f., was Selectman 3 years, and d. May 16, 1761. His wid. Ruth d. Mar. 11, '77, æ. 75.

9. [1]HENRY, Jun., s. of Henry (8), m. Lois Howe, at Hop. 1750, and had 1. HENRY[10], bap. May 6, 1751; 2. GERSHOM, bap. Ap. 22, '52, m. Lydia Wait, Feb. '84, and d. in Boylston; 3.

JOTHAM, bap. Jan. 25, '56, m. —— Goddard, d. in Swanzey, N. H., ab. 1840 ; 4. LOIS, bap. Feb. 26, '58, m. John Steal, Jun., (mistake for Stowell), Oct. 12, '80, and late of Shutesbury ; 5. LUCY, m. Daniel Jones, June, '82 ; 6. RUTH, bap. July, '63, m. Frederick Brown, July, '86, and d. in Petersham ; 7. PETER, bap. July 21, '65, m. Sally Clark, and d. in Petersham, ab. 1814 ; 8. NABBY, bap. Mar. 6, '68, m. Abel Metcalf, Feb. '89, d. at Croyden, ab. 1824 ; 9. LUTHER, bap. June 3, '70, m. in Guilford, Vt., and d. in Marlb., Vt., 1840. Henry Sen. d. in Fram., 1772.

10. ¹HENRY, s. of Henry (9), m. Zuba Haven, Mar. 1, 1781, and had 1. HITTY, b. Nov. 13, '81, m. Abel Eames, Mar. 1804 ; 2. RUTH, b. Mar. 30, '84, m. Nehemiah Howe of Hop., Nov. 30, 1806 ; 3. NABBY, b. July 3, '86, m. Joseph Sanger ; 4. LUCY, b. Mar. 16, '89, m. Lovel Eames ; 5. SUKEY, b. Jan. 16, '92, m. Jona. Eames ; 6. HENRY, b. Aug. 30, '95, d. 1803. Azubah the m. d. Oct. 10, 1820, æ. 67, and her husb. m. 2d wid. Elizabeth Kendall. Henry lived where his son-in-law Abel now lives, and d. Jan. 21, 1829, æ. 78. (G. Stone).

11. ¹JESSE, s. of Henry (8), by w. Betty, had 1. TIMOTHY, b. Sep. 9, 1762, m. Mary Johnson, and d. ab. 1846 ; 2. JESSE, b. June 5, '64, m. wid. Fay, and d. in Strasburg ; 3. BETTY, b. May 1, '66, d. Dec. 31, '76 ; 4. EZRA, b. May 5, '68, d. in Albany ; 5. POLLY, b. Ap. 19, '71, d. Dec. 22, '76 ; 6. SALLY, b. May 3, '73, m. in Strasburg. Jesse the f. was expert in extracting teeth. His w. Betty d. in Fram., Feb. 14, 1776, æ. 34 y., 8 m., after which he moved to Strasburg, and d. there.

12. ¹JOHN, s. of Henry (8), m. Anne Bent ; and had 1. NABBY, d. unm., Dec. 10, 1839, æ. 72 ; 2. JOHN, m. Sarah Littlefield, of Holl., and d. in Fram., May 13, 1838, æ. 61 ; his w. d. Feb. 17, 1827, æ. 40 ; 3. NANCY, lives unm. in Nat. John the f. and his s. John, lived on the farm of Harrison Eames. He m. 2d, Wid. Mercy Fuller ; 3d, Sally Kingsbury, who d. Sep. 27, 1830, æ. 68. John, Sen., d. Mar. 13, 1832, æ. 88.

13. ¹TIMOTHY, s. of Henry (8), m. Sarah Stone ; and had, 1. LUCY, b. May 7, d. 19th, 1758. Timo. m. 2d, Hannah Hill, of Sud., Sep. 26, '63 ; and had, 2. SARAH, b. Feb. 1, '65, m. Benj. Stone, '85 ; 3. PHINEHAS, b. May 14, '66, m. Jane How, of Sud., '88 ; 4. LUCINDA, b. July 30, '68, m. Nathan Smith, '90, moved to Walpole, N. H. ; 5. CHLOE, b. Sep. 3, '70, m. Moses

Haven, '90; 6. HANNAH, b. Dec. 18, '74, m. Matthew Stone. Timo. the f. lived on the border of Sud., his chil. b. or bap. in Fram. He d. in Clinton, N. Y., Sep. 3, 1797. Hannah his w. d. 1795.

14. ^{2}SAMUEL, s. of Thomas (1), m. Mary Death, Jan. 6, 1689-0, and 2d, Patience Twitchell, Ap. 21, 1698; and had, 1. GERSHOM^{15}, b. Dec. 29, '98; 2. PATIENCE, b. Feb. 7, 1702, m. Abr. Rice, Feb. 1, '21-2; 3. MARGARET, b. Jan. 13, '03-4, m. Phinehas Rice, July 26, '27; 4. MARTHA, b. July 9, '06, m. Uriah Drury, Dec. 1, '26; 5. SARAH, b. June 28, '09, m. Dan. Gregory, July 13, '32; 6. JONATHAN, b. Jan. 28, '11-2, m. at Holl., Abigail Golding, 1742, and f. of *Jonathan; Moses*, who went to Upton; and others; 7. SAMUEL^{16}, b. Ap. 16, '14; 8. LYDIA, b. May 1, '16, m. James Clayes, July 24, '35; 9. DAVID^{17}, b. Aug. 26, '18; 10. JOSEPH^{18}, b. Sep. 9, '20. SAMUEL the f. lived near the rail road station, and d. in Fram.

15. ^{2}GERSHOM, s. of Samuel, (14), lived in Holl., m. Susanna Whitney, and had 1. SUSANNA, b. 1725, m. Jos. Cozzens; 2. PATIENCE, 1728; 3. SUSANNA, '30; 4. MARTHA, '32, m. Tho. Drury, '52; 5. LOIS, '34; 6. LYDIA, '36; 7. MARAH, b. and d. '39; 8. REUBEN, '43, m. —— Whipple, and —— Kendall; 9. EZRA; 10. LOIS, '48. Gershom the f. (or son), d. 1762. G.'s w. Susanna d. 1739; he m. 2d, Mary Leland, 1741.

16. ^{2}SAMUEL, s. of Samuel (14), m. Sybilla Haven, Jan. 11, 1738-9; and had, 1. PATIENCE, b. Jan. 6, '40, m. Amos Perry, of Sherb., Feb. 29, '64; 2. SAMUEL, b. Feb. 1, '42, d. unm., prob. in the army; 3. EBENEZER, b. Sep. 1, '44, d. Jan 1, '45; 4. SYBILLA, b. Ap. 3, '47, m. — Leland, of Holl. Sybilla the m. d. Feb. 19, '49, and Samuel m. 2d, Eunice Fuller, of Hop., Dec. 13, 1750; and had, 5. EUNICE, b. Feb. 21, '53, d. Oct. 21, '55; 6. EUNICE, b. June 6, '54, d. Nov. 24, '58; 7. EBENEZER, b. Ap. 26, '56; 8. EUNICE, b. Sep. 9, '58; 9. ALEXANDER; 10. JAMES, both bap. June 26, '63, (one accidentally killed the other while hunting); 11. LYDIA, bap. May 10, '67. Eunice w. of Sam. was adm. to the ch. by letter, from Newton, Mar. 15, 1752. She d. in Nat. Samuel her husb. lived near Mr. Sylvanus Phipps', and d. in Fram.

17. ^{2}DAVID, s. of Sam. (14), m. Elizabeth Butler; and had 1. ELIZABETH, b. Jan. 5, 1745; 2. LYDIA, b. Mar. 28, '48, m. — Baker, lived in Shrewsb.; 3. MOLLY, b. Dec. 16, '50, m. Ezek. Mixter; 4. ANNA, b. Sep. 1, '53; 5. NELLY, b. Oct. 5, '55; 6. NABBY, b. Oct. 28, '58; 7 and 8. SARAH and KATY, b. Oct. 7,

'61; 9. DAVID, b. June 26, '64; 10. WALTER, b. Feb. 27, '67, moved to Peterboro' Slip. D. the f. lived on Mr. Josiah Abbot's place, moved to Peterboro' Slip, and d. ab. the beginning of the Revolution.

18. [2]JOSEPH, s. of Sam. (14), m. Susannah Pike, July 15, 1746; and had, 1. THADDEUS, bap. Nov. 30, 1746, m. — Rice, of Barre, and d. in Westmoreland; 2. MOLLY, b. 1748, m. Nathan Parkhurst; 3. SUSANNAH, bap. Jan. 20, 1750–1, m. Asa Morse, Jan. 15, '77, lives in Fram.; 4. MOSES, bap. Ap. 8, '52, m. Lois Adams, of Holl., Nov. 16, '80, d. in Whitingham; 5. NATHAN, bap. Mar. 9, '55, d. unm.; 6. MEHETABEL, bap. July 3, '57, m. Hon. Needham Maynard, May 6, '81, and d. in N. Y.; 7. MARTHA, bap. Dec. 9, '59, m. Nathan Hemenway, Dec. 3, '78, and d. at Whitestown, N. Y.; 8. SARAH, bap. Aug. 22, '62, m. Jos. Jennings, Jun., Oct. 30, '81, d. at Whitestown; 9. SUBMIT, bap. Oct. 28, '64, m. —— Blodget; 10. ELIZABETH, bap. June 14, '67, d. young; 11. PRUDY, bap. Oct. 7, '70, m. Abner Haven, May '89, d. 1840. Joseph the f. lived near the Railroad, was a Selectman, 1774, and d. in Whitestown, N. Y. ab. 1795. Susannah his w. d. 1788, in Fram.

19. [3]NATHANIEL, s. of Thomas (1), had by w. Anne, 1. LYDIA, b. Dec. 10, 1694, m. Benj. Muzzey of Lexington, Nov. 15, 1716; 2. REBECKAH, b. July 25, '97, m. Daniel Bigelow, June 27, '23; 3. SARAH, b. Nov. 1, 1701, m. Nathaniel Coy, and d. July 23, 1728; 4. NATHANIEL[20], b. Ap. 18, '03; 5. ANNE, b. Jan. 27, '06-7, m. Samuel Knight of Sud., Ap. 23, '40; 6. WILLIAM, m. in Holl. Sarah Perry, 1733, and f. of *Sarah* and *Hannah*, and d. Nov. 1789, æ. 80; 7. DANIEL[21], b. Mar. 20, 1711–2. Nath. the f. lived near the R. Road Station, was Selectman 2 years, and d. Jan. 1, 1746; his w. Anne d. Mar. 12, 1743.

20. [3]NATHANIEL, Jun. s. of Nath. (19), m. Rachel Lovell, of Medfield, Nov. 27, 1735, and had 1. BENJAMIN, b. Sep. 15, '37, d. Nov. 24; 2. NATHANIEL[22], b. July 31, '39, d. Aug. 14; 3. WILLIAM, b. Feb. 21, '40–1, d. Mar. 2; 4. ANN, b. Aug. 6, '44, d. Nov. 30, '48; 5. NATHANIEL, b. Sep. 11, '47; 6. ALEXANDER, b. Oct. 5, '48; 7. BENJAMIN, bap. Mar. 16, '51; 8. RACHEL, m. Richard Gleason, d. in Fitzwilliam. Nath. the f., known as "Corporal Eames," lived where Jona. now lives, and d. Mar. 13, 1796, æ. 93; his w. Rachel d. Oct. 19, 1778, æ. 68.

21. 3DANIEL, s. of Nath. (19), m. Silence Leland, and had in Holl. and Hop., 1. DANIEL, b. 1740, m. Mary Cutler, '61; HOPESTILL, '44; LYDIA, '46, m. Josh. Underwood; ANNA, '48, m. Col. John Gleason, of Fram.; WILLIAM, '49, had 2 w. and d. in Boylston; AARON, '53, m. Sarah Leland. Descendants of Daniel live in Holliston, near Fram. bounds.

22. ³NATHANIEL, s. of Nath. (20), m. Kata Rice, and had 1. ANNA, b. Feb. 5, 1772, m. Amasa Fobes, of Roxbury, Aug. 1, 1802; 2. ALEXANDER, b. July 5, '74, m. Abigail Lovell, of Medfield; 3. ZEDEKIAH, b. Feb. 13, '76, d. Oct. 27, '78, æ. 2; 4. ABEL, b. May 23, '78, m. Hitty Eames, Mar. 1804; 5. RACHEL, b. May 30, '80, m. Seth Fobes, lives in Paris, Me.; 6. STEPHEN, b. July 6, '82, d. Oct. 1, '86; 7. LOVELL, b. Feb. 7, '85, m. Lucy Eames; 8. ZEDEKIAH, bap. Oct. '87, d. in Georgia; 9. PATTY, bap. Aug. '90; 9. JONATHAN, b. July 5, '93, m. Sukey Eames. Nath. the f. lived on the place now of his 's. Jona., and d. Sep. 8, 1820, æ. 73. Kata his wid., d. May 30, 1833, æ. 81.

23. MARY, m. Eben. Frizzell, both of Fram., Jan. 11, 1749. ABIGAIL, of Fram., m. John Newton, Jun., of Southb., Dec. 14, 1772. ASA, of Holl., m. in Fram., Anne Haven, of Holl., 1789. PHINEHAS, m. Isanna Jones, both of Fram., July, 1790.

EATON, JONAS, (perhaps the Jonas of Wat., who, Mar. 23, 1646, sold to Richard Cutting, his house and ground, formerly bought of Simon Onge, (Mid. Deeds), had (Reading Rec) by w. Grace, 1. MARY, b. 1643; 2. JOHN, b. Sep. 10, 1645; 3. JONAS, b. 1647; 4. JONAS, b. Sep. 24. '48; 5. JOSEPH, b. '51; 6. JOSHUA, b. Dec. 4, '53. m. Rebeckah Kendal, and f. of *Joshua*, b. 1683, *Thomas*, and others; 7. JONATHAN, b. Dec. 6, '55, (f. by w. Eliz., of *Jonathan*, who d. 1711, and two drs); 8. DAVID, '57. Jonas, the f.'s will, is dated Jan. 7, 1673. He d. Feb. 24, 1674.

2. JOHN, s. of Jonas (1), had in Reading, by w. Dorcas, 1. JONAS, b. and d. 1677; 2. GRACE, b. 1677, m. —— Boutelle; 3. NOAH. b. 1678; 4. JONAS, b. May 18, '80; 5. JOSEPH, b. and d. '81; 6. MARY, b. '83; 7. DORCAS, b. '88; 8. BENJAMIN; 9. JOSEPH; 10. PHEBE. The est. of John, the f. was settled 1700, and the widow Dorcas m. 2d —— Bryant.

3. JONAS, s. of John (2), a tanner, bought of Geo. Walkup, one half of the "half mile square," and built where is now the old Eaton House, near the Sudb. bounds. By his w. Mehetabel, he had 1. MEHETABEL, b. Feb. 12, 1706-7, m. John Trowbridge; 2. NOAH⁵, b. July 22, '08; 3. JOHN, b. Sep. 3, '10, d. at Plainfield; 4. PHEBE, b. Sep. 28, '12; 5. JONAS, b. Oct. 22, '14; 6. JOSEPH, b. Mar. 12, '16-7, d. at Plainfield; 7. MARY, b. Mar. 12, '18-9; 8. JOSHUA, b. July 1, '21 — his 1st w. d. in Voluntown, Con., 1748-9; 9. BENJAMIN¹⁰, b. Oct. 9, '23; 10. EBENEZER, b. May 6, '27. J. the f. was Selectman '17, and d. Aug. 13, '27, æ. 47.

4. JOSHUA, had in Fram., by w. Lydia, SAMUEL, bap. Feb. 18, 1728, and d. Oct. 8, 1729, æ. 1 y. 7 m. 22 d. Joshua was adm. to the Ch. Aug. 30, 1724, and was Selectman, 1732. [Joshua and w. Lydia, had in Wat. LYDIA, b. Mar. 9, 1711. In 1718, at Weston, Lydia, w. of Joshua, of Wat., now of Worcester, was adm. to the Ch. Joshua, a lawyer at Worc., and after minister of Spencer, was b. at Walth. Dec. 15, 1714. See an interesting notice of him in Willard's address to the Worc. Bar, p. 54.]

5. [1]NOAH, s. of Jonas (3), m. Hannah Vinton, of Stoneham; and had 1. HANNAH, b. Nov. 4, 1731, m. John Cheney; 2. NOAH, b. Aug. 7, '33; 3. ABIGAIL, b. Feb. 1, '35-6, m. Daniel Gregory; 4. JONAS[7], b. Jan. 29, '37-8; 5. JOHN[8], b. July 30, '40; 6. MEHETABEL, b. Ap. 21, '43, m. Deac. Daken, of Sud., and d. ab. 1815; 7. RUTH, b. Feb. 16, '44, m. Peter Parker, d. Mar. 20, 1800; 8. MALTIAR, b. Jan. 15, '47, m. Huldah Haynes, was rated in Fram. 1775, and d. at Athol, 1828; 9. SILAS[9], b. Dec. 1, '50; 10. MARY, b. May 11, '53, m. Sim. Goddard, d. at Ath., ab. 1800. Cornet Noah, the f., lived on the place, now of Ezek. Howe, Jun. and was Selectman 2 years. He d. Oct. 8, 1791, æ. 83. His wid. Hannah, d. Mar. 8, 1795, æ. 87.

6. [1]NOAH, s. of Noah (5), m. Hannah Hunt, and had 1. NABBY, bap. Nov. 20, 1757, m. Jacob Hemenway; 2. NOAH, bap. Nov. 5, '58, m. and d. in Canada; 3. HANNAH, bap. Ap. 6, '60, m. Abel Childs, and d. 1803; 4. LUTHER, bap. Sep. 26, '62, m. Polly Drury, Dec. '89, 2d Nelly Drury, 3d wid. Polly Newton, and f. of *Mary, Nathan, Dexter, Luther, Nancy,* and *William;* 5. NATHAN, bap. Aug. 23, '67, m. Aseneth Fisk, Nov. 18, '94, and d. Ap. 26, 1812. Noah the f. m. 2d Polly Tilton, Feb. 14, '71, and had 6. MOLLY, b. Nov. 11, '71, d. young. Polly the m. d. July, 1803, and Noah m. 3d wid. Martha Abbot, June 12, 1804. Noah was Selectman 2 years, and d. June 12, 1814, æ. 82. His wid. Martha d. Nov. 30, 1834, æ. 82.

7. [1]JONAS, s. of Noah (5), m. Lois Goodnow, of Sud., May 7, 1761, and had 1. LOIS, b. June 16, '62, m. Hon. Jona. Maynard, May 30, 1784, and d. without issue, Dec. 5, 1836, æ. 74; 2. DANIEL, b. Jan. 31, '64, m. Mehetabel Murdock, 1787; 3. JESSE, b. Jan. 27, '66, died suddenly, while in the act of singing at church, Nov. 5, '86; 4. ANNA, b. June 11, '68, d. Nov. '77; 5. NATHAN, d. 1771, and 6. LYDIA, both b. Sep. 28, '70. L. m.

Maj. Lawson Nurse; 7. EUNICE, b. Jan. 25, '73, m. Nathan Henderson, lives in Boston; 8. NATHAN, b. Mar. 4, '75, d. Nov. '77; 9. PERSIS, b. Aug. 23, '77, d. Feb. 5, '96, — suddenly fell dead at the house of Jona. Maynard, Esq., when preparing for a ride; 10 and 11. ANNA, and BETSEY, twins, b. Feb. 23, '80. — A. d. Oct. '87, B. m. Joshua Lane, 1801; 12. JOSEPH, b. May 28, '82. Jonas the f. lived at Salem end; Lois his w. d. Mar. 1819.

8. [1]JOHN, s. of Noah (5), m. Olive Conant, and had 1. REUBEN, b. May 14, 1769, m. Betsey Hunt, lives in Sud.; 2. SALLY, b. Nov. 8, '70, m. Elisha Hunt, d. in Sud, 1842; 3. JOHN, bap. May 23, '73, m. Molly Hunt, Oct. '97, and d. 1846; 4. OLIVE, bap. Ap. 7, '76, m. Reuben Winch; 5. LEVI, bap. June, 14, '78, m. Susannah How, May 16, 1805, and 2d, Eliza Buckminster; 6. ABEL, bap. Oct. 1, '78, m. Sally Hemenway, Mar., 1802, and 2d, Persis How; 7. LUCY, bap, Aug. '82, m. Obad. Perry, of Sherb., May 23, 1803, lives at Sud.; 8. HITTY, bap. Dec. '84, d. young; 9. JESSE, bap. Dec. '86, d. young; 10. ANNA, bap. Mar. '89, d. young; 11. BETSEY, bap. Aug. '93, d. young; 12. NOAH, bap. Feb. '96, d. '98. John the f. d. May 28, 1816, æ. 76; his w. Olive d. Sep. 20, 1842, æ. 93.

9. [1]SILAS, s. of Noah (5), m. Polly Nichols, Feb. 1782, and had 1. JOSIAH, b. Nov. 11, 1782, m. Elizabeth Stever, of Thomaston, Me., and d. in Lynn, 1847; 2. SILAS, b. Oct. 18, '84, m. Nancy Stone, and d. June 23, 1828; 3. MARY, b. Oct. 20, '86, m. Luther Stone; 4. HANNAH, b. Jan. 2, '89, d. Aug. 22, '91; 5. MARTHA, b. Mar. 10, '91, m. Hon. Abner Wheeler; 6. SAMUEL, b. May 14, '94, d. Dec. 18, '97; 7. NABBY, and 8. HITTY, twins, b. May 31, '98, both d. Sep. 24, 1802. Silas the f. lived on the place late of Wid. Nancy Eaton, and d. July 18, 1828, æ. 77. His w. Mary d. Oct. 30, 1818, æ. 61.

10. [2]BENJAMIN, s. of Jonas (3), m. Beulah Stone, Dec. 23, 1747, and had 1. JONAS, b. July 17, '48, lived in Barre, and m. Abigail Allen; 2. EBENEZER[12], b. May 12, '50, m. Rebeckah Stone, May 21, '78; 3. BEULAH, b. Feb. 28, '52, m. Nathan Boynton, Dec. 31, '78; 4. BENJAMIN[11], b. July 27, '54; 5. ANNA, b. Aug. 8, '57, m. Brigham Eaton, of Petersham, May 28, '78. Benj. the f. lived on the place now of Mr. Ebenezer Eaton.

11. [2]BENJAMIN, s. of Benj. (10), m. Mary Stacy, and had

1. ASENETH, b. Oct. 8, 1775, m. Lincoln Brigham, of Southb;
2. NELLY, b. Nov. 28, '76, lives unm. in Fram.; 3. POLLY, b.
May 8, '78, m. Dr. Nathan Rice; 4. FANNY, b. Jan. 14, '80, d.
æ. 18; 5. DAVID, b. Feb. 2, '82, m. Betsey Horn, of Southb.,
and 2d w. at Lake Erie; 6. CYRUS, b. Feb. 11, '84, lives in Warren,
Me.; 7. ANNE, bap. Sep. '89, m. Solo. Nichols, of Whitestown;
8. CHARLOTTE, bap. Sep. '89, m. John Parker, moved to N. Y.,
1810; 9. EMILY, d. young; 10. BENJAMIN, d. æ. 4, (the 2 last
b. in Southb.). Benj. the f. lived on Mr. Charles Capen's farm,
moved to Southb., and d. there. Mary his wid. lives, (1845),
near Lake George.

12. ²EBENEZER, s. of Benj. (10), m. Rebeckah Stone, May
21, 1778, and had 1. NANCY, b. May 28, 1779, m. Rev. Joseph
Emerson, of Beverly, and d. 1804; 2. BETSEY, b. Mar. 19, '81,
lives unm., in Boston; 3. WILLIAM, b. Aug. 18, '83, (Will. Coll.),
ord. at Fitchburg, Aug. 30, 1815, and at Middleborough, Mar.
10, 1824; 4. REBECKAH, b. July 25, '85, lives in Boston; 5.
SUSANNAH, bap. Aug. '87, lives in Beverly; 6. EBENEZER, bap.
Sep. '89, m. Anna Walker, who d. Aug. 14, 1818, æ. 27, and
m. 2d, Sally Spofford; 7. SALLY, bap. Aug., '93, m. Samuel
Witt, d. in Shrewsbury, 1837.

13. REBECKAH, m. James Brown, both of Fram., Oct. 18, 1733.
LYDIA, m. Matthias Clark, Oct. 17, 1729.

SAMUEL and w. Ruth, of Sud., had *Elizabeth*, b. 1731; *Jonathan*,
Thomas, and others. SAMUEL, of Sud., m. Miliscent Wheeler, 1748, and
had *Uriah, Samuel, &c.* JOHN, of Dedham, d. ab. 1658, leaving *John, Mary*, and *Abigail.* WILLIAM, " of Staple," who came over with w. Martha,
three children, and servant, was prob. the Wm. (w. Martha) who had, at
Wat., *Daniel*, b. Jan. 20, 1638-9; *Mary*, 1643. In 1664. they were of
Read., where Martha (prob. the m.) d. ab. 1681, having a s. John. Daniel,
s. of John, m. Mary —, 1664, and had at R., *Daniel, Ann, Martha, Priscilla, Daniel,* and *Mehetabel.*

EDGELL, WILLIAM m. Elizabeth Norman, of Marblehead, and lived
in Woburn and Lexington. His chil. were 1. WILLIAM, (æ. 17, 1743;
see Guardianship, Mid. Prob.), who was a petitioner for Westminster,
Mass., 1759, and d. there, July. 1809, æ. 82; 2 JOHN, m. Rebeckah Winship, of Lexington, Nov. 9, 1762, g. father of Rev. J. Q. A. Edgell, of W.
Newbury. J. the f. d. in Westminster, Vt; 3. SIMON; 4. BENJAMIN, m.
Susannah Wyman. and was f. of *Benjamin, John. Peter, Susannah,* and
Abigail, and d. in Woburn, ab. 1821, æ. 85. Elizabeth, wid of William,
came to Fram., and m. Isaac How, Oct 16, 1739. She d. Oct. 20, 1770,
æ. 73. [Tradition, in the family. supposes William to have come from
England, with a brother, who lived and d. in Phil., and with whom Wm.
learned his trade of a tinman. In Boston, Thomas Edzall, m. Elizabeth
Forman, Sep. 16, 1652, and had s. *Henry,* b. 1654].

2. SIMON, s. of Wm. (1), lived on the farm now of Col. Moses, m. Mehetabel Pike, Mar. 5, 1761, and had 1. MOSES, b. June 1, '62, d. May 10, 1784 ; 2. AARON PIKE, b. Dec. 13, '66 ; 3. MEHETABEL, b. Feb. 13, '70, m. Wm. Bond, of Wat., Sep. '86. Capt. Simon the f. commanded the Co. of Minute men in Fram., and served with reputation in the Revolutionary War ; was Selectman 2 years, and d. Oct. 3, 1820, æ. 87 ; his wid. Mehet. d. Feb. 5, 1835, æ. 91.

3. AARON PIKE, s. of Simon (2), m. Eleanor Trowbridge; and had 1. MOSES, b. Aug. 13, 1792, m. Sophia A. Angier, 1817 — Col. Moses has been 12 years a Selectman, 5 years a Representative, and 22 years T. Treasurer ; 2. NANCY, b. Aug. 23, '94, m. Luther Horn ; 3. MEHETABEL, b. Aug. '96, m. Levi Whitmore. Aaron was 10 years a Selectman, and d. Sep. 28, 1816 ; his w. Eleanor d. Oct. 1840.

EDMUNDS, WALTER, freeman 1639, of Concord, and (under the name of Gualter) with w. Dorothy, admitted to the Charlestown Ch., 1652. He had. 1. JOSHUA, b. ab. 1624, a distiller. at Charlestown, by w. Elizabeth, f. of *William*, b. 1665 Josh. d. Nov. 5, 1683, æ. 59, and his wid. Eliz. m. Richard Martin, Nov. 28, '89. The heirs of Joshua were proprietors of Rutland, 1686 ; 2. DANIEL, b. ab. 1628 ; 3. JOHN, b. July 2. 1640, and by w. Hannah, f. at Charlestown, of *Dorothy*, b. '68 ; *John*, d. '70 ; and *John*, b. '71. John, the f. d. 1677, and his wid. Han., m. Deac. Aaron Ludkin, 1684 ; 4. , a daughter, who m. Potter, of Concord. Walter. the f. d. at Charlestown, July 13, 1667, and his wid. Dor. d. Sep. 14, 1671.

2. DANIEL, s. of Walter, (1), had by w. Marie, 1. RICHARD, b. 1664, d. '68 ; 2. MARY, b. '66, d. '67 ; 3. JONATHAN, b. July 24, '67, (or '69) ; 4. RALPH„ b. Nov. 5, '71 ; 5. MARY, b. Oct. 28, '73, m. Nath. Davis, '92. Daniel (a saltmaker) d. Aug. 22, 1688, æ. near 60. His wid. Mary d. Nov. 26, 1717.

3. JONATHAN, s. of Dan., (2), m. Ruth Frothingham, 1691, and had JONATHAN, b. Mar. 27, 1705.

4. JONATHAN, s. of Jona (3), m. Hannah Gates ; and had 1. JONATHAN, b. Ap. 20, 1728 ; 2. HANNAH, b. '30 ; 3. SARAH, '31, cov. in Fram. July 11, '56, and dism. to E. Sud. Nov. 29, 1761 ; 4. SAMUEL, b. June 29, '35 ; 5. AMOS, d. '41 ; 6. JOHN, d. '44 ; 7. AARON, b. '39 ; 8. ESTHER, d. '43 ; 9. ESTHER, d. '44 ; 10. AMOS, b. Ap. 27, '44, and m. (then of Fram.), Esther Hide, of Newton, Sep. 13, '73 ; 11. ANN, b. 1746 ; 12. ABBY. Jonathan, Jun., the f., was received to the Charlestown ch., 1727,

was of Camb. 1730, and of Newton, 1739; he bought, 1748, of Eben. Winchester, in Fram., where he d.*

5. JONATHAN, Jun., s. of Jona. (4), had by w. Prudence, 1. PRUDENCE, b. July 28, 1760, d. Aug. 18; 2. ANNA, b. Dec. 19, '61, adm. to the ch. Sep. '83, m. Abner How, Sep. 85, moved away, and m. 2d, Timothy Rand; Prudence the m. d. Feb. 24, 1764, and Jona. m. 2d, Huldah Hide, of Newton, Oct. 31, 1765, who was adm. to the ch., Jan. 29, '69, and had 3. HULDAH, b. Mar. 7, '67, m. Samuel Rice, Nov. '88, and d. ab. 1840; 4. PRUDENCE, bap. Oct. 17, '72; 5. ELIZABETH, bap. Oct. 2, '74; Jona. m. 3d, Hannah Ward, of Newton, June 13, '76, who was adm. to the ch. Sep. '88, and had 6. JONATHAN, b. Mar. 6, '77, m. Lucy Nurse, and d. in Fram., Jan. 22, 1830; Lucy his w. d. Jan. 7, 1838. Jonathan the f. was chosen to a Town office, 1777, lived upon his f.'s farm, and d. Jan. 8, 1816, æ. 87; Hannah his w. d. Dec. 26, 1812, æ. 71.

6. SAMUEL, prob. s. of Jona. (4), had in Fram. SARAH, and JOHN, both bap. Nov. 30, 1766. Samuel lived in the house now of Joel Edmunds, was adm. to the ch. Nov. 16, 1766, and recommended to the ch. in Brookfield, Mar. 8, 1772.

7. DAVID, and w. Hannah, had at Marlb., 1. ABIGAIL, b. 1720; 2. HANNAH, b. 1722, m. in Fram. Ezekiel Rice, Jun., Sep. 19, '51; and at Fram. 3. ELIZABETH, b. July 10, 1730. Mr. Swift notes, Ap. 28, 1728, " contribution for neighbor Edmunds." [Lynn Rec. David m. Hannah Hinkson, Aug. 8, 1717.]

8. MARY, was in Fram. from about 1750, to 1760. SARAH, Edmonds, alias Moore, who cov. July 11, 1756, was dismissed to E. Sud., Nov. 29, 1761.

WILLIAM, of Lynn, d. Aug. 4, 1693, leaving *John*, m. Sara Hudson, 1662, (f. of William, John, Jonathan, Mary, Elizabeth, Nathaniel, Joseph, and Benjamin); *Samuel*, m. Elizabeth Meriam, 1675, and prob Elizabeth Bridges, Jan. 27, 1685, (f. of Samuel, Elizabeth, Mary, Abigail, David, b. July 22, 1689, and Jonathan, b. Jan. 7, '92); and *Joseph*, (w. Susanna, d. 1670), f. of William, Joseph, Sara, William, Thomas, and Robert. Mary, w. of William, d. 1657, and he m., the same year, in Boston, wid. Ann (Martine ?). SAMUEL, of Natick, and w. Ruth, had *Jemima*, b. 1748; *Samuel*, b. 1750.

EDWARDS, BENJAMIN, s. of Benj. of Boston, lived in the

---

* Jonathan and Sarah were adm. to the Fram. Church, Oct. 27, 1751. Was this Jona. the f. of the above? Jonathan m. Sarah Malleson, both of Charlestown, Ap. 20, 1732.

Dr. Merriam house, m. Mary Bent of Sud., and had 1. MARY, b. Mar. 27, 1778, m. 1st, Abel Adams, 2d, Eph. Parkhurst; 2. BENJAMIN, b. 1780, d. æ. ab. 10; 3. BATHSHEBAH, b. 1782, d. young; 4. ALEXANDER, m. Anne Haven, d. æ. 29; 5. JONATHAN, d. æ. ab. 30.

ELIOT, DANIEL, m. Hannah Cloyes, and had 1. DANIEL, b. Aug. 17, 1687; 2. EBENEZER, b. Mar. 3, '93; 3. JOHN, b. May 16, '95; 4. JAMES, b. Ap. 2, '97; 5. NATHANIEL, b. Aug. 10, '99; 6. JONATHAN, b. Aug. 16, 1701; 7. PETER, b. Nov. 25, '04. Dan. the. f. was a prop. at Oxford, 1713.

2. DANIEL, Jun., s. of Daniel (1), m. Sarah Provender, Feb. 3, 1707-8; and had HANNAH, b. Nov. 4, 1709. Dan. Jun., was also a prop. at Oxford, 1713.

ELLIS, an individual of this name, a saddler, moved from Fram., ab. 1800.

ESTABROOK, Capt. DANIEL, owned near Tho. Walkup, ab. 1742.

EVERETT, NANCY, m. George Hawes, of Wrentham, Oct. 27, 1796. JESSE, and w. Elizabeth, of Fram., came from Franklin, lived on the Isaac Haven place. Their chil. were, JAMES, d. Mar. 28, 1800, æ. 20; BENJAMIN, d. Aug. 9, 1801, æ. 28. They had also a dr., OLIVE. A son d. in Harv. Coll.

FABER, Miss SUSAN, d. in Fram., Jan. 28, 1834. æ. 77.

FAIRBANK, or FAIRBANKS,* JONATHAN, the N. E. progenitor, d. at Dedham, 1678. His wife's name was Grace. His chil. were 1. JOHN, f. (by w. Sarah), at Dedham, of *Joshua*, b. 1642, d. 1661; *John*, b. '44; *Sarah*, b. '45; *Jonathan*, b. '48; *Mary* and *Martha*, b. '50; *Joseph*, b. '56; *Hannah*, b. '58; *Benjamin*, b. '62, and d. 1694. John, the f. d. 1684; his w. d. 1683. 2. GEORGE; 3. JONAS, of Lancaster, and f. by w. Lydia, of *Mary*, b. 1659; *Joshua*, '61, (killed by the Indians, 1676); *Grace*, b. '63; *Jonathan*, b. '66, (m. Mary Haward, '88, and himself and 2 chil. killed by Indians, and w. made captive, 1697); *Hazadiah*, b. '68; *Jabez*, b. '70; *Jonas*, b. '73. Jonas, the f. was killed by the Indians, 1676, and his est. settled, 1677. (Mid. Co. Rec., 3d vol.) 3. JONATHAN, at Dedham, by w. Deborah, of *Deborah*, b. 1654; *Grace, Sara, Edward, David, Mary*, and *Jeremiah*; 4. MARY, m. Christopher Smith; and 5. ——, who m. Ralph Day.†

2. GEORGE, s. of Jona., (1), had at Dedham, by w. Mary, 1. MARY, b. Nov. 10, 1647; 2. GEORGE, b. May 26, '50, m. Rachel Adams, '71, and a 2d w.; 3. SAMUEL, b. Oct. 28, '52; 4. ELIEZER, b. June 8, '55, and f. at Med-

---

* In this, as in many other instances, modern usage has added a final s to the ancient name. The names of Havens, Stebbins, Sternes, Adams, Woods, Stevens, afford examples of the same change of name.

† RICHARD, who took the freeman's oath, May 14, 1634, had in Boston, (by w. Elizabeth), *Constance*, bap. 1635; *Zaccheus*, b, 1639; and *Zaccheus*, b. and d. 1653.

field, by w. Martha, of *Marie*, b. 1678; and at Sherb., *Martha*, '80; *Lydia*, '83; *Margaret*, '84; *Mercy*, '88; *Eliezer*, '90, d. in Sherb, 1741; 5. JONAS, b. Feb. 23, '56; and at Medfield, 6. JONATHAN, b. May, 1, '62; 7. MARGARET, b. '64. [Geo., sen., was drowned at Medfield, Jan. 10, '82; another account dates the death of Geo., the f., Ap. 6, 1683].

3. JONATHAN, s. of Geo., (2), phys. at Sherb., had by w. Sarah, (who d. 1713), 1. GEORGE, b. Ap. 1685; 2. JONATHAN, b. 89, f. by w. Lydia, (who d. 1724), of *Jonathan*, b. 1714; *Mary*, b. 1717, m. —— White; *Lydia*, 1718, m. Abijah Morse, 1751; *Comfort*, 1720, m. Zebulon Palmer, '37; *Moses*, 1722; *Daniel*, b. 1723, m. Submit Fairbanks, 1747; and by w. Hannah Coolidge, m. 1726, *Joshua*, b. 1727; *John*, 1729, m. Hannah Fisk, '54; *Hannah*, 1731, m. —— Whiting; *Grace*, b. 1734, m. Obadiah Morse, '55; and *Abner*, b. 1736. Jonathan's will was proved Dec. 3, 1754; 3. COMFORT, b. '90, m. Jos. Billings; 4. JOSEPH, b. '92, d. young; 5. SAMUEL, b. '93, m. Susanna Watson, 1718, and f. of *Jonas*, d. 1721; *Samuel*, b. June 21, 1720; *Benjamin; Levi*, and others; 6. JONAS, b. '97, d. young. Jona. had by a 2d w. Anne, 7. BENJAMIN, b. 1715. Dr. Jona., the f. d. 1719, at Sherb.

4. GEORGE, s. of Jona. (3), had by w. Lydia, in Sherb., 1. GEORGE, b. Dec. 2, 1708, m., 1735, Deborah Sawin, and f. of *Reuben*, b. '35; 2. LYDIA, b. '10, m. —— Hayden; 3. JABEZ, b. Oct. 4, '13; 4. SARAH, b. '16, m. —— Hayden. Lydja, the w. d. 1717. George, then of Fram., m. 2d Rachel Drury, Dec. 1718, and had in Sherb., 5. JOSEPH, b. '20, d. '22; 6. RACHEL, b. '21, d. young; 7. ABIGAIL, b. '23, d. young; and in Holliston, 8. ABIGAIL, b. 25, d. young; 9. COMFORT. b. '27, d. '29; 10. SUBMIT, b. '29, m. Dan. Fairbank, '47; 11. MARY, b. '30, m. —— Morse; 12. DRURY, b. '33, d. June 19, 1786, (m. Deborah Leland, '58, and f., at Holl., of *John*, b. '59; *Perley*, b. '61; *Elijah*, b. '70; Rev. *Drury*, b. '72; *Deborah*, b. '75; and *Mary*, b. '81); 13. RACHEL, b. '35, d. 1744. Ens. George, d. at Holl., 1753, and his will was proved Feb. 11, 1754.

5. SAMUEL, s. of Sam. and w. Susanna, and g. son of Dr. Jona. (3), held a town office in Fram., 1748, and lived near the house of W. Nixon, Esq. He m. Hephzibah Nixon, June 6, 1751, and had, 1. HANNAH, b. Jan. 25, 1752, m. —— Rice. The f. m. 2d, Wid. Mary Frizzell, and had, 2. SAMUEL; 3. ZACCHEUS, b. 1759. Samuel the f. d. in F., ab. 1760. His wid. Mary m. (John?) Shattuck, and was buried in Fram., June 14, 1822, æ. 95.

6. ZACCHEUS, s. of Sam. (5), m. Mary Brinley, Mar. 3. 1779; and had 1. ZACCHEUS, bap. Aug. 15, '79; 2. NANCY, bap. May 27, '80, m. Maj. Barzillai Banister, Ap. 23, '98, and 2d, —— Easty, of Southb.; 3. POLLY, d. young; 4. THOMAS, bap. Aug., '83, lives in Nat; 5. —— d. young. Zaccheus the f. m. 2d, Martha Gates, Mar., 1787, and had, 6. POLLY, m. Solo. Rhodes; 7. CATHARINE, m. —— Dunken; 8. DEXTER, d. unm.; 9. CLARISSA, m. —— Nichols; 10. SAMUEL, d. unm.; 11. CHARLES, m. —— Parker; 12. CURTIS, d. unm. Zaccheus mov-

ed to Antrim, N. H., ab. 1799, and had there, PETER W.; SUSANNA; LUCINDA; WILLIAM; and ABIGAIL. Z. the f. d. at Antrim, Jan. 27, 1845, æ. 86.

7. JABEZ, s. of George (4), m. Susanna Corning, and had in Holl., 1. LYDIA, b. 1739; 2. JOSEPH, '41; 3. JOSHUA, '43; 4. ISAIAH, '45; 5. SUSANNAH, '47, d. young; 6. SUSANNAH, '52; 7. JERUSHA, '57; 8. GEORGE, '62. He then moved to Fram., on or near the Brinley farm, and had, 9. DANIEL, b. Mar. 21, '65; 10. COMFORT, bap. Dec. 14, '67.

8. JOSHUA, s. of Jabez, (7), m. Mary Parmenter of Sud., Dec. 3, 1767, and had in Fram., 1. LUCY, b. June 14, '68, m. Eph. Hager, of Marlb., Nov. '89; 2. LUKE, b. May 2, '70, m. Zerviah ——, was f. of *George* and *Sophia*, and was drowned in Sud. River, Aug. 1805; 3. JERUSHA, b. Ap. 8, '72, m. Dan. Allen of Marlb., Feb., '97; 4. ANNA, b. May 13, '74; 5. CORNING, b. Aug. 17, '76, d. Jan. 28, '78; 6. MOLLY, b. May 24, '78, m. Ezra Rugg, Ap. 1, 1802; 7. ASA, b. June 2, '80, d. unm.; 8. ASENETH, b. Mar. 4, '83; 9. HANNAH, b. May 15, '85, m. Eli Fay of Hop., May 11, 1800; 10. DANIEL, b. Oct. 29, '88, drowned in Sud. River, Aug. 1805; 11. SALLY, b. May 15, '90. Joshua the f. moved into Worc. Co., ab. 1804.

FARRAR, JOHN, m. Martha, dr. of the Rev. John Swift, Oct. 13, 1740, and had, 1. MARY, b. Jan. 8, 1741; 2. MARTHA, b. Dec. 15, '44, d. Ap. 3, '45; 3. JOHN, b. and d. May 15, '47; 4. MARTHA, b. June 7, '49. Maj. John the f. m. 2d, Deborah Winch, Oct. 4, 1750, and had, 5. JOHN, b. Aug. 11, '51; 6. DEBORAH, b. Dec. 26, '53; 7. NELLY, b. Nov. 4, '55; 8. JOSEPH, b. Ap. 3, '58; 9. WILLIAM, b. June 22, '60; 10. DANIEL, b. Feb. 19, '63; 11. ANNE, b. Oct. 27, '65; 12. SAMUEL, b. Jan. 22, '69; 13. HITTY, bap. Oct. 14, '71. Maj. Farrar was 10 years a Selectman, and 8 years T. Treasurer, and was Dep. Sheriff, 1769. He moved, with his family, to Fitzwilliam, N. H., where he d.

2. MARGARET (prob. sister to Maj. John), m. in Fram. John Trowbridge, Mar. 27, 1751. "NATHAN Farrow," was in F. 1792.

DANIEL and w. Hannah, of Sud., had *Josiah*, 1722; *Daniel*; and *Phinehas*. JOSIAH, and w. Hannah, of Sud., had *Mary*, 1743; *Phinehas*; *Daniel*, and others.

FAY, ROBERT, m. Mitty Rice, Mar. 1783. MITTY, dr. of David and Jane, was b. May 17, 1783.

This family have been numerous in Southb. THOMAS, sen., of Hingham, d. 1678; there were others in that town.

FESSENDEN, THOMAS, of Fram., m. Mary Cronyn, of Sherb., Sep. 24, 1782. Mr. F. was a saddler. Thomas was prob. in Fram., ab. 1750. (Mss. Journal). He is said to have died in Fram., without issue.

FISHER, SARAH, of Fram., m. David Perry, Jun., of Sherb. Aug. 19, 1773. ABRAHAM, m. Lucy Parkhurst, Jan. 15, 1784. This family came from Franklin.

FISK, or FISKE, NATHAN, of Wat., had by w. Susanna, 1. NATHAN, b. Oct. 17, 1642, and had chil. in Wat., of whom *William*, m. Eunice Jennings, of Fram., 1708, and lived in Weston ; 2. JOHN, b. Aug. 25, '47; 3. DAVID, b. Ap. 29, '50, m. Elizabeth Reed, '75, and had a s. *David*, b. Dec. 11, 1678; 4. NATHANIEL, b. July 12, '53; 5. SARAH, m. Abraham Gale. N., the f. d. June 21, 1676. His will is dated June 19.

2. NATHANIEL, s. of Nathan, (1), m. Mary Child, 1677, and had 1. NATHANIEL, b. June 9, 1678, m. at Sherb., Hannah Adams, Jan. 16, 1706, and was f. of *Nathaniel* ; *Asa*, m. Lois Leland ; *Hannah* ; *Moses*, who d. at Nat., (w. Mehetabel); *Lydia* ; 2. HANNAH, b. 1680 ; 3. SARY, b. '85, m. John Hastings; 4. LYDIA, b. '87; 5. ELIZABETH, b. '92, m.. Benj. Flagg, 1715 ; 6. ABIGAIL, b. '98, m. Allen Flagg, 1717.

3. JOHN, s. of Nath., (2), m. in Sherb., Lydia Adams, July 31, 1706 ; and had 1. JOHN, b. 1709, m. Abigail Babcock, 1731 ; 2. LYDIA, b. '12, d. '15 ; 3. ISAAC, b. Aug. 24, '14 ; 4. DANIEL, b. '16 ; 5. LYDIA, b. '20 ; 6. PETER, b. '23 ; 7. ABIGAIL, b. and d. '27 ; 8. NATHANIEL, b. '30. John, (prob. the f.), d. in Sherb., 1730.

4. ISAAC, s. of John, (3), a weaver by trade, m. Hannah Haven, Nov. 11, 1736, lived first at Worcester, then at Fram., near Addison Dadmun's, after at Guinea end, and finally on Mr. Richard Fiske's place. He had (prob. at Worcester), 1. ISAAC, b. 1736 ; 2. HANNAH, b. 1739, m. Deac. Everett, and d. in Attleboro' ; 3. JOHN, b. 1741 ; 4. RICHARD, b. Feb. 25, 1750 ; 5. DANIEL, a physician, m. Sukey, dr. of Rev. Mr. Thurston, of Medway, and d. in Oxford ; 6. MOSES, d. young ; 7. LYDIA, b. Oct. 25, '53, m. Maj. Lawson Nurse ; 8. MOSES, b. July 12, '55. Isaac the f. d. Dec. 22, 1799, æ. 86. His w. Hannah, (who, after her marriage, was for many years a Teacher), d. Feb. 21, 1800, æ. 85.

5. ISAAC, Jun., s. of Isaac, (4), m. Esther Mann, and had 1. OLIVE, d. æ. 20 ; 2. JAMES, b. Sep. 19, 1773, d. at Savannah, ab. 1799 ; 3. POLLY, b. Aug. 6, '77, d. young. Isaac the f. d. Sep. 19, 1778, æ. 42. His wid. m. Ebenezer Marshall.

6. JOHN, s. of Isaac (4), m. Abigail How, and had 1. NAT, b. Aug. 12, 1772, m. Catharine Slack, of Newton, and lived in

Westmoreland, N. H., and Fram.; Col. Nat d. Aug. 20, 1841, while on a visit to N. H.; he commanded a reg't of militia, ordered to Portsmouth, during the war of 1812; 2. THOMAS, b. Mar. 22, '74, m. Lucinda Trowbridge, of Pomfret, Con.; 3. SALLY, b. July, 17, '76, d. young; 4. JOHN BOYLE, b. at Sherb., Dec. 2, '78, Dart. Coll. 1798, an Attorney in N. Y., d. Dec. 11, 1805; 5. SUSANNAH, b. 1781, m. Eben. M. Ballard; 6. SALLY, b. 1783, m. Wm. Larrabee, Sep. 16, 1806; 7. EDWARD, b. May 25, '86, m. Elizabeth Porter, of Boston, lives in N. Y.; 8. NANCY, b. Jan. 26, '89, m. Col. James Brown; 9. WILLIAM, b. 1791, d. Nov. 19, 1805; 10. GEORGE, b. Sep. 23, '93, m. Wid. Honora Bolton, b. in the W. Indies. John, Esq., the f. lived near Isaac Warren's, and at the Silk Farm, and built the house late of Rufus Brewer, Esq. He held a commission as Justice of the Peace, was Rep. 6 years, and Selectman 12 years. He d. Dec. 17, 1819, æ. 78. Abigail his w. d. Ap., 1829, æ. 77.

7. RICHARD, s. of Isaac (4), built where David Fisk lives, m. Zebiah Pond, and had 1. LUTHER, b. Nov. 12, 1772, m. Sally Wait, of Roxb., and 2d —— Webster, and d. without issue, June 26, 1797; 2. MARTIN, b. Ap. 8, '74, m. —— Gilbert, lived at Norfolk, Va.; 3. PATTY, b. June 3, '76, m. Eben. Freeman, of Barre, (now of Fram.), Dec. 26, 1803; 4. DANIEL, b. Mar. 20, '78, d. in Norfolk, Va., Mar. 23, 1800; 5. NANCY, b. July 6, '80, d. æ. 9; 6. RICHARD, and 7. POLLY, twins, b. Jan. 29, '83. — R. m. Betsey Lovell, and d. Sep., 1841; his w. d. Dec. 2, 1839, æ. 50. — Polly, m. Samuel Valentine, of Hop.; 8. JOSIAH, b. Feb. 22, '85, m. Martha Coolidge, and d. May 3, 1832; 9. DAVID, b. Feb. 16, '91, d. Nov. 24, 1817. Capt. Richard the f., was 5 years a Selectman, and d. Mar. 9, 1824, æ. 80. Zebiah, his w. d. Jan. 25, 1837, æ. 88.

8. MOSES, s. of Isaac (4), m. in Hop. Betsey Bullard, Ap. 13, 1780, and had 1. MOSES MADISON, b. Nov. 25, '80, Dart. Coll. 1802, m. Mary Temple, and d. at Nashville, Tenn.; 2. ISAAC, b. May 26, '82, m. Betsey Johnson, of Nashville, Tenn., lived in Tenn., and in Fram., and d. 1846; 3. HANNAH, b. Aug. 2, '84, m. Joseph Ballard; 4. SENEH, (Aseneth), b. July 29, '86, d. May 9, 1809; 5 BETSEY, b. June 13, '88, d. unm.; 6. OLIVE, b. July 20, '90, m. Elias Temple, Esq.; 7. EBENEZER, b. June 5, '93, m. Emily Willard, d. on a passage from N. Orleans, 1828.

Moses the f. d. in Fram., Mar. 1, 1828; his wid. lives at an advanced age.

9. MICAH, (s. of Jona. and w. Abigail, of Weston), a tanner and currier, m. Lydia Upham, of Weston, and had 1. CHARLES, bap. Sep. 1792, m. Anne Buckminster; 2. CYNTHIA, b. '94, d. æ. 2. Micah the f. was Selectman, 4 years; and d. Dec. 9, 1813, æ. 49; his w. Lydia d. Mar. 1816.

10. MARY, of Fram., m. Zechariah Wilson, of Waltham, June 12, 1777.

Note. — JOHN, of Wat., m. Sarah Wyth, Dec. 11, 1651, and was f. (among others) of *Elizabeth*, b. 1669, m. Simon Mellen, of Fram., Dec. 27, 1688. John, the f. d. Oct. 28, 1685, æ. ab. 65. BENJAMIN, m. Bethshua Morse, 1674, and had *Benjamin*, and others, at Medfield. Deac. JONATHAN, (and w. Abigail), had, in Sud., *Bezaleel, Samuel, William, David, Benjamin, &c.*, and d. Dec. 27, 1742, æ. 63. DAVID, of Camb., d. ab. 1660, leaving *David*, and a dr., who m. —— Fitch. Lt. David, of Camb., surveyor, was, in 1663, æ. 72 years; — his first w. Lydia, d. 1654, and he m. a 2d, Seaborne Wilson, Sep. 6, 1655. David, s. of the latter, was of Lexington, and prob. the only male representative of the family, and had chil. *David, Robert, &c.*

FLAGG, or FLEGG, THOMAS, of Watertown, had by w. Mary, 1. JOHN, b. 1643, m. Mary Gale, '70, f. of *Sarah* and *John*, and d. '97; 2. BARTHOLOMEW, b. Feb. 23, '44; 3. THOMAS, b. April 28, '45, m. Rebeckah Dikes, '67, and d. ab. 1719, at Weston, f. of *Thomas*, m. Rebecca Sanger, 1711, and d. 1719; *Hephzibah, Hannah, Rebecca*, and *Jemima*; 4. MICHAEL, b. Mar. 23, '51; 5. ELIEZER, b. May 14, '53, (prob. of Concord, and f. of *Eleazer*; *Joseph*, m. Mary Tompkins, 1713; and *Priscilla*); his will proved 1722; 6. ELIZABETH, b. Mar. 20, '57, m. Joshua Bigelow, '76; 7. MARY, b. Jan. 14, '57-8; 8. REBECKAH, b. Sep. 5, '60, m. Stephen Cooke, of Newton; 9. BENJAMIN, b. June '25, '62, m. Experience Child, '91, removed to Worcester, f. of *Benjamin*, b. 1691, m. Elizabeth Fiske, 1715, (and had at Worc., Elizabeth, Abigail, Benjamin, (w. Abigail), William, Asa, and Mary); *Experience*, b. 1692, m. Caleb Ball, of Concord, 1713; *Abigail*, b. 1694; *Bathshebah*, b. 1697; *Elizabeth*, b. 1699; *Gershom*, b. 1702; *Ebenezer*, 1706. Benjamin, the f. d. in Worc., May 3, 1741, æ. 79; his w. Experience d. '47; 10. ALLEN, b. May, 16, '65. The f. was living in 1691.

2. MICHAEL, s. of Tho., (1), m. Mary Bigelow, 1673, and had, in Wat., 1. ABIGAIL, b. 1685; 2. MICHAEL, b. '89; 3. MARY, b. '91, m. Wm. Hager, 1711. Michael, the f. m. 2d Mary Earle, 1704, and had 4. EARL, b. Mar. 29, '06; 5. PRUDENCE, b. '08, m. Samuel Frizzell, of Fram., Feb. 1, '26-7; 6. BEZALEEL, m. Susanna Warren, 1730. The will of Michael was proved, 1711.

3. ALLEN, son of Tho., (1), m. Sary Ball, 1684; and had in Wat., 1. SARY, b. 1686, m. Jona. Cutting, 1710; 2. MARY, m. Wm. Pike, of Fram., Nov. 19, 1706; 3. MERCY; 4. ALLEN, b. '91, m. Abigail Fisk, 1717; 5. DELIVERANCE; 6. DANIEL, (f. of *Daniel*, bap. 1722); 7. DINAH, b. '99, d. 1704; 8. JONATHAN, b. May 1, 1704; and 9. DINAH. Allen, the f. d. 1711. His estate was settled, 1714.

4. EARL, s. of Michael (2), came to Fram., and lived prob. in the S. part of the town. He had, by w. Elizabeth, 1. ELISHA, b. May 12, 1728, m. 1st —— Wilson, and 2d a dr. of Rev. Mr.

Mann, of Paxton, and was f. at Petersham, where he d. 1805, of *Earl;* Elijah; Col. *Silas;* Rufus, and others; 2. ELIZABETH, b. Ap. 7. 1734, m. James Sibley, of Hardwick, (now Dana). Earl the f. moved to Petersham, ab. 1736, and was one of the first settlers of that town. Elisha, his son, had a half sister POLLY, who m. Moses Lawrence, of Hardwick.

5. JONATHAN, s. of Allen (3), m. in Wat. Eunice Patterson, Dec. 28, 1726, and had in Wat., 1. LOIS, b. June 7, 1728, (Fram. Rec., 1729); 2. EUNICE, b. May 7, '30, (F. Rec., '31); and in Fram., 3. HEPHZIBAH, b. Aug. 31, '34, m. Grindley Jackson, of Sud., May 30, '53; 4. JONATHAN, b. Mar. 9, '36; 5. JOSEPH, b. Feb. 9, '39; 6. ALLAN, b. May 2, '42, d. in Fram., Dec. 22, 1804; 7. SARAH, b. Jan. 12, '44; 8. MARGERY, b. July 19, '47.

6. JONATHAN, s. of Jona. (5), m. Hephzibah Greenwood, and had in Fram., 1. JONATHAN, m. Esther Ballard, Nov. 28, 1799, and d. in Nat. 1811, æ. 40; his wid. d. in Fram.; 2. HEPSY, m. John Kimball; 3. KEZIAH, m. —— Broad, of Boston; 4. SALLY, m. —— Washburn, of Nat.; 5. POLLY, m. Timothy Kendall of Sherb. Jona. the f. d. prob. in Fram.

7. JOSEPH, m. in Marlb., Abigail Bruce, 1761, and had, in Fram., 1. JOSEPH, b. Mar, 4, 1762; 2. ABIGAIL, b. July 14, '64.

8. JOSEPH, s. of Jona. (5), m. Hannah Tombs, and had, 1. ELIZABETH, bap. July 22, 1764; 2. MARGERY, bap. Feb. 22, '67.

9. ELIJAH, m. in Marlb., Abigail Bruce, 1764, and had in Fram., 1. ALLAN, bap. Nov. 16, 1766; 2. NABBY, bap. Feb. 15, 1768.

ABIJAH, of Sud., m. Mary Stone, 1747, and was f. of *Eunice,* who m. Jos. Darling, 1773. ABIGAIL, of Southb., m. Jona. Rolff, Feb. 14, '50-1. SARAH, of Sud., m. Dan. Drury, of Fram., 1729. MARTHA, m. in Sud., Edward Grout, 1717. MARY, of Marlb., m. Richard Newton, 1768. JOHN, a tanner, of Boston, and w. Abiel, sold land in Woburn, 1699. GERSHOM, m. in Lancaster, Mary Willard, 1750. ASA, (w. Judith,) was of Camb., 1750.

FOSTER, MARY, m. Jonathan Hemenway, Ap. 24, 1744. JEMIMA, m. Jesse Haven, Jan. 22, 1755. JAMES, (s. of James, who came from England, ab. 1750, lived in Brooklyn, and m. a 2d w. here), m. Polly Haven, Dec. 15, 1797. SALOME, adm. to the ch., Aug., 1796. ABIGAIL, from Hop., was in Fram., 1771.

In Sud., PATIENCE m. Tho. Brown, 1667; SARAH, m. Tho. Williams,

1686. In Sherb., ISAAC, and w. Abial, had *Sarah*, 1721, and *Abigail*, '24. JACOB, m. Mary Sheffield, 1728, and was f. in Holl. of *Jacob, William*, and others. In Holl., BENJAMIN, and w. Sarah, 1728; JONATHAN, m. Mary Godding, 1744. Both fam. had chil. In Hop., DAVID, and w. Lydia, 1735, had *David* &c.

FRAIL, SAMUEL, and w. Mary, had in Fram., MARY, b. Ap. 18, 1741; and in Hop., ELIZABETH, b. 1736; GEORGE, b. 1737. Samuel was received from 3d ch. in Salem, 1745. (Hop. ch. Rec.)

Wid. Fraile d. in Salem, 1669. GEORGE, d. in Lynn, Dec. 9, 1663.

FREEMAN, JOHN, came from Boston to Fram, 1775.

FRIZZELL, or FRISSELL, SAMUEL, had in Roxbury, by w. Martha, 1. MARTHA, b. Oct, 1695, m. in Fram., Jonathan Jackson, Mar. 7, 1716-7; 2. EBENEZER, b. Feb. 22, 1697-8; 3. SAMUEL, b. 1700. [DELIVERANCE, (f. not named), was bap. in Fram., May 26, 1717.] Samuel was rated in Fram., 1710, and owned land in the N. W. part of the town, 1716. In 1718, administration on his est., (then of Fram.), was granted to his wid. Martha. Inventory, £156.

JAMES, of Roxbury, had MARY, b. 1656; JAMES, b. '58; EBENEZER, bap. Mar. 12, '70, and perhaps others. James, sen., d. at Roxb., Feb. 6, 1716, æ. ab. 90. Sarah, w. of James, sen., d. Feb. 11, 1712. WILLIAM, of Concord, m. Hannah Clarke, 1667, and had *John* and others.

2. SAMUEL, Jun., s. of Sam. (1), m. in Wat., Prudence Flagg, Feb. 1, 1726-7., and with w. witnessed a deed in Fram., Dec., 1729. [MARTHA, (f. not named), was bap. in Fram., Ap. 15, 1723.]

3. EBENEZER, prob. s. of Sam. (1), conveyed land in Fram. near Warren Nixon, Esq., Dec., 1729; and had by w. Elizabeth, 1. ELIZABETH, b. Dec. 26, 1736; 2. SARAH, b. June 8, '40. The f. m. 2d, wid. Mary Eames, (prob. from Marlb.), Jan. 11, 1749, and had 3. JOHN, b. Oct. 15, '49, m. and lived in Eddington, N. C.; 4. SAMUEL, b. May 3, '51, m. —— Pratt, of Fram., and lived in Heneka, N. H.; 5. MARY, b. June 14, '53, m. Silas Pike, Sep. 30, '77, lived on the farm now of Col. M. Edgell, and moved to Prov.

FROST, THOMAS, of Sud. was living at Lannam, (so called), 1694. His lease from Gov. Danforth, is dated, Mar. 25, 1693. In the survey of Fram., 1750, the ancient house is placed in Fram. near Mr. Tayntor's. He m. Mary Goodridge, Nov. 12, 1678, and had 1. THOMAS, b. Aug. 23, 1679; 2. JOHN, b. Sep.

14, '84, rated in Fram., 1710, and of Groton 1723, when his w. was deranged; 3. SAMUEL, b. Nov. 23, '86; 4. MARY, b. Nov. 8, '90, d. Feb. 20, '90–1. Mary the m. d. Jan. 6, 1690–1. Tho. the f. m. 2d, Hannah Johnson, of Sud., July 9, 1691, who d. in Fram., May 3, 1712. Tho. m. 3d, Sarah Singletary, Dec. 22, 1712. Tho., Sen. was constable of Fram., 1700, and Tythingman, 1712; and his will, made 1717, was proved, 1724. He names in it a dr. SARAH, who m. John Rice.

Elder EDMUND, of Camb., had by w. Thomasine, 1. JOHN, f. of *Thomas*, of Camb.; and *John*, of Salem, (bricklayer, 1696); 2. THOMAS, b. Ap., 1637; 3. SAMUEL, b. Feb , '38, (perhaps the S. of Billerica, f. of *Thomas; Joseph*, of Charlestown, &c. See Mid. Prob., 1718); 4. JOSEPH, b. Jan. 13, '39, of Charlestown, and Billerica, f. by w. Hannah, of *Susanna, Joseph, Stephen, Hannah, Abigail, Miller, and Faith*; and by w. Mary, 5. JAMES,* b. Ap. 9, '43; 6. MARY, b. '45; 7. EPHRAIM, (æ. ab. 39, 1690. Mid. Deeds, vol. X.) His est. was administered, 1718; 8. SARAH, b. 1653. Elder E 's will was proved Oct., 1672; his wid. Roana. THOMAS, of Rox., had a s. *Thomas*, b. 1663. WILLIAM, (w. Mary), was of Salem, 1677.

2. THOMAS, s. of Tho. (1), m. first Mary Gibbs, and 2d, Jane Wight, and had 1. MARY, b. July 29, 1713, m. Deac. Daniel Stone, Mar. 12, '33–4; 2. SYBILLA, b. Sep. 28, '15, m. William Pike, Feb. 21, '38–9; 3. SARAH, b. Dec. 6, '17, d. Dec. 3, 1754; 4. EUNICE, b. May 23, '20, m. Abner Stone, Mar. 10, '40; 5. BEULAH, bap. Aug. 11, '23, m. Bezaleel Fisk, of Sud., Nov. 11, '42; 6. HEPHZEBAH, b. Feb. 22, '29–0, m. Sylvanus Hemenway, 1749–0. Tho. the f. lived where the Methodist ch. formerly stood, and d. Feb. 29, 1751. His w. Jane, d. Jan. 30, 1737. He received from Jos. Sparhawk, of Sutton, Jan. 1739, a deed of lands, before held by lease from Mr. Danforth. He owned, in 1733, a negro man named Gloster.

3. SAMUEL, s. of Thomas, (1), m. Elizabeth Rice, Feb. 1, 1710–1; and had 1. KEZIAH, b. Dec. 1, '11, m. Ebenezer Goodnow, of Sud., Dec. 11, '50; 2. BEZALEEL, b. Sep. 8, '13, and was in Fram., Mar. 1739; 3. SAMUEL, b. Dec. 13, '15; 4. AMASA, b. Jan. 24, '17–8, left town a young man; 5. AMARIAH, b. Oct. 4, '20, H. Coll. '40, pastor at Milford; 6. ELIZABETH, b. May 10, '24, m. Isaac Cutter, of Brookfield, June 18, '43; 7. LOIS, b.

---

* Dea. JAMES, of Billerica, whom Farmer supposes s. of Edmund, d. in Billerica, Aug. 12, 1711, æ. 74? His chil. were *James, Thomas, Samuel, Joseph, Benjamin, Mary, Abigail*, ——, *Hannah*, and *Sarah*. (See settl. of est., Mid. Prob.) He had two wives, Rebeckah, and 2d, Elizabeth Foster, m. 1667.

Oct. 3, '32, m. Phinehas Goodnow, of Sud., Jan. 30, '52. Mr. Samuel, the f., d. Aug. 2, 1736.

4. SAMUEL, s. of Sam. (3), m. Rebeckah How, June 19, 1750, and had, 1. SAMUEL, b. July 2, '51 ; 2. BEZALEEL, b. Sep. 5, '53, moved to Townsend, Vt. ; 3. REBECKAH, b. Sep. 28, '55, m. Daniel Hyde, of Newton; 4. ELISHA, b. Sep. 21, '58 ; 5. HANNAH, b. Jan. 20, '62, m. John Stacy, June, '87 ; 6. ELIZABETH, b. Sep. 6, '64, m. Thomas Rice, Nov., '86, and d. 1823 ; 7. AMARIAH, b. June 13, '68, d. young. Mr. Samuel (the f.) d., Mar. 12, 1799, æ. 82 ? (T. Rec.)

5. ELISHA, s. of Sam. (4), m. Miliscent Winch, Ap. 26, 1781, and had, 1. AMARIAH, b. Sep. 8, '81, d. June 14, '90 ; 2. MILISCENT, b. Nov. 30, '82, m. Elisha Belknap, Dec. 16, 1804 ; 3. ELISHA, b. Ap. 26, '84 ; 4. NANCY, b. Sep. 12, '89 ; 5. ELIZA, b. Jan. 17, '93, m. Jonas Goodnow ; 6. HITTY, and 7. HORACE, twins, b. May 21, '95 — Hitty m. Jesse Lyon, of Newton, lives at Fitchburg ; 8. EDWARD, b. Ap. 1, '98, H. Coll., 1822, m. Sarah Dix, of Littleton, was a physician at Wayland, and d. 1838 ; 9. LUCY, b. Dec. 8, 1800, m. Charles C. Fisk ; 10. NATHAN, b. Aug. 23, 1803, m. Elizabeth T. Stevenson, of N. Y. Elisha occupied the farm of his f. in law, and d. May 10, 1836, æ. 77. His wid. Miliscent, d. Aug. 15, 1837, æ. 74.

6. SAMUEL, s. of Samuel (4), m. Mary Heard, of E. Sudb., and had, 1. SALLY, b. Dec. 28, 1788, m. Thomas Arnold ; 2. REBECKAH, b. Ap. 23, '91, d. æ. 38 ; 3. POLLY, b. Ap. 25, '93, m. Chapin Allen ; 4. NABBY, b. Ap. 4, '95 ; 5. CLARISSA, b. May 23, '97, m. Henry How, of Sud., now a widow ; 6. HANNAH, b. Aug. 15, '99, d. unm. ; 7. HARRIET, b. Feb. 17, 1801, m. Reuben Hunt ; 8. ELIZA, b. Oct. 12, 1803, m. —— Ranson, lives in Me. ; 9. JULIA ANN, m. Joseph Taylor, of Kennebunk. Capt. Samuel the f. was 4 years a Selectman, and a Trustee of the Academy, and d. in Fram., Nov. 1, 1817. He lived near Mr. Tayntor's.

JOSEPH, of Sherb., moved thither from Charlestown, had 2 wives, and by the 2d, besides daughters, had sons *Joseph*, who m. Deb. Estabrook, 1753; and *Jonathan*, who m. Martha Leland, 1760. Jonathan moved to Marlb., N. H., and d. Sept. 25, 1776, æ. 37 ; his s. Jonathan, b. 1765, m. Beulah Stone, ab. 1786, and lived in N. Marlb. JOSEPH, of Charlestown, (w. Sarah), had *Joseph*, b. 1712; *Samuel*, '13; *Joseph*, '19; *Hannah*, '20 ; *Elizabeth*, '25 ; *Joseph*, Ap. 9, '27. EBENEZER, (w. Elizabeth), was of Nat., 1752.

FURBECK, PAUL, cov'd and was bap., May 7, 1721, and was adm. to the ch., Nov. 12, 1721.

GALE, ELIZABETH, m. John Nurse, (both of Fram.), Feb. 21, 1700. HANNAH, m. Jabez Pratt, Ap. 22, 1714. ABIEL, m. Joseph Trumbull, June 18, 1719. ABIGAIL, m. Jona. Cutler, Jan. 10, 1716-7.

ABIJAH, b. at Weston, July 5, 1727, s. of Abraham, and w. (Esther Cunningham), was of Westb., m. Abigail Amsden, 1748, and had many chil.; among them, Capt. *Nahum*, f. of Rev. Elbridge, formerly minister in Wickford and Tiverton, R. I., now of Fram. RICHARD, of Wat., 1640, d. 1679, leaving chil., 1. *Abraham*, m. Sarah Fisk, '73, and d. 1718, f. of Abra., (m. Rachael Parkhurst, 1699); Richard; Ebenezer, m. Elizabeth Green, 1709; John; Joshua, d. 1721; Sarah m. Jona. Pratt, of Fram.; Mercy, m. Samuel Sanderson; Mary; Lydia; Abigail, m. Edward Jackson; 2. *John*, m. Elizabeth Spring, 1677, f. of Elizabeth, John, &c.; 3. *Sarah*, m. —— Garfield; 4. *Mary*, m. John Flagg, 1670. BARTHOLOMEW, of Salem, m. Martha Lemon, 1662, who d. the same year; and he m. 2d, Mary Bacon, and was f. of *Abraham*, b. 1666; *Isaac, Jacob, Bartholomew, Daniel, &c.*

GALLOT, or GALLOP, PETER, a silk weaver, came from France, and lived first where is a cellar hole, on the corner of the Sanger farm, and after moved to the house E. of Mr. Thomas Hastings, which he is said to have built. He m. Priscilla Collar, Jan. 10, 1733-4, and had, 1. PETER, b. Sep. 4, 1734; 2. FRANCIS, b. Sep. 8, '35, d. at Stillwater; 3. JAMES, b. Oct. 18, '38, d. unm., Ap. 27, 1816; 4. JOHN, b. Oct. 2, '41, d. young; 5. JOHN, b. July 28, '43, d. in the Rev. War; 6. PHINEHAS, b. June 28, '45, lived in Stillwater. Peter the f. d. ab. 1763.

2. PETER, s. of Peter (1), m. Lydia Pratt; and had, 1. ELIZABETH, b. June 24, 1762, m. Daniel Bigelow, Mar., '83, moved to Keene; 2. LYDIA, b. June 17, '64, lives unm.; 3. PRISCILLA, bap. Ap. 13, '66, lives unm.; 4. PETER, bap. Mar. 15, '68, m. in Somerset, R. I., and drowned in Taunton, ab. 1820; 5. JOHN, bap. Mar. 25, '70, m. Sally Burnham, Ap., '94, and d. Feb., 1832, f. of *John; Nancy; Nathan; Mary*, and *William;* 6. MARY, bap. Oct. 18, '72, d. young. Peter the f. d. Feb. 15, 1817. Lydia his w. d. Nov. 27, 1821, æ. 91.

7. SARAH, (of another family, probably from Stoneham), m. in Fram., Benjamin Holden, July 9, 1751.

GAMBELL, or GAMBLE, JOSEPH, and w. Lucia, were received to the ch., Mar. 3, 1754; and had THOMAS, bap. May 5, 1754; and JOSEPH, bap. Nov. 30, 1760.

GARDNER, SARAH, w. of Joshua, d. in Fram., Mar. 11, 1750.

Joshua, of Sherb., by w. Sarah, had *Caleb*, b. May 2, 1749. Joshua was s. of Addington and w. Mary, who had in Sherb., *Caleb*, b. 1733; *Peter*, '35; *Elizabeth*, '38; *Aaron*, '41. Hon. Stephen P. Gardner, of Bolton, was g. son of Addington. A. d. in Sherb., Feb., 1754, æ. 57. (G. Stone.) He was b. in Dorch. or Roxbury. PETER had chil. in Roxb., from 1647; and THOMAS from 1652.

GATES, STEPHEN, or Steeven, of Camb., had 1. STEPHEN; 2. SIMON; 3. THOMAS; 4. ELIZABETH, m. John Lazell; 5. MARY, m. John Maynard, of Sud., April 5, 1658.*
Stephen was of Hingham, 1638; he was admitted freeman, 1653. (Farmer.) He signed the Town agreement, at Lanc., Ap. 3, 1654; was constable, 1657, and had a grant of land at Kequassagansett, near Hog Swamp. He also had rights in Groton, on which his g. s , Simon, administered, 1716. (Mid. Prob.) Stephen's will, dated 9 June, 1662, was proved Oct. 7, 1662. He gives to his w. and Simon, his place in Camb., Thomas to continue with them at his pleasure; to Stephen, the house &c. at Nashaway (Lancaster); his land in N. to be divided between Simon and Stephen. ANN, his wid., m. 2d, Richard Woodward, of Wat., ab. 1663, (Mid. Deeds II, 364), and after his decease, she resumed the name of Gates. She d. at Stow, Feb. 5, 1682-3, and her will was proved, Ap. 9.

2. ¹STEPHEN, s. of Steph. (1), had by w. Sarah, 1. STEPHEN; 2. SIMON, b. in Camb. 5 June, 1666-7, m. (then of Stow,) Hannah Benjamin, May 4, '88, and d. 1752, f of *Simon*, d. at Stow, 1736; *Joseph*; *Benjamin*; *Elisha*; *Amos*; *Hannah*, b. Feb. 13, 1688, m. —— Heald; *Mary*, m. —— Haynes; *Susanna*, m. —— Fitch; *Elizabeth*, m. —— Wheeler; 3. THOMAS; 4. Ens. ISAAC, d. at Stow, Nov. 22, 1748, æ 75; 5. NATHANIEL; 6. DANIEL, b. Ap. 25, 1685, d. at Stow, Mar. 22, 1759, æ. 74; 7. SARAH, b. at Marlb., Ap 27, 1679; 8. REBECKAH, b. at M. July 23, '82. Stephen, the f. was of Boston, Feb. 1667. In 1673, he bought of Edward Drinker, of Boston, potter, 300 acres on Elsabeth or Alsabat brook, at Pompquocittacott or Stow, which Benjamin Bowhoe, Indian, quit-claimed to him, 1684, and was among the prop's of Stow, 1681. His will was proved, 1707.

3. ²THOMAS, s. of Steph. (1), m. in Sud., Elizabeth Freeman, 1670, and had in Marlb., 1. ELIZABETH, b. 1671; 2. SARAH, '73; and in Sud., 3. JOHN, b. Ap. 9, '78, d. in Stow, Sep. 19, 1747, æ. 69; w. Mary d. 1752 æ. 69; 4. JOSEPH, b. Mar. 16, '80; and in Stow, 5. JOSIAH, b. Mar. 8, '81; 6. DEBORAH, b. Feb. 22, '83; 7. ANNA, b. July 18, '86; 8. ABIGAIL, b. Feb. 18, '88. Tho's the f., of Lanc., 1670, bought of John Butler, near Hog Swamp. He was of Sud., 1670, and "departed the town," 1679. In 1681, then of Stow, he bought part of a saw-mill in Stow, of Jona. Prescott, of Concord, and in 1683, sold half of the mill to Tho. Ward, of Sud. In 1688, he bought of Eph. Roper and w. Hannah, of Lanc., land in L. Tho. was in Stow, 1693, and constable in that town. (T. Rec.)

4. ³SIMON, s. of Steph. (1), had by w. Margaret, at Camb., 1. ABIGAIL, b. 1671, m. Nat. Sparhawk; 2. SIMON, b. '73, d. '75; 3. SIMON, b. 5 Jan. '75-6; 4. GEORGE, b. '78, d. '79; 5. AMOS; 6. JONATHAN, of Camb. and Worcester, and d. at Worc., 1756, leaving by w. Persis, *Persis*, m. Adonijah Rice; *Margaret*, m, Wm. Bigelow, of Athol, 1753; *Susanna*; *Sarah*; *John*, m. Violata Rice; *Jonathan*, (w. Abigail,) and *William*; 7. SAMUEL, b. 11 Aug., 1685; 8. MARGARET, b. Aug. 13, '89, m. James How. Simon the f., had his chil. chiefly in Camb. In 1686, "of Lancaster," he was on the minis-

---

* In 1657, (Mid. Co. Rec. I. 113), Mary, dr. of Steven, of Lancaster, "was admonished for bold and unbecoming speeches used in the public assembly, on the Lord's day, and especially against Mr. Rowlason, minister of God's word there."

ter's rate; in 1688, a subscriber to build a minister's house. In 1692, "of Muddy River," he bought of Maj. Gookin's heirs, "Okonkonomeset hill," in Marlb. In 1693, "of Boston," he bought of his br. Thomas, land in Lanc. He is sometimes named as of Brookline. His estate was divided among his heirs, 1707. (Mid. Prob.)*

5. ³SIMON, s. of Simon (4), m. in Marlb., Sarah Woods, 1710, and had in Marlb., 1. SIMON, b. Dec. 11, '10, m. Sarah How, '49, and f. in Worc. of *Simon, Asa,* and others ; 2. SARAH, b. Oct. 15, '12, m. —— Church, of Rutland; 3. SUSANNA, b. Dec. 19, '14, m. —— Phelps, of Rutl.; 4. STEPHEN, b. Aug. 8, '18, m. Damaris How, '43, and d. in Rutland, Oct. 5, 1773, f. of *Jonathan,* of Hubbardston ; *Sylvanus,* of Spencer ; *Zadock,* Esq., of Rutl.; *Alfred,* of Me., and others ; 5. SOLOMON, b. May 14, '21, m. Mary Clark, d. in Worcester, 1761, f. of *Samuel,* of Shoreham, Vt. ; *Paul,* of Vt.; *Silas,* of Wardsboro'; *James,* &c.; 6. SAMUEL, b. Feb. 28, '22–3, m. Caroline How, d. in Petersham, f. of *John, Solomon, Samuel, Oliver Cromwell,* and others ; 7. SILAS, b. Feb. '27, m. Elizabeth Bragg, and d. in Marlb., Aug. 25, 1793, f. of *Sarah,* m. Eliezer Holyoke ; *Lydia,* m. Abraham Beman, and d. in Me.; *Silas,* m. Cath. Williams, kept a tavern in Marlb.; *Samuel,* m. Lucretia Willliams, lives in Vt.; *William,* m. Jerusha Goodnow, and Elizabeth How ; *John,* m. —— Ball; *Mary,* (d. young), and *Elizabeth,* (twins); E. m. Apollos Cushing, and lives in Me.; *Susanna,* m. Wm. Arnold ; wid. Elizabeth d. Mar. 20, 1806, æ. 74 ; 8. JOHN, b. Jan. 27, '28–9. Simon the f., bought of his f.'s heirs, 1713, land in Marlb., and d. in M. 1735; his w. Sarah d. 1751.

6 ³AMOS, s. of Simon (4), m. in Camb., May 19, 1703, Hannah, (b. Oct. 10, 1681), dr. of Samuel Oldham, (by his w. Hannah Dana, m. 1670). His chil. (named in his will), were AMOS ; OLDHAM, wounded at Bunker Hill ; SAMUEL ; HANNAH, m. Jonathan Edmunds, of Newton ; MARGARET, m. Thomas Spring of Newton ; ABIGAIL, m. Jonathan Peirson, of Andover ; MARY, m. in Fram., Nehemiah Wright, May 24, 1733 ; SARAH, m. Wm. Jones of Fram., Mar. 31, 1748. Amos the f. lived first in Brookline : was Tything-man in Fram., 1735 ; Overseer of the poor, 1741 ; and Selectman 1740, and prob. for 2 years after. He lived near Mr. Edmond Trowbridge's, and d. in Fram. ; his will was proved, July 22, 1754.

7. ³AMOS, Jun, s. of Amos (6), m. Mary Trowbridge, Nov. 28, 1744, and had 1. AMOS, b. Aug. 29, '45, d. unm. ; 2. MARY, b. Aug. 30, '48, m. Ebenezer Buck, of Upton ; 3. ANNA, b. Jan. 30, '50, m. Samuel Jones, of Fram., moved into N. H. ; 4. GEORGE, b. Aug. 8, '53 ; 5. CHARLES, b. Mar. 4, '55, d. in the Rev. service ; 6. HENRY, b. Mar. 22, '57 ; 7. OLDHAM, b. July 27, '59, m. Deborah Winch, June, '83, d. at Pittsburg, Vt., 1843 ; 8. EDMUND TROWBRIDGE, b. July 23, '61, m. Wid. Tufts, of

---

* "Sept. 1, 1686. Went to Natick Lecture, Simon Gates showing me the way. Mr. Daniel Gookin preached ; were about 40 or 50 men at most and a pretty many women and children." Judge Sewall's Diary.

Malden; 9. MARTHA, b. Ap. 8, '66, m. Zaccheus Fairbanks,
Mar., '87, lives in Antrim, N. H.; 10. RUTH, b. Feb. 12, '68,
m. Ebenezer Hemenway, June, '86, lives in N. Marlb., a wid;
11. SUSANNAH, b. Mar. 9, '70, m. Luther Belknap, Esq., Dec.,
'93, d. '97; 12. JOHN, bap, May 31, '72, m. Eunice Winch, Jan.
5, '95, moved to N. Marlb. Capt. Amos the f. was Selectman, 3
years or more, and moved to Marlb., N. H., ab. 1798, and d. 1799,
æ. 89. Mary his w. d., 1798.

8. ³SAMUEL, s. of Amos (6), m. in Fram., Abigail Blodget,
Ap. 11, 1751, and was adm. to the ch., June 28, '52. He had,
1. ABIGAIL, b. Aug. 5, '52, m. in Rut., Benj. Estabrook, '78; 2.
SARAH, b. Jan. 14, '56, m. Jason Duncan, in Rut., '75; 3.
SAMUEL, b. Nov. 23, '57, m. Susannah Laughton; 4. JOSEPH, b.
Dec. 7, '59, m. Sarah Roper, '89; 5. HANNAH, bap. Dec. 11,
'63, m. in Rut. Sam. Hathorn, '98; and in Rutland, 6. LYDIA,
b. 1770; 7. BENJAMIN, m. Elizabeth Newton. Sam. the f. d.
in Rut., Feb. 19, 1803, æ. 78; his w. Abigail d. 1820, æ. 94.
(G. Stones.)

9. ³HENRY, s. of Amos (6), m. Anne Eames, of Sud., Feb.
12, 1782, and had, 1. PATTY, b. Sep. 17, 1782; 2. CHARLES,
bap. Dec. '83; 3. ANNE, bap. Oct. '87. Henry the f. moved to
Hubbardston, ab. 1789.

10. ³GEORGE, s. of Amos (6), m. Hannah Barret, of Marlb.,
and with w. adm. to the ch. Nov., 1793; and had 1. POLLY, b.
Dec. 9, 1789; 2. PATTY, b. July 23, '91; 3. CHARLES, b. Mar.
18, '93. George the f. moved to Antrim, N. H., ab. 1798.

GIBBS, MATTHEW, had by w. Mary,* 1. MATTHEW; 2. JOHN;[15] 3.
ELIZABETH, m. John Russell, of Duxbury; 4. HANNAH, m. Sam. Winch,
Feb. 11, 1673; 5. MARY, m. John Goodridge, Mar. 23, 1675, and 2d Tho.
Frost, Jr., Nov. 12, 1678; 6. THOMAS, b. Dec. 17, 1656, d. young; 7.
THOMAS, b. Ap. 10, '60, d. Mar. 14, '88. (See Sett. of his est., July 5,
1697. Mid. Prob.) Matthew the f., planter, of Charlestown, sold 1654, his
house, &c., at C. 1655, he was on a committee of the Town, at Sud.; in
1659, had a grant "E. of his house at Landhum;" in 1661, he bought of
Thos. Read, sen., one third of a farm, once of Rev. Edm. Brown, near Doeskin Hill, and in 1673, and 1678, of others, parts of same farm; in 1670,
had a grant E. side of the brook, near his house. In 1681, he bought of
Samuel Howe, 10 acres at Lanham plain. Matth. had deceased 1697.
(See Settlement).†

---

* Mary, dr. of Robert Bradish, of Camb. who d. ab. 1659, m. a Gibbs.
† Farmer notes a Matthew, of N.
Haven, 1639. Prof. Gibbs, of N. H. writes: — "I have not yet succeeded in finding the Matthew Gibbs men-

Note. — GILES took the freeman's oath, March 4, 1632-3. THOMAS, had at Sandwich, *John*, b. Sept. 12, 1634; *Thomas*, b. May 23, '36; *Samuel*, b. June 23, '39; *Sarah*, b. Ap. 11, '52; *Job* and a daughter, twins, b. April 15, '55; J. m. Judith ——, and was f. of Micah and Lydia; *Mary*, b. Aug. 12, '57. See Farmer for others of the name of Gibbs.*

2. ¹MATTHEW, Jr., s. of Mat. (1), m. first, Mary, dr. of John Moore, formerly of Lancaster, 1678, and 2d, her sister, Elizabeth Moore, (b. 1657), and had 1. MATTHEW³, b. Mar. 12, 1680; 2. JOHN, prob. of the Island of Bermudas, 1706, (Mid. Deeds); 3. SAMUEL¹⁰, b. Mar. 1, 1685; 4. JOSEPH¹¹, b. Oct. 7, '87; 5. JONATHAN¹²; 6. JOSIAH¹⁴. Matthew, the f. who lived, 1694, near Lannam Bridge, d. Mar. 9, 1732. His wid. Elizabeth, d. in Fram., Jan. 20, '33-4. M. and w. were rec'd to Fram., from Sud. ch., Feb. 22, 1719. [ELIZABETH, m. in Fram., William Haward, of Mendon, May 16, 1717.]

3. ¹MATTHEW, s. of Mat. (2), m. in Fram., Sarah Page, Ap. 21, 1709, and had 1. SARAH, b. Jan. 20, 1707-8, d. young; 2. SARAH, b. Feb. 12, 1709-0, m. — Jones, and d. young; 3. PHINEHAS, d. unm.; 4. HEZEKIAH, b. June, 12, 1715, m. Elizabeth Pratt, of Bolton, 1745, f. of *Hezekiah*, and d. in B., ab. 1785; 5. ELIZABETH, bap. Oct. 20, '17, m. John Jones, Jun., Nov. 16, 1738; 6. MATTHEW, b. July 26, '20, d. unm. in Fram., Ap. 8, 1804; 7. JONATHAN, b. Mar. 30, '23; 8. MICAH, b. May 9, '27. Matth. the f. and w. were adm. to the ch., Sep. 1, 1723. He lived where is a cellar hole, near Elisha Frost's.

4. ¹JONATHAN, s. of Matth. (3), m. first, wid. Mary Winchester. He had by w. Peggy, 1. POLLY, b. Mar. 24, 1779; 2. HENRY, b. Feb. 9, '85; 3. SALLY, b. Feb. 11, '89; 4. PEGGY, b. May 11, '91. Capt. Jonathan lived at Mr. Phinehas Rice's. He went into the service, 1761.

5. ¹MICAH, s. of Matth. (3), m. Elizabeth Hobbs, of Weston, cov'd Jan. 9, 1755, and was adm. to the ch., Ap. 22, '57. Their

---

tioned by Farmer. He cannot have figured much on the N. H. Records. No other Gibbs than John Gibbs took the oath of allegiance between 1640 and 1660." He adds, that John, who came to N. Haven in 1637 or '38, and d. 1690, m. Hannah Punderson, Oct. 27, 1660; and his will mentions a w. Hannah, and dr. Margaret. He finds a single notice of William Gibbs, hatter. Gibbses have been at numerous places in Con. (MSS. Letter).

* " Gibbe or Gibbs, came originally from Venton or Fenton, in Dartington Parish." "Arms of Gibbs, ar. 3 battle axes, Sable." Mr. Savage's Gleanings, &c. M. Hist. Coll. 3 Ser. VIII. 304.

chil. were, 1. BETTY[1], b. Feb. 28, '55, d. unm., ab. 1777 ; 2. PHINEHAS, b. Oct. 30, '57; 3. MICAH, bap. Nov. 18, '59, d. young; 4. MOLLY, b. June 14, '61, m. Dan. Morse, of Southb., May 9, '81, lived in Vt. ; 5. MICAH, b. May 11, '63, d. young; 6. JONATHAN, b. Aug. 1, '65, d. young; 7. ESTHER, b. June 18, '67, d. young ; 8. SARAH, b. May 10, '69, m. Paul Walker, Feb. 1790, d. in Sud., 1802 ; 9. MATTHEW, b. Aug. 5, '72, d. young. Micah the f. lived on the place now of Matthew Gibbs. His w. Elizabeth d. June 17, 1815.

6. [1]PHINEHAS, s. of Matth. (5), m. Olive Walker of Sud., July 12, 1782, and had 1. HANNAH, m. Jacob Barnes of Marlb. ; 2. PATTY, m. Deliverance Parmenter, d. in Marlb.; 3. MICAH, m. Betsey Nichols, and d. in Fram., Ap. 1, 1831, æ. 43 ; 4. SALLY, b. Oct. 1790, m. Silas Goodnow, d. in Marlb., 1828 ; 5. MATTHEW, b. '91, m. Patty Trowbridge ; 6. ASENETH, bap. June '94, m. Jesse Parmenter of Sud. ; 7 NANCY, bap. July '95, m. Aaron Bailey, of Fram. ; 8. BETSEY, bap. May '97, m. Martin Rice, of Fram.; 9. PHINEHAS, bap. Nov. '99, d. unm., Oct. 1844 ; 10. JOSIAH, b. Feb. 7, '01, m. Sally Walker. Phinehas the f. d., 1846. Mrs. Olive d, ab. 1837, æ. 75.

10. [1]SAMUEL, s. of Matth. (2), m. in Marlb., Lydia Bellows, Aug. 26, 1724, and had in Fram., SAMUEL, b. June 13, '25.

11. [1]JOSEPH, s. of Matth. (2), had in Fram. by w. Mary, or Mercy, 1. MARY, b. Ap. 23, 1716 ; 2. JOSEPH, bap. Sep. 13, '19, m. Hannah Howe, and f. at Rutland of *Daniel ; Joseph ; Elisha ;* and *Asa*. Jos. Jr., the f. d. in Princeton ; and in Sud., 3. CLARK, b. Jan. 30, '21-2, m. Hannah ——, and had at Rut., *Jonas ; Zenas ; Francis*, and *Hannah* ; 4. BEULAH, b. July 2, '24, m. Dan. Parker, '50 ; 5. MARTHA, b. May 14, '27 ; 6. BENJAMIN, b. Sep. 29, '32. Joseph the f., of Fram., m. in Camb., Mercy Clark, July 1, 1722. He bought land in Sud., 1717. Mercy, w. of Jos. d. in Sud., Feb. 28, 1733-4. [A Joseph d. in Fram. insolvent, ab. 1757.]

12. [1]JONATHAN, s. of Matth. (2), had in Fram. by w. Lydia, 1. ESTHER, b. May 26, 1725, d. Oct. 13 ; 2. JAMES, b. May 28, '26, m. Martha Newton, '50, lived in Southb., Holl. and Sturbridge, and f. of *Catharine ; Zephaniah*, m. Lucinda Janes ; *Jonathan*, had 2 wives ; *Levinah*, m. —— Marsh ; and *Martha*, d. unm., and the f. d. ab. '97 ; 3. JACOB, b. Ap. 24, '28 ; 4. LYDIA,

b. Mar. 11, '29-0 ; 5. ESTHER, b. Oct. 22, '31 ; 6. SARAH, b. May 13, '34 ; 7. JONATHAN, (posthumous), b. June 17, '36, d. Sep. 22, '40. Jona. the f. d. in Fram., Sep. 26, '35; (Inventory, £513.17.3.) His wid. Lydia m. Thos. Pierce, of Hop., Jan. 24, '43.

13. ¹JACOB, s. of Jona. (12), m. Sarah Scarber, and had in Southb., RELIANCE, b. Jan. 30, 1762 ; and in Fram., ZENAS, b. Nov. 2, '71.

14. ¹JOSIAH, s. of Matth. (2), had in Fram. by w. Mary, 1. MARY, b. Jan. 27, 1729-0 ; 2. OLIVE, b. Feb. 12, '31-2.

15. ²JOHN, s. of Matth. (1), m. Anna Gleason, of Sherb., 1688, and had in Sud., 1. THOMAS, b. Ap. 19, '89; 2. MERCY, b. Aug. 3, '91; 3. JOHN[18]; and by 2d. w., Sarah Cutler, of Reading, m. May 31, 1694, 4. SARAH, b. Dec. 6, 1701 ; 5. NATHANIEL, m. Bathshebah Parmenter, 1726, and f. in Sud., of *Eunice*, b. '27 ; *Sybilla*, '28 ; *Bathshebah*, '31 ; *Lois*, '32 ; *Nathaniel*, '36, of Marlb.; *William*, '40, of Princeton; *Jesse*, '44, m. Ruth Howe, '65 ; 6. ISAAC[16]; 7. JACOB, f. in Hop., by w. Martha, of *Martha*, bap. 1725 ; *Joseph*, '27 ; *Jacob*, b. '31, m. Phebe Chamberlain, '52 ; *Phinehas*, '33, m. Mary Mellen, '57 ; *John*, '35, m. Hannah Walker, '61 ; *Nathaniel*, '48 ; *Samuel* and *Sarah*, '50. Jacob, sen., was dismissed to Sutton ch., 1759 ; 8. ISRAEL, b. July 11, 1706, m. Mary Hambleton, of Hop. '27, and f. of *Mary*, b. '28; *John*, '30 ; *Rebeckah*, bap. '32 ; 9. EPHRAIM, b. June 12, 1710, d .Aug. 15. John, the f. d. in Sud., Ap. 2, 1718 ; his will proved the same month. Inventory, £623. His wid., Sarah.

16. ²ISAAC, s. of John (15), m. Thankful Wheeler, 1725, and had, in Sud., 1. HEPSEBAH, b. 1726, d. young ; 2. ISAAC[17], b. Jan. 28, '28-9 ; 3. HEPSEBAH, b. '31, m. Jos. Tower, '48 ; 4. ABIGAIL, b. '32, m. Daniel Goodnow, '54 ; 5. SARAH, b. '35, m. David Parks, '55 ; 6. THANKFUL, b. '38, m. Nathan Winch ; 7. JONAS, b. Sept. 9, '40, m. Sally Townsend, lived in Philipston, and d. in N. Y., 1823 ; 8. ANNA, b. '42, m. Gilbert Dench, of Hop., '61 ; 9. URIAH, b. Oct. 20, '44, m. Lucy Townsend, of Stafford, Conn., and f. of *Isaac, Esq.*, now of Fram., b. April 26, '68, and others ; 10. ASAHEL, b. '48 ; 11. MILISCENT, b. '51 ; 12. LOIS, b. '56. Isaac was at Rutland, 1720. He lived near Fram. bounds, and d. æ. 94.

17. ²ISAAC, s. of Isaac (16), m. Lois Townsend in Hop., 1755; and had in Sud. 1. LOIS, b. Nov. '56, m. Timo. Walker of Hop. ; 2. OLIVE, b. May 18, '58, m. Ebenezer Temple, of Fram. ; and in Fram., 3. ANNE, b. Oct. 26, '60, m. Jonathan Ball of Southb. ; 4. MOLLY, b. Oct. 21, '62 ; 5. PATTY, b. June 3, '65, m. John Stow, of Southb ; 6. THANKFUL, b. June 23, '67 ; 7. ELEANOR ; 8. NABBY, bap. Mar. 4, '70 ; 9. EUNICE. Isaac the f. moved to N. Marlb., ab. 1780.

18. ²JOHN, s. of John (15), m. in Fram., Naomi Pike, Mar. 9, 1709-0 ; and had 1. JOHN, b. Sep. 23, 1711, living in 1737 ; 2. NAOMI, b. Jan. 11, '12-3, m. David Winch ; 3. RACHEL, b. Ap. 17, '16, m. Timo. Pike ; 4. HANNAH, b. Mar. 1, '18-9, m. David

Mixer of Southb., Oct. '41. John the f. d. Nov. 23, 1732. [In Southb. wid. Naomi Gibbs m. John Britton, 1738.]
19. JOSEPH of Fram., had by w. Abigail, JOSEPH, b. Feb. 9, 1747.
20. JOSEPH, m. Elizabeth Palmer in Camb., Sep. 11, 1749, and had in Fram., 1. MARY, b. Feb. 28, 1750; 2. ELIZABETH, b. July 14, '52; 3. JOHN BUTTERFIELD, b. May 7, '54; 4. MARTHA, b. Jan. 22, '56; 5. SARAH, b. Nov. 7, '59; 6. BETHIAH, b. Oct. 8, '60. Joseph the f. prob. moved to Hop.

JACOB, of Hop., (15), had a s. *Joseph*, bap. 1727, who, perhaps, was the Joseph above. In Southb., Joseph, m. Sarah Bruce, August 23, 1754. JACOB, of Hardwick, m. Bethia Bacon, 1753. JOSEPH, of Brookfield, m. Anna Clark, 1762.

GLEASON, or GLEISON, GLEZEN, and, (as sometimes written and pronounced), Leesen.

1. THOMAS, early took the oath of fidelity, at Wat., and is named, 1657, on the town record of Camb. He was of Charlestown, Mar., 1662, in the occupation of the "tract of land reserved to Squa Sachem." In 1663, he leased a farm of Capt. Scarlett. He d. in Camb., prob. ab. 1684. He had by w. Susanna, in Camb., MARY, b. Oct. 31, 1657. His other chil. b. before, were (Mid. Co. Rec., I. 158, VI. 13), THOMAS; JOSEPH; JOHN, m. Mary, dr. of James Ross, f. in Sud., of *Mary*, b. 1681; and *Martha*, b. 1668; he d. 1688.

[WILLIAM, of Camb., probably another son of Thomas, had by w. Abiab, 1. WILLIAM, b. 1679, m. in Roxb., Thankful Trowbridge, May 16, 1705, and f. of *Experience*, b. '08; 2. ESTHER, b. and d. 1688. Wm., the f.'s inventory, is dated Feb. '16, '90-1. ELIZABETH, of Camb., m. Sam. Randal, 1709. MARY, m. in Roxb., Jacob Pepper, 1714. JOHN, of Wat., m. Dorothy Godding, 1740. MOSES, of Camb., m. Abigail Brown, 1752. DAVID and w. Mercy, of Camb., had *David*, b. 1744.]

2. JOSEPH, s. of Tho. (1), had in Sud., 1. JOSEPH, b. 1668, d. '69; 2. JOSEPH, b. Oct. 18, '71, m. Hannah Moore, 1705, and d. '11, f. of *Elizabeth*, b. '06, (m. Isaac Allen, '29); *Jason*, (b. '07, m. Mary Curtis, '32, and f. of Jason); *Phinehas*, (b. '10, m. Rebeckah Allen, '32, and f. of Phinehas, b. '32, d. at Westb., Sep., 1808; Benjamin, b. '34; and Jason, b. '35); 3. SUSANNA, b. 1676, m. Sam. Willis, of Sud.; 4. ABIGAIL, b. 1680, m. Noah Morse, of Sherb., 1714; 5. MARY, b. 1682, m. Sam. Biglo, of Marlb., 1716; 6. JOYCE, m. Jacob Newell, of Attleboro'; 7. ISAAC, m. Martha Livermore, and f. of *Isaac*, (who d. at Western, 1751, leaving w. Jerusha. His chil. born at Sud., were Joseph, b. 1731; Isaac, '33; Jonathan, '47; and 5 daughters); *Thankful*, and *Martha*. Joseph, the f. had perhaps three wives, Hannah, Martha, who d. 1684, and 3d, Abigail Garfield, m. Dec. 22, 1686. He d. at Sud., 1711. His heirs' agreement is dated Jan. 18, 1716-7. [JAMES, of Marlb., m. Mary Barrett, 17.13, and was f. of *John*, m. Persis How, '55; *Joseph*, (w. Persis); and several daughters.]

3. THOMAS, s. of Tho. (1), was of Sud. 1665, bought of Benj. Rice, in the S. part, of Fram., was rec'd to Sherb., Oct. 5,

1678. His chil. by w. Sarah, were, 1. SARAH, b. Feb. 6, 1665, m. Jeremiah Morse ; 2. ANNE, m. John Gibbs, 1688 ; 3. THOMAS; 4. ISAAC[5]; 5. PATIENCE ; 6. MARY, b. June 19, 1680 ; 7. JOHN[8]. Thomas, Sen., the f. d. in Fram., July 25, 1705. (See his will. Mid. Prob.) His w. Sarah d. July 8, 1703.

4. THOMAS, s. of Tho. (3), m. Mary Mellen, Dec. 6, 1695 ; and had in Sherb. 1. THOMAS, b. Feb. 26, 1696-7, m. Susannah Haven, Jan. 12, '14-5*; 2. RICHARD, b. Jan. 31, '99, m. Mary Bellows, of Marlb., 1725, and f. at Oxford, of *Richard, Sarah,* and *Patience* — Mary the m. d., 1731 ; 3. JONAS, b. Nov. 6, 1700 ; 4. ELIJAH, b. Oct. 18, '02 ; 5. MOSES, b. Dec. 22, '04, m. Deborah Whittemore, of Malden, 1738, and f. at Oxford of *Moses*, b. 1739 (w. Beulah) ; 6. MARY, b. Feb. 19, '08-9, d. at Oxford, 1736 ; and at Fram., 7. ESTHER, b. Ap. 6, '11 ; 8. SIMON, b. July 26, '13, d. in Oxford, 1793, (w. Charity, chil. *Simon; Bezaleel; Phinehas; Eleazer; Sarah,* and *Adonijah*) ; 9. JAMES, b. Nov. 13, '15, d. in F., May 19, 1722 ; 10. ELIZABETH, b. May 28, '18, m. John Streeter, '49 ; 11. AARON, b. Ap. 26, '20 ; 12. JOSEPH, b. May, 5, '22 ; (and prob. in Oxf.), 13. JOSIAH ; 14. URIAH, (w. Thankful, and chil. *John,* b. 1739 ; and *Lucie,* '42 ; and by w. Abigail, *Peter,* '54) ; 15. DANIEL, m. Martha Bartlett, 1753, and d. at Oxford, Dec. 8, 1794, æ. 64, f. of *Daniel ; Martha ; James ; Stephen ; Josiah ; Sarah ; Abijah ;* and *Hannah ;* 16. PRISCILLA, b. ab. 1731. Administration on Thomas, of Oxford, granted 1732. His. w. Mercy declined it. Inventory, £593. (Worc. Prob.)

5. ISAAC, s. of Tho. (3), m. Deborah Leland, Dec. 11, 1700 ; and had in Sherb. 1. DEBORAH, b. Ap. 27, 1703, m. in Fram. Thomas Winch, Oct. 23, '18 ; 2. ISAAC, b. May 17, '06 ; 3. PRUDENCE, b. Oct. 3, '08 ; and in Fram. 4. FINIUS, (Phinehas ?) b. Aug. 23, '11. Isaac the f. was constable in Fram., 1714, and d. Dec. 5, 1737.

6. ISAAC, Jun., s. of Isaac (5), m. Thankful Wilson, Dec. 9, 1725, and lived near Southb. bounds, in Fram. His chil. were 1. ISAAC, b. Aug. 3, '26 ; 2. ELIZABETH, b. Mar. 20, '28-9, m. John Baker, of Littleton, Mar. 28, '51 ; 3. DEBORAH, b. June

---

* A Thomas and w Priscilla, of Worcester, had *Susanna,* b. 1722; *Isaac,* '24 ; *Phinehas,* '26, m. Eunice Chadwick, '52 ; *Joseph,* '28, m. Lydia Whitney, '51 ; *Patience,* '30 ; *Solomon,* '33 ; *Bezaliel,* '35 ; *Daniel,* '38, m. Patience Stow, '62 ; *Abigail,* '40 ; *Thomas,* '42 ; *Priscilla,* '44.

24, '31, m. John Wheeler, of Nichewaug, Aug. 29, '51; 4. SIMEON, b. Aug. 19, '33, m. Martha Dudley, '64, and lived in Greenwich; 5. THANKFUL, b. Mar. 5, d. Sep. 11, '37; 6. THANKFUL, b. June 17, '38, m. Wm. Dagget, Dec. 27, '59; 7. JAMES, of Westmoreland, N. H.; 8. JOSEPH, b. Feb. 3, '43, m. Sarah Curtis, Aug. 14, '66, and d. in Petersham, 1814 — his w. Sarah, d. 1828, æ. 80; 9. NATHANIEL, bap. Sep. 14, '46, m. Sarah Johnson, and d. in Hardwick; 10. BENJAMIN, bap. May 7, '49, lived in Westmoreland, N. H.; 11. FORTUNATUS, bap. June 7, '52, m. Esther Beman, and lived in Westmoreland. Thankful, w. of Isaac, was recommended to the ch. in Petersham, July 17, 1757, where Isaac d. ab. 1777; his wid. d. at Westmoreland, N. H., æ. ab. 94.

7. ISAAC, s. of Isaac (6), m. Mary Nixon, Nov. 2, 1752; and had 1. LUCIA, bap. June 10, '53, m. John Prouty; 2. DOLLY, bap. Ap. 20, '55, m. —— Sawtell, and 2d, Jesse Healy, and d. 1828; 3. THADDEUS, had 3 wives, and d. in Rockingham, Vt.; 4. WINSOR, Charlestown, N. H., m. Sally Gleason, and d. 1816, æ. 55, f. of Col. *Joseph*, of Langdon; 5. BETSEY, m. John Sawtwell, and d. 1841, æ. 77. Isaac the f. moved to Langdon, N. H.

8. JOHN, s. of Tho. (3), had by w. Abigail, 1. EBENEZER, b. Sep. 1, 1708 (Sherb. Rec.); and in Fram., 2. JOHN,[11] b. Feb. 27, '10–1.; 3. ANNE, b. May 3, '13, m. John Drury, Nov. 22, '33; 4. SAMUEL, b. Dec. 13, '15; 5. ABIGAIL, b. Nov. 23, '17, m. James Cloyes, May 28, '40; 6. MARTHA, b. May 1, '20, m. Jona, Maynard, Nov. 11, '42; 7. SARAH, b. Feb. 6, '23–4, m. John. Crooks, of Hop., Jan. 4, '49; 8. PATIENCE, b. July 7, '29, m. Daniel Ball, Aug. 25, '48, and moved to Athol. Capt. John lived on Mr. Charles Clark's farm, was constable, 1710, and 3 years a Selectman; he d. in Fram., May 9, 1740. Wid. Abigail was adm. to the ch., Aug. 12, 1750.

9. EBENEZER, s. of John (8), m. Thankful Johnson, Dec. 9, 1730; and had 1. EBENEZER, b. Ap. 29, 1735; 2. ELIZABETH, b. Jan. 23, '35, m. Moses Rice, of Rutland, Mar. 21, '55; 3. PETER, b. Feb. 17, '37–8, d. Jan. 26, '54; 4. MICAJAH, b. Oct. 17, '40; 5. CALEB, b. Dec. 7, '43, m. Lydia Rice, Oct. '82, had no issue; w. Lydia d. June 27, 1805; 6. ABIGAIL, bap. July 19, '47, m. Phinehas Whitney, of Sherb, '67. Ebenezer the f. lived at Mr. Charles Clark's, and d. June 29, 1750. His wid.

was adm. to the ch., Aug, 12, '50. Elizabeth, w. of Ebenezer, (prob. a mistake for Samuel), d. in Fram., Feb. 3, 1738. [T. Rec.]

10. MICAJAH, s. of Eben. (9), m. Hannah Drury; and had 1. BETTY, bap. Sep. 2, 1764, m. Jacob Reed, Jun., of Sud., Feb. 5, '81; 2. HANNAH, bap. Ap. 5, '67, m. Abel Reed, of Sud. Jan. 20, '85, and 2d, Asa Clark, of Princeton. Micajah, the f. lived on the place now of Mr. Joseph Angier, and d. while in the continental service, as Capt., at White Plains. His wid. Hannah, (who had kept Tavern while her first husband was in the service, " and made money "), m. Gen. John Nixon, Feb. 5, 1778, and d. in Sud., 1828.

11. SAMUEL, s. of John (8), m. Elizabeth How, Jan. 6, 1735; and had ELIZABETH, who d. æ. 18. The m. d. soon after the birth of the child, — see end of (9). Sam. the f. m. 2d, Dorothy Faux, Mar. 14, 1740, and had 2. WILLIAM, b. June 6, '40, d. July 10, '41; 3. SAMUEL[12], b. Oct. 9, '42; 4. JOHN[13], b. July 22, '46; 5. DOLLY, and 6. MARTHA, twins, b. Oct. 18, '48— D. m. Asa Drury, of Nat., and M. m. Asaph Bigelow, of Fram., and d. 1830; 7. MARY, bap. Feb. 24, '51, m. James Morse. Dorothy the m. d. 1751, and Sam. m. 3d, Abigail Livermore, Ap. 3, '55. He lived on the Charles Clark farm, and d. 1796.

12. SAMUEL, Jun., s. of Sam. (11), m. Elizabeth Brown, and had 1. BETSEY, bap. June 12, 1768, m. John Negus, of Petersham, June 16, '94; 2. EBENEZER, bap. Dec. 4, '68, m. in Putney, Vt.; 3. WILLIAM, bap. Oct. 22, '70, d. young; 4. EDWARD, bap. Aug. 23, '72, m. Sarah Deven, of Wayland; 5. WILLIAM, bap. July 24, '74, m. Ruth Cloyes, Oct. 8, '99, moved to Barnet; 6. ROGER, bap. Oct. 13, '76; 7. DOLLY, bap. Oct. 1, '78, m. —— Bruce; 8. KEZIAH, bap. Oct. 1, '78; 9. SALLY, bap. Sep. '82, went to Holland Purchase; 10. RUTH, bap. Oct. '84, m. Micajah Reed, of Hubbardston; 11. RUHAMAH, bap. Dec. '87. Sam. Jr. was Selectman, 2 years; lived near Mr. Charles Clark's (the farm was divided between him and his br. Col. John); moved into E. Sud., before 1800, then to Vt., and d. at Peacham, 1823.

13. JOHN, s. of Samuel (11), m. Anna Eames, of Holl., and had 1. JOHN, b. Mar. 31, 1771, m. wid. Mitchell, an Englishwoman, and 2d, Jane Paine, of Thomaston, Me., and d. 1832; 2. MOLLY, b. July 27, '73, m. Capt. Nathan Miles, of Barnets-

town, Sep. 21, 1801; 3. LYDIA, b. Mar. 11, '75, m. Jos. Morse, Oct. 11, '95, d. at Union, Me.; 4. MICAJAH, b. Jan. 27, '77, m. Polly Cole, Mar. 22, 1801, d. at Union, Me.; 5. CALVIN, b. Mar. 13, '79, m. Sally Rice, Oct. 18, 1801, lives in Union, Me.; 6. ANNA, (Nancy), b. Jan. 25, '81, m. Joshua Underwood, of Holl., Dec. 15, 1802, lives in N. Y.; 7. REBECKAH, b. Oct. 18, '82, m. Jona. Morse, d. in Union, Me., 1831; 8. OLIVE, b. July 20, '84, m. Micah Stone, of Warren, Oct. 7, 1804, and d. 1812; 9. HITTY, b. Sep. 30, '86, m. John Hemenway, of Royalston, Feb. 8, 1805, lives in Union, Me.; 10. Aaron, b. Feb. 17, '91, m. —— Metcalf, d. in Thomaston, Me., 1829. Col. John, the f., lived at Mr. Charles Clark's, was Selectman in Fram., moved to Union, Me., ab. 1804, and d. 1830; his w. Anne d. 1827.

14. PHILIP, rated in Fram., 1710, m. Martha Brown, May 6, 1714. Wid. Martha d. ab. 1757.

15. PHINEHAS, prob. s. of Isaac (5), had by w. Elizabeth, 1. ELIZABETH, b. Nov. 3, 1733; 2. PHINEHAS, b. July 25, '37, d. Oct. 14, 1755; 3. EZRA, b. Sep. 26, '38; 5. JOANNA, b. July 13, '40. [A Joanna, of Princeton, m. Wm. Gibbs, 1762]; 5. JOHN, b. Oct. 12, '42; 6. THOMAS, b. May 9, '45; 7. PRUDENCE, d. July 12, 1741; 8. PRUDENCE, b. Mar. 20, '47; 9. JESSE, b. May 25, '49; 10. ANNA, b. Oct. 25, '52; 11. DEBORAH, b. Sep. 18, '54. [Phinehas and w. Azubah, cov., Ap. 21, 1754. Deborah, dr. of Phinehas, was bap., Oct. 4, 1753. Phinehas, s. of Phinehas, was bap. Sep. 1, 1754.]

16. JONATHAN, (bap. in Fram., Sep. 10, 1721), m. Lois Flagg, and had 1. a son, d. y.; 2. RUTH, m. — Howe, of Marlb.; 3. LOIS, m. Moses Burnham; 4. MARGARET, d. unm., July 1, 1805. Jonathan the f. lived opposite Mr. Charles Parker's, and d. ab. 1802, æ. over 80; Lois his w. d. 1796.

17. MERCY, bap. May 10, 1719. JONATHAN, bap. Sep. 10, 1721. JOHN, s. of John, Jun., and Thankful, b. Jan. 11, 1730–1.

GLOVER, JAMES, m. Lois Bent, of Sud., Feb. 3, 1762, and had 1. LOIS, b. Nov. 30, 1762, m. Asa Nurse; 2. POLLY, m. Ezra Haven, Ap. 1782, and 2d, Asa Nurse, Dec. 29, 1800; 3. BETSEY; 4. ANNA, bap. June 1, '66, d. young; 5. MARTHA, m. Jonathan Rugg, Jun., Dec. 29, 1800; 6. SARAH, m. —— Thomas, in Me.; 7. EUNICE, d. unm., Sep. 1828, æ. 51.

J. the f. m. 2d, wid. Mary Metcalf, (a Hill), Sep. 23, 1784, and had 8. JERUSHA, b. 1787, m. Thomas Verille, of Vinal Haven, Me., lives a wid.; 9. JULIA, m. Benj. Crabtree, of V. H.; 10. JOHN, b. 1789, m. Martha White, of V. H., now a Shipmaster in Me. James the f. and w. Mary moved to Vinal Haven, Me. 1791, and had there 2 sons and 1 dr. James was b. in Dorchester, had a br. Thomas who d. in Stoughton, and a br. Ebenezer, of Dorch. James lived at Salem end in Fram.

GODDARD, EDWARD, m. Susanna, dr. of Simon Stone, Jun., 1697, and had in Wat. 1. EDWARD, b. May 4, 1698, m. Hephsebah Hapgood, and d. in Shrewsbury, 1777; 2. SUSANNA, b. Feb. 25, 1699–0, m. in Fram. John Drury, May 21, 1719, and 2d, Joseph Haven, Dec. 5, 1760, and lived in Fram. and Athol; 3. SIMON, b. Feb. 18, 1701–2; 4. BENJAMIN, b. Aug. 15, '04, m. Grace Fisk, lived in Shrewsb.; 5. DAVID, b. Sep. 26, '06, adm. to the ch. May 5, '28, grad. at H. Coll. 1731, m. Mrs. Mercy Stone, of Wat., Aug. 19, 1736, and 2d, Mrs. Martha Nichols, of Fram., Dec. 20, 1753, ord. at Leicester, June 30, 1736, and d. on a visit at Fram., during the "great sickness," Jan. 19, 1754, æ. 47 years. His wid. Martha, m. Deac. Daniel Stone, of Fram. (See Worc. Mag. II. 84; Whitney's Hist. Worc. Co.); and at Boston, bap. in 1st Ch.; 6. MARY, bap. June 10, d. Aug. 5, 1711; 7. EBENEZER, bap. 1712, d. young; 8. EBENEZER, b. Feb. 14, '14; and in Fram.; 9. WILLIAM, b. Dec. 10, d. 17th, 1720; 10. HEPHSEBAH, bap. May 8, '23. Edward, b. Mar. 24 or 25, 1674–5, was s. of William, (b. 1653, 7th s. of Edward, a citizen and grocer of London), who m. Elizabeth Miles, and d. ab. 1691. For further particulars, see the "Goddard Genealogy."

Edward came to Fram. from Boston, Mar. 25, 1714, having been a teacher in Boston. He and his w. were admitted to the church by letter, Ap. 9, 1718. He taught, for several years, a grammar school in Fram., and was chosen dea. of the ch., Ap. 14, 1725, but declined. He was several times chosen messenger of the church to Ecclesiastical Councils, and took a prominent part in the religious as well as civil affairs of the town. He was Town Clerk from 1720, in all 18 years; and left proof upon the Records, of his beautiful penmanship. He was Selectman 10 years, and Town Treasurer 2 years. He represented the town at the General Court 8 years, from 1724; was commissioned as Justice of the Peace, and in 1733, was chosen one of his Majesty's Council, in which office he served three years. He also held commissions as Lieut. and Capt. of troop. His skill in drawing legal instruments, rendered him useful as a conveyancer. He was, in his religious opinions, a Calvinist. With others, he withdrew from Mr. Swift's church, without a dismission, and was received to the Hop. ch., Jan. 13, 1732-3. He was afterwards the chief instrument in planting the 2d church in Fram., which declined after his decease, and at length ceased its existence. He was a ready writer, and numerous MSS. sermons, Journals, &c., from his pen, are in preservation. He also printed some controversial papers. He was a zealous and decided man, of undoubted integrity, and possessed considerable talent, exercised chiefly in theological research. He was, perhaps, more strenuous as a defender of religious freedom, than as an advocate for religious toleration, or Christian harmony. The active part he took in the ecclesiastical dissensions which disturbed the church for many years, has probably prevented a just estimation of Mr. Goddard's character. He had many friends, among whom were the Rev. Mr. Bridge, of the 1st ch., in Boston, the Rev. Dr. Prince, and Mr. Secretary Willard; the last two caused to be published an interesting notice of his death in the Boston Gazette, Feb. 16, 1754. Alden also gives a respectful tribute to his memory. (Coll. III. 40.) The Hon. Edward Goddard, d. Feb. 9, 1754, æ. 78 years, 10 m. 14 d., and his w. Susannah d. Feb. 4, 1754, æ. 78 years, 2 m. — both during the great sickness. Mr. Goddard lived W. of Mr. William Temple's, and a cellar hole indicates the spot.

2. SIMON, s. of Edward (1), m. Susannah Cloyes, Nov. 2, 1727, and had 1. MARY, b. Aug. 4, 1728; 2. EDWARD, b. Oct. 31, '29, d. 1742; 3. SUSANNAH, b. July 28, '31, d. 1740; 4. SIMON, bap. in Hop., May 5, '34, d. young; 5. MARTHA, b. Dec. 29, '35, d. 1740; 6. SIMON, b. '38, d. '40; 7. BETTY, b. May 27, '40, m. James Goddard, '67; 8. SIMON, m. Mary Eaton, of F., and 2d wid. Martha Goddard, of F., Nov. 9, 1803, and d. in Gerry; 9. EDWARD, m. Mary How; 10. JOSIAH, m. Ruth Raymond; 11. SUSANNAH. Simon the f. moved early from Fram. His wid. d. in Athol, Nov. 1798, æ. 94.

3. EBENEZER, s. of Edward (1), m. Sybilla Brigham, of Marlb., Jan. 27, 1736, and had in Fram. 1. ABIGAIL, b. Sep. 11, 1737, m. — White, of Charlton; 2. MARTHA, b. Mar. 18, '38, m. Benoni Hemenway, and lived in Athol; 3. SYBILLA, b. Jan. 14, '40-1, m. Jos. Woodward, of Athol; 4. SUSANNAH, b. Sep. 25, '42, m. Phinehas Howe, of Hop.; 5. MARY, b. Aug. 3, '44, m. Rufus Taylor, of Athol; 6. SOPHIA, b. Oct. 3, '46, m. Abner Morton, of Athol; 7. BETTY, b. Jan. 26, '48, m. Nehemiah Howe, of Hop.; 8. ESTHER, b. June 15, '51, m. Sam. Whitney, of Athol; 9. EBENEZER, b. Aug. 9, '53, m. Hannah Death, in Athol, July 6, '75, and d. in N. Y.; 10. BENJAMIN, b. Sep. 2, '55, d. Nov. 6, '71; 11. EDWARD, 12. SAMUEL, twins, b. Ap. 16, '59 — E. m. 1st, Anna Death, 2d, in N. Y., and d. 1844 — S. m. 1st, Keziah Bond, 2d, Betsey Burpee, and d. in Hop., 1846; 13. ABIGAIL, b. in Athol, May 16, '61, m. John Tidd, and lived in Hop. Eben.

the f. was Selectman 4 years, moved to Athol, 1762, and d. Nov. 18, 1762; his wid. Sybilla d. 1807, æ. 89.

4. ELISHA, s. of Robert and w. Mehetabel, of Sutton, and g. s. of Jos. and w. Deborah, of Wat. and Roxb., (Jos. br. of Edward of Fram.), m. in Fram., Mrs. Hannah Haven, Nov. 17, 1748, and had in Fram., 1. ELISHA, b. Dec. 3, '49, d. Oct. 25, '71; 2. SILENCE, b. Nov. 18, '52, m. Maj. Jona. Hale, of Fram., and d. Jan. 15, 1800; 3. MEHETABEL, b. July 17, '55, m. Benj. Heywood, of Worc. Elisha the f. moved to Sutton, m. a 2d w., Mary Thacher, and had ROBERT, MARY, EBENEZER, SAMUEL, and SUSANNAH. E. d. Jan. 19, 1784, and his wid. Mary m. 2d, Jona. Fay, and d. 1796, æ. 61. (God. Gen.)

5. NATHAN, s. of Benj. and w. Grace, of Shrewsb., and g. s. of Edward (1), m. Martha Nichols, of Fram., Dec. 15, '72, and had (b. out of Fram.) 1. NICHOLS, m. Charity White; 2. GRACE, m. Eph. Drury; 3. NATHAN, m. in Fram., Prudence Hemenway, was by trade a painter, and d. in Fram. July 4, 1822. Nathan the f. grad. at Harv. Coll., 1770; removed from Vt. to Fram., where he taught a Grammar School, and d. July 24, 1795.

ELIZABETH, (not Deborah, as in God. Gen.), of Roxb., dr. of Jos. and Deb., m. John Adams, of Fram., June 27, 1706. PETER, was perhaps of Fram., 1749, (Buckminster's Journal). WILLIAM, of Shrewsbury, m. Keziah Cloyes, Jan. 26, 1726-7, and was f. of Deac. *James*, and others, at Marlb. WILLIAM, m. at Sherb., Leah Fisher, Dec. 10, 1685, and had *Elizabeth*, b. Aug. 23, '87, m. Anthony Hancock, of Wrenth., Feb. 25, '08; *William*, b. '89, d. 1703; *Sarah*, b. '93; *Abigail*, b. Dec. 2, '97, m. Sam. Williams, May 14, 1716. Wm. the f. d. Sept. 6, 1708; his wid. Leah, d. Sept. 10, 1720. William of Sherb., was prob. the Wm., s. of Wm. and Eliz., of Wat., b. in London, ab. 1653. In 1693, he sold to Wm. Rider, of Sherb., one half of a tract N.W. part of Quansigamog, (Worcester).

GOODALE, GOODALL, or GOODELL. Wid. *Hannah* (from Lynn, dr. of Richard Haven, and b. Feb. 22, 1645), was in Fram. with a sick child, Ap. 15, 1704. She was buried in Fram., Jan. 1, 1726-7. MARY, probably her dr., was adm. to the Ch., July 31, 1720. MARTHA, of Fram., m. Samuel How, of Sud., Sep. 11, 1704.

Note. — NEHEMIAH GOODALL, m. at Charlestown, Hannah Havens, July 20, 1673, and had at Lynn, *Joseph*, b. 1677; *Mary*, b. Oct. 17, '86, and perhaps others.

JOHN, who went to Marlb. ab. 1702, (w. Elizabeth), d. 1752, æ. 72, and his w. E. d. 1738, æ. 62, and a 2d w. Elizabeth d. 1752, æ. 64. He had, 1. SOLOMON, b. 1707, d. at Brookfield, 1744, (f. by w. Anna, of *John, Solomon,* and *Anna)*; 2. NATHAN, b. 1709, m. Persis Whitney, and f. of Judge *Job, Abner*, &c.; 3. ELIZABETH, b. 1715. ISAAC, of Salem, m. Patience Cooke, 1668, and had chil. THOMAS, (w. Hannah), was of Southb., 1749.

GOODNOW, GOODENOW, or GOODENOUGH, JOHN, of Sud., 1635, made freeman June 2, 1641, selectman of Sud., 1644, d. in Sud., Mar. 28, 1654, leaving a w. Jane, and chil., 1. JANE, m. Henry Wayte, or Wight, of Ded., (and had John, Joseph, Daniel, Benjamin, &c.); 2. ———, m. Andrew Duning. John, sen., d. Mar. 28, 1654, and his will was proved May 24. He names his br. Edmund. His wid. Jane's will was proved, Oct. 2, 1666. She d. July 15, '66. [URSULA d. in Sud., April 23, 1653.]

2. THOMAS, made freeman, May 10, 1643, was prop. of Sud., 1638, and a petitioner for Marlborough, May, 1656. He had by w. Jane, 1. THOMAS; 2. MARY, b. Aug. 25, 1640; 3. ABIGAIL, b. Mar, 11, '42, m. Thomas Barnes; 4. SUSANNAH, b. Feb. 20, '43; 5. SARAH, b. Jan. 20, '43–4, d. '54; 6. SAMUEL, b. Feb. 28, '46, d. 1717, and f. at Marlb., by w. Mary, of *Thomas*, b 1672; 7. SUSANNAH, b. Dec. 21, '47. Thomas, the f. m. 2d, Joanna, 1662, and his will was proved 1664, in which he names his brs. John Rudducke, and Edmund G. [1674, JANE, w. of Chris. Banister, of Marlb., is named as a dr. of Thomas.]

3. EDMUND, br. to the two preceding, made freeman, May 13, 1640, was prop. of Sud., 1638, Selectman, 1641, &c., Rep., '45 and '50, and commissioner to end small causes, 1661. He was Lieut. commanding the Sudb. band, during Capt. Pelham's absence in England. (Johnson's W. W. Prov., p. 193). He had by w. Anne, 1. JOHN, (in 1689, æ. ab. 54. Rev. justified), f. by w. Mary, of *Hannah*, b. 1656, m. James Smith, '80; *Mary*, b. 1659; *Edmund*, '61; *Sarah*, '63; *Sarah*, '66; *Elizabeth*, '72, m. Joseph Haiden, '91; *Joseph*, '74; *Ebenezer*, '77; *Lydia*, '78; *Mary*, '80. John, the f. d. 1721, and his w. Mary d. 1704; 2. HANNAH, b. Nov. 28, 1639, m. James Pendleton, Ap. 29, '56; 3. MARY, b. Aug. 25, '40; 4. SARAH, b. Mar. 17, '42, m. John Kettle; 5. JOSEPH, b. July 19, '45, d. 1676; 6. EDMUND.

4. EDMUND, s. of Edmund (3), m. Dorothy Man, 1688, who d. Ap. 2, '89, leaving a dr. DOROTHY, b. '89; by 2d w. Rebeckah, he had 2. SARAH, b. Mar. 1, 1695–6, m. Daniel Woodward, 1716; 3. JOHN, b. 1698, non compos; 4. JOSEPH, b. Nov. 30, 1700; 5. REBECKAH, b. July 1, 170(2); 6. EBENEZER, b. April 4, '04; 7. CORNELAS, b. Dec. 4, '05, m. Abigail Griffin, '30; 8. JONATHAN, b. Mar. 1, '07, m. Hannah Davis, '37; 9. DOROTHY, b. May '10; 10. DAVID, b. Mar. 10, '12–3, m. Mary Bent, '31; 11. MERCY, b. Mar. 13, '14–5. Edmund, the f. prob. d. ab. 1727.

5. EBENEZER, s. of Edmund (4), m. Elizabeth Allen, 1729; and had 1. PHINEHAS, b. Nov. 24, 1730; 2. REBECKAH, b. Aug. 24, '32; 3. ISAAC, b. Feb. 3, '34–5.

6. PHINEHAS, s. of Ebenezer (5), m. in Fram., Lois Frost, Jan. 30, 1752, and cov. in F., Dec. 17, '52, and had 1. PHINEHAS, bap. Dec., '52; 2. LOIS, bap. Mar. 31, '54; 3. ELIZABETH, bap. Jan. 10, '56; 4. EBENEZER, (posthumous), bap. Dec. 4, '57.

7. ISAAC, s. of Ebenezer (5), m. Martha Hunt, of Sud., Jan. 27, 1757, and had 1. ISAAC, b. Oct. 5, '57, d. unm. ab. 1800; 2. MARTHA, b. Sep. 6, '59, m. Silas Knight; 3. SARAH, b. Sep. 4, '61, m. Eph. Potter; 4. SUBMIT, b. Nov. 5, '63; 5. LEVINAH, b. July 31, '68. Martha the w. d. young. Isaac left town, and d. in Lincoln, ab. 1814.

8. JONATHAN, m. Eunice Tower, and had 1. JOSEPH, b. Oct. 30, 1793, m. Susannah Murdock; 2. LUTHER, b. Feb. 1, '95, m. Polly Newton, and d. 1843; 3. BETSEY, bap. June, '97, m. Dana Bullard, and d. 1826; 4. EUNICE, bap. Sep. '98, m. Nath. Johnson; 5. JONATHAN, d. 1802; 6. LUCY, b. Jan. 14, 1801, m. Cyrus Bullard; 7. EVELINE; 8. GEORGE; 9. WILLIAM; 10. EDWARD, m. Mary B. Trowbridge; 11. WARREN; 12. SARAH.

Jonathan lived in Southb. and Fram. He was b. in Sud., s. of Jona. and w. (Eunice Hastings, who came from Boylston.) Jona. lived where his s. Edward does, and d. 1832, æ. 68.

9. EPHRAIM, (s. of Eph. of Sud.), m. in Fram., Nelly Rice, Nov. 1790, and was f. in Fram., of JONAS; ASENETH; MARY; OTIS; ROXILANA; ELEANOR; and CHARLES. Nelly the w. d., 1834.

10. LYDIA, m. Lawson Moore, in Fram., June, 1784. JOSIAH of Sud., m. Beulah Tredway, of Fram., Aug. 2, 1749. JOSEPH, of E. Sud., m. Martha Stone, of Fram., Nov. 30, 1797. ELIZABETH, m. Daniel Sanger, Jun., in Fram., Nov. 10, 1799. Israel d. in Fram., May 12, 1807, æ. 22.

GOULD, JOHN, of Sud., m. in Sherb., Priscilla Heard, Jan. 2, 1737-8; and 2d Hannah Learned, and had in Fram., HANNAH, b. Aug. 9, 1758, m. and lived in Athol. John the f. d. in Fram., Oct. 7, 1759. His wid. Hannah m. again.

SAMUEL, of Sud., and w. Ruth, had *Samuel*, b. 1715, m. Hannah Brintnal, '37; *John*, b. Aug. 6, '19; *Abraham*, b. '25, m. Hepsebah Maynard, '50, and d. '54; *Thomas*, '28; *Daniel*, '32. JOHN and w. Judith, were of Southb., 1748. GIDEON, of Hop., had *Henry*, bap. 1743. *Susanna*, dr. of Gideon, of Hop., m. in Fram., James Mellen, Jan. 16, 1800.

GRANT, ALEXANDER, rated in Fram., ab. 1738. [Alexander and w. Hannah, of Sud., had *Daniel*, 1711; *Abigail*, b. 1713, d. '26; *Elizabeth*, b. Nov. 22, 1716, m. in Fram., Jabish Pratt, of Sutton, Ap. 10, 1741; *John*, b. 1720; *Samuel*, b. Aug. 29, 1725.]

2. SAMUEL, prob. s. of preceding, m. in Marlb., Priscilla Arthur, 1752, was rated in Fram., ab. 1765, and had RACHEL and HANNAH, bap. Nov. 27, 1774.

WILLIAM and w. (Elizabeth Marshall, m. 1741), had chil. in Holl. BENJAMIN, of Medfield, m. Priscilla Morse, and was in M., 1693. JAMES was of Dedham, 1664.

GRAVES, or GREAVES, JOSEPH, m. Rachel Pratt, May

3, 1723, and had 1. JOSEPH, b. Jan. 21, 1722–3; 2. HANNAH, b. July 5, '25, d. Mar. 2, '38–9; 3. RACHEL, b. July 23, '27, m. Thomas Eames, Jun., Ap. 29, '54; 4. WILLIAM; 5. BENJAMIN, twins, b. Jan. 22, '29–0; (Wm., with w. and 5 chil., was in Fram., 1787); 6. PHINEHAS, b. Feb. 8, '35; 7. BATHSHEBAH, b. June 20, '37, m. Phinehas Butler, Ap. 29, '54; 8. TIMOTHY, b. Oct. 20, '39; 9. JOHN, b. Mar. 31, '42; 10. EBENEZER, b. Oct. 27, '46. Joseph the f. lived near Nat. bounds.

JOESPH, of Sud., (æ. 46, 1689. Rev. justified), probably s. of Admiral Thomas, of Charlestown, m. Elizabeth Maynard, Jan. 15, 1665–6; and had *Samuel*, b. Feb. 14, '66–7, (w. Anne); *Richard*, b. Ap, 7, '72, (w. Johanna); *John*, b. May 10, '74, m. Sarah Loker, 1710; *Deliverance*. Jos. m. 2d, Mary Ross, 1678, and had *Mary*, '80; *Ebenezer*, '81; *Ebenezer*, Feb. 28, '81–2. The descendants in Sud. have been numerous. JOHN, of Roxb., d. 1644, f. of *John, Samuel, Jonathan, Mary*, and *Hannah*. Rear Admiral THOMAS, called by Gov. Winthrop, "an able and godly man," of Charlestown, b. in Ratcliff, Eng., June 6, 1605, d. July 31, 1653, having been commissioned by Cromwell to a naval command. He previously commanded vessels from Boston. His chil. were, *John; Thomas*, (H. Coll., 1656, m. Elizabeth Chickering); *Nathaniel*, bap. 1639, m. Elizabeth Russell; *Joseph; Rebeckah;* and *Susannah*, m. Zechariah Symmes. T. had a br. Abraham. The w. of Thomas was Katharine Coytmore, who d. ab. 1682. (Co. Rec. IV. 34.) ABRAHAM, was of Concord, 1677, and of Andover, 1689.

2. PHINEHAS, s. of Joseph (1), had by w. ——, 1. PHINEHAS, bap. Oct. 12, 1760, m. Sally Mellen, of Hop., 1782; 2. JOSEPH, bap. June 28, '61, m. Sarah Pepper. The f. left Fram.

GREEN, JOSEPH, was in Fram., from Upton, 1769. REUBEN, of Fram., m. Elizabeth Allen, of Natick, 1783. Reuben Green was among the early ministers of the Baptist Society in Fram.

GREENWOOD, JAMES, then of Holl., m. Patience Leland, 1740, and had 1. THANKFUL, m. and d. in Spencer; 2. PATIENCE, b. 1748, m. Joseph Sanger; 3. JAMES, b. 1750; 4. KEZIAH, b. 1753, m. Jona. Flagg, and lived in Nat.; 5. ABEL; 6. POLLY, m. John Kendal, in Fram., June, 1782; 7. WILLIAM; 8. ABIGAIL, b. 1766, m. Nathan Underwood; and in Fram., 9. MARTHA, m. Samuel Frail, of Hop. James the f. was burnt out at Holl., and moved to Fram., ab. 1768, where he died. His wid. Patience d. æ. 96. James was a millwright and cabinet maker, and was employed during the great sickness, to make coffins.

James was b. at Newton, Jan. 27, 1713–4, and s. of James, (m. Thankful Wilson,) b. Dec. 19, 1687, of Thomas and w. Abigail. Tho. (a weaver) d. Sep., 1693; his s. James d. in Holl., 1742. Thankful, w. of James, d. at Newton, Feb. 4, 1713–4. James, sen., was br. to Deacon

William, of Sherb., f. of *William, Caleb, Jonas, Samuel, Joseph,* and others.

2. JAMES, Jun., s. of James (1), m. Experience Harding, and had in Fram., EXPERIENCE, b. Oct. 14, d. Oct. 21, 1777. E. the w. d. Oct. 26, '77, æ. 25. James m. 2d, Hannah Jones, who d. in Fram., Mar. 28, 1812, æ. 62 ; and 3d, Sally Harding.

3. ABEL, s. of James (1), m. Sally Homer, and had 1. SALLY, m. Ebenezer Swift, Sep. 7, 1800 ; 2. ABEL, m. —— Perry ; 3. NANCY, m. Nathaniel Knowlton ; 4. JAMES ; 5. MARTHA, m. —— Hall, of Newton ; 6. BETSEY, m. —— Perry ; 7. HANNAH, m. Elisha Jones ; 8. MARY, m. —— Twitchell.

4. WILLIAM, s. of James (1), m. Mehetabel Jones, Feb. 10, 1789, and had 1. WILLIAM, m. Rowena Weeks ; 2. HANNAH ; 3. MEHETABEL, m. —— Butler, of Hop. Mehetabel the w. d. 1797, and Wm. m. 2d, Sally Winch, Ap. 9, 1799, and had 4. JONATHAN, b. June 18, 1801, m. Candace Hill. Wm. the f. d. in Fram., Aug. 17, 1821. Wid. Sally d. 1843.

DANIEL, of Newton, s. of John (and w. Hannah, who d. 1728, and he m. 2d, Alice Lyons, 1729), m. Sarah Adams, of Fram., May 6, 1728.

GREGORY, DANIEL, m. Sarah Eames, July 13, 1732, and had 1. DANIEL, b. Feb. 16, '33–4 ; 2. JOSIAH, b. July 31, '36, lived in Medway ; 3. LYDIA, b. Feb. 7, '38. Dan. the f. lived near Saxonville, and d. June 25, 1758.

2. DANIEL, Jun., s. of Dan. (1), m. Abigail Eaton, July 1, 1755, and had 1. NOAH, b. May 1, '56 ; 2. DANIEL, b. Oct. 13, '57. Abigail the w. d. June 25, '58 ; and Dan. m. 2d, Persis Newton, of Southb., Jan. 6, '63, and had 3. PERSIS, b. Oct. 15, '63, m. —— Newton, of Southb. ; 4. JOSIAH, b. May 17, '65, d. June 26 ; 5. SARAH, and 6. DANIEL, b. Sep. 24, '66 ; 7. NABBY, b. Sep. 5, '68. Daniel the f. was burnt to death while firing some land in Roger's field, June 15, 1769. His wid. m. and moved to Southb.

3. DANIEL, m. Hannah Buckminster, Oct. 3, 1795 ; and had 1. ABIGAIL, b. July 21, 1797, m. Lowell Mason ; 2. HARRIET, b. Jan. 4, 1801, d. July,'04. Daniel the f. kept a store near the bridge by Mr. Warren's, and d. in Westb. 1822, æ. 57.

Daniel McGregory, (w. Elizabeth), was of Weston, 1710, and d. Mar. 20, 1736. John Gregory was of Sud., 1726.

GROUT, EDWARD, was in Fram., an. ——. His house was

referred to, 1750, as near the New Bridge in the N. E. corner of the town. [Edward of Sud. s. of John, Jun., had by w. Elenor, *Hannah*, d. 1730, and by w. Martha, *Edward*, 1718, (w. Lydia), *Samuel, William*, &c. Edward, Sen. d. at Rutland, Oct. 23, 1743.]

2. ELIAS, b. Feb. 28, 1757, (s. of John, of Medfield, and Sherb., who m. Sarah Mason, 1752, and after, —— Sawin, and a wid. Chamberlain, and d. Mar. 7, 1796, æ. 77), m. 1st, Esther Clap, of Dedham, and had in Sherb. SOPHIA ; ESTHER ; JOHN. He m. 2d, Rhoda Jackson, and had, MARIA ; MARY ; ELIAS ; and ELIAS — the last two prob. in Fram. He m. 3d, Eleanor Dadmun, and had ELEANOR J. ; OLIVIA ; ROYAL ; and ELIAS ; and d. in Fram. 1835, æ. 78.

JOHN, of Sud., received a grant of Cranberry Swamp, 1643 ; was selectman and town clerk several years, and commissioned as a captain. His w. (Dr. Stearns notes) was Sarah Cakebread. He had, 1. JOHN, m. Rebeckah Toll, 1667, and d. 1708, f. of *Sarah*, b. '68; *Rebeckah*, b. '71, m. John Buck ; *Elizabeth*, b. '72, m. James Brewer, 1703 ; *Abigail*, b. '76, prob. d. young ; *John*, b. '82 ; *John*, b. '84 ; *John*, b. '85, (f. of Thomas, Daniel, and Joseph); and *Edward*, b. '88, (wives Eleanor and Martha); J.'s heirs agreed, 1710 ; 2. SARAH, m. John Loker, Jun., and d. 1702; 3. JOSEPH, b. July 24, 1649, of Wat., a carpenter, m. Susa. Hager, and f. of *Joseph*, m. Mary Rogers, 1717 ; *Susannah*, and *Mehetabel* ; 4. ABIGAIL b. Oct. 14, 1655, m. Jos. Curtis, '78 ; 5. JONATHAN, b. Aug. 1, '58 ; 6. ELIZABETH, m. John Livermore ; 7. MARY, b. Aug. 1, 1661, m. Thomas Knap, 1688 ; 8. SUSANNAH, b. 1664. Capt. John d. 1697. His will was proved Aug. 16. Inventory, £690.12s. John, (see Rev. in N. E. Justified), was æ. 70, in 1689 ; a Depos. in the Co. Office, makes him 37, in 1652. JOHN, (w. Mary), of Wat., had *John*, b. Aug. 8, 1641 ; and *Mary*, b. '43. A John took the freeman's oath, 1658. (Co. Rec.) WILLIAM, (w. Sarah), was of Charlestown, 1664.

GRUSHY, BLAYNEY, alias BRIN, a colored servant of Col. Micah Stone, was at Bunker Hill Battle, and d. in Fram., Feb. 8, 1820.

HAGER, WILLIAM, m. in Wat., Mary Bemis, 1645 ; and had 1. MARY, b. Dec. 25, '45, not in the will ; 2. RUHA, who m. Joseph Waight, and 3. SAMUEL, twins, b. Nov. 30, '47—Samuel (w. Sarah, d. ab. 1719), f. of *Samuel*, b. 1698 ; 4. WILLIAM, b. Feb. 12, '58 ; 5. REBECKAH, b. Oct. 29, '61, m. Nathaniel Healey, '81 ; 6. ABIGAIL, m. Benjamin Whitney, 1687 ; 7. HANNAH, m. —— Priest ; 8. SUSANNA, m. Joseph Grout ; 9. SARAH, m. Nathaniel Whitney, 1673 ; 10. MEHETABEL. Wm., the f. d. 1683, and his will was proved Ap. 1, 1684. Inventory, £353.14s. Mary, his wid., d. 1695.

2. WILLIAM, Jr., s. of Wm. (1), m. Sarah Benjamin, 1687, and had in Wat., 1. WILLIAM, m. Mary Flag, 1711 ; 2. SARAH, m. Jona. Flagg, 1712 ; 3. JOHN, b. 1697 ; 4. EBENEZER, b. '98 ; 5. JOSEPH, b. 1701, f. at Walth., by w. Grace, of *Daniel*, b. 1724, m. in Fram., Sarah Travis, Sep. 12, '50 ; *Joseph* ; *Uriah* ; *William* ; *Isaac* ; *Grace* ; *Lydia* ; *Benjamin* ; and *Jonathan* ;

6. MEHETABEL, b. 1704. m. Jos. Travis, of Sherb, '27; 7. MARY, m. —— Cutting; 8. MERCY. William, the f.'s will, was proved, 1732. Sarah, his wid., d. at Waltham, Oct. 26, 1745, æ. 82.

3. EBENEZER, s. of Wm. (2), m. at Wat. Lydia Barnard, 1726, and had in Fram. 1. EBEN'R, b. Mar. 16, 1727-8, a wheelwright, m. Abigail Stow of Marlb., Dec. 26, '53, and f. of *Joel, Ashbel*, &c.; 2. LYDIA, b. Mar. 4, '29-0, lived in Vt.; 3. WILLIAM, b. Ap. 21, '33, m. Sarah Stow, of Marlb., Feb. 12, '61, and d. æ. ab. 78, f. of *Ephraim*, b. Feb. 16, '64; *Lydia ; Eder ; William ;* and *Martin ;* 4. THADDEUS. Eben. the f. came first to Marlb., then moved to Eph. Hager's in Fram.; was for a time on the Brinley Farm, and then returned to Marlb. His w. Lydia d. ab. 1780. Eben. was adm. to Fram. ch., June 9, 1754.

4. THADDEUS, s. of Eben. (3), m. Lois Sawyer, of Bolton, Dec. 9, 1762; and had in Fram., 1. CALVIN, b. Aug. 23, '63, d. at sea; 2. LOIS, b. Jan. 31, '67, m. —— Rumwell, and a 2d w., and lived in Windsor, Vt. Thad. d. in Fram., æ. ab. 40; Lois his w. d. in Bolton.

5. EPHRAIM, s. of Wm., g. son of Ebenezer (3), m. in Fram., Lucy Fairbanks, Nov. 1789; and f. of 1. SALLY, b. Sep. 19, '91, d. young; 2. SOPHIA, b. Jan. 8, '93; 3. LUTHER, b. Dec. 8, '94, d. Feb. 1815, a student in Divinity; 4. LYMAN, b. Jan. 12, '97, d. unm.; 5. EDWARD, b. Dec. 19, '98, m. Mary Knight, of Sud., and d. in Troy, N. H., Mar. 1844; 6. TRUMAN; 7. POLLY; 8. LUCY; 9. WILLIAM; 10. SALLY. Eph. the f. m. 2d, Hannah Adams, of Marlb., and had, 11. HANNAH. He m. 3d, wid. Fanny Angier, of Fram. E. d. Aug. 21, 1843, æ. 79. His w. Fanny d. Ap. 22, 1842, æ. 75.

6. JOHN, and w. Martha, came from Weston to Fram., Ap., 1775. WILLIAM K. of Boston, m. Mehetabel Ballard, of Fram., Oct. 6, 1796. LYDIA, m. Nathan Newton in Southb., 1757. ELIZABETH, m. Ezra Newton in Southb., 1760.

HALE, JONATHAN, m. Silence Goddard, and had 1. NATHAN, d. unm.; 2. MARY, m. Wm. Coolidge, May 19, 1800; 3. ANNA, b. Nov. 14, 1784; 4. JOHN, b. June 16, '89; 5. MEHETABEL; 6. NANCY. Maj. Jonathan and w. were rec'd from the ch. in Newbury, Oct., 1789. He was Selectman from 1788, 3 years; and Trustee of the Academy from 1799, to 1802. He lived at Royal Grout's, and manufactured cards for wool. He moved to N. H.

[Jonathan and w. Martha, of Marlb., had *Elizabeth*, b. 1735.]

HAMILTON, HUGH, and w. were admitted to occasional communion in Fram., Ap. 24, 1724.

Sep. 1744, Ann Camwool, formerly wid. Hambleton, was dism. to ch. in Westboro'. (Hop. Ch. Rec.)

HANCOCK, NATHAN, before 1800 lived in Fram., on the place now of Elias Temple, Esq.

HARDING, SETH, and w. Experience, were received from the Medway ch., 1775. Experience, (b. at Medfield, Oct. 7, 1713), w. of Seth, d. in Fram., Feb. 19, 1782, æ. 68. Seth had chil., SALLY, m. James Greenwood; MEHETABEL, m. Zedekiah Haven, of Hop., Jan. 16, 1783.

HARREY, or HARRY, SIMEON, was adm. to ch. Aug. 28, 1748, m. Violet Lains, in Fram., Feb. 13, '52, and had 1. HANNAH, b. Aug. 6, '54 ; 2. SUSANNAH, bap. Ap. 23, '55 ; 3. PETER, bap. Feb. 27, '56; 4. PETER, b. Jan. 1, '57 ; 5. REUBEN, b. May 2, '59 ; 6. SIMEON, b. Mar. 21, '61. [MARGARET, m. Esau Northgate, of Leicester, Oct. 5, 1749.]

HENRY, and w. Francis, of Sud., had *Simeon*, b. Mar. 9, 1713-4; *Peter*, b. Aug. 26, 1716.

HARRINGTON, or HERENTON, EBENEZER, prob. s. of Thomas, of Wat., m. Hepzebah Cloyes, Feb. 3, 1707-8, and had 1. SARAH, b. Dec. 9, 1708, m. —— Paccard ; 2. REBECKAH, b. Dec. 12, '13 ; 3. THOMAS, b. Nov. 18, '15 ; 4. EBENEZER, b. Mar. 8, '16-7 ; 5. JOSHUA, b. Oct. 11, '18 ; 6. SUSANNAH, b. Sep. 16, '20 ; 7. HEPZEBAH, b. Ap. 10, '22 ; 8. ELIAS, b. Feb. 17, '24-5 ; 9. PHINEHAS, b. Oct. 6, '28. Ebenezer the f. was Selectman, 1742, adm. to the ch., June 15, 1718, his w. adm. Nov. 15, 1719. His will was proved Ap. 8, 1754 ; he names his g. son, Ebenezer Bruce.

Ebenezer was prob. g. son of ROBERT, of Wat., who early took the freeman's oath in Wat., and m. Susan George, Oct. 1, 1649. His chil. were, 1. SUSAN, b. Aug. 18, '49, (in will had m. —— Beers, prob. m. 1st John Cutting, 1671, who d. 1689); 2. JOHN, b. Aug. 24, '51, m. Hannah Winter, '81 ; 3. ROBERT, b. '53 ; 4. GEORGE, b. Nov. 24, '55 ; 5. DANIEL, b. Nov. 1, '57, m. Sara Whitney, '81, and f. of *Daniel*, and *David*, both after of Marlb. ; 6. JOSEPH, b. Dec. 28, '59, had two wives, and was dead 1707 ; 7. BENJAMIN, b. Jan. 26, '61-2, m. Abigail Bigelow, '84 ; 8. MARY, b. Jan. 12, '63, m. —— Bemis ; 9. THOMAS, b. Ap. 22, '65, m. Rebeckah White, '86, and f. of *Ebenezer*, b. June 27, 1686 or '87 ; *Susannah*, '88, m. Joshua Kendall, 1710 ; *Rebeckah*, '90 ; *Thomas*, '91 ; *George*, '95 ; 10. SAMUEL, b. Dec. 18, '66, (w. Grace); 11. EDWARD, b. Mar. 2, '68, m. Mary Ocington, '92 ; 12. SARAH, b. May 10, '71, m. —— Winship ; 13. DAVID, b. June 1, '73. Robert, the f.'s will was proved, 1707. His w. Susan d. 1694.

2. JOSHUA, s. of Ebenezer (1), m. Sarah Nurse, Jan. 11, 1743, and m. 2d, Betty Bent, Oct. 3, 1751, and had 1. JOHN, b. Sep. 2, 1752; 2. SARAH, b. Jan. 14, '54; 3. JOSHUA, b. Sep. 13, '55; 4. HANNAH, b. Aug. 21, '59. Betty, w. of Joshua, was recommended to the ch. in Fitzwilliam, June 26, 1774.

3. DAVID. The w. of David, of Fram., was drowned on returning from Boston, while fording the river near Saxonville, Ap. 29, 1747.

DAVID and w. Mary, of Marlb., had *David*, b. 1719, *Caleb*, &c. CALEB and w. Hepsebah, had chil. in Sud., from 1755. JOSHUA and w. Mary, had at Holl., *Hannah*, 1756, and *Noah*, 1760. Mrs. Ann, wid. of Rev. Mr. Harrington, of Lancaster, formerly wid. of Rev. Mat. Bridge, of Fram., d. in Fram., May 12, 1805.

HARRIS, STEPHEN, m. Mary Angier, May 27, 1752, and had 1. SARAH, b. Mar. 21, '53; 2. JOSEPH, b. Jan. 19, '55; 3. MARY, b. Ap. 25, '57; 4. MITTY, b. July 29, '59; 5. BENJAMIN, b. Feb. 14, '62; 6. ANNA, b. Mar. 28, '64; 7. ANNA, b. Oct. 22, '66; 8. STEPHEN, b. Feb. 25, '69. [STEPHEN was bap. in Fram., Ap. 13, 1746; DANIEL, s. and SARAH, dr. of Stephen, bap. Mar. 25, 1752.] Stephen lived in the N. part of Fram., and moved to N. H., prob. Fitzwilliam.

ERASTUS, (w. Rebeckah), was of Holl., 1754.

HART, CATO, a negro, rated in Fram., ab. 1786.

HARVEY, JOHN, m. Molly Nurse, and had in Fram., 1. ABRAHAM, b. Aug. 29, 1791; 2. JOHN, b. Dec. 5, '93; 3. POLLY, b. Feb. 7, '96, (bap. same mo., as dr. of Moses); 4. SUKEY, b. May 6, '99; 5. SALLY, b. May 21, 1801. [ESTHER, ABRAHAM, and JOHN, chil. of John, were bap. Nov., 1794.] Molly, w. of John, d. June 4, 1801, and he m. Olive Grout, of Sherb, July 3, 1802.

[John was from Southb. John m. Patience Bent, in Marlb., Jan., 1760, and had, in Marlb., *Patience*, b. 1760; and in Southb., *James*, b. June 1, 1768; *Esther*, b. July 28, '70; *Jonah*, b. Oct. 12, '72.]

HASTINGS, WALTER, and w. Lydia, had in F., ABIGAIL, b. Ap. 23, 1727; and in Sud., KEZIAH, b. Ap. 29, 1730.

2. WILLIAM, m. Betsey Abbot, Nov. 1791. THOMAS, m. Nabby Abbot, Ap. 3, 1803. Thomas' father was buried, Nov. 18, 1824. (Buck. Mss. Journal). Wm. and Thomas were sons of Eliphalet, of Walth., who m. Susannah Fiske, Aug. 20, 1761.

HAVEN,* RICHARD, of Lynn, had by w. Susannah, 1. HANNAH, b. Feb. 22, 1645–6, m. Nehemiah Goodall, July 30, 1673, had chil. in Lynn, moved, a wid., to Fram., and was buried Jan. 1, 1726–7; 2. MARY, b. Mar. 12, '47, m. John Tarbox, of Lynn, July 4, '67. [Mary, w. of John T., sen., d. at Lynn, Nov. 17, 1690, leaving a numerous family.] 3. JOSEPH, b. Feb. 12, '49–0; 4. RICHARD, b. May 25, '51, f. by w. Susannah, at Lynn, of *Hannah*, b. Aug. 10, 1677, m. John Parker, July 18, '93; *Joseph*, b. Aug. 17, '80; *Sarah; Susanna*, b. Oct. 1, '86; 5. SUSANNA, b. Ap. 24, '53, m. —— Cogswell; 6. SARAH, b. June 4, '55, m. (John) Whitney; 7. JOHN², b. Dec. 10, '56; 8. MARTHA, b. Feb. 16, '58–9, d. June 14, '59; 9. SAMUEL, b. May, d. Dec. 1, '60; 10. JONATHAN, b. Jan. 18, '62, d. July 3, '64; 11. NATHANIEL¹², b. June 30, '64; 12. MOSES²², b. May 20, '67. [In the Dorchester ch., Goodman Haven was received, Aug. 26, 1680, and in 1691, was bap. Susanna Haven, "now a grown maid, in the family of John Minot. Her f. and m. d. when she was young."] Richard Haven came from the W. of England, and settled at Lynn, in 1645, on a farm near Flax Pond. It is supposed that he had brs. who emigrated to N. E. Richard's will was proved June 14, 1703. His w. Susannah d. Feb. 7, 1682.

2. ¹JOHN, s. of Richard, (1), m. in Lynn, Hannah Hichins, Oct. 3, 1682; and had 1. JOHN, b. June 8, '83, who d. in Fram. unm., ab. 1712. (Mid. Prob.); 2. ELKANAH³; 3. MARY, m. in Sherb. Nathaniel Johnson, Nov. 23, 1708; 4. NATHAN⁹; 5. JOSEPH¹⁰; 6. HANNAH, (æ. 13, 1714), m. Benjamin Burnett, of Harvard, and lived in Hop. (H. Gen.) John the f. was in Fram. 1694, and a member of the ch. at its organization; in 1702, a Selectman; and Representative, 1702 and 3. His est. was adm'd Ap. 2, 1705. His wid. Hannah m. John How, July 1, 1712. [In 1682, John, of Boston, Carpenter, had a deed from Daniel Hutchins and w. Elinor, of Lin, of 30 acres of land in Reading.]

3. ¹ELKANAH, s. of John (2), m. Abiel Barber, of Sherb., Nov. 23, 1708; and had, 1. MEHETABEL, b. Aug. 23, '09, m. Daniel Haven, Dec. 10, '30; 2. ELIZABETH, b. Feb. 3, '10–1. The f. m. 2d, Mary Walker, Dec. 2, '14; and had 3. JOHN. The f. m. 3d, Patience Leland, of Sherb., Feb. 5, '17; and had 4. SYBILLA, bap. Aug. 31, '18, m. Samuel Emmes, Jun., Jan. 11, '38–9, and d. Feb. 10, '49; 5. MICAH, b. June 21, '19; 6. ELKANAH, b. July 21, '21; 7. PATIENCE, b. July 27, '29, d. unm.

---

* It may seem presumptuous in the author to attempt a sketch of this family, after the diligent and successful research of the author of Haven's Genealogy. His only apology is, that he had commenced his labor before the publication of Mr. Adams' valuable work, and could not put it aside without marring his design. He is happy to refer the reader, who may wish for further information than is here given, to that publication. Perhaps a few gleanings may be here found, not wholly without interest.

Elkanah, the f. was Constable, 1720 ; and Selectman, 1730. He lived S. of the old Baptist M. House, and d. in 1765, leaving a 4th w., Lydia.

4. ¹JOHN, s. of Elkanah, (3), m. Susannah Town, (H. Gen.); and had in Fram., 1. TIMOTHY, b. Nov. 22, 1740 ; 2. RUTH, b. Nov. 21, '42 ; 3. LOIS, b. May 29, '45 ; 4. SUSANNAH, b. July 31, '47 ; 5. JOHN, b. Oct. 24, '56 ; 6. KEZIA, b. Nov. 17, '59. John the f. was. Deac. in Sutton. (See H. Gen.)

5. ¹MICAH, s. of Elkanah (3), m. Mary Eames, Jan. 16, 1743-4, and had 1. ELIZABETH, bap. Dec. 8, '45 ; 2. MARTHA ; 3. SILENCE ; 4. WILLIAM, b. June 5, '51 ; 5. ANN ; 6. MARY.

6. ¹WILLIAM, s. of Micah (5), m. Lucy Winch, Nov. 23, 1775. William had by w. Miriam, ANNE, b. Ap. 16, 1778.

7. ¹ELKANAH, s. of Elkanah (3), m. Hephzebah Haven of Hop., Feb. 27, 1752 ; and had 1. SUBMIT, m. Zephaniah Davis, of Chesterfield, N. H. ; 2. TIMOTHY ; 3. ELKANAH, lived in Leicester ; 4. EBENEZER, of Lancaster ; 5. NATHAN ; 6. JOHN, m. —— Low, and went to Canada ; 7. AARON, prob. unm. ; 8. HEPHZEBAH, m. Jonathan Rugg, Nov. 23, 1775 ; 9. CHLOE, m. Joseph Barber, Jun., of Medway, Oct., 1791 ; 10. MICAH ; 11. ANNE, m. Nathan Perry, of Worcester ; 12. SYBILLA, m. Jonathan Curtis, of Charlton. Elkanah the f. lived W. of the S. Burying ground.

8. ¹TIMOTHY, s. of Elkanah (7), m. Lois Pitt, Aug. 1784, and with w. adm. to the ch. June, '89 ; and had 1. LUCY, bap. June, '89, m. Daniel Hemenway ; 2. ASAHEL, bap. June, '89, m. Lydia Stone of Hop. ; 3. BETSEY, bap. June, '89, m. Marshall Stone, of Wayland ; 4. EBENEZER P., bap. Jan., '91, d. æ. ab. 16 ; 5. ASENETH, bap. July, '93, m. John B. Banister ; 6. MARY, m. Nevenson Stone, of Northb. ; 7. SALLY, bap. Nov. '99, d. young. Timothy the f. lived near Mr. Phinehas Rice's, and lives in Wayland. Lois, his w., d. 1804, æ. 46 ; and his 2d w. (a wid. Tucker), d. Jan., 1821.

9. ¹NATHAN, s. of John (2), m. Silence Winch, June 4, 1713, and with w. adm. to the ch. June 15, '18 ; and had 1. SILENCE, b. Dec. 21, '13, d. Dec. 21, '35 ; 2. NATHAN, b. May 7, 1716, H. Coll. '37, d. Nov. 8, '37 ; 3. LOIS, b. Dec. 4, '21, d. Jan. 18, '43 ; 4. PHINEHAS, b. Oct. 6, '23, prob. d. young ; 5. BEULAH, b. Nov. 24, '72, prob. d. young ; 6. ANNAH, b.

May 12, '31, m. (Mrs. Hannah, T. Rec.) Elisha Goddard, of Sutton, Nov. 17, '48. Nathan the f. lived in the old Grout house, near Holl. bounds, was constable, 1729, and d. Mar. 10, 1764, æ. 78.

10. ¹JOSEPH, s. of John (2), m. Mehetabel Haven, Nov. 30, 1721, and cov'd June 9, 1723 ; and had 1. MEHETABEL, b. Sep. 29, 1722, m. Ebenezer Marshall, Feb. 11, '47–8 ; 2. ANNE, b. Ap. 1, '25, m. Josiah Stone, Feb. 25, '46–7 ; 3. SAMUEL, b. Aug. 4, '27, H. Coll., '49, m. at Camb., Mrs. Mehetabel Appleton, Jan. 11, '53, and 2d, Mrs. Margaret Marshal, June 2, '78, was ord. over the So. Parish, in Portsmouth, May 6, '52 ; D. D. Edinburgh and Dart. Coll., and d. Mar. 3, 1806. (See Allen's Biog. Dict. sub nom., and Alden's Coll. ii. p. 192) ; 4. MARY, b. Ap. 14, '30, m. John Nichols, July 17, '51, and 2d, Jonathan Locke, Oct. 2, '61, and d. June 17, 1803 ; 5. MARTHA, b. Feb. 19, '32–3, m. Deac. Simeon Dearborne, and was recommended to the ch. in Wakefield, between 1784 and '87. Mr. Adams states, that she had previously lived in Greenland, N. H. ; 6. JOHN[11], b. June 2, '35 ; 7. SYBILLA, b. Ap. 18, '38, d. young ; 8. DEBORAH, b. Dec. 11, '40, d. young ; 9. SARAH, m. Joseph Bixby, and d. in Sharon. Joseph the f. lived on or near the Joel Coolidge place, was Selectman, 1733, Representative, 1754, and held a commission as Justice of the Peace. Joseph Esq. d. Feb. 27, 1776, æ. 78, and his w. Mehet. d. Jan. 25, 1780, æ. 78. (G. Stones.)

11. ¹JOHN, s. of Joseph (10), m. Anne, dr. of Deac. Daniel Stone ; and had in Fram., 1. OLIVE, b. May 16, 1760 ; 2. ANNE, b. Mar. 12, '63 ; 3. MOLLY, b. July 14, '67 (bap. '66) ; 4. FANNY, b. Sep. 3, '70, m. Rev. Jos. Willard, of Wilbraham ; 5. JOHN, b. Sep. 11, '73, d. Mar. 20, '74 ; 6. SALLY, m.—— Boardman. John the f. was a school-master, adm. to the ch. Feb. 14, '62, and his w. May 4, '66 ; and both recommended to Greenland, Dec. 29, '71. They also lived in Lancaster, N. H.

12. ²NATHANIEL, s. of Richard (1), and w. Elizabeth, had 1. MARTHA, b. Ap. 7, 1690, m. Samuel Wesson, May 7, 1711 ; 2. MOSES, b. Mar. 1, '92 ; 3. ELIZABETH, b. Dec. 11, '93, m. Benjamin Nurse, July 12, '17 ; 4. MERCY, b. Jan. 26, '97, m. Ebenezer Nurse, Ap. 14, 1720 ; 5. SUSANNA, b. Feb. 13, '99, m. Thomas Gleason, Jun., Jan. 12, '14–5 ; 6. MORIAH, b. Sep. 4, 1701, adm. to the ch. Ap. 7, '28 ; 7. EXPERIENCE, b. Ap. 23,

'03, m. Samuel Streeter, July 27, '19; 8. NATHANIEL, b. Sep. 8, '04, m. Hephzebah Rugg, June 10, '24, and f. at Hop., of *Joanna*, b. '25; *Nathaniel*, '26, d. '55; *Jonathan*, '28; *Ebenezer*, '29; *Abraham*, '32; *David*, '34, m. Abigail Prentice, of Sherb., Ap. 23, '61, and lived at Natick; *Hepsibah*, '36. N. m. 2d, Abigail Rice, of Sud., Dec. 7, '41, and had others. Nath. (f. or son), m. Hannah Ware, of Sherb., 1753; 9. JEDIDIAH, b. Aug. 23, '06, with w. Mariam, was of Hop., 1734. [Jedediah, Jun., m. Susanna Vaill, of Hop., Feb. 20, '65]; 10. JAMES[20], b. Mar. 4, 1709-0. Nathaniel, the f. was a member of the Fram. Ch., when constituted; was Constable, 1707; Selectman, 1706. He d. July 20, 1746.

13. [2]MOSES, s. of Nath. (12), m. Sar. Bridges, Ap. 14, 1720, and with w. cov., Jan. 15, '20-1, and had 1. BENJAMIN[14], b. Jan. 22, 1720-1; 2. SARAH, bap. Jan. 12, '23-4; 3. SUSANNA, bap. Jan. 9, 1725-6, m. Jason Rice, of Hôp., Feb. 14, '50-1; 4. MOSES, 4th, b. May 3, '28, d. unm.; 5. ZERUIAH, b. June 23, '30, d. young; 6. JESSE[15], b. Nov. 16, '32; 7. GIDEON[17], b. Mar. 10, '34; 8. LOIS, d. young; 9. ZEDEKIAH, b. Sep. 10, '37, lived in Hop., m. Hitty Harding, Jan. 16, 1783, 2d, a sister of his 1st w.; he also m. wid. Abigail Haven, and d. Sep. 17, 1813, æ. 76. Moses, the f. lived on the place of Mr. E. H. Foster; was Constable, 1734, had his house burnt, 1736. He m. 2d, Susanna Claflin, July 22, 1742, (H. Gen.) and d. ab. 1743.

14. [2]BENJAMIN, s. of Moses (13), m. Ruth Gleason, and had 1. SARAH, b. July 31, 1746, m. Benjamin Haven, and d. 1816, æ. 70; 2. RUTH, b. Oct. 21, '50, m. Gideon Gould, and d. 1786; 3. ZUBAH, b. July 21, '53, m. Henry Eames, and d. 1820, æ. 67; 4. ZERVIAH, b. Feb. 5, '55, m. Andrew Allerd, 1774, (May 1775, H. Gen.), and 2d, Joseph Frail, of Hop., Nov. 25, '84; 5. SUSANNA, b. Aug. 8, '57, m. John Lamb, Mar. 16, '79, and lives a wid. in Philipston, (1847). Benj. had several other chil. who d. young. He d. 1796. Ruth, his wid. d. Sep. 21, 1814, æ. 88. (G. Stone.)

15. [2]JESSE, s. of Moses (13), m. Jemima Foster, Jan. 22, 1755, and had 1. EZRA, b. Dec. 19, '55; 2. MITTY, d. Dec. 30, '57, æ. 1 m. 24 d. Jesse the f. lived on Mr. Joseph Haven's place, was Selectman, 3 years, m. 2d, Hannah Whitney, Nov. 15, 1800, and d. June 11, 1816, æ. 84.

16. ²EZRA, s. of Jesse (15), m. Mary Glover, Ap. 1782, and had 1. WILLIAM, B. U., 1809, d. unm.; 2. JOSEPH, d. unm., 1845; 3. ANN, m. Alexander Edwards; 4. JOHN, m. Martha F. Smith, of Needham; 5. JASON, m. Esther Tucker; 6. OLIVE, m. Seth Drury, of Nat.; 7. MILLY, m. Willard Haven; 8. SALLY, d. unm., æ. ab. 25. Captain Ezra lived on his father's place, and d. Oct. 26, 1794, æ. 38. His w. Mary d. Jan. 31, 1822.

17. ²GIDEON, s. of Moses (13), m. Comfort Pike, Dec. 29, 1757, and had 1. JOTHAM[18], b. Oct. 1, '58; 2. SARAH, bap. Oct. 5, '60, m. Francis How; 3. MARY, bap. Aug. 7, '63, d. unm., ab. '93; 4. MOSES PIKE[19], b. Nov. 14, '65; 5. NATHAN, bap. Nov. 29, '67, m. Mitty Fay, (f. of *Zenas*, bap. Jan. 1797), and moved into N. Y.; 6. ZEDEKIAH, bap. Mar. 11, '70, m. Elizabeth Angier, lives in N. Hartford; 7. JESSE, bap. Ap. 5, '72, lives unm.; 8. ELIZABETH, bap. May 31, '78, m. John Hemenway, and d. 1813; 9. RELIEF, bap: Sep. 10, '78, m. Artemas Conant, May 25, 1800. Lt. Gideon, the f., lived on the place now of his son Moses, was Selectman, 2 y., Deac. of the 1st Ch., m. 2d, wid. Deborah Twitchell, of Sherb., Sep. 25, 1792, and d. Dec. 1829, æ. 95 y., 9 mo.

18. ²JOTHAM, s. of Gideon (17), m. Martha Belknap, Ap. 14, 1779, and, with w. cov., May 28, '80. Their chil. were 1. LUTHER, b. Aug. 26, '79, d. unm.; 2. JOHN, b. Oct. 27, '81, went to sea, and d. young; 3. JEREMIAH; 4. JOTHAM, m. Betsey Spear; 5. GILBERT, bap. July, '91, m. Hannah Burrill, lives in Malden; 6. KITTREDGE, bap. Mar. '93, m. Ruth Harrington, a minister in Vt.; 7. HARRIET, bap. Mar. '97, m. John Smith, d. in Boston; 8. CURTIS, bap. Oct. '99, m. Mary Ann Tilson, lives in Boston; 9. MARTHA; 10. FRANKLIN, m. Sarah Ann Curtis, Pres. of the Merchants' Bank, Boston. Jotham the f. and w., were recom. to the ch. in Fitzwilliam, Jan. 1784, returned to Fram., and he d. in Boston, 1838.

19. ²MOSES PIKE, s. of Gideon (17), m. Chloe Eames, of Sud., May 1, 1790, and had 1. POLLY, b. June 13, '91, d. unm., Nov. 16, 1820; 2. CHLOE, b. June 4, '93. Chloe the m. d. Feb. 3, '94. Moses m. 2d, Submit Horn, Sep. 17, '94, and had 3. ANNA ANGIER, b. Mar. 14, '95, m. Henry G. Foster, of Boston, Mar. 9, 1824; 4. JULIA, b. Nov. 22, '96, m. Joseph Angier, May, 1818, d. 1827; 5. LINCOLN, b. Jan. 14, '99, d. unm. 1836;

6. MOSES, b. Jan. 15, 1801. Moses the f. has been Deac. of the 1st ch., and lives in Fram.

20. [2]JAMES, s. of Nath. (12), had by w. Sarah, 1. JAMES, b. Nov. 24, 1729, d. Dec. '31 ; 2. JAMES[21], b. Sep. 18, '31 ; 3. SQUIRE, b. June 24, '34, m. Hannah Bixby, Mar. 18, '54, moved to Bellingham, ab. 1794, and d. without issue ; 4. ELIZABETH, b. Sep. 2, '36, m. Isaac Hemenway, Nov. 28, '54, and prob. 2d, Israel Leadbetter, Jan. 19, 1782 ; 5. REBECKAH, b. July 26, '43. Sarah, w. of James the f., d. Dec. 19, 1762. James lived on the place late of James Greenwood.

21. [2]JAMES, s. of James (20), m. Mehetabel Bixby, Nov. 16, 1752, and had 1. JAMES, b. July 27, 1753 ; 2. MEHETABEL, b. Oct. 23, '56 ; 3. WILLIAM, b. May 4, '59 ; 4. SAMUEL, b. Jan. 4, '62, m. Desire Cloyes, Aug. '84, and lived prob. in N. Y.

22. [3]MOSES, s. of Richard (1), m. Mary (Ballord, H. Gen.), and had at Lynn, 1. JOSEPH[23], b. Feb. 8, 1688-9 ; 2. SUSANNAH, b. Oct. 20, '90, m. Israel Town, of Fram.; 3. RICHARD[25], b. Jan. 8, '92-3 ; 4. MOSES[26], b. Nov. 11, '95 ; 5. MARY, b. Oct. 1, '98, m. Samuel Stone, Jun., of Fram., Nov. 25, 1725, who d. Aug. 30, 1726, and she m. 2d, Ephraim Ward, of Newton, Sep. 24, 1734 ; 6. MEHETABEL, b. Jan. 30, 1701-2, m. Joseph Haven, in Fram., Nov. 30, '21, and d. Jan. 25, 1780 ; and at Fram., 7. SARAH, b. June 10, '05, m, Ralph Hemenway, Feb. 2, '27 ; 8. DANIEL[30], b. June 16, '08. Mary, w. of Dea. Moses, d. Nov. 18, 1734. He m. 2d Mrs. Elizabeth Bridges, Nov. 27, '35. Moses the f. (then of Lynn), bought Isaac Bowen's lease, Nov. 18, 1702, and obtained from Pres. Holyoke a release of rents, 1767. He was Selectman, from 1710, 4 years ; T. Treasurer, 1717, 2 years. He was chosen Deacon of the ch., Mar. 29, 1717, and d. Nov. 14, 1747, leaving a widow Sarah. (H. Gen.)

23. [3]JOSEPH, s. of Moses (22), m. Martha Walker, in Fram., Jan. 24, 1710-1, and had 1. JOHN[24], b. Nov. 30, 1711, (H. Gen.) ; 2. ELIAS, b. Ap. 16, '14, H. Coll., '33, minister of Franklin, and d. in 1754, (H. Gen.) ; 3. MARY, b. Feb. 11, '15-6, d. May 6, 1727 ; 4. JOSEPH, b. Feb. 7, '17-8, Deac. at Hop., m. Miriam Bayley, '37, f. of *Elias ; Lydia ; Joseph ; Noah ; Obadiah ;* and *John ;* 5. JOSIAH, b. Mar. 23, 1719-0, m. Esther Streeter, Feb. 28, '44, and lived in Hop., (H. Gen.) ; 6. MARTHA, b. Mar. 1, 1721-2, m. George Caryl, of Hop., Feb. 17,

'38; 7. LOIS, bap. in Fram., Ap. 12, '24, m. Moses Adams, of Holl., Nov., 1744, and lived in Fram, and Hop.; 8. ASA, b. June 19, '26, d. Dec. 25, '29; 9. MARY, b. July 30, '28, m. Thomas Pierce, Jun., of Fram., Ap. 26, '50; 10. MOSES, b. Mar. 12, '32, m. in Fram., Abigail Mellen, Nov. 1, '50, and Deacon of the Hop. ch.; 11. HANNAH, bap. July 7, '34, m. Stephen Simson, of Hop., Nov. 8, '53. Joseph the f. was Selectman in 1720, 2 years, and was "dismissed to found a ch. in Hopkinton," Aug. 30, 1724.

24. ³JOHN, s. of Joseph (23), m. Mary Bullard, of Holl., 1732, and had 1. MARY, b. Dec. 5, '32, m. John Stone, Esq. of Holl., and d. Oct. 1, 1809, æ. 77; 2. ZERUIAH, b. Feb. 18, '35–6, d. Dec. 8, '80; 3. ANNA, b. Oct. 12, '37, d. Dec. 30, '53; 4. JESSE, b. Feb. 20, '45, m. Catharine Marsh, '67, and f. of *Anna; Luther*, b. Ap. 15, 1770, m. Experience Parker, Feb. 5, '97, and now Deac. in Fram.; *Catharine;* Deacon *John; Mary; Jesse;* and *Elisha;* 5. SARAH, b. Dec. 17, '50, d. Jan. 3, '54. Lt. John the f. lived in Holl., his first child only recorded in Fram. He. d. Oct. 6, 1785, æ. 73. Mary his w. d. Oct. 26, 1796, æ. 86.

25. ³RICHARD, s. of Moses (22), m. Lydia Whitney, Feb. 4, 1713–4, and with w. adm. to the ch., May 12, '17. Their chil. were 1. LYDIA, b. Feb. 10, '14–5, m. Seth Bullard, of Holl., Oct. 18, '52; 2. HANNAH, b. June 10, '16–7, m. Isaac Fisk, Nov. 11, '36; 3. MARY, and 4. SARAH, twins, b. June 5, '18—M. m. John Hill, of Sherb., July 17, '40, S. d. July 10, '18; 5. SARAH, b. Sep. 11, '19, m. Isaac Hill, of Malden, Dec. 29, '43; 6. RICHARD, b. Dec. 16, '22; 7. ELIZABETH, b. May 24, '24, m. Ebenezer Bullard; 8. JOHN, b. May 7, '26, m. Susannah Drury, Mar. 27, '46, was Deacon of Athol ch., and had at A., *Grace*, b. '47, d. '54; *Susannah*, b. '50, m. Stephen Smith, '66; *Lydia*, b. '51; *Rhoda*, b. '54, m. Samuel Young, '72; *John*, b. '56, m. Martha Death; *Keziah*, b. '59, m. Capt. Wm. Young; *Eunice*, b. '62, m. Abner Sawyer; *Grace*, b. '66, d. '77; *Lydia*, b. '67, d. young. Susannah the m. d. Sep. 2, 1777; 9. REBECKAH, b. Mar. 25, (also recorded Ap. 26), '28, d. Jan. 10, '29; 10. DANIEL, b. Feb. 1, '30; 11. JONATHAN, b. May 3, '32, f. at Athol, by w. Hannah of *Lydia*, b. '61; *Hannah*, b. '62; *Lois*, b. 64; *Jonathan*, b. '67, d. '69; *Mary*, b. '69, d. '70; Jona. the

f. d. Dec. 24, '69; 12. SIMON, b. Mar. 5, '34, d. Ap. 14; 13. ELIAS, b. Feb. 19, '35, d. July 2; 14. SIMON, or SIMEON, had at Athol, by w. Ruth, *John*, b. '62; *Moses*, '64; *Bette*, '66; *Ruth*, '68; *Simon*, '70; *Richard*, '72; *Lydia*, '74; *Chloe*, '76; *Artemas*, (changed to *Daniel*), '78; *Moses*, '81; *Susanna*, '83. Mr. Richard, (prob. f. or son), d. at Athol, Aug. 3, 1770.

26. [3]MOSES, s. of Moses (22), m. Hannah Walker, Nov. 9, 1721, and with w. adm. to the ch., June 30, '22, and had, 1. ABIGAIL, b. Jan. 31, 1723-4, d. Dec. 18, '28; 2. ISAAC[27], b. Ap. 15, '26; 3. HANNAH, b. May 20, '28, m. Joseph Metcalf, of Wrentham, Oct. 23, '51, and 2d Isaiah Whiting, and lived in Me.; 4. DAVID[28], b. May 28, '31; 5. JASON, b. Mar. 2, '32-3, H. Coll. '54, ord. over the 1st ch. in Dedham, Feb. 5, '56, m. Catharine Dexter, Oct. 12, '56, and d. May 17, 1803. Various discourses were published by him; among them one at the Art. Election, 1761, and one at the Gen. Election, 1769. He was f. of Judge Samuel Haven, of Dedham; 6. ABIGAIL, b. June 9, '39, m. John Richardson, of Franklin, and d. ab. 1796. Moses the f. lived on the place now of Mr. Abner Haven, was Deacon of the 1st ch.; his w. Hannah d. Feb. 22, 1749, and he m. 2d, Anna Stow, of Grafton, May 23, 1751, who d. Feb. 12, 1778. Deac. Moses d. Mar. 29, 1778, æ. 82. (G. Stones.)

27. [3]ISAAC, s. of Moses (26), m. Ruth Grant, of Sherb., Nov. 24, 1748, and had, 1. LYDIA, b. July 7, '49; 2. RUTH, b. Ap. 16, '51; 3. MOSES, b. Sep. 5, '54, H. Coll., '82, d. Ap. 3, '85; 4. ISAAC, b. May 16, '56. [ISAAC, d. Sep. 19, '58, æ. 8 mos.]; 5. JOSHUA GRANT, b. June 4, '58, m. Fanny Rice, Aug. 6, '81, and d. young. Ruth, w. of Isaac, d. Oct. 20, '59, æ. 28, and he m. 2d, Molly Jones, and had, 6. LUTHER, bap. Nov. 13, '63, m. Sally Coolidge, of Sherb., lived in Milford; 7. JONATHAN, bap. Mar. '67; 8. JOSEPH, and 9. MARY, both bap. July 10, '68, and both prob. d. young; 10. JASON, bap. Feb. 28, '73. Isaac the f. lived where is a cellar hole, near Washakum Pond; was adm. from Mr. Reed's ch., July 8, '70; his w. Ruth adm. to ch. Sep. 12, '56. Isaac d. July 3, '81, æ. 55; his wid. m. again, and had in all four husbands.

28. [3]DAVID, s. of Moses (26), m. Jerusha Whipple, of Grafton, and had 1. HANNAH, b. Ap. 6, '57, m. Nahum Stone, lived in Grafton, and d. Aug. 30, 1803; 2. JACOB, b. May 17, '59, d.

Jan. 12, '60; 3. DAVID, b. Dec. 10, '60, "slain by the enemy near Saratoga, Oct. 8, '77, æ. 17," (G. Stone); 4. JACOB, b. Ap. 25, '63, H. Coll. '85, ord. at Croyden, N. H., June 18, '88, m. —— Arms, and d. recently; 5. ABNER[29], b. Nov. 15, '65; 6. WHIPPLE, b. Dec. 6, '68, m. —— Powers, lived in Croyden, N. H.; 7. RICHARD, b. Nov. 18, '70, prob. m. Sally Bemis, Nov. 25, '92, lived in Bolton, and d. Nov. 1843; 8. MARTIN, b. June 18, '73, m. Miliscent Metcalf Thompson, Aug. 29, '94, lived in N. Ips., and Montreal, d. prob. in Canada. David the f. occupied the farm now of Abner Haven, and owned land formerly leased to John Whitney; was commissioned as a Justice of the Peace, and d. Dec. 17, 1800, æ. 70. His wid. Jerusha d. Oct. 31, 1811, æ. 75. (G. Stones.)

29. [3]ABNER, s. of David (28), m. Prudence Eames, May 1789, and had 1. JERUSHA, b. Ap. 8, '90, m. Ira Temple, lives in Southb.; 2. DAVID, b. Aug. 30, '91, m. Sarah Coolidge; 3. HITTY, b. June 29, '94, m. John Wenzell; 4. WILLARD, b. Jan. 22, '96, m. Miliscent Haven; 5. LUKE, b. Sep. 24, '97, d. Oct. 17, 1803; 6. ABNER, b. May 2, '99, d. Nov. 3, 1803; 7. CHARLES, b. Aug. 7, 1800, d. Sep. 16, '25; 8. LOUISA, b. Dec. 8, '02, m. Elbridge Gale; 9. ABNER, b. Aug. 11, '06, m. wid. Matilda Lord; 10. EMERSON, b. Mar. 4,'08,m. Susanna Bacheldor. Prudence, w. of Abner, d. 1840.

30. [3]DANIEL, s. of Moses (22), m. Mehetabel Haven, Dec. 10, 1730, and had 1. ABIAL, b. July 1, '32, m. James Metcalf, of Wrentham, Jan. 3, '54; 2. MEHETABEL, b. Aug. 8, '34, m. Col. Daniel Whiting, of Dover, (H. Gen.); 3. EBENEZER, b. Ap. 15, '37, went to Canada in the French War, '59; 4. DANIEL, b. July 15, '39, went to Canada, '59; 5. ASA[31], b. May 27, '42; 6. NATHAN, b. May 7, '45.

31. [3]ASA, s. of Dan. (30), m. Eunice Aldis, of Franklin, Dec. 3, 1767 (H. Gen.), and had in Fram., 1. MEHETABEL, b. Sep. 7, '68, m. (H. Gen.), Paul Sawyer, of Boston. The Haven Gen. adds, JOHN ALDIS, b. Ap. 25, '71; EUNICE, b. Mar. 17, '73; POLLY, b. Dec. 15, '76. Asa the f. d. Ap. 1777; his wid. d. Ap. 15, 1792.

32. BENJAMIN, m. Sarah Haven, and had 1. SALLY, b. 1767, m. Amasa Forrester, of Bellingham, Ap., '93; 2. COMFORT, b. 1771,m. Wm. Bates, of Bellingham, Ap. 21, '96, and d. '98; 3.

Mary, b. 1774, m. James Foster, Dec. 13, '97 ; 4. Elisha, b. '77, d. '82 ; 5. Azubah, b. '79, m. Micah Homer, Nov. 15, 1800 ; 6. Elijah, b. '81, m. Susannah Lamb, and d. in Hop., Jan. 22, 1813 ; 7. Patty, b. '84 ; 8. Betsey, b. '86, m. John Badger, Jun., of Nat., and d. 1819. Benjamin the f. d. May, 1823. Sarah, his w. d. May 16, 1816, æ. 70. 33. SARAH, bap. Sep. 18, 1720. Elizabeth, bap. Aug. 18, 1723. Timothy, bap. Nov. 8, 1724. Ebenezer, bap. Oct. 23, 1726. Susanna, m. in Sherb., Simon Mellen, both of Fram., Oct. 11, 1744. Jacob, s. of David and w. Judith, d. Jan. 12, 1760, æ. 7 mo. Anna, w. of Deac. Luther, d. Sep. 23, 1842, æ. 62. Mrs. Abigail, of Hop., m. John Richardson, of Grafton, July 23, 1789.

HAYDEN, JOHN, m. Nabby Tombs, Mar. 1791.

[John and w. Lucy, were of Hop., 1728. Elisha, of Hop., m. Lydia Fairbanks, 1727. John and w. Louisa, of Hop., had *John*, b. 1740.]

HAYNES, DEBORAH, m. Ebenezer Larned, Oct. 14, 1714. [This family are found early on the Sud. Rec.]

HEALY, WILLIAM, and w. Mercy, cov'd in Hop., and s. William, bap. Sep., 1726. W. and M. in Fram., 1729, lived on the Brinley Farm, and had Phebe, b. Jan. 30, 1730-1 ; Oliver, b. Nov. 5, '33 ; Lily, b. Nov. 11, '36 ; Dorkis, b. May 18, '38. [John Headley, (w. Mary), of Sud., f. of *Sarah*, b. 1722 ; *John*, '23. William of Fram., prob. sprung from the Camb. Healeys].

HEATH, ISAAC, and w. Rachel, had in Fram., 1. Isaac, b. July 24, 1705 ; 2. Ebenezer, b. May 31, '07 ; 3. Anna, b. Sep. 16, '09 ; 4. Rachel, b. Mar. 10, '15 ; 5. Thankful, b. July 5, '17 ; 6. Benjamin, b. Ap. 21, '20. [Martha bap. in Fram., May 22, 1720.] Isaac bought, 1710, of Thomas Reed, of Sud., and w. Mary, 17 1-2 ac. in Weathersfield, part of the estate of John Goodrich, dec. Isaac dismissed to ch. in Coventry, May 19, 1723.

1634, came over in the Hopewell, Isaac, æ. 50, harness-maker ; Eliz., 40 ; Eliz., 5 ; Martha, 30. Elder Isaac was of Roxbury, 1656. William, of Roxb., d. 1652, having had two wives, and leaving chil. *Mary* Spere, (by first wife); *Hannah*; *Isaac*; and *Peleg*. Isaac, of Roxb., had *Mary*, bap. 1653; *Isaac*, '55 ; *Elizabeth*; *Abigail*, '60. Isaac, Jun., m. Anna Fisher, 1681, and had *Anna*, b. 1681 ; *Isaac*, b. July 23, 1683.

HEATON, NOAH, s. of Joseph and w. Keziah, b. in Fram., June 10, 1788. The w. of Noah was adm. to the ch., Nov., 1794.

MILLE, dr. of Lt. Noah and Abigail, d. Jan. 5, 1794, æ. 20, (G. stone.) [The Heatons came to Fram., prob. from Wrentham.]

HEMENWAY, alias Hemingway, Hemmenway, Hiningway, and Heneway.

1. RALPH, or Raph, m. in Roxb., Eliz. Hewes, July 5, 1634, and had, 1. MARAH, b. Ap. 24, (also rec., 30), 1635, buried May 4; 2. SAMUEL, b. June, '36; 3. RUTH, b. Sep. 21, '38; 4. JOHN, b. Ap. 27, '41, m. in Dorch., Mary Trescott, Oct. 6, 1665, and had in Roxb., *Thankful*, b. 1668, m. Jacob Parker, '87; *Marie*, b. '70; *Marie*, b. '74; *Elizabeth*, b. '79; *Sarah*, b. and d '87; *John*, b. '90; John (prob. the f.) d. Oct. 4, 1724; 5. JOSHUA, b. Ap. 9, 1643; 6. ELIZABETH, b. May 31, '45, m. —— Holbrook; 7. MARY b. Ap. 7, '47, d. 1653. Ralph the f. took the freeman's oath, Sep. 3, 1634, and was early a member of the Roxb. ch. He d. June, 1678, and his will was proved in Suff. Prob. Elizabeth, his wid. d. Feb., '84-5, æ. 82. [Rox. Rec.]

2. JOSHUA, Jun., of Roxb., had by w. Joanna, (who was adm. to the Roxb. ch, 1669), 1. JOSHUA, b. Sep. 15, 1668; 2. JOANNA, b. Sep. 21, '70, m. Edward Ainsworth, 1687; 3. SAMUEL, b. 1683. Mary, w. of Joshua, Sen. d. May 5, 1703.

3. JOSHUA, prob. s. of Joshua (2), and w. Margaret, were adm. to the Roxb. ch., 1691; and had in Fram., 1. HEPHZEBAH, 2. BEULAH, (twins), b. Oct. 5, 1691; 3. BENONI, b. Ap. 21, (Marlb. Rec. Ap. 22), 1694, d. unm., Feb. 9, 1754. — Inv. of his est., £190 old tenor. Margaret, w. of Joshua, d. May 12, 1694, and he m. 2d, Rebeckah ——; and had 4. JOSHUA⁴, b. Ap. 2, '97; 5. RALPH⁹, b. Oct. 7, '99; 6. HULDAH, b. Sep. 30, 1702, d. May 1, 1707; 7. REBECKAH, d. Ap. 30, 1707; 8. PHINEHAS, b. Ap. 26, '06, H. Coll. '30, taught school in Fram., '30; ord. at Townsend, and m. Mrs. Sarah Stevens, of Marlb., May 8, '39, and his will was proved, Oct. 19, 1760; he left chil. *Eben.*; *Katharine; Sarah; Phinehas; Elizabeth; Samuel*, and *Joshua;* 9. HULDAH, d. Aug. 1, 1709; 10. EBENEZER¹⁴, b. May 31, 1710; 11. JONATHAN¹⁶, b. Aug. 22, 1712. Joshua the f. was an original member of the ch., and chosen Deacon, at its organization. He was Constable, 1700; Selectman, 1702, — in all, 12 years; T. Clerk, 1702, in all 5 yrs. He was chosen Deputy to the Gen. Court, 1712, and 1717, and was school-master, 1706. He removed his ch. relations to Hop., Sep. 19, 1736, after a protracted controversy with the Fram. ch. He lived near the present "Poor Farm," was living Mar., '54, and d. prob. in Fram. [Joshua m. Abigail Morse, July 1, 1718. T. Rec.]

4. JOSHUA, Jun., s. of Joshua (3), m. Abigail Morse, (dr. of Jos. and w. Elizabeth, of Wat.) Jan. 1, 1718-9; and had 1. JOSEPH⁵, b. Nov. 1, 1719; 2. JOSHUA, b. Nov. 28, '21, m. in

Holl. Anne Twitchell, '49, and f. of *Miriam*, b. '49 ; *John*, b. '52 ; *Anne*, '54, d. '59 ; *Joshua*, b. '55, a school-master ; *Hannah*, '58 ; *Anne*, '60 ; *Rhoda*, '62 ; *Joseph*, '64 ; *Lydia*, '66 ; *Asa*, 68 ; *Levi*, 71 ; *Ezra*, '74 ; 3. ABIGAIL, b. Feb. 29, '23-4, m. William Mellens, Nov. 7, '51 ; 4. SYLVANUS[6], b. August 3, '26 ; 5. HEPHZEBAH, b. Aug. 3, '28, m. John Ballard, and d. at Athol, June 3, 1811 ; 6. ISAAC[7], b. July 17, '30 ; 7. JOSIAH, b. Oct. 5, '33, m. in Holl. Zerviah Mellen, 1761, and f. of *Abigail*, b. '61, d. '66 ; *Josiah*, b. '63 ; *Sarah*, '65 ; *Abigail*, '67 ; *Daniel*, '68, (w. Mary) ; *William M.*, '71 ; *Mary*, '73 ; *James*, '74 ; *Eliphalet*, '76 ; *Zerviah*, '77 ; *Elihu*, '79 ; *Josiah*, '80 ; *Zerviah*, 82 ; 8. BENONI, b. Ap. 20, 1736, m. Martha Goddard, and f. at Athol, of *Sophia*, b, 1759 ; *Abigail*, '61 ; *Asa*, '63 ; and *Martha*, bap. June, '65. Joshua the f. and w. were adm. to the ch. Jan. 2, 1726. Abigail w. of Josh. d. May 25, 1739, and he m. 2d, Jemima, dr. of Tho. and Jemima Rutter of Sud., Mar. 12, 1740. Joshua lived near Loring Manson's, and d. (or his f.) Jan. 30, 1754. (T. Rec. and Mid. prob.) His est. was valued at £2754.12.5.

5. JOSEPH, s. of Josh. (4), m. Mary Adams, July 4, 1743, and had 1. JOHN, b. Sep. 16, '43 ; 2. MARY, b. Jan. 29, '45 ; 3. ABIGAIL, b. Ap. 26, '49 ; 4. ELIZABETH, b. May 24, '53. Joseph the f. was a carpenter, and lived at Mr. Seth Herring's.

6. SYLVANUS, s. of Joshua (4), m. Hephzebah Frost, 1749-0 ; and had 1. EUNICE, b. Jan. 9, 1751 ; 2. THOMAS, b. Feb. 18, '53 ; 3. JOSHUA, b. Ap. 28, '55, d. at Sud. Mar. 1817, and f. at Bolton by w. Miliscent, of *Jesse*, b. 1783 ; *Rebeckah ; Susannah;* and *Betsey* ; 4. SARAH, b. Ap. 23, '57 ; 5. LUTHER, b. Nov. 11, '60. Sylvanus was by trade a blacksmith, lived near Saxonville, and moved from town.

7. ISAAC, s. of Joshua (4), m. Elizabeth Haven, Nov. 28, 1754, and with w. cov'd Dec. 4, '57 ; and had 1. SARAH, b. Sep. 13, '55 ; 2. ABIGAIL, b. Sep. 15, '57 ; 3 JAMES, b. Ap. 12, '60 ; 4. ISAAC[8], b. Oct. 24, '62 ; 5. SARAH, b. Mar. 16, '65 ; 6. REBECKAH, b. Mar. 5, '68, m. Ezekiel Kendall, Ap., '88 ; 7. ESTHER, b. Nov. 25, '71. Isaac the f. lived on the place now of Mr. Amasa Kendall. [Mrs. Elizabeth m. Israel Leadbetter, Jan. 19, 1782.]

8. ISAAC, s. of Isaac (7), m. Patty Maynard, Dec. 1785 ; and had 1. PATTY, b. May 2, '87 ; 2. JAMES, bap. July, '88.

9. RALPH, s. of Joshua (3), m. Sarah Haven, Feb. 2, 1727; and cov'd Ap. 7, 1728. Their chil. were 1. RALPH[10], b. Nov. 20, '27; 2. JOHN[12], b. May 22, '30; 3. BENJAMIN[13], b. Oct. 28, '32; 4. MOSES, H. Coll. 1755, taught school at Lancaster, 1757, and 1759, minister of Wells, Me.; D. D. Harv. 1784, and Dartm. 1792; and d. at Wells, " much lamented," Ap. 11, 1811, in the 76th year of his age, and 52d of his ministry;* 5. JONATHAN, m. in Petersham, Martha Wilder, 1773, and f. of *Sally* and *Lydia;* 6. SILAS; 7. SOLOMON, m. Rebeckah Willson, 1776, and lived near the N. W. bounds of Barre. He was a noted singer; 8. SARAH, m. Joseph Nichols; 9. REBECKAH, m. Alpheus Nichols. Ralph, the f. lived on the farm now of Mr. Wm. Hemenway, and was, (he or his son,) Selectman, 1764. He d. in Fram.

10. RALPH, Jun., s. of Ralph (9), m. Lydia Trowbridge, Jan. 7, 1752, and with w. cov'd, July 26, '52, and himself adm. to the ch., July 8, '70. Their chil. were 1. EZRA, bap. July 26, '52, d. young; 2. WILLIAM, bap. Oct. 28, '53, m. Eunice Parmenter, of Sud., Oct. 21, '81; 3. ABIJAH[11], bap. Oct. 19, '55; 4. DAVID, bap. July 23, '58, m. Polly Davis, of Holden, lived in Hop., and d. at Heath, by the fall of a tree upon him; 5. JOHN, bap. Jan. 11, '61, m. Nabby Henchman, of Athol, and d. in Fram., 1826; his wid. d. Feb. 7, 1845, æ. 73; 6. RALPH, bap. May 28, '63, d. young, of dysentery; 7. MEHETABEL, bap. Mar. 9, '66, d. young, of dysentery; 8. LYDIA, bap. July 10, '68, d. unm., of consumption, ab. 1794; 9. RUTH, bap. Oct. 7, '70, d. young; 10. MOLLY, bap. May 4, '77, d. young. Ralph (known, by reason of his power as a humorist, and also of his gravity, as *Deacon* Ralph), d. in Fram., June, 1800. His w. Lydia d. ab. 1785.

11. ABIJAH, s. of Ralph, Jun. (10), m. Lydia Smith, and had 1. RUTHY, b. May 9, 1780, m. Samuel Winch; 2. BETSEY, b. June 22, '83, m. Samuel Royce, of Marlow, N. H., Mar. 1803;

---

*Dr. Hemenway was an eminent divine, of great metaphysical powers, and the author of numerous publications; among which are 'Dissertations concerning the Church — the Gospel Covenant delineated &c. 8vo. Boston, 1792.' 'Remarks on Emmons' Dissertation on the Scriptural qualifications for the Christian Sacraments, &c., 8vo. Boston, 1794.' 'Dissertation on the Divine Institution of Water Baptism, 4to. Portsmouth, about 1801.' A Funeral discourse was delivered on the occasion of his death, by the Rev. Jos. Buckminster, D. D., of Portsmouth. See Alden's Coll., II. 108, for a notice of Dr. Hemenway.

3. ABIJAH, b. Dec. 21, '87, m. Cynthia Dadmun, and a 2d w. ; 4. MARTIN, m. Eliza Dudley. Abijah, the f. d. Jan., 1826; his wid. Lydia d. a few years since.

12. JOHN, s. of Ralph, Sen., (9), m. Bathshebah Stone, and had MITTY, b. ab. 1760, m. William Dunn, June, 1788. John the f. d. of small pox ; his wid. Bath. m. Lt. Ebenezer Hemenway, Jun.

13. BENJAMIN, s. of Ralph, Sen., (9), m. Lucy Stone, of Sud., Sep. 2, 1762, and with w. cov'd Nov. 24, '63. Their chil. were 1. SARAH, b. May 20, 1763, m. Jonas Hunt, of E. Sud., Feb. '88, and lives ; 2. LUCY, b. May 7, '66, m. Gideon Richardson, and d. in Sud. ; 3. PERSIS, b. Ap. 12, '69, m. Luther Richardson, of Sud., June, '90, and d. in Sud. ; 4. BENJAMIN STONE, b. Dec. 14, '71, m. Patience Hunt, of Sud., was f. of *Curtis, Ezekiel, William,* and *George* ; and d. Feb. 24, 1827, æ. 55 ; 5. PATTY, b. June 20, '77, m. Francis Bogle, of Sud., Jan. 29, 1801, (name entered on T. Rec., as Polly). Benj. the f. lived at William Hemenway's, and d. 1800. Lucy, his w., died 1839.

14. EBENEZER, s. of Joshua (3), m. Deborah Eames, Nov. 29, 1750, and was rec'd to the ch. by letter from Southb., Nov. 3, 1771. His chil., b. in Fram., were 1. ANNA, b. Nov. 10, '52, m. Frederick Manson, and d. on a visit at Camb., 1843 ; 2. NATHAN[15], b. Nov. 6, '55. Dr. Ebenezer was a Physician in Fram., and Selectman from 1768, in all 3 years. He lived near Mr. Loring Manson's, and prob. m. 2d, a wid. Adams.

15. NATHAN, s. of Eben. (14), m. Martha Eames, Dec. 3, 1778, and had 1. BETSEY, b. Ap. 10, '79, d. Sep. 4, '80 ; 2. BETSEY, b. Dec. 8, '80, m. —— Philips, lived at Whitestown ; 3. ABEL, b. May 11, '82, m. in N. Y. ; 4. ANNA, b. Mar. 7, '84, m. —— Goodrich, lives at N. Hartford ; 5. NATHAN, b. Nov. 14, '85, m. Martha Bruce, lives in N. Y. Nathan the f. sold to Mr. Loring Manson, and moved to Whitestown, N. Y.

16. JONATHAN, s. of Joshua (3), m. Mary Foster, Ap. 24, 1744, and had 1. JONATHAN, b. Mar. 18, 1744 ; 2. FRANCIS, b. Sep. 6, '46 ; 3. JACOB, b. May 21, '48 ; 4. MARY, b. Aug. 21, '50, m. at Bolton, John Priest, 1774 ; 5. SIMEON, b. Oct. 4, '52, m. at Bolton, Mary, dr. of Rev. Mr. Goss, 1777, and d. in Fram., May 3, 1818, f. of *Francis*, b. '77 ; *Judith*, b. '80 ; and *Sophia*,

b. '87 ; 6. FRANCIS, b. Ap. 10, '55 ; 7. BEULAH, b. Oct. 10, '57.
17. JONATHAN, m. Thankful Haywood, of Sud., Nov. 3, 1763 ; and had in Fram., AMOS SMITH, b. Nov. 5, 1765.
18. ICHABOD, m. in Roxb., Margaret Brown, 1702, and had in Fram., 1. MARGED (Margaret), b. Mar. 20, 1703–4, d. young ; 2. ICHABOD[19], b. Ap. 20, '06 ; 3. ELIZABETH, b. Aug. 21, '10, prob. d. young ; 4. MARGARET, b. Oct. 13, '15, m. John Ball, '34, and had chil. at Hop. ; she m. 2d, Thomas Shaddock, 1757 ; 5. JOHN[20] ; 6. DANIEL[22]. Ichabod the f. settled on a tract near Mr. Joseph Morse's, which at his death was divided by his sons John and Daniel. He was Constable, 1720, and with w. rec'd to the ch., Oct. 10, '25. He was held in esteem as an amiable man. He was of unusually large stature, and robust. Tradition relates that for a time he lived alone, and often on returning home, found food missing. He at one time encountered, on entering his house, a wolf devouring a pot of beans. He seized the animal, dragged him to the wood pile, and cut off his head with an axe.
19. ICHABOD, Jun., s. of Ichabod (18), m. and had by w. —, BETTY, who m. and lived at Hop. ; and prob. other chil. In 1735, his house is referred to as on the Southb. road ; and he was prob. living in Fram., 1753. Tradition states that he moved " up country."
20. JOHN, s. of Ichabod (18), m. Mary Ran, of Fram., (prob. from Reading), Nov. 26, 1751 ; and had, 1. JOHN[21], b. Sep. 3, '52 ; 2. SUSANNAH, b. Sep. 5, '55, d. 1832 ; 3. RHODA, b. Oct. 11, '57, m. Daniel Hemenway. John (called by reason of his size, " great John,") d. in Fram., ab. 1774.
21. JOHN, s. of John (20), m. Deborah Adams, May 2, 1776 ; and had, 1. JOHN, b. Oct. 6, '76, m. Betsey Haven, Feb. 19, 1801 ; 2. PRUDY, b. Aug. 17, '81, m. Capt. Nathan Goddard ; 3. POLLY, b. Aug. 23, '85, m. John Johnson ; 4. JOSIAH, b. Ap. 23, '91, m. Nancy Rand. John the f. lived at Mr. John Johnson's and d. Jan. 21, 1815 ; his wid. d. July 7, 1846, æ. 88.
22. DANIEL, s. of Ichabod (18), m. Margaret Bellows, and with w. cov'd Dec., 1760 ; and had, 1. MARTHA, b. May 13, 1760, m. David Amsden, and lived in Hop. The m. d. and Dan. m. 2d, Thankful Josselyn, and had, 2. DANIEL, b. Nov. 29, '64, m. Rebeckah Newton, of Southb., Feb., '87, and 2d, Rhoda Hemenway, May, '89 ; 3. ELIZABETH, b. June 22, '66, m. Thom-

as Rand, of Westminster, Nov. '88, and 2d, — Keyes, and d. in Princeton; 4. SARAH, b. Jan. 2, '68, m. Silas Amsden, and lived in Conway; 5. SUBMIT, b. Sep. 27, '69, m. Caleb Stacy, Sep., '88; 6. LEVINAH, b. Feb. 10, '71, m. — Webster; 7. ISRAEL, b. Jan. 3, '73, m. Lavoisie Fay, of Southb., lives in W. Boylston; 8. ANNE, b. Mar. 7, '75; 9. NELLY, b. June 5, '79, m. David Johnson, of Southb., Ap. 3, 1800, lives, (1844), near Lake Erie; 10. MOSES, b. Nov. 29, '81, m. Lucretia Warren, of Westb. [Margaret, dr. of Daniel, bap. Jan. 11, 1761. Ch. Rec.] DANIEL the f. lived on the farm formerly of Patten Johnson, was of great stature, and d. Dec. 1, 1815, æ. 83. His 3d w. was Wid. Desire Cloyes, whom he m. Ap. 1789. Desire d. Feb., 1809.

23. EBENEZER, m. Hannah Winch, May 17, 1711; and with w. adm. to the ch., Feb. 19, 1721. Their chil. were, 1. EBENEZER[24], b. Oct. 24, 1712; 2. HANNAH, b. Feb. 14, '14-5, m. Samuel Hemenway, Mar. 24, '35-6, and moved to " the Manor ;" 3. KEZIAH, bap. Aug. 4, '17, m. Jeremiah Pike, Sep. 14, '43; 4. DANIEL, b. Feb. 2, '19, was of Shrewsbury, 1750, and a housewright; had 3 wives, and was f. of *Daniel*, m. Mary Carrol, and d. in Barre, Aug., 1838, æ. 89; *Jacob*, of Barre, 1782, and Bridport, '97; and *Asa*, who lived in Bridport. Daniel the f. lived at Bridport; 5. JACOB, b. Mar. 20, '21-2, m. Mary Rice, of Marlb., Mar. 29, '48, and f. at Worcester, of *John*, d. 1750; *Samuel*, b. '56; *Jonas*, '59; *Ephraim*, '60; *Sally*, '62; and *Molly*, '65; 6. SAMUEL[27], b. Aug. 3, '24; 7. ELIZABETH, b. June 19, '27, m. Benjamin Robins, of Sturbridge, '47. Hannah, w. of Eben., d. Ap. 27, 1737, and he m. 2d, Thamezin Nurse, (who had an adopted son, Eben. Philips), Feb. 23, 1737-8. Thamezin's est. was administered, 1767. Ebenezer was from Dorchester, and by trade a Weaver; he lived on Deac. Ezra's farm. " Oct. 11, 1716, Mr. Hemenway had his leg cut off" — Dorch. Ch. Rec., which, (with the T. Rec.), afford no entries of births or baptisms of this family.

24. EBENEZER, s. of Eben. (23), m. Mary (Eve, of Roxb.— Tradition), and had, 1. MARY, b. Nov. 4, 1734, was blind, and d. unm., ab. 1814; 2. HANNAH, b. Mar. 26, '37, d. Ap. 19; 3. HANNAH, m. Charles Dougherty; 4. EBENEZER[25], b. May 6, '40; 5. ADAM, lived in Shrewsbury; 6. SAMUEL, went into the army; 7. JACOB[26]. EBENEZER, the f., lived on the N. road to Marlb.,

near Lynd's Rocks, (N. side of the road), and d. 1781; his wid. Mary, d. Nov., 1805. He brought up Jeffry Hemenway as a foster-child.

25. EBENEZER, s. of Eben. (24), m. Wid. Bathshebah Hemenway, and with w. adm. to the ch., Dec. 1, 1765. Their chil. were, 1. FANNY, bap. Ap. 13, '66, m. Josiah Warren, May '89, and d. 1843; 2. LEVINAH, bap. Ap. 12, '67, m. Elijah Cloyes, Mar., '90, lives in Shrewsbury; 3. OLIVE, bap. Ap. 9, '69, d. young; 4. JOSIAH, bap. June 30, '71, m. Polly Parkhurst, Feb., '94, and lives in Fram., f. of *Dexter;* *Winsor;* *Adam;* *Willard;* *Josiah;* *Eliza;* *Josiah;* *Fisher;* *John;* and *Ebenezer;* 5. SALLY, b. Ap., '74, m. Abel Eaton, Mar., 1802; 6. ADAM, b. Mar. 15, '77, m. Catharine Patterson, Mar., 1804, Selectman, 11 years, and Rep.; 7. SAMUEL, b. Oct. 1, '78, m. Becky Stone, Aug. 16, 1801 — a physician, d. ab. 1834; 8. BATHSHEBAH, d. young; 9. LUCY, m. Thomas Larrabee. Lt. Ebenezer lived in the N. part of the town, and d. Dec. 11, 1831. His w. Bathsh. d. July 19, 1828, æ. 90.

26. JACOB, s. of Eben. (24), m. Abigail Eaton; and had, (the first 5 chil. bap. Dec., 1781), 1. LUKE, m. Hannah Ellis, of Dedham, lives in Camb.; 2. MOLLY, d. unm.; 3. ASENETH, m. Artemas Patterson, Ap. 12, 1802; 4. LUTHER, m. Finis Patterson, July 10, 1803, lives in Boylston; 5. HANNAH, m. William Patterson, Sep. 12, 1802, and d. 1802; 6. NABBY, bap. Aug., 1785. Jacob, the f., m. 2d, Sybilla Walker, Dec., 1787; and had, 7. EBENEZER, d. young; 8. RUHAMAH, m. Lewis Allen, of Northb.; 9. CYNTHIA, m. — Hawes, of Northb. Jacob., the f., d. Dec. 19, 1822.

27. SAMUEL, s. of Ebenezer (23), m. Hannah Rice, and with w. adm. to the ch., Sep., 1757. Their chil. were 1. ELIAS, b. Dec. 22, 1757, m. Mary Patterson, and d. Oct. 11, 1834, f. at Marlb., N. H., of *Polly,* b. 1781; *Persis,* b. '83, d. '86; *Hannah,* b. '85; *Elias,* b. and d. '88; *Persis,* b. '89; *Elias,* b. '92; *Enoch,* b. '94; 2. EBENEZER, b. May 26, 1760, m. Ruth Gates, June, '86, and f. at Marlb., N. H., of *Luther,* b. 1787; *Asa,* '90; *Martin,* '92; *Ezra,* '94; *Rowena;* and *Fanny;* 3. RICHARD RICE[28], b. Ap. 24, 1762; 4. HANNAH, b. July 28, 1764, m. Tho. Stone, Dec. 7, '90, lives a wid. in Fram.; 5. SAMUEL, m. Elizabeth Lewis, f. at N. Marlb., of *Samuel,* b. 1793, and the f. moved to

Canada, and d. Dec. 30, 1829; 6. EZRA, b. Sep. 13, 1779, m. Sophia Hill, Aug. 2, 1803, who d. Oct. 24, 1841, æ. 58, and E. m. 2d, Persis Winchester, of Ashburnham, and lives, Deac. of the Hollis Evang. Ch. in Fram. Sam., the f. d. June 18, 1806, æ. 82; Hannah his w. d. Feb. 19, 1814.

28. RICHARD RICE, s. of Sam. (27), m. Rebeckah Parmenter, of Sud., and had, 1. DANIEL, b. May 23, 1780, m. Lucy Haven, and 2d, Polly Johnson; 2. ELIAS, b. May 9, '88, m. Ziba Hill, lives in Fram.; 3. REBECKAH, b. Dec. 5, '89, lives unm. in Newton; 4. RICHARD, b. June 7, '91, m. Lucy Law, lives in Marlb.; 5. EUNICE, b. Nov. 16, '94, m. Willard Bellows, of Southb., and 2d, Eben. Leland, of Grafton. Richard, the f. d. June 7, 1800; Wid. Rebeckah m. Jesse Belknap, Nov. 9, 1803.

29. SAMUEL, m. Hannah Hemenway, Mar. 24, 1735-6, and had SAMUEL, b. May 30, 1743. Samuel, the f. moved to "the Manor."

30. JEFFRY, (see 24), m. Susannah Wright, and had, 1. THADDEUS, b. Feb. 22, 1761; 2. SUSANNAH, b. Jan. 15, '68. Jeffry, the f. lived back of Maj. Buckminster's; m. a 2d w. and d. in Worcester.

31. THADDEUS, s. of Jeffry (30), was bap. Oct., 1782, m. Levina Dudley, Jan., 1783, and had, 1. NANCY, b. June 28, '83; 2. FRANCIS, b. Oct. 22, '84; 3. LAVINIA, b. May 29, '87; 4. LAWSON, b. Ap. 29, '89; 5. CHARLES, b. July 9, '91. Thaddeus, the f. was in the Rev. service, and moved to N. Y.

32. JASON, was in Fram, 1764. JOHN, of Royalston, m. Hitty Gleason, of Fram., Feb. 5, 1805. DANIEL, 2d, m. Lucy Haven, June 3, 1802.

SAMUEL and w. Margaret, were of Woodstock, having s. *Isaac*, (æ. ab. 16, 1732), who had Isaac Johnson for guardian, and m. Mercy ——, and d. ab. 1739. Margaret, his m., d. at W., ab. 1743, leaving an only g. daughter, Margaret, a minor; a s. in-law Samuel Hemenway, a br. Isaac Johnson, and a br. in-law, John Holmes. (Worc. Prob.)

HENDERSON. Mrs. H. d. in Fram., Nov., 1814.

HENRY, JAMES, and w. were in Fram., 1722. (T. Rec.) SARAH, was bap. Feb. 3, 1723. JAMES, bap. Aug. 23, '24, (both prob. chil. of James).

On Sud. Rec., JAMES and w. Elizabeth, had *James*, b. Aug. 16, 1724; *Elizabeth*, b. July 8, '26; *Roby*, b. Mar. 7, '28; *John*, b. June 3, '29.

HERRING, SETH, (b. Feb. 5, 1780, and s. of Benj. and w. Miriam, of Dedham), came to Fram., 1795, m. Deborah Bigelow, Aug. 15, 1802, and was f. of JOHN, CHARLES, &c. [JAMES, and w. Mary of Roxb., had Mary, 1634.]

HERSEY, LEVI, (a native of Hingham), came to Fram., not far from 1800, and d. Dec. 24, 1821, æ. 70. Abigail his wid. d. Ap. 3, 1836, æ. 83.

HIGGINS, HANNAH, relict of Capt. Joseph, d. in Fram., Ap. 30, 1816, æ. 80. JOSEPH d. in Fram., Jan. 4, 1824, æ. 57. Eunice, w. of Capt. Robert K., d. Sep. 21, 1822, æ. 41.

HILL, JONATHAN, (who had relatives in or near Billerica), m. Lois Reed, of Sud., was adm. to the ch., May 8, 1768, and had in Fram., 1. JONATHAN, bap. May 8, 1768, d. unm., 1807; 2. EUNICE, bap. Ap. 8, '70, m. Joseph Clark, of Holl., d. ab. 1810; 3. LOIS, bap. Sep. 6, '72, d. in inf.; 4. LOIS, bap. July 11, '74, m. David Heaton, of Prov., and d. Nov., 1821; 5. LOUIS, b. July 3, '74, m. Mary Winch; 6. LYDIA, d. unm., Mar., 1802, æ. ab. 27; 7. ALFRED, m. Persis Jones, Aug. 15, 1802, d. June, 1822, æ. 42; 8. SOPHIA, m. Ezra Hemenway, Aug. 2, 1803, and d. Oct. 24, 1841, æ. 58; 9. ZEBIA, m. Elias Hemenway; 10. CYNTHIA; 11. ALMOND, d. young. Jona. the f. was a Lieut. at White Plains. He lived in N. E. part of Fram., and d. in F. Lois his w. d. ab. 1813.

2. SHADRACK, m. in Southb., Ruth Graves, Oct. 15, 1767, and had in S., 1. CALVIN, b. Sep. 21, 1768; and in Fram., 2. JABEZ, b. Oct. 19, '74; 3. ENOCH, b. Aug. 14, '74. (T. Rec.) Shad. (s. of Jabez, of Southb., who m. Eunice Johnson, 1743, and had *Shadrack*, b. July 23, '44; *Rachel*, b. Sep. 16, '47), sold May 12, 1774, 23 ac. in the S. W. part of Fram., to Col. Micah Stone.

3. AARON, m. Catharine Hall, both of Sud., June 4, 1778, and had (part b. in Fram.), 1. POLLY; 2. SAMUEL, b. Dec., 1779; 3. ABEL, b. July 22, '87; 4. SALLY. Aaron, the f. d. May 4, 1818, æ. 66. Cath. his w. d. 1846, æ. 87.

NATHANIEL and w. Martha, (prob. from Camb.), had in Sud., *Daniel*, b. 1729; *Sarah*, '32. The Hills of Sherb. and Holl., sprung from JOHN (and w. Hannah), of Medf. and Sherb., who had *Abigail*, b. Feb. 1657; *Samuel*, after of Medfield; *John*, Mar. 14, '61; *Maria*, Oct. 28, '62; *Eliezer*, June, '64, (f. of Eleazer, b. Jan., 1688-9; Sarah, '90; Solomon, '91; Nathaniel, '93, m. Elizabeth Phips, '19; Moses, b. 1700, m. Hannah Hill, of Holl., 1729); *Johnson*, b. '66; and *Ebenezer*, (f. of Ebenezer, b. 1692;

David, '94, (both after of Holl.), and others.) John, sen., d. 1718, leaving wid. Elizabeth. A John Hill was a petitioner in Fram., 1746.

HOLBROOK, DANIEL, "his shop raised, 1788."

HOLDEN, BENJAMIN, and w. Abigail (prob. a Holden), had in Fram., 1. Isaac, b. Ap. 12, 1748, m. and lived in Southb. Benj. m. 2d, Sarah Gallot, July 9, '51, who was adm. to the Ch., June '52, and had 2. Benjamin, b. Aug. 29, '52. Benj., the f. came prob. from Stoneham, lived on the Common, became blind, and d. in Fram., ab. 1790.

2. BENJAMIN, Jun., s. of Benj. (1), m. wid. Elizabeth Ballard, and had 1. Catharine, b. Nov. 22, 1778, m. Benj. Holden, of Southb., 1800; 2. Thomas R., b. July 5, '81, m. —— Jones, of Leverett; 3. Nathaniel, b. Dec. 25, '84, m. —— Harding, of Medway; 4. Betsey, b. Nov. 18, '89. Benj., the f. moved to Leverett, Mass.

3. JAMES, of Fram., m. Abigail Arthur, Aug. 25, 1748. Naomi was adm. to the ch., Feb. 29, 1756, and recommended to the Stoneham Ch., 1789.

John, (prob. s. of Justinian, of Charlestown and Camb., b. 1675,) who m. Grace Denison, of Wat., 1699, had in Weston, *John* and *Judith*, and in Sud., *John*, 1715, and in Concord, *Jonas*, 1721, and others. Jonas and w. Abigail, of Sud., had *Abel*, b. 1752; *Levi*, '54; *Jonas*, '56; *Asa*, '62; *Joel*, 68. Richard, of Wat., and w. Martha, had *Justinian*; *John*, b. 1642; *Martha*, b. 1645, m. Thomas Boyden; *Mary*, m. Thomas Williams; *Steeven*, (his est. sett. 1717, then of Groton); *Sarah*, m. Gershom Swan; *Samuel*; *Elizabeth*; and *Thomas*. (See Mid. Deeds, VII. 154, &c). Richard, the f. 1691, of Groton, "aged, infirm, and a widower," conveyed to s. Stephen, his est. in Groton. Martha, his w. d. 1681. Nathaniel was early of the ch. in Dorch.

HOLLAND, SAMUEL, m. in Marlb., Mary Collar, Jan. 9, 1695, and had in Fram., 1. Samuel, b. Feb. 22, '95–6; 2. Mary; 3. Martha, (twins), b. Aug. 16, '97 — Mary m. Supply Weeks, of Marlb., Mar. 10, 1714–5; 4. Hannah, b. Aug. 27, 1704. Samuel was rated in Fram., 1710; and "wid. Holland" is noticed on the T. Rec., 1712.

John and w. Judith, were early members of the Dorch. ch., and had *John*, (oldest son*); *Nathaniel*, bap. 1638, f. at Charlestown, by w. Mary, of Joseph, b. Oct. 24, 1659; *Deliverance*, bap. '41; *Obedience*, bap. '42, m. Benj. Gamline; *Prudence*, bap. '45; *Relief*, bap. '50, m. John Dowse, and rec'd to the Charles'n ch., May 16, 1675. John, the f.'s will, was dated Dec. 16, 1651, he being "bound for Virginia," and was proved, 1652. His wid. m. Goodman Kinwright. Nathaniel, (prob. s. of John), had by w. Sary, at Wat., *Sary*, b. 1662; *Ruth*, '65; *Nathaniel*, '68; *John*, Ap. 7, '74;

---

* A John d. 1664; his inventory, £3325.17.

Elizabeth, '76; *Mary,* '78. JOHN, m. Elizabeth Park, and had at Newton, *John,* 1699; *Joseph,* 1702, d. '28; *John,* b. '04, m. Elizabeth Angier, '26 ; *Elizabeth,* (m. at Marlb., Isaac Temple, 1725); *Jonas,* b. May 12, 1711, d. 1769, in Marlb., (m. Sarah Banister, 1733, and 2d, Bathshebah Ivory, and f. of Jonas, Ivory, Esther, Park, Luther, Jonas, and Vashti); *Ephraim,* b. 1714; *Sarah,* '16; *Ruth ;* and at Marlb., *Samuel,* b. '21; *Abigail.* CHRISTOPHER and w. Ann, had chil. in Boston, from 1647.

HOLOWAY, DAVID, moved into Fram. from Marlb., m. Lois Walker, Nov., 1787, lived near No. 8, S. House, and was f. of a son and several daughters. He was crushed in excavating a well, and seriously injured.

HOOD, JOHN, a fence viewer, 1712, was dismissed to found a ch. in Hop., Aug. 30, 1724, and was prob. the Capt. Hood, buried at Hop., Aug. 22, 1725. (Swift's Journal). ELIZABETH, m. Josiah Rice, May 6, 1728. [Elizabeth the w. of Thomas Mellen, of Hop., m. ab. 1734, is said to have been a Hood.]

RICHARD, sen., d. at Lynn, 1695 ; f. (by w. Mary), of *John,* b. 1664 ; *Hannah,* '65 ; *Ann,* '72; *Joseph,* '74; *Benjamin,* '77. JOHN and w. Sarah, of Lynn, had *Barbery,* 1694 ; *Hulde,* '97; *Benjamin,* 1700 ; and *Lydia.*

HOPKINS, HANNAH, w. of Capt. Solomon, d. Feb. 19, 1823, æ. 55. Her husb. d. ab. 1835, at an advanced age.

HORN, SUBMIT, m. Moses Haven, Sep. 17, 1794.

ROBERT, Jun., m. in Southb., Thankful Moore, Nov. 1, 1749, and was f. of *Elizabeth,* b. Aug. 28, 1750, m. Moses Newton, '72 ; *Samuel,* b. '53 ; *Robert,* b. '54 ; *Catharine,* b. '57, m. Jedidiah Parker, and d. 1823. Robert was s. of Robert, of Marlb, who m. Elizabeth Maynard, 1723, and had, Robert, b. Aug. 6, 1726. Robert, sen., d. in Southb., in 1760, or '63 ; his wid. Elizabeth d. 1766. JOHN, was early of Salem, and took the freeman's oath, May 18, 1631.

HOUGHTON, ELIJAH, b. in Fram., July 20, 1738. CYRUS, and w. Experience, of Fallam, N. Y., were adm. to the ch., Feb. 14, 1773. EUNICE and ACHSAH, daughters of ——, bap. July 6, 1777.

2. JOHN, m. Susannah Dench, (dr. of Roger, of Waltham), and had 1. EUNICE, b. Feb. 14, 1793 ; 2. SUKEY, b. Oct. 24, '94 ; 3. EMILY, b. Aug. 11, '96 ; 4. EVILINA, b. Sep. 11, '98, (the last 3 b. in Fram.) John the f. built the Centre Hotel, and is probably referred to in Deac. Buckminster's Journal. "Mr. H. raised his house, May 5, 1796." He was a blacksmith, and moved to Providence.

HOW, or HOWE,* JOHN, of Sud. and Marlb., had by w. Mary, 1.

---

* Of the How families of Sud. and Marlb., there appear in those towns, three progenitors, whose families are given in this sketch, — viz. JOHN, DANIEL, and ABRAHAM.

John, b. Aug. 24, 1640, m. Elizabeth ——, 1662, was killed by the Indians, Ap. 20, 1675, (Marlb. Rec.), and f. of *John,* b. 1671, and *Elizabeth,* b. '75 ; 2. Samuel, b. Oct. 20, 1642 ; 3. Sarah, b. Sep. 25, '44, m. —— Ward ; 4. Mary, b. Jan. 18, '46, d. young ; 5. Isaac, b. Aug. 8, '48, m. Frances Woods, 1671, and f. of *Elizabeth,* b. '73 ; *Sarah,* '75 ; *Mary,* '77 ; *John,* '80 ; *John,* '82, (f., by w. Deliverance, of Jesseniah, Matthias, Isaac, [Benjamin, Paul, (of Paxton), Francis, (of Rutland,) &c. ; *Bethiah,* '84, m. Benjamin Garfield ; *Hannah,* '88, m. John Amsden ; *Thankful,* '91 ; Isaac the f. d. 1724, leaving wid. Susanna ; 6. Josiah, m. Mary Haynes, 1671, and had *Mary,* b. '72 ; *Mary,* '74, both d. young ; *Josiah,* '78, m. Sarah Bigelow ; *Daniel,* '81 ; *Ruth,* '84, m. —— Bowker ; *Dorothy,* m. John Prescott. Josiah, the f.'s est., was settled 1711. His wid. m. —— Prescott ; 7. Mary, b. Jan. 18, '54, m. John Wetherby, 1672 ; 8. Thomas, (æ. ab. 35, 1689 — Rev. justified, Dep. Sheriff and Justice of the Peace in Marlb., f. hy w. Sarah, in Marlb., of *James,* b. 1685, m. Margaret Gates ; *Jonathan,* '87, (w. Lydia, and f. of Timothy, Bezaleel, Charles, Eliakim, &c.) ; *Prudence ; Tabitha ; Thomas,* b. '92 ; *Sarah,* '97 ; 9. Daniel, b. Jan. 3, '58 ; 10. Alexander, b. and d. 1661 ; 11. Daniel, b. 1661, not in the will ; 12. Eliezer, b. 1662, m. Hannah How, 1684, and f. at Marlb., of *Martha,* b. '86 ; *Deborah,* '88 ; *Eleazer,* and *Hannah,* b. '92 ; *Gershom,* b. '94, (w. Hannah, f. of Moses, Silas, &c.) ; *Ephraim,* '99, m. Elizabeth Rice, 1722, and d. 1764, and f. of Stephen, Azadiah, &c. ; and *Eliezer,* b. 1707, m..in Fram., Hepzebah Barrett, Jan. 26, 1731–2, f. of Lemuel, Jonas, Levi, Ebenezer, Luther, &c. John, the f. took the freeman's oath, May 13, 1640 ; was an early prop. of Sud. ; Selectman and Marshall, 1642. In 1655, he was appointed by the pastor and selectmen, " to see to the restraining of youth," during public worship. He was petitioner for Marlb., 1656, and a prop. of that town, and lived near the Indian planting field, conciliating, by his great prudence and kindness, his savage neighbors. Sep. 24, 1661, he was licensed to keep a house of entertainment. (Co. Rec. I. 194.) His will was proved June 19, 1689. His wid. Mary d. ab. March, 1698–9.*

2. Daniel,† of Marlb., m. Elizabeth Kerley, 1686, and had 1. Martha, b. 1687, m. Nahum Ward ; 2. Hezekiah, '90, (w. Elizabeth, f. of *Daniel,* and *Abigail*) ; 3. Daniel, b. '92 ; 4. Jonathan, b. '95, (m. Sarah Hapgood, and f. of *Solomon,* b. 1718, m. Mary Howe ; *Elizabeth,* '20, m. Paul How, of Paxton ; *Sarah,* '21, d. young ; *Abigail,* '23, d. young ; *Damaris,* '25, m.

---

* Mr. Allen, in his valuable Hist. of Northborough, (Worc. Mag. II. 130,) gives an interesting notice of John ; and states that " according to a tradition handed down in the family," he was son of a How, of Wat., supposed to be John How, Esq., who came from Warwickshire, in Eng., and who was son of John How, of Hodinhull, and connected with the family of Lord Charles How, Earl of Lancaster, in the reign of Charles 1. Of this tradition, the author of this history has yet failed of discovering confirmation in the Records of Wat. Elder Edward d. at Wat. ab. 1644, and in his will names no sons. Edward came over in the Truelove, in 1634, æ. 60, with Elizabeth æ. 50 ; Jermie, æ. 21 ; Sarah, æ. 12 ; Ephraim, æ. 9 ; Isaac, æ. 7 ; William, æ. 6. This last Edward was prob. of Lynn.

† A descendant from Daniel, (Mrs. Sarah How, of Petersham), of advanced age and approved intelligence, informs the author, that Daniel was of a different family from John ; that he was a clothier, from Devonshire, in England, and brought a brass kettle, long preserved. We give the tradition as we received it, adding, that the author was unable, after much endeavor, to detect in her excellent memory any proof of connection between the descendants of Daniel and John, Sen. A Daniel How, (not the same), came over in the John and Sarah, Nov. 6, 1651. (Boston Records.)

Stephen Gates, of Rutland; *Sylvanus*, b. '27, m. Mary Rice, d. at Petersham, 1802, (f. of Sarah, Stephen, George, Sylvanus, Mary, Washington, and David); *Miliscent*, '29, m. Alpheus Woods; *Ichabod*, '31, went to Me.; *Abigail*, b. '33, m. —— Fox; *Isaac*, '35, of New Ipswich; 5. ELIZABETH, b. 1697, m. Benjamin Bayley; 6. DAVID, b. 1700, lived in Westb.; 7. ZERUIAH, b. 1702. Wid. Elizabeth's acc't of admin. was rendered, 1718, and Daniel's est. was settled, Jan. 12, '21-2.

3. SAMUEL, s. of John (1), m. Martha Bent, 1663, and had in Sud., 1. JOHN, b. July 24, 1664; 2. MARY, b. 1665; 3. LYDIA; 4. SAMUEL, b. 1668; 5. MARTHA, b. 1669, m. Tho. Walker, '87; 6. DANIEL, b. 1672, d. 1680; 7. DAVID, b. Nov. 2, '74, m. Hepsebah Death, 1700, kept the "How Tavern," at Marlb., "when there were but two houses between the tavern and Worcester," and was f. of *Thankful*, b. 1703, m. Peter How, of Hop., '23; *Hepsebah*, b. '06, m. Cyprian Keyes, '29; *Israel*, b. '12, d. in Rutland, 1747; *Eliphalet*, b. '10, lived in Rutland; *Ruth*. '15, m. Hezekiah Stone; *David*, '17, m. Abigail Hubbard, (and f. of Bulkley, Persis, Peter, Abigail, Joseph, Israel, Alice, and David); and *Ezekiel*, b. 1720, d. Oct. 15, 1796, m. Bathsheba Stone, '44, and wid. Sarah Ruggles, who d. 1812, æ. 52, and f. of Ruth, Ann, Hephzebah, Bathshebah, Molly, Ezekiel, Olive, Eliphalet, Adams, and Jane. [An assignment was made, 1714, by the chil. of Samuel, of Sud., and his wid. Sarah. The chil. named were, *John, David, Elisha, Nehemiah, Samuel, Mary, Martha, Hannah, Ebenezer, Micajah, Daniel,* and *Moses*. Moses, (b. Aug. 27, 1695), d. in Rutland, Feb. 16, 1749-0.] Samuel, of Sud., built the "New Bridge," at the N.E. corner of Fram., ab. 1674.

4. JOHN, s. of Sam. (3), m. Elizabeth Woolson, Nov. 3, 1686, and had in Fram., 1. SARAH, b. Dec. 24, 1686, m. Isaac Larned, Nov. 19, 1706; 2. JOHN, b. Aug. 5, 1690, d. in Fram., Jan. 28, 1711-2; 3. ELIZABETH, b. July 24, 1702; 4. MARTHA, b. Mar. 15, 1704-5; 5. PHINEHAS, b. Oct. 10, 1707; 6. EXPERIENCE, d. Feb. 3, 1711-2. Elizabeth, w. of John, d. Dec. 5, 1711, and he m. 2d, Hannah Haven, July 1, 1712. Feb., 1713-4, the name of his w. is given as Sarah. John lived first near Saxonville, and after at the S. part of Fram., near No. 2 School House. He erected a mill on Hop. River; was Assessor, 1700, in all 2 years; Constable, 1702; Selectman, 6 years; T. Clerk, 3 y.; and T. Treasurer, 2 y. He was prob. of Hop., in 1720.

5. SAMUEL, Jun., m. in Wat., Ruth Death, Nov. 23, 1715, and with w. adm. to the ch. in Fram., Feb. 2, 1724; and had in Fram., 1. RUTH, b. Sep. 30, '16, m. James Stone, Feb. 14, '38-9; 2. SAMUEL, b. July 5, '19, moved to Genesee, N. Y.; 3. HEZEKIAH[6], b. June 12, '21; 4. JOSEPH[9], b. Mar. 6, '23-4; 5. ABNER[11], b. Ap. 19, '27. Samuel was clerk of the market from 1709, many years; G. Juryman, 1710; Constable, 1711; and Selectman, 4 y. [Joseph, s. of Samuel and Martha, d. in Fram., Oct. 13, 1723. Samuel m. Elizabeth Sever, both of Fram., Jan. 25, 1738-9. Martha was adm. to the ch., July, 1720. Samuel, of Sud.,

bought of Col. Buckminster, 1706, 100 acres near Joshua Hemenway. Samuel d. in Fram., 1747. Inventory (£570), dated Mar. 30.]

6. HEZEKIAH, s. of Sam. (5), m. Jane Jennison, of Sud., Oct. 31, 1746, and had 1. LUCY, bap. July 19, '47, m. Micah Drury; 2. PARLEY[7], bap. Sep. 24, '49; 3. EUNICE, bap. Oct. 27, '51, prob. d. young; 4. FRANCIS[8], bap. Mar. 31, '54; 5. BEULAH, b. Ap. 16, '58, m. Daniel Campbell, Sep. 20, '80. Hezek., the f. adm. to the ch., July 5, 1747, lived near Mr. Charles Clark's, and d. ab. 1787. His wid. survived him a few years.

7. PARLEY, s. of Hezek. (6), m. Anna Hill, of Medway, and had 1. SETH, b. Sep. 8, 1774, d. young; 2. POLLY, d. æ. 18; 3. BETSEY, d. young; 4. ELIAS, m. Sally Perry, of Nat.; 5. NOAH, m. Betsey McComac; 6. WILLARD, d. unm.; 7. CALINTHA, (Clynshia, T. Rec.), m. John Fisk, Jun., of Sherb., Mar. 7, 1805; 8. AMASA, m. Mary Tombs; 9. LOWLY, m. in Me.; 10. PARLEY, m. Aseneth Perry, of Nat.; 11. SAMUEL, m. —— Wood; 12. LUKE, d. young. Parley, the f. d. in Fram., about 1819. His wid. moved E. with her dr. Calintha, and d. there.

8. FRANCIS, s. of Hezek. (6), m. Sarah Haven, May 7, 1781, and had 1. EDWARD, b. Dec. 25, '82, m. Lois Desper; 2. MICAJAH, b. Mar. 29, '85, lives unm.; 3. FRANCIS, b. Sep. 26, '87, m. Lucy Gay, and is a physician at Dedham; 4. GEORGE, b. Oct. 2, '90, m. Keziah Wait, of Nat., and d. Ap. 21, 1822; 5. MARTIN, b. Feb. 13, '93, d. unm., Mar. 1819; 6. ELIJAH, b. Nov. 1, '95, unm.; 7. RODNEY, b. Aug. 3, '98, d. June 29, 1800. Francis, the f., a shoemaker, was drowned, Aug. 1809. Sarah, his w. d. June 17, 1830, æ. 69 y., 9 m.

9. JOSEPH, s. of Sam. (5), m. Sarah Stone, Nov. 1, 1750, with w. cov'd Feb. 2, '52, and had 1. PRUDENCE, bap. July 12, '52; 2. JOSEPH[10], b. Ap. 8, '54; 3. SARAH, b. Feb. 25, '56; 4. SAMPSON, b. Jan. 12, '58; 5. MIRIAM, b. Feb. 27, '60; 6. NAHUM, b. Mar. 14, '62; 7. DANIEL, b. June 1, '64; 8. MARY, b. Oct. 21, '66; 9. NATHAN, b. Aug. 10, '70; 10. SAMUEL, b. Oct. 19, '73. Joseph and w. were recommended to the ch. in Stow, 1775.

10. JOSEPH, s. of Jos. (9), m. Huldah Stacy, June 15, 1780, was with w. adm to the ch., Dec., '85, and had 1. OLIVE, b. Ap. 1, 1781; 2. SALLY, b. Sep. 25, '82; 3. SAMUEL, b. July 11, '84;

4. Joseph, bap. May, '86. Jos. and w. were recommended to the ch. in Boxboro,' March, 1787.

11. ABNER, s. of Sam. (5), was adm. to the ch., Dec. 10, 1749, m. Hephzebah How, in Hop. 1766, who was rec'd to the ch., 1769. They had in Fram., 1. Billy, bap. Oct. 25, 1767; 2. Peter, bap. Mar. 25, '70, m. in Vt.; 3. Nancy, m. Joel Rice. The f. Abner d. in Fram., and his family moved from the town.

12. ISAAC, m. in Fram., Lydia Jackson, June 26, 1712; and had 1. Jeremiah, b. May 26, '18; 2. Lydia, b. Nov. 18, '21, m. Japhet Perry, June 26, '39; 3. Elizabeth, b. Ap. 14, '23, unm., blind from æ. 18, lived to be ab. 90, and d. in Fram.; 4. Abigail, b. Jan. 28, '25; 5. Isaac,[13] b. Sep. 20, '28, (bap. Nov. 17, '27); 6. Sarah, b. Jan. 28, '30. Isaac, prob. the same, m. wid. Elizabeth Edgell, Oct. 6, 1739; and had 7. Mary, m. Jonas Clark; 8. Joseph, bap. May 3, '47, d. at Holden, unm.; 9. Abraham, m. Anne Edmunds, Dec., '85. Isaac, the f. lived not far from Deac. Jona. Greenwood's; was adm. by letter from Woburn ch., Oct. 16, 1720, and tradition supposes him to have originated at Roxb. He was esteemed as a pious and worthy man, and d. ab. 1752.*

13. ISAAC, s. of Isaac (12), m. Rebeckah Edgell, Aug. 15, 1749, and with w. cov'd Ap. 22, '50. They had 1. Asa[14], bap. Ap. 29, '50; 2. Lydia, bap. Ap. 14, '54, m. —— Buttrick; 3. Simeon, bap. Sep. 12, '56, m. Sally Rice, of Boylston, moved to Vt.; 4. Isaac, bap. Feb. 18, '59, was in the Rev. service, m. Lois Dadmun, June, 1785, and d. 1843, in Holl.; 5. Sarah, b. Dec. 3, 1761, the mother then a wid.

14. ASA, s. of Isaac (13), m. Elizabeth Bettes, of Sud.; and had, 1. Catharine; 2. Mehetabel, bap. Sep. 25, 1768; 3. William, bap. Dec. 1, '70; 4. Asa, bap. Aug. 22, '73. Asa, the f. moved to Holden, ab. 1784.

---

* Alden, in his Coll., III. 39, preserves the following memorandum from the Ms. Journal of Rev. Israel Loring, of Sudb. "Mr. Isaac How, of Fram., departed this life, (ab. 1752,) a man not flowing with wealth. In his house were to be seen no curious beaufet, set out with plates and China ware; no papered, nor painted, nor gilded rooms; no costly dishes; none of these nor such like things there. No! but on the contrary, marks of poverty were there to be seen. However, in this man's house dwelt one of the excellent of the earth, one rich in faith, and an heir of the kingdom, which, with me who was well acquainted with him, there is no doubt he is now in possession of. By his death I have lost a precious, pious, praying friend; but my loss is doubtless his gain; and in that it becomes me to rejoice."

15. DANIEL, and w. Elizabeth, had in Fram., MARY, b. Dec. 9, 1726; DANIEL, b. Mar. 20, 1729-0. [Daniel, of Sud., prob. s. of Sam. (3), m. Elizabeth Johnson, Dec. 17, 1716, and had in Sud., ELIZABETH, b. Sep. 25, 1717, and the same prob. who m. in Fram. Samuel Gleason, Jan. 6, 1735-6; WILLIAM, b. Feb. 11, 1719-0; and JOSEPH, b. May 5, 1723.]
16. JOHN, and w. Mary, had in Fram., 1. REBECKAH, b. Nov. 6, 1742; 2. ELISHA, b. Nov. 6, 1744; 3. SARAH, b. Dec., 1747; 4. JOHN, b. Aug. 27, '52. [John and w. Mary of Sud., had MARY, b. Aug. 21, 1749. Elisha, s. of Samuel (3), had by w. Hannah, a s. John, b. Nov. 29, 1719. John, of Fram. m. Elizabeth Tombs, of Hop., Dec. 10, 1763.]
17. PETER, prob. s. of Samuel, (3), was rated in Fram., 1719. [Peter of Hop., who m. Thankful How of Sud., 1723, had in Hop., *Peter*, '24; *Thankful*, '26; *Lois*, 29; *Jotham*, '33; *Hephzebah*, '41; *David*, '44; *Nehemiah*, '48.]
18. ABRAHAM, m. Elizabeth Perry, June 16, 1749 and with w. adm. to the ch. Feb, 23, 1752, had MERCY, bap. Ap. 5, 1752.
19. EZEKIEL, (b. May 19, 1756, s. of Col. Ezekiel, of Sud.— see No. 3), m. Sally Reed, of Sud., Oct. 15, 1780; and had, 1. SALLY, m. John Trowbridge, of Camb., Mar., 1804; 2. NANCY, m. Lawson Buckminster, Jun.; 3. SUSANNAH, m. Levi Eaton, May 16, 1805; 4. BATHSHEBAH, m. —— Biscoe, and lives in Grafton; 5. EZEKIEL, m. Electa Holden; 6. JACOB; 7. RELIEF, m. Samuel Warren; 8. CURTIS, d. unm. Sep. 1841. Ezek. the f. m. 2d, Sally, wid. of Nathan Eaton, and both live in Fram., at a venerable age.*
20. ISAAC, m. Hannah Howard, Ap. 27, 1727; (and had in Hop. JOHN, b. Feb. 15, 1730-1, m. Mary Atwood, '54.) TABITHA, m. in Fram., Hezekiah Maynard, both of Marlb., June 11, 1739. MATTHIAS m. in Fram., Elizabeth How, both of Marlb., July 31, 1732. EPHRAIM, of Marlb., m. Hannnah Maynard, of Fram., Nov., 1782. LOVEL, of Marlb., m. Nabby Parker of F., June 8, 1803. NEHEMIAH, of Hop., m. Ruth Eames, of Fram., Nov. 30, 1806. ABNER, m. Anna Edmunds, both of Fram., Sep., 1785. JOSEPH, of Sud., m. Hephzebah Belknap, Sep., 1785. JOSEPH, d. in Fram., 1810. LUCY, dr. of David and w. Abigail,

---

* Mr. Ezekiel d. the past winter.

of Sud., d. on a visit at Mr. Isaac Stone's, Oct. 3, 1784, æ. 15. (G. Stone.)

ABRAHAM, who m. at Wat., Hannah Ward, 1657, had at W., 1. MARY, b. 1659, m. —— Bowker; 2. JOSEPH, b. 1661. Ab., the f. moved to Marlb. and had, 3. HANNAH, b. 1663, m. Eliezer How, '84; 4. ELIZABETH, b. '65, m. Sam. Brigham; 5. DEBORAH, b. '67, m. John Barrett, Jr., '88; 6. REBECKAH, b. '68, m. Peter Rice; 7. ABRAHAM, b. '70, killed by French and Indians, at Lanc., July 31, 1704, leaving w. Mary, and only child, Abigail, b. 1702; 8. SARAH, b. '72, m. Jos. Stratton; 9. ABIGAIL; [DANIEL is named as the first son in Abraham's will, 1694.] Abraham, Sen. d. 1695. (Marlb. Rec.) Hannah, his wid., d. ab. 1718. (Mid. Prob.) JOSEPH, s. of Abraham, m. Dorothy Martin, 1687, and his est. was settled, 1706; he had *Sarah*, b. 1688, m. Jerem. Barstow; *Eunice*, '92, m. Tho. Amsden; *Bethiah*, '95, m. Jos. How; *Joseph*, '97, m. Zerviah How, 1722, d. Feb. 18, 1775, f. by w. Zerviah, of Zerviah, and by w. Ruth, (who d. 1776), of Joseph, (d. 1800), Dorothy, Dinah, Thaddeus, Elizabeth, Samuel, Phinehas, Artemas, and Miriam; *Abraham*, '99, (w. Rachel, and f. of Abraham, Asa, Abner, Adonijah, Eunice, Mary, Persis, and Anna); and *Jedediah*, b. 1701. ABRAHAM, of Roxb. (who d. at Boston, 1676), had *Abraham*; *Isaac*, b. 1639; *Deborah*, 1641; *Israel*, 1644; *Hester*, m. —— Mason; *Elizabeth*; and *Sarah*. WILLIAM, of Concord, (w. Mary,) d. ab. 1676.

JOHN, of Marlb., (prob. g. son of John, Sen. (1), through his s. John), d. 1754, leaving a w. Ruth; he had by w. Rebeckah, *Peter*, b. 1695, (f. by w. Grace, of Ezra, Nehemiah, Eben., Peter, &c.); *John*, b. 1697, d. before 1754, (f. by w. Thankful, of Col. Cyprian, Deac. Asa, Anna, and Patience); *Seth*; *Ebenezer*; and drs. *Sarah*, b. 1699, m. Pelatiah Rice; *Rebeckah*, b. 1703, m. John Biglo; *Mary*, b. '05, prob. d. young; *Hannah*, b. '06, m. Jacob Rice; *Elizabeth*, b. '10, m. Matthias How; *Eunice*, b. '12, m. John Sherman; and *Dorothy*, b. '15, m. Joseph Perry.

HOWARD, HANNAH, cov'd Aug. 22, 1725. SAMUEL, s. of Wid. Hannah, b. Jan. 1, 1724. Wid. Hannah adm. to the ch., Oct. 17, 1725. COMFORT, bap. June 19, 1726. HANNAH, m. Isaac How, Ap. 27, 1727.

[DANIEL and w. Elizabeth, had in Sud., *Elizabeth*, b. Sept. 25, 1717.]

HUDSON or HUTSON, DANIEL, and w. Joanna, had in Lancaster, 1. DANIEL, b. May 26, 1651, m. in Concord, Mary Maynard, 1674, who d. 1677, leaving a s. *Daniel*, b. Ap. 15, '77, who m. Mary Orcutt, '97, and d. in S. Bridgewater, 1750, æ. 73. (Hist. of Bridg. Mid. Deeds, X. 89.) Daniel, Jr. was of Boston, 1693; 2. MARY, b. Sept. 7, 1653, m. Samuel Waters (of Woburn, in 1700); 3. SARAH, b. Jan. 1, 1656, m. Jacob Waters; 4. ELIZABETH, b. Jan. 11, 1658; 5. JOANNA, b. Jan. 6, 1660; 6. JOHN, b. March 10, '62, (f. of *Joanna* and *Elizabeth*). (This and the next following entered, prob. by mistake, as children of *John* and Joanna); 7. WILLIAM, b. June 12, '64; 8. ABIGAIL, m. James Atherton, 1684; 9. ANN, b. Jan. 1. '68; 10. NATHANIEL, b. May 15, '71, m. Rebeckah Rugg; (two of N.'s chil. killed by the Indians at Lanc., '97); 11. THOMAS, settled, 1697, at Warwick, R. I., a glover by trade. (Mid. Deeds.) Daniel, the f. was perhaps the Daniel who, with John Hudson, came over in the John and Sarah, of London, Nov. 6, 1651.* (Bos. Rec.) Mr. Willard states that he

---

* Judge Mitchell, (Hist. Bridg.), supposes Daniel to have descended from William, of Boston, 1631. We have been unsuccessful in verifying this conjecture, which derives great authority from its source.

was originally of Watertown, and moved to Lancaster, 1664. (Hist. of Lanc.) He was by trade a bricklayer, and in 1670, bought of Simon Willard a houselot known as Gibson's Hill, and other lands in Lanc. In 1673, he was of Camb., having, in 1672, bought of Wm. Clemance, of Camb., his mansion house, and lands in Camb. and Billerica, the grantee to make provision for Wm. and his w. Ann, during their lives. (Mid Deeds). In 1693, Daniel, Jr. reconveyed to his father land in Lanc., originally of John Moore, and in 1673 given to the son by the f., on the former's approaching marriage. Sept. 11, 1697, " Daniel Hudson, his w. and two daughters," were killed by the Indians at Lanc. (Hist. of Lanc.) Daniel's will, dated 1695, was proved in Mid. Prob.

2. NATHANIEL, of Fram., had bap. May 29, 1726, JOHN; WILLIAM; JOANNA. [NATH., of Marlb., m. Joan Banister, Dec. 20, 1725, and had BENONI, b. June 5, 1726, d. young.]

3. WILLIAM, s. of Nath. (2), m. Dorcas Walkup, Mar. 8, 1747, and with w. cov'd Nov. 26, 1752; and had, 1. NATHAN, bap. Ap. 1, 1752, lived in Monson; 2. THOMAS, bap. Ap. 1, 1752; 3. WILLIAM, bap. May 11, '55.

4. WILLIAM, s. of Wm. (3), m. Tabitha Kibbey, of Con., and had, 1. NATHAN, b. Dec. 15, 1786, m. 1st, Anna Newton, 2d, Martha Drury; 2. SAMUEL, m. Lydia Newton; 3. DORCAS, b. Nov. 1, '91, d. June 18, 1819. William, the f., d. 1810; Tabitha, his w. d. 1798.

5. SARAH, of Fram., m. Daniel Newton, of Southb., Dec. 12, 1728.

JOHN and w. Eliz., of Marlb., had *Miriam*, b. 1745; *Moses*, '49; *Aaron*, '50; *Hannah*, '52; *Ebenezer*, '55; *John*, '57. SETH and w. Mary, of Marlb., had *Seth*, b. 1728; *Joseph*, '29; *Mary*, '32; *Susannah*, '35, d. do.; *Enos*, '36; *Sarah*, '39; *Ezra*, '44; *Jerusha*, '48.

THOMAS, of Southb., who d. 1783, æ. 81, had by w. Mary, *Mary*, b. Sep. 17, 1743, m. Capt. Nathan Brigham, '69. SAMUEL, of Southb., m. Dorothy More, 1737, and had *Jesse*, b. Oct. 2, '40, and *Samuel* who m. —— Angier, and 2d, wid. Ball. In Southb., JOANNA, m. Ezekiel Lennard, May, 1732. SARAH, m. David Witt, Nov. 1744. REBECCA, m. John Lyscom, 1755. DARIUS, m. Dinah Goodnow, of Sud., 1762, and was f. in Sud., of *Abel, Darius*, &c.

HUNT, JOHN, had ELIZABETH, bap. Mar., 1799; and CHARLOTTE. He came from Wat., lived at Lawson Rice's, and removed to Boston. The Hunt family is found on Sud. Rec., also in Holl.

INGERSOL, SAMUEL, had a dr. NANCY, bap. Sep., 1782. He was prob. Capt. Samuel, of Salem, who m., May 31, 1781, Eleanor, dr. of the Rev. Matth. Bridge.

INGLES, JAMES, of Fram., m. Martha Bent, in Sud., Dec., 5, 1782.

INGRAHAM, THANKFUL, w. of PAUL, d. in Fram., Mar. 6, 1837, æ. 63.

IVORY, BERSHABE, of Fram., was m. to Jonas Holland, of Marlb., Feb. 1, 1738-9. (Ms. Rec. of J. Jones, Esq.) DEBORAH, of Fram., was m. to Moses Perry, of Sherb., Feb. 17, 1742. (Sherb. Rec.)

THOMAS, of Salem, m. Mary Davis, 1660, and was f. of *Lois*, b. '60; *Tabithacumi*, '63; *Thomas*, '65; *Hannah*, '67; *John*, '69; *Theophilus*, '70; *William*, '74.

JACKSON, SAMUEL, had, by w. Sarah, in F., 1. ISAAC, b. June 22, 1729; 2. SUSANNAH, b. Feb. 15, 1732-3.

2. JONATHAN, m. Martha Frizzel, Mar. 7, 1716-7, and with w. cov'd Nov. 6, 1720. Their chil. were, 1. MARY, b. Dec. 30, 1716; 2. JONATHAN, b. Dec. 10, '18, "drafted for the W. India service," æ. 22, 1740, (State Files); 3. DAVID, b. May 4, '21; 4. MARTHA, b. Feb. 18, '22-3; 5. DANIEL, b. May 1, '25; 6. ABIGAIL, b. May 18, '27; 7. ELIZABETH, b. Aug. 21, '29; 8. LYDIA, b. Nov. 15, '31; 9. JOSHUA, b. July 1, '34; 10. ANNA, b. Dec. 23, '36; 11. SARAH, b. Jan. 5, '38-9. Jona. the f. owned lands near W. Nixon, Esq., of which he sold to Timo. Stearns. His est. (of Fram. at death), was admin'd by Wid. Martha, and Jona., his oldest son, ———.

3. LYDIA, of Fram., m. Isaac How, June 26, 1712. GRINDLEY, of Sud., m. Hephzebah Flagg, of Fram., May 30, 1753.

GRINDLEY and Hep., had in Sud., *Hannah*, 1754; *Joseph*, '55; *Eunice*, '57; and in Hop., *Jonathan*, bap. '64; *Grindley*, '66; *Molly*, '70. DAVID, of Sud. m. Rebeckah Wyman, 1768, and was f. of *Abigail*. JAMES, RICHARD, and PATRICK came over in the John and Sarah, of London, Nov. 6, 1651. JOHN and w. Margaret had chil. at Camb. from 1647, and EDWARD and w. Margaret, from 1649. See Farmer's Reg.

JAHAH, RHODE, m. Abel Benson, in Fram. Sep., 1784.

JAQUES, JOHN, had settled in Fram., before its incorporation, and a cellar hole near the new road to the Rail Way, indicates where he lived. He was unmarried. "Jaques Hill" derived its name from him. He d. in Fram., Sep. 3. 1746.

ELIZABETH m. in Sud., Richard Chamberlain, Mar. 30, 1672. Nath. Tredway, of Wat., in his will, 1689, names his "kinsman," John Jacuas.]

JENNINGS, STEPHEN, m. in Sud., Hannah Stanhope, Jan. 1, 1685-6; and had, 1. EUNICE, b. 1686, m. William Fiske, of Wat., 1708; 2. STEPHEN; 3. HANNAH, b. Mar. 11, 1690; 4.

MARTHA, b. Sep. 18, 1696, m. Samuel Dedman, May 27, 1714; 5. SARAH, b. Sep. 3, '99, adm. to the ch., Mar. 3, 1722. Stephen, the f. settled near Saxonville, and d. in Fram., Sep. 3, 1701. His est. was administered by Wid. Hannah, of Fram., and Joseph Stanhope, of Sud.

2. STEPHEN, s. of Stephen (1), m. Susannah Biglow, June 9, 1715; his w. was adm. to the ch. Mar. 3, '22; he, Feb., '49. Their chil. were 1. STEPHEN, b. Sep. 6, 1716, and d. Jan. 6, 1798, m. Mary Fessenden of Camb., July 5, '37, and f. at Nat. of *Sarah*, b. July 23, '38; *John*, b. June 6, '40; *Jabez*, b. Ap. 9, '42; *Mary*, b. Ap. 7, '44; *Stephen*, b. Mar. 12, '46; *Martha*, b. May 4, '48, m. Sam. Abbot, of Fram.; *Luther*, b. Oct. 26, '50; *Lois*, b. July 10, '52; *Isaac*, b. July 17, '55; *Jonathan*, (at Sud.), Ap. 29, '58; *Molly*, (at Nat.), Nov. 1, '60; 2. DANIEL, b. Feb. 16, 1717–8, m. Elizabeth Cozzens, of Holl., 1739, and f. of *Daniel*; *Martha*, b. '48; *Patience*, '53; *Susannah*, '61; *Abigail*, '63; (others d. young). D., the f., lived after in Walpole; 3. EPHRAIM, b. May 27, 1720, m. Sybilla Rice, 1743, and f. at Nat., of *Samuel*, b. Mar. 7, '43–4; *Isaac*, Feb. 28, '46–7; *Ephraim*, Sep. 6, '49; *Sybil*, Oct. 28, '52; *Olive*, Sep. 6, '56; *Levinah*, Nov. 7, '59; *Eethel*, Aug. 18, '65; 4. SUSANNAH, b. May 9, 1722, m. Bezaleel Rice, Dec. 2, 1742; 5. ABIGAIL, b. Aug. 28, '24, m. Joseph Maynard, May 29, '46; 6. JOSEPH, b. Mar. 7, '26–7. Mr. Stephen d. Oct. 8, 1763; wid. Susannah d. Oct. 24, 1768. (T. Rec.)

3. JOSEPH, s. of Steph. (2), m. Rachel Drury, Jan. 23, 1752, was adm. to the ch., Dec. '52, and his w. Feb. '53. Their chil. were 1. MARTHA, b. Dec. 14, '52, m. Samuel Abbot, 2d, Noah Eaton, and d. 1834; 2. SUSANNAH, b. Ap. 22, '55, m. Nath. Bigelow; 3. JOSEPH, b. Oct. 24, '57; 4. RACHEL, b. Dec. 18, '59, m. Abijah Abbot, and lived in Paxton; 5. URIAH, b. Ap. 26, '62, moved to Whitestown, m. Ruth Cloyes, of Fram., Dec. 1790; 6. DANIEL, b. Sep. 29, '64, m. Bathsheba Carter; 7. HANNAH, b. Oct. 23, '68, m. Buckminster Rice, July, '86, and d. in Wayland. Joseph, the f. lived at Luther Eaton's, and administration was had on his estate, 1788.

4. JOSEPH, s. of Jos. (3), m. Sally Eames, Oct. 30, 1781, with w. cov'd, Dec. '82, and had in Fram., 1. NATHAN; 2. JOSIAH, bap. Feb. 1784, d. a young man; 3. SUKEY, bap. Ap. '86.

Jos. built near Winsor Moulton's, and moved to Whitestown, N. Y., ab. 1784.

5. STEPHEN, prob. s. of Steph. of Nat., and g. son of Steph. (2), m. Mary Carter, and had 1. BETSEY, b. Sep. 9, 1772; 2. STEPHEN, b. July 30, '74; 3. ISAAC, b. Oct. 2, '77; 4. POLLY, b. Feb. 28, '80; 5. SALLY, b. Sep. 15, '82. Stephen the father moved from town.

WILLIAM, of Charlestown, 1629, was killed by the Pequots, 1633. (Sav. Wint., I. 123). Stephen's w. was taken captive by the Indians at Hatfield, 1677, and after recovered, with other captives, from Canada. (Hubb. Hist. N. E., p. 637.) STEPHEN and BENJAMIN were killed, while making hay in a meadow, at Brookfield, July 20, 1710. Johnson (W. W. Prov., p. 193) speaks of Capt. Jennings as leader of the Wat. band, but then (1651) in Eng. The name was prob. mistaken for Jennison.

JENNISON, ROBERT, a prop. of Wat., had 1. ELIZABETH, b. Ap. 12, 1637, by w. Elizabeth, who was buried Oct. 10, 1638, æ. 30. By his w. Grace, he had 2. MICAEL, (dr.) b. 1640, m. —— Warren; 3. SAMUEL, b. 1642. Robert's will, (in which he names his br. William, and s. in-law, Geo. Read), was exhibited, Oct. 7, 1690. Grace, his w. d. 1686.

2. SAMUEL, s. of Rob. (1), m. Judith Macombe, 1666, and had 1. JUDITH, b. Aug. 13, 1667, m. James Barnard, of Wat., ab. 1697; 2. MERCY, b. Jan. 23, '69; 3. RACHEL, b. Oct. 8, '71, m. Timo. Barron, '99; 4. MERCY, b. Feb. 28, '71-2; 5. SAMUEL, m. Mary Stearns, 1700, (and f. of *Mary*, b. 1700, m. —— Gerrish; *Hannah*, '02, m. Jona. Stone, '24, and 2d, John Goddard; *Samuel*, '04; *William*, '07, H. Coll., 1724, minister of Salem;* *Nathaniel*, '09; *John*, '11; *Lydia*, '13; *Martha*, '19; † 6. ELIZABETH, b. 1676; 7. GRACE, '78, m. Wm. Holden; 8. PETER, b. Oct. 1, '81, d. at Sud., Jan. 17, 1723, (admin. to br. William), f. by w. Jane, of *Peter*, b. 1710; *Sarah*, '11; *Israel*, '13; *Robert*, '15, (m. Sybilla Brintnall, and f. at Sud., of Eunice, 1739, m. Isaac Baldwin, '61; and at Nat., of Phinehas, Lot, Nathaniel and Hannah); *Jane*, '17; *Eunice*, '19; *Samuel*, '22, (m. —— Hayward, and d. at Shrewsbury, ab. 1804, and f. of Joseph B., Deborah, John, Samuel, and Levi). Jane, the m., m. 2d, Jos. Brooks, of Concord, 1725; 9. ROBERT, b. July 25, 1684; 10. LYDIA, b. May 18, '88, m. John Train; 11. WILLIAM, of Sud., 1700. In 1699, a deed of partition of the "Bruswicke, or Horsecraft" Farm, in Sud., was executed by Samuel, of Wat., and his s. in-law, Ja's Barnard. Judith, w. of Sam., d. at Wat., 1723.

3. ROBERT, s. of Sam. (2), had by w. Dorothy, at Camb., 1. JOSEPH, b. Dec. 6, 1720; and at Fram., 2. MARY, b. Oct. 16, '22; 3. ELIAS, b. Sep. 23, '24. Dorothy w. of Rob., was adm. to the ch., Aug. 8, 1725. [Elias m. Hannah Twist, both of Sutton, 1748.]

---

* Rev William of Salem, who m. Abigail, dr. of James Lindall, and d. Ap. 1, 1750, was f. of Lt. *Samuel*, who d. at Oxford, 1790, æ. 57, and Dr. *William*, of Mendon and Douglass, who d. at Brookfield, May 8, 1798, æ. 66.

† Family tradition adds the names of *Mercy, Abigail* and *Eunice*.

4. SAMUEL, of Fram., had by w. Ziba, SAMUEL, b. Ap. 17, 1795.

5. PETER, settled in the S. part of Fram., and had JERUSHA, b. ab. 1755, and others. The mother d. while the children were young.

WILLIAM, of Sud., s. of Samuel (2), had by w. Elizabeth, 1. SAMUEL, b. May 10, 1701, H. Coll., 1720, preached as a candidate at Rutland, 1721, school master at Sud., 1722, and d. Oct. 14, 1729; 2. ABIGAIL, b. Dec., 1702, m. David Baldwin; 3. ELIZABETH, b. July 12, '04, m. John Coggin, and d. Jan. 25, 1725; 4. LYDIA, b. April 11, '06, and d. Aug. 3, 1721; 5. MARY, b. Aug. 21, '08, m. Thomas Stearns; 6. MERCY, b. Mar. 9, '09-0, m. William Johnson. Wm., the f. moved to Worc., was judge of C. C. P. 1731, and d. 1743; his est. divided, 1760. Wid. Elizabeth's will was proved, 1767. (Worc. Prob.) Wm. Jennings (Jennison), was Capt. of the Wat. band, and ab. 1652 was in England. (Johnson, p. 193). WILLIAM, of Charlestown, d. ab. Feb. 1713-4, leaving (by w. Sarah), John, Sarah, Elizabeth, and (prob. sons in law) Tho. Farrand, and Benj. Puzenton.

JOES, WILLIAM, of Fram., m. in Sud., Martha How, June, 1796.

JOHNSON, CALEB, and w. Dorothy, had in Fram., 1. MARY, b. Oct. 24, 1709; 2. MARTHA, b. Sep. 2, 1711; 3. ABIGAIL, b. July 21, '14, d. Nov. 13; 4. ABIGAIL, b. Ap. 14, '16; 5. DOROTHY, b. Jan. 10, '23-4. Caleb, the f. owned a third of the Appleton farm, and lived near Saxonville. Dorothy was adm. to the ch., June 8, 1728. Caleb was of Worcester, in 1730.

[The fol. bap. in Fram., (name of the parent not given) — CALEB, bap. Aug. 2, 1719; PETER, bap. July 7, 1723; DANIEL, bap. Aug. 1, 1725; SARAH, bap. Sep. 26, 1725; MICAJAH, bap. Aug. 27, 1727.]

2. NATHANIEL, of Sherb., m. Mary Haven, Nov. 23, 1708; and had 1. JONATHAN, b. Jan. 30, 1710; and in Fram., 2. JOHN, b. Oct. 26, 1714; 3. HANNAH, b. Feb. 21, '16-7; 4. NATHANIEL, b. Oct. 4, '18, d. July 21, '33.

3. JOHN, and w. Mary, had in Fram., 1. CALVIN, b. Oct. 9, 1755; 2. LUTHER, b. Nov. 14, '57.

4. DANIEL, and w. Eunice, had DANIEL, b. Jan. 3, 1787. [Dan. was adm. to the ch., Ap. 24, 1768, and recommended to the ch. in Harvard, Oct. 8, 1768.]

5. AMOS, m. Elizabeth Child, Aug. 1786, and had 1. ANNA, b. (at Southb.), Mar. 3, 1787; 2. BETSEY, b. Sep. 5, '88; 3. PATTEN, b. Sep. 1, '90; 4. AMOS, b. July 9, '92; 5. SUKEY, b. Dec. 23, '94; 6. EMILY, b. Aug. 30, '96; 7. PEDE, (Experience),

b. Oct. 21, '98. Amos lived near Unionville ; his w. d. Aug. 19, 1835, æ. 69. A. d. 1845, æ. 81.

[Amos descended from Lt. Joseph, who d. at Holl., 1745, having *Lydia*, b. 1710 ; *Moses*, b. 1711, m. Sybilla Plimpton, '32, of Dublin, '64 ; *Isaac*, b. 1714, m. Abigail Leland, '37, (f. of Abner, Isaac, Hannah, Abigail, and Reuben, who m. Lydia Johnson, and was f. of Amos, of Fram., b. 1763); *Joseph*, b. 1716, d. 1729; *David*, b. 1719 ; *Elisha*, b. 1720, m. Mary Gay, '41; *David*, b. 1723, m. Sarah Foster, '49 ; *Sarah*, b. 1727 ; and *Joseph*, b. 1731, m. Mercy Cozzens, '55.]

6. JAMES, b. in Fram., July 21, 1722. THANKFUL, m. Ebenezer Gleason, Dec. 9, 1730. STEPHEN, of Fram., was pub. to Elizabeth Jordan, of Southb., 1783. JEMIMA, of Fram., m. Isaiah Knowlton, of Sherb., May 25, 1796. JONATHAN was rated in Fram., 1780.

NATHANIEL, of Medfield, m. Mary Plimpton, 1671. [A N. d. in Marlb., July 24, 1718, æ. 80] SOLOMON, sen., early took the oath of fidelity, at Sud. S., Jr., took the oath of fidelity July 9, 1645, and owned land at Nashaway, '52. Solomon d. July 28, 1690. CALEB, was s. of Solomon and Hannah, of Sud., and b. Oct 31, 1658; his est , (bounded on Cochit. Brook and Pond), was settled 1718; chil., *Caleb, Solomon*, and *Charles;* perhaps others. JONATHAN, sen., of Marlb., blacksmith, (prob. s. of Wm. (w. Elizabeth), of Charlestown, bap. Aug. 14, 1641), d. Ap. 21, 1712, æ. ab. 70, leaving w. Mary, and chil. *William*, b. 1665 ; *Mary*, b. '64, (m. John Mathes); *Jonathan*, b. '67. JOHN, of Sud., m. Deborah Ward, 1657, f. in Marlb., of *John*, b. 1672.

JONAH, a colored man, rated 1765. THOMAS JONAH, m. Anna Oxford, both of Nat., Nov. 25, 1784.

JONES, JOHN, had by w. Mary, 1. JOHN, b. June 11, 1706 ; 2. JOHN, b. July 15, 1709. John, the f. originally settled near Lanham, was Constable in Fram., 1724, and his w. Mary was adm. to the ch., May 17, 1717.

JOHN, Jun., s. of John (1), m. Elizabeth Gibbs, Nov. 16, 1738; and had, 1. SARAH, b. Jan. 16, '38-9, m. Benj. Stow, Southb., and 2d, Deac. Ward, of Charlton ; 2. ELIZABETH, b. Oct. 16, '41, m. Silas Winch, and d. in Fram., ab. 1830 ; 3. MARY, b. Aug. 7, '44, m. Isaiah Fairbanks, d. in Grafton ; 4. SAMUEL, b. Nov. 18, '46 ; 5. JOHN, b. Nov. 10, '51 ; 6. DANIEL, b. Aug. 31, '55. John the f. lived near Mr. Adam Hemenway's and d. 1798. His w. Elizabeth d., 1776.

3. SAMUEL, s. of John (2), m. Anna Gates; and had 1. BETTY, b. Feb. 28, 1776 ; 2. ANNE, b. Nov. 17, '77, d. July 19, '78. Sam. moved to Dublin, N. H.

4. JOHN, s. of John (2), m. Mary Belknap, Ap. 15, 1779 ; and had 1. PERSIS, b. Feb. 29, 1780, m. Alfred Hill, July 27,

1802, and 2d, Abel Eaton ; 2. JOHN B., b. Aug. 3, 1782, m. Mary A. Bond, lives in Roxbury ; 3. GILBERT, b. Ap. 27, '84, d. young ; 4. DAVID, b. Nov. 7, '85, d. Aug. 26, '86 ; 5. ARTEMAS, b. Oct. 26, '87, m. Martha Childs, d. in Fram., Ap. 2, 1825 ; 6. ELISHA, b. Aug. 11, '89, m. Mary Cheney, of Marlb., d. June 19, 1832 ; 7. GILBERT, b. Nov. 21, '93, d. unm. at Memphis, Vt., ab. 1832 ; 8. JARED, b. Aug. 6, '95, d. unm. in Boston, Dec. 14, 1824. Lt. John, the f. lived at Mr. Nathan Hudson's ; was Selectman, 5 years, and d. July 20, 1826, æ. 75. His w. Mary d. July 13, 1798, æ. 36 y. and 9 m. ; and he m. 2d, Margaret Stone, May 9, 1803.

4. DANIEL, s. of John (2), m. Lucy Eames, June, 1782 ; and had 1. NANCY, b. Sep. 22, 1782, m. Josiah Parkhurst, Ap. 2, 1801, and d. Nov. 1842 ; 2. RUTHY, b. Dec. 10, '83, m. Richard Call, of Boston, 1807, and 2d, Thomas Neville ; 3. LUKE, b. Ap. 4, d. 12th, 1785. Lucy, w. of Dan. d. Ap. 11, 1785 ; and he m. 2d, Mary Dunn, May, 1786 ; and had 4. LUCY, b. Feb. 15, '87, m. Jona. Whiting, of Dover, Mass. ; 5. JOSIAH, b. Sep. 12, '88, d. Jan, 6, 1803 ; 6. BETSEY, b. Ap. 28, '90, m. David Childs ; 7. DANIEL, b. Sep. 7, '92, d. unm. Ap. 25, 1827, æ. 34 ; 8. POLLY, b. June 3, '96, m. Timo. Fife, of Troy, N. H. ; 9. ENOCH, b. July 28, '98, d. Feb. 20, 1827, in Va. ; 10. SALLY, b. Mar. 11, 1800 ; 11. PERSIS, b. Mar. 9, 1802, m. Joseph Taylor, of Worcester, lives in Rutland ; 12. ALMIRA, b. Jan. 5, '04, m. John Emory, of Winchendon ; 13. JOHN, b. Mar. 21, 1807, d. Oct. 4, '28. Dan. the f. was adm. to the ch. May, 1784, lived E. from Adam Hemenway's, and d. suddenly, in the M. House of the 1st ch., Feb. 15, 1818, æ. 62. Mary, his wid. d. Feb. 17, 1838, æ. 75.

5. WILLIAM, m. Sarah Gates, Mar. 31, 1748, and with w. cov'd Nov. 27, '48 ; and had 1. KATHARINE, b. Oct. 14, '48 ; 2. ABIGAIL, b. Dec. 19, '49 ; 3. SARAH, b. Aug. 17, '51 ; 4. FRANCES, b. Aug. 17, '53 ; 5. EZRA, b. Sep. 20, '55 ; 6. WILLIAM, b. Dec. 25, '58. The f. prob. moved to Holl., and had, 7. JESSE, 1760.

6. JOHN, and w. Elizabeth, had in Boston, 1. ELIZABETH, m. Isaac Larned of Oxford, Jan. 1, 1736 ; 2. MARY, b. 1714, m. —— Robinson ; and on Fram. Rec., 3. SIMPSON, b. Dec. 3, 1716 ; 4. SARAH, b. July 9, 1718, m. —— Chapman ; 5.

JANE, b. Nov. 29, 1719; 6. ANNE, b. Nov. 15, 1720, m. Abijah Stone, Oct. 20, 1739, and 2d, Tho. Saltmarsh, of Wat., 1769; 7. JOHN, b. Jan. 9, 1720-1, (Rec.; prob. a mistake for '21-2); 8. ANTHONY, b. June 8, 1723, m. —— Alden, and f. of *John*, (d. 1824, æ. 70); *Anthony ; Isaac*, b. 1757, m. Patty Butler, and d. 1818, æ. 61; *Nathaniel Alden ;* and *Elisha ;* 9. HANNAH, bap. Nov. 8, 1724, m. —— Homes; 10. ABIGAIL, bap. Feb. 9, '26, m. Isaac Smith and Jos. Cozzens. John, the f. of F., cordwainer, executed, in 1720, a deed of partition with Anthony Blount, of 200 acres in Fram., and a dwelling house. He was Selectman in Fram., 1723, and after, a leading man of Hop., where he was rec'd from the ch. in Boston, 1727, and held a commission as Justice of the Peace, and was Col. of the 3d Reg. of Mass. He was much employed in the neighboring towns as a surveyor. His w. Elizabeth was sister of Jane, w. of Steven Arnold, of Warwick, R. I., 1730. He was s. in law of Savil Simpson, Esq., of Hop., and an Executor of his will. He d. Feb. 7, 1773, æ. 82, and his will was presented, Mar. 4; his wid. (named Mary), d. æ. ab. 102. Col. John left several negro servants, among whom were James, Tom, and Bacchus.

7. JOHN, Jun., of Hop., s. of John (6), m. Mary Mellen; and had 1. MARY, b. June 19, 1750, m. Maj. Lawson Buckminster, of Fram., May 4, '69; 2. ELIZABETH, b. Jan. 25, '52, m. Sam. Valentine, Dec. 5, '70, and d. 1828; 3. JONATHAN, b. Nov. 24, '53, d. Mar., '57; 4. ABIGAIL, b. Aug. 15, '58, m. Isaac Clark, Dec. 28, '80, and d. in Fram., Mar. 18, 1838; 5. JANE, b. Mar. 31, '61, m. Gilbert Marshall, of Fram., Oct. 7, '82, and d. Oct. 15, 1836; 6. ANNA, m. Dr. Jerem. Stimpson; 7. OLIVE, b. Ap. 28, '64, m. Rev. N. How, Jan. 3, '91; 8. REBECKAH, b. May 10, '67, m. Rev. Pitt Clark, of Norton, Feb. 1, '98, and d. Mar. 2, 1810. Col. John d. Sep. 5, 1797, æ. 75. (Hop. Rec.)

8. NATHANIEL ALDEN, son of Anthony, g. son of John (6), m. in Hop., Lois Claflin, 1770; and had 1. ALDEN, was in the marine service and lived in Roxb.; 2. POLLY, m. Uriah Day, 2d, William Lovering; 3. LOIS, m. Jeduthan Dadmun, Dec. 18, 1800; 4. LUCY, m. John Parkhurst; 5. BETSEY, m. Josiah Smith, of E. Sud., Mar. 26, 1806; 6. HANNAH, m. Warren Morse; 7. GILBERT D. ; 8. ISANNA, m. Phineas Eames, July, 1790; 9. SALLY, m. Otis Parkhurst; 10. SAMUEL. Nath., the f. moved into Fram. with his chil., lived in the Swift house, and d. in Milford, ab. 1820, æ. 70.

9. SARAH, m. in Fram. James Stone, Dec. 25, 1733. ANNE, m. Phinehas Wilson, Oct. 26, 1739. MEHETABEL, m. Wm. Greenwood, Feb. 10, 1789.

The family of Jones are numerous on Boston Rec. MATTHIAS and w. Anne, had *Elizabeth*, b. 1631; *John*, b. Sep. 16, 1638; *Thomas*, June 18, 1643. JOHN and w. Elizabeth, had *John*, b. Nov. 8, 1665; *William*, 1668; *Jotham*. 1672. JOHN and w. Rebeckah, of Charlestown, had *Thomas*, b. 1673; *John*, 1677, &c. Many of the name were among the early emigrants. (See Savage's Gleanings and Farmer). Concord Records bear many of the name. THOMAS, of Sherb., m. Elizabeth Bullard, Ap. 30, 1701, and was f. of *Jonathan*, *Aaron*, of Holl., *Thomas*, &c. Elder JOHN, was of Holl., 1751. JAMES and w. Sarah, of Sud., 1707. NATHANIEL, and w. Mary, 1708. SAMUEL and w Mary, 1709. SAMUEL, (w. Susannah), of Marlb., 1732, was f. of *Jona.*, *Silas*, *Timothy*, *Nathan*, &c.

KAZER, NATHAN, of Fram.; m. in Sud., Bathshebah Alexander, of Fram., July, 1778. [Eliezer Keazer, of Salem, m. Mary Collins, 1679.]

KELLOGG, DAVID, was m. to Sally Bridge, May 27, 1781, by Rev. Joseph Bridge, of E. Sud., and had 1. MARY, b. Feb. 25, 1782, m. Dr. John Ball Kittredge, July 19, 1801, and d. Aug. 20, 1836; 2. SALLY, b. Sep. 28, 1783, m. Dea. Wm. Brown, Jr., of Boston, May 9, 1805; 3. NANCY, b. July 16, 1785; 4. GARDNER, b. Aug. 28, 1788, m. Wid. —— Fairbanks, and d. Ap. 29, 1842; 5. MARTHA, bap. May, 1787; 6. DAVID, bap. Ap., 1791; 7. CHARLES, bap. Ap., 1793. The Rev. David, b. in Hadley, grad. at Dartm. Coll., 1775, S. T. D., Dartm., was ord. over the 1st ch. in Fram., Jan. 10, 1781, and d. Aug. 13, 1843, æ. 87; Sally his w. d. Feb. 14, 1826, æ. 73. [Joseph Kellock, and w. Joanna, had in Boston, *Edward*, b. Oct. 1, 1660.*]

KENDAL or KENDALL, FRANCIS Kendal, alias Miles,† of Wob., m. Mary Tidd, Dec. 24, 1644, and had, 1. JOHN, b. May 2, '46, (w. Eunice); 2. THOMAS. b. Jan. 28, 1648-9; 3. ELIZABETH, b. 1652; 4. REBECKAH, b. Jan. 2, 1657, m. Joshua Eaton; 5. SAMUEL, b. 1659, m. Rebeckah Mixer, of Wat., f. of *Samuel*, b. 1684; *Isaac*, 86; *Joshua*; *Ebenezer*; *Rebeckah*, m. —— Russell; *Ruth*, m. —— Bancroft; *Abigail*, m. —— Nichols; *Tabitha*, m. —— Richardson. Sam. Sen.'s will was proved 1749, "of Lancaster, formerly of Wob." (Worc. Prob.); 6 JACOB, b. 1660, (w. Persis); 7. MARY, m. Israel Read; 8. HANNAH, m. William Green: 9. ABIGAIL, m. —— Read. Francis, the f. took the freeman's oath, May 26, 1647, and was "released from all ordinary traynings," 1657. (Co. Rec. I. 120.) A deposition given by him, an. 1700, represents him as æ. "ab. 4 score years." His will was proved 1707, in which he names a g. daughter, Mary Peirce. Dea. THOMAS, of Wob., was his brother, who had numerous daughters,

---

* Martin and Joseph Kellogg, (brs.) and a sister, were taken captives at Deerfield, 1703. The brothers escaped. Joseph, Esq. became an interpreter, "the best in his day, that New England had." He d. at Schenectady. Capt. Martin was remarkable for his "courage and bodily strength." He d. at Newington, Conn., 1758.

† The tradition of his descendants represents Francis as having emigrated without the knowledge of his family; and his name was altered to avoid discovery.

but no male issue. Rev. Dr. Kendal, of Weston, supposed the name originally Kentdale, and that the f. of Thomas and Francis was John. A John of Camb., 1646, d. at Camb., March 21, 1660–1. See Inventory in Mid. Prob.

2. THOMAS, s. of Francis (1), of Wob., had by w. Ruth, 1. RUTH, b. Feb. 17, 1674; 2. THOMAS,[3] b. May 19, 1677; 3. MARY, b. Feb 27, '80–1; 4. SAMUEL, b. Oct. 29, '82. (f. by w. Eliz., of Rev. *Samuel*, of N. Salem; *James*, (ancestor of J. Kendall, D.D., of Plymouth); *Josiah* and *Ezekiel*, of Sterling; *Timothy* and *Jonas*, of Lancaster; *Jesse* and *Seth*. of Athol, and several daughters. Sam. lived a time at Athol, and d. at Wob. Dec. 13, 1764.) [Sam., of Wob., bought, in 1725, 60 acres of Dan. Stone, of Hop. Samuel, Jr. bought in Hop., 1731.] 5. RALPH, b. May 4, 1685, a tailor, moved to Lancaster; 6. ELIEZER,[9] b. Nov. 16, 1687; 7. JABEZ, 8. JANE, twins, b. Sept. 10, 1692; 9. ——, b. and d. Dec. 16, '95. Thomas m. 2d, Abigail Broughton, 1696, who d. 1716. Thomas d. May 25, 1730.

3. THOMAS, s. of Tho. (2), m. Sarah, dr. of Rev. Tho. Cheever, of Chelsea; lived in Lex., and had, 1. BENJAMIN[4]; 2. MARY, b. 1711; 3. JOSHUA[5], b. Aug. 7, '13; 4. EZEKIEL, b. Nov. 21, '15; 5. ELIZABETH, b. Mar. 4, '17–8; 6. RUTH, b. June 13, '20; 7. JANE, b. Nov. 14, '22; 8. ELIJAH,[6] 9. ELISHA[8], twins, b. Jan. 30, '24–5. Thomas, the f. moved with his family to Fram., and settled to the N. E. of S. House, No. 9. Mrs. Sarah, w. of Thomas, d. in Fram., Mar. 2, 1761, æ. 75.

4. BENJAMIN, s. of Thomas (3), m. Keziah Leland, of Sherb., Jan. 24, 1732–3. He had in Sherb., 1. BENJAMIN, b. and d. 1736. The m. d. March 21, 1736, æ. 23, and Benj. m. 2d. Eunice Leland, of Holl., 1736, and had, 2. KEZIAH, b. Aug. 7, '37, m. Wm. Boden (Bowdoin), June 16, '57; 3. ASENETH, b. 1740, m. Nath'l Holbrook, May 4, '63; 4. LYDIA, b. '42; 5. BENJAMIN, b. March 18, '45, m. Kezia Twitchell, Ap. '68; 6. ASAPH, b. 1747; 7. EUNICE, b. '50; 8. Timo., m. in Fram., Lucy Rice, June, 1785. Benj. the f. d. in Sherb.

5. JOSHUA, s. of Thomas (3), m. Sarah Dewing, of Nat., 1745, and had in Fram., 1. JANE, b. July 17, 1746, m. Reuben Eames, of Holl., and d. Feb. 2, 1837, æ. 91 y., 8 mos. [Lt. JOSHUA, who was of Holl., unm., ab. 1785, and moved to Wardsboro', Vt., and EZEKIEL, were also chil. of Joshua.] Joshua was rated in Fram., 1755, and prob. left town.

6. ELIJAH, s. of Tho. (3), was adm. to the ch., May 8, 1748, and m. Jemima Smith, of Sud., May 24, 1750. Their chil. were 1. MARTHA, b. Ap. 22, 1751, m. Joseph Drury, of Nat.; 2. ELIJAH, b. June 13, '52, d. Feb. 9, '54; 3. ELIJAH, b. June 20, '54, d. unm., July 11, 1820; 4. CHEEVER[7], b. Aug. 5, '56; 5. NATHANIEL, b. Oct. 22, '58, m. Susannah Haynes, of E. Sud. Sus. d. 1832; Nath. d. in Fram., without issue, Aug. 21, 1844. Elijah, the f. d. in Fram., 1776, æ. 52. His wid. Jemima d. ab. 1810.

7. CHEEVER, s. of Elijah (6), m. Dolly Parish, and with w. cov'd, July, 1781. They had, 1. NANCY, bap. July, 1781 ; 2. BETSEY, bap. May, '84 ; 3. SAMUEL P., bap. Sep., '83.

8. ELISHA, s. of Tho. (3), m. Ruth Payson, of Walpole, and had, 1. SAMUEL, H. Coll., 1782, D D., minister of Weston, Mass.; 2. HANNAH, m. Solomon Marshall, of N. Scotia; 3. ABIGAIL, m. —— Holmes, of Weymouth ; 4. PAYSON, d. young; 5. SARAH, m. Daniel Whitman, of N. Scotia; 6. MARY, m. Joseph Bailey, of Nat., 1788, lives a wid. in Fram.; 7. BETSEY, d. young; 8. SUSAN; 9. RUTH, m. Abijah Mann, of Marblehead; 10. ——, d. in infancy. The f., Elisha, had 4 chil. b. in Sherb. He then removed to Annapolis, N. Scotia, and on the breaking out of the Revolutionary War, returned, lived many years in the family of the Rev. Dr. Kendal, of Weston, and d. at the venerable age of 99 years.

9. ELIEZER, s. of Thomas (2), m. Hannah Rowe, of Lexington, and had 1. THOMAS[10], b. 1715 ; 2. JOHN ; 3. ELEAZER[13] ; 4. HANNAH, m. Simeon Stone, Jan. 1745, and d. at Rutland, 1801, æ. 80 ; 5. JONATHAN, b. Jan. 5, 1728–9, m. Frances Crumpton, of Sud., Mar. 14, '50, and lived in Walpole ; 6. RACHEL, b. Mar. 29, '30, m. Uriah Rice ; 7. SAMUEL, b. Nov. 19, '35, d. young. Eliezer, the f. settled in Fram., at the place of Deac. John Kendall, when the neighborhood was covered with forest. His w. Hannah died, 1761. He m. 2d, wid. Sarah Angier, and executed a deed of settlement to his son Thomas, 1767.

10. THOMAS, Jun., s. of Eliezer (9), m. Hannah Rice, Mar. 27, 1751, and with w. cov'd, Dec. 29, '51, and adm. to the ch., Mar. 4, 1764. His chil. were 1. ELIZABETH, b. Jan. 20, 1752 ; 2. MARTHA, b. Nov. 6, '53, m. Joshua Lamb, May 2, 1776, and d. in Philipston ; 3. JOHN[11], b. May 8, '55 ; 4. HANNAH, b. Sep. 9, '56, m. Joseph Belcher, May '82, lived in Fram. ; 5. NATHAN[12], b. Sep. 12, '59. Tho., the f. lived on the farm of Deac. John, and d. 1795, æ. 80. Hannah, his w., d. 1822, æ. 95.

11. JOHN, s. of Tho. (10), m. Mary Greenwood, June, 1782, and had 1. JAMES, b. Ap. 1783, m. Hannah Wright, at Philipston; 2. ABIGAIL, b. 1785, m. John Eames, of Holl., lives in Dover, Vt. ; 3. NELLY, m. Jonas Bennet, lives a wid., at Canandaigua ; 4. MARY, m. Wm. Gallot, lives a wid., in Holl. ; 5. ANN, d. ab. 1812 ; 6. REBECKAH, b. '93 ; 7. MARTHA, b. '95, m. Nathan Wright, of Philipston ; 8. JOHN, b. 1798, m. Levinah Gibbs, Deac. of the 1st ch. ; 9. SUSAN, b. 1801, m. Silas Hemenway, lives in Prov. ; 10. WILLIAM, b. 1804, m. Milly Perkins,

lives in Wrentham. John, the f. d. in Fram., Nov. 16, 1840, æ. 85. His w. Mary d. Jan. 13, 1837, æ. 76.

12. NATHAN, s. of Tho. (10), m. Betsey Richards, Feb. 1784, and with w. adm. to the ch., Sep. 1786, and had 1. BETSEY, d. æ. 19; 2. AMASA, bap. Nov. 1, 1786, m. 1st, Fanny Esty, 2d, Abigail Mayhew; 3. LUTHER, bap. Aug. '90, m. Mary Case, who d. May 24, 1831, æ. 36, and 2d, wid. Mary Rice; 4. SALLY, bap. Mar. '92, m. Alexander Coolidge, of Nat.; 5. NANCY, bap Ap. 1794, m. Henry Traves. His w. d. May 28, 1846, æ. 87. He survives at an advanced age.

13. ELEAZER, Jun., s. of Eliezer (9), m. Mary Brown, of Sud., Ap. 13, 1749, and had 1. MARY, b. Jan. 10, 1750, m. — Weeks; 2. RACHEL, b. Dec. 28, '51, m. Timothy Darling; 3. COMFORT, b. May 3, '53, d. young; 4. ELEAZER, b. Oct., '56; 5. FANNY, b. July 11, '58, d. young; 6. COMFORT, b. July 10, '60. Eleazer, the f., lived near Mr. Hager's, and moved to Rockingham.

14. SAMUEL, (H. Coll., 1731, see No. 2) — was Schoolmaster in Fram., 1732. Miss SARAH, was prob. in Fram., 1749. THOMAS 3d, was adm. to the ch., 1767. ABIGAIL, dr. of Thomas, was bap. Jan. 26, 1752. MARTHA, m. Nehemiah Wright, Jr., of Fram., Dec. 10, 1778. DANIEL, of Harvard, m. Hannah Rider, of Fram., June 1787. EZEKIEL, m. Rebeckah Hemenway, Ap. 1788. Rev. DAVID, H. Coll., 1794, s. of Jesse, of Athol, was Preceptor of Fram. Academy.

JOSHUA, of Sud., (s. of Joshua, of Burlington), m. Mary Rutter, 1770, and was f. of *Joel*, and *Joseph*. Joshua the f. m. 2d, Betty Stone, who now lives, the wid. of Henry Eames. THOMAS and w. Mary, of Hop., had *Abner*, b. 1739; *Jonathan*, b. '43; *Thomas*, b. '45. Mary, the m. d. 1747. JOHN, of Lanc., (his est. divided, 1741), had chil. *John; Mary.* m. Philip Guss, Jr.; and *Experience*, d. ab. 1747. SARAH, of Marlb. m. Reuben Ward, 1771. JOSHUA, of Southb., m. Mary Morse, Feb. 1773. *Daniel*, s. of Joshua, of Charlemont, was bound to Daniel Stone, of Fram., from 1772 to 1777.

KEYES, OLIVER, of Fram., served under Col. Buckminster, 1722. (State Files.)

KITTREDGE, DR. JOHN B., s. of Benj., of Tewkesbury, and b. Oct. 8, 1771, came to Fram., 1791, and m. Polly Kellogg, July 19, 1801. He still lives in the practice of a profession, he has honorably prosecuted for 56 years.

KNEELAND, (or NELAND), BENJAMIN, and w. Abigail,

had in Fram., JOHN, b. June 18, 1710. Benj., the f. moved to Oxford, where he was among the earliest proprietors.

KNOWLTON, DANIEL, m. Abigail Almy, Feb. 17, 1743, and had in Fram., ELIAS, b. ab. 1744, and 10 other chil. in Hop. Daniel, the f. was rated in Fram., ab. 1765. He lived near the S. House, No. 4, and d. ab. 1782, æ. 65.

2. ELIAS, s. of Daniel (1), m. Elizabeth Jennings, of Holl., and had 1. REBECKAH, b. Oct. 3, 1765, m. Daniel Morse, of Fram., June 29, '90, and went to Holland purchase. D. d. in Holl., 1843; Rebeckah d. in Fram., 1840; 2. ELISHA, b. June 5, 1767, m. —— Chamberlin, of Dublin, and d. there a few years since; 3. DANIEL, m. —— Blake, of Holden; 4. LUTHER, m. Prudence Dadmun, Dec. 28, 1800; 5. JESSE; 6. ELIZABETH, d. unm.; 7. GILBERT, moved E. Elias, the f. lived near the South Burial Ground, and d. in Holl., ab. 1787.

3. ISAIAH, (s. of Jona. of Holl.), m. Jemima Johnson, of Fram., May 25, 1796, and had 1. ISAIAH, b. July 20, '97; 2. LEONARD K., b. 1799, d. young; 3. WILLIAM, b. Dec. 1800. The f. moved E.

4. JONATHAN, and w. Rebeckah, came to Fram., from Holliston, May 27, 1773. (T. Rec.) ANNA, (dr. of Daniel), m. Philip Metcalf, May 26, 1790. RUTH, m. in Fram. Edward Caryel, both of Hop., Sep. 27, 1733. DANIEL, of Holl., m. Abigail Marshall, of Fram., Nov. 11, 1781.

JONATHAN, of Hop., had s. *Jonathan*, bap. 1739. Tradition states that Jonathan and Daniel (1) were brothers, sons of Daniel, whose father emigrated to New England.

LAINS, VILOT, m. Semeon Harry, both of F., Feb. 13, 1752.

LAMB, THOMAS, took the oath of freeman, May 18, 1631, and had by w. Elizabeth, 1. CALEB, b. and d. 1639; Eliz., w. of Thomas, d. 1639, and he m. Dorothy Harbittle, 1640, and had 2. CALEB, b. 1641, m. Mary Wise, 1668, was a mariner, and d. ab. 1697, having *Thomas*, b. 1670; *Caleb*, '71; *Joseph*, '73, d. '92; *Mary*, '78; *Jeremiah*, '79; *Mary*, '82; *John*, '83; *John*, '84; *Eunice*; *Huldah*, '87; 3. JOSHUA, b. 1642; 4. MARY, b. 1644; 5. ABIAL[2], b. 1646. Thomas, the f. was "late deceased," 1651. Dorothy, (prob. his wid.), m. Thomas Hawley, 1651. Farmer states that Tho's, of Roxbury, came over 1630, in the fleet with Gov. Winthrop, and d. April 3, 1645.

JOSHUA, of Roxb., s. of Thomas, m. Mary, dr. of John Alcock, and had *Elizabeth*, b. 1683; *John*, b. and d. '85; *Samuel*, b. Ap. 9, '86; *Thomas*, b. Mar. 23, '89. Mary, wid. of Joshua, d. Oct. 9, 1700. JOSHUA m. Susanna Cary, 1702, and had s. *Joshua*, b. July 14, 1703. Col. Joshua, from Roxb., was an early prop. at Leicester. Hardwick was first called Lambstown from this family. EDWARD, (w. Margaret,) had at Wat., from 1633, *Hannah*, *Samuel*, *Mary*, and others who d. young.

2. ABIAL, s. of Tho (1), had at Roxb., by w. Elizabeth (who was adm. to the Rox. Ch., 1676), HARBUTTLE, bap. Feb. 28, 1674-5; ABIAL³, b. Dec. 23, 1679; JONATHAN⁴, b. Nov 11, 1682. Abial was in Fram. as early as 1695, and occupied land near Doeskin Hill, leased from White and Buckminster. Abial Sen., was Constable, 1700, and Selectman, 1701. He prob. d. in Fram. [One Abial only was rated, 1710.]

3. ABIAL, Jun. s. of Abial (2), m. Hannah Taylor, of Marlb., Oct. 27, 1699; and had, 1. SARAH, b. Ap. 6, 1701; 2. CALEB, b. Oct. 30, 1704; 3. EBENEZER, b. Oct. 19, 1706, (f. at Oxford, by w. Anne, of *Abijah*, b. 1739; *Reuben*, b. '42, d. 1819; *Richard*, '45; *Martha*, '47; *Lucy*, '50) ; 4. ABIAL, b. Jan. 21, 1708-9, (f. at Oxford, by w. Abigail, of *Dorothy*, b. 1741; *Sarah*, '43; *Collins*, '45; *Abigail*, '47; *Levi*, '49, (w. Elizabeth) ; *Abigail*, '51; *Jonathan*, '53; *Zerviah*, '55; *Collins*, '57; *Abiel*, '59; *Edmund*, '61; *Lydia*, '64; *Zerviah*, '67.) [WILLIAM, m. at Ox., Lois Larned, 1743, and Rebeckah Hovey, 1753; SAMUEL, of Ox., m. Sarah Dana, 1753.] Abial was an early prop. of Ox., and was dismissed from Fram., to form a ch. in Ox., Jan. 15, 1721.

4. JONATHAN, s. of Abial (2), m. Lydia Death, in Wat., 1708; and had in Fram., 1. FEBE, b. Mar. 2, 1708-9; 2. LYDIA, b. Dec. 31, 1701; 3. MARY, b. Nov. 8, 1712; 4. JONATHAN, b. Feb. 26, '15; 5. DOROTHY, b. Feb. 3, '17; 6. JOSHUA, b. Jan. 14, '19. Jona., the f. lived in the N. part of the town; was Constable, 1717, and Selectman, 1716, for 3 years. [A Jona. of Leicester, executed, 1745, deeds of gift to his sons Jona. and Josh. His Inventory, (£664), is dated 1749.]

5. SAMUEL, prob. s. of Joshua, (see No. 1), m. Hester Joslin, of Marlb., Feb. 17, 1707-8; and had in Fram., 1. MARY, b. May 31, 1710, m. Phinehas Mixer, of Southb. Nov. 19, '35; 2. BARZILLAI⁶, b. Sep. 12, 1712; 3. SAMUEL⁷, b. Mar. 10, 1721-2. Esther, w. of Sam., d. Mar. 23, 1728-9. [JOSHUA, s. of Sam. and Mary, was b. in Fram., Aug. 15, 1733.] Samuel the f. lived in the west part of the town, near Southb. bounds, and the Turnpike.

6. BARZILLAI, s. of Sam. (5), m. Sarah Knowlton, of Hop., 1734, and had in Fram., 1. JOHN, b. Sep. 23, 1734; 2. ISRAEL, b. ab. 1737, m. Lucy Wheeler, and Hannah Sawyer, and

d. at Templeton, 1836, æ. 91, f. of *Jonas, Asahel, Isaac, Abel, Sally, Levi, Lucy,* and *Deborah ;* and at Hop., 3. SAMUEL, bap. 1741, m. Rebeckah Cozzens, Mar. 18, '62, lived in Philipston; 4. JOSHUA, bap. 1743 ; 5. JOSEPH, bap. 1747, m. Relief Cobleigh, lived in Temp. ; 6. ISAAC, bap. 1749, lived in Philipston ; 7. BARZILLAI, bap. 1752, m. Zuba Bigelow, lived in Philipston ; 8. a daughter, d. young.   Barzillai, the f., d. in Templeton.

7. SAMUEL, Jun., s. of Sam. (5), had in Fram., by wife Sarah*, 1. JOSHUA, b. Oct. 29, 1748, m. Martha Kendall, May 2, '76, d. in Temp. ; 2. BENJAMIN[8], b. Oct. 14, 1750 ; 3. ESTHER, b. May 21, '52, m. Joseph Seaver, and d. in Petersham ; 4. SARAH, b. July 2, '54, m. Manasseh Wilder, of Petersham ; 5. JOHN, bap. July 10, 1756, m. Susannah Haven, Mar. 16, '79, and d. at Philipston, Feb. 5, 1822, f. of *Azubah, Benj. H., Susan, Betsey, Sarah, John, Patty, Ezra, Eleanor* and *Sumner ;* 6. MARY, bap. Sep. 24, 1758, m. Amos Underwood, May '84 ; 7. a son, bap. June 4, '62 ; 8. NATHAN, bap. July 1, '64, m. Lucy Pepper, lived in Guilford ; 9. ELIZABETH, bap. Aug. 17, 1766, m. Timo. Underwood, June 7, '92 ; 10. DAVID, bap. May 29, '68, m. Lydia Barret, and d. in Philipston ; 11. ABIGAIL, bap. Aug. 26, '70, m. Michal Pike, May '93, and d. in N. Y. ; 12. MARTYN, bap. May 1, '74, went to Whitestown, N. Y. [Molly, a dr. of Sam., m. John Parker, of Royalston.] Samuel, the f. and wife Sarah were adm. to the ch., Sep. 1748; and lived where is a cellar hole, between the new road to Southb., and the Turnpike. [Mr. Samuel was buried, Mar. 27, 1793.]

8. BENJAMIN, s. of Sam. (7), m. Nabby Rice, June 23, 1779, and had 1. MARTIN, b. Mar. 13, 1781 ; 2. NATHAN, b. Jan. 25, '82 ; 3. POLLY, b. Nov. 17, '84. Benj. lived on the place of Adam Littlefield, and moved to N. York.

9. ELIZABETH, bap. in Fram., Ap. 14, 1717. ABIGAIL, m. Nathan Underwood, Dec. 27, 1792. SAMUEL, m. in Hop., Mary Atwood, 1747. DOROTHY, of Fram., m. Daniel Johnson, of Marlb., Dec. 23, 1697. MARY, was adm. to the Ch., May 3, 1747.

LAMBERT, PLATO, b. Dec. 1, 1737, was taken when an infant, by Martha Nichols.   (T. Rec.)

---

* Samuel's w., as recorded in the registry of births, was Sarah.

LEARNED, LARNED, or LARNETT, WILLIAM, took the freeman's oath, May 14, 1634, and, with w. Goodeth, was rec'd to the Charlestown church, 1632. He signed a town order, 1634, and in 1637, a remonstrance respecting Mrs. Hutchinson, deemed seditious, for which he made acknowledgments, Nov. 2, 1637, and was made *rectus in curia*. (Col. Rec.) He was one of the founders of Woburn, where he d. Ap. 5, 1646. [Wid. Sarah, d. at Malden, Jan. 24, 1660-1, and wid. Jane d. do., 1660, or, '61.

2. ISAAC, m. in Reading, Mary, dr. of Isaac Sternes, July 9, 1646, and had, 1. MARY, b. Aug. 7, 1647; 2. HANNATH, (Hannah), b. Aug. 24, '49, m. Joseph Farwell, (of Chelmsford), 1666; 3. WILLIAM, oldest son, in 1674, "of Wat.," sold to Tho. Hinchman, land in Chelmsford, (Mid. Deeds, V. 102), and his est. was administered by his brs. Isaac and Benoni, '85. (Co. Rec., IV. 152); 4. ISAAC,[5] b. Oct. 5, 1655; 5. BENONI[3], b. Dec. 4, 1656. Isaac, the f. lived at Wat. and Reading, was of Wob., Ap. 30, 1652, when he sold to Bartholomew Pierson, his house, barn, stable, &c., and 78 acres of land, in Wob. He bought, 1651, of Tho's Dudley, land "six miles N. of Concord," and removed to Chelmsford, where he was selectman, and d. Dec. 4, 1657. His inventory (£222) was presented, April 6, 1658. His wid. Mary m. John Burg, 1662. (Mid. Co. Rec., I. 209).

3. BENONI, s. of Isaac (2), m. at Sherb., Mary Fanning, June 10, 1680, and had, 1. THOMAS,[4] b. Feb. 11, 1681-2; 2. BENJAMIN, b. Aug. 15, '86, m. Hannah Badcock, Feb. 13, 1710, and d. 1712, f. of *James*, b. 1712; 3. MARY, b. Oct. 10, '88, m. George Robinson, of Dedham, Jan. 17, 1707. Mary, w. of Benoni, d. Oct. 14, 1688, and he m. 2d, Sarah ——, and had 4. HANNAH, b. Sep. 10, 1690, m. Eleizer Rider, Sep. 22, 1713; 5. SARAH, b. May 31, '92; 6. ELIZABETH, b. Ap. 28, '94, m. Timo. Leland, Jan. 27, 1710; 7. JOHN, b. May 2, '96; 8. TABITHA, b. Mar. 19, '97-8, m. Jonathan Dewing, Jan. 5, 1721; 9. ABIGAIL, b. July 4, 1700, m. John Woodard, of Sud., Mar. 10, 1739-0; 10. EDWARD, b. Dec. 2, 1705, m. Sarah Larned, Dec. 25, 1728, (f. at Sherb., of *Mary*, b. 1729, m. Abijah Stratton, '47; *Sarah*, b. 1732, m. Jedidiah Phipps, '50; *Daniel*, b. 1734, d. 1752. His w. Sarah d. May 17, '36, and he m. 2d, Abigail Morse, of Sud., 1737, and had *Abigail*, '39; *Benjamin*, '41, of Dublin, 1769; *Abigail*, '45, m. Daniel Grout, '63; his w. Abigail d. Sep. 22, 1745, and he m. 3d, Sarah Pratt, of Newton, Aug. 25, 1748, and had *Edward*, b. July 18, 1749); 11. BATHSHEBA, b. May 3, 1708, m. Josiah Hendee, of Ashford, Jan. 9, 1729. Benoni, the f. was early of Sherb., and on the committee to lay out lots, 1679. He was deacon of the ch., and d. in Sherb., April 10, 1738. His wid. Sarah d. Jan. 25, 1736-7.

4. THOMAS, s. of Benoni (3), settled in Watertown, and had, by w. Mary, 1. JONATHAN, b. Sep. 15, 1708, m. Hannah White, '30, and was f. of *Amariah*, b. '32; *Fanning*, b. Mar. 3, '34, m. Abigail Jackson, of Newton, '59; *Thomas*; *Jerusha*; 2. DAVID, b. Feb. 19, 1710, m. Sarah Mixer, and was f. of *Thomas*, b. 1731; *David*, '33; *Lucy*, '35; *Elisha*, '37; *Mary*, '39; *Sarah*, '41; *Oliver*, '44; *Jesse*, '46; 3. JOSHUA, b. Nov. 22, 1712, m. Elizabeth Goddard, 1731; 4. BENJAMIN, b. Jan. 15, 1713-4; 5. ABIJAH, b. '15, of Camb., m. Sarah Smith, 1736; 6. HENRY, b. 1719; 7. MARY, b. and d. 1720; 8. BEZALEEL, b. 1721, m. Jerusha Bond, '45; 9. HENRY, b. 1722, prob. d. young; 10. MARY; 11. MERCY, b. 1725, prob. d. young; 12. AMARIAH, b. 1726, prob. d. young; 13. JONAS, b. 1728, m. Tabitha Morse, 1753. The will of Thomas, the f. was proved Jan. 12, 1729-0. He had a br. in-law, Joseph Mason. Mary was living a wid., 1736.

5. ISAAC, s. of Isaac (2), m. Sarah Bigelow, July 23, 1679, and had in Fram., 1. ISAAC^6, b. May 10, 1680 ; 2. SARAH, b. Mar. 16, '82; 3. ABIGAIL, b. Mar. 11, '84; 4. MARY, b. Ap. 12, '86, m. William Bond, of Wat., 1712; 5. WILLIAM, b. Feb. 12, '87-8; 6. EBENEZER, b. Sep. (Oxford Rec., Aug. 31), 1690, was a town officer, 1712, m. Deborah Haynes, Oct. 14, 1714, moved to Oxford, and was f. of *Dorothy*, b. 1715 ; *Ruth*, '17 ; *Abigail*, '19 ; *Deborah*, '21, d. '36 ; *Martha*, '24, d. '29 ; *Mary*, '26 ; *Ebenezer*, '28, m. Jerusha Baker, '49 ; *Comfort*, '30 ; *Jeremiah*, '33, (w. Elizabeth, and d. at Oxford, 1812, æ. 79 ; his w. d. 1784). Col. Eben. d. at Ox., Mar. 15, 1772, æ. 81; 7. SAMUEL, b. Oct. 4, 1692; 8. HANNAH, b. Sep. 16, '94, m. Obadiah Walker, of Marlb., May 2, 1715; 9. ELIZABETH, b. July 27, '96 ; 10. MOSES^7, b. Ap. 29, '99; 11. MARTHA, b. May 21, 1702, m. Jacob Cummens, of Oxford, June 27, 1723. Isaac the f. (formerly of Wat.), bought of Thomas Eames, 1679 and 1683, near what is now "Learned's Pond," and was received to Sherb., prob. ab. 1679. He was Selectman in Fram., 1711, and d. Sep. 15, 1737.

6. ISAAC, s. of Isaac (5), m. Sarah How, Nov. 19, 1706, and had, 1. JOSIAH, b. Dec. 1, 1707, (and f. at Oxford, by w. Katharine, of *Katharine*, b. 1733 ; *Josiah*, '35 ; *Samuel*, '38 ; *Moses*, '40 ; *Nehemiah*, '43 ; *William*, '46 ; *Ezekiel*, '49 ; *Sarah*, '53) ; 2. ISAAC, b. Oct. 2, 1709, of Oxford, m. Elizabeth Jones, of Hop., Jan. 1, 1736, and f. at Oxf., of *John*, b. 1741, d. 1830 ; *Elizabeth*, '44 ; *Mary*, '46 ; *Abigail* and *Martha*, '48 ; *Asa*, '50, (w. Mary) ; *Simpson*, '52 ; and by 2d w. Mary, *Hannah*, '54 ; *Hannah*, '57 ; *Isaac*, '60 ; *Lois*, '62 ; 3. EXPERIENCE, b. July 29, 1711. Isaac, the f. was perhaps also of Sherb., and may have been the Isaac, a prop. in Templeton, 1735. Lt. Isaac d. in Oxford, May 20, 1753. [Capt. John who d. in Oxf., 1796, æ. 82, (his wives, Hepsebah—, and Miriam Smith), may have been his son.]

7. MOSES, s. of Isaac (5), had in Fram., by w. Lydia, 1. MOSES^8, b. Feb. 13, 1727-8 ; 2. LYDIA, b. July 6, '30, d. July 9, '92, for many years a schoolmistress; 3. SIMON, b. May 25, '32, said to have d. unm. in the army; 4. SAMUEL, b. Feb. 14, 1733-4, d. Dec. 12, 1751; 5. DANIEL, b. Jan. 2, '35-6, d. Jan. 19, 1742; 6. ELIJAH, b. June 1, d. 22d, 1738 ; 7. MEHETABEL,

b. Mar. 24, 1739–0, d. Ap. 7; 8. HANNAH, b. Mar. 16, '40–1, m. John Gould, and 2d, —— Winter; 9. ELIZABETH, b. Aug. 31, '43, m. Hananiah Temple; 10. DEBORAH, b. Jan. 21, '45, m. —— Adams, (said to have been a cousin, from Truro), and she d. a few years after marriage; her only child d. young; 11. SARAH, b. June 16, '48, d. unm., ab. 1823. Moses the f. was Selectman, 1747 and '48; was for many years Deacon of the first ch., and held in much esteem. He d. May 25, 1769. His w. Lydia d. Oct. 23, 1774.

8. MOSES, Jun., s. of Moses (7), had by w. RUTH, 1. SOLOMON, b. Aug. 17, 1749, went to sea; 2. RUTH, b. Jan. 1, '52; 3. MARY, bap. Aug. 16, '52, d. Nov. 20, '74; 4. MOSES, b. May 15, '54, d. in the service, Sep. 17, '80; 5. SAMUEL, b. June 7, '56, m. Hannah Walker, July 7, '78; 6. SIMON, b. Dec. 11, '58; 7. ANNE, b. Ap. 23, '61; 8. MEHETABEL, b. July 3, '63; 9. THOMAS, b. Jan. 10, '66, m. Lydia Treadwell, 1789, and d. in Templeton; and in Templeton, 10. DANIEL, b. June 18, '68. Moses, the f., moved from Fram. to Templeton.

9. Mrs. ELIZABETH, m. in Fram., Jacob Bancroft Winchester, both of Wat., Mar. 3, 1786.

LAWRENCE, JONATHAN, and w. Elizabeth, had in F., 1. MARY, b. Nov. 30, 1729; 2. SARAH, b. Dec. 15, '31; 3. JONATHAN, b. Feb. 5, '33–4.

JONATHAN, and w. Elizabeth had in Sud., *Elizabeth*, b. Feb. 19, 1727–8. GEORGE, witnessed a deed in Fram., 1723. JONA. and w. Abigail, of Sherb., had *Jonathan*, 1711. JOHN, and w. Susannah, had in Sherb., *Sarah*, b. Oct. 21, 1698; *Mercy*, Mar. 20, 1707; *Samuel*, (in Nat.), Jan. 29, 1712. John, (w. Susannah), d. at Nat., 1712, leaving *Daniel*, *Ebenezer*, *Jonathan*, *David*, *Elizabeth*, *Johanna*. GEORGE, of Wat., m. Elizabeth Crisp, Sep. 29, 1657, and d. 1709, an aged man, leaving sons *George* and *Benjamin*, and several daughters. JOHN, (w. Elizabeth), of Wat., 1635, was f. of *John*, *Peleg*, *Zechariah*, &c.

LEADBETTER, or LEABUTTUR, ISRAEL, and w. Martha, came from Weston, 1775, with these chil., viz; 1. WILLIAM SWIFT; 2. THOMAS, (lived in Holl,); 3. ISRAEL. [ISRAEL, m. Mrs. Elizabeth Hemenway, Jan. 19, 1782. WILLIAM, m. Hepzebah Richards, Dec. 1789.]

2. EZRA, had in Fram., PATTY, bap. Aug. 4, 1776; EZRA, bap. Aug. 23, '78. Both families removed from town.

HENRY, of Dorch., m. Sarah Tolman, Jan. 18, 1658–9, and had *Sarah*, b. '60, m. Henry Withington, '84; *Catharine*, b. '62, m. Eph. Pasin, '84;

Henry, '64, m. Relief Foster, '92; *Deliverance*, '67; *Increase*, '72, m. Sarah Davenport, 1702; *Ebenezer*, '76, of Boston, 1713; *Israel*, '78, (w. Mary), and lived to be æ. over 90.

LELAND, JONAS, of Fram., m. Olive Cole, of Sherb., Oct. 17, 1793. KEZIAH, of Sherb., m. Benjamin Kendal, of F., Jan. 27, 1732-3. This family were early at Sherb., and numerous.

LENNARD, JOHN, was drafted in Fram., 1778.

LEVERETT, REBECKAH, of Fram., æ. over 14, prayed 1792, for the appointment of Col. Micah Stone as her guardian. (Mid. Prob.)

LEWIS, or LEWES, WILLIAM, m. in Southb., Mercy Pike, Dec. 10, 1750, and had in F., 1. WILLIAM, b. Aug. 31, '51; and in Southb., ABIJAH, Mar. 16, '54; WILLIAM, May 14, '62.

JAMES, of Southb., m. Martha Collins, 1753, and had *Mary*, b. '54; *John*, '55. HANNAH, was adm. to the ch. in Fram., July 15, 1753.

LITTLEFIELD, JOHN, and w. Mary, had at Dedham, EXPERIENCE, b. Dec. 17, 1659; JOHN, b. Oct. 5, '64; EBENEZER, b. Oct. 13, '69. John was "late of Wrentham," Ap., 1675, when he sold his houselot, &c., in W., to Henry Wight, of Dedham.

2. EBENEZER, prob. s. of John (1), a housewright, had in Newton, by w. Lydia, 1. JEMIMA, b. 1697; 2. EZRA, b. '99, d. 1703; 3. EBENEZER, b. 1701, d. 1798, m. Abiah Morse, of Medfield, 1728, (and f. at Holl., of *Simeon*, b. 1728, m. Dinah Marshall, '56; *Beulah*, '31; *John*, '37, m. Tabitha Adams, of Medway, (f. of Hannah, Tabitha, Ruth, John, Jotham, and Sarah); 4. PELATIAH, b. 1703, (w. Alice), f. at Holl., of *Elizabeth*, b. '34; *Ebenezer*, '35; *Jeremiah*, '36; *Lydia*, '37; *Huldah*, and *Alice*, '39; *Alice*, '41; *Ebenezer*, '47; *Elizabeth*, '52; 5. LYDIA, b. 1706; 6. JERUSHA, b. 1708, m. John Taylor, 1730; 7. PRAISEVER (son), b. 1710; 8. SUSANNAH, and 9. EPHRAIM, twins, h. 1712 — E. m. Sarah Bullard, of Holl., 1735, and d. 1778, f. at Holl. of *Elizabeth*, d. young; *Sarah*, b. 1739, m. James Perry; *Eliezer*, b. '41, d. young; *Sybilla*, '43, m. Asa Rockwood; *Elizabeth*, '47, m. Thaddeus Lovering; *Ephraim*, Esq., b. '49, d. 1828, m. Sarah Grant, (and f. of Jerusha, b. 1772, m. Aaron Bullard, of Fram.; Eliel, '76, m. Sophia Mellen; Loammi; and Sally, m. John Eames, of Fram.); *Asa*, b. '57, m. Mary Adams, of Holl.; and *Anne*, m. Peletiah Gibbs; 10. SYBIL, b, 1714, m. James Cheney, 1740. Eben, the f. d. at Newton, Jan., 1727-8; his w. Lydia d. Oct. 12, 1717.

3. ASA, s. of Eph. and g. s. of Eben. (2), m. Mary Adams, and had 1. ASA, d. 1790; 2. RUTH, b. Nov. 3, 1780, m. Thomas Temple, Nov. 30, 1797; 3. ADAMS, b. June 30, 1783, m. Mary Morse; 4. POLLY, b. July 20, 1792, m. Grant Fay, of Southb. Asa, the f. came to Fram. from Holl., lived in the west part of the Town, on the Turnpike, and d. Nov. 1837, æ. 80. His w. Mary d. 1838, æ. 88.

LIVERMORE, JOHN, of Weston, m. in Fram., Abigail Stone, June 22, 1731, and had in Weston, 1. ABIGAIL, b. 1731; and in Fram. 2. MARY, b. Oct. 21, 1733; 3. ELIZABETH, b. Jan. 7, '35-6, m. Jesse Stone; 4. JOHN, b. Nov. 7, '38; 5. SUSANNAH, b. May 3, '43, m. Lt. Nathan Smith, of Fram.; 6. MARY, b. July 23, '45; 7. SUBMIT, b. Mar. 19, '48. The wid. Abigail, m. Samuel Gleason, Ap. 3, 1755.

John was b. Ap. 2, 1709, s. of Jos. and w. Elizabeth, (for a time of Sud.), and g. s. of John, who d. in Weston, 1719. John, Sen. d. at Wat., Ap., 14, 1684, æ. 78. Joseph, prob. br. of John, of Fram., (w. Mary) was of Sud., 1731, and had *Samuel*, b. '33, (w. Lois), and others.

LOCKE, or LOCK, JONATHAN, m. in Hop., Mary, wid. of John Nichols, Oct. 2, 1761, and had in Hop., 1. SAMUEL, bap. 1762, d. young; 2. JOHN, b. Feb. 14, '64, H. Coll., 1792, m. Hannah Goodwin, lived in Ashby, and was a Rep. in Cong.; 3. SALLY, b. Ap. 9, '66, m. John Manning, of Ashby, and d. without issue; 4. MEHETABEL; 5. ELIZABETH, b. in Fram., Mar. 5, '70, m. Tho's Heald, Esq., (Dart. Coll., 1794), who was an Att'y in Concord, Mass., and after, a judge in Blakely, Ala., where he d.; his wid. m. Elijah Newhall, of N. Ipswich, and d. 1843; 6. JOSEPH, b. 1772, (Dart. Coll., 1797), m. Lydia Goodwin, was an Attorney at Billerica, State Senator and Counsellor, Chief Just. of the Court of Sessions, and Judge of the Police Court in Lowell; 7. NANCY, b. 1774, m. Imla Goodhue, of Westford. Jona., the f., lived but a short time in Fram., on the Coolidge place. His w. Mary d. June 17, 1803.

EBENEZER, was of Hop., 1732. JOSHUA, (w. Abigail), of Sud., had *Fortunatus*, b. Sep. 26, 1779. SAMUEL, D. D., minister of Sherb., and President of Harv. Coll., d. at Sherb., Jan. 15, 1777, æ. 45. SAMUEL, M. D., d. at Sherb., Aug. 30, 1788, æ. 27.

LOOK, or LUKE, JOHN, m. at Martha's Vineyard, Elizabeth Weaver, and came to Fram. with his chil., viz: 1. ELIZABETH, m. Ephraim Parkhurst; 2. MARY, m. Timothy Stearns, Sep. 3, 1794; 3. EUNICE, m. Josiah Clayes, and d. June 22, 1836, æ. 64; 4. RUTH, m. Enoch Belknap, Oct. 29, 1797. John, the f., d. at sea. His wid. m. 2d, Rev. Edward Clark, of Fram., and d. 1804.

LORING, Mrs. SUSANNAH, d. Dec. 18, 1765. [She was prob. wid. of Daniel Loring, of Boston.]

ISAAC's wife was rec'd to Hop. ch., from Boston, 1756. The Rev. ISRAEL, minister of the W. church of Sud., d. Mar. 9, 1772, æ. 89, and in the 66th year of his ministry.

LOVERING, Lt. JESSE, was in Fram., 1787.

MACCULLOUGH, JAMES, had in Fram., NATHANIEL, b. Jan. 18, 1746; JOSEPH, b. Feb. 28, 1748.

JAMES, of Hop., had *Elizabeth*, bap. 1749; *Agnes*, '51; *James*, '53; *John*, '55; *Jane*, '57.

MACFARLAND, or FARLING, JAMES, had MARGARET, bap. in Fram., Dec. 25, 1748.

EBENEZER and w. Elizabeth had chil. in Hop., from 1776. WALTER, of Hop., (s. of Robert), m. Sarah Richardson, 1778. THOMAS, of Hop., m. Lydia Wires, 1782. ROBERT, of Hop., is said to have emigrated to N. E., æ. 15.

MACKLINTOCK, JAMES, was in Fram., 1727, and signed a petition to the General Court. MARGARET was bap., July 16, 1727.

MACOY. See COY.

MAN. Mr. Man kept school in Fram., 1780, and was prob. from Medway.

MANSON, FREDERICK, b. at Sud., Aug. 16, 1746, (s. of RICHARD, who m. Elizabeth, dr. of the Rev. Israel Loring, June 6, 1746), m. Anna, dr. of Dr. Ebenezer Hemenway, and had in Fram., 1. LORING, b. Dec. 7, 1770, m. Elizabeth Sawin, of Marlb.; 2. RICHARD, b. July 15, '72, m. Polly Hart, of Boston, d. 1802; 3. ANNA, b. Nov. 22, '73, d. Oct. 12, '75; 4. FREDERIC, b. Dec. 2, '75, m. —— Goodwin, of Camb., and lives there; 5. NATHAN, b. Feb. 7, '78, m. —— Hemenway, of Camb.; 6. EBENEZER, b. Dec. 27, '79; 7. POLLY, b. Nov. 5, '81, m. Wm. Barber, of Medway, June 9, 1803, and d. Mar. 1815; 8. JOHN, b. Feb. 13, '84, m. Nelly Nurse, lives in Fram.; 9. SALLY, b. Oct. 2, '85, m. Kellogg Hurlburt, of Utica; 10. DEBBY, b. Feb. 22, '88, m. Cyrus Cobb, of Boston, Aug. 12, 1806, and 2d, Henry Tolman; 11. OTIS, b. Ap. 12, '90, lived in Richmond, Va.; 12. DANA, b. May 14, '94, m. —— Sanger, 2d, —— Newton, lives at Waltham; 13. BETSEY LORING, b. Dec. 26, '97, m. Francis Hurlburt, of N. Hartford. Frederick, the f., learned his trade of shoemaking, at Weston, and came to F., ab. 1767. He first lived at Wm. Hasting's, and after on the Southb. road. He and w. cov'd, May 12, 1771. He d. Oct. 25, 1826, æ. 80. His wid. Anna d. June, 1843, æ. 91.

MARRET, or MERRIT, WILLIAM, m. in Southb., Abigail

Nichols, Mar. 1743, and had 1. ABIGAIL, m. Job Burnham; 2. NATHANIEL, d. unm. Wm., the f. m. 2d, Sarah How, and had 3. SALLY, m. Andrew Newton; 4. WILLIAM, b. July 2, 1753, d. young. Wm. m. 3d, Sarah Cummings, of Southb., 1776. Wm. lived on the Common, and d. ab. 1782.

2. ALVIN, b. ab. 1778, m. Anne Bruce, and had NATHANIEL, WILLIAM, EDWARD, SUMNER, RUTH, and BETSEY. The widow Anne m. 2d, Luther Newton. Alvin lived on the Common.

THOMAS, was of Camb., 1635. JOHN, of Camb., m. Abigail Richardson, 1654, and was f. of AMOS, b. 1657, m. Bethiah Langhorn, '81; JOHN, b. 1664; EDWARD, '70; MARY, '72; LYDIA, '73; others d. young.

MARSH, BETSEY, was b. in Fram., July 30, 1782.

MARSHALL, THOMAS,* m. in Newton, his w. Esther, Nov. 2, 1715, and had, 1. THOMAS, m. in Holl., Beriah Grant, 1744, and d. in Temple, f. of *Aaron*, b. '47; *David*, '50; *Jonathan*, '52, and others who d. young; 2. JOSEPH; 3. EBENEZER,$_2$ b. Sep. 18, 1721; and at Holl., 4. JOHN, b. 1723, m. Mary Farnsworth, and was f. of *Rebeckah*, b. 1750; *Farnsworth*, b. '52, d. a young man; 5. DINAH, b. 1725, d. 1729; 6. EZRA, b. 1729, d. 1732; 7. NAHUM, b. 1732, H. Coll., 1755, m. Martha Lord, of Somersworth, and d. in S.; 8. JAMES,[4] b. 1734. Thomas, the f. was deacon of Holl. ch., 38 years, m. 2d, wid. Abigail Cutler, 1762, and d. Ap. 3, 1766, æ. 75. His w. Esther d. in Fram., Dec. 10, 1761, æ. 71. (G. Stones).

Note.— EBENEZER, of Holl., m. Elizabeth Jones, Jan. 15, 1730, and was f. of *Abigail*, d. 1736; *Dinah*, b. 1737; *Elizabeth*, '42. JOSEPH, of Holl., m. Mary Leland, 1737, and was f. of *Eslcher*, b. '38; *Ezra*, '40; *Ichabod*, '42; and *Joseph*; the f. moved to Milford. BENJAMIN, of Holl., (from Marblehead, prob. nephew of Dea. Tho's), had by w. Sybilla, *Elizabeth*, b. 1761; *Sarah*; *Mary*; *Annes*; *Sybilla*; *Benjamin*; and *Moses*.

2. EBENEZER, s. of Thomas (1), m. Mehetabel Haven, Feb. 11, 1747-8; and had, 1. ANNE, b. Dec. 19, 1748, m. William

---

* Tradition supposes Thomas, of Holl. to have come from Chebacco, (now Essex), a part of Ipswich, and adds that the ancestor was a seafaring man, and in one instance recaptured his vessel from the enemy. The inventory of Thomas, Jun., of Chebacco, (w. Anne), is dated June 19, 1682. One Thomas Marshall commanded a vessel from Boston, 1714. EDMOND, of Newbury, (prob. early at Salem), d. ab. 1673, leaving, (perhaps with other chil.), *Benjamin*, (prob. of Ipswich, 1679, and d. 1716, f. by w. Prudence Woodward, m. 1677, of Edmund. Ezekiel, John, and 4 drs.); *Edmond*, (who sold in 1682, to Thomas Marshall, Jr., late of Ipswich, land in Chebacco). PETER, (w. Abigail), was of Newbury, 1684.

THOMAS, was of Reading, 1640. THOMAS, was of Salem, 1657. JOHN, was of Billerica, 1662, and left a s. John, whose estate was settled 1721. WILLIAM, of Charlestown, 1667, had two wives, and d. ab. 1693, having had *William*, *John*, (of Jamaica, 1697), *Edward*, &c. THOMAS, was of Charlestown, 1684. The Marshalls were early in Boston, where Thomas was chosen Dea. of the first ch., 1650. The name of Thomas is found *passim*. Thomas took the freeman's oath, Sept. 3, 1634. THOMAS, æ. 22, clothworker, came over in the James, 1634. FRANCIS, æ. 20, embarked in the Christopher de London, 1634. WILLIAM, æ. 40, came over, 1634, in the Abigail. JOHN, æ. 14, came over in the Hopewell, 1634.

Ballard, and d. in Fram., ab. 1804; 2. MEHETABEL, b. Oct. 27, 1758, m. Richard Sears, of Chatham, Nov. 25, 1778, lives a wid. in C.; 3. GILBERT, b. Dec. 26, 1760. Mehetabel, w. of Eben., d. Feb. 19, 1776, æ. 53; and he m. 2d, Wid. Dixon, of Boston; 3d, Esther Fisk, Ap. 25, 1781; and 4th, Wid. Mary Haven, Oct. 23, 1783. Ebenezer was a millwright and iron-worker in Fram., on Hop. River; was selectman 1764, for 2 years; and d. Nov. 15, 1802, æ. 81. (G. Stone.)

3. GILBERT, s. of Eben. (2), m. Jane Jones, of Hop., Oct. 7, 1782; and had, 1. EBENEZER, b. May 1, '83, d. 1803; 2. MARY, b. Jan. 9, '86, m. Thomas Danforth, of Norton, Ap. 26, 1804; 3. MEHETABEL, b. Jan. 30, '88, m. Samuel Danforth, and lives in Bristol, N. H.; 4. NANCY, b. May 8, '90, d. unm., 1834; 5. ALETHENE, b. Mar. 28, '92, m. Richard Sears, of Chatham; 6. REBECKAH, b. Oct. 1, '94; 7. Jane, b. 1796, m. Cha's Scudder, of Boston; 8. ELIZABETH, b. 1798; 9. JOHN JONES, b. May 24, 1800, m. Elizabeth Taber, of Roxb.; 10. FEAR SHEPARD, b. Jan. 23, 1806, m. Calvin Shepard, Jun. Gilbert, the f. d. Feb., 1842; Jane his w. d. Nov., 1836.

4. JAMES, s. of Thomas (1), then of Fram., m. Lydia Harrington, 1756; and had, 1. LYDIA; 2. OLIVE, m. in Fram., Jacob Pepper, Feb. 25, 1780; 3. ABIGAIL; 4. JULIA. J. of F. m. 2d, Wid. Sybil Holbrook, of Sherb., May 16, 1786, and d. in Sherb.

JACOB, of Nat., m. Mary Morse, 1775, and had *David, William, Pelatiah,* and *Mary.*

MASTRICK, or MISTRICK, JOHN, m. Sarah Coy of F., Aug. 12, 1747. He was probably a native of Wales; was in F., 1767, lived near Long Pond, and was wild and eccentric in his habits. He had a s. *Joseph,* b. in Hop., June 19, 1752.

MATTHEWS, or MATHES, JOHN, of Marlb., m. Mary Johnson, and had, 1. LYDIA, b. Mar. 16, 1691, d. 1706; 2. RUTH, b. May 9, '93; 3. JOHN, b. Jan. 18, '94, m. Jerusha Bigelow, 1718, and was f. in Southb., of *John,* b. Oct. 17, 1719; *Joseph,* d. young; *Jerusha,* b. '24; *Mary,* '26; *Sarah,* d. young; *Barnabas,* b. 30, m. Anna Munroe, '55; *Sybil,* '32; *Paul,* '34, m. Lucy Rice, '59; *Jabez,* '36; *Thankful,* '39; 4. DANIEL, b. Mar., 1697, m. Eunice Morse, 1724, and was f. of *Solomon,* b. '29; *Eunice,* '30; *Asahel,* '32, m. Elizabeth Woods, Nov. 25, '60; *Samuel,* '34; *Persis,* and *Hannah,* '35; *Silas,* '37, *Phinehas,* '39, d. '40; *Thankful,* '41; *Aaron,* '43; *Phinehas,* 44, d. '56; and *Grace,* '48. Mary, w. of John, d. June 22, 1710, and he m. 2d, Sarah Garfield, 1713. John was prob. of Marlb., 1681.

Note. — JOHN, of Roxb., had *Gershom,* b. 1641; *Elizabeth,* '43. Farmer supposes him to have moved to Springfield.

2. JOHN, g. s. of John (1), m. in Southb., Susanna More, Dec., 1743; and had in Fram., 1. JABISH, b. Ap. 27, 1745; 2. HANNAH, b. May 4, '47; 3. SARAH, b. Mar. 20, '48; 4. JOHN, b. Mar. 3, '50; 5. SAMUEL, bap. Sep. 23, '53; 6. SUSANNAH, bap. Aug. 22, '56. J., the f. lived at Guinea End, and left town.
3. OLIVER, (b. June 3, 1765), s. of Asahel, (see No. 1), m. Olive Nurse, of Fram., Mar., 1790, and had bap. in Fram., Dec. 1795, chil. ANNE, and SALLY.

MAVERIC, or MABRIC, JAMES, cov'd in F., Aug. 4, and was bap. Aug. 18, 1717; he had, by w. Mary, in Sherb. 1. SARAH, b. Aug. 13, 1718, m. John Putnam, Ap. 25, 1737; and in Sud., 2. MARY, b. Mar. 4, 1720-1, m. David Mellen, of Fram., June 20, 1744; 3. ABIGAIL, b. June 4, 1725, m. Moses Hill, Aug. 10, '49; 4. JAMES, b. Aug. 4, 1729; 5. ESTHER, b. Ap. 30, '32; 6. SILENCE, b. Ap. 16, '35, m. (then of Fram.), Jedediah Parmenter, of Sud., Feb. 5, 1755; 7. ESTHER. Mary, w. of James, d Nov. 17, 1740; and he m. 2d, Lydia Sanderson, Ap. 28, 1742. "Mr. Maveric" was prob. of Fram., 1748. He d. Nov. 17, 1750. [MARTHA of Fram., m. Thomas Bellows of Marlb., May 29, 1716.]

MAYHEW, JOHN, of Shrewsbury, m. in Fram., Hannah Rugg, Feb. 21, 1743; and had in Southb. 1. JOHN, b. Ap. 28, 1747; 2. JONATHAN, b. Mar. 14, '49; and in Fram., 3. MOLLY, b. Jan. 17, 1752. John was prob. for a time of Hop.

2. JOHN, s. of John (1), had in F., by w. Abigail, 1. JOHN, b. Dec. 24, 1775; 2. WALTER, b. Feb. 22, '82; 3. POLLY, b. July 22, '87; 4. NABBY, b. Sep. 2, '91; 5. MARTIN, b. Mar. 17, '95. Lt. John the f. and w. were adm. to the ch., 1780; he d. in Fram., Feb. 27, 1832, æ. 84; his w. Abigail d. Nov. 9, 1825, æ. 73.

THOMAS, (w. Jane), was of Wat., 1635. John Mayo, of Roxb., was f. of *John*, (b. 1658, w. Sara); *Eleazer, Joseph, Thomas, Benjamin*, &c.

MAYNARD, JOHN, of Sud., who m. Mary Axdell, 1646, had the following chil.: 1. JOHN[2]; 2. ZACHARY, b. June 7, 1647; 3. ELIZABETH, b. May 26, '49, m. Joseph Graves, Jan. 15, '65-6, and d. 1676; 4. HANNAH, b. Sep. 30, '53, not in the will; 5. MARY, b. Aug. 3, '56, m. Daniel Hudson, Jun., '74, and d. 1677; 6. LYDIA, m. Joseph Moore. John was of Camb., 1634, and took the freeman's oath, May 29, 1644. He was a petitioner for Marlb., 1656. He d. at Sud., Dec. 10, 1672, and his will was proved Ap. 1. '73. [LYDIA m. in Charlestown, Samuel Hale, Mar. 19, 1668.]

2. JOHN, Jun., s. of John (1), m. Mary Gates, 1658, and had, in Marlb., 1. JOHN, b. 1661, d. 1731; his chil. by w. Lydia, were *John*, b. 1690, m.

Hepsebah Brigham, 1719 ; *Daniel*, b. '92, (w. Mary), d. 1760 ; *James*, b. 1694, m. Mary Morse, 1719, and lived at Westb., f. of Phinehas, James, &c. ; *Mary*, '96 ; *Reuben*, '98 ; *Abigail*, 1701; *Phinehas*, '03, d. '25 ; *Bethiah*, '05, d. 1720; *Hezekiah*, '08, m. Tabitha How, of Marlb., in Fram., June 11, 1739, and f. of Bethiah, Hezekiah, (w. Hannah), and Adam ; 2. ELIZABETH, b. 1664, m. —— Brigham ; 3. SIMON, b. 1666, d. young ; 4. SIMON, b. 1668, f. by w. Hannah, of *Hannah*, b. 1694 ; *Simon*, '96, m. Sarah Church, 1718 ; *Elizabeth*, '98, m. Robert Horn, 1723 ; *Tabitha*, 1701 ; *Elisha*, 1703 ; *Eunice*, 1705 ; *Ephraim*, 1707, w. Sarah, (f. of Tabitha, Sarah, Ephraim, Simon, Joseph, Benjamin, and Eunice); *Benjamin*, b. 1709, and prob. of Shrewsbury, (f. of Seth, Jonah, Benjamin, Simon, Sarah, and Abigail); 5. DAVID, b. 1669, d. at Westb., ab. 1757, f. by w. Hannah, (who d. 1725), of *Keziah*, b. 1703; *David*, '04 ; *Ruhamah*, '06, m. Deac. Josiah Newton ; *Jonathan*, '08 ; *Martha*, '10, m. Daniel Mason ; *Jesse*, '12 ; *Jotham*, '14, prob. of Bolton ; *Ebenezer*, '16 ; *Nathan* ; *Hannah*; and *Mercy* ; 6. ZECHARIAH, b. 1672 ; 7. HANNAH, m. —— Davenport ; 8. SARAH, b. 1680 ; 9. LYDIA, b. 1682; 10. JOSEPH, b. 1685, m. Elizabeth Price, 1707, and f. of *Persis*, b. 1713 ; *Elizabeth*, '16 ; *Benjamin*, '21. Elizabeth, his w. d. at Worcester, 1732. John, Jr., early took the oath of fidelity, at Sud. He d. at Marlb., and his will was proved, Jan. 9, 1711–2. He left a w. Sarah.

3. ZACHARY, or ZECHARIAH, s. of John (1), m. Han. Coolidge, 1678, and had, 1. ZECHARIAH, b. Ap. 30, 1679, f. by w. Sarah, at Sud., of *Zebadiah*, b. Jan. 17, 1701–2, m. Sarah Mosman, 1734, and d. Feb. 18, 1775 ; *Sarah*, 1703 ; *Jonathan*, '06 ; *Lucy*, Ap., 17(09), m. John Hayden, of Hop., 1726 ; *Timothy*, 1712 ; *Nathan*, 1714, m. Betty Jewell, 1741 ; *Zechariah*, b. Jan. 15, 1719–0, m. Sybilla Brigham, 1738, who d. Feb., 1778, and wid. Mary Walker, 1778, (father of Daniel, Gideon, William, &c.,); 2. JOHN, b. Jan. 26, 1680–1, d. 1740, m. Elizabeth Neadom, of Camb., 1713, and d. Mar. 12, 1740, æ. 60, f. of *John*, b. 1721, m. Esther Rice, '47, and d. 1809, f. of Caleb, Abel, Israel, Reuben, &c. ; 3. HANNAH, b. Jan. 25, 1683 ; 4. JONATHAN, b. Ap. 8, 1685 ; 5. DAVID, b. May 22, 1687 ; 6. ELIZABETH, b. Jan. 3, 1691–2, m. Thomas Walker, 1717, and d. 1723 ; 7. ABIGAIL, b. Mar. 13, 1700. Zechariah, the f. d. in Sud., 1724. His w. Hannah d. 1719.*

4. JONATHAN, s. of Zachary (3), m. Mehetabel Neadom, of Camb., Dec. 10, 1714 ; and had in Fram., 1. MEHETABEL, b. Mar. 4, 1715–6, m. Caleb Drury, May 27, 1735 ; 2. JONATHAN[5], b. Jan. 1, 1717–8 ; 3. ZECHARIAH, b. Nov. 23, 1719, d. July 15, 1741, æ. 21.7.22 (G. stone) ; 4. JOHN, b. Sep. 29, 1721, lived in Grafton ; 5. JOSEPH[8], b. Nov. 20, 1725 ; 6. WILLIAM, b. Dec. 4, 1727, d. July 24, 1740, æ. 12.7.20. (G. stone). Jona. the f. came from Sud. to Fram., occupied the Aaron Bullard farm, was constable, 1718. His will was dated, Dec. 15, 1760. Mehetabel his w. d. Oct. 19, 1767, æ. 77. (G. stone.)

5. JONATHAN, Jr., s. of Jona. (4), m. Martha Gleason,

---

* Moses, of Sud. m. Lois Stone, of Fram., 1734, and d. March 26, 1782, æ. 85, f. of *Samuel* ; *Moses*, who m. Tabitha Moore, 1752, and moved to Rutland, where he d. Dec. 1796, æ. 67. About 16 months before his death, he weighed 451 pounds. (Rut. Rec.) ; Capt. *Micah* ; *Daniel* ; *Josiah* ; *Nathaniel* ; *Abigail*, and *Lois*.

Nov. 11, 1742, and with w. rec'd to the ch., Nov. 4, 1750; and had, 1. WILLIAM⁶, b. Mar. 29, 1745; 2. JONATHAN⁷, b. May 22, 1752. Jona. the f. m. 2d, wid. Sarah Hill, (a Muzzey), of Sherb., by whom he had no chil. He lived in the Dr. Stone House, and d. in Fram., 1782. His w. Sarah d. ab. 1789.

6. WILLIAM, s. of Jona. (5), m. Mary Pepper, was with w. adm. to the ch., Oct. 13, 1771, and had in Fram., 1. JOHN, b. Oct. 3, 1766, m. at Santa Cruz, Mary Durant, and d. in Scarboro' Me., June, 1818; 2. MARTHA, b. May 8, 1768, m. Isaac Damon, of E. Sud., Jan. 1, '98; 3. MARY, b. June 2, '70, m. Eph. Carter, of Lancaster, and d. June, 1827; 4. BENJAMIN, b. Ap. 4, '72, d. unm. in Demarara, ab. 1810; 5. WILLIAM, b. Mar. 11, '74, m. Eunice Dench, Mar. 12, '97. and d. Nov. 15, 1804, (f. of *Lawson Dench*, b. June 22, 1798, and *Mary;* his w. Eunice d. July, 1822; 6. THOMAS, b. Dec. 25, '75, d. unm. in Demarara, ab. 1808. Lt. William was T. Clerk in Fram. 6 years, and lived in Mr. Elias Temple's house. His w. Mary d. in Fram. Mar. 12, 1780, and he went to Carolina, ab. 1788, taught school and d. there.

7. JONATHAN, s. of Jona. (5), m. Lois Eaton, May 30, 1784, and had no issue. The Hon. Jonathan, (Harv. Coll., 1775), served as an officer in the army of the Revolution; was a Trustee of the Fram. Academy; Selectman, 5 y.; T. Clerk, 2 y.; Representative 1800 and 1805; and after, chosen a Senator. He enjoyed to a high degree the confidence and esteem of his fellow townsmen, and d. July 17, 1835, æ. 83. His wid. Lois d. Dec. 5, 1836, æ. 74.

8. JOSEPH, s. of Jona, (4), m. Abigail Gennings, (Jennings), May 29, 1746, and had, 1. MEHETABEL, b. May 28, '47, m. Caleb Winch, and lived in Fitzwilliam; 2. SUSANNAH, b. Oct. 22, '48, m. and d. in Fitzw.; 3. JOSEPH⁹, b. May 17, '50; 4. ABIGAIL, b. Dec. 2, '51, m. and d. in Fitzw.; 5. JOHN, b. May 14, '53, m. Martha Wilder, of Lanc., Ms., and d. at L. æ. 89; 6. NEEDHAM, b. Aug. 15, '55, served as aid to Gen. Warren at Bunker Hill, m. Hitty Eames, May 6, '85, removed to Whitestown, N. Y., where he was raised to the Bench, and d. a few years since; 7. SARAH, b. Mar. 28, '57, m. Matthias Felton, of Fitzw., Oct. 18, '81, and d. there; 8. HANNAH, b. Ap. 2, '59, m. Eph. How, of Marlb., Nov., '82, and d. in M.; 9. ELIZABETH, b, Ap. 24, '61, m. Jason Winch,

and d. in Fitzw.; 10. ANNE, b. May 4, '63, m. Nath'l Polly, Oct. 18, '81, and d. in Sherb.; 11. MARTHA, b. Mar. 31, '65, m. Isaac Hemenway, Dec., '85, and moved to Whitestown. Ensign Jos., the f. lived at Mr. Aaron Bullard's, and d. Aug. 3, 1769, æ. 43. His wid. Abigail moved to N. Y., with her son Joseph.

9. JOSEPH, son of Jos. (8), m. Deborah Twitchell, of Sherb., May 5, 1775, with w. cov'd, Mar., 1782, and had 1. POLLY, b. Nov. 6, 1775, d. Jan. 1, '78, burnt to death; 2. DEBBY, b. Dec. 19, '77; 3. TABBY; 4. JOSEPH, bap. Ap. 1782; 5. NABBY, bap. May, '82, d. Dec. 14, '84; 6. NELLY, b. May 20, '82.; 7. JOHN, b. Aug. 1, '84; 8. NATHAN, b. May 14, '87; 9. POLLY, bap. Ap. 1790. Joseph occupied his f's place, and moved, ab. 1788, first to Goshen, and after to Whitestown.

10. BILLY, (William), was b. in Fram. Mar. 26, 1784.

MELLEN, variously written MELLENS, MILLENS, MALING, MELLING, MELEN and MELES.

1. RICHARD, had at Charlestown, (the f.'s name on Boston Rec., written Mellers*), JAMES, b. June 3, 1642; and at Weymouth, SARAH, b. Ap. 4, 1643. [MARY, m. at Charlestown, Daniel Whittemore, 1662.] Richard took the freeman's oath, Sep. 7, 1639. The Hon. Christopher Webb writes that Richard Maling had land granted him at Weymouth, on the back side of Kingoak Hill, &c., between 1642 and '44, but his name disappears after from the Records of that town. (Ms. letter). He doubtless left that town, and probably removed to Charlestown or its vicinity.

2. JAMES, m. Elizabeth, dr. of Richard and Bridget Dexter, and had in Charles'n, 1. ELIZABETH, b. Sep. 4, 1659, m. Tho. Barlow, 1681; 2. MARY, b. July 8, 1661; 3. JAMES, b. Ap. 14, '63; 4. MARY, b. 1664, m. Phinehas Upham; 5. RICHARD, b. Ap. 24, '65; 6. JOHN, b. Sep. 17, '66, m. Elizabeth ——, and in 1695, was Master of the Brigantine Sarah, (Mid. Co. Rec.), and d. ab. that time, leaving a daughter; 7. SARAH, b. Nov. 27, '68; 8. THOMAS, b. May 11, '70, m. Mary (prob. dr. of Bartholomew) Threadneedle, of Boston, 1693, and was f. in Boston, of *James*, b. 1694; *Thomas*, '98; *Elizabeth*, 1700; *Benjamin*, '02; *Susanna*, '04; *William*, '07; *Ruth*, '09; *Ruth*, '13; *Deborah*, '17. The descendants in Boston, of the next generation, wrote " Melling;" 9. WILLIAM, b. Aug. 22, 1671, m. and was f. of *Deborah*, who m. in Malden, John Brintnal, 1712. James, the f. d. at Malden or Charlestown, and his wid. Eliz. had the administration of her husband's est. granted her, June 15, 1680. She m. 2d, Stephen Barrett, 1680.

3. SIMON, had by w. Mary, 1. SIMON[4], b. at Winesimit, Sep. 25, 1665; and at Malden, 2. THOMAS[11], b. Aug., 1668; 3. RICHARD, b. Jan. 2, 1671-2; 4. MARY, m. Thomas Gleason, of Fram. Dec. 6, 1695; 5. JAMES, (æ. 15, 1696, and chose br. Tho. as

---

* The name " Mellers " does not appear in the Hist. or Rec. of Charlestown; and of the family of Mellowes, we fail of finding a Richard.

guardian); 6. JOHN, b. at Watertown, Jan. 29, 1685-6. Simon, the f., settled in the S. part of Fram., ab. 1687, and enjoyed civil privileges at Sherb. He d. Dec. 19, 1694, and in the settlement of his est., 1695, all the above chil. are named. His wid. Mary d. in Fram., June 1, 1709, æ. 70.

4. ^{1}SIMON, s. of Simon (3), m. Elizab. Fisk, of Sherb., Dec. 27, 1688; and had 1. SIMON^5, b. May 16, 1690; 2. MARY, b. June 4, '95, d. Ap. 30, 1711; 3. JAMES^7, b. Mar. 8, '98. Simon, the f., was Constable, 1700; Tythingman, 1703, and Selectman, 1704. He d. Aug. 30, 1717, æ. 52, (T. Rec.) and a funeral discourse was preached by Mr. Swift, Sep. 1. His Inventory amounted to £629. See Will — Mid. Prob.

5. ^{1}SIMON, Jun., s. of Simon (4), m. Esther Town, Ap. 23, 1711, and was with w. adm. to the ch., Ap. 23, 1721. Their chil. were 1. MARY, b. Mar. 28, 1712, m. Jonathan Mores, Sep. 30, 1731; 2. JOHN, b. May 13, '14 — (prob. the John, after called Dr. Mellen, who in 1748, received a Town grant, for doctoring John Provender); 3. SIMON, b. June 10, 1716, m. Abigail Ball, Ap. 27, 1742, and f. at Hop. (where he d. 1795), of *Jonathan*, bap. 1745; *Susannah*, '55; *Abigail*, '57; *Edward*, '61; 4. JONATHAN, b. Nov. 25, 1718; 5. DAVID^6, b. Mar. 10, 1721-2; 6. ESTHER, 7. ISRAEL, twins, b. Mar. 22, 1724-5. Simon, the f., was Selectman, 1741. [Simon m. in Fram., Susannah Haven, Oct. 11, 1744. She was prob. a 2d wife.]

6. ^{1}DAVID, s. of Simon (5), m. Mary Maveric, of Sud., June 20, 1744; and had in Fram., ANN, b. Feb. 8, 1744; and in Oxford, JOHN, b. 1750; MARY, '53; LUCY, '56; DAVID, '59.

7. ^{1}JAMES, s. of Simon (4), m. Abigail Sanderson, of Wat., Sep. 29, 1720, with w. cov'd Aug. 14, 1721, and had in Fram., 1. ELIZABETH, b. Aug. 21, '21, m. in Holl., Elias Whitney, 1746; 2. ABIGAIL, b. Ap. 18, d. Ap. 24, 1723; 3. JAMES, b. Ap. 6, '24, d. Ap. 26, 1732; 4. ABIGAIL, b. Feb. 21, '26-7; 5. ABNER, b. Oct. 25, '29, d. Ap. 28, 1732; 6. JAMES^8, b. Mar. 10, '32-3; 7. ANNE, b. June 28, '35, d. Oct. 15, 1736; 8. JOSHUA, b. Jan. 16, 1737-8. [A Joshua m. Rebeckah Mellen, at Hop., 1771, and d. at Oxford, Jan. 30, 1828]; 9. ABNER, b. Aug. 17, 1740, prob. d. young. James, the f., was Selectman, 1740, and d. prob. in Fram. His w. d. ab. 1771.

8. ^{1}JAMES, s. of James (7), m. Martha Battle, of Dedham,

Nov. 28, 1754, and had 1. JAMES⁹, b. Dec. 1, '55; 2. NATHAN-IEL, b. Feb. 21, 1758, m. Anne Nutt, of Hop., f. in Fram., of *Anna* and *Patty*, and at Upton of *Nathaniel, Nancy*, &c., moved to Vt., and d. æ. 72; his s. *Nathaniel* was a Rep. in Vt.; 3. ABNER¹⁰, b. Mar. 25, '60; 4. ABIGAIL, b. Oct. 14, '62, m. Capt. William Nutt, of Hop.; 5. JOSHUA, b. Sep. 14, '65, had by 1st w. Elizabeth Valentine, *Joshua, John, Clarissa;* and by 2d w. Elizabeth Comey, *Elizabeth, Emily, Edward*, B. Un. 1823, lawyer at Wayland, *Harriet* and *Abigail*. Joshua was Rep. from Hop., 4 years, and lives in Westboro'. James, the f., lived on the Silk Farm; was a Baptist preacher, ord. at Brimfield, and d. at Dover, 1769. His wid. Martha, of Fram., m. Michael Homer, of Hop., Nov. 5, 1777.

9. ¹JAMES, s. of James (8), m. Lydia Marshall, and had in Fram., 1. JAMES, b. Oct. 28, 1776, m. Susanna Gould, Jan. 16, 1800, lives in Vt. (1844); 2. MOSES, b. May 19, '78, d. ab. 1798; 3. LYDIA, b. Jan. 20, '80, m. John Golden, of Hop.; 4. AARON, b. Ap. 24, '82, m. —— Newton, of Southb., and d. ab. 1838; 5. NATHANIEL, b. Sep. 17, '84, m. —— Brown, and d. in Wrentham; 6. ABIGAIL, b. Jan. 30, '88, m. in Vt., Dr. —— Mathews, 2d, Daniel Fay; 7. PATTY, b. Nov. 2, '89, d. young. Capt. James, the f., d. in Fram.

10. ¹ABNER, s. of James (8), m. Deborah Homer, of Hop., Nov. 11, 1784, and had in Fram., 1. BETSEY, b. Aug. 27, 1786, m. John Dadmun, lives in Fram.; 2. MICHAEL, b. Sep. 20, '88, m. Sarah Holden, of Dorch., lives in Brookline, a merchant in Boston; 3. JOHN, b. July 16, '90, m. Harriet Homer, of Boston, lives in Madison, Indiana; 4. ABIGAIL, b. Sep. 6, 1792 (twin to the next), m. Samuel Murdock, d. in Fram., young; 5. DEBORAH, b. Sep. 6, '92, m. John Hopkins, lives in Boston; 6. MARTHA, b. Ap. 17, '95, m. Ebenezer Tombs, lives in Hop.; 7. MOSES, b. Sep. 2, '97, m. Mary Brett, of Bridgewater, lives, a merchant, in Boston; 8. NANCY, b. Feb. 13, '99, m. Josiah Norcross, of Hop., lives in Fram.; 9. ABNER, m. Helen Cadwell, of N. Y.; 10. MARIA, m. Wm. Banks, of N. Y. Abner, the f., lived in the house now of Rev. Elbridge Gale, and d. 1831, æ. 71. His w. Deborah, d. Dec. 23, 1820, æ. 55.

11. ²THOMAS, s. of Simon, had by w. Elizabeth, 1. HENRY¹², b. Aug. 12, 1691; 2. THOMAS, b. Aug. 12, 1693, d. Feb. 4,

1711–2; 3. LYDIA, b. Ap. 12, '95; 4. SARAH, b. Mar. 22, '97, m. Ephraim Twitchell, of Sherb., Sep. 28, 1721; 5. MARY, b. Oct. 16, '99; 6. RICHARD[15], b. Nov. 10, 1701; 7. TABITHA, b. Jan. 4, 1703–4, m. Mark Whitney, of Hop., Jan. 4, 1726–7. Thomas, the f., was Tythingman, 1704.

12. [2]HENRY, s. of Thomas (11), m. Abigail Pratt, Mar. 24, 1711–2, and had in Fram., 1. THOMAS[13], b. May 15, 1713; 2. DANIEL,[14] b. Mar. 6, 1714–5; 3. SYBILLA, b. July 20, 1717; 4. ABIGAIL, b. Nov. 20, '19; 5. JOHN, bap. June 3, 1722, H. Coll. 1741, taught school same year at Sud., for £85, ord. at Sterling, Dec. 19, 1744, where he continued, "probably at the head of the clergy of the county," until Nov. 14, 1774. He was installed at Hanover, Feb. 11, 1784, and retired Feb. 1805. (See Worc. Mag., II. 213.) He m. Rebeckah, dr. of Rev. John Prentice, of Lanc., and was f. of *John*, b. 1752, H. Coll., 1770; *Henry*, b. 1757, Harvard College, 1784; *Prentice*, b. 1764, Harvard Coll., 1784, and Chief Justice in Me. John, the f., d. in Reading, July 4, 1807, the author of many printed discourses. His w. Rebeckah d. at Hanover, Jan. 11, 1802;* 6. MARY, bap. June 28, 1724, m. John Jones, Jun., of Hop., 1749; and in Hop., 7. LYDIA, b. Ap. 20, 1726, m. Jacob Chamberlin, of Hop., 1747; 8. JOSEPH, b. May 20, 1728, m. Ruhamah Butler, and d. 1772; 9. ELIZABETH, b. July 1, 1730, m. James Nutt, of Hop., 1747; 10. MARTHA, (twin), b. July 1, 1730, m. Samuel Chamberlin, 1749; 11. JAMES, bap. 1732. Henry, the f., was adm. with his w. to the ch., Mar. 11, 1720, dismissed to Hop. Ch., Dec. 27, 1724, and rec'd there, Jan. 3. He was chosen Deac. at Hop., 1732, and d. May 13, 1767, æ. 75. His wid. Abigail, d. July 30, 1781, æ. 88.

13. [2]THOMAS, s. of Henry (12), had in Hop., by w. Elizab., 1. HENRY, bap. 1735, 'd. 1813, a tanner, f. at Hop., by w. Sarah, of *Susanna*, bap. 1757; *Elizabeth*, '60, m. Winsor Stone; *Sarah*, '62, m. Phinehas Graves, of Fram., 1782; *Ruhamah*, '65; *Mary*, '67; *Abigail*, '71; *Henry*, '73; and

---

* Rev. John Mellen, according to the inscription on his monument, was born Mar. 14, 1722. He and the next child, were bap. in Fram., and the birth of neither is recorded in Fram. or Hop. His f. was received to the Hop. ch., Jan., 1724–5. The presumption that he was born in Fram., may be removed by the tradition, (if true), that the Trustees of the Hopkins' Fund, having offered to educate, gratuitously, at Harv. Coll., the first male child born in Hop., the father of John removed his family to Hop., soon before, the birth of the latter, who accordingly received the promised gratuity.

by 2d w. (wid. —— Abbe), *Rhoda* and *Thomas*, b. '75 ; *Lydia*, '78 ; *Anne*, '81 ; 2. ELIZABETH, b. 1737, m. —— Torrey ; 3 Col. JAMES, b. 1739, m. —— Russell, lived in Milford ; 4. MARY, bap. 1742 ; 5. SARAH, bap. 1744, d. young ; 6. LUCY, bap. 1746, m. Abner Stone, 1763, d. at Fitzwilliam, Jan. 27, 1824, æ. 77 ; 7. SARAH, bap. 1749, m. Ephraim Richardson, of Lancaster, 1766, and 2d, W. McFarland, Esq. ; 8. MEHETABEL, bap. 1751, m. Dr. Freeland ; 9. Maj. THOMAS, bap. 1754, of Hop. and Wat., f. of *Leonard*, *Lovel*, and *Alanson*, and d. 1805. Capt. Thomas, the f. m. 2d, wid. —— Wilson, and had, 10. JOSEPH, lives at Milford. Capt. Thomas d. in Hop., 1782.

14. ²DANIEL, s. of Henry (12), m. in Fram., Hannah Adams, Feb. 3, 1735–6, and had 1. ROBERT, b. Nov. 5, 1736, m. Sarah Holbrook, and f. at Holl., of *Joel*, b. 1764, lived in Swanzey, N. H. ; Col. *John*, b. 1766, m. Mary Bullard, and d. 1837 ; *Sarah*, b. 1768, m. —— Holbrook, of Grafton, and 2d, Joel Brooks, of Petersham, and d. July, 1846. Robert, the f., d. June 17, 1803, æ. 67, his w. Sarah d. Nov. 10, 1799, æ. 65 ; 2. JOSEPH, b. Mar. 17, 1737–8, m. Mary Parker, and f. at Holl. of *Hannah*, b. 1764, m. Joseph Forrestall, lived in Troy, N. Y. ; *William*, b. 1766, m. Lydia Underwood, and d. Sep. 4, 1807, æ. 41 ; *Henry*, b. 1769, m. Abigail Day, lived in Belchertown ; *Mary*, b. 1774, m. Joseph Messenger ; *Sophia*, b. 1779, m. Eliel Littlefield ; *Joseph*, (who d. young), and *Joanna*, (twins), who m. —— Town, of Charlton. Lt. Joseph, the f., d. in Holl., Nov. 12, 1787, æ. 49 y., 8 m. ; 3. JOHN, bap. in Hop., 1744, m. Sarah Fisher, of Medway, went to Fitzwilliam, ab. 1769, and f. of *John*, m. Ursula Cutter, and Olive Chamberlain, (and f. of John and William) ; *Elihu* (twin to John), d. without issue ; *Ruth*, m. David Stone, and d. 1808 ; *Puah*, m. Sam. Stevens, of Vt., and d. 1845 ; *Lois*, m. Isaac Bullard, of Medway ; *Julia*, m. Eben. Pierce, of N. Y. ; and *Lucretia*. John, the f., d. July 25, 1784, æ. 40 ; his wid. m. Rev. Benj. Brigham, of Fitzw., and d. Feb. 4, 1821, æ. 75 ; 4. ELIZABETH, bap. July 5, 1747, m. John Reed, of Dedham ; 5. DANIEL, bap. Ap. 6, 1749, lives (1846), at Fitzwilliam, m. 1st, —— Farwell, 2d, —— Goodrich, and f. of 5 daughters ; and at Holl., 6. HANNAH, b. 1751, m. Asa Johnson, of Attica, N. Y. ; 7. JAMES, b. 1753, m. Deborah Rockwood, and f. at Holl., of *James*, d. young ; *Deborah*, d. æ. 2 ; *Timothy*, b. 1780, m. Betsey Underwood, and d. 1845, leaving daughters, and no sons ; *Elizabeth*, (twin to Timothy), m. Martin Cutler, and d. young ; 8. ZERVIAH, (date of birth unknown), m. Josiah Hemenway, of Holl., 1761.

Daniel, the father, moved from Fram., to Holl., ab. 1750, and d. there, Jan. 17, 1784, æ. 68; his w. Hannah, d. May 27, 1794, æ. 83.

15. [2]RICHARD, s. of Thomas (11), and w. Abigail, cov'd June 20, 1725, and his w. adm. to the ch., June 8, 1728. Their chil. were 1. JOSIAH, b. Aug. 24, 1725, unm., mentally deranged; 2. WILLIAM[16], b. Sep. 14, 1728; 3. RICHARD, b. Aug. 30, 1730; 4. SAMUEL[17], b. Oct. 15, 1732; 5. MARY, b. June 23, 1739. Richard, the f., prob. lived at Mr. Davis', where his house was destroyed by fire.

16. [2]WILLIAM, s. of Richard, (15), m. Abigail Mellen, Oct. 18, 1750, and 2d, Abigail Hemenway, Nov. 7, 1751, and had 1. ABIGAIL, b. Oct. 10, 1752, m. Darius Monger, Esq., Rep. from S. Brimfield; 2. LUCY, b. June 15, '55, prob. d. young; 3. RICHARD, b. Feb. 20, '58; 4. NATHAN, b. June 4, '51; 5. WILLIAM, b. June 3, '55. (These 2 as recorded; perhaps an error of 10 years); 6. ANNA, b. — 4, 1767. William, the f., moved to Draper, Vt., ab. 1777.

17. [2]SAMUEL, s. of Richard (15), m. Submit Stone, and had in Fram., 1. MARTHA, b. June 5, 1760; 2. EZRA, b. May 7, 1762; 3. GILBERT, b. Aug. 15, 1764.

18. ABIGAIL, of Fram., m. Moses Haven, of Hop., Nov. 1, 1750. ABIGAIL, m. William Mellen, both of F., Oct. 18, '50.

SARAH, m. in Hop., Nathaniel Pike, 1765. MARY, m. in Hop., Phinehas Gibbs, 1757. THOMAS, of Petersham, m. wid. Catharine Dyer, and was f. of *Nancy*, b. Mar. 13, 1783, and a son; both d. young. JOHN, of Hop., had a s. *Samuel*, bap. 1762. Some of the early Mellen families in Fram., lived on the fields to the E. of Mr. Joseph Merriam's.

MERRIAM, Dr. TIMOTHY, a native of Concord, Mass., m. Huldah Darling, of Bellingham, and had in Concord, 1. TRYPHENA, m. Wm. D. Hills, of Charlestown; 2. MARY, m. Jesse Hall, of Camb.; and in Fram., 3. TIMOTHY, b. Ap. 26, 1791, lost at sea, Jan. 1827; 4. JOSEPH, b. Nov. 23, 1793, m. Alice, daughter of Nathaniel and Rhoda Thayer, of Franklin, lives in Fram.; 5. GALEN, b. Dec. 5, 1797, m. Silence Baxter, a merchant in Boston; 6. HANNAH, (twin to Galen), m. Joseph Fisher, a native of Belchertown, of the U. S. Navy. She was lost at sea, Oct. 1841; 7. ROSALINE A., b. Nov. 14, 1805, m. Elbridge M. Jones, of

Fram. Dr. Timothy practiced many years in the medical profession at Fram., and d. Sep. 17, 1835, æ. 76. His wid. d. Jan. 22, 1840, æ. 73.

METCALF, or MEDCALFE, LEVI, (who came from Franklin, 1783), m. Lois Biglow. Their chil. were OLIVE, m. in Fram., Aaron Pratt, of Sherb., Oct. 1790; LOIS, m. Peter Cloyes; SALLY, b. '79, m. Obed Daniels. Levi, the f., d. 1832, æ. ab. 86. 2. PHILIP, (br. of Levi, and son of Barnabas, of Franklin,) m. Anna Knowlton, May 26, 1790, and had 1. DANIEL, b. Mar. 4, 1791, m. Eliza Knowlton; 2. HEALY, b. May 18, '93; 3. LEWIS, 4. LUCY, (twins), b. Jan. 29, '96. 3. OBED, (s. of Samuel, of Franklin,) m. in Fram., Nabby Park, Feb. 4, 1790. ABEL, (br. of Obed), m. in Fram., Nabby Eames, Feb. 1789. JOSEPH, of Wrentham, m. Hannah Haven, of Fram., Oct. 23, 1751. JAMES, of Wrenth., m. Abiel Haven, Jan. 3, 1754. Mrs. MARY, m. James Glover, both of Fram., Sep. 23, 1784.

This family prob. descended from MICHAEL, of Dedham, who d. 1664, leaving w. Mary, (who had a dr., Martha Bullard), and chil. *Thomas; John*, of Medfield; a dr. Wilson; drs *Elizabeth* Bancroft; *Joane* Waker; *Rebeckah* Mackentoth; *Sarah* Onion; *Martha* Stow, (her first husband, William Brignall); and g. chil., Michael Metcalfe, Jun , (or sen.), John Mackentoth, and Robert Onion. Michael took the freeman's oath, May 18, 1640; a Michael, also, May 18, 1642, and May, 1645. JOHN took the oath, Mar. 4, 1634-5.

MATTHEW, Esq., of Hop., had by w. Deborah Bullard, *Fisher;* and *Matthew*, m. Punh Tilton. SETH, of Southb., m. Hannah Bancroft, 1773. BARNABAS, of Franklin. had brs. *Michael*; *Pelatiah*; *James*; Dr. *Ebenezer*; and *Samuel*, whose s. Caleb lives in Boston.

MIDDLESEX, SALEM, m. Kata Benson, Sep. 1783, and d. in Fram., Aug. 16, 1816. See the notice of Peter Salem, in the preceding history.

MIXER, MIXSER, MIXTER, or MIXTURE, ISAAC, early took the oath of fidelity in Wat. where he d. His will is dated, May 8, 1655; and his chil. were ISAAC; and SARAH, who m. John Sternes. Wid. Sarah d. in Wat., Nov. 24, 1681. 2. ISAAC, s. of Isaac (1), m. Mary Cooke, Sep. 19, 1655, and had, 1. MARY, b. May 18, 1656, m. George Manning, 1680; 2. SARAH, b. Nov. 29, '57, m. (Samuel?) Hager. Isaac's w. (named Sarah, on the Wat. Rec.), d. July 2, 1660; an f he m. Rebeckah Garfield. Jan. 10, 1660-1; and had 3. REBECKAH, b. Mar. 9, '62, m. Samuel Kendall; 4. ISAAC, (in f's will "oldest son") m. Elizabeth Pierce, 1684; his will proved, Jan., 1725-6; he had prob. no issue; he brought up his cousin, Isaac Peirce; 5. ELIZABETH, b. June 18, '65, d. 1685; 6. JOANNA, b. Dec. 14, '66, m. —— Ward;

7. John, b. Mar. 1, '68, m. Abigail Fisk, '95, a tanner, and f. of *Abigail*, b. '96; *John*, Jan. 22, '98-9 : *Elizabeth, Dec*. 30, 1702; *George*, Dec. 27, '04; 8. George, b. Dec. 12, '70, (not in the will); 9. Abigail, b. Nov. 4, '72, m. Samuel How, Dec. 11, 1690-1; 10. Joseph, b. Aug 7, '74, m. Anne Jones, Deac. at Wat., and f. of *Rebecca*, b. 1703, d. 1704; *Joseph*, b. 1705, m. Mary Ball, 1726, lived in Shrewsbury; *Sarah*, b. 1708, m. David Learned, 1730; *Lydia*, b. 1710, m. —— Warren; *David*, b. and d. 1713; *Mary*, b. 1714; *Josiah*, b. 1716, d. ab. 1789, m. Mary Gearfield, 1741, (and prob. 3 other wives), and f. at Waltham, of Mary; Samuel, (m. Elizabeth Bigelow, and d. at N. Braintree, father of Jason, Esq. of Hardwick, and Hon. Samuel, of N. Braintree); Josiah; Ann; and by 2d w. Sarah Mead, m. 1754, Sarah; Persis; and Lois; *Anne*. b. 1719, m. Isaac Rice, '41; *Abigail*, b. 1721. Deac. Joseph's est. (£874), was adm'd, 1723; w. Anne d. ab 1736; 11. Daniel[4], b. Feb. 21, 1675-6; 12. Mehetabel, b. and d. 1677; 13. Benjamin[3], b. Mar. 23, 1679; 14. Dorothy, b. Sep., 1680, m. Wm. Davis, of Roxb., 1710; 15. David, d. 1683. Rebecca, w. of Isaac, d. Mar. 16, 1682, and he m. 3d, in 1687, Mary French, of Billerica, prob. wid of John Sternes, of Billerica. (Mid. Deeds, vol. X, deed of Mary Mixer, to son Sam. Sternes). Isaac, the f. d, " an aged man," 1716, leaving wid. Mary. (See Will in Mid. Prob.)

3. BENJAMIN, s. of Isaac (2), bought in 1701, of Isaac How, of Marlb., S. side of Stoney Brook, in what is now Southb., and m. Rebeckah Newton, of Marlb., Nov. 27, 1711. Their chil. were, 1. Phinehas, b. Dec. 26, 1712, m. Mary Lamb, Nov. 19, 1735, and f. of *Abigail*, b. Oct. 27, '36. He moved from Southb.; 2. Benjamin, b. Mar. 23, 1715, m. Sarah Garfield, and f. of *Sarah*, b. July 23, '38, m. —— Newell, of Dudley; *Benjamin*, deaf and dumb; *Joseph*[9], b. Mar. 7, '42; *Ezra*. b. Aug. 10, '48, d. young; *Levinah*, b. 1751, d. 1754; Sarah, the m. d. 1754; he m. 2d, Dinah Newton, 1755, who d. without chil., æ. over 90; Benj. d. æ. over 80; 3. Isaac, b. Nov. 26, 1716; 4. David, b. Dec. 22, 1718-9, m. Hannah Gibbs, Oct., 1741, and f. of *Rebeckah*, b. Sep. 10, '42; *Naomi*. '44; *David*, July 18, '49; *Hannah* Ap. 27, '52; the f. moved prob. to Sutton; 5. Joseph, b. and d. 1724; 6. Ebenezer, b. May 23, 1729, (prob. posthumous) went to L. Island. The f. d. 1728 — his Inventory, £568.15.9. The wid. m. 2d, Moses Newton, Oct., 1743.

4. DANIEL, s. of Isaac (2), had in Fram., by w. Jude, or Judith, 1. Elizabeth, b. Oct. 12, 1704; 2. Daniel, b. June 4, 1706, d. Jan. 20, 1721-2; 3. John[6], b. Nov. 4, 1711; 4. Isaac[5], (see will of Isaac, of Wat., proved Jan. 1725-6.) Daniel, the f., was Constable, 1705; and Selectman, 1722, 3 years. He was prob. living in Fram., near Southb. line, 1735. "Old Mrs. Mixer, w. of Daniel," was adm. to the ch., Feb. 4, 1749.

5. ISAAC, s. of Dan. (4), had in Fram., by w. Anne, 1. Judith, b. July 6, 1735, m. Joseph Nichols, of Needham, Oct. 28, '55; 2. Anne, b. Nov. 25, '36; 3. Daniel, b. Oct. 21, '38. Isaac, the f., lived near the Poor Farm; was Selectman, 1745, 2 years.

6. JOHN, s. of Dan. (4), m. Mary Lyscom, of Southb., Dec. 25, 1739, and had in Fram., 1. Lydia, b. Nov. 7, 1741, m. John

Harrington, of Marlb., 1768; 2. RUTH, b. June 27, '42, d. y.; 3. RUTH, b. Ap. 2, '44; 4. JOHN⁷, b. Nov. 10, '45; 5. MARY, b. May 27, '47, adm. to the ch., Aug. 1790, d. unm. in F.; 6. NATHAN, b. Aug. 1, '49, d. at the battle of Bennington; 7. EZEKIEL, b. June 9, 1752, m. Anne Pepper, moved to Fitzwilliam, N. H. John the f., lived in the house late of Royal Stone, on the Southb. Road, and d. in Fram. His wid. lived to a great age.

7. JOHN, s. of John (6), m. Thankful Puffer, and with w. cov'd May 31, 1772, and with w. adm. to the ch., Feb. 1781. Their chil. were 1. DANIEL, bap. June 1, 1772; 2. SALLY, bap. Dec. 18, '74; 3. ANNE, bap. June 14, '78; 4. NATHAN, bap. May, '86; 5. LYSCOM, bap. May, '90. John the f., occupied his father's farm, and moved to Whitestown, N. Y.

8. TIMOTHY, had in Fram., by w. Molly, 1. JOSEPH, b. Feb. 11, 1770; 2. POLLY, b. Jan. 31, 1772.

9. JOSEPH, s. of Benj. and Sarah, of Southb., (see No. 3,) m. Jane Newton, 1765, and had in Southb., 1. LEVINAH, b. Feb. 11, 1766, m. Jeremiah Newton, and d. 1840; 2. SARAH, b. Sep. 28, '67, m. Wm. Stow, of Southb., lives (1845); and in Fram., 3. EBENEZER B. bap. Oct. 8, 1769, m. Phebe Stow, of Southb., and d. in N. Y.; 4. WILLIAM, bap. July 21, '71, d. æ. 3 mos.; 5. JOSEPH, bap. Jan. 10, '73, d. young; 6. ANNA, bap. Mar. 30, '74, m. Luther Angier, of Southb., and d. young; 7. JOSEPH, bap. Ap. 7, '75, m. Nancy Fay, of Southb., lives in Oxford, Me.; 8. THEODAD, bap. Sep. 1777, m. Hollis Jewel, lived in Southb., and St. Albans, Vt., and d. young; 9. WILLIAM, bap. Aug. 1, '79, m. Patience Churchill, lives in Paris, Me.; 10. BENJAMIN, bap. Jan. 1783, m. Betsey Shepard, of Marlb., lives in Hillsborough, N. H. Lt. Joseph, the f., was Ensign in Capt. Tho. Drury's Co. in the Rev. war. He lived near Mr. Temple's, on the Goddard place; moved to Southb., ab. 1785, and d. in Boston, æ. ab. 60. His w. Jane d. in Fram., 1785.

10. JOSEPH and POLLY were bap. Oct. 4, 1772. BENJAMIN was adm. to the ch., 1775.

MOHEAG, ABIGAIL, was prob. living in Fram., 1749. (Deac. Buckminster's Journal.)

MONTGOMERY, Capt. M., was living in Fram., 1750, on the road from Saxonville to Marlb., and was rated by the name of Gomery, 1760. His name was Robert.

MOORE, MORE, or MORES, SAMUEL, m. in Sud., Sarah Haynes, Dec. 8, 1714, and had in Sud., 1. DOROTHY, b. Sep. 6, 1715, m. Peter Goodnow, '36; 2. ELIZABETH, b. Mar. 24, '16–7, adm. to the ch., Nov. 19, 1752; 3. HANNAH, b. May 31, '19; and in Fram., 4. SUSANNAH, b. May 13, '21; 5. MARY, b. Mar. 14, '22–3, m. Samuel Clark, of Sherb., Jan. 15, '46; 6. THANKFUL, b. Feb. 10, '24–5; 7. SAMUEL, b. Mar. 30, '27, d. young; 8. JOSIAH, b. Ap. 10, '29; 9. MARTHA, b. Mar. 17, '30–1; 10. SARAH, b. Ap. 12, '32; 11. PETER^2, b. June 6, '34; 12. SAMUEL, b. May 11, '40. Capt. Samuel, the f., was Constable in Fram., 1728, and Selectman from 1737, 6 years. He was adm. to the ch., Nov. 4, 1750.

2. PETER, s. of Sam. (1), had in Fram., by w. Hannah, 1. REBECKAH, bap. Jan. 3, 1762, m. Benj. Collins, of Southb.; 2. SALLY, bap. Mar. 13, '65, d. unm., at Philipston, 1837; 3. SAMUEL, bap. Ap. 14, '65, m. Anna Underwood, Oct. 6, '95, d. in Philipston, 1841; 4. LUTHER, bap. Aug. 24, '66, had 2 wives; 5. FANNY, bap. July 31, '68, m. Joseph Angier, Mar. '91, 2d, Eph. Hager, and d. 1842; 6. MARTHA, bap. Ap. 22, '70, m. Charles Stockwell, of Leverett; 7. MOLLY, bap. Nov. 8, '72, m. Josiah Stockwell, and d. in Philipston; 8. GRACE, bap. June 2, '76, m. Wm. Howe, of Philipston. Peter the f., lived on the old Littlefield place, with w. cov'd, Jan. 3, 1762, and moved into the country. He d. ab. 1816. His w. Hannah d. ab. 1794.

3. JONATHAN Mores, resident in Fram., m. Mary Mellen, Sep. 30, 1731. WILLIAM was of Fram., Ap. 6, 1748. POLLY, m. Samuel Hawes, of Wrentham, Nov. 13, 1796. PERSIS m. Abner Stone, Mar. 5, 1776. LAWSON, m. Lydia Goodenough, June, 1784.

JOHN, sen., of Sud., (perhaps of Camb., 1637), who left a numerous posterity, early took the oath of fidelity, at Sud. He bought, Sep., 1642, a house and land of Edmund Rice; and in 1645, a houselot and town rights of John Stone. His will was proved, 1674. He had chil., *John, Lydia, Jacob, Joseph, William, Elizabeth, Mary.* His w. was Elizabeth. JOHN, of Lancaster, (perhaps his son), m. in Sud., An Smith, Nov. 16, 1654; had, in Lanc., *Mary*, b. 1655, m. Matthew Gibbs, '78; *Elizabeth*, '57, m. the same; *Lydia*, '60, m. —— Witherby; *John*, '62; *Joseph*, '64; *Ann*, '66, m. —— Hildrick; *Jonathan*, '69. John, the f. was of Sud., 1682, and returned to Lancaster, where he d. at or before 1705, leaving a wid. Mary.

MOQUET, (pronounced Mucket), FRANCIS, prob. a native of France, m. in Medfield, Ap. 7, 1721, Mrs. Elizabeth Symmes, and had no issue. He kept a house of entertainment in Fram., as early as 1729, at the house late of Deac. Buckminster. He afterwards lived in (prob. built or enlarged) the house E. of Mr. Tho. Hastings'. He was in Stow, Aug. 1754, in the family of the Rev. Mr. Gardner, in a destitute state, and assistance was asked from Fram. He is noticed on the Sud. Rec., as in that Town, Oct. 1754. This is the latest notice of him known. His name is not unfrequently repeated in the Town, at the present day, in connection with past events.*

MORSE, JOSEPH, of Wat., m. Elizabeth Sautle, 1691, and had, 1. JOSEPH, b. 1693; 2. ABIGAIL, b. 1696, m. in Fram., Joshua Hemenway, July 1, 1718; 3. ZECHARIAH, b. 1699; 4. SAMUEL, b. 1702; 5. JONATHAN, b. Feb. 10, 1704-5; 6. DANIEL, b. Ap. 24, 1707; 7. ELIZABETH, m. in Fram., John Clayes, Dec. 10, 1730. Joseph, the f. d. at Guilford, on a visit there, June 24, 1709. He wrote a letter, dated two days before his death, (now in the possession of Mrs. Eben. Freeman, of Fram., a descendant), in which he speaks of a cousin Jones. His est. was assigned to Joseph, his eldest son, 1714. His wid (with several of the chil.) moved to Fram., she having m. 2d, Benjamin Nurse, sen., of Fram., Feb. 16, 1713-4. A s. of Jos. lived in Franklin.
Joseph was prob. g. son of Joseph, (and w. Esther), of Wat., (living 1685), who had *Joseph*, b. Ap. 30, 1637, m. Susanna Shattuck, Ap. 12, '61, and d. 1677; *John*, b. Feb. 28, '38-9. Deac. at Wat., d. 1702; *Esther*, '45; *Jeremiah*, m. Abigail Woodward, 1681.†

2. JONATHAN, s. of Joseph (1), m. Mary Cloyce, May 16, 1734, and had, 1. ZERUIAH, b. June 25, '35, m. Abraham Nurse, Oct. 24, '53 ; 2. JONATHAN³, b. Feb. 10, '36-7 ; 3. ELIZABETH, b. Nov. 17, '38, prob. d. young; 4. JOSEPH, b. Dec. 17, '40, d. unm., of apoplexy ; 5. NATHAN, b. Nov. 13, '42, d. young ; 6. JAMES⁴, b. May 19, '46 ; 7. ASA⁵, b. Feb. 24, '47 ; 8. NATHAN, b. Feb. 16, '50, m. Wid. —— Hill, of Grafton, d. in Alstead ; 9. MOLLY, b. Nov. 25, '52, m. William Arnold. Jona. the f. occupied the farm now of Mr. Ebenezer Freeman; was Selectman, 1759, 3 years ; was chosen Deac. of the first ch., Aug. 29, 1751 ; and d. Mar. 5, 1801, æ. 96, " an honest man." Mary his w. d. Mar. 27, 1785, æ. 72.

3. JONATHAN, Jun., s. of Jona. (2), m. Mehetabel Nurse, and had, 1. DANIEL, b. Nov. 25, 1765, m. Rebecca Knowlton,

* Miss Nancy Bent has in her possession a volume of Appleton's Sermons, with a preface by President Wadsworth, printed 1728; on which is written, "Elizabeth Moquet, her book, given by the Rev. Jos. Baxter, Boston, 1744."

† 1634, embarked in the Increase, Samuel, æ. 50; w. Elizabeth, æ. 48 ; Joseph, æ. 20. In the James, came over (1635), Anthony, and William, of Marlborough. (Savage's Gleanings).

June 29, '90, and moved to W. part of N. Y. ; 2. LEVINAH, b. Dec. 17, '67, m. John Murray, Vt., and d. there, leaving 4 chil., who with the f. m'd to Me. ; 3. JOSEPH, b. Mar. 27, '71, m. Lydia Gleason, Oct. 11, '95, 2d, —— Mitchell ; 4. CALVIN, b. Nov. 22, '73, m. at the Eastward ; 5. JONATHAN, b. Mar. 24, '76, m. Rebecca Gleason, lives in Union, Me. Jonathan, the f. lived towards the Common, and d. young.

4. JAMES, s. of Jona. (2), m. Mary Gleason, and had 1. JOSIAH, b. July 6, 1773, d. Sep. 19, '75 ; 2. DOROTHY, b. Sep. 1, '75, m. Micajah Cloyes, Jan. 26, 1800, moved to N. Y.; 3. ANNA, b. June 23, '79, m. Reuben Dunton, lives in Boylston ; 4. JOSIAH, b. Dec. 9, '81, d. Aug. 17, 1800 ; 5. POLLY, b. May 28, '84, m. Adams Littlefield ; 6. ABIGAIL, b. Dec. 27, '86, m. Ebenezer Freeman ; 7. BETSEY, b. Mar. 27, '91, d. Oct. 8, '99 ; 8. JAMES, b. June 12, '94, d. July 11, '98. James, the f. lived on his father's est., and d. Sep. 15, 1822, æ. 76. His wid. Mary d. Dec. 7, 1842, æ. 92.

5. ASA, s. of Jona. (2), m. Susannah Eames, Jan. 15, 1777, and had, 1. JOSEPH, b. 1778, d. 1782 ; 2. NATHAN, b. 1779, d. 1780 ; 3. BETSEY, b. 1780, d. young ; 4. ASA, b. Mar. 27, '82, m. Julia A. Carpenter ; 5. JOSEPH, b. Mar. 3, '84, lives in Fram., unm. ; 6. ASENETH, b. Dec. 15, '85, m. Elijah Cloyes, of Fram. ; 8. MEHETABEL, b. Jan. 27, '88, lives in Fram., unm. ; 8. GILBERT, Nov. 8, '90, lives unm. (1844), in N. Orleans ; 9. SUSANNA, b. Jan. 4, '92, m. Col. Jonas Cloyes, of Fram. ; 10. DEXTER, b. Dec. 14, '97, m. in Alabama. Asa, the f. lived at Mr. Joseph Morse's, and d. Feb. 19, 1831, æ. 83. His wid. d. in Fram., at the extreme age of 96 years.

6. JACOB, of Fram., m. Abigail Ball, of Wat., Feb. 26, 1728, and had, (Sud. Rec.) 1. LYDIA, b. Nov. 11, 1728 ; 2. ABIGAIL, b. Jan. 10, 1731 ; 3. OLIVER, b. Aug. 12, 1734, m. Elizabeth Osborn, 1759 ; 4. HANNAH, b. Dec. 19, 1736, d. 1739 ; 5. ISAAC, b. June 31, 1739 ; 6. DANIEL, b. Feb. 25, '41, d. 1742 ; 7. SAMUEL, b. Jan. 19, '42–3. Before 1740, Jacob was in the occupation of land under Eben. Winchester, and Isaac Howe, at the N. part of the town ; and was sued at law by Col. Buckminster. (Suff. Co. Rec.)

7. BENJAMIN, m. Mary Jones, Oct. 26, 1750, and had in Southb., 1. JOHN, b. Nov. 11, '52 ; and at Fram., 2. DANIEL, b.

Feb. 8, '55; and at Southb., 3. a son, b. Oct. 30, '59; 4. MARY, b. Feb. 18, '62; 5. ANNE, b. Mar. 24, '64; 6. CHARLOTTE, b. Dec. 4, '65.

Benjamin, was s. of Zechariah, who m. in Fram., Huldah Whitney, Nov. 16, 1724, and had, at Southb., *Benjamin*, b. Dec. 3, 1725; *Mary*, b. Dec. 25, '28; *Elizabeth*, b. June 20, '31.

8. DAVID, m. Esther Sanger, and moved from Holliston into Fram. Their chil. were 1. SARAH, m. —— Lyman, of Winchester, N. H.; 2. BENJAMIN[9]; 3. LUTHER, bap. in Fram., Nov. 21, 1773; 4. ANNE, bap. Ap. 7, 1776; 5. ESTHER, bap. Oct. 1, '78, m. —— Dodge, of Winch.; 6. DAVID, d. unm., injured by a lever while at work on the highways, at the E. part of Fram.; 7. JOHN, bap. Sep., '83, m. —— French, of Winch.; 8. WILLIAM, bap. Oct., '91. David, the f. and w. were adm. to the ch. Aug., '91; lived near Wid. Eaton's, moved to Winchester, N. H.

9. BENJAMIN, s. of David (8), m. Sarah Claflin, Nov. 29, 1792; and had in Fram., 1. JOEL, b. June 25, '93, m. Mary Scott, of Newton, and d. in Fram., July 24, 1825; 2. BETSEY, b. Jan. 20, '95; 3. CORNELIUS, m. Clarissa Haven; 4. BENJAMIN, m. Louisa Temple; 5. SARAH, m. Nathaniel Merrit; 6. PERSIS, d. young; 7. HANNAH, d. young. Benj. the f. lived at Winchester, N. H., and at Dover, and d. in Fram., ab. 1827; his w. Sarah d. a few years before.

10. MARY, w. of Daniel, was adm. to the ch., Ap. 26, 1752. ABIGAIL, of Sherb. m. Benj. Bruce, of Fram., July 1, 1718. THOMAS, of Sherb., m. Mary Treadway, of Fram., Mar. 29, 1736–7. DANIEL, of Marlb. m. Polly Gibbs, of Fram., May 9, 1781.

The family of Morse extended widely in Medfield, Sherb., and Holl. They are generally to be traced back to Samuel and w. Elizabeth, of Dedham. The descendants are too numerous to be here given. SAMUEL, prob. s. of Jos., of Dedham, m., in Sud, Elizabeth Moore, Feb. 10, 1664, and had chil. in Medfield. BETHIAH, (prob. from Dedham), m. in Sud., John Perry, May 23, 1665. JONATHAN, and w. Mary, had chil. at Marlb., from 1717.

MOULTON, CALEB, was rated for the highways in Fram., 1775. DANIEL, JESSE, and JOSEPH, were also residents here ab. 1790.

Caleb, of E. Sud., d. Jan. 11, 1800, æ. 91; his w. Sarah d. June 1, 1786, æ. 69. Capt. Caleb d. at E. S., Sept. 19, 1821, æ. 76. ROBERT was early a freeman at Salem. ROBERT, m. at Salem, Mary Cook, 1672, and had *Mary; Robert*, 1675; *Ebenezer*, '78; *Abigail*, '82. JACOB was of Charlestown, 1663.

MUNN, JOHN, and w. Abigail, came from Sherb. to Fram., Ap. 7, 1774. (T. Rec.)

MUNROE, ANNA, of Fram., m. Asa Nurse, June 3, 1778.

MUNSELL, JACOB, and w. Mary, had in Fram., MARY, b. Aug. 9, 1731; ESTHER, b. July 31, 1733. Mary was a member of Mr. Bridge's ch., 1746.

MUZZEY, or Mussey, BENJAMIN, of Lexington, m. in Fram., Lydia Eames, Nov. 15, 1716; prob. lived in Sherb., or on the borders of Fram., and was living 1753; his w. Lydia, a wid. ab. 1762, d. Oct. 21, 1775, æ. 81.

Benjamin, prob. descended from BENJAMIN, who had at Malden, 1. BENJAMIN, b. Ap. 16, 1657, had at Camb., by w. Sarah, *Mary*, b. 1683; *Benjamin*, b. Feb. 20, '89; *Amos*, Jan. 6, '99-0; *Bethiah*, 1701; and d. at Lexington, May 17, 1732, æ. 74. He bought, 1693, of Edward Pelham, of Newport, 206 ac. between Camb. and Concord; 2. JOSEPH, b. Mar. 1, 1658-9. Benjamin, the f. of Rumney Marsh, 1673, had w. Alice. In 1677, a deed speaks of his w. as dr. of Richard Dexter, of Malden. He sold half a farm of 300 ac., in Boston, on Charlestown line, to Thomas Brattle, 1673, and bought, 1680, of Timothy Brooks, rights in Billerica. Robert Muzzey took the freeman's oath, Sep. 3, 1634.

2. JOSEPH, was in Fram., 1719; and in 1721, signed a receipt of money from Jonathan Rice, of Fram., "for the purchase of his (Joseph's) land in said town."

Joseph, of Sud., m. Patience Rice, 1721, and was f. of *Benjamin*, b. June, 1729, (w. Mary, and had chil. at Sud.); *Joseph*, 1731; *William*, '33; *Nathaniel*, '36, (w. Jane, and lived in Sud. and Rutland); and several drs. THOMAS m. Abigail Cuzzens, 1736, and d. 1754, f. at Holl., of *Robert*, b. 1745, (who went to England, and had the small pox there. He had by w. Martha, Robert, 1769); *Thomas*, 1750; *Abigail*, '53. THOMAS, a joiner, d. at Mendon, and his est. was settled, 1756. (Worc. Prob.) His w. was Huldah, and he left many drs. JOHN and w. Abigail, had chil. in Rutland, from 1740.

NEGUS, WILLIAM, m. in Marlb., Persis Maynard, 1730; and had in Worc., 1. BENJAMIN, b. 1730, m. Elizabeth Woodcock, 1755, and f. at Petersham, of *Jonas*, b. 1754, &c.; 2. WILLIAM, b. 1732; and in Fram. 3. SAMUEL, b. June 23, 1735. The f. moved to Petersham, and had 4. PERSIS, b. 1737; 5. JOHN, b. 1740; 6. JOSEPH, b. 1742, m. —— Mellen, and f. of *John*, m. in Fram., Betsey Gleason, June 16, 1794; *Joel ; Paul ; Sally ; Catharine ; Fanny ; Mary ;* 7. MARTHA, b. 1745; 8. LUCY, b. '47; 9. SILAS, b. '50; 10. SOLOMON, b. '53.

BENJAMIN took the freeman's oath, May 10, 1648, and was f. by w. Elizabeth, at Boston, of *Elizabeth*, b. 1640. m. Richard Barnard, '59; *Benjamin*, 1641; *Mary*, 1643; *Samuel*, 1645; *Hannah*, 1653. JONATHAN took the freeman's oath, Sep. 3, 1634. In 1675, ISAAC, of Taunton, cooper, was sole heir of Jonathan, late of Boston. (Mid. Deeds, VIII. 21.)

NELAND, see Kneeland.

NEWTON, SOLOMON, from Southb., m. Hannah Dudley, and had in Fram. 1. SOLOMON, b. Nov. 11, 1772, was seriously injured in a well, d. unm. in N. Y.; 2. THANKFUL, b. Aug. 22, '79, went to N. Y. Solo. the f. d. in the Rev. service. His w. Hannah d. in Fram., ab. 1810.

2. EPHRAIM, br. of Solo. (1), m. Abigail Claflin, Mar. 1784, and had in Fram., 1. PAMELA, b. May 2, 1785, m. in Medway; 2. AMOS, b. Ap. 13, '87. The f. lived on the Common, and moved to N. Y., ab. 1800.

3. JONAS, (b. Ap. 25, 1763), s. of Amos Jr. and Jane, of Southb., m. Olive Tozer, and had in Fram., 1. LYDIA, b. Ap. 17, 1788, m. Samuel Hudson, of Fram.; 2. PHINEHAS, b. May 7, 1790, m. —— Onthank, of Southb., and d. 1843; 3. POLLY, b. July 14, 1792, m. Luther Goodnow, of Fram.; 4. PETER, b. July 19, 1795, m. Mary Ann Bixby, and 2d, Maria Dunton. Jonas the f. lived on the Common, and d. 1843; Olive his w. died Sep. 1820.

4. ANDREW, s. of Andrew and Mehetabel, of Southb., m. Sarah Merritt, and had in Fram., 1. WILLIAM, b. 1773, m. Abigail Newton, of Worcester, lives in Shrewsbury; 2. a son, d. young; 3. LUTHER, b. Jan. 21, '79, m. 1st. Patty Bruce, who d. Oct. 13, 1835, æ. 56, and 2d, Anna Merritt, 3d, wid. Ruha. Godey; 4. SHUBAEL, b. 1781, m. Abigail Pike, of Hop.; 5. MARTIN, d. in Boston of small pox; 6. SALLY, m. Edward Rawson of Westboro'; 7. FANNY; 8. ANNA, m. Nathan Hudson, and d. in Fram. Andrew the f. d. in Fram., ab. 1792. He owned on Fiddle Neck, a forge and corn mill, (which his father Andrew had owned and occupied before him), beyond Bigelow's mill, at the fall. [Andrew of Southb., (who m. Mehetabel Bellows), had besides Andrew, Jun., *Mehetabel*, b. 1745; and *James*, b. Aug. 24, 1751, and was living in Fram., 1778.]

5. GERSHOM, "warned out of town," 1721. GERSHOM, was rated in Fram. ab. 1757. ZERVIAH, was adm. to the ch., Ap. 5, 1747. ZERVIAH, bap. June 14, 1747. ABIGAIL, dr. of Jason,

bap. May 14, 1758. SUSANNA, m. Ebenezer Singletary, Ap. 5, 1713. DANIEL, of Southb., m. Sarah Hutson, of Fram., Dec. 12, 1728. WILLIAM, of Marlb., m. Elizabeth Wright, of Fram., Dec. 1, 1737. RICHARD, of Southb., m. Martha Pike, of Fram., Jan. 27, 1743. NATHAN, (from Southb.) m. Polly Nichols, July 1784. EBENEZER, m. Sally Rice, June, 1785, (lived in the N. part of the town, and d. in Southb.) HANNAH, m. Nathan Tombs, Nov. 24, 1792. REBECCA, of Southb., m. Dan'l Hemmenway, Jun., of Fram., Feb. 1787. JAMES, of Fram., m. in Hop. Bathshebah Nurse, 1769. SHADRACK, b. in Fram., July 19, 1783.

RICHARD took the freeman's oath, May, 1645, was one of the early prop. of Sud., and a petitioner, 1656, for Marlb., of which he was a prop., and to which (in the part now Southb.) he removed from Sud. He d. in Marlb., leaving a wid. Hannah, Aug., 1701, "almo-t a hundred years old." (T. Rec.) His chil. by w. Anne, were, 1. JOHN, b. Oct. 20, 1641, m. Elizabeth ——, 1666, and f. of *John*, b. 1667; *Samuel*, '68; *Zachary*, '71; *Elizabeth*, '72, m. Zechariah Eager; *Thomas*; *Sarah*, b. '79, m. Jonathan Rugg, of Fram. ; and *Silence*, m. Elisha Bruce; 2. MARY, b. June 12. 1644, m. Jona. Johnson; 3. MOSES, b. Mar. 26, 1646, m. Joanna ——, '68, and had *Moses*, (w. Sarah); *David*, b. 1672; *Jonathan*, b. 1679, d. 1753; *James*; *Josiah*; *Edward*; *Hannah*; *Mercy*; *Jacob*; *Ebenezer*. Moses, sen., d. in Southb., May 23, 1736; 4. JOSEPH, w. Kath.; 5. DANIEL, d. Nov. 29, 1739. f. of *Daniel*, *Benjamin*, *Susanna*, *Isaac*, *Abraham*, *Mary*, *Samuel*, *Nathaniel*, *Lydia*, and *Mercy*; 6. ELIZABETH, m. —— Dingley; 7. SARAH, m. —— Taylor; 8. ISAAC; 9. HANNAH, d. young. (Mid. Prob. and Deeds). Deac. JOSIAH d. at Westb., Feb. 9, 1755, æ. 66. JOHN, took the freeman's oath, Mar. 4, 1632. The family of Newton has been most numerous in Southb. Willard Newton, Esq., has occupied the farm originally owned by Richard.

NICHOLS, NATHANIEL, m. Isabel (Hayes), and had at Reading, 1. MARY, b. Ap. 20, 1717; [a Mary m. in Fram., Josh. Train, of Weston, Mar. 25, 1743]; 2. NATHANIEL, b. Mar. 6, 1719, m. in Fram., Mary Philips, of Southb. Sep. 12, 1745, and prob. d. same year; see Inventory, dated Nov. 12; 3. ABIGAIL, b. July 13, 1721, m. William Marret, in Southb., Mar. 1743; and in Fram., 4. JOSEPH, b. Ap. 6, 1727; 5. BENJAMIN, b. Aug. 8, 1729; 6. ISABEL; 7. ANNA, b. July 4, 1733. Nath., the f. was chosen Constable, 1733. His will was proved May 20, 1745. Inventory, £684.

RICHARD, of Reading, d. 1674, leaving w. Ann, and chil., *John*, *Thomas*, *James*, *Mary*, and *Hannah*. JOHN, of Reading. (w. Abigail, m. 1676,) whose will was proved 1721, had *John*, b. 1677, d. 1721; *Richard*, 1679; *Richard*, '82; *Thomas*; *Kendall*, '86; *James*, '88; *Nathaniel*, '91; *Abigail*, '94; *Samuel*, '96; *Benjamin*, 99; *Joseph*, 1702. RANDALL, was of Charlestown, 1642.

JOHN, (w. Lydia), had chil. at Topsfield, from 1663. JAMES, of Malden, m. Mary Felt, 1660, and his est. was settled, 1707, — his chil., *James, Nathaniel, Mary, Elizabeth, Anna, Samuel, Caleb.*

2. JOSEPH, of Needham, m. Judith Mixer, of Fram., Oct. 28, 1755; and had in Fram., 1. JOSEPH, b. Dec. 19, 1755, m. Thankful Winch, Aug. 26, 1779; 2. ANNE, b. Nov. 30, '57, m. Jesse Cheney, of E. Sud; 3. FORTUNATUS, b. Jan. 30, 1760, m. Sally Cloyes, Sep. 1783, and lived in Westboro'. Joseph the f. was a schoolmaster, taught in Fram. 1776, and 1783, and at one time in Weston. Jos. and w. were adm. to the ch., Nov. 24, 1763. Joseph d. in Westb., Sep. 15, '96; his w. Judith d. at do., Aug. 21, 1796.

3. ABRAHAM, had bap. in Fram., SARAH, June 1, 1746; JOSEPH, Nov. 27, 1748. Ab. was living back of John Trowbridge, (a cellar hole remains), 1750.

4. THOMAS, m. in Sud., Eunice Parmenter, 1752; and had THOMAS, bap. in Fram., Oct. 21, 1753; and EUNICE, b. in Sud. Aug. 24, 1755, d. May 10, 1766. Eunice was adm. to the Fram. ch., Sep. 9, 1753. [1781, Thomas, of Grafton, sold to Peter Gallot, land in Fram.]

4. JOSEPH, had in Fram. by w. Martha, 1. JOHN, b. Ap. 7, 1731; 2. MARTHA, b. Ap. 30, 1733; 3. JOSEPH, b. Oct. 8, 1738; 4. ALPHEUS, b. Nov. 5, 1742; 5. MITTY, b. 1752, d. unm. in Utica, N. Y. Mrs. Martha, wid. of Joseph, m. Rev. David Goddard, of Leicester, Dec. 20, 1753.

5. JOHN, s. of Joseph (4), m. Mary Haven, July 17, 1751; and had, 1. ABIGAIL, bap. June 7, 1752, m. —— Chamberlin; 2. JOSEPH, bap. Aug. 4, 1754; 3. JOHN, bap. Dec. 31, 1758; 4. MARY, m. Silas Eaton, Feb. 1, 1782. Mary, w. of John, was adm. to the ch., Ap. 26, 1752.

6. JOSEPH, Jun., s. of Jos. (4), m. Sarah Hemenway, cov'd Feb. 29, 1756, and with w. adm. to the ch. Feb. 27, 1763. Their chil. were 1. MARY, b. Oct. 16, '62, m. Nathan Newton, July, '84; 2. JOSEPH, b. Mar. 17, '64; 3. BENJAMIN GODDARD, b. Aug. 18, '65; 4. How, b. May 27, '67; 5. JOHN, b. July 17, '69, m. Hannah Nixon, who d. 1810, æ. 38, and 2d, the wid. of Samuel Nichols, of Holl. (a Leland); 6. MITTY, b. Jan. 21, '71, unm.; 7. DANIEL, b. Dec. 15, '72; 8. SARAH, b. Jan. 1, '75; 9. LABAN WHEATON, b. Mar. 30, '77; 10. NABBY, bap. Oct. 17,

'79 ; 11. ALPH, b. Dec. 11, '80 ; 12. PATTY, b. Dec. 12, '82. Lt. Joseph the f. was Selectman, 1779, and with w. recommended to the ch. in Fitzwilliam, May 3, 1781.

7. ALPHEUS, s. of Jos. (4), m. Rebecca Hemenway, and with w. adm. to the ch., Sep. 18, 1768. Their chil. were 1. SARAH, b. July 19, '67, m. —— Forbush, of Westb.; 2. LUCINDA, b. Nov. 27, '68, unm. ; 3. PATTY, b. Nov. 5, '73, d. young ; 4. JULA, b. May 6, '75 ; 5. RUHAMAH, b. Jan. 28, '78, m. — Orin, now of Westb. ; 6. BECKY, bap. Oct. 17, '79, m. Deac. Brigham Fay, of Southb.; 7. MATILDA, b. Dec. 11, '81, m. Winsor Horn ; 8. SOPHIA, b. June 28, '85, m. Elisha Fay, of Southb. ; 9. EUSIBIA, b. Mar. 19, '87, m. Nathan Brown. Alpheus, the f. d. in Southb.

ZECHARIAH, and w. Rebecca, had at Sherb., Sarah, b. 1745 ; Lydia, '47. MORDECAI and w. Alice, had at Boston, John, b. Aug. 18, 1653. ISAAC (w. Sarah), d. at Sutton, ab. 1756, f. of Henry, Isaac, William, Benjamin, Mary, Abigail and Anna. Capt. JOHN, (who m. Jerusha Moore, 1755), d. at Oxford, 1812, æ. 78; and WILLIAM, (who m. Mary Willson, 1745), d. at O, 1794, æ. 72; ALEXANDER, (w. Margaret), was of O., 1743, all having chil.

NIXON,* also written, NICHSON, NICKSON, and NICK-ERSON, CHRISTOPHER, m. Mary Sever, and with w. cov'd, May 5, 1728. Their chil. were 1. JOHN, b. Mar. 1, 1727 ; 2. ELIZABETH, b. Mar. 3, 1728–9 ; 3. MEHEPZEBATH, b. June 20, '31, m. Samuel Fairbanks, June 6, '51 ; 4. MARY, b. Dec. 24, '33, m. Isaac Gleason, Jun., Nov. 2, '52, and 2d, —— Sawtwell, and d. in Langdon, N. H. ; 5. THOMAS, b. Ap. 27, '36 ; 6. ELIZABETH, b. Dec. 31, '38 ; 7. ABIGAIL, m. David Andrews. Christopher, the f., came from the South, and lived on the Joseph Belcher place. He m. a 2d w., Mrs. Mercy Collar, Aug. 16, 1748, and d. in Fram.

Richard Nixon, b. in Middlesex Co., N. J., Oct. 1758, was in a corps of dragoons commanded by his brother, Maj. Robert. Richard d. in N. Y. city, 1844, whither he removed, 1795; and was nearly 30 years in the Custom House. (N. Y. paper.)

2. JOHN, s. of Chris. (1), m. Thankful Berry, Feb. 7, 1754, and with w. cov'd, Mar. 25, 1759. Their chil. (recorded chiefly in Sud.), were 1. JOHN, b. Aug. 25, 1757, bap. in Fram., Mar.

---

* Thomas Nixon, D. D., b. prob. near 1660, was a prebendary of Canterbury, in England. (Berry's Gen's. of Co. of Kent, p. 380.)

25, '59, m. —— Moore, lived in Sud.; 2. SARAH, b. Nov. 19, '58, m. Abel Cutler, '79; 3. HEPHZEBAH, b. Aug. 31, '60, m. Timo. Moore, '80; 4. MARY, b. Sep. 16, '61, m. in Fram., Capt. Peter Clayes, Jan. 1785; 5. JOSEPH, b. July 27, '63, lived in Waltham; 6. KEZIAH, m. in Fram., Ebenezer Brown, Nov. '88; 7. ANNE, b. May 6, '66, m. in Fram., Thomas Richardson, Feb. 1789; 8. ARTEMAS, b. Sep. 3, '67, lived in Waltham; 9. BENJAMIN, b. May 13, '70; 10. BETSEY, b. Oct. 5, '75, m. John Warren, '98. John, the f., m. 2d, wid. Hannah Gleason, of Fram., Feb. 5, 1778, who d. in Sud., Sep. 26, 1831, æ. 90. John served in the French War, as Capt., 1756; commanded the Co. of minute men in Sud., 1775. In Nov., 1775, he was appointed Lt. Col., and Aug. 9, 1776, was commissioned as Brig. General. He was in command with his regiment at Bunker Hill, and served with much honor there, and during the War. He lived generally within the bounds of Sud., near Fram., moved to Vt., ab. 1806, and d. in Middleboro', ab. 1815.

3. THOMAS, s. of Chris. (1), m. Bethiah Stearns, and had in Fram., 1. CATE, b. July 31, 1758, m. Wm. Stowell, of Worc., moved to Paris, Me., and d. 1842; 2. THOMAS, b. Mar. 19, '62; 3. ASA, b. Aug. 17, '67, d. Dec. 1, '71; 4. HANNAH, b. Sep. 21, '72, m. John Nichols, of Southb.; 5. BETHIAH, d. in Southb., Mar. 19, 1823. Col. Thomas, the f., served as Ensign in the French War, 1756. He commanded a Co. of minute men, in 1775, and was commissioned as Colonel. He was reputed a brave and efficient officer, and served through the war. He removed from Fram. to Nichol's Mills, in Southb., ab. 1784, and d. on his passage by water from Boston to Portsmouth, Aug. 12, 1800.

4. THOMAS, Jun'., s. of Tho. (3), m. Lydia Hager, May 16, 1790, and with w. cov'd Dec. 1795. He had 1. WARREN, b. Mar. 9, 1793, m. Salome Rice, of Wayland, has been Selectman in Fram., 11 years, and Justice of the Peace; 2. OTIS, b. Mar. 11, '96, m. —— Swain, of Nantucket, moved to Morgan, O., and m. a 2d w. in N. Y.; 3. SUKEY, b. Nov. 23, '97, d. unm., Aug. 3, 1828; 4. RENY, b. Nov. 25, '99, d. unm., Jan. 29, 1824. Lydia, w. of Tho., d. May 21, 1822, and he m. 2d, wid. Sarah Stone. Capt. Tho. was Selectman 2 years, and d. in Fram., Jan. 4, 1842, æ. near 80. He was fifer in the Rev. war, and appointed prob. Quarter Master.

NORCUT, RICHARD, and w. Naomi, had NAOMI, b. Oct. 31, 1723. RICHARD, d. Jan. 20, 1726-7. PRISCILLA was b. Feb. 1, 1721-2.

NORTHGATE, ESAU, whose w. Peggy was bap. July 10, 1756, had HANNAH, bap. June 19, 1757; SUSANNAH, bap. May 6, '59; ESAU, bap. Sep. 30, '59.

NURSE,* NURS or NOURSE, BENJAMIN, prob. s. of Francis, had by w. Thamezin, 1. THAMEZIN, b. Nov. 13, 1691, m. Ebenezer Hemenway, Feb. 23, 1737-8, and d. ab. 1767, (see admin.); 2. BENJAMIN, b. Jan. 20, '94; 3. WILLIAM, b. Mar. 8, '96, was living 1767, (prob. the Wm. of Shrewsbury, who m. Rebecca Fay, of Westb. 1723, was f. of *Daniel, Zerviah,* &c.; he lived at the " Shoe," called also " Nurse's corner," annexed in 1762 to Westboro', (Worc. Mag. II. 3.), and d. Ap. 15, 1779; his w. Reb. d. June 22, 1776; 4. ELIZABETH, b. Sep. 18, '98, m. Theophilus Philips, in Hop., 1732; 5. EBENEZER, b. Mar. 27, 1700-1; 6. MARGARET, b. Ap. 24, '03; 7. MOSES, b. Mar. '04-5; 8. AARON, b. Jan. 11, '08. Benjamin, the f., received in 1707, a deed from Col. Buckminster of 110 ac., then in Benj.'s possession. He lived prob. at Mr. David Fiske's, was Selectman, 1702, and d. in Fram., his will proved Feb. 13, 1748, having m. 2d, Elizabeth, wid. of Joseph Morse, of Wat., Feb. 16, 1713-4.

NOTE — FRANCIS, Sen., d. at Salem, 1695, his est. administered, Dec. 23d. He had by w. Rebecca, 1. JOHN, who d. 1719, f. by w. Elizabeth (Smith, m. Nov. 1, 1672, d. '73), of *John,* b. Oct. 12, '73; and by w. Elizabeth (Verry, m. Aug. 17, '77), of *Elizabeth,* m.——Douty; *Samuel,* b. 1679; *Sarah,* '80, m. —— Twist; *Jonathan,* b. May 3, '82, m. a dr. of John Hardenden; *Joseph,* '83; *Benjamin,* Feb. 20, '86; *Hannah,* '87, m. —— Verry; *Deborah;* 2. SAMUEL, m. Mary Smith, 1677, and f. of *Samuel, Mary, George, Mary, Rebecca, Ebenezer,* (m. Eliz. Mitchell, 1722, and f. of *Caleb, Eben.,* &c.); 3. FRANCIS, b. Feb. 3, 1660-1, his est. settled (of Reading), Oct. 8, 1716, leaving w. Sarah, and chil., *Benjamin,* b. Jan. 28, 1689-0; *Jonathan,* '92, d. 1717; *Josiah,* '94, d. 1718; *Joshua,* d. 1717; *Caleb,* d. 1727; *Nathaniel,* b. '97, d. 1717; *Abigail;* a s. *Francis,* b. 1686, d. '88; 4. BENJAMIN, b. Jan. 26, 1665, prob. the B. of Fram., above; 5. MICHAEL, m. —— Bouden; 6. REBECCA, m. Tho. Preston, 1670; 7. MARY, m. John Tarbell, 1678; 8. ELIZABETH, m. William Russell. Francis, the f., administered, with John How, the estate of Edmond Bridges, of Salem; his w. Rebecca was one of the victims of the Witchcraft delusion, although ample testimonials were given of her private character, and domestic virtues.—(See the preceding history; p. 32.) Rebecca was sister of Sarah, w. of Peter Clayes.

---

*The family of Nurse is noticed as in Sussex, Eng. Sir D. Nurse, (b. in the 17th century), was of Chitingstone, in that Co. (See Berry's Gen's. of the Co. of Kent.)

2. BENJAMIN, Jun., s. of Benj. (1), m. Elizabeth Haven, July 12, 1717, and with w. cov'd Ap. 27, 1718, and adm. to the ch. Sep. 1, 1723. His chil. were 1. THAMEZIN, b. June 7, 1718, m. Jedidiah Bigelow, of Grafton, Jan. 27, 1736–7; 2. EXPERIENCE, b. Nov. 21, 1723. [BENJAMIN, m. Mary Belknap, both of Fram., June, 1737. BENJAMIN, m. Bethiah Bridges, Nov. 22, 1749. BENJAMIN was recommended to the ch. in Partridgefield, Oct. 2, 1774.]

3. EBENEZER, s. of Benj. (1), m. Mercy Haven, Ap. 14, 1720, and had EBENEZER, b. in Sherb., Oct. 3, 1720, who with MERCY, was bap. in Fram., Sep. 30, 1722.

4. JOHN, prob. s. of John, and g. son of Francis, m. Elizabeth Gale, Feb. 21, 1700, who was adm. to the ch., Oct. 5, 1718. Their chil. were 1. JOHN, b. Aug. 27, 1701; 2. JOSEPH, b. Oct. 7, 1703; 3. SARAH, b. May 2, 1705, m. William Weston, or Wesson, in Hop., '43; 4. ELIZABETH, b. Nov. 26, '08, m. Thomas Biglo, of Marlb.; 5. MEHETABEL, b. Ap. 12, '12, m. John Belknap, of Westb., and d. before 1747; 6. SAMUEL, b. Feb. 18, '13–4; 7. THAMEZIN, b. Aug. 20, 1716, m. Abner Bixby, of Hop., 1734. John, the f. rec'd a deed from Col. Buckminster, of land where Mr. Curtis Child lives, Mar. 20, 1696. He lived in advanced age with his s. in-law, Abner Bixby, on the David Fiske farm; a cellar hole remains. He d. in Fram.

5. JOHN, Jun. s. of John (4), m. Bathsheba Rugg, and with w. adm. to the ch. Ap. 29, 1722. Their chil. were 1. JOSEPH[6], b. Jan. 6, '23–4; 2. SARAH, b. Jan. 15, '24–5, m. Joshua Harrington, Jan. 11, '43; 3. ABRAHAM, b. Sep. 22, '27, d. Dec. 17, 1729; 4. ZERVIAH, b. Mar. 8, '29–0, adm. to the ch. July 27, 1746, and recom. to Rutland ch. May 18, 1760; 5. ABRAHAM[7], b. July 27, '32; 6. HANNAH, b. Feb. 4, '34, m. Thomas Reed, of Rutland, Dec. 12, 1754; 7. JOANNA, b. June 14, '37, was adm. to the ch. May 1, 1774; 8. MEHETABEL, b. Aug. 9, '39; 9. JONATHAN, b. Dec. 28, '41. John, the f. moved to Waterford, Me., an aged man.

6. JOSEPH, s. of John (5), m. Sarah Walkup, Feb. 27, 1746, and his w. adm. to the ch., May 6, 1750. He had, 1. SARAH, bap. Feb. 14, 1748; 2. MOLLY, bap. Sep. 17, '49; 3. JONATHAN, bap. Feb. 10, '51; 4. BATHSHEBAH, bap. Nov. 12, '52, m. in Hop., James Newton, 1769; 5. JOSEPH, bap. June 14,

'54; 6. HANNAH, bap. Mar. 20, '57; 7. REUBEN, bap. June 7, '61; 8. EBENEZER, bap. June 19, '63; 9. KATY, bap. Dec. 28, '66. Joseph, the f. was by trade a shoemaker, and with w. was recommended to the ch. in Fitzwilliam, Ap. 21, 1776. (Several of the first chil. are recorded at Hop.)

7. ABRAHAM, s. of John (5), m. Zerviah Morse, Oct. 24, 1753, and with w. was adm. to the ch. Mar. 31, 1754. Their chil. were 1. ASA[8], b. Sep. 10, '54; 2. JOHN[9], b. Mar. 10, '56; 3. BETTY, b. Nov. 19, '57, d. 1761; 4. LAWSON[10], b. June 6, '61; 5. JOSIAH, b. June 2, '63, d. unm. at Rehoboth, Sep., 1777, while returning from the army; 6. PETER, b. Mar. 23, '65, d. 1781; 7. OLIVE, b. Feb. 21, '67, m. Oliver Matthews, of Southb., Mar. 1790, and d. 1795; 8. MOLLY, b. Nov. 2, '68, m. John Hervey, of Southb., Jan. 1789, and d. June 4, 1801; 9. BETTY, b. Sep. 11, '70, m. Thomas Richards, May, '91, and d. 1791; 10. ANNE, b. July 3, '72, m. Nathan Burnet, of Barre, Aug. 23, '92, and d. Ap. 1805; 11. SALLY, b. Dec. 23, '74, m. Silas Davis, of Shrewsb., Dec. 29, 1800, and lives in Prov.; 12. NATHAN, b. Aug. 4, '77, prob. m., and d. Sep. 20, 1805. Abraham, the f. lived at Curtis Child's, was Selectman, 1782, and d. Feb. 1793. His wid. Zerviah d. Nov. 6, 1805, æ. 70. (T. Rec.)

8. ASA, s. of Abr. (7), m. Anne Munroe, of Fram. (prob. from Lex.), June 3, 1778, and had 1. JOSIAH, b. Mar. 13, 1779, d. unm. in Boston. The f. m. 2d, Lois Glover, May 3, 1781, and had 2. ——, b. May 3, '82, d. at birth; 3. JAMES, b. July 6, '83, d. young; 4. MARY, b. May 7, '85, m. Rufus Brewer, Esq.; 5. CHARLOTTE, b. June 12, '87, m. Aaron Hadley, lives in Charlestown; 6. ——, b. Feb. 16, '89, d. young; 7. MILISCENT, b. Feb. 3, '91, m. 1st, Aaron Eames, 2d, Edward Childs, lives a wid.; 8. NEWELL, b. Mar. 21, '92, m. Harriet Bullard, of Holl., lives W.; 9. OLIVE, b. Dec. 3, '93, m. David Brewer; 10. SARAH, b. Sep. 9, '95, m. Nathan Fairbanks, of Holl., and d. 1819; 11. SUSANNAH, b. May 11, '97, m. Henry Brewer; 12. ——, b. Feb. 14, 1800, and d. young. The m. d., and he m. 3d, Polly, wid. of Ezra Haven, (a Glover), Dec. 29, 1800, and had, 13. ELIZABETH, b. Dec. 19, 1801, m. Charles Haven. Asa, the f. d. in Fram. July 23, 1803. His wid. Polly d. 1822, æ. 57.

9. JOHN, s. of Abr. (7), m. Susannah Brown, Nov. 8, 1781,

and had, 1. LUCY, b. Feb. 1782, m. Jonathan Edmunds, and d. Jan. 7, 1838; 2. JOHN, b. Feb. 22, '84, d. unm. Mar. 21, 1825; 3. NELLY, b. Feb. 28, '86, m. John Manson; 4. JOEL, b. May 27, '88, d. Oct. 24, 1805; 5. SUSANNAH, b. Sep. 24, '90, d. young; 6. ANNE, b. Oct. 16, '92, d. young; 7. ANNE, b. Ap. 8, '97, d. young. The m. d. July 15, '97, and the f. m. 2d, wid. Anne How, (a Tayntor, of Marlb.), Ap. 25, '99, and had, 8. SALLY, b. Mar. 7, 1800, m. Larkin Brewer; 9. ANNE, b. Nov. 18, 1801, m. Wm. Eaton; 10. SUSANNAH, b. June 7, 1803, m. Curtis Child; 11. GEORGE, b. Ap. 3, 1806. Capt. John the f. lived at Curtis Child's, was Selectman from 1795, 4 years, and d. æ. ab. 72. Anne his w. d. 1827, æ. 65.

10. LAWSON, s. of Abr. (7), m. Lydia Fisk, in Hop, 1779; and had 1. NATHAN, b. Mar. 13, '80, w. Esther; 2. LAWSON, b. Dec. 15, '81, lives in Tenn., a physician; 3. NANCY, b. Mar. 21, '84; 4. FORTUNATUS, d. Feb. 25, 1816. Maj. Lawson the f. m. 2d, Lydia Eaton, Jan. 1, 1799, was Selectman, 1804, 4 years, and d. Sep. 11, 1832, æ. 71. His wid. Lydia, d. July 15, 1838, æ. 68. He lived on Mr. Daniels' farm.

Capt. SAMUEL, of Bolton, b. Ap. 25, 1715, o. s., (s. of —— (name not recorded), Jun., of Salem, who m. Dorothy Faulkner, 1708), m. Elizabeth Kellogg, and had 1. JOHN, b. Nov. 17, 1740, m. 1st, Hazadiah Hapgood, of Marlb., '66, and f. of *Samuel*, b. Sep., 1766; and m. 2d, —— Sawyer; 2. DAVID, b. Jan. 19, '41-2, m. Rebekkah Barrett, '62, and f. of *David, Stephen, Oliver, Rebecca, Elizabeth, Abigail, Sarah,* and *Catharine*; 3. ELIZABETH, b. Jan. 22, '43-4, d. '45; 4. a son, b. and d. Feb. '45-6; 5. ELIZABETH, b. Jan. 4, '46-7, m. Amos Merriam, '67; 6. JONATHAN, b. Dec. 18, '48, m. Ruth Barret, and f. of *Peter*, b. Oct. 10, '74, H. Coll. 1802, m. Mary Barnum, minister at Ellsworth, Me.; Deacon *Jonathan; Silas; Samuel;* Dr. *Amos,* H. Coll., 1812, &c.; 7. SARAH, b. Jan. 8, '50, m. Phinehas Moor, '70; and by 2d w. Abigail Barnard, of Marlb., 8. BENJAMIN, b. Jan. 16, '55, m. Sybil Bailey; 9. ABIGAIL, b. Jan. 7, '57, m. Abr. Holman, '84; 10. EUNICE, b. July 5, '60, m. Jasoniah Houghton; 11. PHEBE, b. May 9, '62, m. Jona. Atherton; 12. ABIGAIL, b. '64; 13. ABIGAIL, b. 1765; 14. LUCY, b. June 28, '69, m. Eph. Fairbanks; 15. Maj. BARNARD, b. June 10, '91, m. Hannah Barret, '93. Capt. Samuel, the f. d. at Bolton, May 8, 1790, æ. 75 years and 2 days.

ODEL, SAMUEL, rated in Fram., ab. 1786.

ONTHANK, JOHN, rated in Fram., ab. 1724.

ORDWAY, JOSEPH, and w. Susannah, had in Fram., ABIGAIL, b. June 17, 1753. SAMUEL, a shoemaker, was rated in Fram., ab. 1782, and moved from town ab. 1805.

OXFORD, CUFFEE, m. in Waltham, Nelly Donahew, Dec. 12, 1758, and had in Fram., 1. ZERUIAH, b. May 31, 1760; 2.

PATTY, b. Nov. 20, '61 ; 3. PARLEY, bap. Jan. 1, '64 ; 4. NANNY, bap. Sep. 15, '65, m. Thomas Jonah, Nov. 25, '84.

PADELFORD or PADELFOOTE, JONATHAN, of Camb., m. Mary Blanford, Oct. 5, 1652, and had 1. JONATHAN, b. July 6, '53, d. Oct. 29 ; 2. MARY, b. Aug. 22, '54 ; 3. JONATHAN, b. Aug. 13, '56 ; 4. ZECHARIAH, b. Dec. 16, '57 ; 5. EDWARD, b. June 14, '60. Mary, wid. of Jonathan, m. Thomas Eames, ab. 1662, and was killed by the Indians, in Fram., Feb. 1, 1675-6.

2. ZECHARIAH, s. of Jon. (1), chose 1674, Edward Wright for his guardian, was of Sherb., 1679, having settled near Farm Pond, and cleared what is now known as *Zachary's Point.* He d. in Fram., prob. unm., July 7, 1737.

Dr. JOHN, Jun., (Y. Coll. 1768), and w. Bethshua, were of Hardwick, 1770.

PAGE, JOHN, of Fram., m. Susannah Leland, of Sherb., Ap. 24, 1712, and had in Fram., 1. EXPERIENCE, b. Jan. 11, 1712-3, m. —— Buck ; 2. JOHN, bap. May 18, 1720 ; 3. JONATHAN, b. ab. 1723. John, the f., removed to Sutton. Admin. on the est. (£542) of John, Physician, was granted, July, 1731.

2. SARAH, m. in Fram., John Gibbs, Ap. 20, 1706. MARIAH, was in Fram., ab. 1765.

JOHN, (his w., —— Mash), d. in Haverhill, Nov. 1687, his w. d. Feb., 96-7. JOHN, Jun., who d. at H., June 27, 1714, m. Sarah Davis, June 18, 1663, and had *Sarah*, b. July 7, '80. BENJAMIN, of H., m. Mary Whittier, Sep. 21, 1666, and had 9 chil. JOHN, Sen. d. at Wat., 1676, æ. ab. 90 ; his w. Phebe d. 1677, æ. 87. J. was f. of 1. *John*, Jun., who m. Faith (probably niece of President) Dunster, sold at Wat., 1669, owned at Groton, and was f. of John, Jonathan, Joseph, Mary, and a dr. who m. —— Boardman. John, Jun., was dec'd, 1712; his w. Faith, d. 1699; 2. *Samuel*, of Concord, 1669; and prob. 3. *William*, of Wat., whose wid. Hannah, in 1665, m. Nicholas Wood, of Boggestow.

PALMER, ELNATHAN, and w. Mercy, had in Fram., SAMUEL, b. Ap. 29, 1703. The f. was not rated, 1710. He lived the S. side of the River, not far from the Town's centre. POLLY and BETSEY, were adm. to the ch., Nov. 1793. CATHARINE H., dr. of Joseph, bap. Mar., 1791.

MARY, m. in Sud., James Pendleton, Oct. 22, 1647. In Marlb., SARAH, m. Joseph Ward, 1743.

PARK, or PARKS, GIDEON, m. Hannah Fuller, both of Newton, Aug. 31, 1758, and had in Newton, 1. JOHN, b. 1759 ; 2. LOIS, m. in Fram., Daniel Usher, Dec. 26, '85 ; 3. ABIGAIL,

b. 1763, m. in Fram., Obed Metcalf, Feb. 4, '90; 4. SAMUEL, b. 1766, rated in Fram., '87; and prob. in Fram. (in part), 5. HANNAH, m. Samuel Perry; 6. MOSES, d. æ. 10; 7. SARAH, m. Joseph Whitney, of Sherb., Oct. 3, '92; 8. ESTHER, m. Reuben Fay, Jun., of Southb., July 24, '96; 9. GIDEON, d. unm., Dec. 15, 1817, æ. 41. Gideon, the f., d. in Fram., July 28, 1794. His wid. Hannah d. July 16 or 17, 1805, æ. 70.

2. JOHN, s. of Gideon (1), m. Sally Richardson, and had 1. LUCY, b. July 13, 1792; 2. JOSEPH, b. Jan. 6, '94; 3. GIDEON; 4. SUSAN; 5. GIDEON. John, the f., was Collector, 1789, and Selectman, 1802, 7 years. He d. Ap. 10, 1828. His wid. lives in Boston.

WILLIAM took the freeman's oath, May 18, 1631, and had, at Roxb., *Theoda*, b. 1637; *Hannah*, '39; *Martha*, '41; *Sarah*, '43. RICHARD, of Camb., 1647, d. 1666, leaving a w. and s. *Thomas*, and two drs. (See Mid. Prob.) THOMAS, of Camb. (Newton), m. Abigail Derkes, 1653; and had 1. THOMAS, b. '54, d. 1681; 2. JOHN, b. Sep. 6, '56, and d. 1718, f. by w. Elizabeth, at Newton, of *John*, b. 1696, and d. 1747, (m. Abigail Lawrence, 1720, and f. of Lois, b. 1732, and Gideon, of Fram., b. April 7, '34); *Solomon*, b. '99, d. at Holl., Jan. 3, 1754, (f. by w. Lydia, of Keziah, Lydia, and Solomon, H. C., 1753, d. Dec. 29, '53, æ. 22; and Samuel, Esq., who m. Mary Russell, 1758, and had Solomon, James, Samuel, &c.); *Elizabeth*, b. 1701, m. Jos. Moss, '20; *Abigail*; *Joseph*, b. 1705; *Mary*, b. 1708; 3. ABIGAIL, b. Mar. 3, 1658, m. John Fisk, '79; 4. EDWARD, b. Ap. 8, 1661; and d. Aug. 11, '90; 5. RICHARD, b. Dec. 21, '63, (perhaps the R. of Sherb., 1707), f. by w. Sarah, at Newton, of *Richard*, who m. Sarah Fuller, 1717, and had Jerusha, Huldah, William, Thomas, and Priscilla; 6. SARAH, b. Mar. 21, 1666, m. —— Knap; 7. REBECKAH, b. Ap. 13, 1668, m. John Sanger; 8. JONATHAN, b. Aug. 27, 1670, d. at Newton, 1719, had three wives, and chil., *Jonathan*, b. 1695; *Lydia*; *Mindwell*; *Margery*; *Eunice*; and *Hannah*; 9. ELIZABETH, b. July 28, 1679, m. John Holland. Tho. the f. d. 1690, and his estate was settled, Mar. 12, '93-4.

PARKER, HANANIAH, of Reading, m. w. Elizabeth, Sep. 30, 1663, and had, 1. JOHN, b. Aug. 3, '64; 2. SAMUEL, b. Oct., '66; 3. ELIZABETH, b. June, '68; 4. SARAH, b. '72, d. '73; 5. HANANIAH, b. Nov. 2, '74, d. æ. 11 mos.; 6. EBENEZER, b. Feb. 13, '75-6, w. Rebecca; 7. MARY, m. —— Poole. Hananiah, the f. d. Mar. 10, 1723-4, æ. 86, leaving a wid. Mary. (See will, Mid. Prob.)

2. JOHN, s. of Han. (1), by w. Deliverance, had (on record at Reading and Lexington), 1. HANANIAH, b. Oct. 10, 1691, d. at Port Royal, 1711; 2. ANDREW, b. Feb. 14, '92-3, m. Sarah Whiting, 1720, f. of *Sarah*, b. 21; *Jonas*, '22; *Amos*, '23; 3. Lt. JOSIAH, b. Ap. 11, '94, d. Oct. 8, 1756, m. Anne Stone, Dec. 8, 1718, and f. of *Anna*; *Deliverance*; *Mary*; *Josiah*; *Lois*; *John*, (w. Lydia Morse); *Thaddeus*, (w. Mary Reed); and *Joseph*; 4. MARY, b. Dec. 4, 1695, d. 1709; 5. EDEE, b. Aug. 19, '97, d. 1709; 6. JOHN, b. Nov. 8, 1703. John, the f. d. at Lexington, Jan. 22, 1740-1, æ. ab. 78. His w. Deliverance d. at Lexington, Mar. 10, 1717-8.*

---

* Mrs. Fay, of Fram., has a Bible which once belonged to John, of Lexington. It bears his name, and the date 1709.

3. JOHN, s. of John (2), m. in Fram., Experience Cloyes, and had 1. PETER, b. Oct. 3, 1738 ; 2. SUBMIT, b. Dec. 3, 1742, m. Thomas Bent, and d. ab. 1784; 3. NATHAN, bap. Mar. 2, 1745-6, prob. d. young. John, the f., settled in Fram., at or near Mr. Abijah Fay's. He was Selectman, 1756, and d. Feb. 23, 1783, æ. 79. His w. Experience d. Oct. 13, 1780, æ. 77.

4. PETER, s. of John (3), m. Ruth Eaton, Dec. 8, 1761; was with w. admitted to the ch., May 22, 1763, and had 1. JOHN, b. Nov. 16, 1762, m. Deborah Lamb; 2. NATHAN[5], b. Oct. 23, '64; 3. ABIGAIL, b. Dec. 15, '66, m. Lovel How, of Marlb., June 8, 1803 ; 4. RUTH, b. Jan. 8, '69, m. Joseph Bigelow, of Holl., Nov. 8, '85; 5. EXPERIENCE, b. Feb. 19, '71, m. Luther Haven, of Holl., Feb. 5, '97; 6. PATTY, b. Ap. 15, '73, m. Eleazer Bullard, of Holl., Nov. 1, '93; 7. SALLY, b. May 25, '75, m. Wm. Eames, of Holl., Ap. 21, 1800 ; 8. PETER, b. Mar. 16, '77, d. Dec. 17, '84 ; 9. JOSIAH, b. Ap. 26, '79, m. Olive Stone, Ap. 8, 1804, f. of *Charles*, b. Mar. 6, 1805. Olive the w., d. July 4, 1826, æ. 47 ; the f. lives in Fram. ; 10. ARTEMAS, b. Dec. 20, '81, m. Almy Clark, Jan. 21, 1806 ; 11. ANNE, b. Ap. 25, '84, d. Jan. 8, '85 ; 12. PETER, b. July 10, '87, d. May 7, '88. Peter, the f., was Selectman, 1777, 4 years ; and Town Treasurer, 1783, 4 years ; and d. Nov. 5, 1803, æ. ab. 65. His w. Ruth d. Mar. 20, 1800, æ. 55.

5. NATHAN, s. of Peter (4), m. Catharine Murdock, and had 1. HARRIET, b. Oct. 10, 1793, m. Josiah Bigelow ; 2. PRESTON, b. May 20, '96, d. Oct. 10, '98; 3. MARIA, b. Ap. 16, '99, m. Abijah Fay ; 4. PRESTON, b. Nov. 4, 1802, d. Aug. 20, '04 ; 5. PETER, b. June 18, 1804, Y. C., 1831, M. D., missionary to China, m. Harriet Webster. Nathan was adm. to the ch., Aug. 1792, (w. *Abigail* received at the same time.) He d. Aug. 17, 1826, æ. 62.

6. MOSES, m. Keziah Bellows, Ap. 3, 1747, and with w. cov'd Ap. 1749. They had in Fram., 1. ASA, b. Mar. 5, 1747.; 2. ELIAS, bap. Feb. 21, '49. Moses lived in the N.W. part of Fram., '50. [MOSES m. in Fram., Elizabeth Wait, July 5, '22.]

7. JOSEPH, rated in Fram., 1710, was here 1717. SARAH and child were warned from the Town, 1719. ROBERT of Fram., m. Eunice Parmenter, of Sud., Mar. 8, 1748, and was prob. in Fram., 1749. BENJAMIN was drafted in Fram., 1778.

8. JAMES, H. Coll. 1763, studied Divinity, and relinquished it for the medical profession. He was adm. to the ch. in Fram., Nov. 11, 1764, and was School-master, 1769. He m. in Southb., 1st, Sally Smith, Nov. 1771, and had MOLLY and SALLY; and by 2d w. Grace, ROBIE, and JAMES.

JAMES was s. of James (w. Anna), who came to Southb., and d. at S. April 8, 1754. His chil. were, JAMES; Deac. ABNER; BENJAMIN, who m. Abigail Taylor, and d. 1797, æ. 56, f. of Rev. *Jeroboam*, b. Ap. 3, 1769, H. Coll., '97, minister at Southb.; *Anna; Benjamin; Heman*, d. 1818, æ. 40; *Daniel P.*, merchant in Boston, and *William*; SARAH, m. Nathan Bridges, 1755; HANANIAH, m. Abigail Ward, Dec. 2, 1755, f. at Westb., of *Pierpont, Hepsebah, Harvey, &c.*; JEDEDIAH, b. Aug. 10, 1749, m. Catharine Horn, and f. of *Swain*, and *Temple*; TIMOTHY, b. Jan. 1, 1752, lived in Templeton; ANNA, b. 1753, d. 1754; and JOSIAH, who went to Coos. JOHN and w. Jane, had chil. in Southb., from 1749. TIMOTHY, of Newton, (s. of John and w. Esther, g. s. of John (w. Mary), whose est. was settled 1714), m. Keziah Hammond, 1743, d. at Holl., Jan. 5, 1754, æ. 36, f. of several drs. JOHN (w. Mary), had chil. in Marlb., from 1753. WILLIAM, was of Sud., 1638. JOSHUA had chil. in Sud., from 1714. JACOB was of Hop., 1746, and m. Lydia Park.

PARKHURST, sometimes written Parkis, GEORGE, and w. Susanna, had, 1. GEORGE, b. ab. 1618; 2. PHEBE, who m. Thomas Arnold, of Wat. In 1651, George, then of Boston, had m. Susanna, widow of John Simson, of Watertown. George took the freeman's oath, May 10, 1643, and sold, in 1645, land in Wat., bought of Hue Mason, near Wm. Page. He was living in 1655.

2. GEORGE, s. of George (1), of Wat., m. Sary Browne, Dec. 16, 1643, and had, 1. JOHN, b. June 10, '44; 2. DANIEL, bap. in 1st church, Boston, 1649; 3. SARY, b. Sep. 14, '49. George, of Wat., m. Mary Pheza, 1650. He d. in Wat., 1699, æ. 81. His w. Mary d. Mar. 9, 1680.

3. JOHN, s. of Geo. (2), had, by w. Abigail, 1. JOHN, b. Feb. 26, 1671; 2. ABIGAIL, b. Sep. 10, '74; 3. SARY, b. Nov. 26, '76; 4. RACHEL, b. Dec. 30, '78, m. Abraham Gale, '99; 5. ELIZABETH, b. Sep. 18, '81; 6. MARY, b. Dec. 23, '83; 7. GEORGE, b. Jan. 17, '85–6, (prob. f. at Weston, of *Daniel*, b. 1726, who m. Martha Gamage, of Camb., 1746, and f. of Daniel, b. 1755, d. young, f. of Wm., M. D., of Petersham; *Jonathan*, b. '28; *William*, b. '31, (perhaps the W., of Holl., who m. Martha Perry, 1757, and f. of Jonathan, Alpheus, William, Amos, Joel, and Nahum); and *George*, b. 1733, who moved to German Flats. (See letters of G. ship, 1739); 8. SAMUEL, b. Ap. 11, 1688, m. Sarah Shattuck, 1716; 9. HANNAH, b. Ap. 17, '90, m. John Newton, of Marlb., 1717.

4. JOHN, Jr., s. of John (3), m. Abigail, dr. of Dea. John Morse, and had at Wat., 1. JOHN, b. and d. 1695; 2. JOHN, b. Ap. 29, '97; 3. ABIGAIL, b. June 20, '99; 4. LYDIA, b. 1701; 5. ELIZABETH, b. 1704, d. Dec., 1732; 6. JOSIAH, b. July 9, '06; 7. ISAAC, b. July 19, 08, m. Lydia Bigelow, 1733; (Isaac, Jun. of Mendon, d. ab. 1761); and at Weston, 8. MARY, b. July 10, '10; 9. JONAS, bap. 1712; 10. JEMIMA, bap. June 19, 1715. John, the f. was received to Weston church, 1708, and chosen Deac., 1710.

5. JOSIAH, s. of John (4), m. at Weston, Sarah Carter, Oct. 23, 1735, and had 1. JOSIAH, b. Mar. 8, 1737; 2. NATHAN, b. Nov. 1, (also entered 2d), '38, and with w. Mary, and dr. Elizabeth, "came from Weston to Fram., Mar. 16, 1769," and prob. left town; 3. MARY, b. Mar. 11, '44; 4. SARAH, b. Sep. 21, '47; 5. AMOS.

6. JOSIAH, s. of Josiah (5), m. Elizabeth Bigelow, of Fram.; and had, 1. HANNAH, m. Jonathan Adams, Feb. 25, 1779, and moved into Penn.; 2. JOHN, b. ab. 1760; m. Sally Bullard, Dec. 1783, had in Fram., *John*, b. Dec. 30, 1784; in N. H., he had *Daniel*, May 6, '87; *Josiah*, Mar. 12, '89; and *Sally*, Ap. 10, '93; then moved to Penn.; 3. AARON, m. Sally Thompson, in Bellingham, moved to Stafford, Con.; 4. ELIZABETH, b. Feb. 28, 1763, m. Samuel Walker, May, '84; 5. EPHRAIM, b. Jan. 16, '65; 6. LUCY, b. June 19, '66, m. Abraham Fisher, Jan. 15, 1784, lived in Claremont, and d. 1845; 7. SALLY, b. Jan. 6, '68, m. Micah Morse, lived in N. H., and d. 1814; 8. EUNICE, b. Nov. 20, '69 m. —— Becket, lived in Unity, N. H., d. ab. 1829; 9. MOLLY, b. Nov. 15, '71, m. Josiah Hemenway, 1793, lives in Fram.; 10. LYDIA, b. June 28, '75, m. Solo. Brackett, Aug 19, '94, lives a wid. in Fram.; 11. JOSIAH, b. May 25, '78, m. Nancy Jones, Ap. 2, 1801, lives in N. H. Josiah, the f. lived on the place of his g. son Charles, moved twice to Marlb. N. H., and d. there 1832, æ. 95. His w. Eliz. d. Jan. 22, 1816, æ. 79.

7. EPHRAIM, s. of Josiah (6), m. Elizabeth Luke; and had 1. JOHN LUKE, b. Sep. 7, 1789, m. Persis Goodale, of Marlb., 1819; 2. NANCY, b. May 20, '92, d. unm. Feb. 16, 1816; 3. JEREMY, b. July 19, '94, d. unm., 1843; 4. EMILY, b. July 29, '96, m. Winthrop Morse, of Hop., lives in Worcester; 5. EDWARD, b. Aug. 6, '98, m. Cordelia James, 1827, lives in Ohio; 6. LOUISA, b. 1800; 7. WILLIAM, b. June 30, '03, lives in Ill.; 8. SUSAN, b. 1805, m. —— Colburn; 9. CHARLES, b. Mar. 5, 1808, m. Mary Goodale; 10. HENRY, b. Oct. 20, '13, lives in Boston. Betsey, w. of Eph., d. Dec. 25, 1825, æ. 58; and he m. 2d, wid. Mary Adams. He lives in F.

PARKMAN, ALEXANDER, m. Keziah, dr. of Deac. Wm. Brown, and with w. cov'd Dec. 3, 1769; and had in Fram., 1. BETTY, bap. Dec. 3, 1769; 2. ROBERT BRECK, d. in Parkman, O. The. f. moved to Marlb. N. H., of which he became a Representative, and had POLLY, b. 1779; and JOHN, 1782. He removed to Whitestown, N. Y.

Alexander was s. of the Rev. EBENEZER, of Westboro', who was b. in Boston, Sep. 5, 1703, (H. C., '21), ordained at Westb., Oct. 28, '24; had by his first w. Mary, *Mary*, b. Sep. 14, 1725; *Ebenezer*, Aug. 20, '27, d. in Westb., July 5, 1811; *Thomas*, July 3, '29; *Lydia*, Sep. 20, '31, d. June 21, '33; *Lucy*, Sep. 23, '34. Mary, the m. d. Jan. 29, 1735-6, and the f. m. 2d, Hannah, dr. of the Rev. Rob. Breck, of Marlb., and had, *Elizabeth*, b. Dec. 28, '38, d. Jan. 14, (or 19), '38-9; *William*, b. Feb 19, 1740-1, (Deacon);

Sarah, b. Mar. 20, '42–3; *Susanna*, b. Mar. 13, '44–5; *Alexander*, b. Feb. 17, '46–7, of Fram., &c. ; *Breck*, b. Jan. 27, '48–9, d. in Westb.; *Samuel*, b. Aug. 22, '51, a distinguished merchant in Boston; *John*, b. July 21, '53, d. unm., Sep. 10, '75 ; *Anna Sophia,* b. Oct. 18, '55, m. Hon. Elijah Brigham, and d. Nov. 26, '83; *Hannah*, b. Feb. 9, '58, d. Oct. 14, '77 ; *Elias*, b. Jan. 6, '61, d. in Milford. The Rev. Ebenezer d. at Westb., Dec. 9, 1782. His wid. Mad. Hannah, d. Aug. 20, 1801, æ. 84.

PARMENTER, variously written Permenter, Parmiter, Parmeter,* JOHN, sen., with his son John, was among the first settlers and proprietors of Sud., and took the freeman's oath, May 13, 1640. He was selectman, 1641, and he (or his son), was on a committee of inspection into the moral condition of families, &c., Feb. 28, 1655, and selectman, 1660. In 1654, he was agent at Sud., for Herbert Pelham, Esq., and Capt. Wm.; also for Thomas Walgrave, Esq. He removed from Sud. to Roxb., where, in 1670, he sold to Tho's Rice, of Marlb., several parcels of land in Sud. (Mid. Deeds, VII. 102). His w. Bridget, d. Ap. 6, 1660. His will was proved, 1671. He names his w. Annie, s. in-law, John Woods, (whose wife's name on other records is Mary), and g. s. John Parmeter. Capt. Isaac Johnson, of Roxb., his g. s. John, and his cousin Cheeney, shoemaker, were executors. (His s. John had deceased, in Sud., 1666). John m. in Roxb., Annis Dane, Aug. 9, 1661.

2. JOHN, Jr., s. of John (1), was among the first prop. of Sud., and took the freeman's oath, May 10, 1643. He bought in Sud., Henry Prentice's houselot, 1642; and in 1649, sold his house, &c., in Sud., to John Goodnow. He, or his father, was one of Maj. Willard's troopers, at Dedham, 1654, and the "major's man." In 1665, he was allowed to keep a house of entertainment, at Sud. (Co. Rec., I. 59.) His chil. (all named in his will), were, 1. JOHN, b. ab. 1639 ; 2. JOSEPH, b. Mar. 12, 1642 ; 3. GEORGE ; 4. MARY, b. June 10, 1644 ; 5. BENJAMIN. John, the f. d. at Sud., April 12, 1666, and his will was proved the same year. (Inventory, £310.15.) His wid. was Amee, who d. in Sud., 1681.

Note.—JAMES d. in Sud., 1678. MARY, m. Richard Burke, 1670. LYDIA, m. Thomas Pratt, Jun., of Sherb., June 5, 1681.

3. JOHN 3d, s. of John (2), æ. ab. 50, 1689, (Rev. in N. E. justified),had by w. Elizabeth, in Sud., 1. SARAH, b. Aug. 29, 1668, m. Edmund Bowker, '88 ; 2. MARY, b. Oct. 15, '70, m. —— Bennit; 5. ELIZABETH, b. Dec. 9, '72, m. —— Garfield ; 4. JOHN 4th, b. Ap. 9, '78, f. by w. Martha, of *Sam.,* b. and d. 1707 ; *Submit,* b. May 18, '08, m. Jona. Garfield, '30 ; *Silence,* b. Oct. 9, '10 ; *Martha,* June 21, '13 ; *Deliverance,* Nov. 10, '17 ; *Joshua,* Nov. 20, '19 ; *Caleb,* Ap. 9, '22 ; and by 2d w. Mehetabel Livermore, *Nathaniel,* b. Nov. 9, 1729; *John,* b. June 11, '31, (had 2 wives Ruth and Abigail); John 4th, d. Oct. 17, '68; 5. JOSEPH, b. Aug. 24, 1685, m. Lydia Rice, 1717, and was f. of *John,* b. Dec. 31, '17 ; *Lidiah,* b. June 17, '20 ; *Elizabeth,* b. May 17, '22 ; *Peter,* b. Sep. 11, '24 ; *Jason,* b. July 6, '30, (w. Sarah); *Rebecca,* b. Nov., '37 ; *Thankful,* b. Oct., '41. The will of John, the f. was proved, Nov. 10, 1719.

4. BENJAMIN, s. of John (2), m. Thamazin Rice, 1680, and was f. in Sud. of 1. LYDIA, b. Sep. 29, 1681, m. —— Griffin ; 2. BENJAMIN, b. Jan. 21, '82, m. Mary Adams, 1708, and f. of *Tamson,* b. Oct. 1713; and *Freelove,* b. Ap. 30, '25 ; 3. DAVID, b. 1685 ; 4. DAVID, b. Ap. 12, '86, (d. Mar. 6,

---

* Dr. Stearns (Mss.) states that the name is of French origin, and denotes "a mountaineer," and that the early settlers of this name, in Sud., were proverbially small of stature.

1742–3), m. Abigail Brewer, 1713, who d. June 6, 1758, and was f. of *Abigail*, b, Jan. 21, 1713–4; *Edmond*, b. Jan. 30, '15–6, d. Dec. 27, 1792, m. Miliscent Rice, '48, and 2d w. Mary, and 3d Sarah, who. d. 1820, æ. 97, (f. of Joel, Eben., Asa, &c.); *James*, b. May 4, 1719, m. Mary, f. of James, Eleanor, (m. Abel Tower, &c.); and *Samuel*, b. May 11, 1722, m. Mary (Tower?) (and f. of Ezra; b. 1760, whose son William, of Camb., has been a Representative to Congress); 4. MERCY, b. Dec. 8, 1687, m. Tho. Burk, 1718; 5. THANKFUL; 6. JONATHAN, b. Jan. 15, 1702–3, d. 1734, and f. by w. Mary, of *Susanna, Mary, Jonathan*, and *Abigail*; Benj. had other chil. who d. young. He d. 1737, and his will was proved in May, his w. Tamson surviving him.

5. GEORGE, s. of John (2), m. Hannah Johnson, 1679; and had in Sud., 1. GEORGE, b. May 5, 1679, m. Mary Bent, 1701, and d. Oct. 25, 1727, f. of *Uriah*, b. Nov. 1702, m. Sarah Dunton, '22, f. of Elijah, (who m. Lydia) and others; *Elias*, b. Mar. 1705–6, w. Thankful, lived at Hop., (and f. of John, of Petersham, Elias and several drs.); *Deliverance* and *Thankful*, b. Dec. 16, '09; D. m. Ruth Hayden, '31, (and f. of Elizabeth, Jason, Persis, Josiah, &c.); *Zebulah*, b. Ap. 1716, m. in Fram, Phinehas Parmenter, '36; and *Hannah*, b. Jan. 1721; 2. JOSEPH, b. May 19, 1681, f. by w. Mary of *Bethsheba*, b. 1705; *Mary*, '09; *Adonijah*, Nov. 1, '15; *Joseph*, Nov. 24, '18, prob. of Rutland; *Charles*, Sep. 21, '21; 3. SOLOMON, b. June 17, 1683, d. 1755, rated in F., 1705, m. 1st, Dorothy, and had *Dorothy*; m. 2d, Deb., dr. of Tho. Pratt, of F., July 1, 1717, and had *Zeruiah*, b. 1718, m. Nat'l Hayden; *Abigail*, '19; *Solomon*, Sep. 14, '21, m. Elizabeth Craigie, '48, moved to Rutland; *Deborah*, b. 1724, m. Gideon Brown, '54; *Ezekiel*, b. Ap. 3, '26; *Jedidiah*, b. July 19, '28, m. Silence Maveric, '55; *Grace*, b. 1730; *Lucea*, b. 1732; *Hephzebah*, b. 1735; 4. JOHN[6], b. Ap. 17, 1685; 5. DANIEL, b. Aug. 3, 1688, m. Rebecca Adams, 1714, and f. of *William*, b. July 16, '19, m. Mary Pepper, of Fram. Sep. 24, '40, (f. of Daniel, Isaiah, Jacob, Mary, Lois, William, Thomas, and Eunice, m. in Fram., Bathshebah, m. in Fram., and Rebecca); *Aaron*, b. June, 1723, m. Jane Craigie, 1747; 6. AMOS, b. Mar. 12, 1693–4; 7. HANNAH, b. July 17, 1696; 8. ABIGAIL, b. Feb. 17, 1702–3. George, the f. d. in Sud., 1727.

6. JOHN, s. of Geo. (5), m. in Sud. Abigail Burk, June 1, 1709; and with w. cov. in Fram., July 28, 1717. He lived in the N. part of the town. His w. Abigail d. Ap. 11, 1757. He d. in Fram. No chil. are recorded.

7. AMOS, s. of Geo. (5), m. in Sud. Mercy (or Mary) Wood, Dec. 21, 1715, and with w. cov. in Fram., May 12, '17; and had 1. PHINEHAS[6], b. Feb. 7, '16–7; 2. ASA, b. Mar 12, '18, d. Nov. 3, 1739; 3. MARTHA, b. Oct. 18, '19, d. Jan. 21, 1741; 4. KEZIAH, b. June 24, '22, m. Joseph Stanhope, of Sud., Jan. 24, '39–0; 5. ———, b. May 7, '24, d. young; 6. DINAH, b. June 4, '25, m. Samuel Stanhope, July 7, '42; 7. JOSHUA[10], b. Feb. 26, '27–8; 8. LYDIA, b. June 14, '30, m. Abigail Walker, of Sud., Mar. 1, '50; 9. RUTH, b. Sep. 13, '32, m. Elisha Bruce, of Southb., Jan 8, '54. Amos the f. lived in the N. part of the town, near Mr. Ezek. How's. Mary his w. d. Oct. 21, 1739.

8. PHINEHAS, s. of Amos (7), m. Zebulah Parmenter, of Sud., June 3, 1736, and had in Fram., Amos[9], b. Dec. 5, 1736. Phinehas lived near Mr. Vose's, and moved from town.

9. AMOS, s. of Phin. (8), m. Mary Berry, and with w. cov. Aug. 17, 1761. His chil. were 1. MOLLY, b. Aug. 29, '61, m. Joshua Parmenter; 2. ABIJAH, b. Mar. 12, '63, m. Polly Drury, July, 1790, d. without issue, and his wid. m. again ; 3. OLIVE, b. Feb. 23, '66 ; 4. NELLY, bap. Oct. 8, '69, m. Peter Smith, of Medfield, May 20, '95; 5. AMOS, bap. Oct. 8, '69, m. Tryphena Banister, Ap. 8, '98, lived in N. H. ; 6. PHINEHAS, bap. May 4, '77, m. —— Tuttle, and lived in Upton. Amos, the f. lost a leg by disease, and d. in Fram., Feb. 26, 1785.

10. JOSHUA, s. of Amos (7), m. Persis Parmenter, with w. cov. July 26, 1752; and had in Fram., 1. REUBEN[11], b. Mar. 3, 1752, m. Sarah Potter of Marlb.; 2. MERCY, b. Ap. 27, '54, m. John Dunken, of Rutland, Nov. 27, '75 ; 3. DINAH, b. Ap. 9, '56, m. Geo. Baker, lived in Gardner, and d. ab. 1822; 4. ELIZABETH, b. Jan. 23, '59, m. Peter Stanhope, and d. in Me. ; 5. JOSHUA, b. Mar. 23, '61, d. in Sep.; 6. ——, b. Dec. 21, '62, d. Jan. 2, '63 ; 7. JOSHUA[12], b. Feb. 23, '64; 8. EZRA[13], b. Jan. 31, '67 ; 9. PERSIS, b. May 22, '69, m. Isaac Hunt, of Sud., Aug. 13, '95 ; 10. STEPHEN, b. Sep. 12, '71, m. Deb. Gates, of Stow ; 11. KEZIAH, bap. June 26, '74, m. Ezek. Parmenter, of Sud., Jan. 15, '97 ; 12. ELIAS, b. July 8, '76, m. Eunice Brown of Sud., June, '97, and d. Dec., 1821 ; 13. ARTEMAS, b. Nov. 11, '78, m. Lucretia Parmenter, and d. 1833. [Luke, s. of Joshua, bap. June 24, 1770, said not to have been of the same family.] Josh., the f. m. 2d, —— Gates, and 3d, —— Winch, lived near Mr. Ezek. Howe's, and d. in Fram.,.Oct. 19, 1822.

11. REUBEN, s. of Joshua (10), m. Sarah Potter, and with w. cov. Oct. 10, 1773. They had, JOEL, bap. Oct. 17, '73 ; REUBEN, and RACHEL, bap. Aug., 1781. The parents were recommended by the ch. Mar. 1783.

12. JOSHUA, s. of Josh. (10), m. Polly Parmenter, Aug. 1785, and with w. cov'd Mar. '94. They had bap., Mar., '94, SUMNER, OLIVE, WINTHROP, and RHODA. The f. moved to N. Y., ab. 1800.

13. EZRA, s. of Josh. (10), m. Susannah Brown, of Sud., and with w. cov. June 1792. Their chil were ELEANOR ; SUSAN-

NAH; NABBY, d. æ. 5; SYLVIA, d. æ. 3; SUSANNAH; NABBY; SYLVIA; WARREN; ELEANOR; JEWELL.

14. POLLY, m. Eleazer Smith, of Walpole, Nov. 1793.

PARRIS, MARY, relict of Samuel, of Wayland, d. Ap. 24. 1805, æ. 34. (G. stone.)

PATTERSON, PATTESON, or PATTISON. Nov. 6, 1651, embarked in the John and Sarah, of London, for N. E., JAMES Pattison and DAVID Patterson.

1. JAMES, m. Rebecca Steevenson, of Camb., May 29, 1662, had in Billerica, 1. MARY, b. Aug. 22, '67, m. Peter Proctor, of Chelmsford, Jan. 30, '88; 2. JAMES, b. Feb. 28, '68, d. Oct. 3, '77; 3. ANDREW, b. Ap. 4, '72, m. Elizabeth Kebbe, of Charlestown, '97; 4. JOHN, b. Ap. 8, '75, m. in Concord, Joanna Hall, of Bill., Dec. 29, 1702; 5. JOSEPH, b. Jan. 1, '80–1, a tailor, m. in Sud., Mary or Mercy Goodnow, Sep. 22, 1701, and his will proved 1736, f. at Wat., of *Mary*, b. 1702; *Mary*, b. Aug. 16, '04, m. —— Haas; *Lydia*, b. Oct. 9, '06; *Eunice*, '08, m. Jona. Flag, '26; *Joseph*, b. Aug. 27, '10, m. Lydia Merean, of Newton, 1737, (f. at Wat., of Joseph, Elizabeth, Beulah, Abigail, and Amos); *Hepsebah*, b. Dec. 7, '13; *Sebilla*, m. —— Ball; *Lydia*, b. 1718; and *Elizabeth*, b. 1727, (by 2d w. Rebecca Livermore, m. 1724); 6. JAMES, b. Ap. 13, '83; 7. REBECKAH, b. 1682, d. 1683; 8. JONATHAN, b. Jan. 31, 1685. The will of James, of Billerica, "a Scotchman," was proved, 1701. He speaks of a br. in-law, Andrew Stevenson.

2. JAMES, (whose father is said to have been James), prob. g. s. of James (1), was b. Aug. 13, 1707, m. Lydia Fisk, October 14, 1730, and had in Sud., 1. JONATHAN, b. Nov. 30, '35, unm., killed in the French war, by the Indians, July 20, '58; 2. DAVID, b. May 17, '39; 3. ANDREW, b. Ap. 14, '42, m. Elizabeth Bond, of Worcester, Oct. 21, '61, and f. at Sud., of *Sarah*, b. May 15, '64; and *James*, b. Feb. 22, '68. The f. moved to Princeton and Petersham. James, the f. d. in Princeton, May 4, 1766. His w. Lydia d. Sep., 1776, æ. 66.

3. DAVID, s. of James (2), m. Beulah Clark, of Fram., and with w. cov. Nov. 16, 1759. Their chil. were, 1. DAVID, b. Aug. 7, 1760, m. in N. Haven, and d. in S. C., 1798; 2. LYDIA, b. Dec. 8, '61, m. Ezra Rice, of Northboro', and d. in Concord, 1832; 3. MOLLY, b. Sep. 30, '63, m. Elias Hemenway, moved to N. Marlb.; 4. JONATHAN, b. Sep. 3, '65, m. Sarah Rice of Northboro,' lived there, in Vt., Canada, and Conn., and d. lately in Northb.; 5. JAMES, b. Sep. 3, '67, m. Lavoisie Wyman, of Northb., d. South, 1836; 6. ISAAC, b. Mar. 9, '69, m. Persis Wyman, of Northb., lived in Boylston, was infirm, and killed by a wagon, 1795; 7. NANCY, b. Feb. 18, '71, m. Jabez M. Parker, of Westb., moved to Philipston, and d. 1843; 8. ENOCH, b. Sep. 30, '72, m. Mary Adams, lives in Boston; 9. ARTEMAS, b. Mar. 30, '74, m. Aseneth Hemenway, Ap. 12, 1802, lives in Northb.; 10. SALLY, b. Ap. 12, '75, d. Sep. 23; 11. SALLY, b. July 31,

'76, m. Gill Bartlett, of Northb., and d. ab. 1826; 12. BEULAH, b. June 20, '79, m. Henry Hastings of Northb., and lives there; 13. CATHARINE, b. Feb. 7, '81, m. Adam Hemenway, of Fram., Mar., 1804; 14. WILLIAM, b. Ap. 19, '82, m. Hannah Hemenway, Sep. 12, 1802, 2d, Eliza Adams, and was killed by the cars on the B. and W. R. Road, 1835; 15. FINIS, b. Sep. 1, '85, m. Luther Hemenway, July 10, 1803, lived in N. H. David, the f. lived at Mr. Brackett's, moved to Boylston, 1783, and returned to Fram., 1799. He. d. Nov. 28, 1809, æ. 70. His w. Beulah d. May, 1829.

PEPPER,* ROBERT, took the freeman's oath, May 10, 1643, and was early a memb. of the Roxbury ch. He m. in Roxb. Elizabeth Johnson, 1642; and had 1. ELIZABETH, bap. Mar. 3, '43-4, d. Ap. '44; 2. ELIZABETH, b. 1645, m. John Evered of Dedham, May 13, '62; 3. JOHN, b. Ap. 8, '47, m. Bethiah Fisher, of Dedham, '69, who d. 1669. John d. 1670; 4. JOSEPH, bap. 1648; 5. JOSEPH, b. Mar. 8, '49-0, m. Mary ——, who m. 2d, Joshua Sever. Joseph was slain by the Indians, at Sudbury, Ap. 21, 1675, in Capt. Wadsworth's Co.; he left a dr. *Bethiah*, b. 1676; 6. MARY, bap. 1651, m. Samuel Evered, in Dedham, 1669; 7. Benjamin, bap. May 15, 1653, d. 1658; 8. ROBERT, b. Ap. 21, 1655, was taken captive by the Indians, at Northfield, Sep. 1675, and was prisoner to Shoshanim, Sagamore of Nashaway; 9. SARAH, b. Ap. 28, 1657, m. —— Mason, of Boston; 10. ISAAC, b. Ap. 26, '59; 11. JACOB, b. July 25, (Rox.; 28, Bos.Rec.)'61. Robert's will was proved July 17, 1684, his w. Eliz. d. Jan. 5, 1683-4.

2. JACOB, s. of Rob. (1), m. Elizab. Paine, 1685; and had, 1. Robert, b. and d. 1685; 2. ROBERT, b. Mar. 16, '86-7; 3. REBECCA, b. July 11, 1702; 4. ANNA, b. '05; 5. MARY, b. '07, d. '08; 6. BENJAMIN, d. '13.

3. JACOB, m. in Roxb. Mary Glezen, 1714; and had, 1. MARY, b. Mar. 30, 1715, d. Ap. 6; and at Fram., 2. MARY, b. Oct. 25, '17, m. Wm. Parmenter, of Sud., Sep. 25, '40; 3. BENJAMIN, b. Oct. 30, 1719. Jacob, the f., d. in Fram., Ap. 10, 1739.

4. BENJAMIN, s. of Jacob (3), m. Abigail Pratt, of Fram., Jan. 6, 1741-2, with w. adm. to the ch. Jan. 19, 1752; and had 1. BENJAMIN, bap. July 19, 1752, d. unm.; 2. ANNE, bap. Mar. 17, '54, m. Ezekiel Mixer; 3. JACOB, bap. Dec. 28, '55, m. Olive Marshall, May 4, '80, had a s. *Benjamin*, and d. in Weston, ab. 1785; 4. STEPHEN, bap. Mar. 22, '60, d. young; 5. PRUDENCE, bap. Oct. 25, '61, m. Azariah Walker, Aug. 16, '81, and d. at Needham; 6. SARAH, bap. Nov. 6, '63, m. Joseph Greaves, moved to Me.; 7. LUCIA, bap. Feb. 22, '67, d. young; 8. ABIGAIL, m. 1st, Capt. Elijah Cloyes, and 2d, Maj. Healey, of Dud-

---

* Berry's Genealogies of the Co. of Kent, England, names one Richard Pepper, who was born ab. 1600.

ley; 9. LUCY, m. Nathaniel Lamb ; 10. MOLLY, m. Wm. Maynard; 11. BETSEY, d. young; 12. a dr., d. young. Capt. Benjamin kept for some time a public house, at the Dr. Stone place. He was m. in Mr. Swift's house. He afterwards occupied the house, and on the spot where he was married, placed his bed, on which both he and his wife died, and they were buried in the same grave. Abigail, w. of Benj. d. Sep. 7, 1807; Capt. Benj. d. Sep. 9, 1807. (T. Rec.)

5. ROBERT, prob. s. of Jacob (2), had in Fram., by w. Sarah, 1. JOSHUA, b. Jan. 18, 1720–1 ; 2. ROBERT, b. Feb. 28, 1722–3. [Sarah, prob. dr. of Robert, (or Jacob), was bap. Ap. 11, 1725.] Robert, "our Schoolmaster," cov'd, Jan. 29, 1721; his w. was adm. July 2, 1721. Robert kept school in Sud., 1728.

RICHARD, and w. Mary, were early members of Roxb. ch. JOSEPH, of Roxb., m. Anne Youngman, 1720, f. of *Joseph, Rebecca*, and *Anna*. JACOB, of Hardwick, m. Abigail Foster, 1754.

PERKINS. Dr. Perkins, (prob. RICHARD, Harv. Coll., 1748, s. of Rev. Daniel, of Bridgewater, and br. of the w. of Rev. Matthew Bridge), was rated in Fram., 1758. He m. Mary Hancock, sister of Gov. Hancock, and dr. of his own m. in-law. He prob. remained but a short time in Fram. A Dr. Perkins, (prob. Daniel, son of the above), was a Physician in Fram., 1789, and Collector that year. He lived in Mr. Geo. Eames' house. He "had his vendue," Jan. 1792, and Feb. 14, "moved to the Mohawk." Mrs. Polly Perkins began school, June 15, 1789. (Dea. Buckminster's Ms. Journal.)

PERRY, JAMES, had by w. Mary, JOSEPH, b. Jan. 15, 1703–4. JAPHET, m. Lydia How, June 26, 1739, and their dr. *Lydia* was bap., July 17, 1746. (Japhet had a dr. *Sarah*, at Sud., b. Aug., 1740). . SAMUEL, Jun., of Nat., m. Olive Rice, of Fram., Oct., 1789. SAMUEL, 3d, m. in Fram. Hannah Park, both of Nat., Oct., 1793. This family is numerous on Sherb., Holl. and Sud. Rec.

PETERATTUCKS, JACOB, was in Fam., 1730, and worked for Col. Buckminster. NANNY was m. to Prince Yongey, May 19, 1737. The name savors of Indian origin.

PETTES, ANNE, m. Timothy Pike, Feb., 1783.

PHILIPS, EBENEZER, m. Abigail Pratt, and had EBENEZER,

b. Aug. 12, 1766. Wid. Abigail cov'd May 10, 1767. MARY, of Southb., was m. to Nathaniel Nickols, of Fram., Sep. 12, 1745. HENRY, Esq., was moderator of a Town Meeting, in Fram., June 12, 1728. This family is found on the Southb. Rec.

PIERCE, or PEIRCE, JOHN, had by w. Elizabeth, JOHN, b. Ap. 12, 1730; SUSANNA, b. Feb. 24, '32–3. John, the f. lived at the E. part of the town.

2. THOMAS, of Hop., m. Lydia Gibbs, of Fram., Jan. 24, 1743, and had in F., 1. ELIZABETH, b. Nov. 30, 1744; 2. JONATHAN, b. Dec. 4, 1745. [THOMAS, of Fram., m. Mary Haven, of Hop., Ap. 26, 1750.]

3. JONATHAN, prob. s. of Tho. (2), had by w. Lydia, in Fram., JONATHAN, b. July 28, 1788.

4. ELIZABETH, m. Abraham How, both of F., June 16, 1749. HANNAH, m. Wm. Ballard, Jun., both of F., Aug. 25, 1741.

JOHN, was in Sud., 1655. MOSES, of Sud., and w. Mehetabel, had chil. from 1752; DAVID and w. Sarah, from 1764. WM. and w. Sarah, of Southb., had *Hannah*, 1736, and *Seth*, 1738. JOSEPH, of Wat., (w. Hannah) had *John*, 1699; *William*, 1707.

PIKE, JEREMIAH, prob. s. of James and w. Rachel, had at Reading, 1. JEREMIAH², b. Jan. 15, 1673–4; 2. JAMES, b. May 2, '76, d. 1676; 3. ELIEZER, (or Ebenezer) b. and d. 1677; 4. MICHAEL⁴, b. Ap. 7, '78; 5. JAMES, b. Nov. 7, '79; 6. RACHEL, b. Dec. 14, 1681; 7. JAMES, b. Sep. 15, '82, rated in Fram., 1710, [perhaps of Weston, where Sarah w. of James was adm. to the ch. 1714, and d. '23. James' est. was settled, 1727, f. of *John, James, Sam., Benj., Nath'l, Jona., Onesiphorus,* and 2 drs.] 8. NATHANIEL³, b. May 4, '85; 9. WILLIAM¹², b. Mar. 14, '87–8; 10. NAOMI, b. Feb. 14, '88–9, m. in Fram., John Gibbs, Mar. 9, 1709–0. Jeremiah and his family came to Fram., prob. before its incorporation, and with his sons, settled on the road by Deac. M. Haven and L. Belknap, Esq., which was called "Pike Row." Jerem. Sen. was Selectman, 1700, 4 years, and d. Jan. 9, 1710–1.

JAMES, (and wives Naomi and Sarah), was of Reading, and perhaps the James rec'd to Charlestown ch. 1647; prob. also of Cambridge, where he had s. *John*, b. Jan. 1, 1653–4; and at Reading, *Zachariah*, and others who d. y'ng. JOHN, of Langford, came over in the James, 1635. JOHN, Sen., of Salisb., d. 1654, (his will proved Oct. 3), leaving *John,* (w. Mary, and f. of John, &c.); *Robert,* (w. Sarah, f. of John and several drs.) [A Robert was Commissioner to Me., 1668, and after of the Council. Hutch. i. 262];

Dorothy ; Ann ; and dr. *Israell.* JOSEPH, a Dep. Sheriff, was shot by the Indians near Haverhill, Sep. 4. 1694. The estate of Joseph, of Newbury, was administered Ap. 1697, (w. Susanna, chil. *Sarah, Mary, John, Joseph,* (m. Hannah. dr. of Lt. Isaac Smith, who d. in the Canada expedition) ; *Benjamin, Hannah,* and *Thomas.*) RICHARD, lived, 1675, W. side of Muscle Cove, at Falmouth. At Charlestown, JOHN, m. Elizabeth Engleshie, 1671, and JOSEPH, m. Susannah Smith, 1680—both had chil. at C.

2. [1]JEREMIAH, s. of Jerem. (1), m. in Concord, Susanna Wooster, May 6, 1701, and had in Fram., 1. MOSES[3], b. Sep. 1, 1702 ; 2. AARON, b. July 11, 1709, m. Comfort Pike, Aug. 23, 1733, and d. in Fram., prob. without issue, Ap. 26, 1774. Jer. the f. was Selectman, 1719, for 14 y. ; and T. Treasurer 12 y. He d. in Fram. Feb. 3, 1746. His w. Susanna d. Mar. 11, 1746. (T. Rec.)

3. [1]MOSES, s. of Jerem. (2), m. Mehetabel Pratt, July 13, 1727, and cov'd Mar. 3, 1728. His chil. were, 1. ASA, b. July 12, '28, d. Ap. 12, 1731 ; 2. SUSANNAH, b. Jan. 31, '29–0, m. Joseph Eames, July 15, '46 ; 3. SARAH, b. Nov. 6, '31, adm. to the ch., July 5, '52, and d. Mar. 24, '61. Mehetabel the m. d. Jan. 30, 1733–4. Moses m. 2d, Mrs. Relief Stacy, Dec. 29, 1737 ; and had, 4. MOSES, b. Sep. 9, '38, d. May 15, '41 ; 5. COMFORT, b. Mar. 11, '40–1, m. Deac. Gideon Haven ; 6. MEHETABEL, b. Oct. 13, '43, m. Capt. Simon Edgell ; 7. MOSES, b. July 14, '46, d. Jan., 1748. Moses, the f., lived on the place now of Deac. Moses Haven, was Deacon of the 1st ch., Selectman, 1746, 14 years, and T. Treasurer, 1746, 14 years. He d. much respected, Aug. 4, 1759, æ. 56. His wid. Relief, d. Ap. 23, 1770, æ. 63.

4. [2]MICHAEL, or Michel, s. of Jerem. (1), m. Mehetabel Brown, in Roxb., May 28, 1706 ; and had in Fram., 1. MEHETABEL, b. Dec. 15, 1707, m. John Winch, Jan. 27, 1743 ; 2. TIMOTHY[5], b. Jan. 24, 1709–0 ; 3. ABRAM[6], b. Feb. 12, 1712. [Abram, s. of Mich., is said to have had a br. JOHN[9].] Michael the f. was Selectman, 1729, and adm. to the ch., Ap. 30, 1749.

5. [2]TIMOTHY, s. of Mich. (4), m. Rachel Gibbs ; and had, 1. NAOMI ; 2. RACHEL, m. Asa Pike. Timo. lived at John Newton's, was with w. adm. to the ch., Oct. 7, 1750. Rachel, wid. of Timo., d. June 18, 1805. (T. Rec.)

6. [2]ABRAHAM, s. of Mich. (4), m. Martha Bellows, of Southb., Jan. 27, 1742 ; and had, 1. NAOMI, bap. Ap. 26, '47 ; 2. DANIEL[8], bap. Aug. 9, '47 ; 3. SILAS[7], bap. Aug. 5, '50 ; 4.

Moses, b. Feb. 12, '52, " slain by a cannon ball, shot by the ministerial troops, on Plowed Hill, Aug. 28, 1775, and buried on the S. Westerly part thereof, æ. 22 y. 6 m. 16 d." (T. Rec.) Abr., the f., lived on the farm now of Col. M. Edgell, having exchanged farms with Deac. Balch. He d. Jan., 1810, æ. near 98.

7. ²SILAS, s. of Abr. (6), m. 1st, Hannah Parmenter, July 19, 1772; and had, 1. Nelly, b. Oct. 11, '72, m. Obad. Osborne, of Sud., Oct. 26, '97. S. m. 2d, Molly Frizzel, in Sud., Sep. 30, 1777; and had, 2. Polly, b. June 26, '79; 3. Moses, b. May 16, '83, unm. Molly, w. of Silas, was bap. and adm. to the ch., Aug. 15, 1779. Silas lived at Col. Edgell's, moved to Prov. ab. 1804. His w. Molly, d. in Fram., 1824.

8. ²DANIEL, s. of Abr. (6), m. Lois Underwood; and had Luther, bap. Dec. 15, 1770. He, with his w., was adm. to the ch., Dec. 16, 1770, and recommended to Royalston, Oct. 13, '71.

9. ²JOHN, said to have been br. of Abr. (6), m. Sarah Balch, and with w. adm. to the ch., Feb. 26, 1758, and had, 1. Timothy, b. Oct. 7, '59, m. Anna Potter, Feb., '83; 2. John, b. Nov. 15, '61, went into the service, and d. there. Sarah his wid., d. Jan. 28, 1823, æ. 88.

10. ³NATHANIEL, s. of Jerem. (1), had by w. Mary, in Fram., 1. Nathaniel, bap. in Fram., (with Timothy and Sarah), Dec. 6, 1719, m. in Fram., Abial Pratt, Nov. 8, 1734; and f., at Hop., of *Nathaniel*, b. 1744; *James*, b. 1746; *Timothy*[11], 1748; *David*, 1752; *Jonathan*, 1755; 2. Sarah, b. in Fram., Jan. 15, 1715–6; and in Hop., 3. Timothy, b. 1717; 4. Dinah, bap. in Fram., Mar. 13, 1720; 5. Hannah, bap. in Fram., Jan. 7, 1722; 6. Eunice, b. in Hop., 1723; Ebenezer, 1726; James, 1728; Samuel, 1730, f. at Hop., by w. Abigail, of *Abigail, Mary, Rachel, Reuben, Samuel, Aaron,* and *Moses;* Rachel, 1733; Submit, 1735; Mary, bap. in Hop., 1736. Nath., the f. d. in Hop., ab. 1735. Mary, prob. his w., was adm. to the Fram. ch., Mar. 17, 1717, and perhaps, (under the name of Sarah,) rec'd to Hop. ch., and her child James bap., 1728.

11. ³TIMOTHY, prob. s. of Nath., Jun., and g. son of Nath. (10), had at Hop., by w. Abigail, (prob. a Boyden), Asa; Abner; Chloe, b. 1775; Timothy, b. 1779; all of whom came from Hop. to Fram., Ap. 18, 1782, lived on the Common, and moved to N. York.

12. [4]WILLIAM, s. of Jerem. (1), m. Mary Flagg, of Sherb., Nov. 14, 1706; and had in Fram., 1. EBENEZER[13], b. Jan. 22, 1707-8; 2. COMFORT, b. Feb. 20, '09-0, m. Aaron Pike, Aug. 23, '33; 3. WILLIAM[14], b. Nov. 28, '13; 4. MARY, b. Jan. 21, '15, m. John Willis, of N. Sherb., July 17, '35; 5. JEREMIAH[16], b. Mar. 19, '17-8; 6. JACOB[17], b. Feb. 26, '20-1; 7. ABIGAIL, b. May 26, '24, m. Charles Ward, of Southb., August 25, '42; 8. SARAH, b. Oct. 6, '27. Mary, (prob. w. of Wm.), was adm. to the ch., Nov. 15, 1719. William adm., Ap. 30, 1749.

13. [4]EBENEZER, s. of Wm. (12), m., in Marlb., Sarah Fay, of Southb., 1729. In 1737, he lived towards Stone's end. [Rebeckah, wid. of Ebenezer, of Hop., and her dr. Rebeckah, were at Wilmington, 1765.]

14. [4]WILLIAM, s. of Wm. (12), m. Sybilla Frost, Feb. 21, 1738-9, who was adm. from Sud. ch., 1755. Their chil. were, 1. ASA[15], b. Jan. 24, 1739; 2. EXPERIENCE, b. Nov. 9, '43; 3. JANE, b. July 1, '53, m. — Wheeler, of Concord. Wm., the f., lived E. of Mr. N. Hudson's.

15. [4]ASA, s. of Wm. (12), m. Rachel Pike, who was adm. to the ch., Oct. 2, 1763. They had, 1. MICHAEL, bap. Nov. 13, '63, m. Abigail Lamb, May, '93; 2. AARON, bap. Dec. 22, '65, m. Bethiah Brindley, Feb., '94; 3. RACHEL, bap. Oct. 16, '68, m. Stephen Bigelow, of Boylston, June, '90; 4. MARY, bap. Dec. 1, '71; 5. WILLIAM, b. Sep. 4, '74. Asa, the f., occupied the Town's house for the poor, and m. 2d, Sarah Blodget, Feb. 1792.

16. [4]JEREMIAH, s. of Wm. (12), m. Keziah Hemenway, Sep. 14, 1743, and with w. adm. to the ch., Feb. 23, 1752. They had, 1. MARY, b. July 28, '44; 2. JEREMIAH, b. July 20, '49, m. — Childs, of Sturbridge, and d. there; 3. RUTH, bap. Jan. 27, '52, prob. d. young. The f. m. 2d, Mary, wid. of Elkanah Haven, (an Eames), and had, 4. KEZIAH, b. May 29, '58, m. Wm. Fay; 5. COMFORT, b. July 30, '64, m. Lemuel Robinson, of Rutland. Jerem., the f. was a bone setter, lived at Nathan Hudson's, and moved to Rutland, ab. 1780.

17. [4]JACOB, s. of Wm. (12), m. Elizabeth Britton, of Southb., Jan. 7, 1742, and had 1. JOHN, b. Jan. 23, '42-3; 2. NATHAN, b. Dec. 24, '44; 3. ELIZABETH, bap. Aug. 27, '47; 4. JACOB, b. June 18, '51. [1761, a commission was ordered on the real est. of Jacob, late of Shrewsbury. Worc. Prob.]

18. JOHN, m. Mary Eames, Sep. 8, 1726, and with w. cov'd, July 2, 1726, and had GERSHOM, b. July 15, '27. Mary, the m. d. July 31, '27, and he m. 2d, Abigail Parkhurst, of Weston, Sep. 23, 1728.

19. HANNAH, was bap. Jan. 7, 1722. BENJAMIN, bap. Sep. 29, 1723. MARTHA, bap. May 7, 1723. MARTHA, m. Richard Newton, of Southb., Jan. 27, 1743. JOSEPH, of Newbury, m. Lydia Drury, Dec. 5, 1722. LOIS, m. Isaac Allerd, Mar. 17, 1752. ELIJAH, of Hop., m. in Fram., Sally Clark, of Hop., Feb. 25, 1796. SHADRACK, bap. Aug. 1786.

PITCHER, MOSES, was paid for mending the M. House windows, 1766.

PITT, LOIS, m. Timothy Haven, Aug. 1784.

POLLY, NATHANIEL, in Fram., 1778, and said to have been of Sherb., m. Anne Maynard, Oct. 18, 1781, and had 1. JOHN, b. Aug. 5, '82; 2. WILLIAM, b. Jan. 10, '84. Anne, the m. d. of the small pox, and N. m. 2d, in Sherb., Eleanor Tyler, Nov. 18, 1793. [JOSIAH, æ. 11 years, came to live with Deac. T. Buckminster, June 6, 1781.]

POWERS, JONAS, (who prob. lived at the N. part of the Town), and w. Lydia, cov'd May 1, 1763, and their dr. MARY was bap. May 1, 1763.

PRATT, or PRAT, THOMAS, had 1. THOMAS^2, b. ab. 1656; 2. JOHN^5; 3. EBENEZER^6; 4. JOSEPH^8; 5. PHILIP^9; 6. DAVID^{11}; 7. JABEZ^{14}; 8. NATHANIEL^{16}; 9. ABIAL, m. Daniel Bigelow; 10. EPHRAIM^{27}; 11. JONATHAN^{23}. Tho., the f., took the freeman's oath, May 26, 1647, and was early at Wat. He bought of Tho. Eames, in 1679, land not far from Gleason's Pond, in Fram., and became an inhabitant of Sherb. Administration on his est. was granted, 1692, to his wid. Susannah, and s. John. Jona., David, and Jabez, were the 3 youngest. The Inventory of his est., £142.2, is dated Dec. 14, 1692.

2. ^{1}THOMAS, Jun., s. of Tho. (1), m. Lydia Parmenter, June 5, 1681, and had 1. THOMAS^3, b. July 16, '82; 2. LYDIA, b. Jan. 15, '84, m. Jonathan Rice, Nov. 18, 1714; 3. DANIEL^4, b. Mar. 24, '87; 4. ABIGAIL, b. Oct. 11, '92, m. (Deac.) Henry Mellen, Mar. 24, 1711-2; 5. DEBORAH, b. Sep. 15, '94, m. Solo. Parmenter, of Sud., July 1, 1717. Tho. Jun., bought in 1678, of Tho. Eames, near the Pond; was an inhabitant of Sherb., 1679,

and appears on Sud. Rec., 1693-4. He was *chosen* Representative from Fram., 1710 (did not serve), and was Selectman, 1713. By a deposition he appears to have been æ. 80, 1736. He lived on the road from Mr. Charles Clark's, N., and d. in Fram., Feb. 6, 1741, æ. ab. 85.

3. ¹THOMAS, s. of Tho. (2), m. Sarah Willard, Jan. 24, 1710-1, and had in Fram., 1. BENJAMIN, b. Sep. 12, '11; 2. ABIGAIL, b. Jan. 10, '12-3; 3. FINNIS, (Phinehas?), b. Mar. 27, '15; 4. LYDIA, b. Nov. 23, '18. Tho., the f. was of "Hasanamisco, part of Sutton," 1724. His will (made at Grafton) was proved, 1761, wife not named. (Worc. Prob.)

4. ¹DANIEL, s. of Tho. (2), m. Elizabeth Rice, May 23, 1723, and with w. cov'd, Jan. 26, '24, and had 1. ELIZABETH, b. Feb. 29, '23-4, m. Peter Brewer, of Southb.; 2. LOIS, b. June 7, '26, m. Samuel Dadmun; 3. MARTHA, b. Dec. 15, '28, m. Daniel Bigelow, and d. in Fram., ab. 1785; 4. LYDIA, b. Nov. 14, '29, m. Peter Gallot. Daniel, the f. bought 1718, 11 ac. N. of Tho. Pratt's, and rec'd from his father Tho., 172-, a deed of land near Larned's Pond, the same Tho. Gleason bought of Benj. Rice, he to pay his 3 sisters certain sums. He was by trade a blacksmith, was Constable, 1726, and d. ab. 1778. His w. survived him several years.

5. ²JOHN, s. of Tho. (1), had by w. Ruth, 1. JOHN, b. Nov. 27, 1691, m. in Marlb., Bathshebah Fay, 1716, and was f. of *Phinehas*, b. Feb. 28, 1716-7, d. 1717; and at Westb. of *Silas*, b. Feb. 27, '21; *Isaiah*, Feb. 14, '23; 2. SUSANNAH, b. Mar. 12, '93, prob. m. Obadiah Allen, of Hop., May 17, '20; 3. ISAAC, b. Aug. 6, '96, m. in Marlb., Eunice Fay, of Westboro', Ap. 17, 1721, and was f. at W. of *Mary*, b. '21; *Isaac*, Jan 4, '25-6; 4. AMOS, b. May 26, '99, m. in Marlb., Ann Allen, of Shrewsb., Dec. 12, 1722, and was prob. the Amos of Shrewsbury, 1750, f. of *Elnathan, Alpheus, Mercy*, (m. Jotham Death), *Anna*, and *Mary*, (see Conveyance — Worc. Prob.); 5. RUTH, b. Feb. 6, 1701; 6. ELEAZER, b. Jan. 10, '02-3; 7. HEZEKIAH, b. Nov. 27, 1705, f. at Westb., by w. Rachel, (who d. Aug. '51), of *Rachel*, b. 1736, *John*, '37, *Nathan*, d. young, *Ruth*, b. '41, and other drs. [A Hezek. m. in Marlb., Mary Cutler, 1754.] John, the f. was rec'd to Sherb., Jan. 13, 1677-8. He bought, 1694, of Sam. How, 50 ac., bounded on John Adams, &c., and of Matth.

Rice, 30 ac. near Indian Head. He sold, 1703, to John How, 30 ac. swamp and upland, on the highway from Sherb. to Sud. He was Selectman in Fram., 1709, and prob. moved to Marlb.

6. ³EBENEZER, s. of Tho. (1), settled near the W, and had at Sherb., by w. Mary, 1. SARAH, b. Nov. 7, 1693, m. Ebenezer Twitchell, Dec. 3, '17; 2. EBENEZER, b. June 13, '95, f. by w. Mary, at Sherb., of *Mary*, b. Oct. 3, 1721, and *Jacob*, b. Mar. 1, '24; 3. JACOB, b. Nov. 7, '97; 4. GERSHOM, b. Sep. 18, 1700, m. Abigail Rice, of Fram., July 3, '29, and f. at Sherb. of *Sarah*, b. Ap. 22, '33, *Jacob*, b. Oct. 3, '35, d. 1811, (m. Lydia Eames of Fram., and f. of Eben., Henry, Aaron, and Jacob), *Abigail*, b. Ap. 3, '38, *Ebenezer*, b. May 13, '41, *Mary*, b. Nov. 10, '43, *Anna*, b. Mar. 24, '46. This family have lived for many generations near the W, by Fram. bounds. Eben., the f. was rated in Fram., 1710.

7. EBENEZER, and w. Charity, had in Fram., 1. ESTHER, b. Nov. 20, 1748; 2. ABIGAIL, b. Ap. 20, '50, d. in Fram., Jan. 18, 1837, æ. 86, 9; 3. EBENEZER, b. Sep. 22, '53.

8. ⁴JOSEPH, s. of Tho. (1), m. Hannah Provender, 1696; and had in Fram., 1. HANNAH, b. Jan. 31, 1696; 2. PRUDENCE, b. Ap. 22, '98; 3. RACHEL, b. Nov. 6, 1703, m. Jos. Graves, May 3, '23; 4. MARY, b. Mar. 4, '05-6, m. Jeremiah Belknap, Aug. 10, '32; 5. BARSHEBAH, b. Ap. 24, '08, m. David Sanger, of Sherb., May 27, 1736. Joseph, the f. was a housewright by trade; was constable, 1716, and d. Oct. 31, 1747. (T. Rec.) His w. Hannah d. May 20, 1745. Jos., of Sherb., sold, 1689, to his br. Tho., 6 ac. of upland (in Fram.), bounded S. on Nat., the same he bought of John How. The Inventory of Jos. of Fram., is dated Nov. 16, 1747.

9. ⁵PHILIP, s. of Tho. (1), m. Rebecca, wid. of Isaac Newton, of Marlb.; and had, 1. JEMIMAH, b. Dec. 12, 1698, in Fram., 1764, prob. unm.; 2. PHILIP, b. Sep. 10, 1701. Phil., the f. was Constable, 1719. Rebecca, (prob. his w.), d. Sep. 3, 1728. Philip d. Feb. 12, 1739, (T. Rec.), and his son Philip adm. on his est.

10. ⁵PHILIP, Jun., s. of Philip, (9), m. in Newton, Mary Osland, June 26, 1726, and cov. July 14, '28; and had 1. JOHN, b. Aug. 15, '28; 2. JOHN, b. Aug. 1, '30, d. Mar. 25, '31; 3. ISAAC, b. Aug. 26, '32; 4. JONATHAN, b. July 21, d. Aug. 26,

1733; 5. JOHN, b. Oct 13, '34, m. Sarah Dyer, of Nat, 1756; 6. PHILIP, b. Mar. 25, '41.

11. ⁶DAVID, s. of Tho. (1), had by 1st w. Rachael, 1. DAVID¹², b. Jan. 28, 1702. He m. 2d, in Reading, Sarah Bancroft, Dec. 14, 1704, and had 2. RACHEL, b. Oct. 18, '06, m. Daniel Claflin, Dec. 21, '26; 3. MEHETABEL, b. July 4, '08, m. Moses Pike, July 13, '27; 4. TIMOTHY, b. June 4, '10; 5. ELISHA, b. Feb. 16, '15-6; 6. HEPHZEBAH, b. Oct. 11, '12; 7. JONATHAN, b. June 25, '18; 8. SARAH, b. Feb. 29, '19-0; 9. ABIGAIL, b. Sep. 26, '22; 10. PRUDENCE, b. Feb. 17, '24-5. David, the f. was Selectman, 1723, and d. 1731. Moses Pike was appointed, 1733, guardian of Elisha and Prudence.

12. ⁶DAVID, Jun., s. of Dav. (11), m. Sarah Claflin, Mar. 10, 1723-4, and with w. cov. Dec. 20, '24, and had, 1. DAVID¹³, b. Jan. 30, '24-5; 2. JONATHAN, b. Sep. 23, '35, (perhaps the "Jona. late of Fram. deceased." T. Rec. 1782); 3. RACHEL, b. Sep. 6, '39; 4. NATHAN, b. Nov. 5, '43. David, the f. d. in Oxford, 1777, æ. 75; his w. Sarah d. 1783, æ. 78.

13. ⁶DAVID, s. of David, (12), m. Elizabeth Brewer, May 20, 1745, cov. Dec. 8, '45; and had, 1. DAVID, b. May 13, 1745; 2. SILAS, b. Sep. 26, '47; 3. BETSEY, b. Mar 13, '48; 4. SARAH, b. Ap. 2, '50.

14. ⁷JABEZ, s. of Tho. (1), m. Hannah Gale, Ap. 22, 1714; and had, 1. ABIEL, b. Sep. 24, '16, m. Nathaniel Pike, of Hop., Nov. 8, '34; 2. JABEZ, b. July 7, '18; 3. BENONI¹⁵, b. Ap. 3, 1720. Jabez m. (prob 2d w.) Rebecca Stratton, Mar. 31, 1726. [Jabish, of Sutton, m. Elizab. Grant, of Fram., Ap. 10, 1741.]

15. ⁷BENONI, s. of Jabez (14), m. Hannah Parmenter, of Sud.; and had 1. ABNER, b. Ap. 24, 1738, m. Mary Wright, Jan. 22, '95, had a dr. Hitty, who m. —— Temple. Abner d. in Fram., ab. 1820; Molly his wid. buried May 26, 1825; 2. ABIGAIL, b. Mar. 9, '39, d. Nov. 5, '46; 3. SARAH, b. Ap. 2, '41, d. Nov. 3, '46; 4. MARY, b. Mar. 25, '45, d. Nov. 10, '46; 5. ABIGAIL, b. Nov. 12, '47, m. Ebenezer Philips; 6. SARAH, b. Mar. 5, '49, d. unm.; 7. NAHUM, b. Aug. 26, '52, d. unm. in Philipston; 8. MARY, b. Ap. 28, '55, m. George Baker; 9. JESSE, b. Sep. 30, '59, m. Polly Dalrymple, of Sud., f. of *Jesse*, &c. and d. in Fram. Mar. 15, 1819; 10. JOHN, b. Nov. 25, '62, d. unm. Benoni, the f. lived near Rufus Hosmer's.

16. ⁸NATHANIEL, s. of Tho. (1), had by w. Abigail, at

Wat., 1. NATHANIEL[17], b. July 10, 1702; 2. MARTIN, b. Dec. 13, '03, m. in Fram., Lydia Biglo, Sep. 30, 1731, and f. at Hop. of *Lydia*, b. '34, and *Benjamin*, '36 — the m. recommended to the ch. in Westb. from Hop., 1738, and had *Joseph*, b. Ap. 7, '38; 3. THOMAS, b. Feb. 14, '05; 4. PHILIP, d. young; 5. ABIGAIL, b. Aug. 15, '07; 6. PHEBE, b. Dec. 22, '09. Nath'l m. 2d, in Marlb., Abigail Wait, Aug. 18, 1712; and had in Fram., 7. MARTHA, b. Dec. 18, '13, prob. the M. who m. Seth Tomlin, of Windham, Sep. 16, '41; 8. DEBORAH, b. Dec. 14, '16, adm. to the ch. Aug. 31, '46, and d. unm., 1791; 9. BERIAH, b. Aug. 27, '21, d. ab. '43; 10. SIMON[18], b. Jan. 24, '25-6; 11. ABIGAIL, b. May 21, '31. Nath'l, the f. was apprenticed to Sam. Allen, of Sud., shoemaker, 1680, and 1707, of Wat., bought of Benj. Bridges, of Fram., 32 ac. between Collar's meadow and Sud. River. His will was proved 1736, in which he speaks of three chil. by a former marriage, Nath'l, Martin, and Phebe. His est. was settled, June, 1749.

17. [8]NATHANIEL, Jun., s. of Nath., (16), and w. Margery, had DANIEL, b. Nov. 5, 1733, d. Oct. 31, 1740.

18. [8]SIMON, s. of Nath. (16), m. Mercy Chamberlin, of Holl., Jan. 3, 1750; and had 1. BERIAH[19], b. Sep. 30, '50; 2. MARY, b. Mar. 9, '52, m. John Pratt, and d. in Leverett, ab. 1838; 3. SIMON[20], b. Mar. 24, '54; 4. ABIGAIL, b. Aug. 20, '56, d. unm. ab. 1800; 5. MARTHA, b. Nov. 22, '58; 6. NATHANIEL[21], b. Mar. 1, '60; 7. EPHRAIM, b. May 23, '63, m. Anne Bullard, Dec. '85, and moved to N. Y.; 8. JOHN, b. Sep. 29, '65, m. Betty Hager, and moved into Penn.; 9. JONATHAN[22], b. May 8, '69.; 10. WILLIAM. Simon, the f. lived on the Common; was struck by lightning, at Mr. J. Cloyes, June, 1777. He d. 1790; his w. Mary d. 1788.

19. [8]BERIAH, s. of Simon (18), m. Molly Dudley; and had 1. DANIEL, b. Oct. 11, 1774, d. Oct. 2, '77; 2. POLLY, b. Aug. 1, 1777; 3. DANIEL, b. May 30, '79; 4. BERIAH, b. Aug. 9, '81. The f. moved to N. Y.

20. [8]SIMON, Jun., s. of Sim. (18), m. Martha Pratt, Nov. 26, 1778, and had 1. MILLY, b. May 8, '80, m. Daniel Pratt, lived in N. Y.; 2. FANNY, b. Sep. 1, '84, lives unm.; 3. LUTHER, b. Ap. 28, '87. The f. moved to N. Y.

21. [8]NATHANIEL, s. of Sim. (18), m. Elizabeth Bullard, 1784, and had 1. MOSES, b. 1785, d. 1802; 2. CYNTHIA, b. 1789,

m. Curtis Billings, of Sharon, lives a wid.; 3. CALVIN, b. Dec. 7, '92, m. Betsey Smith, of Welfleet, lives in Fram.; 4. PATTY, b. June 14, '96, d. unm. 1823; 5. HITTY, b. May 10, '99, m. Charles Jones, of Fram., and lives in Nat.; 6. LUKE, b. Oct. 15, 1801, m. Betsey Tufts, of Lynn; 7. ELIZA, b. 1806, m. Charles Knowlton, of Fram. Nath., the f., a Pensioner, d. in Fram., 1834. His wid. lives in Fram.

22. ⁸JONATHAN, s. of Sim. (18), m. Sally Holden, of Southb., who was adm. to the ch., Nov. 1798. Their chil. were 1. LEVI, b. May 27, '94; 2. LESY, (Lizzy?), b. May 8, '96; 3. LUSENE, b. Aug. 5, '98; 4. LUCINDA, b. Dec. 14, 1800. Jona., the f., moved to Leverett, ab. 1805.

23. ⁹JONATHAN, s. of Tho. (1), m. Sarah Gale, of Wat., and had 1. JONATHAN, b. Ap. 21, 1701;* 2. ABRAHAM, b. Mar. 2, 1702–3; 3. SARAH, b. Oct. 18, 1704. Admin. on Jonathan's est. was granted, 1735.

24. JOHN, m. Mary Pratt, May 7, 1778, and had MARY, b. Feb. 19, 1781.

25. Baptisms in Fram., (names of parents not given), BEULAH and SUSANNAH, Oct. 20, 1717. ABIGAIL, Oct. 5, 1718. ELIZABETH, Mar. 8, 1724. MEHETABEL, July 23, 1727. ASA and ANNE, chil. of John, bap. Oct. 9, 1774.

26. MARY, m. Sam. Putnam, of Sud., July 27, 1748. ABIGAIL, m. Benj. Pepper, Jan. 6, 1741–2. ABIGAIL, m. Peter Brewer, Dec. 22, 1748. ABIGAIL, m. Joshua Barton, of Leicester, Mar. 28, 1750. MARTHA, m. Simon Pratt, Jr., Nov. 26, 1778. EPHRAIM, (prob. of Wayland), m. Hannah Belcher, June, 1788. AARON, of Sherb., m. Olive Metcalf, of Fram., Oct., 1790. JONATHAN, "late of Fram., deceased, who is supposed to have been b. in Hop." (T. Rec. 1782.)

27. ¹⁰EPHRAIM, s. of Tho. (1), was perhaps the Ephraim, of Sud., who by w. Elizabeth, had 1. JOSIAH, b. March 6, 1700. [A Josiah m. in Shrewsb., Sarah Wilson, 1724. Josiah, of Sud., who d. 1759, and w. Ketura, had *Samuel*, b. Ap. 25, 1735, d. 1755; *Josiah*, b. Aug. 17, '37; *James*, b. Mar. 17, '39; *Sarah*, b. Aug. 18, '42]; 2. EPHRAIM, b. Nov. 30, 1704, m. Martha Wheelock, in Shrewsb., 1724; (Dr. Stearns notes him as

---

* Jonathan, of Oxford, had by w. Lydia, who died 1729, *Keziah*, born 1727; *Lydia*, b. '28, d. '29; and by 2d w. Ruth, who d. 1731, *Ruth*, b. 31; and by 3d w. Deborah, who d. 1793, *Mellison; Lydia; Huldah; Jonathan*, b. 1741, (f. by w. Abigail, of Esther, Nahum, Abigail, Meliscent, Alice); *Elias*, '43, d, 1816; *Elisha; Esther; Deborah*.

f. of *Michael*); 3. PHINEHAS, b. July 8, 1706, m. Martha Puffer, of Lancaster, 1726, and had *Mary*, b. June 26, '26-7; *Rebecca*, b. Ap. 19, '29; *Ephraim*, b. Jan. 10, '31-2; *Beulah*, b. Mar. 5, '34-5; *Susanna*, b. Feb. 3, '36-7; *Thankful*, b. Mar. 11, '40; and *Phinehas*, b. May 3, '43; 4. ELIZABETH, b. Ap. 25, 1711; 5. MARY, b. Dec. 2, 1718. Of Ephraim, the f. who probably moved to Shrewsbury, see note below.* [EPHRAIM, Jun., of Shrewsbury, m. Abial Leland, 1752.]

PHINEHAS, "one of the first planters of N. E., Joiner," d. at Charlestown, Ap. 19, 1680. (Charles. T. Rec.) JOHN, of Charlestown, d. ab. 1708, f. of *Thomas, Ebenezer, Joseph, William, Caleb, Joshua, Mary, Hannah*, and *Abigail*. There are several families of Pratts on the Oxford Records. JOSEPH d. there, 1790, æ. 84.

PRINCE. See YONGEY.

PROVENDER, JOHN, held leased lands from Col. Buckminster, was rated in Fram., 1710, and his will was proved, 1712. He left chil. 1. JOHN, prob. a prop. of Templeton, 1735, and d. in Fram., ab. 1759; 2. JONATHAN, rated in Fram., 1710; 3. ISAAC, rated in Fram., 1708; 4. DAVID; 5. HANNAH, m. Joseph Pratt, Mar. 19, 1695-6; 6. SARAH, m. Daniel Elliot, Feb. 3, 1707-8. [BENJAMIN, (prob. another son), was rated in Fram., 1710, and d. in the expedition to Cape Breton.]

PUFFER, WILLIAM, of Sud., m. Abigail Treadway, of Fram., June 8, 1742, and had in Sud., 1. JABEZ, b. July 16, 1743; and in Fram., 2. MARY, bap. Nov. 29, '47; 3. THANKFUL, b. June 16, '49, m. John Mixer.

2. JABEZ, or JABISH, s. of Wm. (1), m. Rachel (Morse?), and had 1. WILLIAM, b. Mar. 4, 1764; 2. BENJAMIN, b. Ap. 6, '65; 3. MARY, b. July 22, '66; 4. JOHN, bap. Ap. 30, '69; 5. RACHEL, bap. Oct. 28, '70; 6. NATHAN, bap. Mar. 22, '72. The f. moved to Dublin, N. H.

---

* Of Ephraim, son of Thomas (1), who was living at his father's decease, 1692, we have found no trace, after much research, unless we adopt the natural supposition, that he was the Ephraim of Sudbury. Farmer states that Eph. of Sud. was g. son of JOSHUA, of Plymouth. [Joshua and Phinehas came over in the 3d ship Ann, and were among the forefathers at Plymouth]. He adds that he was b. in E. Sud., Nov., 1687, and d. in Shutesbury, Mass., May, 1804. Another account states than he d. æ. 116 years, and could count 1500 descendants (?); that he took no animal food for 40 years, and that his health was so good that "he was able to mow a good swarth, 101 years in succession." By an examination of the minutes above, taken from the Sud. and other Rec., the reader will discover a serious discrepance with these statements of the age of Ephraim. The additional statement by Farmer, that Ephraim's *son* Michael d. 1826, æ. 103, is obscured by the probable fact that Michael was grandson of Ephraim, Sen.; and as his f. Eph. Jr. was not married until 1724, the age of Michael is probably exaggerated. If the Ephraim who d. at Shutesbury, was the f. of Michael, instead of being 116 years old, his age was but 99 years and 5 months.

There is a pond in Sudbury, covering an area of ab. 36 acres, called Pratt's Pond.

The Puffer family lived at Mr. Amasa Kendall's, and sprung from JAMES, (w. Mary, who d. Dec. 29, 1751, æ. 80), who came to Sud., and d. Nov. 11, 1749, æ. 86. JAMES, of Dorchester, m. Abigail Newton, of Milton, Dec. 17, 1695. JAMES was of Braintree, 1655. (Farmer.) James, s. of MATTHEW, was b. at Mendon, June 4, 1668.

PULLEN, JOSEPH, came from Boston to Fram., 1770.

PUTNAM, JOHN, m. in Sud., Sarah Maveric, Ap. 25, 1737, and had in Fram., JASE (Jesse ?), b. Mar. 25, 1743. Jesse was on the roll of a militia Co. at Sud., 1759.

JOHN, (w. Sarah), had at Sud., *Elizabeth, Samuel, James, Mary, John, Nathan, Enos, Daniel, Asa, Sarah,* and *Abel.* DANIEL, (w. Thankful), had at Sud., *Lucy,* 1748, and *Relief,* '51. SAMUEL, of Sud., m. in Fram., Mary Pratt, July 27, 1748. SAMUEL, of Salem, (who m. Mary Leach, 1709), had *Samuel,* b. 1711, *John,* '15, *Daniel,* '17, &c., and d. in Sud. SAMUEL, the f. was prob. s. of John, (m. Hannah Cutler, 1678), and g. son of *Nathaniel,* (w. Elizabeth), and g. g. son of JOHN, (w. Priscilla), who came from Abbots-ason, Rockinghamshire, Eng., and d. in Salem, 1662. (Salem Rec.)

RAN, or RAND, MARY, m. John Hemenway, Nov. 26, 1751.

THOMAS, of Westminster, m. Elizabeth Hemenway, Nov. 1788.

TIMOTHY, m. in Fram., (date unknown, prob. ab. 1780), Anne Edmunds, and had a daughter ANNE, who m. —— Holt, a hatter, in Fram.

RAWSON, JOHN, and TURNER, were in Fram., 1790.

READ, ISAAC, Jun., m. in Sud., Lydia Goodnow, Jan. 16, 1755, and had in Fram., NATHAN, b. Feb. 5, 1756.

Isaac prob. descended from THOMAS, sen., of Sud., who owned land in Fram., 1689. His s. Thomas m. Mary Wood, May 30, 1677. The family are numerous on Sud. Records. THOMAS, of Rutland, m. Hannah Nurse, in Fram., Dec. 12, 1754.

REED, SOLOMON, m. Abigail Houghton, of Con., and had in Fram., 1. SARAH ; 2. JOHN, b. Nov. 11, 1751, Y. Coll., 1772, Chaplain in the U. S. Navy, ord. at W. Bridgewater, June 7, 1780, Rep. to Cong. 1794, 6 years, and author of an " Apology for Infant Baptism," and various printed Discourses. He received the degree of D. D. at Brown Un., 1803. He m. Hannah Sampson, 1780, who d. 1815, and he m. again. He d. Feb. 17, 1831, æ. 79. He was f. of the Hon. John Reed, M. C., and Lt. Gov. of Mass. ; 3. SOLOMON, b. 1752, Y. Coll., 1775, ord. at Petersham, m. Susannah Willard, and f. of *Solomon, Susannah, Mary, Josiah, Hannah, Sally, Samuel, John, William,* and *Catharine.* He d. in Petersham, Feb. 2, 1808, æ. 55 ; 4. SAMUEL, b. 1754, Y. Coll., '77, ord. at Warwick, Mass. ; 5. TIMOTHY, b.

'56, Y. Coll., '82, m. Hannah Kingman, '88, was a lawyer in W. Bridgewater, where he d. 1813. Solo., the f., was b. in Abington, ab. 1718, grad. at Harv. Coll., '39; was ord. over the 2d Cong. Ch. in Fram., Jan. 1746–7. His connection with the Ch., was dissolved 1756, and he was afterwards installed over the N. Parish in Middleborough, Mass., where he remained until his death, in 1785.

RHYNE, ANNE, adm. to the ch., Nov. 1782. Her chil. ANNE and HANNAH, were bap. Nov. 21, 1782.

RICE, EDMOND, had by his w. Thamezin, 1. HENRY[10]; 2. EDMUND[8]; 3. EDWARD[2], b. 1618; 4. THOMAS[3]; 5. MATTHEW[4]; 6. SAMUEL[6]; 7. JOSEPH[7]; 8. BENJAMIN[5], b. May 31, 1640.* Thamezin, the m. d. June 18, 1654. Edmund m. 2d, Mercy Brigham, Mar. 1, 1655, and had, 9. RUTH, b. Sep. 29, 1659; 10. ANN, b. Nov. 19, 1661. Edmund, the f. came from Barkhamstead, in Hertfordshire, South Britain, took the freeman's oath, May 13, 1640, was one of the first proprietors of Sudbury, and was rated the sixth in the number of acres granted him. He was selectman in Sud., 1644, and Deacon, 1648. He, in 1652, obtained grants within the bounds of Fram., and leased the Glover Farm, 1647, and the Dunster Farm, 1653. In May, 1656, he was a petitioner for Marlb., and in 1662, was empowered to marry. He was frequently appointed by the General Court to locate grants, and appears conspicuous in the transactions of his time. Edmund, sen., whom a deposition represents as æ. 62, in 1656, was buried at Sud., May, 1663. (Marlb. Rec.) The same year, administration was granted to his wid. Mercy. (Co. Records, I. 224.) (Inventory, £567.14.8.) The settlement (Co. Files, the same year) proposes that the wid. pay to the eight elder chil., (not named), to the eldest £40, to each of the others, £20; and to the two younger chil., had by the said widow, £10 each.

2. EDWARD, s. of Edmond (1), m. 1st, Agnes Bent, by whom he had no chil. He m. 2d, Anne ——, and had. 1. JOHN, who m. Tabitha Stone, Nov. 27, 1674, and was f. of *John*, b. 1675, m. Eliz. Clap, of Milton, 1700; *Anna*, '78; *Deliverance*, '81, m. John How, '03; *Tabitha*, '83; *Prudence*, '85; *Abigail*, '87; *Edward*, Dec. 23, '89, d. in Rutland, Sep. 27, 1756, æ. 66; *Dinah*, '91; *Moses*, '94; *Tamar*, '97, m. Wm. Moore, '17; *Aaron*, Aug. 13, 1700, of Rutland; 2. LYDIA, b. July 30, 1648; 3. LYDIA, b. Dec 10, '49; 4. EDMUND, b. Dec. 9, '53; 5. DANIEL, b. Nov. 8, '55. d. 1737, f. by w. Bethiah, of *Daniel, Luke, Eleazer, Hopestill, Bethiah,* and *Judith*; 6 CALEB, b. Feb. 8, '57, d. 1658; 7. ANNE, b. Nov. 9, '61; 8. DORCAS, b. Jan. 29. '64; 9. BENJAMIN, b. Dec. 22, '66, m. Mary Graves, Ap. 1, '91, and d. Feb. 23, 1748, f. of *Azariah*; *Lydia*, b. 1695; *Elizabeth*, '97, m. Eph. How; *Simon*, or Sim-

---

* The identity of the eight sons of Edmond, above given, is fully proved by deeds and wills which the author has inspected. Three of the sons, (not all, as tradition supposes), are known to have died at a very advanced age, and many of the descendants have been remarkable for longevity. The connection, supposed by Farmer, of the Rices of Sud. and Marlb., with RICHARD, of Concord, is not verified. Richard, by will (dated 1708), gives to his chil., *Paul, Mary, Hannah* Wilcoson, *Elizabeth* Billings, *Abigail* Read, *Peter, Sarah* Cookworthy. Richard was of Camb.,1635, and "agreed with to keep 100 cows." (Camb. Rec.) ROBERT, of Boston, (w. Elizabeth), had *Joshua,* 1637; *Nathaniel*, '39; *Patience*, '42.

eon, '99, of Northboro'; *Zerubbabel*, '02, d. Aug. 2, '75, (w. Elizabeth);
Rachel, '03, m. Ab. How ; *Matthias*, '06, Deac. at Marlb., d. Feb. 3, '64, (w.
Anna m. 2d, Abr. Rice); *Priscilla*, '08, m. —— Partridge ; *Damaris*, '11, m.
Jona. Brigham ; 10. ABIGAIL, b. May 9, '71. Deac. Edward, the f. had a
deed from his f. 1654, of lands and houses near the S. bounds of Sud.,
part "between the spring and John Bent's," formerly belonging to Philemon Whale, Hugh Drury, &c. He was a petitioner for Marlb., 1656, and
Deacon there. He was b. at Barkhamstead, Hertfordshire, S. Britain,
1618, and d. at Marlb., Aug. 15, 1712, æ. ab. 93 years, having had 142 descendants, of whom 119 were living at his death. (See Marlb. Records ;
and Boston News Letter, Aug. 25, 1712.] Anne, w. of Deac. Edward, d.
1713, æ. 83.

3. THOMAS, s. of Edmond (1), had by w. Mary, at Sud., 1. GRACE, d.
1654 ; 2. THOMAS, b. June 30, 1654, m. Anna, 1681, and f. of *Jedidiah*, b.
1690, m. Dorcas Wheeler, '13 ; *Abiel, Anna, Ashur,* *Adonijah, Perez,
Vashti, Beriah, Jason, Thomas,* and *Charles* ; 3. MARY, b. Sep. 4, 1656, m.
Josiah White, '78 ; 4. PETER, b. Oct. 24, '58, (w. Rebecca, who d. 1749),
and d. at Marlb., Nov. 28, 1753, æ. 95.1.4, f. of *Elisha*, b. 1690, d. in Brookfield, 1788 ; *Zipporah*, b. '91 ; *Cyprian*, m. Lydia Rice, 1721, d. at Brookfield, '88, æ. 95 ; *Pelatiah*, b. '94, d. at Northb., Ap. 7, 1775 ; *Elnathan ;
Peter ; Abigail*, m. —— Bouker ; *Deborah ; Rebecca*, m. —— Eager ; *Abraham*, b. '09, m. Persis Robinson, '36, d. Jan. 22, '86, f. of Elizabeth, Lucy,
Joel, Miriam, Persis, Peter, Samuel; Persis, the m. d. 1755, and Ab. m.
Anna, wid. of Deac. Matthias Rice, of Northboro' ; 5. NATHANIEL, b.
Jan. 3, '60, and d. Nov. 13, 1726, m. Sarah ——, and 2d, wid. Patience
Stone, 1704, and f. of *Nathaniel, Mary,* and *Patience* ; 6. SARAH, b. Jan.
15, 1662, m. (John) Adams ; 7. EPHRAIM, b. at Marlb., '67, d. 1732, m. Hannah Livermore, Feb. 21, '89, and f. at Sud., of *Hannah,* d. young, *Ephraim,*
(m. Mary Noyes, 1725), *Mary, Josiah,* (dead before 1732), *Grace,* d. young,
Thomas, Gershom (m. Elizabeth Battle, 1728,) *John, Isaac,* (d. 1793), *Hannah* ; 8. JAMES, b. 1669, d. in Worcester, 1730, f. of *Jotham, Zebediah,
Cyrus, Frances, James, Jasoniah. Grace,* and *Berzela,* (who d. at Worcester,
1741, æ. 27.) See Par. 8 ; 9. JONAS, b. 1673. [A Jonas, "the 1st settler
in Worcester," d. at W., Sep, 22, 1753. Rec.] ; 10. GRACE, b. 1675, m.
Nathaniel Moore, 1702 ; 11. FRANCES, m. —— Allen. Corporal Thomas,
was selectman of Sud., 1662, and prop. of Marlb., 1657. He had a deed,
1654, from his f., of land on Pine Plain. His will was proved, 1681. (Inventory, £370.) His wid. Mary's will, was proved 1715.

4. MATTHEW, s. of Edmond (1), m. Martha Lamson, Nov. 2, 1654,
and had in Sud., 1. SARAH, b. Sep. 9, '55, m. —— Loker, and was deceased, (leaving four children), 1718 ; 2. MARTHA, b. Aug. 17, 1656, m.
John Bent ; 3. DEBORAH, b. Feb. 14, 1659-0, m. Thomas Sawin, Jan. 23,
'84 ; 4. RUTH, b. Ap. 2, '62, (not in the will) ; 5. ELIZABETH, b. May 20,
'63, (not in the will) ; 6. DOROTHY, b. Feb. 14, '64-5, m. —— Wares ; 7.
ISAAC, b. '68, d. 1718, owned a farm at Indian Head, in Fram., prob. the
300 acres, bought 1694, of Gookin and How, and was f. by w. Sybilla, of
Sybilla, b. 1691, m. Phinehas Brintnal, '16, *Martha, Mary, Abigail,* and
Ruth, m. John Goodnow. In Isaac's will, proved June, 1718, he gives
half of the Indian Head farm to his man, Benj .Dudley, whom he "brought
up ;" 8. PATIENCE, b. Mar. 5, 1671, d. 1722, (had m. —— Leland. See f.'s

---

* Ashur, the above, (or another), is said to have been taken captive by the Indians, and afterwards returned, m., and was of Worcester, where he chose a wild life in the woods. Ashur and w. Tabitha were of Westb. 1735.

will.) Matthew's will was proved (he of Sud.), Dec. 30, 1717. He was an extensive prop. of lands in Fram., on the road from " Sherb. to Stone's Mills," and was rated there, 1708. He received, in 1654, a deed from his f. Edmond, of land on Pine Plain, &c. He prob. lived not far from Cochituate Pond.

5. BENJAMIN, s. of Edmond (1), m. Mary, dr. of Deac. Wm. Brown, of Sud., ab. 1662. (See Mar. Sett.—Mid. Deeds.) His only child was EBENEZER, b. May 1, 1671, and his (E.'s) will proved, July 1, 1724. Ebenezer m. Bethiah Williams, of Dorchester, 1698, and was f. at Sud., of *Mary*, m. — Loker, *Sarah*, *Bethia*, *Elizabeth*, *Catharine*, *Ebenezer*, *Grace*, and *Abigail*. Benjamin, the f. rec'd from his f. Edmond, (date not noted), 80 ac. of land, S. W. of Cochituate Brook, " on the path to Quintecok." He had the grant of a houselot, at Marlb., Nov. 26, 1660, and in '73, lived " near unto Sud." His w. Mary d. Jan. 3, 1690-1.

6. SAMUEL, s. of Edmond (1), m. Elizab. King, Nov. 8, 1655, and had, 1. ELIZABETH, b. Oct. 26, '56, m. —— Haynes; 2. HANNAH, m. —— Hubbard; 3. JOSHUA, f. by w. Mary, of *Samuel*, b. 1693, *Nahum*, '95, *Sarah*, '98, *Zephaniah*, 1700, (w. Mary, of Worc.), *Andrew*, '03; 4. EDMOND, m. Ruth Parker, of Roxb., Nov. 15, '92, and d. at Westb., 1726, (will proved Sept. 12, and names w. Hannah, and br. Joshua), and had, at Marlb., by w. Ruth, *Dinah*, b. 1693, m. —— Brigham; *Silas*, '95, and *Timothy*, '97, both in captivity, in 1726; *Nahor*, '99, slain by the Indians, 1704; *Huldah*, '01; *Moses*, b. and d. '04; *Seth*, '05; *Thankful*, '07; *Eleazer*, '09; *Ruth*, '12; *Eben.* b. and d. '14; *Anna*, '16; and in Marlb., 5. ESTHER, b. 1665, m. —— Hubbard; 6. SAMUEL, b. '67; 7. MARY, '69; 8. EDWARD, '72. (Edward, Jr., of Marlb., m. Lydia Fairbanks, May 25, 1702, and had *Gideon*, and nine drs.) 9. ABIGAIL, b. 1674; 10. JOSEPH, prob. m. Mercy Kerley, 1708, and had *Jesse*, and drs. Samuel, the f. was a prop. of Marlb., 1657, and he d. there. His will, of which his brs. Edward and Joseph were overseers, was proved, Ap. 7, 1685. Inventory, £349. [Mary, w. of Samuel, d. June 18, 1678. Abr. Brown, s. in-law to Samuel, d. May, 1678.]

7. JOSEPH, of Sud., s. of Edmond (1,) m. Mercy King, 1658. By w. Martha, he had MARTHA, b. Jan. 14, 1662; JOSIAH, b. May 3, '63; CALEB, b. '66, m. Mary Ward, '96, (who d. 1742), Deac. at Marlb., and d. Jan. 5, 1738-9, f. of *Martha*; *Mary*, m. —— Beman; *Josiah*, d. at Northboro', 1792; *Jabez*; *Nathan*, d. at Marlb., 1764; *Rebecca*; *Sarah*; *Caleb*; *Hepsebah*; *Keziah*. Martha, w. of Joseph, d. Jan. 4, 1668-9; and by w. Mary, he had, JOSEPH, b. June 5, 1671, who d. at Marlb., Dec. 3, 1745, æ. 74, and his w. Elizabeth d. Oct. 13, 1733, æ. 48; ELEAZER, b. Oct. 26, '72; MARY, Aug. 15, '74; PHINEHAS, b. 1682. [Phinehas, (w. Eleanor), was of Worc., 1728.] Joseph, the f. had the grant of a houselot at Marlb., Nov. 26, 1660.*

8. EDMUND, s. of Edmond (1), early received a deed of land from his father; but no information respecting him subsequently appears.†

---

* Joseph, of Wat. had a w. Mary, who d. May 13, 1677; by a w. Sary he had in Wat., besides a dr. Sary, b. and d. 1681, a s. *Jonathan*, b. Mar. 26, '79, who m. (then of Wat.) Anne Darby, of Stow, 1702, was deacon at Sud., and f. of Bethulia, m. Benj. Gates, 1727; Persis, Wm., m. Hannah Graves, 1733,; Dorothy, Katharine, Ann, and Esther. A Joseph took the freeman's oath, 1673. Mid. Co. Rec. III. 54.

† Administration was granted, Ap. 12, 1714, on the estate of Edmund, " sometime of Marlb., who d. intestate," to Matthew and Isaac. It

9. JAMES and w. Sarah, had at Fram., DANIEL, b. Mar. 13, 1704–5. [This may have been the same James (w. Sarah), s. of Thomas, who d. in Worc. See Thomas (3).]
10. HENRY, oldest son of Edmond (1), m. Elizabeth Moore, Feb. 1, 1643, and had 1. MARY, b. Sep. 19, 1646; 2. ELIZABETH, b. Aug. 4, '48, m. John Brewer; 3. JONATHAN[11], b. July 3, '54; 4. ABIGAIL, b. June 17, '57, m. Thomas Smith; 5. DAVID[31], b. Dec. 27, '59; 6. THAMEZIN, b. Feb. 2, '61, m. Benj. Parmenter, '80; 7. RACHEL, b. May 10, '64, m. Thomas Drury, Dec. 15, '87; 8. LYDIA, b. June 4, '68, m. Samuel Wheelock; 9. MERCY, b. Jan. 1, '70, m. Elnathan Allen, and d. 1727; 10. HANNAH, m. —— Taylor. [The will names a g. dr., Mary Brigham. It is prob. that Jonas Houghton m. a dr. of Henry.]

Henry, the f. was b. in S. Britain, took the oath of fidelity at Sud., July 9, 1645; had a grant from Sud., ab. 1643, in the S. part of the town bounds, butting E. on Mr. Dunster's farm; Jan., 1658, was "admitted freeman for special considerations." In 1659, he received from his father, a deed of land in the wilderness, at "New Trouble," and about the same time, from do., land S. of Cochituate Brook, confirmed to him by an Indian deed, Mar. 10, 1672–3. In 1679, his br. Benjamin conveyed to him, (living near unto Sud.), land near his (Henry's) dwelling house. Henry lived very early at what was termed Rice's End, in Fram., and his dwelling house was given in his will to his s. Jonathan. He d. in Fram., Feb. 10, 1710–1, and being older than his br. Edward, could not have been less than ab. 93 years of age. He is noticed in the Boston News Letter, Aug. 25, 1712, in connection with his br., as "both men of virtuous lives." His will was proved at Mid. Prob. His w. Elizabeth d. in Fram., Aug. 3, 1705.

11. [1]JONATHAN, s. of Henry (10), m. Martha ——, who d. 1675, and had 1. MARTHA, b. June 27, '75, d. young; the f. m. 2d, Rebecca Watson, Nov. 1, 1677, and had 2. JONATHAN[12], b. 1678; 3. DAVID, b. '80, m. in Concord, Elizabeth Cutler, of Sud., Nov. 7, 1707, and was f. of *Israel*, b. Aug. 20, '08, (m. Sarah Rose, '30, and f. at Sud., of Grace, David, Henry, Rebecca, Sarah, Sarah, and Lydia); *David*, b. Nov. 23, 1713; 4. ANNA, b. 1683, m. Wm. Cutler, of Camb.; 5. HENRY, b. '85, m. Elizabeth Moore, Dec. 27, 1716, lived in Nat., and f. of *Elizabeth*, m. Hezekiah Coller, Mar. 1, '43. Reb., the m., d. Dec. 22, 1689, and he m. 3d, Elizabeth Wheeler, Feb. 12, '91, and had 6. MARTHA, m. James Whitney, Feb. 2, '14–5; 7. HEZEKIAH[13], b. ab. 1694; 8.

---

prob. referred to undisposed lands and rights, accruing to the heirs of Edmund, sen. EDMUND m. Joyce Russell, in Sud., Oct. 13, 1680; and had *Joyce*, b. '81, m. Samuel Abbot, '05; *Edmund*, b. July 9, '88; *Lydia*, b. May 24, '90.

Abraham[21], b. ab. '97; 9. Ezekiel[23], b. Oct. 14, 1700; 10. Elizabeth, b. Feb. 28, 1702-3, m. Daniel Pratt, of Fram., May 23, '23; 11. Phinehas[29], b. June 24, '05; 12. Sarah, b. in Fram., Sep. 24, '07, d. 1727; 13. Richard[30], b. Jan. 31, '09-0; 14. Abigail, b. Mar. 23, '13-4, m. Gershom Pratt, (who lived near the W), July 29, '31. Jonathan, the f., lived and kept a public house in E. Sud., where his chil. were recorded until 1705. He moved soon after to Fram., (his aged father was that year a widower), and was Selectman, 1708, 10 years, and Representative, '11 and '20. His father gave him by will his dwelling house, and for some years he kept in Fram. a public house.* Tradition supposes him to have lived at the late Thomas Rice's. He d. in Fram., Ap. 12, 1725, æ. 70. (G. Stone.) His will was proved at Mid. Prob. The will of his wid. Elizabeth, was proved 1744. All but the first five chil. were by Elizabeth.

12. [1]JONATHAN, s. of Jona. (11), m. (then of Sud.), Lydia Pratt, of Fram., Nov. 18, 1714, and had in Sud., Bulah, b. Dec. 11, '16, and Jonathan, bap. in F., Jan. 6, '22-3. Jona. and w. cov'd in Fram., Jan. 6, 1722-3, and he had deceased before 1744.

13. [1]HEZEKIAH, s. of Jona. (11), m. Mary Haynes, of Sud., Ap. 30, 1719, and had in Marlb., 1. Mary, b. Feb. 24, '19-0, d. Mar. 30; 2. Hezekiah, b. Feb. 27, '20-1, bap. in Fram., Mar. 5. He d. in Fram., Sep. 5, 1745, prob. unm.; 3. Uriah, b. Oct. 17, '23, d. in Fram., Dec. 31, 1733; 4. Jonathan[14], b. Oct. 8, '25; 5. Peter[18], b. ab. '27; 6. Mary, b. in Fram., Sep. 5, '28, d. in Fram., Dec. 13, 1733. Lt. Hezekiah, the f., moved from Marlb. to Fram., between 1725 and 1728, was Selectman '28, 13 years, was chosen Deacon, May 17, '51, but declined serving. He occupied as a tavern, the house now in possession of his aged g. son Uriah, which, the latter says, was originally built by a Frenchman. He d. in Fram., Nov. 16, 1761, æ. 67. (G. Stone.) (See settlement at Mid. Prob.) His wid. Mary d. Dec. 16, 1785, æ. 95. (G. Stone.)

---

* The following note preserved among the Mss. papers of Jonathan, we give as a characteristic of the times.

"Cousin Jonathan Rice, — I know not what my wife's business was to your house to-day, unless it were to get you to buy something considerable for her. Therefore these may give you to understand, that I dont allow of your laying out any money for (her), unless it be for a few pins or papper, or such like things; so I remain your loving friend, ———.
Nov. 18, 1708."

14. ¹JONATHAN, s. of Hezek. (12), m. Ruth Eames, Oct. 29, 1746, and had 1. HEZEKIAH[15], b. Sep. 19, 1748; 2. MARY, b. Feb. 4, '49–0, m. Daniel Newton, and moved to Vt.; 3. CATA, b. Sep. 5, '51, m. Nathaniel Eames; 4. GRACE, b. June 25, '53, m. Thomas Drury, Dec. 21, '80; 5. RUTH, b. Ap. 4, '55, [bap. recorded probably by mistake, as of *Hannah*,] m. Nathaniel Fay, of Southb.; 6. JONATHAN[16], b. May 14, '57; 7. FANNY, b. Oct. 18, '58, m. Joshua Grant Haven, Aug. 6, '81, and d. young; 8. LUCIA, bap. Mar. 28, '60, m. Timo. Kendal, of Sherb., June '85; 9. PHINEHAS[17], b. Nov. 23, '61; 10. STEPHEN, b. May 24, '63, d. young; 11. SUBMIT, b. Jan. 31, '65, m. Robert Fay, Jr., Mar. '83, and 2d, Caleb Putnam, of Croydon, N. H.; 12. ABEL, b. Oct. 20, '66, m. Nelly Belknap, Ap. '91, and moved to N. Y.; 13. OLIVE, bap. Ap. 29, '70, m. Samuel Perry, of Nat., Oct. '89. Jona., the f., lived next S. from Uriah Rice's, and d. ab. 1777. His wid. Ruth d. May 16, 1805, æ. 78.

15. ¹HEZEKIAH, s. of Jona. (14), m. Abigail Eames, of Hop., 1773, with w. cov'd Ap. 10, '74, and had in Fram., RUTH, bap. Ap. 17, '74. The f. lived in Dublin, came to Fram., and went into the army. He lost 3 chil. by the Canker-rash, and d. in Hop., near Westb. He was recommended to the ch. in Hop., Aug. 1793.

16. ¹JONATHAN, s. of Jona. (14), m. Anne Belknap, Ap. 1782, and with w. adm. to the ch., Sep. '88. Their chil. b. in Nat., and bap. in Fram., were 1. FANNY, b. Aug. 11, '84, bap. Sep. '88, m. Eben. Kimball; 2. NANCY, b. July 15, '86, bap. Nov. '88; 3. PATTY, b. Nov. 25, '88, m. —— Thurston, of Union, Me.; 4. CHLOE, b. Sep. 25, '90, bap. Sep. '90, m. Leonard Leland, of Sherb.; 5. ASENETH, (Nat. Rec., Sena), b. Ap. 19, '93, bap. Ap. '93; 6. CAROLINE, b. Nov. 11, '95, bap. Nov. '95; 7. EUNICE, b. July 20, '99, bap. Aug. '99, d. 1840. Jona., the f., lived beyond Joel Rice's, on the borders of Nat. He died, Feb. 25, 1838, æ. 80. His w. Anne, d. Mar. 4, 1834, æ. 70.

17. ¹PHINEHAS, s. of Jona. (14), m. Ruth Perry, of Nat., 1784, with w. cov'd June '87, and had 1. STEPHEN, bap. June, '87, m. Mary Eaton; 2. MICAJAH, bap. June, '87, m. Lucy Bannister, and 2d, wid. Abigail Page; 3. PHINEHAS, bap. July, '89, m. Sally Rutter, and d. Jan. 1, 1826; 4. NABBY, bap. Nov. '91, m. Oliver Shed, and lives in Weston; 5. RUTH, bap. Feb. '94, m.

Luther Brown, and lives in Worcester ; 6. SALLY, m. Abel C. Smith, lives in Dover, N. H. ; 7. MARY, bap. Nov. '98, d. unm., Oct. 3, 1825 ; 8. LAWSON, m. Elizabeth Murdock, of Wesminster. Ruth, w. of Phin., d. Oct. 28, 1832, æ. 69, and he m. 2d, wid. Susan Bullard. Phinehas, the f., lived near S. House No. 10 ; was Selectman, 1817, 8 years, and d. May 17, 1842, æ. 80. His wid. lives in Fram.

18. [1]PETER, s. of Hezek. (12), m. Ruth Trowbridge, with w. cov'd July 3, 1757, and adm. May '81. Their chil. were 1. URIAH[19], b. July 7, '57 ; 2. PETER, b. Feb. 7, '61, d. in Hackensac, N. Y., in the service, Sep. 1780 ; 3. ELEANOR, b. Sep. 22, '63, d. '75 ; 4. EZRA[20], b. Nov. 14, '65 ; 5. MEHETABEL, b. Mar. 4, '68, d. '75 ; 6. JONAS, b. May 20, '70, d. '75 ; 7. JOEL, b. Mar. 27, '72, d. '75; 8. HITTY, b. June 11, '78, d. June 12, 1837, æ. 59. Peter, the father, lived at Mr. Uriah Rice's, and d. June 28, 1805, æ. 78. His wid. Ruth d. May, 1822, æ. 86.

19. [1]URIAH, s. of Peter (18), m. Mary Eames, June 1784, and had 1. ELEANOR ; 2. MARY ; 3. CLARISSA, bap. Oct. 1791, m. Capt. Eliphalet Wheeler. Uriah, the f., was Selectman, 1796, 2 years, and lives, with his w., having been united in marriage 63 years.

20. [1]EZRA, s. of Peter (18), m. Ruth Eames, July, 1790 ; and had, 1. JOEL, b. Dec. 2, '91, m. Nancy Howe ; 2. JOHN, b. Ap., '93, m. Dolly Ball, lives in Chelsea ; 3. PETER, b. '95, m. Marshy Roby, lives in Wayland ; 4. PERKINS, m. Maria Goodnow ; 5. LOUISA, m. —— Dixon, lives in N. Y.; 6 ALMIRA, m. Francis Bowers ; 7. ABIGAIL. Ezra, the f. lived next N. of Widow Eaton's, and d. Feb. 2, 1833, æ. 67. Ruth his w. d. Nov. 8, 1832, æ. 67.

21. [1]ABRAHAM, s. of Jona. (11), m. Patience Eames, Feb. 1, 1721-2, and with w. cov. Nov. 4, '22. They had 1. JONATHAN, b. Nov. 4, '22 ; 2. ABRAHAM[22], b. May 9, '25 ; 3. SARAH, b. Ap. 9, '27 ; 4. SAMUEL, b. May 10, '30 ; 5. PATIENCE, b. July 22, '32, m. Daniel Tombs ; 6. HENRY, b. Aug. 3, '36 ; 7. DAVID, b. Jan. 13, '38, m. Mary Sanger, Oct. '59, d. without issue, Feb. 1, '90, æ. 51, (G. Stone), and his wid. Mary moved to Littleton ; 8. RICHARD, b. Sep. 28, '43, d. Sep. 26, 1746. Cornet or Capt. Abraham, the f. lived in the S. W. part of Fram., was Selectman

1743, 5 years, and was killed by lightning June 3, 1777, æ. 80. (G. Stone.) His wid. Patience d. Jan. 2, 1796, æ. 94. (G. Stone.)

22. [1]ABRAHAM, s. of Abr. (21), had by w. ——, who kept school in Fram., SARAH, bap. May 5, 1754; ABRAHAM, bap. July 1, '64; SUSANNAH, bap. Aug. 3, '66; and NATHAN.

23. [1]EZEKIEL, s. of Jona. (11), m. Hannah Whitney, Jan. 23, 1722-3, and was adm. to the ch. Mar. 4, '49. He had, 1. EZEKIEL[24], b. Oct. 29, '23; 2. JOHN, b. Ap. 9, '25; 3. JAMES, b. July 13, '26, lived near Natick; 4. HANNAH, b. Oct. 15, '27, m. Thomas Kendall, Mar. 27, '51, and d. 1822; 5. DANIEL, b. Aug. 10, 1729, d. unm.; 6. RICHARD[16], b. Oct. 20, '30; 7. MARTHA, b. Aug. 8, '32; 8. URIAH[28]; 9. MOSES, m. Mary Sparawk, in Nat., 1766, and lived in Nat. Ezekiel lived between Corn. Morse's and the wid. Sanger's. The house was purchased and moved by Dr. Kittredge. He m. 2d, Prudence Bigelow, May 10, 1753. [Ezekiel of Fram. (f. or son) m. Mrs. Margaret Pond, of Nat., 1769, and wid. Ruth Chapen of Sherb., Jan. 8, '72.]

24. [1]EZEKIEL, s. of Ezekiel (23), m. Hannah Edmunds, Sep. 19, 1751, and with w. adm. to the ch. May 3, '52. Their chil. were, 1. Ezekiel[25], b. June 20, '52; 2. HANNAH, b. Mar. 26, '54, m. Thomas Stone, of Southb.; 3. DANIEL, b. Nov. 24, '55; 4. ABIGAIL, b. Dec. 29, '57, m. Benjamin Lamb, June 23, '74, moved E.; 5. ANNE, b. Oct. 8, '59, m. Jacob Belcher, Mar., '82, d. 1838; 6. ELIZABETH, b. Oct. 13, 1761, m. —— Wilder, and 2d., —— Brigham; 7. MARY, b. Sep. 20, '63; 8. SARAH, b. Dec. 19, '65; 9. AARON, b. Nov. 16, '67; 10. PERSIS, bap. June 3, '70; 11. SARAH, bap. Oct. 4, '72. Ezekiel, the f. lived at the wid. Sanger's, and d. May 12, 1806, æ. 82 1-2. (T. Rec.)

25. [1]EZEKIEL, s. of Ezek. (24), m. Lydia Bullard, May 1782, and had 1. LOWELL, b. June 29, '83, m. —— Partridge; 2. JESSE, b. Aug. 31, '85, m. —— Maynard, and d. in Westb.; 3. WILDER, b. Feb. 14, '88, m. —— Goodnow, of Nat., and lived there; 4. JOHN, b. Ap. 21, '90; 5. BETSEY, b. July 18, '92, m. John Morse, and lives in Nat. Lydia, w. of Ezekiel, d. Ap. 25, '93. (T. Rec.) Ezek. lived at Amasa Kendall's.

26. [1]RICHARD, s. of Ezek. (23), m. Sarah Drury, Jan. 16, 1755, and with w. cov. Mar. 21, '56. They had, 1. MARTHA, b. May 7, '56; 2. JAMES[27], b. June 24, '58. Richard d. prob. in Fram. His w. d. at the E.

27. ¹JAMES, s. of Rich. (26), m. Sarah Perry, in Nat. 1780, and with w. adm. to the ch. Oct. '94 ; and had, 1. SALLY, b. in Nat., Ap. 17, '81, m. Calvin Gleason ; 2. NATHAN D., b. in F., Aug. 29, '84, m. Deborah Banister. James lived prob in Nat. and in Fram., near Wid. Eaton's at Mr. Loker's. His w. d., and he moved, taking his mother, to the E.

28. ¹URIAH, s. of Ezek. (23), had by w. Rachel, (both adm. to the ch. Aug. 28, 1763), 1. PRUDENCE, b. Ap. 22, '62; 2. JOHN, b. Feb. 22, '64. Uriah lived with his f., and left town.

29. ¹PHINEHAS, s. of Jona. (11), m. Margaret Eames, July 6, 1727, and cov'd July 7, '28. He had, 1. JOSEPH, b. June 27, '28, d. unm. in Fram., Dec. 21, 1781 ; 2. LYDIA, m. Caleb Gleason, Oct. 1782 ; 3. ZERVIAH, m. Caleb Drury, Oct. '82. The est. of Phinehas was adm'd 1764. The homestead was N. of "Drury Lane," and the "Royal Close" was also named.

30. ¹RICHARD, s. of Jona. (11), m. Hannah Bent, 1734, and had HANNAH, b. Nov. 10, '35, m. Samuel Hemenway, and d. Feb. 19, 1814. Richard, the f. d. 1737. His wid. Hannah m. Jeremiah Belknap, Nov. 30, 1738.

31. ²DAVID, s. of Henry (10), m. Hannah Walker, Ap. 7, 1687, and had, 1. ELIZABETH, b. Sep. 8, '89, m. Samuel Frost, Feb. 1, 1710–1 ; 2. HANNAH, b. Jan. 5, '91–2, m. John Bent, Nov. 15, 1711 ; 3. BEZALEEL³²; 4. JOSIAH⁴⁰, b. Aug. 19, 1701. Hannah, the m. d. Dec. 18, 1704. "Deac. (David) Rice d. Oct. 16, 1723. *Proh! dolor.*" (Swift's Journal.) David was one of the original members, and first Deacons of the ch. in Fram., was Selectman, 1700, 4 years, and T. Treasurer, 1708, 2 years. He prob. lived near Deac. Luther Haven's. The agreement of his heirs is on Record in the Mid. Prob.

32. ²BEZALEEL, s. of Dav. (31), m. Sarah Buckminster, June 23, 1720, and with w. cov. Feb. 19, '21, and w. adm. to the ch. May 5, '22. Their chil. were 1. BEZALEEL³³, b. May 19, '21 ; 2. DAVID³⁶, b. Sep. 17, '23 ; 3. SARAH, b. Sep. 1, '25, m. David Stone, '45, and d. in Petersham, Oct. 22, 1815, æ. 90 ; 4. ZERUIAH, b. Feb. 14, '27–8, d. Mar. 4, 1739–0 ; 5. JOSIAH³⁸, b. Nov. 23, '34 ; 6. MARTHA, b. July 9, '37, m. —— Drury, and lived in Shrewsb. Bezaleel, the f. was a physician in Fram., and lived in the red house near Mr. Elisha Belknap's ; Selectman, 1742. No notice is preserved of the decease of himself or w.

33. ²BEZALEEL, s. of Bezaleel (32), m. 1st, Susannah Gennings, Dec. 2, 1742, and had 1. BEZALEEL, b. Ap. 11, '44, d. Aug. 10, '48; 2. HEZEKIAH³⁴, b. Oct. 2, '45; 3. SUSANNAH, b. July 6, '48, m. Ezra Twitchel; 4. SARAH, b. Sep. 5, '50, m. — Brewer. Susannah the m., d. Sep. 15, 1750, and he m. 2d, Sarah Bent, Mar. 13, '51, who was adm. to the ch., Jan. 13, '54, and had 5. BEZALEEL, b. Dec. 5, '51, d. unm. (non compos mentis); 6. JOHN, b. Feb. 9, '54; 7. NATHAN, b. Aug. 18, '56; 8. MARY, bap. Mar. 28, '62; 9. SAMUEL³⁵, bap. Sep. 23, '64. Bezaleel, the f. lived in the house late of Joseph Goodnow, and d. ab. 1795.

34. ²HEZEKIAH, s. of Bezaleel (33), m. Abigail Eames, of Hop., 1773, and with w. cov. Ap. 10, '74, and had 1. RUTH, bap. Ap. 17, '74. The f. lived in Dublin — returned to Fram., and was in the service; 3 of his chil. d. of the Canker-rash. Hez. and w. were recommended to the ch. in Hop., Aug. 1793. Hez. d. in Hop. [Hez., of Fram., m. Elizabeth Eames, of Hop. 1775. Hop. T. Rec.]

35. ²SAMUEL, s. of Bezaleel (33), m. Huldah Edmunds, Nov. 1788, and with w. adm. to the ch., Oct. '96. They had 1. HANNAH, b. '89, d. young; 2. SALLY; 3. CYNTHIA, m. Luther Bailey; 4. SAMUEL, d. unm. ab. 1836; 5. ELIZABETH, m. Joseph Bailey; 6. MARTIN, bap. 1797, m. Betsey Gibbs; 7. JONATHAN EDMUNDS, bap. '99, d. unm. Sam., the f., lived near Col. Brown's, and d. Oct. 1800.

36. ²DAVID, s. of Bezaleel (32), m. Hannah Winch, Sep. 27, 1750, and with w. adm. to the church, June 30, '51, and had 1. HANNAH, b. Jan. 19, '52, m. Deac. Tho. Buckminster, and d. 1793; 2. ANNE, b. Mar. 29, '55, m. Jonas Ryder, June 17, '79; 3. DAVID, b. May 2, '57, m. Lucy Ryder, Aug. 2, '80, and died Ap. 5, 1817; 4. DEBORAH, b. Sep. 26, '59, m. James Stone, s. of John, Esq., of Holl., Nov. 24, '79; 5. MARTHA, b. Ap. 17, '62, d. young; 6. THOMAS³⁷, b. May 2, '64; 7. MARTHA, b. Sep. 8, '66, m. John Brown, May '86, lived in Williamstown; 8. NATHAN, bap. Ap. 9, '69, m. Polly Eaton, Sep. 29, '96, was a physician at Wayland, and d. Feb. 23, 1814; his w. Mary d. 1818; 9. ZERVIAH, bap. July 12, '72, m. John Dudley, May 3, '92, and d. in Petersham; 10. WILLIAM, bap. May 7, '75, m. Anne Johnson, of Wayland, lived in N. Salem. Cornet David, the f., d. Mar. 1802. His w. Hannah d. Jan. 1816.

37. ²THOMAS, s. of Dav. (36), m. Elizabeth (Betsey) Frost, Nov. 1786, and with w. cov'd Nov. '98. They had 1. MILISCENT, bap. July '98, m. Nathaniel Reeves, and 2d, Sylvester Reeves, lives in Wayland ; 2. PATTY, bap. July '98, m. John Wilson ; 3. THOMAS, bap. July '98, kept a store in Fram., m. Eliza Lane, and d. Feb. 12, 1844, æ. 53 ; 4. LUTHER, bap. July '98, m. Mary Clifford, d. in Fram. ; 5. KEZIAH, bap. July '98, m. Deac. Henry H. Hyde, of Fram. ; 6. PRESCOTT, bap. Oct. '98, m. 1st, ———, 2d, Mary Hyde, and lived in Boston ; 7. CURTIS, bap. Oct. '98 ; 8. ANNE, d. young ; 9. GEORGE, m. in Boston ; 10. SOPHIA. Thomas, the f., lived near Deac. Luther Haven, and d. ab. 1828 Betsey, his w. d. July 8, 1821, æ. 55.

38. ²JOSIAH, s. of Bezaleel (32), m. Mary Underwood, and with w. adm. to the ch., Feb. 29, 1764. They had 1. ELISHA³⁹, b. Mar. 12, '64 ; 2. BUCKMINSTER, b. July 19, '65, m. Hannah Jennings, July '86, and lived in Wayland and Stow ; 3. NELLY, b. Sep. 19, '67, m. Eph. Goodnow, Nov. '90, and d. in Fram. ; 4. JOSIAH, b. Sep. 29, '68, m. Charlotte Bacon, of Nat. ; 5. JOHN, b. Mar. 27, '70, m. Anne Bigelow, Mar., '95, lived in Leominster; 6. MICAJAH, b. Jan. 13, '72 ; 7. NAHUM, bap. June 26, '74, d. young ; 8. JONAS, bap. Oct. 6, '76, d. young ; 9. DANIEL, b. Mar. 29, '79, went off; 10. POLLY, b. Dec. 20, '81, d. unm., æ. ab. 18 ; 11. AMOS, b. Feb. 16, '82, d. of lockjaw, while learning a trade. Josiah, the f., lived where is a cellar hole, near the wid. Banister's, in the E. part of Fram. He was buried, Nov. 29, 1799.

39. ²ELISHA, s. of Josiah (38), m. Abigail Corey, and with w. adm. to the ch., Nov. 1789. They had bap. RUHAMAH and NABBY, Dec. '89, and moved to Sud. He was a tailor.

40. ²JOSIAH, s. of David (31), m. Elizabeth Hood, May 6, 1728, and was of Hop., 1732.

41. JOHN, adm. to the ch., Jan. 15, 1748. HANNAH, adm. May '81. Wid. Mary adm., Oct. '90. JOHN HOLBROOK, bap. Mar. 4, 1759, and d. in the continental service, at Danbury, Conn. JABEZ, m. Hannah Brigham, both of Marlb., June 7, 1732. JASON, of Hop., m. Susanna Haven, Feb. 14, '50–1. MOSES, of Rutland, m. Elizabeth Gleason, Mar. 21, '55. SALLY, m. Eben. Newton, June '85. OLIVE, m. Alvin Bent, Mar. '89. POLLY, m. Wm. Arnold, of Marlb., Jan. '90. SARAH, m. Asahel

Knights, of Sud., Ap. 14, 1799. DOROTHY, m. Amos Davis, July 28, '99.

RICH, ELISHA, was before 1780, a Baptist preacher in F. He was by trade a gunsmith. He removed to Chelmsford, and from thence to the West.

RICHARDS, JOSEPH, of Southb., had by w. Mary, 1. WILLIAM, b. Feb. 25, 1729-0; 2. JOSEPH, b. Ap. 1, '31. [A Jos. m. in Holl., Mary Cobb, 1760, and was prob. in Fram., 1778.] 3. MARY, b. Sep. 27, '33; 4. EBENEZER, b. Feb. 25, '38; 5. MARTHA, b. Jan. 31, '40; 6. JOHN, b. Dec. 10, '42, m. Hepsebah Amsden, '75; 7. HANNAH, b. Jan. 24, '44; 8. ESTHER, b. Feb. 25, '46. Joseph, (prob. the f.), d. in Southb., June 4, 1748. (T. Rec.)

JOHN, of Lynn, m. Mary Bruer, 1674, and was f. of *Mary*, '75; *John*, '77; *Edward*, '79; *Crispas*, '81; *Elizabeth*, '83; *Joseph*, '85; *William*, '88; *Abigail*, '91. Joseph, of Lynn, m. Mary Bouden, 1726. Farmer notes from Lewis, that EDWARD, of Lynn, d. Jan. 26, 1690, æ. 74, leaving a s. John. EDWARD, (w. Susan), of Dedham, 1639, d. ab. '84, f. of *John, Nathaniel, Mary, Dorcas, &c.*

2. WILLIAM, s. of Jos. (1), m. Elizabeth Knap, Nov. 21, 1753; and had in Southb., 1. WILLIAM, b. Jan. 17, '56. Col. Wm. d. in Partridgefield; the m. d. 1756, and the f. m. 2d, Sarah Bixby, Feb. '57, and had, 2. SARAH, b. Aug. 12, '57, d. young; 3. ELIZABETH, b. Feb. 4, '60, bap. in Fram. (as Betsey), May 27, '80, and m. Nathan Kendall, Feb. '84; 4. JOSEPH, b. Mar. 16, '62; 5. THOMAS, b. Ap. 16, '64; 6. HEPHZEBAH, b. July 9, '66, m. in Fram., Wm. Leadbetter, Dec. '89, and lives (1844) in Richmond, Mass.; 7. ALICE, b. (perhaps in Fram.) '68, d. young. William, the f. was adm. from the Southb. ch., Mar. '88.

3. JOSEPH, s. of Wm. (2), m. Rhoda How, of Hop., and had in Fram., 1. JOSEPH, b. Sep. 29, 1782; 2. RHODA, b. Aug. 8, '84; 3. SUSANNA, b. Aug. 13, '86. Joseph, the f. was rec'd from Fram. at Hop. '90, and afterwards lived in Richmond.

4. THOMAS, s. of Wm. (2), m. 1st, Betsey Nurse, May 1791, and 2d, Polly Chamberlain, with whom he was adm. to the ch. Oct. 1796. Their chil. were, 1. SULLIVAN, b. June 20, '94; 2. BETSEY, b. May 29, '95; 3. CURTIS, b. June 10, '96; 4. HOLLIS, b. Mar 9, '98; 5. WILLIAM, b. May 7, '99; 6. MARIA, b. Aug. 28, 1800; 7. EMERY, b. Ap. 2, '02; 8. WILLARD, b. Aug. 6, '03; 9. MARY C., b. at Brookfield, Feb. 16, '05. Polly, w. of Thomas, d. at Brookfield, Feb. 18, 1805, and he m. 3d, Lucy Wood, and lived (1844) in Sturbridge.

5. TIMOTHY, and Betsey cov'd in Fram., May. 28, 1780.

RICHARDSON, THOMAS, m. Anne Nixon, Feb. 1789.
LUTHER, of Sud., m. Persis Hemenway, of Fram., June, 1790.
RIDER, WLLIAM, of Wat., m. Hannah Lovet, Aug. 11, 1674, and had, 1. WILLIAM, b. in Camb., July 29, 1675, f. by w. Deborah, (who d. at Sherb., a wid., July 15, 1750,) of *Mary*, b. Aug. 13, 1706, m. Asa Morse, '28; *Deborah*, b. June 22, '10, m. Richard Sanger, '30; *William*, b. Oct. 24, '15, m. Elizabeth Hill, Ap. 10, '46, (was prob. T. Clerk of Natick, 1723, and f. of Aaron, '48, William, '50, &c.); 2. HANNAH, b. Ap. 4, 1678; 3. HANNAH, b. May 28, '80, m. William Johnson, '99; and at Sherb., 4. DANIEL, m. Elizabeth Adams, May 16, 1711, (who d. 1724), and had *Hannah*, b. Aug. 17, 1712; *James*, Mar. 9, '15; *Daniel*, Aug. 13, '17; *David*, Aug. 15, '19; *Peter*, b. '22, d. 1745. Dan., (f. or s.) had by w. Esther, *Joseph*, b. Feb. 13, '31. Daniel cov'd in Fram., Feb. 4, 1728; 5. ELEAZER, b. Jan. 22, 1687, m. Hannah Lerned, 1713, and had *Eleazer*, b. Oct. 21, '14; *Gideon*, Oct. 9, '21; *Ebenezer*, Dec. 14, '23, of Hop., 1745; *Jonas*, Dec. 27, '25; *Preserved*, Mar. 16, '28; *John*, Aug. 12, '29; *Hannah*, July 18, '31, d. 1744. Wm., sen., of Sherb., bought, 1693, one-half of a tract N.W. part of Quansigamog, alias Worcester. He d. in Sherb., Aug. 27, 1724. His Inventory, £347.1.

ESTHER, who came from Sherb. to Fram., 1771, æ. ab. 75, (T. Rec.), was prob. dr. of William. DAVID, (w. Elizabeth), was f. at Sherb., of *Phinehas*, 1724. THEODORE, (w. Sarah), at Sherb. and Holl., was prob. s. of WILLIAM, sen., and had *Joseph*, b. May 21, 1729, who d. 1819, æ. 90; *Mary*, *Deborah*, and others. THOMAS, was taxed in Fram., ab. 1733. THOMAS, (w. Sarah), was of Wat., 1694. THOMAS, (w. Elizabeth), was of Boston, 1654. PHINEHAS, was of Falmouth, 1667, and JOHN, of do., at Back Cove, 1675. JAMES, and w. Hannah, had at Camb., *Hannah*, Mar. 1, 1650; *James*, Jan. 3, '53–4; *Thomas*, Mar. 1, '57. EPHRAIM was of Medford, 1695. JAMES, of Billerica, m. Mary Abbot, 1703.

2. GIDEON, g. son of Wm. (1), m. in Hop., Lucy Smith, (b. in Ipswich), Oct. 11, 1744; and had 1. ELIZABETH, b. 1746, m. Aaron Johnson, of Holl., and d. in Lancaster; 2. JONAS, bap. 1749, m. in Fram., Anne Rice, June 17, '79, and d. without issue in F. Aug. 25, 1818, æ. 69; 3. GIDEON, bap. 1751, m. his cousin Anne Rider, June '82, moved to Hop. and Sterling; 4. ASA, bap. 1754, d. æ. 5; 5. LUCY, bap. 1756, d. æ. 3; 6. ANNE, m. Nathaniel Bigelow, Jun., Oct. '82, and d. at Leominster, a widow, Dec. 1845, æ. 87; 7. LUCY, bap. 1760, m. David Rice, Aug. 2, '80, and lived (1844) in Nat. All the above were born in Hop.; and 8. HANNAH, (b. prob. in Sherb.), m. Daniel Kendall, of Harvard, June '87, and was living (1844) a wid. in Boston. Gideon, the f. moved into F., before 1782, and d. July 28, '94, æ. 72. (G. Stone.) His wid. Lucy was adm. to the ch. Aug. 1795, and d. Mar. 1807, æ. 87 1-2. (G. Stone.) [JONAS d. Dec. 15, 1826, æ 73. G. Stone.]

ROBINSON, JONATHAN, had in Fram., by w. Martha, 1. MARTHA, d. Dec. 12, 1729; 2. MARTHA, b. July 10, 1730; 3.

SARAH, b. Jan. 24, '32–3 ; 4. JONATHAN, b. Mar. 9, '34–5, at Crown Pt. 1762; 5. ELIAKIM, b. Aug. 16, '37; 6. HEPHZEBAH, b. Oct 6, '45; 7. MARY, b. Mar. 26, '48; 8. ELISHA, b. Aug. 27, '51. Martha, w. of Jona. d. Ap. 28, 1752 (T. Rec.), and he m. 2d, Patience Hunting, of Needham, and had, 8. PATIENCE, b. May 7, 1754, m. Nath'l Prentiss Russell, of Marlb., May 1, 1794; 9. EUNICE, bap. Sep. 7, 1760. Patience, w. of Jona., d. Aug. 11, 1768. (T. Rec.) He had a 3d w. Abigail, who d. (prob. in Sud. or Marlb.) Dec. 28, 1806, æ. 96 y. 10 m. Jona. the f. prob. lived on " the Leg," which was set off to Marlb. Dr. Stearns notes that Jona. d. Feb. 24, 1793, æ. 87.

GEORGE, of Wat., m. Sarah Behony, 1703, and had *George*, b. May 15, 1704, and *Jonathan*, Feb. 14, 1705–6. JONATHAN, of Wat., m. Ruth Morse, 1706, and had, at Lexington, *Jonathan*, b. Feb. 25, (Camb. Rec., Feb. 21,) 1706–7, and others.

2. ELISHA, s. of Jona. (1), m. Eunice Rice, of Sud., Nov. 25, 1773, and had in Fram., 1. ELISHA, b. Sep. 3, '74; 2. JOEL, b. Dec. 7, '75. The f. moved from the Town.

3. SAMUEL, was of Fram., before Feb. 1726, when his son SAMUEL, then in his 19th year, chose a Guardian. (Mid. Prob., XVII, 398.) The son SAMUEL m. in Southb., Mercy Lennard, May, 1732, was in Hardwick, '36, and had in H., *Elizabeth, Lenard Samuel, Moses* (afterwards Gov. of Vt.), *Paul, Silas, Mercy, Sarah, David, Jonathan* and *Anne.* He moved to Vt., ab. 1765. (Hardw. Rec.)

SAMUEL, (3), was prob. the Sam., of Camb., who m. Sarah Manning, 1703, (she d. 1709), and had *Samuel*, 1707, and *Dorothy*, '09. WILLIAM, (w. Elizabeth), had at Concord, *Hannah*, July 13, 1671; and at Camb., *William*, '73; *Mercy*, '76; *David*, '78; *Samuel*, '80; and *Jonathan*, Ap. 20, 1682. WILLIAM, of Southb., m. Judith Newton, Jan. 3, 1754. DR. JEREMIAH, of Marlb., m. Eunice Amsden, 1746, and d. Oct., '71, æ. 58, f. of *Thomas A., Eunice, Bradbury, Cain, Lydia, Winthrop.*

RUGG, JOHN, of Lancaster, subscribed the town covenant, Feb. 12, 1654–5. He had by w. Martha, two chil., b. and d. 1655. He m. w. Hannah, May 4, 1660, and had, 3. JOHN, b. June 4, '62; (his w. Elizabeth administered, 1712, and his real estate was settled, 1716). The chil. were, *John*, (dead); *Samuel ; Nathaniel*, b. 1701; *David ; Jonathan*, (prob. m. at Shrews., Dorothy Griffin, Jan. 14, 1724–5, and had in Southb., Alpheus, b. Mar. 6, 1729–0); *Benjamin ; Elizabeth ; Mary;* and *Abigail ;* 4. MARCA, (Mercy), b. July 11, '64, (prob. d. before 1712); 5. THOMAS, b. Sep. 15, 1666, prob. of Lexington, and had by w. Elizabeth, *Thomas*, b. Dec. 6, 1691, (Camb. Rec., 1690); *William*, Nov. 16, '93; *Elizabeth*, Jan. 20, '95; *Hannah*, Ap. 26, '97; *Abigail*, Mar. 15, '99; *Sarah*, Feb. 12, 1701–2; *Mary*, May 30, '03; *Ruth*, Sep., '06; *Tabitha*, Sep. 10, '08; *Miliscent*, Nov. 11, '10; and *Martha*, Nov. 10, '13; 6. JOSEPH, b. Dec. 15, 1668, who with w. and three children, and the "wid. Rugg," was killed, 1697, at Lancaster.

See Willard's Hist., Worc. Mag., II. 296). His brother John administered on his estate, 1697, and a settlement was executed, 1712, his daughter Hannah then a captive in Canada. (Mid. Prob.); 7. HANNAH, b. Jan. 2, 1670-1, m. in Concord, John Ball, 1690; 8. REBECKAH, b. May 16, 1673, m. Nathaniel Hudson; 9. DANIEL, b. prob. 1679, m. Elizabeth Priest, of Lancaster, 1704; 10. JONATHAN, b. prob. 1680. The will of John, sen., of Lancaster, was proved 1696. His wid. Hannah was killed by the Indians, as above.

2. JONATHAN, s. of John (1), m. in Marlb., Sarah, dr. of John Newton, and had 1. BATHSHEBAH, b. in Marlb., Oct. 26, 1703; and in Fram., 2. SARAH, b. Oct. 2, '05, adm. to the ch. Feb. 11, '28, and m. Hachaliah Bridges, Nov. 11, '28; 3. HEPHZEBAH, b. Jan. 18, '07-8, m. Nathaniel Haven, June 10, '24; 4. ABRAHAM, b. Ap. 27, '10, d. May 4. Sarah, w. of Jona., d. May 7, 1710, and he m. 2d, Hannah Singletary, Dec. 11, 1710, and had 5. MEHETABEL, b. Sep. 15, '11, adm. to the ch., Feb. 11, '28, and m. Joseph Bixby, of Hop., Mar. 30, '32; 6. HANNAH, b. Nov. 28, '13, m. John Mayhew, of Shrewsb., Feb. 21, '43; 7. JONATHAN, b. Nov. 27, '16, prob. d. young; 8. JOHN, b. June 10, '18; 9. EBENEZER, b. July 22, '20, d. Aug. 10; 10. JONATHAN, b. ab. '22. (See G. Stone.) Jonathan, the f., was youngest son of John, of Lancaster, and chose John Houghton as his Guardian. He received by his father's will, "half of the meadow at Wataquadock," and meadows on Nashua River, &c. He settled in Fram., at the W. part, near Southb. bounds, where his descendants have continued to live until quite recently. He was Constable 1722, and d. in Fram., Dec. 25, 1753, (T. Rec.); his wid. Elizabeth was living 1754.

3. JONATHAN, s. of Jona. (2), m. Hannah Walkup, Feb. 17, 1743, and was with w. adm. to the ch., June 1, '46. Their chil. were 1. HANNAH, b. Nov. 9, '46, m. — Warner, of Westmoreland; 2. ELIZABETH, b. May 13, '48, m. Alpheus Reed, of Westmoreland; 3. DANIEL[4], b. Ap. 19, '51; 4. JONATHAN[5], b. May 6, '53; 5. MOLLY, b. Aug. 14, '56, m. Ira Newton, of Southb., '76; 6. JOHN, b. Aug. 31, '64, lived prob. in Chesterfield. Jona., the f., lived on his father's place, and d. suddenly, Mar. 6, '76, æ. 54. (G. Stone.) Hannah, his w. d. May 30, 1786, æ. 63. (G. Stone.)

4. DANIEL, s. of Jona. (3), m. Sarah Bancroft, of Southb., and was with w. adm. to the ch., Ap. 24, 1774. Their chil. were 1. ELIJAH, b. May 3, '75; 2. NATHAN, b. June 8, '77; 3. DANIEL,

b. June 11, '79; 4. JOHN, b. May 18, '82; 5. SALLY, b. Ap. 10, '85; 6. BETSEY, b. June 22, '89; 7. HANNAH, b. Dec. 26, '92. Daniel, the f. lived opposite his father's house, and moved to Chesterfield, ab. 1793.

5. JONATHAN, s. of Jona. (3), m. in Sud., Hephsebah Haven, of Fram., Nov. 23, 1775, and with w. was adm. to the ch., May 7, '80. Their chil. were 1. JONATHAN, b. May 20, '77, and d. July 4, 1843, m. Patty Glover, Dec. 29, 1800, who d. Aug. 1, 1824, and 2d, Lucinda Marsh, of Holl., Ap. 26, 1825; 2. HEPZEBAH, b. Feb. 3, '79, d. unm., Ap. 19, 1815; 3. EZRA, b. Mar. 20, '81, m. Polly Fairbanks, Ap. 1, 1802, and d. July 2, '10. Polly, his w., d. May, 1812, æ. 34; 4. MARY, bap. Oct. 1786, m. Levi Cutting, Oct. 21, 1806, and lived in Fram. Lt. Jona., the f. m. 2d, wid. Rachel Tucker, in Sherb., May 25, 1809. He was Selectman, 1785, 4 years, and d. Nov. 20, 1833. His wid. Rachel d. at Brimfield, Dec. 6, 1843, æ. 80.

RUSS, JOSEPH, was in Fram., before 1720.

RUSSELL, THOMAS, was prob. in Fram., 1749. (Deac. Buckminster's Journal.) [Deac. JONATHAN, was of Sherb., his w. Mary d. 1771, æ. 70. Deac. James, of Holl., d. Sep. 16, 1777, æ. 62.]

SABIN, THOMAS, was rated in Fram. ab. 1786.

SALEM, PETER, see a notice of him in the preceding history.

SALMON, FRANCIS, was rated in Fram. ab. 1754.

SALTER, SAMUEL, and w. Judah, had SARAH, b. Dec. 3, 1735. Wid. (Judah) Salter, m. Joseph Angier, June 16, 1743.

SAMPSON, JOSEPH, m. Desire Symonds, Jan. 18, 1738-9.

SANDERS, Wid. MEHETABEL and child, were of Fram., Jan. 2, 1788. T. Rec.

SANDERSON, THOMAS, was rated in Fram., ab. 1738. [A Thomas (w. Anna) was of Waltham, and had ABNER, 1739, and others.]

2. NATHANIEL, of Fram., m. Mary Drury, Oct. 4, 1739, moved to Petersham, and had at P. 1. JONATHAN, b. Sep. 1740, d. æ. 92, m. Molly Curtis, and f. of *John, Susanna, Curtis, Sally, Polly* and *Joel;* 2. MARY, m. Charles Wilder; 3. JOSHUA, d. 1757, æ. 6; 4. MOSES, m. Sophia Jackson; 5. JOEL, m. and d. 1774, æ. 28; 6. NATHANIEL, m. Betsey McLellan; 7. EUNICE, m. John Rogers; 8. LOIS, m. Geo. Cutting, and Sam. Young; also

Susanna, and Grace, who d. young. Nath. d. at Pet., Sep. 7, 1774, æ. 61 years, 2 m. 27 d. His w. Mary d. Sep. 8, 1805, æ. 85.

Nathaniel, Deac. David, (who d. at Pet., f. of *David, Ebenezer, &c.),* and Thomas, of Walth., were sons of Jonathan, who m. in Wat., Abigail Fisk, 1699, and d. at Waltham, Oct. 4, 1743, æ. 70, f. of the above, and *Jonathan, Abigail,* (m. Jas. Mellen, of Fram.), *Margaret,* m. Benj. Whitney, of Fram.; *Eunice.* Jonathan, (sen.), of Camb., bought at Wat., 1682. In Dec., 1695, he gave a deposition, then æ. ab. 49, and stated that he lived, æ. 17, with Justinian Holden, of Camb. (Mid. Deeds, XI.) He was Deac. at Wat., and d. 1735, (his w. Abiah, d. 1723), leaving *Thomas, Samuel, Edward, Abiah, Hannah, Jonathan,* and *John,* d. in Leicester, 1750. The name is frequently written Saunders. Robert, was of Camb., 1642. Robert, of Wat., had *Benjamin,* bap. July, 1649, and *Robert,* bap. 1652. Robert, sen., of Boston, had m. (date not given, very early) Mary, wid. of John Cross, of Wat. Edward, was early of Wat. William, who m. at Wat., 1666, had a s. *William,* b. 1670, (who settled in Sud., and by w. Anne, had Amos, m. Ruth Hoar; Isaac, and others); and a s. *John.*

SANGER, Richard, and w. Mary, had, at Wat., 1. Mary, b. Sep. 26, 1650, m. John Harris, '70; 2. Nathaniel, b. Feb. 14, '51–2, f. by w. Mary, at Sherb., of *Mehetabel,* b. 1680; and at Roxb., *Mary,* '81; *Jane,* '83; a son, '84; *Nathaniel,* '85; and *Benjamin,* '88. [Nathaniel d. at Woodstock, ab. 1735, leaving w. Ruth, and chil. *David, Benjamin, Mehetabel, Jane, Elizabeth, Jonathan, Eleazer,* and *Nathaniel*]; 3. John, b. Sep. 6, '57, m. Rebecca Park, and f. at Watertown, of *John,* b. Dec. 19, 1685; *Rebecca,* b. March 7, '88–9, m. Tho. Flegg, 1711; *David,* b. Mar. 21, '97, m. Patience Benjamin, 1720, (and f. of *Patience, Lydia,* (both d. young), *John, David, William, William, Nathaniel, Samuel,* m. Mary Fairbanks, 1757, *Solomon,* and *Lydia,* d. young); and *Elizabeth,* b. June 2, 1703; 4. Sary, b. and d. 1661; 5. Sary, b. Mar. 31, '63; 6. Richard, b. Feb. 22, 1666–7; 7. Elizabeth, b. July 23, '68; 8. David, b. Dec. 21, '70, d. 1695, probably unm. Richard, the f. was a blacksmith, was in Sud., 1646, and "removed his habitation to Watertown, the 8th or 9th mo. anno, 1649." (Sud. Rec.) He d. in Wat., Aug. 20, 1691.

RICHARD, s. of Richard (1), m. Elizabeth Morse, and had, at Sherb., 1. Elizabeth, b. Ap. 2, 1693, d. Jan. 25, 1775; 2. Mary, b. Ap. 11, '95; 3. Hannah, b. Feb. 7, '97, m. Ephraim Twitchell, Feb. 9, '26–7; 4. Esther, b. Oct. 20, '98; 5. Deborah, b. Aug. 5, 1701; 6. Sarah, b. Feb. 10, '05, m. Nathaniel Holbrook, Aug. 20, '28; 7. Richard, b. Nov. 4, 1706, d. 1786, m. Deborah Rider, Feb. 19, 1729–0, and had *Zedekiah,* d. 1736; *Deborah,* b. 1733, d. young; *Samuel,* b. July 7, '35, had two wives; *Deborah,* b. Nov. 12, '37, m. —— Twitchell, 2d; —— Fawcett, and 3d, Dea. Gideon Haven, of Fram.; *Daniel,*[5] b. Feb. 13, '40; *Mary,* b. Sep. 30, '42; *John,* had two wives; *Zedekiah,* b. Oct. 4, '48, H. Coll., 1771, and D. D., m. Irene Freeman, 1771, ord. at Duxbury, July 3, 1776, and installed at S. Bridgewater, Dec. 17, 1788, where he d. Nov. 17, 1820. His s. Ralph, H. Coll., 1808, is pastor at Dover; *Jedidiah,* went to Whitestown, Feb., 1789, and became a judge in New York; *Asa,* m. —— Dana; 8. Abigail, b. July 3, 1709; 9. David,[3] b. Feb. 22, 1712. Richard, the f. d. at Sherb., 1731.

3. DAVID, s. of Richard (2), m. Bathshebah Pratt, of Fram., May 27, 1736, and had in Fram., 1. Joseph[4], b. Ap. 19, '37; 2. Mary, b. Dec. 19, '38, m. David Rice, Oct., '59; 3. Esther, b.

Dec. 17, '40, d. Dec. 2, '41; 4. ESTHER, b. Nov. 23, '42, m. David Morse; 5. SARAH, b. Dec. 25, '45, d. unm. æ. ab. 25; 6. HANNAH, b. June 23, '47, m. Nathan Dadmun; 7. DAVID, b. May 9, '51, m. Ruhamah Nutt, of Hop., and lived in Hop., Fram., and Littleton, N. H. David, the f., lived near the wid. Eaton's, 1750. He "d. at Albany in defence of his country, Dec. 15, 1755, æ. 45." (G. Stone.) His wid. Bath. d. Nov. 20, 1783, æ. 76.

4. JOSEPH, s. of David (3), m. Patience Greenwood, May 19, 1779, and had 1. JEDUTHAN, b. Ap. 13, 1780, lived in Roxb. unm.; 2. JOSEPH, b. Nov. 23, '81, m. Abigail Eames, and d. in Fram., Feb. 5, 1830; 3. LYDIA, b. Oct. 15, '83, lives unm.; 4. ADONIJAH, b. Oct. 4, '85; 5. OBADIAH, b. May 7, '88, m. —— Belknap; 6. NABBY, b. Sep. 1, '90, lives unm. Joseph, the f., d. in Fram., Mar. 13, 1805. (T. Rec.) His widow Patience, " was found dead in her bed," July 17, 1805. (T. Rec.)

5. DANIEL, s. of Richard and g. son of Richard (2), m. Olive Hooker, of Sherb., Nov. 4, 1761, and was with w. adm. to the ch., Nov. 4, '65. They had 1. DEBORAH, b. Jan. 7, '62, m. Joseph Brown, Nov. 8, '81; 2. BETTY, b. Ap. 6, '63, m. Samuel Bigelow, of Walth., Jan. '90; 3. DANIEL, b. July 3, '65, m. Persis Phipps, of Sherb., Sep. 27, '89, 2d, Elizabeth Goodnow, Nov. 10, '99, 3d, Clarissa Johnson, of N. H. He d. Dec., 1839; 4. OLIVE, b. Mar. 26, '67, d. unm. in Fram., 1829; 5. RICHARD, b. Dec. 26, '69, m. at Whitestown, N. Y.; 6. HEZEKIAH, b. July 27, '71, m. —— Dench, of Hop.; 7. REBECCA, bap. Mar. 13, '74, m. John Stone, of Holl., Oct. 23, '96, and 2d, Dr. Walker, of Barre; 8. BENJAMIN, bap. Oct. 13, '76, d. young. Daniel, the f., m. 2d, Esther Goodnow, of Sud. He kept a tavern near the R. Road Station, to the N.; was Selectman, 1771, 6 years, and d. Sep. 27, 1807. (T. Rec.)

Eleazer, (s. of Nathaniel?), d. at Keene, N. H., March, 1765, æ. 66, and his wid. Mary, 1783, æ. 80. He lived, previously, at Hardwick and Petersham.

SARGEANT, MARGARET, alias Peggy, was in Fram., 1717, and her support was the occasion of a lawsuit between Fram. and Weston.

SAVAGE, HABIJAH, s. of Habijah, was bap. in Fram., Sep. 10, 1775.

SAWIN, or SAWING, DEBORAH, of Fram., m. George Fairbanks, of Holl. May, 1735.

THOMAS was of Sherb., 1679, a house carpenter, and in 1691, sold to Matthew Rice, land on Wachitua (Cochituate) Brook. He was prob. s. of John, of Wat., b. Sep. 27, 1657, and m. Deborah Rice, 1684.

SAWTELL, SYBIL, was m. to Jesse Belknap, July, 1788.

SEAVER, or SEVER, JOSEPH, m. in Sud., Mary Reed, Dec. 10, 1701; and had, 1. ROBERT; 2. MARY, b. Oct. 5, 1706, m. Christopher Nixon; 3. NATHANIEL, b. Ap. 1, 1709; 4. HANNAH, b. 1712, m. Jonathan Belcher, and d. in Fram. 1796, æ. 84; 5. ELIZABETH, b. Jan. 31, 1714, m. Samuel How, Jan. 25, '38–9; 6. ABIGAIL, m. Azariah Walker. Joseph, the f. is said to have originated in Roxbury. He was rated in Fram., 1710, and Constable, 1716. He lived near Mr. Eben. Eaton, bought land of Capt. Robert Montgomery, and d. 1754, his will proved, Aug. 26.

SHUBAEL, of Roxb., (w. Hannah), had *Robert*, b. 1670; *Joseph*, '72; *Hannah*, '74; *Abigail*, '77; *Shubael*, '79; and *Thankful*, '84. Shubael was s. of Robert, who took the freeman's oath, Ap. 18, 1637, and had *Shubael*, b. 1639; *Caleb*, and *Josiah*, 1641; *Hannah*, 1650. Caleb, sen., d. at Roxb., Mar. 6, 1713, his w. Sarah, Jan. 31, 1708, leaving *Caleb*, *Nicholas*, *Thomas*, *Elizabeth*, and *Sarah*. JOSHUA, (w. Elizabeth), d. in Dorchester, 1716.

2. ROBERT, s. of Joseph (1), had by w. Eunice (on Sud. Rec.), 1. JOSEPH, b. June 10, 1727; and on Fram. Rec., 2. BENJAMIN, b. Oct. 8, '28; 3. THANKFUL, b. Oct. 6, '31; and on Sud. Rec. 4. SAMUEL, b. Ap. 8, 1747. Robert was a bricklayer, and his house was consumed by fire, Oct. 1749. He, with two sons, was at the taking of Louisburg. He moved to Narraganset No. 2 (Westminster). His wid. Eunice administered on his estate 1752.

3. NATHANIEL, s. of Joseph (1), m. in Sud. Rebecca Willis, Feb. 23, 1737–8; and had 1. ELIJAH, b. June 16, 1739; 2. ANN, b. Jan. 3, 1739–0; and on Fram. Rec., 3. JOSIAH WILLIS, b. July 18, 1742, prob. lived in Sterling; 4. REBECCA, b. Feb. 3, '43; 5. JOSEPH, 6. MARY, twins b. Jan 26, 1746; 7. CATHARINE, bap. Aug. 28, 1748, m. —— Dyer, and 2d, Tho. Mellins, and lived in Petersham. Nathaniel lived, 1749, near Moses Cutting's, and was of Westminster, July 17, 1754, when he m. (2d w.) Judith Treadway, of Fram., and had, LUTHER, CALVIN, FANNY, ROBERT, BETTY, RICHARD, and JOHN REED. He d. of the small pox in Petersham, 1777. He is said to have had 8 chil. by his first wife.

4. MOSES, and w. Lucia cov'd Mar. 4, 1759, and dr. LUCIA was bap.

5. JOSEPH, prob. from Roxb., and a distant relative of Nat'l (3), m. Elizabeth Lamb, and was with w. adm. to the ch., Oct. 1781. He had, 1. JOSEPH, b. July 26, 1775; and the three following bap. Jan. 1783, 2. ESTHER, m. Lemuel Twitchell, of Athol; 3. WILLIAM, d. at Malaga; 4. KEZIAH, m. Samuel Twitchell; 5. ABRAHAM, m. —— Cole, was living (1846) in Philipston; 6. BETSEY, m. James Cheney; 7. ABIGAIL, d. young; 8. POLLY, m. —— Haskell. Joseph the f. moved to Philipston, and m. 2d, Abial Rich, and had other children. Joseph was by trade a blacksmith.

6. SHUBAEL, br. of Joseph (5), had bap. in Fram., 1. PATTY, July 23, 1769; 2. RUTH, Sep. 1, '71; 3. SHUBAEL, July 11, '73; 4. LUCY, Oct. 13, '76; 5. WILLIAM, Sep. 1781. Shubael was a blacksmith, lived at Mr. Charles Capen's, and left town. [A Shubael m. in Newton, Deliverance Hide, Dec. 8, 1764.]

7. JOHN, was bap. in Fram. Nov. 1754. RICHARD, of Roxb., m. Mary Ballard, of Fram., Nov. 13, 1745.

SHATTUCK, SHADDUCK, or SHADWICK, EPHRAIM, m. Elizabeth Jackson, 1747, with w. cov'd in Fram., Nov. 27, 1748, and had bap. in Fram., EPHRAIM, July 17, 1748; SAMUEL, Jan. 21, 1749-0.

EPHRAIM, and w. Elizabeth, prob. the same, moved to Templeton, (now Philipston), and had chil. *Ephraim, Samuel,* after of Conway, *Abigail, Betsey, Polly,* d. young, *Patty, John, Lucy,* and *Sarah.* Ephraim, Sen., m. 2d, wid. —— Jordan. SILAS, and w. were of Temp., 1762. They were both chil. of JOHN, (w. Silence), of Marlb., who had *Abigail,* 1717; *John,* 1722; *Thomas,* 1723; [A Thomas m. at Hop., Margaret Ball, 1757. A Thomas was of Petersham, 1760, and had chil. by w. Elizabeth Parmenter.] *Samuel,* 1726; *Ephraim,* 1728; *Silas,* 1738. John, of Marlb., prob. descended from William, of Wat., who d. Aug. 14, 1672, æ. 50.

2. JOHN, was Warden in Fram., 1772, and Selectman, 1777, and adm. to the ch. Sep. 1781. He came from Marlb., and lived, and prob. d. in the N.W. part of Fram. " Old Mrs. Shattuck," (his wid.) was buried June 14, 1822, æ. 95. A Wid. Saunders, (a sister) had lived with the latter.

John, was prob. the John Jun. of Marlb., who by w. Abigail, had at M., *Joseph,* b. 1745; *Lucy,* '47; *Thaddeus,* '52; *Susanna,* '55; *John,* '58; *Anna,* '60; and *Chloe,* '64.

SHAYS, DANIEL, noted as having given a name to the insurrection of 1786, is said by Lincoln, (Hist. of Worcester), to have been born in Hop., 1747, and to have worked with Mr. Brinley, a respectable farmer of Framingham.

Daniel was a captain in the revolutionary service, m. wid. Eunice Hayden, and d. in Sparta, N. Y., Sep. 29, 1825, æ. 78, having, in 1820, received a pension from the U. S. Government. " Oct. 3, 1758, a child of Patrick Shay was bap. in his own house, on account of the dangerous state of the child, which was bap. on account of their other children being bap. in the Church of England ; ye name of the child was Roger." (Hop. Ch. Rec.) PATRICK, of Hop., m. wid. Rebecca Cozzens, of Sherb , Oct. 30, 1765. MARY, of Sherb., m. Elijah Barnes, of Shutesbury, Oct. 17, 1775.

SHEARS, JOHN, and w. Earls, (prob. Alice), had a son, THOMAS, who d. in Fram., Jan. 9, 1708. THANKFUL, (prob. his dr.), m. in Fram., Joseph Berry, Jan. 27, 1719-0. John, the f. was rated, 1710, and for many years chosen Tythingman, as late as 1724. He lived at Mr. Ezekiel How's, and was probably the John, who m. at Camb., Alice Mitchelson, Ap. 9, 1688.

SAMUEL, (w. Mary), of Dedham, had *Mary*, 1664, and *John*, '66. JOHN, (w. Mary), of do., had *Mehetabel*, 1668.

SHEFFIELD, MERCY, m. Nathan Dudley, Mar. 30, 1786.

This family in Sherb. and Holl., sprung from WILLIAM, received at Sherb., 1679, who settled at Chabboquassit. (See deed of John Awansamug, of 500 acres to him, 1675. Mid. Deeds, vol. XI) He d. at Sherb., Dec. 6, 1700 ; his will proved, 1701 ; his est. settled, 1708. His chil., by w. Mary, were *Hannah*, b. Ap. 18, 1663 ; *Daniel*, b. Mar. 3. '65 ; *William*, b. Mar. 19, '67, m. Hannah Bullard, May 30, '92, and f. of Hannah, Isaac, (d. at Holl., 1777, æ. 79), William, (w. Mary), d. at Holl., 1732, Rachel, Sarah, and Mary ; *Martha*, b. Jan. 8, 1668 ; *Joseph*, b. Mar. 3, '71, (had, of f. 1691, land in Dover); *Thamezin*, b. May 25, '73, m. Jonathan Adams ; *Susanna*, b. Dec. 12, '75, m. Zuriel Hal, Sep. 1, '97 ; *Elizabeth*, b. Nov. 28, '78 ; *Nathaniel*, b. Mar. 7, '81, (f. by w. Mary, at Holl., of Nathaniel, Mary, Rachel, &c.); *Mary*, m. John Clark ; *Rachel*, m. and had chil. ; and *Elizabeth*. WILLIAM, had a dr. Susanna, b. Dec. 11, 1675. (Hingham Rec.) EDMUND, was early of Braintree, and d. 1705, æ. 90, f. of Edmund, Isaac, Matthew, and Samuel. (Farmer.)

SIBLEY, JOHN, was in Fram., ab. 1790.

SIMONDS, DESIRE, m. Joseph Sampson, Jan. 18, 1738-9.

SIMPSON, SIMSON, or SIMPTSON, SAVIL, or SEVILL, was of Boston, cordwainer, as late as 1708, where he had, JANE, b. Sep. 13, 1680, m. Steeven Arnold ; SAVIL, Oct. 15, '81 ; SAMUEL, Feb. 23, '82 ; ELIZABETH, Mar. 5, '84, m. John Jones, May 12, 1713. He bought July 4, 1687, the land granted to Col. Crown, which was included in Fram., 1700, and after embraced in Hop. He was rated in Fram., 1710, and made Justice of the Peace in Hop. His will, prepared June 8, 1716, was proved

Jan. 3, 1725-6. He d. Aug. 22, 1725. (Swift's Journal). He names in his will, his sons-in-law, Anthony Blount, (a Tallow Chandler, in Boston, 1720) and John Jones, and his g. chil. Thomas Eyre, (the parents probably Thomas and Deborah, of Boston,) Anne and Sarah Lawson, and Mary and Elizabeth Jones.

SINGELTARY, or SINGLETARY, RICHARD, of Salem, 1637, took the freeman's oath, Sep. 7, 1638. He was after (1638) of Newbury, and later of Salisbury, and had a son John, and prob. others. (Hist. of Newb.) RICHARD received a division of land in Haverhill, Jan. 20, 1653, and was selectman, 1655. Richard, f. or son, had by w. Susanna Cooke, in Hav., BENJAMIN, b. Ap. 4, 1656, who m. Mary Stockbridge, Ap. 4, 1678, and had *Susanna*, b. Jan. 27, '78; *Richard*, Mar. 16, '80-1; *Jonathan*, Aug. 28, '83; *John*. July 6, '86; *Brawten*, Mar. 25, '89; *Joseph*, Feb. 9, '92-3; and *Mary*, July 14, '95. Richard, the f. d. in Hav., Oct. 25, 1687, æ. 102. Susanna, w. of Richard, d. Ap. 11, 1682.

2. NATHANIEL, prob. s. or g. son of Richard (1), m. in Hav., Sarah Belknap, Dec. 22, 1673, and had, 1. JOHN, b. May 7, 1675; 2. JONATHAN, b. Nov. 18, d. Nov. 24, '78; 3. SARAH, b. Oct. 23, '79, m. in Fram., Thomas Frost, Dec. 12, 1712; 4. SUSANNA, b. Sep. 19, '81; 5. RICHARD, b. Aug. 5, '83. [A Richard was killed by the Indians at Lancaster, Aug. 19, 1707. Worc. Mag. ii. 299]; 6. HANNAH, b. May 23, '85; 7. HANNAH, b. May 23, '85, m. in Fram., Jonathan Rugg, Dec. 11, 1700; 8. EBENEZER, b. June 18, '87. Nathaniel, the f. was killed by the Indians at Hav., Aug. 13, 1689, and a posthumous child, 9. was b. Aug. 20, '89. A part, at least, of his family moved to Fram.

3. JOHN, s. of Nath. (2), m. in Haverhill, Mary Grelee, Dec. 17, 1700, and lived after in "Hampton, alias, Salisbury," 1709, when he bought of Col. Buckminster, land in Fram., N. of Stoney Brook, bounded on Jona. Rugg. His chil. b. in Fram., were RICHARD, b. May 27, 1710; and MEHETABEL, b. Mar. 10, 1714-5. John, the f. was rated in Fram., 1710, and dismissed to the ch. in Sutton, Sep. 11, 1720, and his wife was dismissed, Jan. 29, 1720-1. [NATHANIEL signed a document as an inhabitant of Fram., 1727, and may have been s. of John. JOSEPH, of Sutton, (perhaps another s. of John), d. ab. 1748, when a nuncupative will was proved in Worc. Prob. He left a w. Martha and no issue. Mrs. Singeltary d. in Fram., Sep. 8, 1816.]

4. EBENEZER, s. of Nath. (2), m. in Fram. Joanna Newton, Ap. 5, 1713, and had 1. JOANNA, b. Ap. 22, 1714, m. Richard Smith, of Hop. May 22, 1734; 2. EBENEZER, b. Sep. 9, 1716.

Eben the f. prob. d. 1723, when administration, (his Inventory being £483.13), was granted to his wid. Joanna, who m. Deacon James Brewer, of Sud., May 20, 1731.

5. EBENEZER, s. of Eben. (4), m. Dorothy Smith, in Hop., 1742, and had, 1. EBENEZER, b. Dec. 25, 1742, d. young; 2. DOROTHY, b. Mar. 13, '44; 3. EBENEZER, b. July 8, '45; 4. DANIEL, b. Aug. 22, '47; 5. NATHAN, b. Feb. 18, '49; 6. ZIPPORAH, b. Sep. 0, 1753. Eben., the f. was a Miller, and lived on the Richard k place, and d. ab. 1785. His wid. Dorothy was sick for many rs in Fram. Ebenezer who d. in Hop., 1812, æ. 61, was . his son. Rhoda w. of Eb. of Hop., d. 1839, æ. 87.

ITH, NATHAN, m. Susannah Livermore, of Weston, and Marlb., LYDIA, b. Sep. 2, 1763; NATHAN, Dec. 3, '65; Sud., JOHN, m. in Providence; RUFUS, b. Feb. 14, '72; a ram., SUSANNA, b. Oct. 27, '80; [a Sukey m. in Fram., Geo. Smith, of Rehoboth, R. I., Jan. 1, 1799.]

2. NATHAN, s. of Nathan (1), m. Lucinda Eames, in Sud., May 11, 1790, and had in Fram., 1. RUFUS EAMES, b. Ap. 29, 1791; 2. BETSEY, b. Mar. 18, '93; 3. SUKEY, b. Jan. 7, '99. Nathan, the f., moved to Walpole, N. H.

3. GEORGE, of Rehoboth, R. I., m. Sukey Smith, in Fram., Jan. 1, 1799, and had POLLY, b. Mar. 13, 1799.

4. ABIGAIL was bap. in Fram., May 15, 1726. RICHARD, of Hop.; m. Joanna Singletary, of F., May 22, 1734. ESTHER, æ. 13, came to live with Deac. Buckminster, July 9, 1781. ELIEZER, of Walpole, m. Polly Parmenter, Nov. 1793. PETER, of Medfield, m. Nelly Parmenter, May 20, 1795.

JOHN, (w. Sarah) and RICHARD, (w. Mary), were of Sud., ab. 1647, and had descendants. SETH, (w. Mary), was of Medfield, 1662; and SAMUEL, (w. Elizabeth), 1670. Not less than seventeen of this name, (as variously spelled), took the freeman's oath, between 1630 and 1647.

SNOW, SIMEON, was among the early Baptist ministers in Fram.

SPEAR, LYDIA, was prob. in Fram., 1749.

STACY, or STACE, JOHN, and w. Relief, cov'd in Fram., Aug. 13, 1726, and Relief adm. to the ch., Mar. 10, 1728. Their chil. b. in Fram. were 1. FORTUNATUS, b. Oct. 9, 1726; 2. NATHANIEL, bap. June 16, '28; 3. MOLLY, m. John Bent, Oct. 23, 1751. Administration on John's est., was granted to wid. Relief and Gideon Bridges, 1733. The wid. m. Deac. Moses Pike, Dec. 29, 1737, and d. Ap. 23, 1770, æ. 63.

2. NATHANIEL, s. of John (1), m. Mary Witherby, in Southb., Jan. 10, 1751, and was adm. to the ch., Dec. 29, '51, his w., Feb. 16, '52. Their chil. were 1. ANNE, b. Dec. 27, '51, m. Samuel Stone; 2. MARY, b. Ap. 13, '53, m. Benj. Eaton; 3. JOANNA, b. May 18, '55, m. Jesse Hayden, and lived in Fitzwilliam; 4. JOHN, b. June 15, '57, m. Hannah Frost, June '87; 5. CALEB, b. Oct. 14, '58, m. Submit Hemenway, Sep. '88; 6. HULDAH, b. Sep. 27, '60, m. Joseph How, '80. Nathaniel, the f., lived on Mr. Daniels' land, at Salem end, and d. Dec. 28, 1760. (T. Rec.) His wid. m. Nathaniel Bigelow.

Thomas, of Ipswich, 1648, d. 1690, had *William*, (m. Priscilla Buckley at Salem, 1679, and had chil.); *Thomas*; *John*, 1658; *Joseph*, 1661, d. Oct. 15, '90; *Symon*, 1664; *John*, 1666; *Elizabeth, Mary, Susanna*. HENRY, was of Salem, 1677. See Farmer for others.

STANHOPE, ELIZABETH m. Caleb Bridges, Sep. 23, 1731. SAMUEL, m. Dinah Parmenter, July 7, 1742. JONATHAN was prob. in Fram., 1750. SUSANNA witnessed a deed in Fram., 1717.

Ens. JONATHAN, of Sud., (æ. ab. 57, 1689; Rev. justified, pp. 31, 32), sold, in 1663, to John Hains, a town right, bought of Thomas Islinge; he had, by w. Susanna, 1. JONATHAN, m. Sarah Griffin, May 11, 1674, and f. of *Isaac*, b. 1675; and *Jonathan*, d. young; 2. HANNAH, m. Stephen Jennings, Jan. 1, '85; 3. SARAH, b. Mar. 25, '58; 4. JOSEPH, b. Sep. 13, '62, m. Hannah Bradish, Jan. 1, '85, and f. of *Susanna*, 1685; *Jonathan*, 1687, (w. Abigail, chil. Joseph, m. Keziah Parmenter, 1740, Anna, Samuel, and Abigail); *Jemima*, 1691; *Isaac*, 1696; 5. JEMIMA, b. 1665; 6. MARY, b. '67; 7. REBECCA, b. 1670. Jonathan, the f. d. Oct. 22, 1702, and his will was proved at Mid. Prob. The ancient Stanhope place is between Mr. Ezek. How's and the How Tavern.

STEARNS, STERNES or STERNE, TIMOTHY, m. Bethiah Adams, of Medway, and had 1. SARAH, b. Dec. 1, 1729, d. unm. Feb. 8, 1825; 2. TIMOTHY, b. Aug. 28, '31, d. unm., Jan. 3, 1820, æ. 88, eccentric and hermit-like in his habits; 3. NATHAN, b. Aug. 22, '33, d. unm., drowned in Sud. River, Feb. 28, 1778; 4. BETHIAH, b. Oct. 6, '35, m. Col. Thomas Nixon; 5. JOSHUA, b. Aug. 8, '37, d. July 24, 1751; 6. JONATHAN, b. Sep. 19, '39, d. unm., May 10, 1807; 7. JOHN, b. June 5, '41, m. —— Newton, d. in Southb.; 8. ACE, (Asa), b. May 3, '44, d. Aug. 13, 1751; 9. HANNAH, b. May 20, '46, m. Benj. Flagg, of Worc., and d. 1843. Timothy, the f., came from Wat., was in Fram.,

1724-5, and occupied land formerly of Isaac Heath ; (on the lease are endorsed payments by Timo., and previously by Samuel Stearns.) He lived opposite W. Nixon, Esq., and d. ab. 1757.

 Timothy prob. descended from ISAAC, of Wat., (said to have come over with Gov. Winthrop), took the freeman's oath, May 18, 1631, and d. 1671, and had by w. Mary, (who d. 1677), *John*, m. Sarah Mixer, was of Billerica, f. of Samuel, Isaac, John ; *Isaac*, b. 1632, (w. Sarah) had deceased, 1677 ; *Sary*, 1635, m. Samuel Stone, June 7, 1655 ; *Mary* ; *Samuel*, b. 1638, m. Hannah Manning, 1662, (whose s. Samuel was b. Mar. 29, 1672, m. Mary Hawkins, 1698, and had Samuel, Joshua, Sarah, Jonathan, Prudence, Eunice) ; *Elizabeth*, m. —— Manning ; *Abigail*, m. John Morse, 1666. Isaac, the f. was one of Maj. Simon Willard's troopers, at Dedham, 1654. He had a "kinsman," Charles Sternes. [Isabel, w. of John, d. at Wat., 1639, æ. 60.]

2. TIMOTHY, came from Reading to Fram., he had 3 wives, Lydia Walton, wid. —— Williams, and Molly Bowers. His chil. (prob. by 1st w.,) b. in Reading, were 1. TIMOTHY, b. Sep. 14, 1767, m. in Fram., Mary Look, Sep. 3, '94 ; 2. LYDIA, b. Mar. 16, '69, m. Nathan Parker, and d. at Reading ; 3. ELIZABETH, b. Ap. 2, '71, m. Samuel Peters, of Reading ; 4. AMOS, b. Aug. 27, '74, m. Sally Watts, of Boston ; 5. RUTH, b. Mar. 26, '77, m. Wm. Johnson, and was m. of 18 chil. Timothy and w. were adm. to the ch., Feb. 1790.

 JONATHAN, and w. cov. at Hop., 1738, and had bap. s. *Jonathan*. DAVID, s. of David, bap. at Hop., 1743.

STEVENS, or STEPHENS, JOSEPH, s. of Cyprian, came with w. Prudence, from Sud. to Fram., ab. 1714. They had in Sud., 1. PHINEHAS, b. Feb. 20, 1706-7 ; 2. AZUBAH, b. Oct. 21, '08 ; 3. SAMUEL, b. Sep. '11 ; and in Fram., 4. MINDWELL, b. Feb. 24, 1713-4 ; 5. ISAAC, m. Marcy Hubbard, 1743, and Abigail Parling, '48 ; 6. MARY, d. 1739 ; and on Rutland Rec., 7. DOROTHY, b. 1721, m. Andrew Lennard ; 8. JOSEPH, b. 1723, m. Dinah Rice, '47 ; 9. LUCE, b. 1725, m. Isaac Bullard, '53.

 Ens. Jos., the f. moved from Fram. to Rutland, ab. 1720, where, at its incorporation, in 1722, he was chosen selectman, assessor, and town treasurer. He was afterwards chosen deacon. Aug. 14, 1723, his sons Joseph and Samuel, with the Rev. Jos. Willard, were killed by the Indians at R., and Phinehas and Isaac were taken captives to Canada, (the f. having escaped in the bushes.) For the redemption of the latter, a contribution (£15.5.) was taken up in the Fram. ch., Ap. 19, 1724. A letter from Mr. Wm. Brintnal, (State Files), dated Aug. 19, 1725, states. "Ens. Stevens is arrived with his son from Canada." Phinehas, one of the captives, m. Eliz. Stevens, 1734, and was f. of *Samuel, Willard, Simon, Enos, Mary, Phinehas*, and *Katharine*. He moved to Charles'n, N. H., and became distinguished in the Cape Breton war, and for his brave defence of that plantation, Ap. 4, 1747, with a command of about thirty men, against an attack from 400 French and Indians, under Mons. Debeline. Deac. Jos. the f. d. at Rutland, 1769.

THOMAS,* of Charlestown, iron-monger and blacksmith, had a grant from Sud., Mar. 2, 1662, he to do the smithwork for the town. In 1664, he was offered land "for his encouragement to keep a free school." He was also town clerk for several years. By w. Mary, he had *Anne*, b. Mar. 20, 1664; *Thomas*, b. Ap. 14, '65, of Plainfield; *John*, b. Ap. 23, '67, m. Abigail Walker, 1714, also of Plainfield; *Jacob*, b. Mar. 1, '74, d. in Stow, 1754; *Cyprian*, b. Ap. 19, '70. In 1681, Thomas sold to his brother, John Greene, his house, land, &c., in Sud., and moved to Pompasiticut, (Stow,) where he is noticed as proprietor the same year. His son Thomas was prop. at Stow, 1684. CYPRIAN, (æ. ab. 28, 1677), m. Mary, dr. of Maj. Simon Willard, Jan. 22, 1671, and was f. of *Mary*, m. Sam. Wright, Esq., of Sud.; *Dorothy*; *Simon*, of Lanc., Marlb., and Plainfield; *Elizabeth*, m. Capt. Ephraim Wilder; and *Joseph*, of Sud., Fram., and Rut. CYPRIAN, (w. Ruth), was of Lanc., 1693. Cyprian and Jacob, were prop. of Rut., 1686. CYPRIAN, of Stow, m. Damaris Whitney, 1726, and had in Stow, *Ephraim*; and in Rut., *Thomas*, b. 1728; *Anna*, 1733. JOSEPH, of Mendon, m. Sarah Tayre, July 2, 1671.

STIMSON, or STIMPSON, GEORGE, m. Abigail Clark, in Hop., 1751, and had 1. JEREMIAH, m. Anne Jones, of Hop., was a physician at Hop., and Trustee of the Fram. Academy; 2. ABIGAIL, b. 1753, unm.; 3. EXPERIENCE, m. Abigail Stone, of Hop., 1776; 4. GEORGE; 5. BETSEY; 6. SARAH, m. in Fram., Increase Claflin, Ap. 1782; 7. EPHRAIM. George, the f. lived near the Paper Mill; was taxed in Fram. 1770, and moved with his family to N. Y., ab. 1790.

GEORGE, (from Ipswich), had at Hop., *Alice*, bap. 1738; *Nathaniel*, '43; *Ephraim*, '45; *Samuel*, '47. CHARLES, of Hop., had bap., ——, 1739; *Sarah*, 1740. He m. Elizabeth Thomson, 1741, and had bap. *Mercy*, 1744, *Amos*, '45; *Alexander*, '47; *Ephraim*, '50; *Melatiah*, '53. JAMES, m. Sarah Cutler, in Weston, 1729. Dr. James, (w. Sarah), was of Sud., 1764. ANDREW, and w. Abigail, of Charlestown, 1695. GEORGE, of Ipswich, had *George*, b. 1672, d. '78; *Mercy*, '82; *Alice*, '84; and at Chebacco, *Prudence*, b. '86.

STONE, or STON, GREGORY, (who, and his b. Simon, were early emigrants to N. E.), was admitted freeman, May 25, 1636, was dea. of the church, at Camb., Representative, 1638, and a prop. of Wat. He lived near Mt. Auburn, and d. at Camb., Nov. 30, 1672, æ. 82. He m. in England, wid. Lydia Cooper, who d. June 24, 1674. His chil. were, 1. JOHN,

---

* The f. of Thomas was Col. THOMAS, of Devonshire, England, who moved to London, and was f. of WILLIAM, who lived in London, THOMAS, RICHARD, and CYPRIAN, and three daughters, of whom MARY only came to New England, and m. Capt. Whipple, of Ipswich. Thomas and Cyprian came to New England with Capt. Green, ab. 1660. Cyprian was of Chelsea, and after, of Lancaster. RICHARD came to New England after his brothers, and was already married; he was f. of Deac. Samuel, of Marlb. After his death, his wid. with her only daughter, returned to Eng. [Jos. Willard, Esq.'s Mss.]

b. ab. 1619; 2. DANIEL, (w. Mary), f. of *Mary*, b. Mar. 22, 1644, (a M. m. in Concord, Isaac Hunt, May 14, 1667); *Sarah*, b. Sep. 22, '45; *Daniel*, b. Jan. 2, '46-7; *David*, d. 1646; *Elizabeth*, b. Jan. 1, '48-9; *Abigail*, b. Ap. 28, '53; 3. DAVID, f. by w. Eliz., of (all bap. in Camb.), *David*, b. Ap. 6, 1649; and by w. Dorcas, of *David*, m. Sarah Hildreth, Dec. 31, 1674, and d. Aug. 21, 1679, æ. 29; *Daniel*; *Dorcas*, b. Dec. 18, '52; *John*, 1654; *Samuel*, b. June 19, '56, (w. Hannah); and *Nathaniel*; 4. ELIZABETH, m. —— Potter, and lived in Ipswich; 5. SAMUEL, was at Dedham, in Maj. Willard's troop, 1654, m. Sarah Sternes, of Wat., June 7, 1655, was deac. at Lex., and d. 1715, æ. 80, f. of Deac. *Samuel*,* b. 1656; *Isaac*; *Sarah*, b. '60, m. Edward Converse, 1684, and 2d, —— Hills; *John*, b. '63, m. Rachel Shepard, 1687, and d. 1712, f. of John, Anna, Rachel, and Ruth; *Lydia*, b. '65; *Mary*, b. '67; ——; *Anna*, b. '73; and *Joseph*; 6. SARAH, m. —— Meriam, of Concord. Lydia, w. of Gregory, had by her 1st husband, *John*, and *Lydia* Cooper; the last m. David Fisk.

2. JOHN, s. of Gregory (1), had by w. Anne, 1. HANNAH, b. June 6, 1640, m. John Bent, July 1, 1658, and prob. d. young; 2. MARY, m. Eliphalet Fox; 3. DANIEL[3], b. Aug. 31, 1644; 4. DAVID[20], b. Oct. 31, '46; 5. ELIZABETH, m. Samuel Stow; 6. MARGARET, b. Oct. 22, '53, m. William Brown, Jan. 11, '76; 7. TABITHA, b. May 29, '55, m. John Rice, Nov. 2, '74; 8. SARAH, b. Sep. 22, '57, m. Jacob Hill; 9. NATHANIEL[32], b. May 11, '60; 12. JOHN, unm., and particularly provided for in the f.'s will.

John, the f. was an early Prop. of Sud., and shared in the first three divisions of land there. In 1643, he had a grant of six ac. " in Natic bounds." About 1645, he sold to John Moore, his dwelling house, and houselot (in Sud.), with all other lands and meadows belonging to the said J. S., or that shall hereafter be due. In 1654, he was appointed " to see to fences on his side of the River." 1655, he was T. Clerk; 1656, he had confirmed by the General Court, a purchase from the Indians of land " at the

---

* SAMUEL, Jun. was f. of Capt. Samuel, who m. Abigail Reed of Woburn, 1706, and had at Concord, *Abigail*, b. April 21, 1707, m. Micah Stone, of Fram., and 2d, Col. Jos. Perry; *Samuel*, b. Dec. 8, '08, m. Mindwell Stevens, 1732, (and f. at Rutland, of Samuel; Isaac, (d. in the French war); Mindwell; Stevens; Stevens, and Elijah); *Jonas*, b. Dec. 3, 1710, (and lived at Rutland and Lexington); and at Sud., *Elizabeth*, b. Dec. 21, '13, m. John Stone, of Fram. and Rutland; *Tabitha*, b. Jan. 9, '15-6; *Mary*, b. Mar. 9, '17-8, m. Abijah Flagg, '47; *Susanna*, b. Ap. 24, '20; *Nathan*, b. Ap. 28, '22, and his will proved 1758, (f. by w. Mary, at Sud. and Rutland, of Mary, Thankful, Nathan, Jeaduthan, Lois, and Rebecca); *Eunice*, b. July 2, 1724; *Isabel*, b. Sep. 9, '27; and *Isaac*, b. Ap. 5, '30. Capt. Samuel lived at Concord, Sud., and Rutland, and d. in Lexington, April 5, 1769, æ. 84. His w. d. Jan. 16, 1767, æ. 80. (Lex. Rec.) He had prob. a son *Joseph*.

falls of Sudbury River," which, the same year, he had "just broken up and fenced in." He had other lands granted, which were laid out, 1658. 1659, the road " from Sud. to John Stone's house," prob. at the Falls, is referred to in a description of the bounds of Natick Plantation.* He was also Elder of the ch. in Sud., and was known as Deacon, and often as Elder John Stone. In 1665, he was freeman at Cambridge, and he represented that town in 1682 and 3. In 1679, he was one of a com. to settle the disputed location of the meeting house in Sherb., and the same year was with Capt Tho. Prentice and Wm. Bond, commissioned by the Co. Court, (Rec. iii. 306), " for to order and settle the rebuilding of Lancaster." He d. at Camb. May 5, 1683, and his estate was settled June 9. (Mid. Deeds, B. 16, p. 190.) His will was dated Ap. 16, 1683, (he then æ. ab. 64), and recorded June 1st. John's w. was prob. related to Elder Edward How, of Wat.

3. [1]DANIEL, s. of John (2), m. Mary Ward, Nov. 2, 1667; and had, 1. DANIEL[4], b. Nov. 22, 1668; 2. ANNE, b. Jan. 15, 1670; 3. TABITHA, b. May 4, '72, m. David Haynes; 4. SARAH, b. Feb. 14, '75, m. James Rice; 5. MARY, b. Aug. 10, '77, m. Jonas Rice, Feb. 10, 1701–2; 6. ELIZABETH, b. Nov. 9, '78, m. Joseph Livermore; 7. ABIGAIL, b. Feb. 13, '80, m. Dr. John Sherman of Springfield; 8. JOHN[14]. Daniel, the f. was Deacon of the ch. in Sud., and Selectman in Fram., 1700, 2 years. His w. Mary d. June 10, 1703, and he m. 2d, Abigail Wheeler, Feb. 8, 1703–4, who d. Oct. 28, 1711, and he m. 3d, Ruth Haynes, of Sud., Nov. 18, 1712. Dea. Daniel d. 1719, æ. 75. Administration was granted Ap. 11, 1719, to his son John. His funeral charges were £60. His wid. lived with his g. son, Deac. Daniel Stone.

4. [1]DANIEL, Jun., m. Patience Brown, dr. of Maj. Thomas of Sud.; and had 1. PRISCILLA, m. James Fox, of Dorchester; 2. BEULAH, b. Aug. 23, 1695, m. Josiah Brown, Jan. 14, 1719; 3. KEZIAH, b. July 29, '97, m. Eliab Moore, Mar. 5, 1728; 4.

---

* W. F. Stone, Esq., of Cambridge, who has made diligent research into the history of his family, obligingly writes, that Elder John first built at *Otter Neck*, a half mile down the river, a "fordway" being near it. He probably built again on the hill by the Lannum road, near Mr. Fisk's, on the spot from which was removed, to the mill village, the house recently sold by Mr. Abner Stone to the prop. of the Railroad. Two or three rods S. from that spot, he built what was called in ancient deeds, "the old house," whose cellar hole is still remembered. He is supposed also to have built at the Ox-bow, and, soon after, another house nearer the mills.

Micah⁵, b. Mar. 1699; 5. Lois, b. Nov. 21, 1701, m. Moses Maynard, of Sud., Mar. 18, 1723-4. Daniel, Jun., was Selectman and T. Treasurer, 1702, and d. Dec. 22, 1702, æ. 34. Administration was granted to his wid. Patience, who m. 2d, Nathaniel Rice, and d. Nov. 13, 1722, æ. 52.

5. ¹MICAH, s. of Dan. (4), m. Abigail, dr. of Sam. Stone, of Lexington, Ap. 2, 1724; and had, 1. Josiah⁶, b. Dec. 23, '24; 2. Daniel⁹, b. Ap. 11, '27; 3. Micah¹¹, b. May, 1729; 4. John, b. Mar. 1731, unm., d. in the army, Dec. 6, 1755; 5. Moses¹³, b. June 26, 1734; 6. Eliab, b. May 5, 1737, H. Coll. 1758, taught school in Sud., adm. to Fram. ch. Nov. '59, and dismissed to Reading ch. Ap. 12, '61, was ord. at Reading, May 20, '61, m. Sarah Hubard, of Concord, and d. Aug. 31, 1822.* He was f. of the Rev. Micah Stone, D.D., H. Coll., 1790, Tutor 1794, and minister at Brookfield. Micah the f. lived for some time on " the Island," at Sud. He was Selectman in Fram. 5 years from 1732 to his death, and Representative 1734 and 1735. He d. of small pox, Oct. 13, 1738, æ. 39, and his wid. Abigail m. 2d, Col. Joseph Perry, Jan. 22, 1752, and d. Oct. 4, 1796, æ. 90.

6. ¹JOSIAH, s. of Micah (5), m. Anne Haven, Feb. 25, 1746-7, was adm. to the ch. Oct. 25, 1761, and had, 1. Beulah, b. Nov. 22, '47, d. May 7, 1752; 2. Abigail, b. Nov. 11, '49, adm. to the ch. June, 1710, m. Moses Adams, and was m. of the Rev. Moses, of Acton; 3. Lucy, b. Ap. 11, '52, d. Ap. 52; 4. Luther⁷, b. Ap. 11, 1753; 5. Josiah⁸, b. Feb. 22, '62; 6. Micah, (and 7. Anne, a twin who d. young), b. May 30, 1766, m. Mary Coggswell, and moved from F. The Hon. Josiah was a Selectman, 1756, 18 years; T. Treasurer, 1769, 8 years; T. Clerk, 1769, 7 years; was Representative, '71, 3 years, and a Delegate to the Provincial Congress 1775 and 1776, and afterward a State Senator and Counsellor. He was active and prominent in the transactions of the Town, and was held in general esteem. He held also several military commissions, and was a Justice of the Peace, and in 1782, a special Judge of the C. C. Pleas. He was suddenly

---

* Dr. Flint, in his bi-centennial address at Reading, 1844, says, (p. 39), " And let me here acknowledge, that I owe the first awakening desire to obtain an education, to the influence emanating from the higher cultivation and taste, that distinguished the character and family of my spiritual father, the honored and excellent pastor of my native parish, the late Rev. Eliab Stone."

killed in his saw-mill, at Sud. falls, by falling from the carriage of the mill while placing a log, Ap. 12, 1785, æ. 60. (G. Stone.) His w. Anne d. May 20, 1819, æ. 94.

7. ¹LUTHER, s. of Josiah (6), m. Mary Trowbridge, with w. adm. to the ch. Dec. 1789, and had, 1. MARGARET, b. July 29, 1779, m. Gilbert Taylor, of Southb., and 2d, Heman Parker; 2. NANCY, b. May 29,'81, m. Maj. Josiah Flint of Shrewsb.; 3. THEODORE, b. July 20, '83, lives in Douglass; 4. HARRIET, b. July 29, '90; 5. PATTY, m. James Farwell; 6. MARY, m. Maj. Josiah Flint, (his 2d w.); 7. EUNICE; 8. SOPHIA, went to N. Y.; 9. HARRIOT, m. Capt. Alpheus Kimball, of Fitchburg; 10. LUTHER, m. Diadema Hunt, of Douglass. Luther, the f. lived where is now the Factory yard, and moved to Northborough, &c., ab. 1795. He d. in Fitchburg, 1837, æ. 84. His w. d. the same year.

8. ¹JOSIAH, s. of Josiah, (6), m. Elizab. Fiske, of Waltham. Their chil. were 1. WILLIAM FISKE, b. Ap. 10, 1784, m. Harriet Brigham, of Westboro', was educated as a Physician, and has been Register of Deeds in Mid. Co. He lives in Camb.; 2. LUTHER, b. May 6, '86, m. Mary Eaton, and lives in Fram.; 3. NANCY; 4. ABIJAH, m. Martha Buckminster, and lives at Westboro'; 5. ASENETH, d. unm., May 30, 1842, æ. 52; 6. MARY, m. Jabez G. Fisher, of Westb.; 7. MICAH, a merchant in Fram., and at his decease, President of the Fram. Bank. He d. Oct. 25, 1838, æ. 40, greatly esteemed, and left large legacies to the first Parish and the Fram. Academy; 8. ELIZA F., m. Jos. Lothrop, and d. on her return from Europe, in the Straits of Gibraltar, Oct. 28, 1844; 9. JOSIAH, m. Sophia Brigham, of Wayland. Josiah m. 2d, Nancy Stone, and had 10. SEWALL; 11. SUMNER. Maj. Josiah owned the mills at Sud. falls, was Selectman 1801, 3 years, and d. in Fram., Sep. 3, 1836, æ. 74.

9. ¹DANIEL, s. of Micah (5), m. Persis Haynes of Sud.; and had, 1. PERSIS, b. July 17, 1750, d. Mar. 1, 1752; 2. NAHUM, b. Nov. 25, '52, m. Hannah Haven, and d. at Grafton, ab. 1805; 3. JOHN, b. Feb. 17, '57, m. Ann Hunt of Sud. June 25, '78; 4. DANIEL¹⁰, b. Sep. 5, 1760; 5. PERSIS, b. Aug. 15, '62, m. Buckley Adams, Feb. 1785. Capt. Daniel, the f. was Selectman 1767, 2 years, and d. in Fram., Ap. 3, 1813, æ. 86; his w. Persis d. May.7, 1804, æ. 76.

10. ¹DANIEL, s. of Daniel (9), m. Sally Buckminster, of Fram., July, 1788, and had 1. DEXTER, b. Ap. 12, 1791, m. ——, and 2d, Ellen Kittredge, was a merchant in Phila., and d. on a visit at Fram., 1846; 2. ELIZABETH, b. May 23, 1794, m. William H. Knight, and lives in Fram.; 3. PERSIS; 4. MARY, m. Henry H. Fuller, Counsellor at Law, in Boston; 5. ELMIRA, m. Rev. Bezaleel Frost, of Concord. Daniel, the f., was Selectman, 1797, 5 years, lived N. from the falls, and d. Nov. 9, 1834, æ. 74. His wid. Sally d. Ap. 19, 1845, æ. 75.

11. ¹MICAH, s. of Micah (5), m. Rachel Haynes, of Sud., Oct. 11, 1748, and had 1. ABEL, b. Jan. 1749, d. young; 2. MICAH, b. Aug. 28, '53, d. Jan. 9, 1768; 3. RACHEL, b. May 7, '71, d. Feb. 28, 1772; 4. RACHEL, b. Aug. 8, '74, was burned to death, Sep. 22, 1775; 5. ABEL¹². Rachel, the m., d. June 18, 1794, æ. 64, and Micah m. 2d, wid. (Sarah) Bachelder, of Grafton, who was buried Sep. 26, 1820. Col. Micah was Selectman 1784, 2 years. He was commis'd as Lt. Col., Feb. 4 (or 14) 1776. He was highly respected in the Town, and left in his will a large fund for the support of the poor, having previously made the donation of a bell for the first Parish. (See Hist.) He d. Sep. 1813, æ. 84.

12. ¹ABEL, s. of Micah (11), m. Margaret Trowbridge, and with w. cov'd, Nov. 8, 1772. Their chil. were 1. MARTIN, bap. Nov. 15, '72, d. young; 2. MARGARET, bap. July 28, '74, died young; 3. PATTY, bap. Mar. 9, '77, m. Joseph Goodnow, of E. Sud., Nov. 30, '97; 4. MICAH, bap. Mar. '82, m. Olive Gleason, Oct. 7, 1804, lived in Warren and Fram.; 5. POLLY, bap. Feb. '84, m. John Newton, Ap. 10, 1803, and 2d, Luther Eaton; 6. ANNE, bap. Oct. '86, m. Maj. Josiah Stone, lives a wid. in Millbury; 7. JOHN TROWBRIDGE, bap. Dec. '87, m. Lucy Richardson, lives in Fram.; 8. ABIGAIL, m. Sam. Murdock, and d. in Rochester, 1841. Abel, the f., moved to Canada. His w. Margaret m. 2d, John Jones, of Fram., May 9, 1803.

13. ¹MOSES, s. of Micah (5), m. Hannah Moore, of Sud., Nov. 14, 1754, and had in Fram., 1. JACOB, b. May 13, 1755, d. prob. unm.; 2. JOSIAH, b. May 1, '58, m. Abigail Cheney, '81; and in Sud., 3. MOSES, b. Mar. 7, '67, m. Ruth Morse, 1789; 4. HANNAH, b. Dec. 27, '70, m. David Lincoln, 1804; 5. ELIAB, b.

Dec. 28, '74, m. Hannah Osborn, 1804. Moses lived in Fram., and at Sud., on or near " the Island," and d. in Fram.

14. [1]JOHN, s. of Deac. Daniel (3), m. Anne Tileston (from Dorchester, dr. of Timo.), Jan. 31, 1706–7. Their chil. were 1. DANIEL[15], b. Oct. 21, 1707 ; 2. JOHN, b. Mar. 31, '09, d. Feb. 5, 1730 (Family Rec.) ; 3. JAMES[18], b. July 5, 1711 ; 4. URIAH, b. May 16, 1713, and had at Oxford by w. Mary, Mary, b. 1740 ; Uriah, '44 ; Elizabeth, '46 ; John, '50 ; Katey, '52 ; Samuel, '54 ; Sarah, '57 ; Abijah, '59 ; Isaac, '63, and Anne, '66 ; 5. ANN, b. Jan. 21, d. Feb. 13, 1715–6 ; 6. ABNER[19], bap. Aug. 18, 1717 ; 7. ABIJAH, b. June 17, '19, m. Ann Jones, of Hop., Oct. 20, 1739, and d. Nov. 5, 1758, f. at Hop. of Anna, bap. 1741, m. Tho. Saltmarsh, '69 ; Abijah, 1749, m. Experience Stimson, of Fram., '76 ; Elizabeth, 1752 ; Mary, 1755, m. Samuel Clark, '72 ; John, 1758 (m. Lydia Jones, 1783, and f. of John, bap. 1784 ; Elizabeth, '86 ; Anne, '87 ; Abijah, '89 ; and Lydia.) John the f., " d. at my house, Nov. 26, 1719," (Swift's Journal ; whose w. was sister to John's wife). The wid. Anne d. Mar. 25, 1733 ; her son Daniel administered on land at " the Gore." John in 1716, held as a slave, one Jone Jackson, whose husband John, was of N. London.

15. [1]DANIEL, s. of John (14), m. Mary Frost, Mar. 12, 1733–4 ; and had 1. ANNE, b. May 12, 1735, m. John Haven, Mar. 28, 1759 ; 2. ELIJAH[16], b. Sep. 28, '36 ; 3. DANIEL, b. Oct. 13, '38, d. Feb. 25, 1754 ; 4. MARY, b. Aug. 4, '41, m. James Page, Nov. 24, 1764, lived in Hardwick, and d. Jan. 6, 1770 ; 5. PHINEHAS, b. Nov. 2, '43, d. Sep. 3, '51 ; 6. JOHN, d. Sep. 19, '51, æ. 8 ; 7. JANE, d. Sep. 22, '51, æ. 2 ; 8. ABNER[17], b. Feb. 2, '51 ; 9. BEULAH, b. Dec. 1, '52, d. unm. Feb. 22, 1824, æ. 72, (G. Stone) ; 10. EUNICE, b. Ap. 14, '55, m. Nathan Stone, Dec. 14, 1773, and 2d, Moses Fisk, of Nat. Mary, w. of Dan., d. May 26, 1760, æ. 46, (G. Stone), and he m. 2d, Nov. 27, 1761, Mrs. Martha, wid. of Rev. David Goddard, of Leicester. He was Selectman, 1740, and elected Deac. of the ch., Jan. 29, 1763. He lived near Mr. Abner Stone's, and his house was destroyed by fire. He d. May 15, 1783, æ. 75. (G. Stone.)

16. [1]ELIJAH, s. of Daniel (15), m. Elizabeth Lyndes, of Leicester, and was adm. to the ch., Aug. 3, 1766. Their chil.

were 1. ELIZABETH, bap. Aug. 3, 1766, m. Jos. Banister; 2. ELIJAH, bap. Mar. 31, '71, m. —— Rawson; 3. LYNDS, b. Jan. 1, 1770, d. Ap. 22, '90; 4. DANIEL, b. Nov. 18, '73, H. Coll., 1791, m. Hitty Bixby, Nov. 30, 1802, 2d, Sophia Coolidge, 3d, —— Hawes, and d. at Sharon, where he was in practice as a Physician, 1842, f. of Prof. *Daniel*, of the Univ. of Penn., who d. 1846; 5. FORTEN, (Fortunatus), b. Sep. 27, '75, m. Sally Cutler, of Sud., and d. in N. Y., 1840; 6. POLLY, b. Ap. 18, '77, d. Sep. 16, '78; 7. OLIVE, b. July 22, '79, m. Josiah Parker, and d. July 4, 1826; 8. JOANNA, b. Nov. 29, '80, m. Silas Eaton; 9. JONATHAN, b. May 30, '83, m. —— Upham, of Canton, and a 2d w., and lives in Illinois; 10. POLLY, b. Ap. 18, '85. Dr. Elij., the f. was a Physician in Fram., lived S. of the wid. Eaton's, and d. Aug. 10, 1804, æ. 68. (G. S.) His w. Eliz. d. July 24, 1830, æ. 89. (G. S.)

17. [1]ABNER, s. of Dan. (15), m. Persis Moore, (b. in Boston), Mar. 5, 1776, and had 1. PHINEHAS, m. Mary Jarvis, of Camb., and d. ab. 1802; 2. ABNER, m. Sally Russell, of Weston, and lives in F.; 3. MARTIN, m. Sarah Coolidge, of Wat.; 4. BETSEY, bap. Feb. 1785, m. Nathan Stone, lives in Fram.; 5. JESSE, bap. May, '97, d. unm., æ. 7 1-2. Abner, the f., was a miller, lived at Mr. Abner's, was Selectman, 1789, 3 years, and d. Oct. 1, 1829. His w. Persis d. June 17, 1837, æ. 79.

18. [1]JAMES, s. of John (14), m. Ruth How, Feb. 14, 1738-9; and had 1. JOTHAM, b. Jan. 29, 1741, d. young; 2. RUTH, b. Nov. 17, '46, d. young; 3. ABNER; 4. EUNICE, both bap. Jan. 3, '49, and d. young; 5. BEULAH, bap. May 21, '50, d. young; 6. LUCY, bap. Sep. 9, '53, m. Joseph Tower, and d. Dec. 9, 1835. James d. in Fram., Jan. 17, 1754. Wid. Ruth was adm. to the ch., Sep. 4, 1757.

19. [1]ABNER, s. of John (14), m. Eunice Frost, March 10, 1740, and d. in Fram., Sep. 10, 1745. His w. d. Mar. 23, 1746.

20. [2]DAVID, s. of John (2), had by w. Susanna, 1. SUSANNA, b. Jan. 29, 1677; 2. MARY, b. Feb. 19, '82, m. Ephraim Curtis, May 10, 1705; 3. SAMUEL[21], b. May 23, '85; 4. THOMAS[28], b. Mar. 11, 1687-8. David the f., lived on what is called the Thomas Stone place. He bought 1683, 200 ac. of Gookin and How, on Sud. River, and Deer Swamp, was Selectman 1713, and d. 1737; his will proved in May.

21. ²SAMUEL, s. of David (20), had by w. Bathshebah, 1. PRISCILLA, b. May 15, 1708, d. Aug. 29; 2. ZEDEKIAH²², b. Mar. 4, 1709–0; 3. ABIGAIL, b. Ap. 3, 1712, m. John Livermore, June 23, '31, and 2d, Sam. Gleason; 4. DAVID, b. Jan. 30, 1716–7, m. Sarah Rice, Mar. 26, 1745, and f. at Rutland, of *Sarah*, b. May 27, '46, d. unm., æ. 22; and at Petersham, *Zeruiah*, b. Nov. 24, '48, d. unm., æ. 64; *David*, Feb. 1, '51, m. Nancy Felton; *Susanna*, Ap. 10, '53, went to N. Y.; *Hannah*, Mar. 24, '55, unm., bedridden 40 years, d. 1814; *Josiah*, Mar. 12, '57, d. unm.; *Anna*, June 19, '59, unm.; *Martha*, Oct. 7, '61, d. young; *Buckminster*, Jan. 18, '63, d. æ. 6; *Ashbel*, May 12, 17—, d. æ. 4; *Buckminster*, Aug. 26, 17—, m. Lucinda Keith, and d. of canker-rash, Dec. 23, '95, æ. 26. David, the f. exchanged farms with his br. Samuel, and with w. was recommended to ch. in Nitchewaug, Jan. 23, 1748. He d. at Pet., Oct. 12, 1807, æ. 90. His w. Sarah d. Oct., 1815, æ. 90; 5. EPHRAIM²³, b. May 21, '19; 6. JOSEPH²⁴, b. June 16, '21; 7. BATHSHEBAH, Aug. 16, '23, m. Ezekiel How, of Sud. 1744; 8. SUSANNA, b. July 12, 1726; 9. SAMUEL²⁵, m. Rebecca Clark, June 14, 1737. Sam., the f., lived on the Bennet place. He became blind, and d. ab. 1750. His w. survived him.

22. ²ZEDEKIAH, s. of Sam. (21), had by w. Martha, NATHAN, b. Dec. 12, 1734. Zedekiah was 1745, among the early settlers of Nichewaug, and on a Parish committee there, that year and in 1754.

23. ²EPHRAIM, s. of Sam. (21), m. in Sud., Joanna Eames, of Fram., July 24, 1745; and had JOSEPH, bap. May 18, 1746. The f. is said to have lived after in Middleton, Con.

24. ²JOSEPH, s. of Sam. (21), m. Dorcas Hobbs, of Weston, in Sud., May 4, 1747; and had in F., 1. EPHRAIM, b. July 3, 1747; 2. JOSIAH, b. Feb. 6, '50; 3. SUSANNAH, b. Mar. 25, '55, m. — Carter; 4. SAMUEL, b. Nov. 24, '56; 5. DORCAS, b. May 8, '59, m. Samuel Dadmun, Oct. '87, and lived in Princeton and Templeton; 6. JOSEPH, b. Dec. 13, '60; 7. NATHAN, b. at Sud. July 8, '64; 8. ELIZABETH, b. Oct. 9, '67, d. young. Joseph, the f. was Selectman, 1755, and adm. to the ch., Ap. 3, 1757. He lived some time at the Eastward, and d. in Fram., on the Bennet Farm., ab. 1770.

25. ²SAMUEL, s. of Sam. (21), m. Rebecca Clark in Fram.,

June 14, 1737, and was with w. adm. from Nitchewaug, July 5, '47. Their chil. were 1. JASON[26], b. Dec. 28, 1737; 2. BATHSHEBAH, b. Sep. 30, '39, m. Ebenezer Hemenway; 3. SUSANNA, b. May 10, '41, m. Jona. Ward, Esq., of Southb., and d. 1790; 4. LUCY, b. Jan. 1, 1742, m. Mark Moore, Feb. 9, '74, and lived in Warwick; 5. SARAH, b. Mar. 4, '45, adm. to the ch. 1771, m. Moses Fisk, and d. ab. 1799; 6. MARY, b. May 2, '47, m. Peter Bent, of E. Sud., and d. at Northboro'; 7. REBECKA, b. Ap. 9, '49, adm. to the ch. 1771, m. Eben. Eaton, May 21, '78; 8. SAMUEL, b. Nov. 13, '50, m. Anne Stacy, and d. at Fitzwilliam; 9. ANNE, b. Oct. 1, '52, m. Joshua Trowbridge, and d. 1836; 10. WINSOR[27], b. May 30, '54. Lt. Samuel, the f. d. in Fram., ab. 1787, and his wid. survived several years.

26. [2]JASON, s. of Sam. (25), m. Deborah Goodnow, of Nat. and with w. cov'd Aug. 17, 1776. Their chil. were 1. DEBORAH, b. Nov. 18, 1765, m. near Canada; 2. THADDEUS, b. Feb. 2, '68, d. young, scalded; 3. REBECKAH, b. Oct. 14, '69, m. Isaac Abbot, of Holden, Feb. 19, 1801. Jason, the f., moved to Fitzwilliam, ab. 1770.

27. [2]WINSOR, s. of Sam. (25), m. Betsey Mellen, of Hop., 1778, and with w. cov'd, May 28, '80. They had 1. LUTHER, and 2. WINSOR, twins, bap. Oct. 1, '78; 3. NANCY, bap. May 27, '80; 4. HENRY, bap. Sep. '82; 5. SAMUEL, bap. Sep. '84; 6. BETSEY, bap. May '86; 7. SALLY, bap Aug. '88; 8. HENRY, bap. Feb. '91; 9. GARDNER, bap. Oct. '93. The f. moved to Tyringham, ab. 1799.

28. [2]THOMAS, s. of David (20), m. Mary Curtis, of Sud., Dec. 14, 1710, and had 1. MARY, b. Feb. 25, 1711-2, m. Isaac Clark, Ap. 21, '40; 2. THOMAS[29], b. Ap. 29, '14, d. young; 3. ABIGAIL, b. Mar. 19, '16, d. young; 4. BEULAH, b. Sep. 22, '18, d. young; 5. SABILLA, b. June 26, '21, d. young. The f. m. 2d, Elizabeth Andrews, of Camb., June 18, 1730; and had 6. THOMAS[29], b. Jan. 28, '31-2; 7. JOHN, b. Jan. 18, '33-4, d. young; 8. ABNER[31], b. Ap. 8, '36. Tho., the f., was Selectman, 1726, 5 years, lived on the Bennet Farm. His death (in Fram.) is not on record.

29. [2]THOMAS, s. of Tho. (28), m. Alice Coller, and had, 1. THOMAS[30], b. Jan. 26, 1760; 2. BETTY, b. Mar. 18, '62, m. Joshua Kendall, 2d, Henry Eames, and lives in Fram., having been

many years infirm, and crippled. To her intelligent memory the author is greatly indebted. Thomas, the f. lived in the old house of Mr. Eben Stone, was Selectman, 1782, and d. Nov. 13, 1812, æ. 83. His w. Alice d. Feb. 1782, æ 55.

30. ²THOMAS, s. of Tho. (29), m. Hannah Hemmenway, Dec. 1790; and had, 1. HANNAH, b. Sep. 9, '93, m. Nathan Underwood, Ap. 29, 1819, lives in Athol; 2. THOMAS, b. Aug. 26, '95, m. Nancy M. Hawes of Westboro', and d. in Prov. 1836; 3. EBENEZER, b. July 4, 1797, m. Jane Walker, Selectman in Fram. 1837, 3 years; 4. JOHN, b. Ap. 17, '99, m. Mary Dodge, of Boston, and lives in B.; 5. DAVID, b. Sep. 16, 1803, m. Anne M. Mann of Dedham, and d. 1839; 6. GILMAN, b. Aug. 20, 1805, m. Emily Amesbury of Prov., lives in P. Tho., the f. occupied his father's farm, and d. July 1, 1826. His wid. Hannah d. a few months since.

31. ²ABNER, s. of Tho. (28), m. Lucy Mellen of Hop., 1763, and with w. cov'd May 26, '65. They had 1. MOLLY, b. Jan. 31, 1764, d. young; 2. JOHN, b. June 6, '65, d. young; 3. BEULAH, b. Feb. 22, '67, m. Charles Bowker, and d. in Fitzwilliam; 4. DAVID, b. Feb. 8, '69, m. Ruth Mellen, 1792, and 2d, Ruby Hatch; 5. LUCY, b. Ap. 17, '71, m. David Pelton, of Lyme, N. H.; 6. SALLY, bap. Aug. 1, '73, d. unm.; 7. NABBY, bap. Sep. 17, '75, m. Nahum Pierce, of Lyme, N. H.; 8. BETTY, bap. Nov. 2, '77, m. Tho. Durkee, of Alden, N. Y.; 9. ABNER, d. 1812; 10. MARY, m. Ezekiel Rand, of Greensboro', Vt. Abner, the f. and w. were recommended to the ch. in Fitzwilliam, Ap. 1781, and he d. there Dec. 8, 1826. He lived on the Bennet farm in Fram., which he sold to Mr. B.

32. ³NATHANIEL, s. of John (2), m. Sarah Wayt, (of Malden), Ap. 25, 1684; and had, 1. NATHANIEL³³, b. Oct. 15, '85; 2. EBENEZER³⁵, b. Ap. 16, '88; 3. JONATHAN³⁶, b. Mar. 24, '90; 4. ISAAC; 5. JOHN³⁸, b. Ap. 13, 1702; 6. MARY, b. Dec. 19, 1705, m. —— Coggin; 7. SARAH, b. Oct. 12, '08, m. —— Carter; 8. HEZEKIAH³⁹, b. Mar. 5, 1710-1. Nath., the f. was Selectman, 1706, 4 years. He was adm. to the ch., May 16, 1725. His will is dated June 23, 1732, and was entered Nov. 2.

33. ³NATHANIEL, s. of Nath. (32), m. Mary Cutler of Sud. Aug. 10, 1711, and had 1. JAMES³⁴, b. July 2, 1712; 2. JOSEPH, b. Jan. 1, 1716-7. [A Jos. (w. Sarah) had at Bolton, *Betty*,

b. 1744.] The f. d. June 9, 1729, æ. 43, (G. S.), and his w. was adm. to the ch. Oct. 16, 1720.

34. ³JAMES, s. of Nath. (33), was adm. to the ch. May 7, 1727, and m. Sarah Jones, Dec. 25, 1733. He had NATHANIEL, b. Nov. 17, 1734.

35. ³EBENEZER, s. of Nath. (32), m. in Concord, Prudence Pratt, May 10, 1721, cov'd with w., Dec. 24, '21, and was with w. adm. to the ch., Sep. 15, '23. Their chil. were 1. EBENEZER, b. Feb. 5, 1721-2, m. in Sherb., Mary Estabrook, Ap. 11, 1752; 2. JOSEPH, b. Nov. 8, 1723, d. Dec. 20, '30; 3. PHINEHAS, b. Mar. 7, 1725-6, d. Jan. 7, '30-1; 4. SILAS, b. Ap. 29, 1728 m. in Sherb., Elizabeth Russell, Jan. 25, 1750, and was f. in Natick, of *Silas*, b. July 14, '50; *Amos*, Nov. 20, '51, *Elizabeth*, Oct. 21, '53; *Nathan*, Mar. 28, '54; *Silas*, Ap, 5, '55; *Jeduthan*, Feb. 26, '57, d. 1759; *Ebenezer*, Jan. 26, '59; *John*, June 30, 61; *Judith*, Ap. 9, '63. The f. prob. was the Silas at Dublin, 1763; 5. PRUDENCE, b. July 11, '30 — (she or the following m. John Badger, of Nat.); 6. SARAH, b. Sep. 28, '32; 7. HANNAH, b. Nov. 18, '33, m. Joseph Hill of Sherb., Mar. 9, '52. Eben'r, the f. is said to have lived between Hollis Hastings' and the Turnpike, and d. early in 1743. His wid. Prudence, m. 2d, Daniel Bigelow, of F., July 17, '46, who d. 1752, and she m. 3d, Ezekiel Rice, May 10, 1753. Eben. received from his f. by will, Wait's Meadow, S. of Sud. Riv., near the 2d M. House.

36. ³JONATHAN, s. of Nath. (32), m. Abiel Bigelow, Oct. 11, 1716. Her chil., all bap. Feb. 9, 1724, were, 1. JONATHAN. [He was perhaps the J. and w. Ruth at Worcester, f. of *Daniel*, b. 1752; and *Mary*, '62]; 2. REUBEN; by w. Mary, he had at Rutland, *Mary*, b. 1746, m. Ezra Perry, '65; *Reuben*, '47, m. Grace Munro, 1768; *Jesse*, '49, m. Azubah Sibley, '74; *Sardius*, '51; and at Petersham, *Jonathan*, '53, d. young; and *Rachel*, m. Aaron Hager. Reuben, the f. d. in Petersham; 3. SIMEON, m. in Southb. Hannah Kendall, Jan. 1745, and had in Marlb., *Hannah*, b. Jan. 15, '45-6, m. Joseph Wilson, '70; and in Rutland, *Daniel*, b. 1748, d. 1754; *David*, '49; *Jonas*, '52; *Lucy*, '54; *Daniel*, '57; *Susanna*, '60. Simeon, the f. d. at Rutl. May 12, 1785, æ. 63; his w. Hannah d. 1801, æ. 80; 4. LEVI. Jonathan, the f. d. young; his "wid. Abiel," was adm. to the ch.

Nov. 17, 1723, and m. Samuel Walker, of Nat., June 15, 1743. J.'s heirs received from his f. by will, a tract of land bounded on Sud. Riv., Square meadow Brook, and land formerly of Sam. Winch and Tho. Frost.

37. ISAAC,* m. Elizabeth Brown of Sud., in Wat. July 24, 1722, and with w. cov'd Oct. 14, 1722, and w. adm. Aug. 1, '25. They had, 1. EUNICE, b. Nov. 21, 1722; 2. JONAS, b. Aug. 12, '25. [Lt. Isaac, d. at Shrewsbury, Ap. 22, 1776, æ. 78 y. 8 m. Mrs. Elizabeth d. at the advanced age of 96.]

38. [3]JOHN, s. of Nath. (32), m. Elizabeth Stone, (dr. of Sam. and Abigail, of Sud. and Rut.), Jan. 13, 1731, moved to Rutland, and had 1. JOHN, b. Dec. 18, '32, and d. at Rutland, 1819, by his w. Lucy, (who d. 1824, æ. 89), f. of *Hezekiah*, b. 1756, d. '61; *Elizabeth*, '58; *Lucy*, '60; *John*, '63; *Hezekiah*, '69; *Susanna*, '74; 2. ELIZABETH, b. June 16, 1733; 3. ABIGAIL, b. Oct. 5, '34, d. '55; 4. SARAH, b. Dec. 14, '36; 5. EUNICE, b. Mar. 21, '39, m. —— Bellows; 6. BEULAH, b. 1741; 7. ELIZABETH, b. 1743; 8. DORCAS, b. 1745, d. 1747; 9. HEPSEBAH, b. 1747; 10. ISRAEL, b. 1749. John, the f. built on the hill at Rut., where is now the Hotel. He was deac. of the church, and Justice of the Peace, and a prominent man in the town. He d. Oct. 11, 1776, æ. 73. His first w. d. 1751, æ. 37.

39. [3]HEZEKIAH, s. of Nath. (32), m. Ruth How, of Sud., and had 1. ELIPHALET, b. Dec. 5, 1735, m. Lydia Goddard, was Dea. at Marlb., N. H., and f. of *Calvin; Beulah*, b. 1762, m. Jona. Frost, and d. 1808; *John* b. 1764, (lives at Dublin (1846) f. by w. Elizabeth, of John, Polly, Betsey, Nabby and Andrew); *Cynthia*, m. John Farrar; *Ruth*, m. —— Raymond; *Shubael*, m. Polly Rogers, (f. of Jesse, Cyrus, Parley, Lydia, Jeremiah, &c.); *Nabby*, b. Sep. 18, '72, m. Phinehas Farrar; *Luther*, b. Nov. 17, '74, unm.; *Patty*, b. Jan. 13, '79, d. young, drowned; *Asa*, b. Dec. 1, '80, d. young; 2. JESSE[40], b. Sep. 28, 1737; 3. HEPHZIBAH, b. July 8, '41, m. Jeremiah Belknap; 4. RUTH, b. Feb. 10, '43, m. John Eames; 5. SARAH, b. Feb. 24, '46, m. —— Davis, of Oxford; 6. LOIS, b. Aug. 3, '49, m. (Uriah) Stone, of Oxford; 7. ISRAEL, b. Jan. 2, '52, d. in Ward — (prob. the I. and w. Tryphena at Oxford, f. of *Calvin*, b. 1777); 8. HEZEKIAH, b. May 27, 1755. Capt. Hezek., the f., received from his f. the homestead, "Bridgefield," and his interest in "Baiting Brook meadow;" lived near Maj. J. Stone's, where was lately a cellar

---

* The parentage of Isaac is uncertain. He may have been son of Joseph, of Lexington, and a descendant of Gregory, through his s. Samuel.

hole. He was Selectman, 1759, 2 years, moved to Oxford, and d. July 18, 1771, æ. 60. His wid. m. Deac. Bancroft, of Ward. 40. ³JESSE, s. of Hezek. (39), m. Elizabeth Livermore, and was with w. adm. to the ch., Oct. 5, 1760. They had 1. WILLIAM, b. (in Fram.), May 3, '60 ; 2. JOHN, lived in Worthington ; and on Oxford Rec., JESSE, b. '65, lived E. ; ELIZABETH, '68 ; ISAAC, '69, lived in Ward ; ELIZABETH, '72 ; JEREMY, '76. Jesse, the f., was recommended by the ch., Ap. 1775.

41. SIMON, br. of Gregory (1), æ. 50, came over in the Increase, 1634, with w. Joan, æ. 38, and chil., 1. FRANCIS, æ. 16; 2. ANN, æ. 11 (not in the will); 3. SYMON,⁴² æ. 4 ; 4. MARIE, æ. 3 ; 5. Jo. (John), æ. 5 w., (d. young.) (Mr. Savage's Gleanings.) He had, at Wat., 6. JOHN, b. Aug. 15, 1635, Deac. at Wat., and f. by w. Sary, at Wat., of *John*, 1666 ; *Samuel*, 1674 ; and several daughters. He d. Mar. 26, 1691. 7. ELIZABETH, b. Ap. 5, 1639. Simon, the f. took the freeman's oath, May 25, 1636, and was deac. at Wat. He m. 2d, Sarah, wid. of Richard Lumkin, of Ipswich, who d. 1663. (Inventory, £570.) In her will, she refers to kinsmen John and Daniel Warner, and Thomas Wells. Simon, the f. d. at Wat., Sep. 22, 1665, æ. ab. 80. (T. Rec.) His will was proved Oct. 3, 1665. Inventory, £127.17.

42. SIMON, s. of Simon (41), m. Mary (Whipple), and had, 1. JOHN, b. July 23, 1658 ; 2. MATTHEW,⁴³ b. Feb. 16, '59-0 ; 3. NATHANIEL, b. and d. Feb., '61-2 ; 4. EBENEZER,⁴³ b. Feb. 27, '62-3 ; 5. MARY, b. Jan. 6, '64 ; 6. NATHANIEL, Har. Coll., 1690, ord. at Harwich, (now Brewster) m. a dr. of Gov. Hinckley, d. ab. 1755, æ. 88, and was f. of *Hannah; Nathan*, H. Coll., 1726, ord. at Southb ;* *Nathaniel ; Mary ; Reliance ; Thankful ; Aresa ; Keziah ; Eunice ;* and *Huldah ;* 7. ELIZABETH, b. Oct. 9, '70 ; 8. DAVID, b. Oct. 19, '72, m. Mary Rice, 1710 ; 9. ——, b. and d. 1674 ; 10. SUSANNA, b. Nov. 4, '75, m. Edward Goddard, Esq.; 11. JONATHAN, b. Dec. 26, '77, m. Ruth Eddy, '99 and others. Simon, the f. was representative from Wat., in 1678 and 1679, and d. Feb. 27, 1707-8. His w. Mary d. 1720.

43. MATTHEW, s. of Simon (42) was of Lancaster, 1693, and in 1697, of Sud., when he exchanged lands with Isaac Lewis, of Rumney Marsh, receiving rights, &c., at Lancaster. He was deac. of the church, and d. at Sud.; his will proved Aug. 9, 1743. He had a w. Mary, and chil. 1. JOSEPH ; 2. ADAMS, m. Sarah Wight, 1717, and had at Sud., (where he was deac.), *Benjamin*, b. Feb. 20, 1717-8, m. Beulah Fisk, '37, and d.

---

* NATHAN, b. at Harwich, Feb. 18, 1708, was ordained at Southb., Oct. 21, 1730, and d. May 31, 1781. (G. Stone.) His chil. by w. Judith were *Nathaniel*, b. Sep. 3, 1735, d. 1759 ; *Reliance*, b. Oct. 22, '36 ; *Nathan*, b. Sep. 30, '37 ; *Huldah*, b. Dec. 19, '38 ; *Judith*, b. July 12, '40, d. 1771 ; *Mary*, b. July 23, '42 ; *Hannah*, b. Ap. 21, '44 ; *John*, b. June 22, '45 ; *Joanna*, b. Ap. 22, '47·; and by a 2d w. Mary, *Thomas*, b. May 1, 1752, m. Lydia Twitchell, '76, and moved E. ; *Peter*, b. Nov. 28, 1757. Rev. N.'s w. Judith, d. Feb. 9, 1748-9, æ. 36. JONATHAN, of Southb. m. Judith Newton, Sep. 21, 1737, and had, *James*, d. young ; *Judith*, b. Dec., 1740, d. in Sud., unm. ; *Abigail*, b. June 5, '43 ; *Jonathan*, b. May 3, '46, disordered in mind ; *Rachel*, b. Ap. 7, '49 ; *Joseph*, b. Mar. 28, '52 ; *James*, b. Feb. 23, '55. Jonathan, the f. d. ab. 1772.

STONE.

1745, (f. of Benjamin, Lucy, and Sarah); *Bathshebah*, b. 1721, m. Ezek. How, '44; *Elizabeth*, b. 1723, m. Nathaniel Rice, '41; *Isaac*, b. Feb. 18, '35-6, m. Sarah Moulton, '57. Deac. Adams m. 2d, wid. Hannah Barber. 3. MARY; 4. RACHEL, m. Thomas Cobb, of Barnstable, June 1, 1710.

43. EBENEZER, s. of Simon (42), m. Margaret Trowbridge, 1686, and had, 1. EBENEZER, b. Dec. 21, '86, m. Sarah Bond, 1713, and f. at Wat., of *Josiah, William, Nathan*, &c., and d. 1784, æ. 97; 2. MARGARET, b. Aug. 1, 1688, m. Nathaniel Hammond, and d. at Newton, 1776, æ. 88; 3. SAMUEL,[44] b. July 1, 1690; 4. JOHN,[45] b. Sep. 18, 1692; 5. NATHANIEL, b. Sep. 6, '94, d. 1713; 6. MINDWELL, b. June 26, '96, m. Eben. Woodward, 1716, and d. '74; 7. DAVID, b. May 15, '98, d. 1725; 8. MARY, b. Ap. 19, 1700. [A M. m. at Newton, Dan. Woodward, May 16, 1739]; 9. SIMON, b. Sep. 14, 1702, and d. 1760, m. Priscilla Dike, 1732, (who d. 1760), and f. of *Ephraim*; *James*, m. Sarah Billings, of Lincoln, Dec. 31, 1767; and several daughters; 10. JAMES, b. June 8, 1704, H. Coll., 1724, school master in Fram., 1725, ord. at Holl., Nov. 20, 1728, m. Elizabeth, dr. of Rev. J. Swift, of Fram., Ap. 15, 1731, who d. Ap. 12, 1739, æ. 35. He d. July 28, 1742, æ. 38, (G. Stones), f. of *John*, Esq., b. June 21, 1732, and d. in Fram., Aug. 1, 1817, æ. 85, (f. at Holl., by w. Mary, who d. Oct. 1, 1809, æ. 77, of James, b. 1754; John, m. Rebecca Sanger, of Fram., Oct. 23, 1796, and Sarah, m. John Bent, of Fram., and d. Sep., 1843, æ. 83); *Elizabeth*, b. May 13, 1735; *Nevinson*, b. Mar. 17, 1737; 11. EXPERIENCE, m. Joseph Ward, 1733, and d. in Spencer. Margaret, w. of Eb., d. May 4, 1710. He m. 2d, Abigail ——, (prob. Wilson), who d. 1723, and he m. 3d, wid. Sarah Livermore, Ap. 8, 1722, who d. 1741. The Hon. Ebenezer, was a man of much influence, and held many public offices. A letter, in the author's possession, from him, to his br. in-law, E. Goddard, Esq., dated Feb. 27, 1748, (his 85th birth day), is written in a good and firm hand.

44. SAMUEL, s. of Eben. (43), m. Hannah Searle, of Roxb., in Wat., May 21, 1716; and had in Fram., 1. HANNAH, b. Ap. 29, 1717, m. William Marean, Jr., of Newton, 1737; 2. MARY, b. Jan. 23, 1718-9, m. Daniel Woodward, Jr., of Newton, 1739; 3. ESTHER, b. Aug. 3, 1721, m. Ebenezer Hammond, and lived near Oxford, 1748; 4. MATTHIAS, b. Oct. 21, 1723, m. at Worcester, Susanna Chadwick, 1749, and f. at W., of *Priscilla*, b. 1753; *Susanna*, 1755; 5. NEHEMIAH, b. Oct. 24, 1724, m. in Newton, Hannah Lock, 1748, and lived at the "Country Gore," near Oxford. Hannah the m., d. Nov. 4, 1724 (T. Rec.) and Sam. m. 2d, Mary Haven, Nov. 25, 1725, and had a posthumous s., 6. SAMUEL, b. Oct. 5, 1727, d. æ. ab. 20. Samuel, Jr., the f., d. in Fram., Aug. 30, 1726. (T. Rec.) His wid. Mary m. Ephraim Ward, of Newton, Sep. 24, 1734. The f's est. (bounded on Deac. J. Adams), was sold by the heirs to Hezekiah Rice, 1748. Samuel was Selectman in Fram., 1722, 3 years.

45. JOHN, s. of Eben. (43), m. Lydia Hydes, of Newton, 1717, and was with w. adm. to the ch., July 20, 1718. They had 1. MARGARET, b. Oct. 24, 1718. Lydia, the m., d. Nov. 3,

1718. (T. Rec. Mr. Swift's Journal notes, Nov. 4, "John Stone's wife dying.") The f. m. 2d, Abigail Stratten, of Wat., Nov. 4, 1719, and had 2. ABIGAIL, b. Sep. 2, 1720; 3. JONAS, b. Sep. 5, 1722, m. Anne Stone, 1745, became a Deacon and was f. at Newton of *Samuel*, b. 1747, (m. Elizabeth Clark, 1774, and f. at Petersham, of Hannah, Samuel, Clark, Betty, Sally, and Gardner); *Jonas*, b. 1749, m. Martha Winchester, '75; *Seth*, b. 1751, (m. 1st, Esther Clark, 1775, had at Petersham, Norman; Eben., d. young; Moses; and Aaron; m. 2d, Zerviah Bragg, 1784, and had Lydia and Ebenezer; m. 3d, Sally Parling, 1791); *Amos*, b. 1753, Deac. at Petersham, and d. June 19, 1802, æ. 50; his w. Anna d. Feb. 6, 1788, æ. 34, and he m. 2d, Susanna Hawes, 1789. His chil., Samuel, d. young; Nancy, m. Jonas Tower, and d. young; *Anna*, b. 1755; *Ebenezer*, (m. Mindwell Richardson, 1788), and *Aaron*, twins, b. 1759; and *Sarah*, b. 1760; 4. on Newton Records, LYDIA, b. 1724, m. Jacob Chamberlain, of Worc., 1744; 5. ABIGAIL, b. Ap. 24, '26; 6. DAVID, b. Sep. 24, '28; 7. MINDWELL, b. Jan. 25, '30-1; 8. SARAH, b. Mar. 30, '33; 9. ANNA, b. 1734; 10. JOHN, b. Jan. 12, '36-7, m. Martha Craft, 1762. Deac. John, the father, d. at Newton, 1765; his w. Abigail d. 1788. John and w. were dismissed from Fram. to Newton ch., Sep. 27, 1724.

46. JAMES, (s. of John, Esq., of Holl., see No. 43), m. Deborah, dr. of David Rice, of Fram., and with w. cov'd, Feb. 1782. Their chil. were 1. POLLY, b. June 20, 1781; 2. HANNAH, (Hop. Rec.), b. 1783; 3. NATHAN, bap. in F., Nov., 1789; 4. NEVENSON, bap. Oct., 1794, m. Polly Haven. James, the f. moved to Northboro'. Anne, wid. of James, d. Jan. 1846, æ. 84.

47. JOSEPH*, m. Lydia Parkhurst, of Weston, Ap. 11, 1723, and had in Fram., 1. LYDIA, b. Jan. 15, 1723-4; 2. ABIGAIL, b. Feb. 3, 1724-5, m. Matthias Bent, Feb. 26, '46; 3. LUCY, b. Jan. 17, '27-8; 4. LUCY, (or Lucia), b. Jan. 17, '27-8, m. Job

---

* Joseph was s. of Joseph, of Lex., who d. Jan. 17, 1702-3, æ. 32, and his estate was settled, Dec. 13, 1705, leaving w. Sarah, and chil. *Isaac, Lydia, Joseph, Abigail, Sarah*, and *Tabitha*. Jos., sen., was prob. g. son of Samuel, s. of Gregory, who, in a deed, names his s. Joseph's son Joseph. JOSEPH, of Lex., whose will was proved May 21, 1753, (his w. Mary, and chil. *Ephraim*, of Stow, *Joseph*, of Brookfield, *Samuel, James*, of Weston, *Sarah*, m. Jonas Stone, *Marcy*, or Mary, m. William Keyes, *Dorcas*, m. Benj. Stow, *Elizabeth*, m. Benj. Lamson, ——, m. Josiah Shattuck), was prob. s. of Deac. Samuel, of Lexington, and g. s. of Samuel, s. of Gregory.

Cushing of Shrewsb., (s. of Rev. J.), Feb. 20, 1752, and was dism'd to Shrewsb. ch. Nov. 19, '52. Job kept a publick house at S.; 5. KEZIAH, b. May 19, 1730; 6. JOSEPH, b. Aug. 27, '31, built at Mr. Cornelius Morse's, and prob. d. without issue at Harvard; 7. ISAAC[48], b. Ap. 10, 1735; 8. SUBMIT, b. June 30, '38, m. Samuel Mellen; 9. MARTHA, b. Mar. 18, '41, m. Oliver Miles, of Concord; 10. PURCHASE, b. July 24, 1744; 11. NATHAN, b. Aug. 14, '46, m. Eunice Stone, dr. of Deac. Daniel, and f. at Nat. of *William*, b. Dec. 18, 1774, m. Betsey Fisk, '96; *Hitty*, b. May 10, '77, m. Wm. Johnson, 1796; *Nathan*, b. Aug. 11, '79, m. Betsey Stone, of Fram., Nov. 21, 1805, and lives in F. ; *Polly*, b. 1782; *Nancy*, '84; *Joseph*, '89; *Lucy*, '92. Lt. Nathan, d. at Nat., July 3, 1793. Joseph, Jun., of Lexington, was a blacksmith, and in 1719, bought 150 ac. in F., at Indian Head, and was Selectman 1732, 3 years. He lived at Mr. Abner Wheeler's, and d. in Fram., near 1780.

48. ISAAC, s. of Jos. (47), m. Persis Howe, Sep. 28, 1763, and with w. cov'd Mar. 11, '64, and adm. May, '81. Their chil. were 1. PERSIS, bap. Ap. 8, '64, d. young; 2. PURCHASE[49], b. Nov. 25, '65; 3. JOHN, b. Dec. 10, '67, d. unm.; 4. PERSIS, b. Dec. 4, '70, m. Isaac Damon, of E. Sud.; 5. ISAAC, b. Mar. 9, '73, m. Grace Whiting, was lately living in Quincy; 6. JOSEPH, b. Nov. 17, '74, m. Sarah (Briar?), an Englishwoman; 7. DAVID, and 8. PETER, twins, b. Ap. 4, '77, both d. in the Provinces; 9. REBECKAH, bap. Aug. 1, '79, m. Samuel Hemenway, 2d, Aug. 16, 1801, d. in N. Y. June 11, 1840, and buried in Fram. Isaac, the f. lived at Mr. Abner Wheeler's, and d. Jan. 5, 1815, æ. 79 y. 8 m. (G. S.) His w. Persis d. May 7, 1806, æ. 62 y. 5 m.

49. PURCHASE, s. of Isaac (48), m. Lois Damon, and had, 1. MARSHALL, b. Jan. 14, 1790, m. Betsey Haven (dr. of Timo.), and d. 1828; 2. SEWALL, b. Dec. 10, '91, d. æ. 4; 3. BUCKLEY, b. Ap. 18, '93, m. Mary Pierce, of Boston, and lives in Fram.; 4. PERSIS, b. Aug. 29, '95, m. Nathaniel Parker, of Shrewsb., lives in Canada. The f. moved to Wayland, near Fram., (where he now lives), ab. 1800, and had 5. LUCY, m. John A. Ingraham; 6. EVELINE, m. —— Munro, of Vt.; 7. SUSAN, m. Eph. Farwell; 8. GEO. WASHINGTON, d. unm. prob. in S. C.

50. DAVID, s. of David* and w. Mary of Sud., m. Elizabeth Bent, Oct. 17, 1771, and had in Fram., 1. BETSEY, b. Oct. 18, 1772, lives unm.; 2. AARON, b. Aug. 30, '74, m. 1st, Elizabeth Cutting, and 2d, Sally Cutting; 3. EPHRAIM, b. Dec. 16, '76. David, the f. lived at Mr. Charles Fiske's, d. young, and his wid. m. again.

51. THOMAS, lived in Fram., and according to tradition was killed in the French war. He had, 1. THOMAS, who lived N. of Deac. Moses Haven, where is a cellar hole, and d. unm. ab. 1814, at an advanced age; 2. SARAH, unm., lived with her brother, and d. Nov. 24, 1829, æ. 90. The m. lived many years with Thomas, Jun. The family were eccentric in their habits.

52. JOSEPH, was bap. Mar. 30, 1718. EBENEZER, bap. Oct. 12, 1718. HANNAH, adm. to the ch. May 17, 1717. ABIGAIL, adm. Mar. 31, 1728. SUBMIT, bap. May 2, 1762. MARY adm. to the ch. July 5, 1772.

53. DANIEL, (w. Mary), was of Boston, 1658. DANIEL, of do., 1680, Chirurgeon, sold house and land in Camb. to Sam. Andrews. NICHOLAS, Ship Carpenter, (w. Hannah) had at Bos., *Josiah*, 1653, &c. (his dr. *Mary* m. Isaac Johnson, of Charlestown, 1671). NATHANIEL, (w. Hannah), of Bos. had *Benjamin*, 1663. JOHN, (w. Mary), of Boston, 1659. Wid. Mary m. Roger Wheeler, in Boston, Nov. 23, 1659. JOHN, of Hull, N E., died 1659—left by will to w. Jane, and £60 to his br. Simon's chil., "which some time lived in Cousingstone, Somersetshire, O. E." ROBERT, (w. Sarah), had at Salem, *Samuel*, 1657, *Robert*, *Benjamin*, &c. SAMUEL m. (at Beverly?) Elizabeth Herrick, Mar. 2, 1657. ELIAS, (w. Abigail) had chil. at Charlestown from 1687. There were Stones at Rowley, before 1700. THOMAS and others were of Roxb., 1639. HUGH, of Andover, had *John*, 1668, &c. DANIEL m. at Hop., Mary Wood, Jan. 11, 1726, and had *Josiah*, b. July 29, 1730; *Daniel*, Dec. 6, '32; *Benjamin*, bap. 1743; *Sarah*, do. June '45; *Samuel*, do. June '51. Daniel sold, in 1725, land and house in Hop., to Sam. Kendall, of Wob. Daniel and w. were rec'd at Hop. from Westboro', 1747, and dismissed to N. Braintree, 1761. JOHN, the architect of Charles River Bridge, d. 1791, æ. 62.*

STOWELL, ABIJAH, had bap. in F., June, 1784, SAMUEL, DAVID, SALLY, and POLLY; Ap. 1785, ASA; Oct. 1787, ISAAC. "Mr. Stowell moved away, Ap. 10, 1786," [Deac. Buckmin-

---

*David d. at Sud., Feb. 6, 1801, æ. 84. He m. Mary Moore, May 24, 1743, and was f. of *Lydia*, d. young; *John*, b. 1745, lived in Wayland; *David*, b. May 13, 1747, of Fram.; *Joel*, b. '51, m. Sarah Stone, and Hannah Adams; *Deborah*, m. Rufus Babcock; *Mary*, d. unm., æ. over 70.

† The family of Stone is numerous in Eng. Berry gives the genealogy of THOMAS, of Framfield, Essex, whose s. *Nicholas* had chil. from 1620. Sir WILLIAM, Knight, was of London, before 1600. JOHN, of London, was f. of *Andrew*, whose son Symon was counsellor at the Middle Temple, prob. before 1600. (Sussex and Kent Genealogies.)

ster's Journal.) He moved prob. into N. H., and is spoken of by the aged, as a pious and worthy man.

STRATTON, REBECCA, m. Jabez Pratt, Mar. 31, 1726. ELIZABETH, m. to Abraham Temple, both of Marlb., Ap. 12, 1732. SAMUEL, of Mendon, m. Mary Walker, Nov. 17, 1737. SAMUEL, rated in Fram., 1760.

JOSEPH, (w. Sarah), of Marlb., had *Joseph*, b. 1696; *Sarah*, 1700; *Elizabeth*, '10; *Jonathan*, '14. JABEZ, of Sherb., (w. Tabitha Coolidge, m. at Wat., 1725), had *Ebenezer*, b. 1742. ABIJAH, of Sherb., m. Mary Learned, June 3, 1747, and had in Nat., *Jonathan, Abijah, Samuel*. This family were early in Wat. and Concord.

STREATER, or STREETER, SAMUEL, m. Experience Haven, July 27, 1719, and with w. cov. May 14, 1721. They had 1. JOSEPH, bap. May 14, 1721; and on Hop. Rec., EXPERIENCE, bap. 1728; REBECCA, b. Nov. 24, '32; JAMES, '34; SUSANNA, '37; DANIEL, '39; JONATHAN, '41; and MERCY, '43. Sam., the f. moved to Hop. He bought, May, 1742, the place now occupied in Hop. by Mr. Augustus Phipps, T. Clerk, and sold the same, 1745, to Tho. Butler. Sam. and w. were dismissed from Hop. to Sutton ch., 1747.

2. STEPHEN, and w. Katharine, cov. in Fram., Feb. 7, 1725; and had, 1. ESTHER, b. Jan. 13, 1724–5, m. Josiah Haven, Feb. 28, '44; 2. STEPHEN, b. Feb. 14, '26–7; 3. ABIGAIL, b. Jan. 15, '28–9; 4. ELIZABETH, b. Jan. 9, '29–0; 5. JOHN, b. Feb. 14, '31–2; 6. URSULA, b. Nov. 9, '33; 7. ADAMS, b. Dec. 31, 1735. Stephen, the f. prob. lived at the N. part of Fram., where is a cellar hole, on the farm of the late Mr. John Eaton.

3. MARY, adm. from Reading to the ch., Sep. 24, 1721. DEBORAH, m. Jedidiah Belknap, ab. 1730.

STEPHEN, took the freeman's oath, May 29, 1644, and with w. Ursula was rec'd to the Charlestown ch., Oct. 21, 1652; and had there *Hannah*, b. 1644. His will was executed ab. 1681? (See Mid. Deeds, VII). He left w. Ursula, and chil., STEPHEN, SAMUEL, and JOHN. STEPHEN and w. Rebecka, were of Muddy River, 1679. STEPHEN, and w. Deborah had at Wat., *Stephen*, b. June 20, 1667; *Sary*, Oct. 2, '69; and at Camb., *Rebeckah*, 1683; *Deborah*, '85; *Joseph*, '87; *Benjamin*, '89, d. 1690. Deborah the m., d. 1689. JOHN, (w. Mary), had at Camb., Hannah, 1700. SAMUEL, (w. Mary), had at Concord, *Judah*, 1666; *John*, d. '67; *John*, b. 1671; and *Eleazer*, 1668.

SWIFT, JOHN, m. Sarah, (b. Sep. 7, 1671), dr. of Timothy Tileston, of Dorchester, and w. Sarah; and had, 1. SARAH, b. Sep. 16, 1702, adm. to the ch. Mar. 24, 1728, m. Eben. Roby, of Sud. June 6, 1729. She had deceased before 1745; 2. ELIZ-

ABETH, b. Mar. 26, 1704, adm. to the ch. Mar. 24, 1728, m. Rev. James Stone, of Holl., Ap. 15, 1731, and d. Ap. 12, 1739; 3. ANNE, b. July 5, 1706, m. Rev. Philips Payson, of Walpole, Dec. 5, 1733; 4. MARY, b. Nov. 16, 1708, unm. 1745; 5. JOHN, b. Jan. 14, 1713-4, H. Coll., 1733, and school-master in Fram. the same year. He was ord. at Acton, m. Abigail Adams, of Medway, and had son *John*, H. Coll, 1762, Physician at Acton, and d. of small pox, 1775. Rev. John of Acton d. of small pox, Nov. 7, 1775, æ. 61, and in the 37th year of his ministry — (Shat. Hist. of Concord); 6. MARTHA, m. Maj. John Farrar, of Fram., Oct. 13, 1740, and d. ab. 1749. Rev. John, of Fram., d. Ap. 24, 1745, æ. 66, and in the 45th year of his ministry; (see Hist.) His will was proved in May. He left a considerable estate, and gave to his son his Library, and his rights of land in Dorchester, Canada, "derived on account of his br. Wm. Swift, who perished in the first expedition against Canada." The witnesses of the will were Wm. Pike, Stephen Ballard, and Mary Farrar. Sarah, his w. d. Feb. 1, 1747, æ. 73.

THOMAS, came over with the first settlers of Dorchester, in 1630, and took the freeman's oath, May 6, 1635. He signed the ch. covenant, 1636. His chil. were 1. THOMAS, b. May (or June) 17, 1634 (or '35); 2. JOAN, m. John Baker, Nov. 5, 1657; 3. OBADIAH, b. July 16. '38, m. Rest, dr. of Maj. Humphrey Atherton, Mar. 15, 1660, (or '61), and d. Dec. 27, 1690, f. of *Rest, Obadiah, Hopestill, Elizabeth, Elizabeth, Abigail,* and *Elizabeth;* 4. ELIZABETH, b. June 11, (or Ap. 20). 1640; 5. RUTH, b. July 2, (or Aug. 24), 1643, m. William Greenow, Oct. 10, 1660; 6. MARY, b. Sep. 21, 1645, m. John White, Jan. 11, 1663-4; 7. ANNA, b. Nov. 14, 1647; 8. SUSANNA, b. Feb. 11, 1651, m. Hopestill Clap, Ap. 18, 1672. Thomas, Sen., d. May 4, 1675, æ. 76, and his will was proved, July 30; in it he names his brs. in-law, Wm. Sumner, and John Capen. His w. Elizabeth d. Jan. 26, (G. Stone, May 30), 1677, æ. 67.

THOMAS, Jun., was a member of the ch. of Milton, when gathered, 1678. He m. Elizabeth, dr. of Robert Vose, Dec. 9, 1657; and had THOMAS, b. July 30. 1659; ELIZABETH; WILLIAM, b. May 5, 1670, d. in the first expedition to Canada; JOHN, b. 1678, [Mar. 14, 1678-9,] of Fram.; SAMUEL, b. 1683, was commissioned as Col., and chosen Representative; he d. Oct. 13, 1747, æ. 64; *Ebenezer*. third son of Col. Samuel, d. at Fram. The Rev. Mr. Swift notices in his Journal, that his f. was buried Feb. 3, 1717-8, and the next day his mother died.* Tho. prob. m. 2d, Sarah Clap, Oct. 16, 1676.

---

* For several of the above particulars, the author is indebted to the late Rev. Dr. Harris. On revising the minutes of the latter, in connection with the author's own notes, several discrepancies were discovered, which will be noticed above, the author's memoranda, in those instances, being inclosed in brackets. Dr. H. noted, that Tho., sen., m. Elizabeth Vose, 1657, and that his dr. Ruth, d. Nov. 16, 1657.

2. EBENEZER, of Fram., (prob. g. son of Col. Samuel — see the note above) m. Martha Rice of Nat., 1775, and d. in Fram., Sep. 3, 1775, æ. 23. (G. Stone.) EBENEZER, m. Sally Greenwood, Sep. 7, 1800, and lived at Unionville, where he d.

TAYLOR. Capt. Taylor is referred to as in Fram., 1759. EZRA do., 1760. [EZRA Esq., and w. Abigail, were of Southb., f. of *Ezra*, b. 1743, &c. JOHN, Jun., was adm. to Hop. ch. 1741.]

TEMPLE, THOMAS, had by w. Sarah, 1. THOMAS, b. Jan. 29, 1738; 2. HANANIAH, b. Oct. 12, '40, m. Elizabeth Learned, and d. in Orange, ab. 1820; 3. JOSIAH, b. Ap. 10, '42; 4. RICHARD, b. Ap. 18, '44; 5. SARAH, b. Ap. 14, '46, m. —— Tucker, and d. in N. H.; 6. JOSEPH, b. Oct. 9, '48; 7. PHEBE, b. Ap. 1, '50, m. —— Newton, of Southb., and d. in N. Marlb.; 8. JONATHAN, b. Feb. 17, '52, d. in Westminster, Vt., ab. 1806; 9. EBENEZER, b. Mar. 15, '54, m. Olive ——, and d. in Marlb. N. H.

Thomas, the f. is said to have originated at Reading, and came to Fram. ab. 1745. He first lived near Eph. Hager's, and after at Mr. Wm. P. Temple's. He was Selectman, 1760, 12 years, and T. Treasurer, 1767, 2 years. He was a prominent member of Mr. Reed's ch., of which there are indications of his having been chosen Deacon; but he probably declined. (Mss. letter.) He d. in Fram., Feb. 28, 1773, æ. 58. (G. Stone.) His w. Sarah d. June 20, 1768. (T. Rec.)

2. THOMAS, s. of Tho. (1), m. Martha (Brewer), who cov. Jan. 24, 1782. Their chil. on record are, 1. ANNE, b. May 26, 1761; 2. ARABELLA, b. Feb. 24, '62; 3. NICANOR, b. Mar. 29, '64.

3. JOSIAH, s. of Tho. (1), m. Elizabeth Pitts, of Camb., (b. in Townsend), and was with w. adm. from the ch. in Camb., Feb. 1789. They had at Camb., 1. JOSIAH, d. unm. Nov. 17, 1800, æ. 28, (G. Stone); 2. JOHN, m. Abigail Johnson of Southb.; and at F., 3. THOMAS, b. Nov. 24, '75; 4. ELIZABETH, b. Ap. 2, '78, d. unm., 1798; 5. DAVID, b. Aug. 15, '80, d. unm., May 7, 1800; 6. POLLY, b. July 11, '82, m. Moses M. Fisk, of Knoxville, Tenn., Sep., 25, 1803, and d., 1806; 7. ELIAS, b. Aug. 8, '85, m. Olive Fisk, Selectman, 1829, 4 years, Representative, 1833, and T. Clerk from 1832, 15 years; 8. NELLY, b. May 13, '87, d. unm., 1810; 9. WILLIAM PITTS, b. Oct. 17, '89, m.

Betsey How. Lt. Josiah, the f. lived where his son William P. does, and d. Oct. 5, 1824. His w. Elizabeth d. July 2, 1829, æ. 83.

4. THOMAS, s. of Josiah (3), m. Ruth Littlefield, Nov. 30, 1797, had ELIZA, b. Ap. 27, 1798, and the f. d. Aug. 27, 1798, æ. 22. (G. Stone.) [RUTH, m. Luther Rockwood, of Holl., Dec. 22, 1806].

RICHARD, of Charlestown, had by w. Joanna, *Abigail*, b. 1647, m., at Concord, Tho. Babcocke, '69; *Richard*, 1654; *Isaac*, 1657; Joanna, w. of Richard. d. at Concord, 1689. Richard and w. Sarah, of Concord, had *Richard*, b. 1692, d. 1705; *Joseph*, 1694. Richard d. at Concord, Feb. 16, 1698. ABRAHAM, of Concord, m. Deborah Hadlock, 1673, and had, *Richard*; *Abigail*; *Mary*; and *Joseph*, m. Abigail Sterns, 1717. ABRAHAM, m. Elizabeth Stratton, both of Marlb., in Fram., Ap. 12, 1732, and had in M., *Joseph*, b. 1732; *Jonathan*, '35, m. Dorothy Morse. '60; *Sarah*, 1737. RICHARD, (w. Deborah), of Reading, had *Thomas*, b. 1696; *Jonathan*, '99; *John*, 1704; *Elizabeth*, '06; *Jabez*, '09; *Ebenezer*, '16. The f. of Richard is said to have been killed at Biddeford. ABRAHAM is on Salem Rec., 1637.

THAYER, LEVI, claimed the Brinley Farm, 1785, and had the possession of it.

THOMAS, JOHN, was in Fram., 1716.

THOMSON, ——, owned the farm of Mr. Cornelius Morse, and was buried, May 18, 1787; he left no issue. MILISCENT METCALF m. Martin Haven, both of Fram., Aug. 29, 1794. WILLIAM HENRY, b. Nov. 16, 1799, (in Boston), was taken by Mr. Joel Coolidge to bring up. (T. Rec.)

TILESTON, or TILESTONE, ANNE, m. John Stone, both of Fram., Jan. 31, 1706-7.

Anne was dr. of TIMOTHY, of Dorch., Cooper, and Representative, 1689, who m. Sarah ——, Ap. 28, 1659, and had, *Timothy*, (w. Hannah); *Elizabeth*, b. Mar. 29, 1666; *Cornelius*, Sep. 4, '68; *Sarah*, Sep. 7, '71, m. Rev. J. Swift, of Fram.; *Thomas*, Oct. 19, '75; *James*, July 2, '78; *Anne*, Dec. 7, '81. The father's est. was divided, 1698, (Suff. Prob.) THOMAS took the freeman's oath, Mar. 9, 1636-7.

TINDY, CUFF, was in Fram., 1795. He was servant to Dr. Jones, of Hop.

TITAS, CATO, rated in Fram., ab. 1770.

TOMBS, or TOMMS, NATHAN, m. Hannah Newton, Nov. 29, 1792, and had, 1. DEXTER, b. Jan. 29, '95, d. a young man; 2. SUKEY, b. Jan. 17, '97, m. Abijah Hemenway; 3. REBECCA, b. Sep. 19, '99, m. Jonas Bacon; 4. HOLLIS, b. Dec. 4, 1801, drowned, a young man; 5. ZOBIDY, b. Nov. 20, 1803, m. Jabez Tombs, and —— Hayden, of Milford; 6. EMILY, m. —— Clark, of Medway. Nathan, the f. lived between Salem End and Unionville, and d. 1842. His w. Hannah, d. Aug. 1834.

DANIEL, of Hop., m. Elizabeth Coller, 1739; and had, 1. ELIZABETH, bap. 1743, m. John How, of Fram., Dec. 10, '63; 2. LUCRETIA, bap. 1745, prob. d. young; 3. DANIEL; 4. JOSEPH, b. 1751, d. in Hop., 1831, æ. 80, m. Mary Homer, who d. 1835, æ. 71, having had *Joseph, Mary, Elizabeth, Hannah, Michael,* (of Boston), *Ebenezer, Abiah B., Jonathan H.,* and *Fanny;* 5. WILLIAM, m. Anne Clark; 6. EBENEZER, bap. 1760; 7. MARY, m. Amasa How; 8. HANNAH, m. Joseph Flagg; 9. NATHAN, of Fram.; 10. ABIGAIL, m. John Hayden; the last 2, by a 2d w., Patience Rice. Daniel the f. is supposed to have emigrated to N. E., and settled in Hop., where he d. Mar. 27, 1804, æ. 90. Mrs. Tombs d. May, 1795, "an aged woman." (Hop. Rec.)

TOMLING, —, and child warned out of town, 1744. (T Rec.)

TORREY, REUBEN, came to Fram., ab. 1800, and d. there. His dr. ABIGAIL m. —— Ballard.

TOWER, JOSEPH, (s. of Joseph and Rebecca, of Southb.), m. Lucia Stone, (dr. of James), cov. June 20, 1773, and his w. adm. to the ch., July, 1781. They had, 1. EUNICE, b. Sep. 3, 1772, m. Jona. Goodnow, and d. Nov. 14, 1832; 2. LUCY, b. May 25, 1778, lives unm. [2 sons of Joseph d. young.] Joseph, the f. lived at Mr. Charles Trowbridge's, and elsewhere, and d. Feb. 26, 1812, æ. 64; his w. L. d. Dec. 1835, æ. 81.

JOSEPH, of Sud., m. Hephzibah Gibbs, 1748, and had *Thankful, Joseph, Isaac, Jeduthan, Jonathan,* and *Molly.* AMBROSE, of Sud., m. Jerusha Clap, 1751, and 2d, Elizabeth Davis, 1782, and was f. by 1st w. of *Silas, Silence, Asahel, Abel, Mary, Sarah, Jerusha,* and *Daniel.* BENJAMIN, (w. Anne), of Sud., had chil. from 1762.

TOWN, or TOWNE, JACOB, of Topsfield, m. Katharine Symons, June 26, 1657; and had, 1. JACOB, d. 1659; 2. JOHN, b. 1658; 3. JACOB, m. Phebe Smith, June 24, 1684, f. of *Joshua,* b. '84; *John,* '85; *Abigail,* '89; 4. KATHARINE, b. Feb. 25, '61, m. Elisha Perkins, Feb. 23, '80; 5. DELIVERANCE, b. Aug. 5, '64, m. John Stiles, '84; 6. EDMOND, b. July 21, '66; 7. RUTH. Jacob's will was proved, Jan. 1, 1704–5. Inventory, £196.2.6. (Essex Prob.)

Note. — Besides Jacob, there were at Tops., EDWARD, had *William,* b. 1658. SARAH, m. Edmond Bridges, Jan. 11, 1659. EDMOND, m. Mary, dr. of Thomas Browning, and had *Thomas,* m. Sarah French, 1685, and d. ab. 1720, (f. of Edmond, Thomas, Richard, Experience, Sarah, Ednah and Mercy); *Joseph,* b. 1661, m. Phebe —, and 2d, Eamy Smith, '87, and d. 1717, (f. of Benj., Daniel, Nathan, Jesse, Nath'l, Amos, and Emmy); *Abigail,* m. Jacob Peabody, '86; *Rebecca; William,* m. Margaret Willard, 1694; *Samuel; Mary; Sarah; Elizabeth.* JOSEPH, had *Phebe,* b. 1666; *Joanna; Mary; Susanna; Joseph,* b. Mar. 22, 1673; *Sarah; Martha.*

2. JOHN, s. of Jacob (1), had by w. Mary, at Topsfield, 1. MARY, b. June 23, 1681; 2. JOHN, b. Nov. 25, 1682, d.

young; 3. ISRAEL, b. Nov. 18, 1684; 4. ESTHER*, m. Simon
Mellen, of Fram., Ap. 23, 1711 ; 5. EPHRAIM, rated in Fram.,
1710 ; 6. DAVID, b. ab. 1694, his w. Priscilla d. at Oxford,
1741 ; his w. Margaret d. 1778, æ. 78. He d. at Belchertown,
Sep. 20, 1781, æ. 87. [Ox. Rec.] ; 7. SAMUEL ; [a Sam. m. at
Ox., Bathshebah Moors, 1743, and had *Lucie*, and *Samuel*] ; 8
EDMUND, b. (Fram. Rec.), May 7, 1699, and d. ab. 1745 — his
Inventory, £537 ; f. at Oxford, by w. Elizabeth, of *Edmund*, b.
1733, (4 others d. young), who m. Hannah Sparhawk, 1756,
(and had Zaccheus, Hannah) ; and *Elizabeth* — See Settlement
1755 ; 9. JOHN, b. at Fram., May 31, 1702, f. by w. Lydia at Oxf.
of *Thomas*, b. 1729 ; *Abner*, '31 ; *Isaac*, '33 ; *Febe*, '37, d. 1741 ;
Lidya, '40 ; *Rachel*, '42 ; *Hannah*, '44 ; *Simon*, '48 ; *Lydia*,
'52 ; 10. ZERVIAH, m. John Cloyes, of Fram. (his 2d w.), Nov.
22, 1748 ; 11. JONATHAN. [Katharine, w. of Deac. Jonathan,
d. at Oxford, 1757.]

John came to Fram. from Topsfield, and bought, 1707, of Col.
Buckminster, 211 1-2 ac., bounded E. by John Swift, elsewhere
on Moses Haven and Bare Hill. He occupied where Aaron Bullard has lived, and his house was prob. near there. He was
Selectman from 1700, to 1712, in all 3 years. He was dismissed
to form a ch. in Oxford, Jan. 15, 1721, and was one of the 4
who met at O. to form a church, and was the first Deacon chosen.
He was in 1713, a Grantee and Prop. of the Oxford Township.
His will was proved, 1740. (Worc. Prob.)

3. ISRAEL, s. of John (2), m. Susanna Haven, (dr. of Dea.
Moses), and had in Fram., 1. MARY, b. Nov. 16, 1709 ; 2. SU-
SANNA, b. Sep. 11, 1711; [Mr. Adams notes that Susanna m.
Deac. John Haven, and d. at Sutton, Oct., 1806, æ. 91 ; Haven
Gen.] ; 3. JOSEPH, b. Jan. 20, 1713, (d. young ; Haven Gen.) ;
and at Oxford, LOIS, b. May 18, 1729 ; [a Lois m. at O., John
Wilson, 1749.] Mr. Adams adds to the above, MOSES, who settled in Oxford, (prob. the Moses who m. Bethiah Reed, 1747, and
f. of *Joseph*, *Esther*, *Elias*, and *Sarah*) ; ELIJAH, who d. without
issue ; and ISRAEL, who removed to Belchertown. He adds that
one dr. of Israel, Sen., m. a Larned of Oxford, and d. æ. over
100, and another m. a Kingsbury of O. Israel came to Fram.,

---

* An Esther, b. 1686, is entered as daughter of John and Katharine.
Essex Co. Rec.)

prob. with his father ; and was also, in 1713, a Grantee and 'Proprietor of Oxford Township. The first church meeting at Oxford was held at his house. Ensign Israel d. at Oxford, Oct. 29, 1771, æ. 86. His wid., says Mr. Adams, moved to Belchertown, and d. Jan. or Feb., 1787, æ. 96. [EDMUND, of Hoosac Fort, m., in Fram., Abigail Brewer, Jan. 16, 1755.]

Note. — WILLIAM, of Camb., 1635, was chosen to register births, &c., 1639, and bought of David Stone a house, &c., 1653 ; he d. in Camb., 1685, æ. 80, and his w., Martha, d. 1673. They had *Peter*, bap. in England, (a cooper, had w. Joanna, 1687); and *Mary*, b. Sep., 1637.

TOWNSEND, JOSEPH, and w. Sarah, had in F., JERUSHA, b. May 29, 1717.

JOSEPH, of Southb. m. Hannah Bruce, May 3, 1731, and had, in Marlb., *Lydia*, b. 1731 ; *Joseph*, 1734.

2. JACOB, and w. Sarah, had in Fram., 1. SARAH, b. Sep. 12, 1731 ; 2. JACOB, b. Ap. 7, '36 ; 3. MARY, b. Jan. 22, '38 ; 4. NATHAN, b. Sep. 2, '42 ; 5. SAMUEL, b. Feb. 2, '44.

3. TIMOTHY, m. Hannah Foster, and had, (part entered at Hop.), 1. LOIS, b. June 11, 1738, m. in Hop., Isaac Gibbs, of Sud., 1755 ; 2. HANNAH, b. Jan. 7, 1740–1, m. in Hop., Nath'l Gibbs, Jun., of Sud., 1761 ; 3. JERUSHA, b. 1743, d. young ; 4. SARAH, b. 1746, m. Stephen Crossman ; 5. DEBORAH, b. 1748, m. Israel Walker ; 6. MARY, b. 1751, m. Jacob Chamberlain ; 7. ABIGAIL, bap. in Fram., July 9, 1754, m. Samuel Chamberlain ; 8. TIMOTHY, m. Priscilla Sanger, 1784, and f. of *Alanson, Pamela, Fanny,* and *Hannah,* d. young. Timothy, the f., prob. lived near Hop. and Fram. bounds, and was received at Hop. from the ch. in Fram., 1758.

MARTIN, of Wat., m. Abigail Trayne, 1668, who d. 1690. His est. was settled, 1712. His surviving chil. were, *Jonathan*, b. 27 April (or July), 1688 ; *Martin* ; and *Abigail*, b. Sep. 18, 1669, m. Nath'l Pratt. BENJAMIN, (w. Susanna), was of Westboro', 1721. NATHAN, (w. Sarah), had, at Westb., *Jacob*, 1768, *Nathan, John, Aaron, Samuel*.

TOZER, RICHARD, of Boston, m. Judith Smith, 1656, and had THOMAS, b. May 5, 1657. Farmer supposes him the Richard killed by the Indians, in Maine, according to Hubbard, in Oct., 1675, [WILLIAM, m., in Boston, Elizabeth Pickering, Sep. 22, 172(0).]

2. SIMON, and w. Mary, adm. to the ch. in Weston, 1710, had MARY, b. Aug. 16, 1693 ; JOHN, b. Oct., 1695, m. Experience Jackson, of Newton, 1718, and f. of *Mary*, b. 1720, m. Joseph Cheney, 1747 ; ABIGAIL, and RICHARD, twins, b. ab. 1700 ; SUSANNA, b. Jan., 1702 ; JUDITH, b. Jan., 1704. Simon, the f., d. ab. 1718, (see Inventory), and his wid. removed from Weston, 1719.

3. RICHARD, of Southb., s. of Simon (2), had by w. Elizabeth, 1. RICHARD, b. Oct. 13, 1732, m., in Fram., Mary Belknap, Feb. 14, '53, and f., at Southb., of *John*, b. Ap. 23, '54, m. Mary Fry, (and f., at N. Marlb., of John, Eben. and Ruth); *Mary*, b. May 14, '56; *Peter*, b. July 6, '58, went to Vt.; *Anna*, b. Sep. 30, '60; *Patty*, b. Oct. 26, '62; *Deborah*, b. Oct. 6, '64. Richard, Jun., prob. moved to Marlb., N. H., and had 9 chil. by a 2d w., Lydia Lewis. He is said to have had a br., a comb maker, at Rox.; 2. HANNAH, b. at Westh.. July 4, 1737; 3. THANKFUL, b. Oct. 22, 1739; 4. SIMON, b. Nov. 7, 1743. Richard, the f., and his w. Elizabeth, d. at N. Marlb.

4. SIMON, s. of Richard (3), m. Lydia Cloyes, and had, in Fram., 1. JOSIAH, b. Sep. 1, 1764, m. — Fay, and d. in Southb.; 2. OLIVE, bap. Jan. 21, 1770, m. Jonas Newton, Sep., 1786, and d. 1820 ; 3. LYDIA, m. Joel Brewer, of Southb., and d. ab. 1839. Simon and w. Lydia were adm. to the ch. Dec. 1, 1765.

TRAIN, TRAYNE or TRAINE, JOHN, of Wat., had by w. Margaret, 1. ELIZABETH, m. John Stratton, 1658; 2. REBECCA, m. — Basto; 3. MARY, b. 1642, m. — Memory; 4. SARAH, b. Jan. 31, '46–7, m. Jacob Cole, Oct. 12, 1679, (Charles. Rec.); 5. ABIGAIL, b. Jan. 31, '48–9, m. Martin Townson, 1668 ; 6. JOHN, b. May 25, '51 ; 7. HANNAH, b. Sep. 7, '57, m. Richard Child, 1678; 8. THOMAS, f. by w. Rebecca (Sterns, m. 1692–3), of *Benoni*, d. young ; *Deborah ;* and *Rebecca.* Margaret, the m., d. Dec. 18, 1660, æ. ab. 44; (T. Rec.) The f. m. 2d, Wid. Abigail Bent, 1675, who d. 1691. He came over in the Susan and Ellyn, 1634, then æ. 25, and in the same vessel came Margaret Dix, æ. 19,* He early took the oath of fidelity, at Wat., and in 1680, " was released from all ordinary traynings," (Co. Rec., III. 327.) He d. at Wat., 1681, and his will was proved, Ap. 4, of that year.

2. JOHN, s. of John (1), m. Mary Stubs, 1674, and had, at Wat., 1. JOHN, b. and d. 1675; 2. ABIGAIL, b. '77; 3. ELIZABETH, b. '79 ; 4. JOHN, b. '82 ; 5. MARY, b. '85; 6. THOMAS, b. '88. John, the f., d. in Weston, 1718.

3. JOHN, s. of John (2), m. Lydia, dr. of Samuel Jenison, 1705, and had at Wat., (Weston), 1. JOHN, b. Feb. 9, 1705–6, m. Anne Cunningham, Oct. 4, '37, f. of *Jonathan*, b. 1742 ; *Silas*, b. '47 ; 2. JUDITH, b. 1708, m. Josiah Upham, '32; 3. SAMUEL, bap. 1712; 4. EBENEZER, bap. Aug., '15 ; 5. JOSHUA, 6. JONATHAN, (twins), bap. Sep. 1718; 7. WILLIAM, bap. '21; 8. PETER, bap. Jan., 1725.

4. SAMUEL, s. of John (3), m. Rachel Allen, of Weston, and had, 1. LYDIA, m. Thaddeus Spring ; 2. SAMUEL, b. Aug. 11, 1745, m. Deborah, dr. of Arthur Savage, and had *Arthur*, b. Feb., 1772, m. Betsey Seaverns ; *Isaac*, b. Oct., '78, m. Sarah Harrington ; *Charles*, b. Jan. 7, '83, of Fram.; *Samuel*, b. June 29, '85, m. Harriet Seaverns; *Betsey*, b. '87, d. æ. 10. Sam. d. at Weston, 1839, æ. 93; his w. Deb. d. Mar. 1828, æ. 81 ; 3. EPHRAIM, m. Mary Hammond, lived in Hillsboro', N. H.; 4. EUNICE, m. Thomas Hill, of Goldsboro', Me. ; 5. RACHEL, m. David Crabtree, of Fox Island ; 6. MARTHA, m. Abijah Allen, and lived (last), in New Ipswich, N. H. ; 7. NAHUM, m. Loisa Fisk; 8. ENOCH, m. Hannah Hewing, (whose f. was a native of Scotland, and Chaplain in the British Army), and was f. of *Enoch*,

---

* The author has failed of discovering the entry of John's marriage. From the correspondence, in age, of his w. Margaret, and Margaret Dix, that he married her, becomes a plausible conjecture.

a merchant in Boston. Sam., the f., d. in Weston, 1806, æ. 94; his w. Rachel d. ab. 1802.

Note. — DAVID, (w. Hannah), had at Athol, in the part annexed to Philipston, David, b. 1777, Oliver, Lydia, Hannah, Molly; and united with the community at Lebanon. JONATHAN, of Athol, m. Mercy Baits, 1770, and had chil.

5. JOSHUA, s. of John (3), m.. in Fram., Mary Nichols, Mar. 25, 1743, and prob. resided here. No chil. are on record. Joshua was rated in Fram., 1746 and 1752. A wid. Train was rated in Fram., 1756.

6. CHARLES, g. s. of Samuel (4), grad. at Harv. Coll., 1805, was ord. at Fram., Jan. 30, 1811. He m. Elizabeth Harrington, who d. in Fram., Sep., 1814, æ. 30. He m. 2d, Hephzibah Harrington, by whom he had ARTHUR SAVAGE, B. Univ., 1833, ord. at Haverhill; CHARLES R., B. Univ., 1837, Attorney at Fram.; ALTHEA, d. Sep. 11, 1845, æ. 24; LUCILLA, d. 1841, æ. 18; and SARAH. Mr. Train was Preceptor of the Fram. Academy, 1808, and has been a Trustee since 1832; Representative, 1822, 6 years, and after, a State Senator.

TRAVIS, or TRAVERS, JAMES, and w. Mercy, had in F., 1. JOSEPH, b. Dec. 3, 1700, m. Mehetabel Hager, of Wat., Feb. 28, 1726-7, and f. in Sherb., of *Sarah*, b. Ap. 21, 1728, m. in Fram., Daniel Hager, of Weston, Sep. 12, 1750; *Asa*, b. May 28, '29, m. Sarah Dunten, 1753, and had, at Nat., Asa, 1754; *Zerviah*, b. July 10, '33; 2. JAMES, b. Ap. 12, 1703, m. Rebecca Squire, of Sherb., Feb. 10, 1725, and was f., at Holl., of *James*, b. 1732; *Daniel*, '34; *Thankful*, '37 — Wid. Rebecca d. 1757; 3. MERCY, b. Jan. 26, 1705-6; 4. JOHN, b. Aug. 16, 1710; 5. MERCY, b. Oct. 26, 1729. James, the f. lived near Salem End, was rated 1710, and signed a petition to the General Court, from Fram., 1727. He prob. moved to Holl. Mercy, w. of James, d. at H., 1744.

2. JOHN, s. of James (1), m. Anne Maxwell, in Holl., 1741, and had in Fram., 1. SUBMIT, b. Mar. 14, 1742, d. 1745; and in Holl., ISAAC, b. and d. '46; JOHN, '47; MARY, '49, d. 1751; MERCY, '51; SARAH, '53; MOLLY, '62; and ELIZABETH, '65.

NICHOLAS, of Woburn, had *Samuel*, b. 1643. DANIEL, of Boston, (w. Esther), had *Ephraim*, b. Sep. 13, 1659. DANIEL, sen., of Boston, d. January 19, 1682, æ. 76. JAMES, of Salem, m. Marcy Peirce, 1667, and had *Elizabeth*, b. 1667. MERCY, m. Benjamin Whitney, of Fram., October 24, 1701. JAMES, of Hop., m. Elizabeth Wesson, 1745, and had *Eliz-*

abeth, b. 1747. DANIEL, of Nat., (w. Thankful), had *Polly*, 1767, *Daniel, Betty, Sally.* JOSEPH, of Nat., (w. Sarah), had *Susanna*, b. 1741, *Daniel*, '42.

TREDWAY, TREADWAY, or TREADAWAY, NATHANIEL, of Wat., had by w. Sufferanna, 1. JONATHAN, b, Nov. 11, 1640; 2. JAMES; 3. JOSIAH, m. Sarah Sweetman, 1674, (who d. 1697), and had *Josiah*, b. 1675, d. 1683; *James*, b. '76, m. Sarah Bond, 1702, and f. of James, b. '03; William, Jan., '05-6; Josiah, '07; *Sarah*, b. 1679; *Bethiah*, '81; *Abigail*, '83; *Tabitha*, '90; — the f. m., at Charlestown, Dorothy Cutler, 1698, and had *Catharine*, b. 1703; 4. MARY, b. Aug. 1, 1642, m. — Hawkins; 5. ——, a dr., m. — Hayward; 6. LYDIA, m. Josiah Jones, 1667; 7. ELIZABETH, b. Ap. 3, 1646, m. Sydrach Habgood, 1664; 8. DEBORAH, b. Aug. 2, 1657, m. Joseph Goddard, '80. Nath'l, the f., a Weaver, lived in Wat., and with w. was legatee of Elder Edward How, of Wat., 1644. He conveyed, in 1688, land, house, &c., at Wat., to his s. Josiah, a Weaver. He d. July 20, 1689, his will being on record, His w., Sufferanna, d. July 22, 1682.

2. JONATHAN, s. of Nath'l (1), m., at Medfield, Judith Thurstane, Mar. 1, 1666, and had at M., 1. LYDIA, b. Sep. 8, '67, d. Mar. 29, 1703; and at Sud. 2. NATHANIEL, b. Dec. 2, '68, d. 1668; 3. JONATHAN, b. 1670; 4. JAMES, b. Oct., 26, '71; 5. HANNAH, b. June 14, '80; 6. EPHRAIM, b. Nov. 14, '81; 7. HULDAH, b. Nov. 1, '87, m. Benj. Lumbert, of Barnstable; 8. BENJAMIN. Jonathan, the f. who was disordered in mind, 1695, d. at Sud., May 28, 1710. His wid., Judith, d. in Fram., Oct. 12, 1726. (T. Rec.)

BENJAMIN, s. of Jona. (2), m. Mary Maynard, Ap. 19, 1714; and had in Fram., 1. HANNAH, b. Mar. 19, 1714-15, m. Jabish Puffer, of Sud., Oct. 18, 1738; 2. MARY, b. May 16, 1718, m. Thomas Morse of Sherburne, Mar. 29, '36-7; 3. ABIGAIL, b. Dec. 2, '19, m. William Puffer, of Sud., June 8, '42; 4. JONATHAN, b. May 21, '21, m. Elizabeth Hayden in Hop., 1744, [and f. in Hop., of *Lucy*, bap. 1751. *Hannah*, dr. of Wid Treadway, bap. 1758.] Jona. was living, 1752, and charged in an acct. book in Fram.; 5. a child, still-born, Ap. 3, 1724; 6. JUDITH, b. Oct. 29, '26, d. July 19, '27; 7. JUDITH, b. July 5, '28, m. Nathaniel Sever, of Naraganset No. 2 (Westminster), July 17, '54; 8. JAMES, b. Aug. 18, '30, d. Sep. 3; 9. BEULAH, b. Jan. 26, '32-3, m. Josiah Goodnow, of Sudb., Aug. 2, '49. Mary, w. of Benj. d. in Fram. Nov. 27, 1766; (T. Rec.) and he m. 2d, Hannah Tracy, of Southb., 1770. He lived at Mr. Amasa Kendal's, and the "Treadway Meadow" probably derived its name from him. He was Selectman, 1737. No entry is made of his death.

TROWBRIDGE, JAMES, of Dorchester, s. of Thomas, (prob. of Dorchester), m. Margaret, (dr. of Maj. Humphrey Atherton), Dec. 30, 1659, and had, in Dorch., 1. ELIZABETH, b. Oct. 12, '60, m. John Mirick, at Newton, 1682; 2. MINDWELL, b. June 20, '62, m. —— Fuller; and at Camb., (Newton), 3. JOHN, b. May 22, 1664; 4. MARGARET, b. Ap. 30, 1666, m. Ebenezer Stone, of Newton; 5. THANKFUL, b. Mar. 4, 1667-8, m. —— Ward; 6. HANNAH, b. June 15, 1672, m. (John) Greenwood, and d.

1728; 7. THOMAS, b. Dec. 10, 1677; 8. DELIVERANCE, b. Dec. 30, 1679, m.
—— Ward; 9. JAMES, f. by w. Hannah, of *Margaret*, b. 1707; *Daniel*,
1711, m. Hannah Spring, 1734; and *Hannah*, 1713; 10. WILLIAM, deac. at
Newton, and d. 1744, f. by w. Sarah, (who d. 1720), of *Huldah*, b. 1711, d.
æ. 3; *William*, b. and d. 1713; *Huldah*, 1715, m. Isaac Steadman, 1738;
James, b. April 28, 1717, m. Jerusha Park, 1740, and lived in Worcester,
(f. of William and several daughters); *Abigail*, d. 1738; *Sarah*, b. 1722, d.
1735; *Margaret*, b. 1724; *Beulah*, 1726; and *Thaddeus*, 1728; 11. CALEB,
b. Nov. 7, 1692, Harv. Coll., 1710, ord. at Groton, m. Mrs. Hannah Walter, of Roxb., 1718; 12. MARY, m. —— Steadman; 13. EXPERIENCE, m.
Samuel Wilson, and d. 1705; 14. ABIGAIL. James moved from Dorchester to Newton, ab. 1664, when his w. Margaret was dismissed from
the church in D., to form a church at Nonantum. (Dorch. Ch. Rec.) He
was deacon of the church at Newton. His w. Margaret d. at Newton,
1672, when he m. a 2d w. Margaret, who, as his wid., d. Sep. 16, 1727. (N.
T. Rec.) Dea. James d. May 22, 1717. (T. Rec.) In his will, he speaks of
his f. in-law, Humphrey Atherton, refers to rights he (James) had in
Dorchester, by his f. Thomas, also names his brothers John Ward, and
John Hides. He was also brother-in-law to Elyas Kendrick. (See Mid.
Deeds. Vol. VI.)

2. THOMAS, s. of James (1), had, at Newton, 1. JOHN; 2. EDMUND, b.
1709, Harv. Coll., 1728, after a judge, and d. Ap. 2, 1793 (Farmer); 3.
LYDIA, b. 1711; 4. MARY, b. 1715. Thomas, the f. d. ab. 1725. (See
Mid. Prob., same year.) [A *Thomas*, m. at Newton, *Susanna*, Jan. 7,
1716. A Thos., " late of N. London," Nov., 1727.]

3. JOHN, s. of Thomas(2), m. Mehetabel Eaton, of Fram., dr.
of Jonas, cov. Mar. 20, 1726, and was adm. to the ch. Feb. 4,
1749. His chil. were 1. MEHETABEL, b. Jan. 26, 1725-6, m.
—— Gates, (her heirs referred to in the will); 2. MARY, b. July
27, '28, m. Amos Gates in Sud., Nov. 28, 1744, lived in Fram.;
3. JOHN[4], b. May 22, 1730; 4. LYDIA, b. Dec. 24, 1731, m.
Ralph Hemenway, Jan. 7, '52; 5. THOMAS[7], b. Ap. 1, 1734;
6. RUTH, b. Mar. 3, '36, m. Peter Rice of Fram. John, the f.
bought of Sam. Bullen, and lived at or near Mr. Matthew Gibbs'.
He was Seclectman, 1750, 2 years, and d. May 19, 1762. (T.
Rec.) His will was proved soon after. Mehetabel, his wid. was
buried Mar. 26, 1777. (Mss. Journal). John was brother to
Judge Trowbridge.

4. JOHN, Jun., s. of John, (3), m. Margaret Farrar, Mar.
27, 1751, and was adm. to the ch. Jan. 12, 1752. His chil. were
1. JOHN[5], b. Feb. 12, 1752; 2. PEGGY, b. Mar. 17, '54, m. Abel
Stone, and 2d, John Jones of Fram.; 3. JOSHUA[6], b. Feb. 20,
'56; 4. MARY, b. July 10, '58, m. Luther Stone; 5. MARTHA,
b. Feb. 8, 1762, d. May 6; 6. DANIEL, b. Feb. 1, '64, m. Prudence Badger, June 1785, moved to N. Y., and d. Mar. 1825;

7. MARTHA, b. Oct. 7, '66, m. Dr. Gambell, of Amherst, and 2d, —— Dunbar; 8. NELLY, b. Feb. 7, '69, d. Feb. 18; 9. LYDIA, (d. young, of canker-rash), and 10. NELLY, (twins), b. Oct. 4, 1770. N. m. Aaron P. Edgell, of Fram., and d. a wid., Oct. 22, 1840. Col. John, the f. lived at the N. part of the Town. He served as Major at R. I. in the Revolution, was Selectman, 1769, 6 years, and T. Treasurer, 1799, 7 years. He d. May 1807, æ. 77. His w. Margaret d. Mar. 6, 1774, æ. 45.

5. JOHN, s. of John (4) m. Mary Bent, of Fram., in Sud., Ap. 23, 1776, and with w. cov. Sep. 10, '80. Mary was adm. to the ch. Jan. '90. Their chil. were, 1. EDMUND, b. Ap. 30, 1777, m. Hannah Wheeler, of Western, Mass., Mar. 1800, and lives in Fram.; 2. JOHN, b. June 12, 1778, m. (then of Camb.,) Sarah How, May 6, 1804; 3. JOSIAH, b. Sep. 28, '85, m. Margaret Wintermute, lives, a Physician, at Buffalo, N. Y., of which he has been Mayor; 4. WILLIAM, b. June 20, '91, m. Eliza Jordan, lives at St. Mary's, N. S. Col. John, the f. was an orderly Sergeant in the Rev. War, Selectman, 1783, 8 years, T. Treasurer, 1806, 19 years, Representative 1809, 10 years, and Delegate to the State Convention, 1820. He was trustee of the Academy 1804, 20 years, and gave the sum of $500, as a fund, the interest to be appropriated in aid of students from Fram. at the Academy, preparing for College. He was held in general esteem and confidence and d. 1826. His w. Mary d. 1844. æ. ab. 89.

6. JOSHUA, s. of John (4), m. Anne Stone, had chil., was Selectman in Fram., 2 years, and d. Dec. 9, 1824.

7. THOMAS, s. of John (3), m. Hannah Perry, was adm. to the ch., Mar. 29, 1752, and his w. do. July 9, '58. Their chil. were 1. LUTHER, b. June 3, 1756, m. in Albany, and d. 1802; 2. HANNAH, bap. Dec. 23, '59; 3. EDMOND, bap. Mar. 8, '62; 4. POLLY, bap. June 15, '66; 5. THOMAS, bap. June 12, '68; 6. JOSEPH, bap. June 3, '70. Thomas, the f. moved to N. H., prob. Fitzwilliam.

TRUMBULL, TRUMBLE, or THRUMBLE, JOSEPH, m. Mary Cloyes, and had in Fram., ABIGAIL, b. Feb. 23, 1697.

2. JOSEPH, m. Abial Gale, June 18, 1719, and had 1. ABIGAIL, bap. Aug. 28, 1720; 2. JOHN, bap. Sep. 29, 1723.

JOHN, took the freeman's oath, May 13, 1640, and had at Camb., by w. Elizabeth, 1. ELIZABETH, b. June, 1638; 2. JOHN, b. Aug. 4, 1641, and f.

at Charlestown, by w. Mary, of *James*, 1681; and *Samuel*. (See Mid. Deeds, 1685.) 3. HANNAH, b. Dec. 10, 1642; 4. MARY, b. Feb. 9, 1644-5; 5. JAMES, b. Dec. 7, 1647. John, sen., was of Charlestown, 1677 and 1685, where his wid. Elizabeth d. 1696, æ. 86. Farmer gives DANIEL, of Lynn, 1647; JOHN, of Rowley, 1643.

TUCKER, JOHN, prob. in Fram., 1735. Mr. Tucker was buried in Fram., July 29, 1797. ABEL, was adm. from the ch. in Milton, Feb. 1799, kept a store at the N. E. part of Fram., near Mr. Moulton's, and by w. Rachel, had WILLIAM, b. Sep. 10, 1801, and ESTHER, m. —— Haven. Rachel the m., m. 2d, Jonas Rug, 1809, and d. in Brimfield, Dec. 1843.

TURNER, AMOS, was rated in Fram., ab. 1756, and Constable, 1759.

TUTTLE, JOSEPH, was b. in Fram., May 27, 1755. May 23, 1793, "Dr. Tuttle began to board with us." (Deac. Buckminster's Journal.)

TWITCHELL, AMOS, was rated in Fram., 1780. EZRA, (w. Susannah) had the following, who d. on the days named, and were buried all in one grave; SUSANNA, d. Dec. 19, 1776, æ. 8 y., 1 m.; ANNA, Dec. 18, æ. 6 y.; CALVIN, do. æ. 3 y., 6 m.; CYNTHIA, do. æ. 1 y., 5 m. (G. Stone.)

UNDERWOOD, SAMUEL, m. at Wat., Mary Knap, 1741; and had in Fram., 1. MARY, b. May 15, '43, m. Josiah Rice; 2. RUTH, b. Aug. 10, '45; 3. LOIS, b. June 4, '48, m. Daniel Pike; 4. SAMUEL, b. Mar. 12, '50; 5. RUTH, b. Feb. 7, '54; 6. AMOS, b. Oct. 14, '57, m. Molly Lamb, May '84. The wid. Mary was adm. to the ch., Oct. 25, 1767. [A Samuel was rated in Fram., 1775.]

2. JONAS, m. Naomi (Pike?), and with w. cov'd Ap. 15, 1764, and adm. July 1781. Their chil. were 1. NAOMI, d. æ. over 70; 2. ANNE, bap. Aug. 3, 1766, m. Samuel Moore, of Gerry, Oct. 6, '95; 3. TIMOTHY, bap. June 12, 1768, m. Betsey Lamb, June 7, '92, and d. in Athol; 4. NATHAN, bap. July 8, '70; 5. LUCIA, b. July 6, '72, prob. d. young; 6. LUTHER, bap. Sep. 7, '74, d. young; 7. LUCY, bap. Oct. 13, '76; 8. OLIVE, bap. Sep. 10, '78, m. Joseph Moulton, of E. Sud., June 28, 1804. Jonas, the f. d. in Fram., Sep. 28, 1800, æ. 67. Naomi, his w., d. Dec. 25, 1783.

3. NATHAN, s. of Jonas (2), m. Abigail Greenwood, and had in Fram., 1. LUCY, b. Oct. 21, 1793, m. Joshua Underwood;

2. NATHAN, b. July 26, '95, m. Hannah Stone; 3. LUTHER, b. Sep. 27, '97, m. Aseneth Stone, of Wayland; 4. ABIGAIL, b. July 22, '99; 5. NANCY, b. Ap. 26, 1801, d. 1804; 6. GEORGE, b. Mar. 9, '03, d. Sep. '04; 7. GEORGE, b. Oct. 20, '05, m. Martha Smith, of Holl. [Nathan, m. Abigail Lamb, Dec. 27, 1792.]

4. JONATHAN, m. Priscilla Bailla, Jan. 22, 1740, and had in Nat., *John*, b. '42; *Mary*, '45; *Mercy*, '47; *Abigail*, '51; and in Sud., *Hannah*, '55, m. Enoch Johnson, '76.

Lt. JOSHUA, of Sherb., m. Mercy Fairbanke, Jan. 13, 1708, and had *Mercy*, m. Eli Jones, 1729; *Jonathan*, (probably the J. who m. Priscilla Bailla, 1740); *Joshua*; *Joseph*, m. Jemima Leland, 1739, and d. 1759, (f. in Holl., of Reuben; David; Joshua, m. Lydia Eames; Elizabeth; Timothy; Miliscent, d. young; Joseph, d. young; Asa, of Wardsborough; Joseph, went to Vermont); *Thankful*; *David*, d. æ. 21; *Mary*. JONATHAN, of Sud., m. Lydia Muzzey, June 4, 1744, and had *Keziah, Jonathan, Reuben, Samuel, Jonas, Lydia.* TIMOTHY, of Sud., m. Susanna Bond, 1752, and had *Timothy, David, Elizabeth.* JOHN, of Sud., m. Bathshebah Rice, 1763, and had *Isaac, Jonas, Anna, Asahel.* JOSHUA, d. at Mendon, ab. 1743, leaving wid. Hannah.

THOMAS, of Dorchester, moved to Wat., ab. 1651, and his will was proved, Ap., 1668; he left a w. Magdalen, who d. Ap. 10, 1687. æ. ab. 80; and a son Thomas, who d. 1680. JOSEPH, of Wat., (br. of Thomas), was f. by w. Mary, (who d. Feb. 13, 1658-9), of *Joseph*, who d. 1692, (w. Elizabeth, and chil. John, b. 1676, m. Reb. Shattuck, 1701; Elizabeth, b. 1679; Joseph, b. May, '81; Joshua, b. Jan. 31, '82-3, perhaps the J. of Sherb.); *Thomas*, b. Oct. 11, 1658, m. Mary Palmer, 1679, and had Thomas, Mary, Elizabeth, Jonathan, b. 1686, (of Camb. and Lex., w. Ruth), Abigail, Martha, and Thomas. Joseph, the f. who prob. had other chil., m. Mary How, of Dorch., 1662, who d. 1667. Joseph, d. Feb. 16, 1676-7, æ. ab. 62. MARTIN, d. at Wat., 1672, had a w. and prob. no issue. WILLIAM, of Concord, 1639, d. in Chelmsford, 1693, leaving drs.; (his wives were Sarah and Ann.) PETER, æ. 22, embarked in the Rebecca, for N. E., 1634.

UPHAM, WILLIAM, m. Elizabeth Robinson in Newton, Mar. 3, 1740-1, and had in Fram., 1. WILLIAM, b. Aug. 7, 1747, m. Anne Shepard, 1770; 2. ELIZABETH, b. Mar. 31, 1750; 3. NAOMI, b. Feb. 18, '52, d. 1769; 4. FRANCIS, b. Sep. 15, '54; 5. DANIEL, b. Jan. 28, '57; and at Newton, 6. BENJAMIN, b. Feb. 18, 1762, d. 1771; 7. EPHRAIM, d. 1765. William, the f. lived near Mr. Rufus Hosmer's; a cellar hole remains. His w. Elizabeth was adm. to the ch., Aug. 18, 1754. [ABIGAIL, dr. of ———, bap. in Fram., Ap. 8, 1750.]

PHINEHAS, of Malden, had a s. Phinehas, b. 1659, who d. 1720, and had, by w. Mary, *Mary*; *James*; *Jonathan*; *William*, b. Oct. 30, 1697; and *Elizabeth*.

USHER, DANIEL, m. Lois Park, Dec. 26, 1785.
VICKERY, JOHN, and family, warned out of Town, 1725.
(Fram. Rec.)

WAIT, WATE, WAITE, WAYT, WAYTE, WEIGHT, and WAIGHT, RICHARD, of Wat., had by w. Mary, 1. STEEVEN, buried Mar. 8, 1638, æ. 8 days; 2. JOHN, b. May 6, 1639; 3. THOMAS, w. Sarah, and had, at Wat., *Richard*, b. Jan. 29, 1674-5, d. Oct. 5, 1690; *Phebe*, b. 1676; *Thomas*, b. Mar. 7, '77; *John*, Feb. 16, '80; *Joseph*, Feb. 4, '81-2, d. at Worcester, Oct. 5, 1753, æ. 71, (w. Sarah, and had at Wat. and Worc., Priscilla, b. 1707, m. Charles Adams; John; and Rebecca, m. — Curtis); *Sary*, b. 1687; *Mary*, 1689; *Richard*, 1691; *Abigail*, 1697; 4. JOSEPH, prob. of Marlb., m. Ruhamah Hager, and had, *Ruhamah*, d. 1714, æ. 38; *William*, b. 1679, (m. Abial —, and had at Marlb., Gershom, b. 1700; Jason, '02; Sarah, '04; and at Sherb., Hepsebah, b. Nov. 25, 1707; Rebecca, June 29, '09; Abial, Nov. 18, '11; Betty, Aug. 31, '14); *John*, b. and d. 1692; *Joseph*, b. 1695, m. Mary Holland, 1721. Richard, the f., d. at Wat., Jan. 16, 1668, æ. 60; (T. Rec.) His wid., Mary, d. 1678, æ. ab. 72; (T. Rec.) See administration on Mary's est., Mid. Prob., 1679.

Note.—RICHARD (Wayte,) of Boston, (not, as Farmer supposes, the same with Richard, of Wat.), took the freeman's oath, Mar. 9, 1636-7, and was prob. the Richard, "Marshal," who obtained a grant of 300 ac. S. of Sud. River, in Fram., 1658, which he sold to Mr. Danforth. His will was proved, 1680, his br. GAMALIEL, an Executor. His chil. were, by w. Elizabeth, 1. JOSEPH, d. Nov. 20, 1651, æ. 14; 2. ISAAC, b. and d. 1638; 3. RETURNE, b. July 8, 1639; 4. HANNAH, b. Sep. 14, 1641, (not in the will); 5. NATHANIEL, bap. 1643, [a N. was in Medford, 1696]; and by w. Rebecca, 6. JOHN, b. Nov. 1, 1653; 7. RICHARD, b. 1658 — [a R. and w. Elizabeth, at Medford, 1720]; 8. JOHN, b. Feb. 9, 1660; 9. ABIGAIL, (in the will), m. — Jones. GAMALIEL Wate, (br. of Richard, of Boston), took the freeman's oath, Mar. 4, 1634-5; had, according to a deposition, a grant near Sentry Hill, in Boston, (d., says Farmer, Dec. 9, 1685, æ. 87), and was f. by w., Grace, of MOSES, b. 1637, d. 1638; GRACE, b. Jan. 10, 1638-9; MOSES, b. 1640, d. 1641; SAMUEL, b. 1641; and JOHN. JOHN, of Malden, took the f.'s oath, May 26, 1647, Speaker of the House, 1688, d. 1694, and had *Samuel*, b. Oct. 11, 1650; *Rebecca*, 1662; *Thomas*; and perhaps *Joseph*. JOSEPH, of Malden. m. Mercy Tufts, of Charles., 1688, and d., leaving *Joseph*, *Thomas*, *Peter*, and *Jonathan*; his wid., Mercy, m. — Jenkins. HENRY (Wayte or Wight), of Dedham, m. Jane Goodnow, of Sud., and d. ab. 1662, f. of *John*, *Joseph*, *Daniel*, *Benjamin*, (perhaps the B. Weight, f., at Sud, of Hannah, b. Dec. 6, 1702), and a son, name unknown. JOHN, of Ipswich, had, by w. Katharine, *John*, 1686. THOMAS (Weight) took the freeman's oath, Oct. 8, 1640. Some of this last name were of Concord.

2. JOHN, of Wat., s. of Richard (1), m. Mary Woodward, Jan. 13, 1663, and had in Wat., 1. JOHN, b. and d. 1665; 2. MARY, b. Dec. 9, '66, m. prob. — Randall; 3. JOHN, b. Dec. 27, '69, f. by w. Mary, at Wat., of *John*, b. 1694; *Mary*, '96; *Robert*, '99; *Sarah*, 1704; *Lydia*, 1706; 4. SARAH, b. 1672, (not in the settlement); 5 AMOS, b. 1679; 6. REBECCA. John, the f., d. at Wat., 1691, and his est. was settled 1705. (Mid. Prob.)

3. AMOS, s. of John (2), m. at Wat., Elizabeth Cutting, 1701, and had in Wat., 1. ELIZABETH, b. Jan. 11, 1701-2, m. in Fram., Moses Parker, July 5, 1722; 2. SUSANNA, b. Oct. 26,

1704; and at Fram., 3. AMOS, b. Dec. 27, 1707; 4. EZEKIEL[4], b. Sep. 11, 1710; 5. JOHN[6], b. June 8, 1713; 6. JOSIAH[7], b. Feb. 19, 1715–6. Amos, the f. lived in the N. part of Fram., and was Constable, 1728.

4. EZEKIEL, s. of Amos (3), m. Lydia Stanford, of Sherb., Ap. 20, 1738, and had 1. BARECHIAS, b. Ap. 18, 1739; 2. MARY, b. Nov. 28, 1740, d. Dec. 10. Lydia, w. of Ezek., d. Dec. 13, 1740, (T. Rec.); and he m. 2d, Rebecca Frost, in Sherb., June, 1743, and had 3. REBECKA, b. Mar. 16, 1743–4, taught a school in Holl.; 4. THOMAS, bap. May 18, 1746; 5. THOMAS, b. June 26, 1748, d. Feb. 14, '48–9; 6. LYDIA, Dec. 20, 1749; 7. THOMAS, bap. Aug. 2, 1752; and at Holl., 8. THOMAS, b. 1753; 9. THADDEUS, 1755; 10. SILAS, 1758. Rebecca, w. of Ezek., d. at Holl., 1779. Ezek. lived at the N. W. part of Holl.

5. BARECHIAS, s. of Ezek. (4), m. (prob. a Woodward); and had 1. LYDIA, bap. Oct. 17, 1762, m. Gershom Eames, Feb., 1784; 2. ELIAS, bap. Oct. 6, '65; 3. NANCY, m. Joseph Blanchard, Oct., 1789; 4. JAMES, bap. May 1, 1770, a blacksmith; 5. MARY, d. unm.; 6. HANNAH, a cripple. The f. was by trade a blacksmith, lived near the burying ground, and is said to have moved to the E.

6. JOHN, s. of Amos (4), m. Hannah Graves, of Southb., Oct. 18, 1739, and had in Fram., 1. HANNAH, b. July 16, 1740; 2. SARAH, b. Mar. 17, '41; 3. JOHN, b. Nov. 15, '44; 4. DANIEL, b. May 28, '48; 5. ELIZABETH, bap. May 3, '52; 6. RUTH, 7. MARTHA, both bap. Aug. 30, '55.

7. JOSIAH, s. of Amos (3), m. Sarah Stanford, of Sherb., 1743; and with w. cov. July 29, 1746. They had 1. JOSIAH[8], b. Ap. 25, 1743; 2. SARAH, b. Dec. 16, '44; 3. AMOS, b. Aug. 26, '46, m. at Marlb., Abigail Townsend, 1768; 4. SARAH, b. Sep. 19, '48; 5. SUSANNA, b. Oct. 14, 1750; 6. DAVID, b. July 26, '52; 7. JOSEPH, b. Mar. 1, '54; 8. BETTY, b. Ap. 23, '56; 9. LEVERESE, b. Oct. 29, '58; 10. PHEBE, b. Jan. 5, '61; 11. SAMUEL, b. May 23, '63.

8. JOSIAH, s. of Josiah (7), m. Mary, dr. of Joseph Adams, and with w. cov. Nov. 1771, and had, 1. ANNE, bap. Ap. 5, 1772; 2. POLLY, bap. Sep. 20, '72; 3. JOSIAH, bap. Ap. 24, '74. The f. is said to have d. in the Rev. War. None of this name (Wait) now remain in Fram.

JOHN, (w. Anna,) had at Sud., *Anna*, b. Ap. 8, 1728; *John*, '30; *Joseph*, '32; *Benjamin*, '36–7; *Sarah*, '39; *Lydia*, '41. The estate of GAD, of Poquioge, (Athol), was settled, 1753, the chil., *Benjamin, Nathan, Reuben, Simeon*, and a dr. who m. Richard Moreton. JOSIAH, (w. Sarah), at Athol, had *Eunice*, b. Oct. 29, 1776; *Rhoda*, b. Jan. 28, 1780.

WALKER, THOMAS, and w. Mary, (who was 14 years younger than her husband), had in Sud., 1. MARY, m. Rev. James Sherman, 1680; 2. THOMAS, b. May 22, 1664; 3. WILLIAM, b. July 22, 1666, m. Sarah Goodnow, 1686, and d. 1732, f. of *William*, b. 1687; *Sarah*, d. young; *Thomas*, b. Aug. 15, 1689, m. Elizabeth Maynard, 1717, (f. of Hezekiah, b. 1718; Sarah, 1720; Nathan, 1722); *John*, b. Sep., 1693, m. Jemima Stanhope, 1717, (f. of William, John, James, Phinehas, (the last two of Rutland), Sybilla, Abigail, and Micah); *Abigail*, b. Aug. 15, 1702; *Mary*, b. Oct. 30, '06; *Hezekiah*, b. Oct. 8, 1711, m. Hannah Putnam, 1738, f. of Reuben; 4. HANNAH, b. November 26, 1668, d. same year; 5. HANNAH, b. 1669, m. Deac. David Rice, of Fram., Ap. 7, 1687; 6. DANIEL, b. Nov. 2, 1672, d. Nov. 8; 7. DANIEL, b. Feb. 10, 1673–4, d. 1755, (f. by w. Dorothy, of *Daniel*, b. Oct. 27, 1710, m. Hannah Wood, '47; *Eliphalet*, b. Feb. 11, 1711–2; *Jabez*, b. July 18, '14; *Dorithy*, b. Mar. 12, '16–7, m. Isaac Livermore, '46; *Mary*, b. Oct. 11, '18; *Josiah*, b. Sep. 13, '21; *Bezaleel*, b. May 7, '24, m. Deborah Barnes, '55); 8. SARAH, b. July 25, 1677, (not in the will); 9. ABIGAIL, b. Oct. 29, 1679, m. John Stevens, 1714; 10. JOHN, d. young; 11. ELIZABETH, prob. d. young. The will of Thomas, the f. was proved at Mid. Prob., 1697. His descendants are numerous on the Sud. Rec. THOMAS, and w. Mary, (prob. the same) were of Boston, where they had *Mary*, b. Aug. 9, 1661, and a Thomas, (his son?) d. 1659. In 1664, the town of Sud. considered if they would give Mr. Walker land, for his encouragement to keep a free school in Sud. (T. Rec.) In 1672, Thomas, ordinary keeper at Sud., renewed license. (Co. Rec., III. 20.)

2. THOMAS, s. of Tho. (1), m. Martha How, 1687; and had 1. THOMAS, b. Sep. 1688, d. young; 2. SAMUEL, b. Sep. 24, 1689; 3. OBADIAH, m. Hannah Learned, May 2, 1715, had at Marlb., *Silas, Hannah, Obadiah*; 4. MARTHA, m. Joseph Haven, Jan. 24, 1710–1; 5. MARY, m. Elkanah Haven, Dec. 2, 1714; 6. THOMAS, b. ab. 1700, with w. Mary, adm. to Hop. ch. 1724, and d. at Hop., 1773, æ. 73, — (T. and Ch. Rec.); 7. ASA, b. June 7, 1702, d. Feb. 24, 1722–3; 8. HANNAH, b. June 17, 1705, m. Moses Haven, Nov. 9, 1721; 9. JASON, b. Oct. 28, 1708, Deac. at Hop., and d. 1787, æ. 78, f. by w. Hannah, (who d. 1803, æ. 82), of *Jason*, bap. 1733; *Thomas*, bap. '35; *Asa*, bap. '37; *Joseph*, bap. '39, Deac. at Hop. and d. 1813, æ. 75; and *Hannah*, bap. '41; 10. JOHN, b. Feb. 1, 1713–4. Tho. Jun., then of Sud., bought, 1688, of Gookin and How, 60 ac. on both sides of the highway from Sud. to Sherb., bounded on John Adams and John Bent. Feb. 1693–4, his wife is prob. referred to on the Sud. Records, as teaching a school. He was held in great respect in Fram., where he was T. Treasurer, 1700, and Constable,

1703. He d. Oct. 25, 1717. (T. Rec.) Mr. Swift notices his burial, Oct. 27 — "*Hodie Sepultus* Tho. Walker; *proh! dolor.*" His will was proved Dec. 2. He owned lands at Billerica and Wells. MARTHA, (prob. his wid.) m. John Whitney, (his 3d. w.) Nov. 10, 1718.

3. SAMUEL, s. of Tho. (2), m. Hannah Jennings, Nov. 3, 1715, and with w. cov. Sep., 15, 1717. They had 1, MARY b. June 19, 1716, m. Samuel Stratton of Mendon, Nov. 17, '37; 2. SAMUEL, b. June 4, '18, m. Mary Carlile, Sep. 28, 1738, f. at Marlb., of *Mary, Hannah, Lois, Vashti, Sarah,* and *Lydia*; 3. HANNAH, b. Ap. 18, 1720, d. Feb. 27, 1720-1; 4. AZARIAH, bap. June 24, 1722; 5. LOIS, bap. June 19, 1726. [Sam. of Nat. m. Wid. Abiel Stone, of Fram., June 15, 1743.]

4. AZARIAH, s. of Sam. (3), m. Abigail Seaver, and cov. Mar. 30, 1746. He had 1. ABIGAIL, bap. Feb. 24, 1759, m. Jonathan Hemenway; 2. MARTHA, bap. Feb. 24, 1759, m. Aaron Brown, 2d, —— Cutting; 3. AZARIAH, bap. June 10, 1764, m. Prudence Pepper, Aug 16, 1781, and d. at Nat.; 4. SAMUEL, m. Elizabeth Parkhurst, May, 1784; 5. HANNAH, bap. July, 1766, m. Samuel Larned, July 7, 1778; 6. MARY, m. Tho. Parmenter, of Sud., 1780; 7. LOIS, bap. July, 1766, m. David Holloway of Marlb., Nov. 1787; 8. SYBIL, m. Jacob Hemenway, Dec. 1787; 9. MATTHIAS, m. Jane Moulton, was f. at Fram., of *Hannah, Jane, Azariah, Matthias, Mary, Sophronia,* and *Horace,* and left town. Azariah lived where is a cellar hole in a pasture, in the N. E. part of Fram., owned by Henry Richardson, Esq. He d. at Needham, ab. 1804. His wid. Elizabeth d. Dec. 15, 1815.

ISRAEL, of Hop., d. May 29, 1798, æ. 87, f. of *Lois, Abigail, Israel,* b. 1743. Wid. MARY d. at Hop., 1813, æ. 91. Wid. SARAH d. at Sherb., Mar. 10, 1751. JOHN, (w. Lydia), d. at Weston, 1718. PAUL, of Sud., m. Sally Gibbs, of Fram., Feb., 1790. In 1634, embarked in the Elizabeth de London, Richard, æ. 24; William, æ. 15; James, æ. 15; Sara, æ. 17. RICHARD, shoemaker, came over in the James, 1635. Walkers were early in Lynn, Woburn, and Reading.*

WALKUP, GEORGE, m. Naomi Stevenson, both of Reading, Nov. 4, 1688. (Co. Rec.) They had 1. THOMAS[5], b. (Fram. Rec.) Mar. 16, 1689; 2. GEORGE, b. (Reading Rec.), Jan. 6, 1690-1; and at Fram., 3. NAOMI, b. Mar. 28, 1692, d. young;

---

* In 1650, one William was imprisoned a month for "courting a girl without leave." (Col. Rec.)

4. RACHEL, b. Jan. 29, 1703-4, m. James Boutwell, Mar. 9, '43-4; 5. NAOMI, b. Ap. 1709, m. —— Grant; 6. THANKFUL, adm. to the ch. May 16, 1728, m. Ebenezer Boutwell. George, the f. was Grand Juryman, 1722, and lived on Nobscut Hill. A cellar hole remains on Mr. Eben. Warren's farm, where he is said to have lived. He d. 1748, and his will was proved Nov. 28. The author has discovered no earlier trace of this family, who are said to be of Scotch extraction.*

2. GEORGE, s. of George (1), m. Sarah Graves of Sud., Ap. 29, 1725; and had, 1. GEORGE, b. Ap. 30, 1727, m. Jemima Very, of Worcester, 1759, and had a dr. *Molly*, who d. unm. in Coleraine, ab. 1795; 2. JONATHAN, b. July 17, 1732, prob. d. young; 3. HENDERSON, b. Sep. 4, 1735; 4. WILLIAM, b. Sep. 24, 1740. George, the f. lived near Mr. John Eaton's, and d. Nov. 3, 1748. His wid. Sarah d. 1792, æ. 98.

3. HENDERSON, s. of Geo. (2), m. Susannah Clements of Hop., who was bap. June, 3, 1759, and with her husb. cov. May 20, 1759. They had 1. HANNAH, b. May 27, 1759; 2. GEORGE, b. Ap. 4, 1762; 3. LUCY, b. Nov. 26, 1763; 4. SARAH, bap. Nov. 24, 1760; 5. SUSANNAH, bap. Oct. 30, 1763. They had also PEGGY, THOMAS, &c. The f. moved to Coleraine, ab. 1763. He m., in all, 5 wives, was the f. of 17 (or 19) chil., and f. or f. in law to 28 chil. He lived where is a cellar hole on Mr. John Eaton's farm.

4. WILLIAM, s. of Geo. (2), m. Elisabeth Stimson of Hop., 1765, who cov. Nov. 29, 1766. They had 1. BETTY, bap. Nov. 29, 1767, m. William Dougherty, Jan. 1788; 2. LUTHER, bap. Dec. 18, 1768, d. young; 3. MOLLY, bap. Sep. 23, 1770, d. unm., ab. 1841; 4. LUTHER, bap. Feb. 14, 1773, d. unm., a young man; 5. MILLY, bap. Aug. 4, 1776, m. Gideon Willis, of Weston, Nov. 7, 1803, lives in Swansey, N. H.; 6. LYDIA, b. Aug. 7, 1777, lives unm.; 7. BEULAH, bap. July 18, 1779, m. Justin Granger, of Con., and d. in Camb. ab. 1834; 8. WILLIAM, b. Mar. 4, 1781, m. Esther Moore, dr. of John and Anne of Sud., and lives in Fram., 9. RUFUS, m. Nancy Belcher, dr. of John,

---

* A tradition exists, that the progenitors of this and the Winch family, came over by mistake. Having visited a ship in which their friends had embarked, during a night passed on board, the ship sailed with them, and the morning found them on their way to N. E..

and lives in Fram. William, the f. lived by Mr. John Eaton's, and d. May 1836, æ. 96. His w. Elizabeth d. Mar., 1807.

5. THOMAS, s. of Geo. (1), and w. Hannah cov. in Fram., July 10, 1720. They had 1. DOROTHY, b. June 19, 1717, m. Samuel Britton in Southb., 1740; 2. DORCAS, b. Feb. 5, 1719, m. William Hudson, Mar. 18, 1747; 3. WILLIAM, b. Jan. 30, 1721, d. young; 4. HANNAH, b. Jan. 28, 1723, m. Jonathan Rugg, Feb. 17, 1743; 5. SARAH, b. July 1, '25, [a Sarah, bap. July 5, 1724], m. Joseph Nurse, Feb. 27, 1746; 6. THOMAS, b. Sep. 11, 1727, probably unm., lived on Nobscut, and at Mr. Bailey's, and afterward dug a cave near Mrs. Gordon's house, where he lived alone. He was out in the wars, and is said to have incurred the particular enmity of the Indians. Thomas, the f. and w. were adm. to the ch. Ap. 23, 1721. He is said to have d. in Fram.

WARD, Wid. JOANNA, was in Fram., 1720, with a son. [She was prob. the wid. of Obadiah, who m. Joanna Harrington, of Wat., Dec. 20, 1693.] WILLIAM, of Worcester, m. Mary Coggin, of Fram., Feb. 20, 1732-3. EPHRAIM, of Newton, m. Mary Stone, of Fram., Sep. 24, 1734. CHARLES, of Southb., m. Abigail Pike, of Fram., Aug. 25, 1742. ABIGAIL, of Fram., m. Joseph Bellows of Southb., Sep. 14, 1749. TIRZA, m. Benjamin Angier, both of Fram., Mar. 1785.

SAMUEL, of Hop., m. Hannah Cody, 1739. The Ward family is found on Marlb. and Sud. Rec.

WARREN, JOSIAH, m. Hephzibah Hobbs, Mar. 3, 1737; and had in Fram., 1. HEPHZIBAH, b., Oct. 28, 1741; 2. SARAH, b. Sep. 1, '43; 3. LYDIA, b. May 16, '45; 4. JOSIAH, b. Mar. 29, '47; 5. ESTHER, b. Jan. 24, 1748; 6. HANNAH, bap. Feb. 3, 1751; 7. ISAAC, b. July 17, '53, (bap. Aug. 23, 1752); 8. JOHN, b. Dec. 25, 1755, (bap. Dec. 29, 1754).

Josiah, the f. was b. Feb., 1715, at Weston, and was s. of John, who m. Abigail Livermore, 1708. He prob. descended from John, sen., of Wat., who d. Dec. 13, 1667, æ. 82, f. of *Daniel*, m. Mary Barron, 1650; *John*; *Mary*, m. John Bigelow; *Elizabeth*, m. —— Knap; *Margaret*, d. 1662; and prob. a dr., who m. —— Bloyce.

2. JOSIAH, m. Fanny Hemenway, May, 1789, and had 1. EBENEZER, b. June 9, 1790, m. Abigail Stow, of Marlb.; 2. SAMUEL, b. Oct. 12, '93, m. Relief, dr. of Ezekiel How, — Selectman, 1832, 4 years, Post Master in Fram., and late proprie-

tor of the Fram. Hotel; 3. DANA, b. June 11, 1795, m. Lucy Tayntor, of Fram.; 4. JOSIAH, b. Jan. 27, 1798, m. Almira Manson; 5. ANNA, unm.; 6. JOHN, m. Maria Gale. Josiah, the f. was b. July 10, 1756, and d. Nov., 1840, æ. 84, 4. His wid. d. Dec. 2, 1843, æ. 79.

JOHN, m. in Fram., Zipporah Brigham, both of Marlb., June 7, 1733. SAMUEL, of Marlb., had by w. Rebecca, *Daniel*, b. 1712, *Timothy*, 1715. THOMAS, of Southb., by w. Lydia, had *Lydia*, b. May 12, 1728.

WATSON, OLIVER, was adm., by letter, from the ch. in Leicester, to occasional communion, Feb. 14, 1724. (Ch. Rec.) OLIVER, (prob. his son), was bap. Sep. 15, 1723.

WEBB, Mr. (said to have been an old countryman), was in Fram., 1754. He taught a school in Fram.

WEEDG, (prob. for WEDGE), SILENCE, b. Ap. 4, 1709.

WENZELL, JOHN, m. Hephzibah Bigelow, in Holl., 1790, and had 1. HENRY, b. Mar., 1791, m. Lucy French, of Boston, and d. at Sherb., 1833; 2. JOHN, b. Jan. 5, '93, m. Mehetabel, dr. of Abner Haven, Selectman, 1833, 5 years; 3. HEPHZEBAH, b. May 20, '95, lives unm.; 4. CATHARINE, b. Oct. 31, '98, m. Curtis Hartshorn, of Holl., 2d, Ezra Dearth, and d. ab. 1839; 5. ELIZA, m. Selah Higley. John, the f. was b. in Boston, 1765, and had a br. *Jacob*, and sister *Susanna*. His f. was a foreigner, b. prob. in Holland. John was a wheelwright and farmer, and came, 1792, from Holl. to Fram., where he d. 1830, æ. 65. Hephzebah, his wid. d. Dec. 1841, æ. 75.

WESSON, or WESEN, SAMUEL, m. Martha Haven, May 7, 1711, and had JOHN, b. Dec. 1, 1711. [Martha Weston, (prob. wid. of the above), m. in Fram. Isaac Cusans, of Sherb., Jan. 12, 1714–5. She d. 1746, in Sherb.]

2. JOHN, m. Ruth Death, of Sherb., Jan. 22, 1740, and had SAMUEL, b. July 14, 1741.

3. "Mr. Wessen here to make plows," 1789. May 7, 1790, "Mr. Wesson moved away." (Dea. Buckminster's Journal.)

JEREMIAH, of Sud., m. Sarah Bent., 1729, and had *Jonathan*, b. June 22, 1730; *Sarah*, b. Feb. 10, '32–3; *James*, b. Ap. 2, '34. WILLIAM, of Southb., m. Mary Bruce, 1765, and had *Josiah*, 1767. WILLIAM, of Hop., m. Mrs. Sally Bixby, of do., Feb. 9, 1789.

WETHERBE, or WITHERBY, JOSEPH, had by w. Elizabeth, 1. HEPHZEBAH, b. Feb. 14, 1706–7; 2. DEBORAH, b. Feb. 14, 1709; 3. ELIZABETH, b. Sep. 15, 1714. Jos., the f. was in Fram., 1708, and Constable, 1712. He lived in the N. part of the town.

JOHN and Mary Wethersby, had in Sud., *Thomas*, b. Jan. 5, 1678. CALEB, of Southb., and w. Joanna, (J. d. 1736), had *Joanna*, b. and d. July, 1734.

WHEELER, ABNER, s. of Abner and w. Elizabeth, who lived near the bounds of Lincoln and Concord, came from Concord to Fram., 1798, opened a store, and in 1801, bought the public house built by John Houghton, which he occupied many years, with much credit and success. He was Selectman, 1809, 8 years, a Representative, and one of the Hon. Board of Co. Commissioners, several years. He was a man of sound judgement, attractive manners, and estimable character, and contributed much to the prosperity and growth of the centre village. He m. Polly Bennet, Dec. 23, 1798, and had *George, Horatio*, (both d. unm.,) and *Abner Bennet*, Harv. Coll., 1831, a Physician in Boston. Polly, w. of Abner, d. Ap. 10, 1836, æ. 58, and he m. 2d, Miss Martha Eaton. He was buried in Fram., Oct. 13, 1843, æ. 71.

[Maj. BENJAMIN, br. to Abner, came to Fram., 1801, and m. Rebecca Bennet, Dec. 11, 1804. Capt. ELIPHALET, another br., came to Fram., 1806, m. Clarissa Rice, and has for many years held the office of Deputy Sheriff. PATTY, (a sister), of Lincoln, m. in Fram., Stephen Buttrick, of Concord, Dec. 6, 1801. HANNAH B. (a sister), m. Nathaniel Swift Bennet, of Fram.]

2. ABIGAIL, m. Deac. Daniel Stone, Feb. 8, 1703–4. JOHN, of Nichewaug, (Petersham), m. Deborah Gleason, of F., Aug. 29, 1751. ISAAC, of Holden, m. Sarah Darlin, Aug. 18, 1752.

WHISTON, EZRA, was rated in Fram., ab. 1782.

WHITE, JOSEPH, was joint proprietor with Col. Buckminster 1st, of land in Fram., 1693.

2. JOHN, m. Sybilla, dr. of Jos. Buckminster, Jan. 24, 1728, and had in Fram., 1. JOHN, b. Oct. 17, 1728 ; 2. THOMAS, b. July 27, '31 ; 3. REBECCA, b. Feb. 5, '33–4 ; 4. SARAH, b. June 22, '37 ; 5. SYBILLA, b. Oct. 29, '41. This family prob. left Fram.

MARGARET, w. or dr. of THOMAS, d. at Sud., Nov. 17, 1649. RICHARD, (of Sud., 1639), ANTHONY, and THOMAS, (selectman, 1642), shared in the first three divisions of land in Sud. Anthony, m. Grace Hall, 1645, and d. at Wat., his will dated Nov. 16, 1685, and left *John,** *Abigail*, m. ——

---

* John, s. of Anthony, was convicted of having a pack of playing cards, at the Co. Court, 1677. (Co. Rec., Vol. 3.)

Butters, and *Mary*, m. Jacob Willard, Oct. 23, 1677. JOHN, of Sud., and w. Elizabeth, had *John*, b. Aug. 8, 1653; *Elizabeth*, 1658; and *Hannah*, 1669. JONATHAN, of Sherb., (w. Susanna,) had *Jonathan*, b. Oct. 10, 1704. DAVID, (w. Abigail), had *David*, 1731, *Sarah, Peter*, and *Abigail*. JAMES, of Southb., (w. Joanna), had Mary, 174–.

WHITNEY, JOHN, æ. 35, embarked, 1634,* in the Elizabeth and Ann, for N. E., with 1. Jo. (John), æ. 11, m. Ruth ——, and d. at Wat., (his est. settled, 1693), and had at Wat., *John*, b. Sep., 1643; *Ruth*, b. Ap. 15, '45, m. Enos Lawrence; *Nathaniel*, b. Feb. 1, '46–7, m. Sary Hager, 1673, (f. at Weston, of Nathaniel, Sary, and William); *Samuel*, July 28, '48; *Mary*, Ap. 23, '50; *Joseph*, b. Jan. 15, '51–2, m. Martha Beech, '74, (f. of Joseph, 1675; John, '80, prob. d. at Weston, 1749; Isaac, d. young; Benjamin, b. 1684; Mary; and Martha, d. young); *Sarah*, b. Mar. 17, '53, m. Daniel Harrington; *Elizabeth*, b. June 9, '56, m. Daniel Warren, '78; *Hannah*; and *Benjamin*, b. Nov. 28, '60, m. Abigail Hager, '87, and 2d, w. Eliz., his will proved 1736, (leaving Benjamin, Samuel, Joseph, and Elizabeth); 2. RICHARD, (æ. 9), m. Mary Coldam, 1650, and had, at Wat., *Sary*, Oct., 1653; *Moses*, Aug. 1, '55; *Joanna*, Jan. 16, '56–7; *Deborah*, Oct. 12, '58; *Rebecca*. Dec. 15, '59, d. 1660; *Richard*, Jan. 13, '60; and *Elisha*, Aug. 26, '62. Richard, sen., and Moses, were among the prop. of Stow, ab. 1681. Richard, sen. (f. or son), d. at Stow, 1723; the descendants numerous there.† 3. NATHANIEL, (æ. 8); 4. THOMAS, (æ. 6), m. Mary Kedell, 1654, and had at Wat., *Thomas*, b. 1656; *John*, d. young; *John*, d. young; *Eliezer*, b. 1662, (m. Dority Ross, of Sud., and had Sarah, 1688, and at Wat., James, Eliezer, Dority, Elnathan, and Jonas); *Elnathan*, b. 1662; *Mary*, Dec. 22, '63; *Bezaliel*, b. Sep. 16, '65; *Sary*, Mar. 23, '66; *Mary*, Aug. 6, '68; *Isaiah*, b. Sep. 16, '71, (f. by w. Sarah, at Camb., of John, Isaiah, John, Nathaniel, Sarah, Elijah, and Jonas); *Martha*, b. 1673; 5. JONATHAN,[2] (æ. 1); and by w. Elinor, the f. had at Wat., 6. JOSHUA, b. July 15, 1635. (A Joshua, prob. the same, m. Abigail Tarbell, at Wat., 1672, and had, *William*, b. Feb., 1677–8; *Joshua, Cornelius, David*; his drs. in the will, were *Mary, Martha, Elizabeth*, dr. Hutchins, dr. Woods. Joshua, of Groton, 1697, sold to Nathan Fiske, land in Wat. His will was dated, Ap. 17, 1713, then æ. ab. 76;) 7. BENJAMIN.[3] Elinor, w. of John, d. May 11, 1659, and he m. the same year, Judah Clement. John took the freeman's oath, Mar. 3, 1635–6, and d. 1673, æ. 74. His inventory is dated June 4, and his will was proved in the Mid. Prob.

2. JONATHAN, s. of John (1), m. Lydia Jones, Oct. 30, 1656, and had at Wat., 1. LYDIA, b. July 3, 1657, m. at Sherb., Moses Adams, April 15, 1684, and d. May 27, 1719; 2. JONATHAN, b. Oct. 20, 1659, had a lot, and built near Chestnut Brook, in Sherb., 1691 or 2, and had by w. Sarah, at Sherb., *Sarah*, b. March 2, 1693, m. —— Warren; *Jonathan*, b. Sep. 27, '94, d. young; *Tabitha*, b. Aug. 22, 1696, m. —— Parks; and at Wat., *Shadrack*, b. Oct. 12, '98; *Jonathan*, b. Nov. 25, 1700 — [a Jonathan d. at Mendon, 1755, (Isaac administered,) leaving w. Lydia, and chil. Jesse, Jonathan, Sarah, David, Susanna, m. Isaac Tenney, and Lydia, m. Sam. Bowker]; *Anna*, b. May 24, 1702, m. —— Cutler; *Amos*, b. 1705; (and in the will,) *Isaac*; *Timothy*; *Zaccheus*. (b. at Sud. Nov. 16, 1707); Jonathan was of Concord, when he d., and his will was proved, 1735. He left a w. Sarah; 3. ANNA, b. Ap. 28, 1660, [prob. the dr. who m. Cornelius Fisher];

---

* See Mr. Savage's Gleanings. M. H. Coll.

† The will of Richard, of Stow, was proved Dec. 23, 1723. He left children Richard, Jonathan, Joshua, Hannah Farr, Elizabeth Wetherby, Sarah, Ruhamah, and Hephzibah.

4. John[6], b. June 4, 1662; 5. Josiah, b. May 19, 1664; 6. Elin, b. Oct. 12, '66, d. 1678; 7. James, b. Nov. 25, 1668, d. in Sherb., Nov. 30, 1690; 8. Isaac, b. Jan. 12, 1670, d. in Sherb., Dec. 2, 1690; 9. Joseph, b. March 10, '72, prob. f. by w. Rebecca. at Sherb., of *Jonas*, b. 1708; *Joseph*, '10; *Sylvanus*, '12; *James*, '14; and *Ephraim*, '16; 10. Abigail, b. Aug. 18, '75; 11. Benjamin, b. 1678, m. (as Benj. Jun.) Mercy Traves, in Sherb., Oct. 24, 1700, and d. 1718, prob. without issue. (See his will, 1718.) Jonathan, the f. was in Sherb. 1679, and d. there ab. 1702, in which year his will was proved.

3. BENJAMIN, s. of John (1), had by w. Jane, at Wat., Jane, b. Sep. 29, 1669, m. at Sherb., Jonathan Morse, Jan. 4, 1692–3; and at Sherb. Joshua, b. Sep. 21, 1687. Jane, w. of Benj., d. at Sherb. Nov. 14, 1690.*

4. BENJAMIN, of Fram., m. in Marlb., Mary Poor, Ap. 11, 1695. He was prob. the same, who, in 1698, occupied land of Mr. Danforth, in F., bounded on Isaac Bowen and John Whitney. [Benjamin was Constable in F., 1723, and '25; and Tythingman, 1726.]

5. BENJAMIN, m. in Wat., Margaret Sanderson, Feb. 24, 1731–2, and had in Fram., 1. Jonathan, b. Sep. 25, 1734; 2. Persis, b. Aug. 20, '39; 3. Amos, b. Sep. 27, '46.

6. JOHN, s. of Jona. (2), m. Mary Hapgood, 1688; and had 1. Mary, b. Mar. 27, 1689, m. Daniel Moore, Feb. 1, 1709; 2. Elizabeth, b. Jan. 29, '90–1, m. Jona. Willard; 3. James[7], b. Dec. 28, '92; and by w. Sarah, 4. Lydia, b. Ap. 18, '95, m. Richard Haven, Feb. 4, '13–4; 5. Hannah, b. Sep. 27, '97, adm. to the ch. May 17, 1719, m. Ezek. Rice, Jan. 23, '22–3; Sarah, the m. (prob. a Haven), d. Ap. 23, 1718; John m. 3d, Martha Walker, Nov. 10, 1718, who d. Nov. 14, 1721. John, the father leased of Mr. Danforth, Mar. 25, 1699, at the S. part of the town, land he already had occupied; was Selectman, 1714, in all 3 years; Constable, 1718; Tythingman, 1719 and '24. He was adm. to the ch. July 26, 1719. His inventory bears date, May 22, 1735.

7. JAMES, s. of John (6), m. Martha Rice, Feb. 2, 1714–5, and was with w. adm. to the ch., Sep. 22, '17. They had in F., 1. John, b. Ap. 10, 1716, m. Abigail Perry, of Sherb., Feb. 8, '38–9, and d. in F., 1741, (will dated, Oct. 31), prob. without issue; 2. James[8], b. June 4, '18. James, and w. were dism. to Sherb. Ch. Mar. 28, 1728, where he was chosen Deac., and d. Ap. 10, 1770, æ. 77; he m. 2d, Elizabeth Twitchell, 1732, who

---

* It is quite probable, that Benj. had at Sherb., *Benjamin*. b. May 22, had other chil. Benj. (w. Hester), 1709. Benj. d. at Sherb., 1723.

d. Mar. 31, 1782, æ. 85. His other chil. were, MARY, b. May 12, 1720; MARTHA, b. Nov. 9, '21; BENJAMIN, b. June 13, '23; MICAH, b. June 4, '25; EZRA, b. Feb. 22, '30; DANIEL, b. Dec. 13, '33.

8. JAMES, s. of James (7), m. Patience Leland, Mar. 18, 1742; and had in Fram., 1. JOHN, b. Mar. 10, 1742; and in Sherb. 2. JOSEPH, b. Mar. 7, '45; 3. MARTHA, b. Aug. 16, '47.

9. EPHRAIM,* and w. Mary were adm. to the Fram. ch. Sep. 6, 1767, and had, 1. PERSIS, bap. Sep. 6, 1767; 2. BASSOM, (or Bascom), b. Nov. 9, '68; 3. MARTHA, b. Feb. 9, '71; 4. JOHN, b. July 9, '73; 5. EPHRAIM, b. Jan. 6, '76. Eph. d. in Camb., by the accidental discharge of a gun, Sep. 16, 1775. T. Rec.

10. JONATHAN, m. Susanna (Whitney?), and had in Sherb., 1. SUSANNA, b. Jan. 20, 1703, m. Gershom Eames; 2. KEZIA, b. July 31, '06, m. —— Jones; 3. DOROTHY, b. Aug. 28, '08, m. —— Hunt; 4. MARY, b. May 28, '10, m. Jos. Jones, May, '35; 5. LYDIA, b. Mar. 3, '12, m. Isaac Hill, May 2, '45; 6. JESSE, b. '14, and 7. HANNAH, b. '15, neither in the f.'s will; 8. ELIAS[11], b. Nov. 14, '16; 9. MEHETABEL, b. Dec. 27, '19, m. —— Cutler; 10. GEORGE, b. Aug. 12, '21, d. 1752, f. by w. Sarah, of *Isaac, Hannah, Marsy*, and *Sarah*. Jona., the f., of Holl., d. 1753, his will dated Feb. 2.

11. ELIAS, s. of Jona. (10), m. Elizabeth Mellen, 1746, and had in Holl., 1. ABIGAIL, b. 1747; 2. ELIAS, b. '50; 3. AMRILLEN, b. '53; and in Fram., 4. JONATHAN, b. Jan. 25, '60, killed in the Rev. war.

12. MARK, of Hop. m. in Fram., Tabitha Mellen, Jan. 4, 1726-7; and had 1. LOVE, m. Jona. Battle, of Dedham, Jan. 2, '54; 2. MARY, m. —— Cody; 3. THOMAS, bap in Hop., 1737; 4. TABITHA; 5. SARAH, bap. '39; 6. ESTHER; 7. MARK, bap. 1746. Mark was adm., by letter, to Fram. Ch., Feb. 10, 1754, and d. at Nat., his will dated June 17, 1760. His w. Tabitha taught school in Hop.

13. ISAAC, m. in F. Elizabeth Bridges, Sep. 27, 1722, (had at Hop., *Judith*, 1727). HULDAH, m. in F., Zech. Morse, of Marlb., Nov. 16, 1724. ABIGAIL, m. in F., Ebenezer Chapin, of Mendon, Mar. 29, 1743. JOSEPH, of Sherb., m. Sarah Park, of F., Oct. 3, 1792. ELENOR, was early in Fram.. JOHN, d. in Fram., June 18, 1805.

---

* Tradition supposes Eph. to have been son of Abraham, a blacksmith, who had a br. John, and lived in the S. part of the town, and was living, 1796; his widow is noticed, 1797. T. Rec.

BENJAMIN, of Marlb., m. Sarah Barret, 1710, (who d. 1730), and his est. was divided, 1749; he left w. Abigail, and chil. *Solomon*, b. 1721; *Sarah*, '23; *Dinah*, '27; *Job*, '29; *Abigail*, '31; *Benjamin*, '32; *George*, '33; *Samuel*, '34; *Anna*, '36. ISRAEL, of Oxford, (w. Hannah), d. 1746. EZEKIEL, of Sutton, d. 1753. NATHANIEL, (w. Sarah), of Sherb., had *John*, b. 1716. NATHANIEL, of Westb., d. Jan. 27, 1776, æ. 79, and had by w. Mary, (d. Dec. 3, '76, æ. 76.) *Ephraim*, b. 1722; *Oliver*, '24; *Mary*, '27; *Nathaniel*, '28; *Anna*, '30; *Lucy*, '34. ELI, of Westb., (w. Elizabeth, who d. 1777,) had *Eli*, b. 1765; *Elizabeth, Benjamin, Josiah*. JOHN, of Weston, (w. Sarah,) d. 1749, f. of *Joseph, Isaac, Zechariah, John, Abraham*. THOMAS, of Southb., m. Ann Gould, 1753. JASON, (w. Arabella,) of Sud., had *Micah*, 1730; *George*, '33. JOHN, of Sud.,(w. Bethiah,) had *Ephraim*, 1740. JOHN, of Bolton, (w. Elizabeth,) d. 1747.

WILDER, ELIZABETH, adm. to the ch., Nov. 1789.

WILLARD, BENJAMIN, b. ab. 1665–6, s. of Maj. Simon Willard, of Concord, m. Sarah, dr. of John Lakin, of Groton, was of Sud., 1693, and had in Sud., SEMIONE, b. Ap. 27, 1701, m. Phœbe Newton, June 10, '29; HANNAH, b. 1702; DOROTHY, b. 1706; HANNAH, b. Jan. 19, 1707, m. Eph. Brigham, of Marlb., 1730; BENJAMIN, b. Jan. 19, 1708. His other children were JOSEPH; SARAH, m. Tho. Pratt, of Fram., Jan. 24, 1710–1; MARGARET, m. Nehemiah How, and 2d, James Miller; and ESTHER, m. Thomas Boyle. Benj. was rated in F., 1710, and with w. Sarah, adm. to the ch., May 12, 1717. He removed to Hasanamisco (Grafton), where he was a prominent man, and d. June 16, 1732, æ. 66. His will was proved at the Worcester Prob. Inventory £663. He was a Grantee of Princeton, 1686, was "very serviceable to his country, in his younger days, as Capt. of a Co. against the Indians," declined the office of Lt. Col., in Col. J. Chandler's Reg., and held a commission as Justice of the Peace. N. E. Weekly Journal, June 26, 1732.

2. JOSEPH, s. of Benj. (1), m. in Fram., Martha, dr. of Capt. Isaac Clark, Jan. 5, 1715–6, with w. cov'd, June 30, 1717, and had in Fram., BENJAMIN, b. Nov. 13, 1716, m. Sarah Brooks, of Concord, May 17, 1739; SARAH, (prob. his dr.), bap. Oct. 12, 1718, m. Noah Brooks. The f. moved from Fram. to Grafton, where he was known as Maj. Joseph, and d. ab. 1774. His other chil. were JOSEPH, m. Hannah Rice; ISAAC, m. Sarah Whipple; JOSIAH, m. Dinah How; DANIEL, m. Sybill Willard; SIMON, d. unm.; SOLOMON, d. unm.; MARTHA, m. David Harrington, and was drowned in Sud. River, in F., during a freshet, Ap. 29, 1747; HANNAH, m. Richard Roberts; PHOEBE, unm.; MARY,

m. Daniel Goddard. In an obituary notice of Maj. Joseph, it is said, that " very few men have left behind them a fairer moral character."

JONATHAN, of Sud., m. Mary Cook, of Camb., Jan. 23, 1728-9; and had in Sud., *Samuel*, b. Nov. 7, 1729, d. 1733; *Elizabeth*, b. Mar. 12, 1734-5, d. at Sherb., May 22, 1744; *James*, d. at Sh., July 4, 1744 ; *Susanna*, d. do., June 26, '44. JOHN, and w. Elizabeth, had chil. in Sud.

WILLIAMS, ABRAHAM, (from Sandwich), a native of Marlb., m. Mrs. Anna Buckminster, of Fram., Sep. 11, 1751. (Mss. Rec. of J. Jones, Esq.); and had (on record, in Fram.) 1. SARAH, b. Sep. 5, 1752, N. S., m. Rev. Mr. Fuller, of Princeton, and d. in Boston, Feb. 22, 1796 ; and at Sandwich, 2. ABRAHAM, b. 1754, and d. at Sandwich, Feb. 22, 1796 ; 3. ELIZABETH, b. 1756, m. Dr. —— Smith, of Sandwich, and d. in Boston ; 4. ROBERT BRECK, b. 1757, d. in the prison ship, at N. Y.; 5. ANNA, b. 1759, m. Rev. —— Smith, of Martha's Vineyard ; 6. JOSEPH, b. 1761, m. in Me., and d. in Boston ; 7. MARTHA, b. 1762, m. Capt. Tobey, of Sandwich, and d. in Me. ; 8. WILLIAM, b. 1765, m. —— Atwood, and d. in Fram. ; 9. THOMAS, b. 1768, m. —— Atwood, and d. in Boston ; 10. CAROLINE, b. 1770, m. Josiah Dwight, of Stockbridge, and had two sons, one killed in a privateer. Abraham, the f., was grad. at Harv. Coll., 1744, and S. master in Sud., do.; ord. at Sandwich, June 14, 1749, and d. Aug. 8, 1784, æ. 58.

2. EZEKIEL, and w. Sally, had in Fram., 1. EZEKIEL, b. Jan. 8, 1782 ; 2. NANCY, b. Nov. 29, '84 ; 3. POLLY, b. Oct. 9, '87. The f. moved to N. Y., May 11, 1790.

3. THOMAS, (said to have been br. of Ezek.), was with w. Susanna adm. to the ch. from Roxb, 1782, and had in Fram., 1. THOMAS, b. June 4, 1782; 2. PATTY, b. June 1, '85 ; 3. BILLY, b. Oct. 12, '87. Thomas, the f., moved to N. Y., May 11, 1790.

3. HANNAH, (not related to the above, but a connection of the w. of Timothy Stearns, of Fram.), m. in Fram., John Belcher, June, 1787.

ABRAHAM, of Marlb., (w. Joanna), before 1692, had sold lands to John How, sen., and was prob. the same who d. 1712, and had been representative from that town. ABRAHAM, of Marlb., m. Prudence How, 1715, (she d. 1725), and had *Isaac*, b. 1716 ; and *Elizabeth*, 1723, d. young. He had a son *William*, bap. 1731. WILLIAM, of Marlb., had by w. Elizabeth, *Thomas*, b. and d. 1692; and *Abraham*. THOMAS, of Sud., m. Sarah Foster, Sep. 23, 1686. WILLIAM, of Sud., m. Elizabeth Jennison, 1767. NEHEMIAH, of Sud., (w. Hepzibah), had *William*, b. 1745, &c. SAMUEL, of

Sherb., m. Abigail Goddard, 1716. WILLIAM, of Southb., m. Sarah Drury 1769, and had a numerous family. JOSEPH, (w. Zerviah), of Southb., 1767.

WILSON, or WILLSON, NATHANIEL, of Roxbury, m. Hannah Crafts, 1645, and had HANNAH, b. May, 1647; JOSEPH, and BENJAMIN, twins, b. 1655; ISAAC, b. 1658, m. Susanna Andrews, 1685, d. at Newton; his estate settled 1720 — his chil., *Samuel, Ebenezer, Susanna, Hannah*, and *Abigail*. Nathaniel and w. Hannah, of Muddy River, had MARY, b. May 22, 1661; ABIGAIL, b. 1663. Administration on Nathaniel, of Newton, æ. ab. 70, was granted, in 1692, to his oldest son *Nathaniel*, and his youngest s. *Samuel*. (Mid. Prob) Hannah, w. of Nathaniel, d. at Newton, Aug., 18, 1692. (Newton Rec.) The est. of N., sen, was settled April 9, 1694; his chil., *Benjamin*, (dec'd); *Nathaniel; Joseph; Samuel; Isaac*; the w. of Tho's Oliver; the w. of Tho's Gill; Rebeckah, w. of Shubael Sever; the w. of Edward Jackson.

BENJAMIN, (prob. s. of Nathaniel), had at Roxb., *Benjamin*, b. 1678. B. (w. Sarah, who d. 1689), had at Newton, *John*, b. Ap. 17, 1688. B.'s est. was settled, 1705; his chil. *John, Benjamin, Joseph, Sarah*, and *Mary*. JOSEPH, of Newton, (prob. s. of Nathaniel), bought land, 1678, of Richard Parks, (both of Cambridge Village). He d. 1725, and had by w. Deliverance, (who d. 1718), *Hannah*, b. June 10, 1685, m. —— Turner; *Deliverance*, Oct. 1, 1687, m. at Wat., Daniel Squier, 1710; *Margaret*, b. Oct. 1, 1689, m. —— Pitte; *Sarah*, m. (William?) Trowbridge; *Thankful*, b. 1692; *Mary*, b. 1694; *Experience*, b. 1696, m. —— Willcains; *Elizabeth*, m. Wm. Ward; *Abigail*, m. —— Smith; *Josiah*. SAMUEL, of Newton, (whose chil. had letters of g. ship, 1717), had by w. Experience, (who d. 1705), *Experience*, b. 1697; *Margaret*, '99; *Samuel*, 1701; *Thomas*, 1703; *Experience*, '06. ROBERT, of Camb., m. Deborah Stevenson, and had *Deborah*, 1666; *Sarah*, '68; *Andrew*, Ap. 17, '70. ANDREW, (w. Hannah), had chil. at Camb., *Andrew*, b. 1696, *Hannah, Deborah, John, Mary*. JOHN, of Newton, (who m. —— Mayhew), had a s. *John*, who m. Mehetabel Metcalf, and d. in Sutton, 1784, æ. 48, f. of Maj. John, of Petersham, b. 1765.

2. NATHANIEL, Jun., s. of Nath. (1), m. Hannah Jackson, and had in Newton, 1. NATHANIEL³, b. Dec. 4, 1682; 2. ELIZABETH, b. Nov. 9, 1684; 3. HANNAH, b. Oct. 18, 1686; 4. SUSANNA, b. Nov. 6, 1688, d. unm. in Fram., Dec. 7, 1746; 5. EDWARD, b. Oct. 3, '89, signed a dissent, on the T. Records of Fram., as an inhabitant, Mar. 4, 1716-7, and was of Shrewsbury, a bricklayer, Feb., 1746-7. Besides these, Nath. was f. (by the same wife), of 6. MARY, m. in Fram., Gideon Bridges, May 23, 1723; 7. RELIEF, m. John Stacy, and 2d, Deac. Moses Pike, Dec. 29, 1737; 8. THANKFUL, adm. to the ch., Mar. 14, 1725, m. Isaac Gleason, of F., Dec. 9, '25, and d. in Westmoreland, N. H., æ. over 90; 9. ABIGAIL, (half sister to the former chil.), m. Richard Mellen, of F. (See Mid. Prob. files.) Hannah the m. d. in Newton, Sep. 26, 1690, and the f. m. 2d, Elizabeth Osland, Mar. 11, 1692-3. In 1698, N., bricklayer, and w. Eliza-

beth, executed a deed of house, &c., in N. to James Benton. Nath. Sen., was rated in Fram., 1710, and d. Dec. 26, 1721. (T. Rec.) His w. Elizabeth d., Mar. 10, 1715. (T. Rec.)

3. NATHANIEL, s. of Nath. (2), m. Elizabeth Reed, Dec. 28, 1709, was adm. to the ch., June 8, 1728, and had in Fram., 1. PHINEHAS, b. Aug. 19, 1710, m. Anne Jones, Oct. 26, 1739; 2. MARY, b. Dec. 10, 1713; 3. ELIZABETH, b. Feb. 24, 1714–5; 4. BENJAMIN, suddenly killed by a fall from a cart. Nath'l, the f., was Constable, 1724, and Selectman, 1728. He d. in Fram., his Inventory, (£1690-1-6), bearing date, Ap. 8, 1751. His wid. Elizabeth, (who had a dr.-in-law, Rush or Rust), was living, very aged, 1763.

4. JAMES, (prob. b. in Newton), m. Deliverance Bridges, Jan. 21, 1719–0, and with w. cov'd, Sep. 1721, and adm. to the ch., Feb. 2, 1724. They had in Fram., 1. JOHN, b. Oct. 17, 1721, H. Coll., 1741, Physician, m. Elizabeth Overing, and f. of *John*, O., m. Nancy Dench; and *Mary Ann*, m. Dr. John Money, of Prov.; 2. JESSE, b. Ap. 4, 1724, d. prob. unm. in Hop., ab. Jan., 1759. James and w. D., were received from Fram. to the Hop. ch., 1729. They had in Hop., ELIZABETH, bap. 1726, d. unm.; JAMES, b. July 8, 1730, m. Elizabeth Bowker, 1754, and f. of *James*, b. '64, d. in Fram., 1833, m. Mary Tilton; *Elizabeth*, m. Peter Clark, of Newton, and lives a wid. in Fram.

JOHN, of Hop., had *Benjamin*, bap. 1741; *Mary*, bap. 1743. JAMES, m. 2d, Mary Barret, 1751, and had, in Hop., *Nathaniel*, bap. 1753, of Winchendon. JOSIAH, of Hop., br. of James, m. in Fram., Hannah Cloyes, Ap. 22, 1735, and had at Hop., *Lydia*, b. 1737.]

5. ABIGAIL, dr. of —, bap. Mar. 4, 1749–0. ANNE, m. Jona. Clark, May 2, 1745, and d. in Fram., 1797, æ. 81. Lt. Wilson lived in the N. part of Fram., 1737.

JOHN, came over in the John and Sarah, of London, 1651. JOHN, d. at Medfield, 1691, f. by w. Sarah, of *Thomas*, b. Nov. 12, 1652; *Elizabeth*, 1653; *Elizabeth*, 1656; *John*, '60; *Thomas*, Nov. 18, '62; *Susanna*, Dec., '64. JOHN, of do., and w. Sarah, had *John*, b. May, 1686; *Elizabeth*, Oct., '89; *Roger*, '91. MICHAEL, (w. Mary), of Medfield, 1675. HENRY, (w. Mary), of Dedham, had *Michael*, b. Aug. 7, 1644; *Sarah, Mary*, and *Elizabeth*. JOHN, of Sherb., d. 1756, æ. 44, having by w. Mary, a son *John*, b. 1747, and four drs. older. BENJAMIN, of Hop., d. 1751, left w. Rebeckah, and chil. *Joseph, Samuel, Jonathan* and *Nathaniel*. NATHANIEL, (w. Thankful), was of Charlestown, 1684. Deac. Edward d. at C., 1706, f. of *William, John*, and four daughters. There were Wilsons early at Malden.

WINCH, SAMUEL, m. Hannah Gibbs, Feb. 11, 1673; and had, 1. JOHN, b. 1674, d. young; 2. SAMUEL, b. Mar. 27, 1677;

3. John, b. Jan. 8, 1679 ; 4. David, b. Mar. 15, 1684, d. at Annapolis Royal, and his br. John administered, 1711; 5. Hannah, b. Jan. 16, 1687-8, m. Ebenezer Hemenway, May 17, 1711 ; 6. Silence, b. Nov. 10, 1690, m. Nathan Haven, June 4, 1713 ; 7. Thomas[7], b. 1694. Samuel, m. Sarah Barnard, of Wat., Jan. 11, 1698-9, and had, 8. Mary, b. Nov. 23, 1700, m. Benoni Adams, of Sherb., May 14, 1724, and d. in Holl., a wid., ab. 1744 ; 9. Daniel[14], b. June 28, 1702. Samuel, the f., appears on Sud. Rec., 1671. He bought, 1683, of Wid. Anne Stone, 56 ac. at Wolfe Swamp, a part of Corlet's Farm, (prob. at the Frost place*). In 1689, "Winch's old house" is referred to as on Mr. Danforth's land. He was among the original members of the ch. in Fram., Oct. 8, 1701 ; was Selectman, 1709, and Tythingman, 1716. " Aug. 3, 1718, our brother, Sam. Winch, was buried, who died of a cancer." Swift's Journal.

Note. — The only early notice of this family, is the marriage of Mary Winch, at Springfield, to Richard Everett, June 4, 1643.

2. [1]JOHN, s. of Samuel (1), was adm. to the ch., Sep. 22, 1717, and his w. Elizabeth, Sep. 29. They had, 1. Elizabeth, b. Dec. 21, 1706, d. unm., æ. ab. 20 ; 2. John, b. July 10, 1710 ; 3. David[4], b. Dec. 9, 1714 ; 4. Jonathan, b. July 3, 1716 ; 5. Deborah, b. Dec. 27, 1717, d. unm., ab. 1727. John, the f., d. Jan. 19, 1718-9, (T. Rec.), (æ. 46). His w. Elizabeth had administration on his est.

3. [1]JOHN, s. of John (2), m. Mehetabel Pike, Jan. 27, 1743 ; and had Mehetabel, b. July 7, 1744, m. Thomas Brown, and lived at Mrs. Swan's, near Saxonville.

4. [1]DAVID, s. of John (2), m. Naomi Gibbs, and had, in F., 1. Sarah, b. July 12, 1735 ; 2. John, b. July 17, '36, m. Keziah Goodale, and lived in Holden ; 3. Naomi, b. May 16, '38 ; 4. Elizabeth, and 5. Silence, twins, b. Mar. 13, '39 — S. m. Ebenezer Belknap ; 6. David, b. Mar. 10, '43, unm., lived and d. at Winchendon ; 7. James, b. May 31, 1746, lived at Holden, and d. unm., young ; 8. Aaron[5], bap. Oct. 23, '48. David and w.

---

* Samuel is said to have lived where is a cellar hole, nearly opposite the old Frost house ; this last, tradition supposes to have been built by Sam. and a son, near 150 years since.

were recommended to the ch. in Shrewsbury, Sep. 14, 1761, and lived in Boylston.

5. [1]AARON, s. of David (4), m. Ruth Winch, and had RHODE, bap. May, 1781. The f. moved from Fram., ab. 1787, to Barre and Winchendon.

6. [1]JONATHAN, s. of John (2), m. Elizabeth Clements, of Reading, and with w. cov. Dec., 1746. They had 1. RUTH, b. Mar. 23, 1746, m. Aaron Winch, and d. in Winchendon, 1838; 2. DEBORAH, bap. Jan. 20, '50, d. young; 3. SUSANNA, bap. Nov. 19, '52, adm. to the ch., Feb. '81, and d. unm., 1821; 4. JONATHAN, bap. Mar. 9, '55, d. young; 5. SARAH, bap. Aug. 22, '62, d. young; 6. SARAH, bap. Nov. 17, '65, m. William Greenwood, Ap. 9, '99, and d. 1843; 7. ANNA, m. Samuel Cutting, and d. ab. 1840, in Fram.; 8. ELIZABETH, bap. Nov. 28, '73, prob. d. young. Jonathan, the f., lived at Deac. Jona. Greenwood's, and d. 1770. His w., Elizabeth, survived many years.

7. [2]THOMAS, s. of Sam. (1), m. Deborah Gleason, Oct. 23, 1718, and was with w. adm. to the ch. May 5, 1722. They had 1. DANIEL, bap. Ap. 10, 1720, (not in the will); 2. THOMAS[8], b. June 25, '23; 3. SAMUEL[9], b. June 7, '26; 4. DEBORAH, b. Jan. 27, '28-9, m. Maj. John Farrar, of Fram., Oct. 4, '50; 5. HANNAH, b. July 15, '31, m. David Rice, Sep. 27, '50; 6. JOSEPH[11], b. Mar. 1, '33-4; 7. NATHAN[13], b. Nov. 9, '37. Lt. Thomas, the f., was Selectman, 1733, and d. in Fram., Sep. 22, 1761, æ. 67. (G. Stone). He left, by his will, a negro girl, Jenny.

8. [2]THOMAS, s. of Tho. (7), m. Elizabeth Drury, Dec. 20, 1743, and had, 1. CALEB, b. Sep. 26, 1744, m. Mehetabel Maynard, and lived in Fitzwilliam. [Caleb, and w. Mehetabel, of Monadnoc, were adm. to the ch. in Fram., July 28, 1770. Ch. Rec.]; 2. CATHARINE, bap. Dec. 8, 1745, m. Eldad Atwood, of Medway, May 4, 1780, and lived in Holl.; 3. SYBILLA, bap. Feb. 14, 1748, m. Timo. Dadmun, and d. in Fram.; 4. HANNAH, bap. Oct. 15, '49, m. Daniel Belcher, and d. 1805; 5. JASON, bap. Sep. 1751, m. Elizabeth Maynard, and moved to Fitzwilliam; 6. JOEL, bap. June 10, '52; 7. SAMUEL, bap. Jan. 15, '55; 8. REUBEN, bap. Nov. 20, '57; 9. SAMUEL, bap. Feb. 3, '60; 10. THOMAS, bap. Ap. 27, '62; 11. ELLICK, bap. June 29, 1766. [Thomas m. Elizabeth Drury, July 17, 1754.] Thomas, Jun., the f. lived on land belonging to Deac. J. Greenwood.

9. ²SAMUEL, s. of Tho. (7), m. Mary, dr. of Eben. Winchester, Nov. 22, 1751, and was with w. adm. to the ch., Aug. 30, 1752. They had, EBENEZER[10], b. Feb. 12, 1753. Samuel, d. Mar. 17, 1754, æ. 26 ? (G. Stone.)

10. ²EBENEZER, s. of Sam. (9), m. Esther Brinley; and had 1. POLLY, b. Feb. 27, 1776, d. young; 2. NATHANIEL, b. Oct. 7, '78, d. 1779; 3. KATY, b. Feb. 19, '82; 4. NATHANIEL, b. May 9, '84. Eben. the f. lived in Deac. Buckminster's house, and left town, ab. 1786, for Newton.

11. ²JOSEPH, s. of Tho. (7), m. Mary Beals, of E. Sud., and with w. cov. Feb. 15, 1756. They had 1. MOLLY, b. Mar. 28, '56, m. Wm. Beals; 2. LUCY, b. Oct. 13, '57, m. Wm. Haven, of Fram., Nov. 23, '75, and lived at Wayland; 3. JOSEPH, b. June 25, '59, m. Anne Philips, of Lexington, lived in Lex. and Fram., and moved E.; 4. ABIJAH, b. May 31, '61, m. Anna Warner, moved off, and d. 1843; 5. PATTY, b. Mar. 12, '63, m. Dan. Bemis, of Weston, and d. 1838; 6. JESSE[12], b. May 6, '65; 7. LUTHER, b. Mar. 19, '67, m. Lydia Beals, and a 2d w., and moved from town; 8. NELLY, b. Dec. 15, '68, m. Leonard Cummings, of Cornish, lately living at C.; 9. EUNICE, b. Oct. 26, '70, m. John Gates, Jan. 6, '95, and d. in Marlb., N. H., 1814; 10. REUBEN, b. Sep. 22, 1772, m. Olive Eaton, Sep. 26, '94, and d. in Fram., 1846; 11. SAMUEL, bap. Ap. 7, '76, m., then of Marlow, N. H., Ruth, dr. of Abijah Hemenway, Mar. 12, 1801, and d. in Boston ab. 1836. His w. Ruth d. Sep. 22, 1820. Joseph, the f. served as a Capt. in the war of the Rev.; was noted as a superior marksman, and for his ready wit. He d. in Fram., Ap. 7, 1815.

12. ²JESSE, s. of Jos. (11), m. Patty Brown, Mar., 1788, who was adm. to the ch., Sep. 1796. They had, 1. ENOCH, bap. Sep., 1796, m. Dorcas Greenwood, and was shot at a Turkey shooting; 2. LUCY, bap. Sep., 1796, m. Charles Morse; 3. NANCY, bap. May, '97, m. —— Barker, of N. H.; 4. MARTHA, m. Wm. Flagg, of W. Needham, a Tavern Keeper. Jesse, the f. d. at Princeton, ab. 1804. His w. Patty m. 2d, —— Jackson, of Newton, and d. in Nat.

13. ²NATHAN, s. of Tho. (7) m. Thankful Gibbs, of E. Sud., and was, with w. adm. to the ch., Nov. 24, 1759. They had 1. THANKFUL, b. Ap. 19, '60, m. Joseph Nichols, Aug. 26, '79, and lived in Grafton; 2. NELLY, b. Jan. 27, '62, d. young;

3. DEBORAH, b. May 6, '65, m. Oldham Gates, June, '83, and lived in N. Y. and N. H. ; 4. NATHAN, b. Feb. 28, '67, m. Lydia Rollins, of Dublin, N. H., Nov. 22, '92 ; 5. MILISCENT, b. Nov. 22, '63, m. Elisha Frost, Ap. 26, 1781. The f. m. 2d, Abigail Brown, Feb. 8, 1769, and had, 6. HEPHZEBAH, bap. Oct. 1, '69, m. Samuel Rollins, of Dublin, N. H., Nov. 22, '92; 7. ABEL, bap. Aug. 11, '71, d. young; 8. JOEL, bap. July 28, '73, d. young ; 9. LUCY, bap. Nov. 2, '77, m. John Palmer ; went to Littleton, N. H. ; 10. DAVID, left town; 11. ABEL, b. Mar. 15, '80, moved to Littleton, N. H.; 12. ANNE, m. Sylvanus Phipps, Feb. 1802, and d. 1835 ; 13. JOEL, m. Sally Sessions, of Weymouth. Lt. Nathan, the f., was buried, Sep. 5, 1803.

14. ³DANIEL, s. of Sam. (1), m. Sarah Gibbs, Mar. 4, 1731; and had 1. DANIEL, b. Jan. 12, 1731-2. Sarah, the m. d., Feb. 2, 1733-4, and the f. m. 2d, Abigail Reed, of Sud., Mar. 11, 1742, and had 2. SILAS[15], b. July 29, 1744 ; 3. MARY, b. Oct. 28, '47 ; 4. SARAH, d. unm., Oct. 9, 1805 ; 5. ABIGAIL. [One of the drs. m. prob. —— Childs, of Concord.] Daniel the f. lived back of Ezra Hemenway's. He was adm. to the ch., Sep. 2, 1750 ; his w. Abigail, do., Mar. 4, 1749. Daniel's will was proved Sep. 4, 1758.

15. ³SILAS, s. of Daniel (14), m. Elizabeth Jones, and with w. cov. Jan. 31, 1768. They had 1, JOSIAH[16], bap. Mar. 6, 1768 ; 2. LEVINAH, bap. Sep. 10, '69, prob. d. young ; 3. OLIVE, bap. June 23, '71, d. unm.; 4. JOHN, bap. July 18, '73, m. — Gould, of Malden, and lived there and at Fram. ; 5. ELIZABETH, bap. Oct. 6, '76, m. Peter Woodbury, of Walth., Mar. 24, '96, and lived at Bridgewater ; 6. ANNE, bap. Ap., 1781, m. Jason Belcher, Nov. 9, 1800, and 2d, Benjamin Dudley, d. in Sud. ab. 1841, had in Fram., a dr. *Charlotte.* Silas, the f., d. Sep. 19, 1834, æ. 90 y. and 2 m. His w. Elizabeth, d. Ap. 2, 1833, æ. 91 y., 6 m.

16. ³JOSIAH, s. of Silas (15), m. Polly Moulton, May, 1789, and had 1. MARY, b. May 14, '90, m. Lewis Hill of Fram. ; 2. JOSIAH, b. Sep. 1, '92, m. — Robinson, and — Dutton ; 3. LUTHER, b. Mar. 17, '96, m. — Stone, lives in N. Y. ; 4. JOHN, b. Aug. 5, '98, m. in Sag Harbor, N. Y. ; 5. SALLY, b. June 21, 1801, m. Micah Claflin, and 2d, Wm. Hyde ; 6. BETSEY, b. Dec. 12, '03, m. Alden Jones, of Vt. ; 7. LUCINDA, b. Aug. 13, '06,

m. John Jennison, of Bellingham; 8. WALTER, b. May 10, '11, m. Nancy Davis. Josiah the f. d. in Fram., Ap. 22, 1833. Polly, his w. d. Dec. 11, 1841, æ. 71.

17. THOMAS, m. Abigail Hager, of Waltham, Feb. 22, 1759; and had 1. THOMAS, b. Dec. 1, '61; 2. SAMUEL, b. Jan. 31, 1763.

18. DANIEL, of Fram., m. Rebecca Reed, of Rutland, 1761. HANNAH m. Jabez Nichols, in Worc. Co., 1740. ELIZABETH, bap. in Fram., Jan. 11, 1746. LEONARD C. d. Sep. 11, 1805. (T. Rec.)

WINCHESTER, EBENEZER, m. Martha Buckminster, Feb. 13, 1717-8, with w. cov. June 7, 1719, and the w. adm. to the ch., Aug., 1725. They had 1. MARTHA, b. Aug. 11, 1719; 2. MARY, b. Aug. 26, '22, m. Samuel Winch, Nov. 22, 1751, and 2d, Capt. Jona. Gibbs; 3. EBENEZER, b. Aug. 30, 1725, Harv. Coll., 1744, adm. to the ch., Oct. 11, 1747, Selectman, 1741, 2 years. He was a physician, and d. unm., in the family of Dr. Ezek'l Hersey, of Hingham, ab. 1756; on his estate (£183.7.4) Jona. Gibbs, of Fram., Gent. administered; 4. prob. JOSHUA, who was bap. May 14, '27, m. Mary Whipple, of Grafton, 1750; 5. ELIZABETH, b. Oct. 21, 1727, (bap. Oct. 8); 6. SARAH, b. Mar. 8, '30; 7. BEULAH, b. Aug. 21, '33. Ebenezer, the f., lived near the Brinley Farm, and was Constable, 1726. Administration on his estate was granted, Nov. 17, 1744, to his s. Eben'r. One of his drs. prob. m. Caleb Hitchens. His wid., Mrs. Martha, m. Rev. James Bridgham, of Brimfield, Nov. 1, 1739.

2. NATHAN, had BEULAH, bap. in F., Sep. 26, 1756.

BENJAMIN, of Sud., had by w. Elizabeth, *Prudence*, b. 1734; and at Westb., *Ann*, b. '38; *Mary*, '39. BENJAMIN, of Brookline, m. at Camb., Eliz. Chamberlain, 1726. WILLIAM, of Southb., (b. ab. 1737, near Dorchester, whose mother, Elizabeth Whiting, d. at S., 1733), had by w. Hannah, *Jacob B. P.*, b. July 6, 1762; *John*, Oct. 5, '64; *John*, July 6, '69; *Submit*, Jan. 13, '72; *Bridget*, June 8, '73, CALEB, of Marlb., m. Anna Smith, Sep., 1761, and had *Rufus*, and *Mary*, both d. young; *Caleb, Rufus, Stephen*, and *Samuel*. STEPHEN, (w. Hannah), had at Newton, *Stephen*, b. 1723; *Charles, Hannah*, &c. Most, if not all these, were probably descendants of JOHN, of Muddy River, who d. Ap. 25, 1694, æ. four score and upwards, leaving w. Hannah, and had *John, Josiah, Mary*, and *Jonathan*. JACOB B. Winchester, m. in Fram., Mrs. Elizabeth Learned, both of Wat., Mar. 3, 1786,

WOOD, or WOODS, THOMPSON, had by w. Martha, in Fram., 1. ISAIAH, b. May 29, 1701; 2. THOMAS, b. Nov. 20,

1704; 3. HANNAH, b. Jan. 20, 1707-8. The f. was rated in Fram., 1710, Constable, 1723. Martha, his w., was dismissed to the ch. in Pomfret, Dec. 5, 1725.

2. JOHN, m. Elizabeth Buckminster, Mar. 3, 1704-5, and had in Fram., 1. JOHN, b. July 24, 1707, m. at Hop., Mary How, '27; 2. MARY, b. Aug. 4, 1709, m. at Hop. John Chamberlin, '44; 3. ELIZABETH, b. Mar. 3, 1711-2, d. Ap. 13, 1714; 4. BENJAMIN, b. Ap. 15, 1714, m. at Hop., Martha Chamberlin, '37, had *John*, bap. '39; 5. ELIZABETH, b. Aug. 4, 1716; 6. THOMAS, b. Sep. 9, 1719, m. at Hop., Mary Taylor, '40, f. of *Thomas, Samuel, Mary, John, Benjamin;* 7. JOSEPH, b. Aug. 3, 1722, m. Martha Gibson, '42, had *William,* '45. Capt. Jos. d. at Hop., 1785, æ. 63; his w. Martha, d., 1754, æ. 33.

Deac. BENJAMIN, of Westb., had by w. Sarah, *Benjamin Buckminster,* d. young; *Matthew,* b. 1770; *Buckminster,* b. '76.

3. MARY, of Fram., m. Amos Parmenter, in Sud., Dec. 21, 1715. LOUIS, of Newton, m. Thomas Drury, of Fram., Sep. 15, 1794.

JOHN, of Sud., pin-maker, (æ. 54, 1664), was a petitioner, 1656, for Marlb., and d. there, July 10, 1678, (his will proved Oct. 1), f. by w. Mary, (d. 1690, æ. 80), of 1. JOHN, b. May 8, 1641, (w. Lydia), Deac. at Marlb., his est. settled Aug. 17, 1716, his chil. *John,* b. 1670, m. Martha ——, (d. 1697), and Patience ——, f. of David, John, Ephraim; *Lydia,* b. '72, m. Abr. Eager; *Hannah,* '77, m. Moses Leonard; *Joseph,* d. young; *Joseph,* '82; *Sarah,* '85, m. Simon Gates, 1710; *Silence,* '89; *Benjamin,* '91, m. Elizabeth Morse, 1717, f. of Benjamin, Fortunatus, Alpheus, John, &c.; Benjamin, Esq., d. 1740; *James,* '94; 2. ISAAC, his will proved Aug. 17, 1720, f. by two wives, of *Isaac, Joseph, Charles, Solomon, Dinah, Mary,* and *Elizabeth;* 3. JAMES, b. July 18, 1647, deac. at Marlb., d. at M., 1718, f. by w. Hopestill, (d. 1718, æ. 73), of several children, many of whom d. young; 4. KATHARINE. The will of John, sen., names his g. child, Hannah Levins, and his s. in-law, John Bellows, (his w. prob. Mary.)

MICHEL, of Concord, 1642, d. before 1677, leaving 7 chil. SAMUEL, of Groton, d. ab. 1712, (w. Hannah), f. of *Samuel; Thomas,* b. 1663, &c. DANIEL, (w. Sarah), of Topsfield, had *David,* 1670, *Daniel, John,* &c. JOSIAH, of Charlestown, d. 1691, f. of *Josiah, Samuel, Joseph.* Woods are numerous on Marlb. and Sud. Rec.

WOOLSON, NATHAN, m. Miriam ——, of Holl., and had in Fram., 1. JOSEPH, b. Sep. 19, 1770; 2. SIMEON, b. Sep. 3, 1772. The f. moved to Hop., where Nathan, Sen. d., 1843. He had also a son Isaac. The f. of Nathan is said to have belonged to Weston, and to have d. in Fram.

2. CYRUS, (br. of Nathan), m. in Fram., Persis Angier, June, 1784, and had 1. SALLY, b. Mar. 26, 1785, m. Elijah Bemis,

Oct. 9, 1805, and lives in Fram.; 2. John, b. July 15, '87, m. Martha Rice, and lives in Fram.; 3. Levinah, b. Jan. 9, '90, m. Ezra Bemis, and lives in Southb. Cyrus, the f. d. 1792. His wid. Persis yet lives.

Thomas, of Camb., 1653, and of Wat., 1666, d. ab. 1713. (See will.) He m. Sarah Hide, Nov, 20, 1660, and had 1. *Sarah*, b. 1661, m. —— Bond; 2. Thomas, b. Feb. 28, 1666-7, (w. Elizabeth, f. at Wat., of *John*, b. July 8, 1694; *Elizabeth*, Aug. 17, '98; and at Camb., of *Jonas*, 1711); 3. Elizabeth, b. Ap. 30, 1668, m. at Sud., John How, Nov. 3, 1686; 4. Mary, b. Nov. 28, 1673, m. Samuel Jones, 1700; 5. Joseph, b. Nov. 16, 1677, f. at Wat. and Sud., by w. Hannah, of *Joseph*, b. Dec. 13, 1699, (f.* at Weston, by w. Elizabeth, of Elizabeth, bap. Feb., 1739); *Hannah*, b. Aug. 8, 1704; *Thankful*, b. at Sud., June, 1708; *Isaac*, 1711. Joseph, the f. moved from Sud. to Weston. Sarah, w. of Thomas, sen., d. at Sud., Sept. 11, 1721. Nathaniel, of Sud., m. Elizabeth Reed, 1709. Joseph, (w. Sarah), of Wat., had *Mary*, b. 1701.

WOOSTER, SUSANNA, was m. in Concord, to Jeremiah Pike, both of Fram, May 6, 1701.

Ebenezer, of Sud., m. Hannah Ross, 1704.

WRIGHT, Widow Rite shared in the division of meadow, in Sud., 1639, and was prob. the widow Dorothy, who m. John Blanford, Mar. 10, 1642. Edward; Samuel, who m. Lydia Moores, 1664, and d. 1664, his inventory dated Aug. 30; and Lydia, who m. James Cutler, 1665, were prob. her chil.

2. EDWARD, of Sud., m. Hannah Axsell, (Axdell), June 18, 1659; and had 1. Hannah, b. Jan. 9, 1660; 2. Dorothy, b. Oct. 20, '62, m. Benjamin Moore, 1666; 3. Sarah, b. Jan. 17, 1664-5; 4. Mary, b. Jan. 2, '66, m. Noah Clap, July 28, '90; 5. Elizabeth, b. Mar. 6, 1668; 6. Samuel, b. 1670; 7. Abigail, b. Sep. 15, '72; 8. Edward, b. Mar. 16, 1677; 9. Martha, b. Dec. 25, 1681. Capt. Edward, the f. d. at Sud., Aug. 7, 1703. His wid Hannah, d. May 18, 1708.

3. SAMUEL, s. of Edward (2), m. Mary, dr. of Jonathan Willard, and g. dr. of Maj. Simon, and had at Sud., 1. Mary, b, Feb. 10, 1703-4, m. Col. Aaron Willard; 2. Dorothy, b. Mar. 7, 1705-6, m. Robert Phelps, 1729; 3. Abigail, b. Feb. 19, 1707-8, m. Rev. Samuel Willard, of Biddeford, Oct. 29, 1730, (f. of Pres. Willard, of Harv. College) and m. 2d, Rev. Richard Elvins, of Scarboro', Me., and d. at Petersham, in the family of her son. Deac. William Willard, Sep. 19, 1785, æ. 77; 4. Isabel, b. Feb. 3, 17(09-0), m. Rev. Thomas Frink, 1729; 5. William, b. Dec. 22, 1712. The following in the will, (Worc. Prob.) 6. Cyprian, drowned in Muscopog Pond, June 29, 1729, (Rutl. Rec.), f. by w. Hannah, of *Samuel*, and *John*; 7. Hannah, m. Aaron Rice, 1726. Samuel, Esq., the f. moved from Sud. to Rutland, where he was a prominent man, and held a commission as Justice of the Peace. He d. Jan. 15, 1739-0. Mary, his w. d. May 18, 1739. (Rut. Rec.)

4. EDWARD, Jun., s. of Edw. (2), and w. Hannah had 1, Nehemiah, b. at Sud., May 23, 170(7); and on Fram Rec; 2. Zerubbabel, b. Aug. 14, 1708; 3. Bezaleel, b. July 22, 1710;

---

* A Joseph m. at Malden, Elizabeth Upham, 1726.

4. WILLIAM, b. Sep. 21, 1711, m. Mary Ball, Jan. 22, 1737-8;
5. TABITHA, b. Mar. 27, 1713, m. James Arms, of Leicester,
Oct. 14, 1742; 6. ELIZABETH, b. Mar. 11, 1716-7, m. William
Newton, of Marlb., Dec. 1, 1737; 7. HANNAH, b. Ap. 15, 1719,
m. Thomas Ball, Feb. 7, 1739-0; 8. EDWARD, b. Mar. 10,
1720-1; 9. MEHETABEL, d. Mar. 18, 1743-4; 10. LOIS, d.
unm. in Fram., 1813, æ. 85.

[MARY, dr. of Edward and Mary, (perhaps by mistake for E.
and Hannah), b. Nov. 17, 1714. T. Rec.] Edward the f. moved
from Sud. to Fram., and was rated in Fram., 1710. In 1735,
he was living near the centre of the town. His death is not on
record.

5. NEHEMIAH, s. of Edw. (4), m. Mary Gates, May 24,
1733, and had in Fram., 1. MARY, b. Oct. 24, 1733, d. unm.;
2. THOMAS, b. Ap. 25, 1737, prob unm.; 3. PATTY, b. Aug. 18,
1739; 4. HANNAH, b. Ap. 9, 1741; 5. NEHEMIAH, b. July 6,
'48, m. Martha Kendall, Dec. 10, '78, lived and d. in Philipston, f. of *Nathan, William, Artemas, Hannah,* and *Patty*; 6.
SARAH, b. Dec. 7, 1745; 7. MEHETABEL, bap. Mar. 30, 1751;
8. MARGARET, bap. Aug. 30, 1755, m. —— Whitcomb; 9.
MARY, bap. Mar. 12, 1758. Nehem. the f. owned a farm W. of
Dea. Moses Haven's, which was bought of him by the Buckminsters. He afterwards lived on the centre Common, and d. in
Fram.

6. BEZALEEL, and w. Susannah, cov. June 19, 1757, and
had 1. BEZALEEL, b. Sep. 2, '57; 2. JOSEPH, b. Feb. 1, 1759.
Bezaleel, (f. or son), d. Sep. 10, 1759. A letter from Bezaleel
to Capt. Buckminster, dated Mar. 3, 1759, leads to the belief
that he then lived in Spencer.

7. MARY, m. Abner Pratt, Jan. 22, 1795. MOLLY, adm. to
the ch., June, 1783. SARAH, dr. of JOSIAH, bap. Oct. 2, 1748.
A Wid. Wright lived in Fram., 1798.

EDWARD, of Roxbury, had *Zachary,* b. Aug. 5, 1642; *Samuel,* b. Jan. 26,
1644-5. EDWARD, of Boston, m. Mary Powell, May 27, 1657, and had
Mary, Jan. 19, 1657. ROBERT, of Boston, and w. Mary, had *John,* d. Mar.,
1645; *Joseph,* b. Nov. 14, 1655. Robert was prob. the R. in Maj. Willard's
troop, at Dedham, 1654. SAMUEL, was made free at Springfield, Ap. 13,
1648. (Sav. Winth., II. 375.) EDWARD, of Concord, who d. 1691, (his w.
Elizabeth, d. 1690), made, Jan. 26, 1683, a settlement of his estate. His
children were *Samuel,* (w. Mary, had Mary, 1693); *Edward,* b. Jan. 21,
1657; *Peter,* m. Elizabeth Lambson; and three daughters. (See Mid.

Deeds, Vol. VIII.)* SAMUEL, of Braintree, (w. Mary) had *Mary*, b. Nov. 21, 1698; *Joseph*, and *Benjamin*, b. Ap, 16, 1700; *Hannah*, b. Dec. 7, 1701. JOSEPH, of Marlb., m. Mary Holland, January 1, 1721. For others, see Farmer.

YONGEY, PRINCE, m. Nanny Peterattucks, May 19, 1737. Prince is prob. the same as Prince Jonar, rated ab. 1767, and Prince, colored servant of Col. and Deac. Buckminster, who d. Dec. 21, 1797, æ. 99 y. 4. m. For a further account of Prince, see the preceding Hist.

YOUNGMAN, FRANCIS, of Roxb., m. Anna Heath, 1685, and had JONATHAN, b. Oct. 9, 1686; CORNELIUS, b. Sep. 1, 1688; EBENEZER; b. Nov. 2, 1690, m. in Boston, Mercy Jones, 1713; ANNA, 1695; ELIZABETH, 1699; a dr. (prob. Leah), b. 1701; Leah d. May 28, 1701.

2. JONATHAN, s. of Francis (1), had by w. Sarah, at Fram., SARAH, b. June 9, 1713; LEA, b. Ap. 14, 1715; JONATHAN, b. May 20, 1722. [On Sud. Rec. they had JOHN, b. June 1, 1724; and on Roxb. Rec., ——, b. July 23, 1710; ANNA b. Feb. 29, 1716-7; MARY, Feb. 15, 1718-9; DANIEL, Mar. 12, 1725-6.] Francis lived in Fram., where is a cellar hole, beyond the house of Warren Nixon, Esq.

---

* In a deed of John Hoare, of Concord, to Edward Wright, of Concord, 1682, reference is made to rights of the latter, "to houses, lands, &c., in the Lordship of Castle Bromwich, Co. of Warwick, Eng., by virtue of a deed of gift, by Edward Wright, of C. B., to feoffees in trust, for the use of Francis Wright, son and heir apparent of said Edward Wright, and of Mary Wiggin, dr. of John Wiggin, of Addridge, Co. of Stafford, before the solemnizing of a marriage between the said Francis and the said Mary, and to their heirs, &c.; said deed of gift being now in the hands of said John Hoare, and beareth date, 27th June, 10th year of the reign of King James." (Mid. Deeds, sub. eod. an.) A suit for the non-fulfilment of this covenant, for exchange of lands in Eng., was entered in Mid. Court. (Co. Rec. III. 18.)

SUPPLEMENT.

BENT, JOSEPH, and w. Rachel, were at Milton, 1697, and had 1. MARY, b. 1700; 2. Capt. JOSEPH b. 1701, d. at Albany Dec. 7, 1755, æ. 54, f. by w. Martha (who d. Dec. 4, 1766 æ. 65) of Capt. *Lemuel*, b. 1727, d. 1774, (w. Melatiah d. 1796); *Abigail*, b. 1730; *Eunice*, b. '31; *Joseph*, b. '35, (f. of Ruth, Eunice, Lois and Joseph); *William*, b. 1738; *Martha*, b. '39; *Rufus*, b. '41; 3. JOHN, b. 1703, (w. Elizabeth) f. at Milton, of *John*, b. 1729; *Rebecca*, '31; *Elizabeth*, '32-3; *Prudence*, '35; *Susanna*, '37; *Lydia*, '41; *Sarah*, '43; *Rachel*, '45; *John*, '47; *Noah*, '49; 4. RACHEL, b. 1705; 5. ELIZABETH, b. 1708; 6. SARAH, b. 1710; 7. EBENEZER, b. 1712, f. at Milton, of *Ebenezer*, b. 1737; *Samuel*, '40; *Nedobiah*, '42; *Mary*, '44; *John*, '46; *Deborah*, '48; *Sally*, '50; *Betsey*, '52; 8. EXPERIENCE, b. 1714; 9. THANKFUL, b. 1716. Admin. on Joseph, of Milton, blacksmith, was granted to his son John, Ap. 15, 1728.*

BIGELOW. Of JONATHAN, (named as son of Jonathan,† and g. son of John (1), in the preceding sketches,) who d. in Weston, ab. 1745, leaving chil. *Benjamin, Jonathan, James,* &c., some doubt exists. He may have been of the family of Joshua.

CLARK, JONAS, of Camb. d. (his will dated Dec. 19, 1699), leaving chil. *Jonas, Timothy, Joseph, Samuel, Susanna, Abigail;* he names also his dr. Bonner, dr. Dickaloon, and dr. Green.

CLOYES. *Susanna* and *Mercy*, adults, were bap. at Charlestown, in 1698.

---

* Joseph, of Sud , who d. 1675, had a s. Jos., b. 1675, who disappears from that place, or the neighborhood; but of his identity, as the Joseph of Milton, no proof has presented itself. The author possesses a traditionary account of one EXPERIENCE Bent, of Plymouth, who had the grant of a square mile tract of land, at Hobbs' Hole, so called. His s. *Joseph*, lived in Middleborough, and d. æ. over 80, having chil. Joseph, John, William, and three drs. William, son of John, lives at Paris, Me., æ. ab. 80 years.

† A Jonathan is said to have settled in Weathersfield Lane, Hartford, Conn., ab. 1668, and d. Jan. 10, 1710, æ. 62. Jona., son of John, of Wat., was b. in 1646, which presents a discrepance in the age, although the identity of the two is not improbable.

DRURY. The descent of Thomas, Sen., of Fram. from Hugh, seemed to the author very clear. A more recent examination of Hugh's will, has disclosed a singular ambiguity. Thomas being called *his* "oldest son," and also the oldest son of his (Hugh's) son John, then deceased, the same Thomas probably being referred to. In the Suff. Deeds XV, 193-4, is recorded an agreement of the heirs of Hugh and John, dated April 28, 1692, to which Thomas, then of Sudbury, and a son of John, was a party. Thomas, Sen. of Fram., it is presumed, therefore was *grand son* of Hugh. Hugh, of Boston, was prop. of the Castle Tavern, and land near Mill Bridge, &c.

JENNINGS. RICHARD Jennyns, "late of Bermuda," had deceased, 1692, leaving claims in Boston. (Suff. Deeds).

JENNISON, WILLIAM, referred to in the preceding Register, was of " Colchester, O. England," April 8, 1657, when his br. Robert, as his attorney, conveyed to Edmund Rice, 200 ac. (before granted by the Gen. Court to Wm.) bounded W. by the Dunster farm ; N. by Sud. line ; E. by Wat. line ; S. near Dedham bounds.

KENDALL. English authorities suppose this name to have been originally Candale. Magna Brit. VI. 19.

RICE, JACOB, of Marlb. d. Oct. 30, 1746, æ. 86, having had by w. Mary (who d. Oct. 6, 1752, æ. 80) *Amos*, b. 1693 ; *Martha*, '96 ; *Obadiah*, '98 ; *Esther*, 1701 ; *Eunice*, '02 ; *Mercy*, '05 ; *Jacob*, '07, f. of Capt. Amos ; *Gershom*, 1710, d. Oct. 11, 1790, f. by w. Lydia, of Thomas, Gershom, Solomon, &c. ; *Bethiah*, b. 1712, m. — Brigham ; and *Mary*. Mr. Allen (Hist. of Northb.) supposes Jacob to have been son of Edward, who was son of Edmond. ROBERT, of Boston, had by w. Elizabeth, *Joseph*, b. 1637 ; *Nathaniel*, b. 1639 ; *Patience*, b. 1642. JOSHUA (w. Bathshebah) was of Boston, 1664.

THE NAME OF FRAMINGHAM.

The origin of this name in England, is thus accounted for. The place originally so called having been subject to Britons, Romans, Saxons and Danes, was inhabited by a great mixture of various nations ; and hence was denominated, Friendlingham or Framlingham, i. e. a house, or habitation of strangers — Friendling signifying, in Saxon, a stranger, and Ham, a dwelling or house. — Magna Britannia, V. 223.

OLD AND NEW STYLE.

Before 1752, the year began March 25th, (called Lady Day) ; although in Catholic countries, after 1582, it commenced Jan. 1. Hence between Jan. and March, it was common to double-date. The difference between the Julian and Gregorian year in the 18th century, was 11 days ; after 1800 it was 12, which is to be added to any date in Old Style, to reduce it to the New.

INDEX.

A.

Academy, 79. Trustees, 81. Preceptors, 82.
Adams, Josiah, 86.
Agriculture of Fram., 140.
Ammunition, town stock of, 87.
Appleton's Farm, 12, note.
Ashland, 1, 23, 163.
Awansamug, Indian, 18, 19.

B.

Bank of Fram., 153.
Baptisms, 127.
Baptist Society, 119, n., 128.
Beaver Dam Bridge, 54.
Bills of Credit, 45.
Birds, &c., bounty on, 48, n.
Boman, Wm., 5, 18. Brook, 5, n., 8.
Brewer, Col. Jona., 93.
Bridge, Matth., settlement, 113. Life, 119.
Bridge, Indian, 6. Charles Riv., 46. New, 16. Horse, 16. Bridges, 50.
Brinley, Nath'l, 138. Edward, 138. Farm, 137.
Brown, Rev. Edmund, 2, n. His land, 7, 12, n.
Buckminster, Col. Jos., 12, 34, 55, 70, 87, 89, 137. Joseph, Jun, 89. Col. Wm., 93.
Bunker Hill Fight, 93.
Burying Grounds, 131.

C.

Canada Expedition, 48.
Carpet Factory, 150.
Casualties, &c., 64.
Catholic Church, 131.
Chapman, Rev. Geo., 126.
Church, First, 106. Members, 127. Second, 116.
Cochituate, 4, 5. Pond, 144. Brook, 3. Ford, 15.
Cold-Spring, 10.
Colored Persons, 63.
Common, lands, 36, 135. Centre, 136.
Concord Fight, 93. River, 1, 141.
Corlett, Elijah, 6, 7, n.
Crown, Col., 9.

D.

Danforth, Thomas, 6, 8. Grants, 8. Life, 9, n. Sells in F., 35. Death, &c., 36.
Deacons of First Church, 126.
Deer, 43, 46.
Dunster Farm, 3, n., 145.

E.

Eames, Thomas, Grants, 11. Committee, 16. Indian assault on his house, 24. Inventory of loss, 27.
Earthquake, 66.
Ecclesiastical History, 95.
Education, 34, 74.
Emigrations from F., 72.
Ephraim, Peter, Indian, 28.

F.

Factories, 148.
Fiddle Neck, 38.
Fire, disasters by, 68.
Fisheries, 61.
Fitzwilliam, 73.
Flood, great, 31.
Framingham, bounds, &c., 1. Part set off to Ashland, 1; to Hopkinton, 10; to Southborough, 38; to Marlborough, 38; grants in, 3; settlement, 12; name, 14; surveys, 38, 39, n.; incorporation, 34; Township, 41; difficulties with Sherburne, 44 : with Weston, 45; petition for new county, 46; receives grant of New Fram., 46; action on excise bill, 48; statistics, 151; early list of taxable polls, 162.
Free Masons, 153.

G.

Garrison houses, 87.
Gleason, widow, 49.
Glover Farm, 3. Rev. Jesse, 3, n., 12, n.
Goddard, Edward, 107.
Gookin, Sam., 11, n. Dan., 11, n., 37.
Gore's survey, 38, 42.
Graduates, 84.
Guinea-End, 135.

456 INDEX.

H.

Half-mile-square, 36, n.
Health, &c., 132.
Highways, 15, 31, 51. Grants, 60.
Hills in Framingham, 141.
Hollis Ev. Soc., 131.
Holliston, 72.
Hop-Brook, 12.
Hopkinton, 47, 72, 108, n.

I. J.

Indian, bridge, 6; graves, 17, 55; head, 11; history, 16; wars, 86; praying towns, 22.
Jethro, Indian, 18, 19; field, 19.

K. L.

Keith, Omen S., 86.
Kellogg, Rev. David, 121; character, 123.
Knight, Wm. H., 146, 150.
Lanesborough, 46, n.
Leg, the, 38.
Longevity, 132.
Lynde's land, 11; rocks, 12.

M.

Maguncook, 10, 12, n., 15, 22, 23.
Marlborough, 2, 15, 16, 46, 73.
——————— Association, 110.
Meadows, 148.
Meeting Houses, 38, 95; Mr. Reed's, 116, 128.
Mills, 148.
Ministers, 105.
Mortality, 131.

N.

Natick, 2, 15, 22, n., 38, 46, n.
Nero, 63.
Netus, 7, n., 17, 24.
New Bridge, 16.
New Framingham, 46, n., 47.
Nipmucks, 18.
Nipnap Hill, 17.
Nipnox, 5, 6, 15.

O. P. Q.

Okommakamesit, 22.
Otter Neck, 13.
Oxford settled, &c., 72.
Physicians, 85.
Pond Farm, 3, n.
Poor, 69.
Population, 62.

Pounds, 60.
Prince, 64.
Quabuog, 16.

R.

Reed, Solomon, 116.
Revolution, 89.
Rice Abraham, killed, 67; Edmond, 3, 4, 5, 7, n., 8, 12; Henry, 13.
Rice's End, 135.
Ripley, Rev. Ezra, 121, n., 123, n.
Rivers, &c., 141.
Russell, Richard, 6.
Rutland settled, 72, n.

S.

Salem, Peter, 64, n.
Salem End, 32, 135.
Saxonville, 134; church, 130.
Schools, 74; teachers, 79.
Shay's Rebellion, 94.
Sherburne, 11, 23, 29, 34, 44, n.
——— Row, 135.
Sherman's land, 12, n.
Shrewsbury, 72.
Sickness, great, 66.
Simpson, Savil, 10.
Singing, 61, n, 119, 122.
Small Pox, 68.
Soldiers from Framingham, 156.
Southborough, 38.
Statistics, 151.
Stocks, 45.
Stone, Col. Micah, 71, 103; John, 5, 12, 16; Josiah, 49.
Stone's End, 134.
Straw manufacture, 151.
Sudbury, 2, n., 17, 25, 30, 31, 33, 34, 46, 154.
Sudbury Farms, 37, 41.
Surveys of Fram., 38, 39, n., 50.
Swift, Rev. John, 105; J. Jr., 114.

T. V. W.

Tom, Capt., Indian, 20; his hill, 21.
Topography of Fram., 134.
Train, Rev. C., 128.
Valuation, 62, 153.
Wayte, Richard, 5; Mount, 24.
Weld, Daniel, 7.
Westborough, 49.
Wheaton, Laban, 121, n.
Wheeler Farm, 140.
Willard, Rev. Joseph, 72, n.
Winter, severe, 35, 66.
Witchcraft delusion, 32.
Wolves, 44.
Workhouse, 70.
Wuttusacomponum, Indian, 18.

www.ingramcontent.com/pod-product-compliance
Lightning Source LLC
Chambersburg PA
CBHW071222230426
43668CB00011B/1268